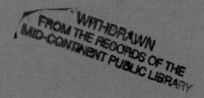

AMERICAN SECRETARIES OF THE NAVY

AMERICAN SECRETARIES OF THE NAVY

VOLUME II 1913–1972

EDITED BY PAOLO E. COLETTA

NAVAL INSTITUTE PRESS
ANNAPOLIS, MARYLAND

Copyright © 1980
by the United States Naval Institute
Annapolis, Maryland

Printed in the United States of America

Library of Congress Cataloging in Publication Data
Main entry under title:

American Secretaries of the Navy.

  Includes bibliographical references and index.
  1. United States. Navy—Management—History.
2. United States. Navy Dept.—History. 3. United
States. Navy Dept.—Biography. I. Coletta, Paolo
Enrico, 1916–
VB23.A57   353.7′092′2 [B]   78-70967
ISBN 0-87021-073-4 (set)
ISBN 0-87021-067-X (v. 1)
ISBN 0-87021-068-8 (v. 2)

CONTENTS

PREFACE

This study presumes to be neither a text nor an operational history of the United States Navy. Rather it seeks to bring into proper perspective the men and measures responsible for the administration of the Navy, for making it or keeping it an adequate instrument of national power. It deals with more than the decisions and efforts that provided the men and materials needed to win battles and wars, for during most of its history the United States Navy has been at peace. It encompasses all the myriad factors that compose "sea power." Since the Navy often worked with the land and air forces, its relations to the other military arms are considered. Since the Navy is but one recipient of budgeted funds, military-civilian relations are not overlooked. And since the Navy has been a decisive factor in the formulation of American foreign policy or in turn has been greatly affected by such formulation on the strictly diplomatic level, its impact upon foreign policy and the impact upon it of foreign policy naturally play a large part in its development.

While a basic outline is followed by each author, no attempt has been made to restrict the story to the outline or to deny the writer free use of his treatment and style. All deal with at least the following topics: 1) a short biographical sketch of each secretary, including his political career, if any, and the reasons for his appointment; 2) problems facing the secretary when he assumed office; 3) the degree of success in his resolution of problems; 4) administrative competence and plans for departmental reorganization, if he had any; 5) the influence of domestic policy, foreign policy, strategy, and tactics on naval administration; and 6) a summary of achievements in both operational and administrative fields.

In dealing with how a secretary attempted to solve his problems, the writers include his relations with the president, members of the cabinet, the other military services, and the public. In handling plans for reorganization they stress domestic needs, overseas requirements, and aid to allies. And with respect to the actual administration of the Navy they deal with at least manpower, training and education, ships, armament, logistics, naval aviation, the Marine Corps, research, the Reserve components, and the impact of nucleonics. Each author acknowledges any aid received from others in "The Contributors" section.

This is not an official U. S. Navy history. In the essays on secretaries of the Navy who served after passage of the National Security Act, 1947, the opinions or assertions expressed therein are the personal ones of the authors and do not necessarily reflect the views of the Department of Defense.

INTRODUCTION

> History shows that without sea experience as a guide to Naval Administration afloat and ashore no country can have a good fighting Navy.
>
> Rear Admiral Julius A. Furer, USN (Retired)

From 1797 until 1947, a secretary of the Navy both advised the President as a member of his cabinet and administered a department. The President had the final power of decision, but much depended upon his character, that of the secretary, and also upon circumstances. Strong Presidents such as Theodore Roosevelt and Franklin Delano Roosevelt acted as their own secretaries, whereas weak ones such as Warren G. Harding readily delegated responsibility for naval policy. Similarly, the power of the Office of the Secretary of the Navy varied in accordance with whether the nation was at peace or at war; whether the Congress favored or opposed administration policy; whether times were good or bad. Also much depended upon whether the secretary had civilian and professional aides who gave him expert advice or, on the other hand, sought to detract from his power; and on whether the secretary really wanted to be a leader or not. One secretary, John D. Long, for example, who served under William McKinley and Theodore Roosevelt, stated that "I make a point not to trouble myself overmuch to acquire a thorough knowledge of the details pertaining to any branch of the service. My plan is to leave all such matters to the bureau chiefs, or other officers. . . ."[1] Hence, Theodore Roosevelt could say of his secretary that he was "a high-minded man: but one "wholly unfit to be Secretary of the Navy" because of his ignorance of naval matters.[2]

Over the years, too, opinion has varied on the qualities a secretary of the Navy was expected to have. In declining the offer to be the first secretary of the Navy, George Cabot wrote:

It is undoubtedly requisite that the officer at the head of the naval department should possess considerable knowledge of maritime affairs; but this should be elementary as well as practical, including the principles of naval architecture and naval tactics. He should also possess skill to arrange systematically the means of equipping, manning, and conducting the naval force with the greatest possible despatch, and with the least possible expense; and, above all, he should possess the inestimable secret of rendering it invincible by an equal force. Thus a knowledge of the human heart will constitute an essential ingredient in the character of this officer, that he may be able to convert every incident to the elevation of the spirit of the American seaman. . . .

It is not to be expected that a man will be found possessing the ability to perform at once all the duties of an office, new and difficult; but I trust men may be found—and it seems to me indispensable that such should be found—who will, by industrious application of genius and talents, soon acquire the requisite qualifications.[3]

A century and a half later, the "Gates Report" set forth the "professional qualifications" of a secretary:

When judged on the basis of *professional qualifications*, the individuals chosen by the President and his Congress to fill the position of Secretary are usually men having a broad understanding and appreciation of public and political affairs. With this ability is often present a broad business background, but seldom does it include specific knowledge of, or experience with, professional naval matters. Furthermore, "policy control" is a task which requires broad specialization obtainable only in limited degree by direct experience in the Naval Establishment, and it is therefore a task which should be performed by an "outside" executive and one whose tenure in Navy need not be of prolonged duration.[4]

For the early decades of the Navy Department's existence, when fighting ships differed little from merchant ships, experience as a merchant ship captain, or at least some mercantile experience, appeared to be desirable in a secretary, and an Eastern man was most likely to be chosen because most of the states fronted the Atlantic Ocean. Since then, lawyers, journalists, authors, and businessmen have been appointed. In the early days, merchant ship owners were favored as Navy agents, civilian representatives of the Department who acquired and outfitted naval vessels; today naval officers of high rank and industrial managers administer the combined military-industrial complex of the Shore Establishment. Geography and personal friendship may play a part in the selection of a secretary. So may a President's obligation to reward a particularly effective campaign aide or interest group, or his need for demonstrated administrative capability, as in the case of Frank Knox. In consonance with the principle of civilian supremacy established when President John Adams approved the creation of the Navy Department in 1797, naval officers have not acted as secretaries except as *ad interim* appointees.

The conduct of naval operations and naval administration is a dynamic process, with operations and administration often overlapping, as in the formulation of broad strategic plans. Until 1815 the Secretary of the Navy sought advice where he might, from naval officers as well as elsewhere. The early squadrons, which served at home and on distant stations in the 19th century, chastized pirates, showed the flag, occasionally engaged in exploratory and scientific expeditions, and fought in the War of 1812, the Mexican War, the Civil War, and the Spanish-American War. During the first half of that century, warfare changed little either in methods or instruments: wood and sail were only slowly challenged by iron and steam; merchant seamen could be made into men of war in short order; and naval officers occasionally acted as diplomats and executive agents. Yet by 1815, with the age of steam aborning, the need to improve naval administration was answered by the creation of the Board of Navy Commissioners, which joined the help and advice of three senior regular officers of the Navy to the few clerks who served the secretary.

In 1842 the Board was replaced with a bureau system which originally encompassed five bureaus: Bureau of Yards and Docks; Ordnance and Hydrography; Construction, Equipment, and Repair; Medicine and Surgery; and Provisions and Clothing (later Supply and Accounts). In 1862 the Bureau of Navigation (later Personnel), of (Steam) Engineering, and of Equipment were added, and Aeronautics in 1921. In 1940 Construction and Repair was merged with Engineering to become the Bureau of Ships. These and later changes are discussed in the text. It should be noted that, in the absence of an advisory officer or council until the advent of the Office of the Chief of Naval Operations in 1915, the secretary leaned more upon the Chief of the Bureau of Navigation than upon any other individual for advice. But with the passage of time he was also aided by the U. S. Naval Institute (1873), which provided an excellent forum for discussing naval matters; the U. S. Naval War College (1884); and the General Board of the Navy (1900), which was formally enjoined to "advise" the secretary on naval policy but not to undertake any administrative or operational duties. In the meantime, the shift from sail to steam and recognition of the heightened need for professional training of officers had resulted in the establishment of the U. S. Naval Academy in 1845.

The greatest requirements for competence in a secretary of the navy have come in times of war, times of rapid technological change. In 1846 and again in 1917, except for aircraft in the latter period, the Navy played a supporting role with ships and weapons at hand, whereas in 1861 and 1941 adjustment to rapid technological change paralleled great expansion of the Navy itself. Fortunately, bewhiskered Gideon Welles, enigmatic Josephus Daniels, voluble Frank Knox, and intense, determined James V. Forrestal proved capable of providing the equipment and men and of creating the distant bases needed for far-flung operations in which the Navy was engaged during their terms of office. In the meantime, the "Three Williams"—Hunt, Chandler, and Whitney—and Benjamin F. Tracy rebuilt a navy which had been permitted to deteriorate drastically during the generation following the Civil War.

Following the Spanish-American War, the United States became a world power. How large should its navy be? How should it be administered? Because the bureau chiefs were immersed in those areas over which they had cognizance, the bureau system was ill suited to provide professional direction to plan and control naval operations. Moreover, various naval secretaries, congressional committees, and the staff corps—medical, supply, civil engineering, chaplains, and the like—feared loss of power if a general staff on the German army pattern were adopted. A compromise solution for providing the secretary with professional advice was the General Board of the Navy, 1900, an outgrowth of the Naval War Board of the Spanish-American War. A secretary could now take the board's advice into consideration when he advised the President on what policies he should follow in supporting the national interest and also offer recommendations on such matters as the size and makeup of the Navy in both materials and men. Once the size and composition of the Navy was determined by Congress, a secretary then usually engaged in a battle royal to obtain what he considered to be the Navy's rightful share of the nation's resources and industrial facilities. The quality of the advice the secretary received from the General Board may be evaluated by noting the names of some of its members who served with great distinction—Admirals George Dewey, Henry Clay Taylor, Robley D. Evans, Charles E. Clark, French Ensor Chadwick, Harry Shepard Knapp, Bradley A. Fiske, Joseph Strauss, Mark Bristol, Thomas G. Hart, and Ernest J. King.

Nevertheless, by 1905 demands for reform in naval administration resulted in Senate investigations. In consequence, under Secretary George von L. Meyer (1909–1913), four line officer aides—for Operations, Material, Inspection, and Personnel—were superimposed upon the bureau system. While Daniels (1913–1921) let that arrangement lapse, he was the first Secretary to live with a Chief of Naval Operations (CNO), a post created in 1915 to specialize in systematic planning, in coordinating the work of the Navy Department, and in suggesting how cooperation could be achieved with the Army, other government departments, and private industry. Beginning in 1942, the functions of the General Board were taken over first, by the CNO and, later, by the Joint Chiefs of Staff. Yet, with the exception of Admiral Ernest J. King, who held the office during World War II, the CNO had no command authority over either the commanders of the fleets or over the bureaus and officers of the Department.

Until World War I, entrenched politics kept most of the repair work and new construction in the East Coast navy yards, and little interest could be generated in building needed yards and bases at Pearl Harbor, Guantánamo, Cavite, Guam, and elsewhere. As a result, there was excessive duplication of facilities within the various departments in the navy yards, but this was lessened somewhat beginning during Meyer's term by the provision of a technical manager, responsible under the commandant for the industrial part of the work. Such improvements were of inestimable value when, following the doldrums in naval building during the Washington Conference "holiday" beginning in 1922, President Franklin D. Roosevelt, who had been Assistant Secretary of the Navy from 1913 to 1920, gave his full support to the rebuilding plans initiated by Carl Vinson, chairman of the House Naval Affairs Committee. While such naval operations as the Neutrality Patrol revealed the need for a larger navy in the Atlantic, materials were acquired to implement legislation calling for a "Two-Ocean Navy." The death of Secretary Claude A. Swanson in 1940 left an opening for the bipartisanship Roosevelt wished to illustrate; in consequence, in July 1940, two Republicans, Frank Knox, a newspaperman from Chicago, became Secretary of the Navy, while Henry L. Stimson took over the post of Secretary of the Army that he had once held under President William Howard Taft. Knox engaged a management engineer to bring to the Department the efficiency methods common in big business. Forrestal, the first Under Secretary of the Navy, meanwhile developed new administrative machinery for procurement and drew upon the business and industrial worlds for civilian experts to help cope with problems of coordination with the Army and other government agencies. After Knox's death in 1944, Secretary Forrestal supervised the last great reorganization of the Navy undertaken while its secretary still had cabinet status. It was Forrestal who, in the first year following the War, caused studies to be made for the reorganization of the postwar Navy and, finally, took a leading part in the three-year battle, 1944-1947, looking to a unification of the three branches of the military services, Army, Navy, and Air Force. In view of Forrestal's excellent service, it was fitting that, under the National Security Act of 1947 which unified the armed forces, President Harry S. Truman appointed him to be the first Secretary of Defense.

Henceforth, problems of naval administration were solved within the framework of a Department of Defense. Although the Secretary of the Navy no longer enjoyed cabinet status, he still had to seek the cooperation of the Bureau of the Budget, the Appropriations committees, and the vitally important Armed Services committees, which in 1947 replaced the old Naval Affairs committees.

The congressional committees not only could affect policy but could investigate and, in the Senate, had to approve nominations to the officer corps and particularly to flag rank, while the Bureau of the Budget, in supervising departmental estimates and program management, could most effectively control internal naval policy. Finally, naval administration had to reflect the policies of the President and Congress. Presidential policy has varied from the crippling retrenchment of a Thomas Jefferson and Richard M. Nixon to the great support given to the Navy by the two Roosevelts. It has often been said that the life of a ship is in greater jeopardy on Capitol Hill than it would be in actual battle.

The degree of effectiveness of the many secretaries has varied greatly. A host of secretaries are all but forgotten or, as in the cases of Robert Thompson and Edwin Denby, are remembered for their peccadillos or failures rather than for their positive accomplishments. The first secretary, Benjamin Stoddert, won a crown in the naval firmament because of the wisdom with which he laid down administrative policy. By not attempting to usurp presidential power, by offering sage advice and getting it accepted, he was in effect able to initiate and carry out his own policies. But even he noted the difficulty of finding time to think about policy amid the increasing demand for his attention to administrative details. Equally capable as secretaries were Benjamin W. Crowninshield; Gideon Welles; Hunt, Chandler, Whitney, and Tracy, who sponsored the New Navy of the 1880s; and Meyer, Daniels, Knox, and Forrestal. Each had to forge his own way, for there was no formula for the office, no way of training for it.

Unlike the President and congressmen, moreover, a secretary of the navy had no constituency. His record had to be assessed by the way in which he carried out policy laid down by the people's elected representatives. On the one hand, Congress established the size of the Navy, funded it, approved departmental reorganization plans and nominations to office, and investigated any facet of the service. On the other hand, the secretary was constantly subjected to demands from pressure groups—from industrial organizations desiring to make sales, reserve officer organizations demanding changes in reserve policies, fathers seeking appointments to the Naval Academy for their sons, or mothers worried about the morals of their young sons in the service. In addition to being an administrator, the secretary had to be the Navy's chief public relations man and keep the Navy image well burnished before the public as well as Congress, be its chief recruiter, and defend the power of his office against the other military services. Finally, because of the worldwide range of naval operations, he acted in an executive capacity while carrying out the orders of the President or, often, policies established by the Department of State.

Since 1947 the Secretary of the Navy has rarely been included in that small number of men who must make the crucial decisions that mean peace or war, life or death, for nations as well as for individuals. Yet he controls an awesome military power that may be used to determine the fate of millions of people. Today he is tested not only by his ability to obtain men and materials for the Navy but also by his performance as a member of the triple-headed team that constitutes our military establishment.

NOTES

1. Lawrence S. Mayo, ed., *America of Yesterday as Reflected in the Journal of John D. Long* (Boston: Atlantic Monthly Press, 1923), pp. 157, 169–70.
2. Roosevelt to Munroe Smith, 24 Mar. 1915, Elting Morison and others, eds., *The Letters of Theodore Roosevelt*, 8 vols. (Cambridge, Mass.: Harvard University Press, 1951–1954), 8:912–13.
3. C. W. Upham, *Life of Timothy Pickering* 4 vols. (Boston, 1867–1873), 3:319–20.
4. *Recommendations Concerning the Executive Administration of the Naval Establishment* (Gates Report) (Washington: GPO, 7 Nov. 1945).

THE CONTRIBUTORS

ROBERT GREENHALGH ALBION is Professor Emeritus, Harvard University, from which he obtained his Ph. D. in 1924. He also has a Litt.D., Bowdoin, 1948; Litt.D., Southampton College, 1970; and LHD, University of Maine, 1971. In addition to teaching two generations of civilian and naval students he has written a five-foot shelf of his own on naval and maritime subjects. Among his best known works are *Forests and Sea Power* (Harvard University Press, 1924); *The Rise of New York Port* (Charles Scribner's Sons, 1937); *Sea Lanes in Wartime* (Norton, 1941); with Robert H. Connery, *Forrestal and the Navy* (Columbia University Press, 1962); and *Five Centuries of Famous Ships* (McGraw-Hill, 1978). From 1943 to 1950 he served as historian of naval administration in the Navy Department.

K. JACK BAUER received his Ph.D. from Indiana University in 1953. He served as a member of the staff of the National Archives in the historical sections of the Marine Corps and Navy. In the latter he was an assistant to Samuel Eliot Morison for the writing of the *History of United States Naval Operations During World War II*. Among his books are *Surfboats and Horse Marines* (Naval Institute, 1969); *Ships of the Navy, 1775–1969: Combat Vessels* (Rensselaer Polytechnic Institute, 1970); *The Mexican War 1846–1848* (Macmillan, 1974); and *Soldiering* (Presidio, 1977). Following a year as John F. Morrison Professor at the General Command and Staff College, Leavenworth, Kansas, he returned to his post as Professor of History at Rensselaer.

JOHN J. CARRIGG obtained his Ph.D. from Georgetown University in 1953. Since 1948 he has taught at the College of Steubenville, Ohio, where he is chairman of the History Department.

PAOLO ENRICO COLETTA obtained his Ph.D. at the University of Missouri. He taught at the University of Missouri and at Stephens College before obtaining a commission in the naval reserve, in which he served for three wartime years and then in an inactive status prior to retiring in the grade of Captain after thirty years of service. After teaching at South Dakota State College and the University of Louisville, he moved to the U.S. Naval Academy. In addition to numerous reviews and articles, he has written *William Jennings Bryan*, 3 vols. (University of Nebraska Press, 1964–1969); *The Presidency of William Howard Taft* (University Press of Kansas, 1973); *The American Naval Heritage in Brief* (University Press of America, 1978); *The U.S. Navy and Defense Unification, 1947–1953* (University of Delaware Press, 1979); and *Admiral Bradley A. Fiske and the American Navy* (Regents Press of Kansas, 1979).

EDWIN MALBURN HALL obtained his Ph.D. from Pennsylvania State University. After teaching in several preparatory schools during the Great Depression and then at his alma mater, he began a long tour at the U.S. Naval Academy, from which he retired in 1974. He has contributed to E. B. Potter, ed., *The United States and World Sea Power* (Prentice Hall, 1955), and also to E. B. Potter and C. W. Nimitz, eds., *Sea Power: A Naval History* (Prentice Hall, 1960).

PAUL THAYER HEFFRON obtained his Ph.D. at Fordham University. He taught at Boston College for sixteen years, where he was also chairman of the Department of History and Government. Since 1966 he has been associated with the Manuscript Division, Library of Congress, of which he is at this writing the acting chief. His major publications include "Wiretapping and the Law," *Catholic World*, May 1954; "Theodore Roosevelt and the Appointment of Mr. Justice Moody," *Vanderbilt Law Review*, v. 18, March 1965; "Secretary Moody and Naval Administrative Reform," *American Neptune*, v. 29, January 1969; "Manuscript Sources in the Library of Congress for a Study of Labor History," *Labor History*, v. 10, October 1969; "Felix Frankfurter: Manuscript Historian," *Manuscripts*, v. 23, Summer 1971.

ROGER KENNETH HELLER obtained an A.B. and M.A. degree from the University of California, Berkeley. Since completing thirty-three years of active and reserve duty with the U.S. Army, he has taught Modern Military History, U.S. Diplomatic History, The Ascent of Man, and a Social Science Seminar at San Jose State University. His *History of the 361st Infantry Regiment, 1917–1954* appeared in 1955.

WALTER R. HERRICK obtained his Ph.D. from the University of Virginia. After teaching at Rollins College, Winter Park, Florida, for five years, he moved to Quinnipiac College, Hamden, Connecticut. In addition to various book reviews, he is the author of *The American Naval Revolution* (Louisiana State University Press, 1966).

HAROLD D. LANGLEY obtained his Ph.D. at the University of Pennsylvania in 1960. He has taught at Marywood College, Scranton, Pa., Montgomery Junior College, Takoma Park, Md., and the Catholic University of America. Since 1969, following a tour of six years as a diplomatic historian at the Department of State, he has been an Associate Curator with the Division of Naval History, The Smithsonian Institution, and also an adjunct professor at Catholic University. His major publications include *Social Reform in the U.S. Navy, 1798–1862* (University of Illinois Press, 1967); *To Utah With the Dragoons* (University of Utah Press, 1974); and, as co-editor, *Roosevelt and Churchill: Their Secret Wartime Correspondence* (New York and London: The Saturday Review Press/Dutton, 1975).

GEORGE H. LOBDELL obtained his Ph.D. in 1954 from the University of Illinois. He taught first at Carthage College; for the past twenty-three years he has been at Ohio University, Athens. An Army veteran of World War II and Korea—he was separated as a lieutenant colonel in 1967—he has written with Arlan Helgeson and Richard Brown, *The United States of America: A History for Young Citizens* (Silver Burdette, 1964), and the article on Frank Knox that appears in the *Dictionary of American Biography*.

JOHN NIVEN, a naval veteran of World War II, obtained his Ph.D. at Columbia University in 1954. He taught at Mitchell College and then for six years was the Assistant to the Chairman and Director of Publications at the General Dynamics Corporation. Since 1960 he has been in the History Department of the Claremont Graduate School. His major publications include *Connecticut for the Union: The Role of the State in the Civil War* (Yale University Press, 1965); with Courtlandt Canby and Vernon Welsh, eds., *Dynamic America: A History of the General Dynamics Corporation* (Doubleday, 1960); *Gideon Welles: Lincoln's Secretary of the Navy* (Oxford University Press, 1973); and *Connecticut Hero Israel Putnam* (Connecticut Bicentennial Commission, 1978).

FRANK LAWRENCE OWSLEY, JR., obtained his Ph.D. from the University of Alabama. He taught at the U.S. Naval Academy from 1957 to 1960 and has taught at Auburn University since 1960, where he is a Professor of History. He was a visiting Professor at the University of Nebraska in 1967–1968. He has authored *The C.S.S. Florida: Her Building and Operations* (University of Pennsylvania Press, 1965) and *The Struggle for the Gulf: The War of 1812 in the Gulf States*, forthcoming from the University of Florida Press. He has also edited and annotated editions of H. S. Halbert and T. H. Ball, *The Creek War of 1813 and 1814*, and John Reid and John Henry Eaton, *The Life of Andrew Jackson*, both published by the University of Alabama Press.

STEPHEN TALLICHET POWERS obtained his Ph.D. from the University of Notre Dame in 1965. He is an Associate Professor and chairman of the Department of History at the University of Northern Colorado, in Greeley. His article, "Robert Morris and the Courts Martial of John Manley and Samuel Nicholson of the Continental Navy," appears in *Military Affairs*.

PAUL BRENNAN RYAN is a naval historian at the Hoover Institution on War, Revolution and Peace at Stanford University. He is a graduate of the U.S. Naval Academy and holds master's degrees in International Relations (Stanford) and History (San Jose State University). A career naval officer, he served in submarines in World War II, saw service afloat in the Far East and Mediterranean, and held three commands at sea. In addition he was posted as naval attaché to pre-Castro Cuba (1950–1952) and also to Canada (1956–1959). Two tours at the Pentagon gave him a first-hand look at policy-making at the highest level. His last active duty was as Deputy Director of Naval History, at the Navy Department. His major publications include *The Lusitania Disaster*, with Thomas A. Bailey (Free Press, 1975), *The Panama Canal Controversy* (Hoover Institution Press, 1977), and, with Thomas A. Bailey, *Hitler vs. Roosevelt: Their Undeclared War in the Atlantic, 1939–1941* (Free Press, 1979).

ALLISON SAVILLE obtained his Ph.D. at the University of Washington. He has taught at the U.S. Naval Academy, Texas A&M, and University of Hawaii. In addition he has been a research fellow at the Smithsonian Institution and Curator of the Submarine Force Library and Museum at the Submarine Base, Groton, Connecticut. His latest book is *The Gazela Primeiro* (Leeward Publications, 1978).

PAUL RICHARD SCHRATZ obtained a B.S. from the U.S. Naval Academy, an M.A. from Boston University, and a Ph.D. from Ohio State University. After retiring from the naval service in 1968, he joined the University of Missouri as Director of International Studies. From 1973 to 1975 he served as a Foreign Affairs-Defense Policy specialist with the Commission on the Organization of the Government for Foreign Policy. Following a year as Visiting Scholar at the Brookings Institution, he joined Georgetown University, from which he is currently on contract to the Air War College, Montgomery, Alabama, as Professor of International Affairs. A heavily decorated naval veteran, he served on both the Naval and National War College faculties and in policy positions in the Defense Department. For many years he has been an editorial writer for *Shipmate*, the publication of the Naval Academy Alumni Association, and a frequent contributor to the Naval Institute *Proceedings*. He edited the recent George C. Marshall Foundation study, *Evolution of the American Defense Establishment Since World War II*, and has authored or contributed to many other books and professional journals.

He hereby acknowledges the support of Vice Admiral Stansfield Turner while President of the U.S. Naval War College, and of Vice Admiral Edwin B. Hooper, USN, Retired, former head of the Naval History Center, support without which the essays on Secretaries Connally, Korth, and Nitze might not have appeared.

MARSHALL SMELSER obtained his Ph.D. from Harvard University. After teaching for several years at St. Louis University, he served in the Army from 1944 to 1946. He then taught at the College of St. Thomas for a year before moving on to the University of Notre Dame, where he was sometime head of the Department of History. He was a Forrestal Fellow at the U.S. Naval Academy, 1956–1957, and a Guggenheim Fellow in 1963–1964. His publications include *The Campaign for the Sugar Islands* (Chapel Hill, N.C., 1955), *The Congress Founds a Navy* (University of Notre Dame Press, 1959), *The Democratic Republic, 1801–1815* (Harper and Row, 1968), *Winning of Independence* (Chicago: Quadrangle Books, 1972), and *The Life that [Babe] Ruth Built* (Quadrangle/New York Times Book Co., 1975). He is now deceased.

W. PATRICK STRAUSS obtained his Ph.D. at Columbia University. He taught at Columbia University, San Francisco State College, and Michigan State University before moving on to Oakland University, Rochester, Minnesota, in 1970. In the meantime he served as a Fulbright Lecturer in American History at the University of Hong Kong for two years, 1964–1965 and 1970–1971. In addition to numerous articles and reviews, he has published *Americans in Polynesia, 1783–1842* (East Lansing, Mich., 1964), *Isolation and Involvement: An Interpretive History of American Diplomacy* (Waltham, Mass., 1972), and has edited *Stars and Spars: The American Navy in the Age of Sail* (Blaisdell Publishing Co., 1969).

JOHN R. WADLEIGH received a B.S. degree from the U.S. Naval Academy in 1937. During thirty-four years as a commissioned officer he served primarily in cruisers and destroyers, and was a survivor of the aircraft carrier *Yorktown*, sunk in the Battle of Midway, 1942. He retired in 1971 in the rank of rear admiral as Commander, Training Command, Atlantic Fleet. He has written for the U.S. Naval Institute *Proceedings, Shipmate*, and other maritime publications. He is currently collaborating on a centennial history of the U.S. Naval War College.

GERALD EVERETT WHEELER obtained his A.B., M.A. and Ph.D. degrees from the University of California, Berkeley. After teaching at the University of California, he moved east to the U.S. Naval Academy, then back west, to the San Jose State University, San Jose, California. He was chairman of the Department of History and also served in various other administrative posts, culminating in Dean of the School of Social Sciences. He is the author of *Prelude to Pearl Harbor: The United States Navy and the Far East, 1921–1931* (University of Missouri Press, 1963), and of *Admiral William Veazie Pratt, U.S. Navy: A Sailor's Life* (Office of Naval History, 1974). In addition to contributing reviews and articles to many military and historical journals, he is working on a biography of Admiral Thomas C. Kinkaid.

JOSEPH ZIKMUND obtained his Ph.D. from Duke University. He has taught political science at Duke University, Temple University, and Albion College. At the last he was chairman of the political science department before moving on to the Illinois Institute of Technology in Chicago, where he is chairman of the Social Science Department and Director of the Masters Program in Public Administration. His books include *The Ecology of American Political Culture: Readings* (T. Y. Crowell, 1975); *Black Politics in Philadelphia* (Basic Books, 1973); and *Suburbia: A Guide to the Literature* (Gale Research Co., 1978).

Abbreviations Used in the Footnotes

ADM	Admiral
AEC	Atomic Energy Commission
AF	*Air Force Magazine*
AFJ	*Armed Forces Journal*
AFM	*Armed Forces Management*
AHR	*American Historical Review*
AN	*American Neptune*
ANAFJ	*Army, Navy, Air Force Journal*
ANAFR	*Army, Navy, Air Force Register*
ANC	*Army and Navy Chronicle*
ANJ	*Army and Navy Journal*
APSR	*American Political Science Review*
App.	Appendix
ARR	*American Review of Reviews*
ARSN	*Annual Report of the Secretary of the Navy*
ASECNAV	Assistant Secretary of the Navy
ASP:NA	*American State Papers: Naval Affairs*
AUQR	*Air University Quarterly Review*
AW	*Aviation Week*
BGEN	Brigadier General
BOB	Bureau of the Budget
BUAIR	Bureau of Aeronautics
BUC&R	Bureau of Construction and Repair
BUEQ	Bureau of Equipment

BUNAV	Bureau of Navigation
BUORD	Bureau of Ordnance
BUPERS	Bureau of Naval Personnel
BUSANDA	Bureau of Supplies and Accounts
BUSHIPS	Bureau of Ships
CAPT	Captain
CDR	Commander
CH	*Current History*
CHS	Connecticut Historical Society
CINC	Commander in Chief
CNO	Chief of Naval Operations
COL	Colonel
COMMO	Commodore
CR	*Congressional Record*
DDR&E	Department of Defense Research and Engineering
DOD	Department of Defense
EML	Eleutherean Mills Library
ENS	Ensign
FA	*Foreign Affairs*
FADM	Fleet Admiral
FR	*Papers Relating to the Foreign Relations of the United States* (with year[s])
GEN	General
GB	General Board of the Navy
GPO	Government Printing Office
Ex. Doc(s).	Executive Document[s], Congress
HAHR	*Hispanic American Historical Review*
HASC	House Armed Services Committee
HCA	House Committee on Appropriations
H. Ex. Doc(s).	House Executive Document(s)
HL	Huntley Library
H. Misc. Doc(s).	House Miscellaneous Document(s)
HL	Huntington Library
H. Rpt.	House Report
IND	*Independent*
JAH	*Journal of American History*
JCS	Joint Chiefs of Staff
JSH	*Journal of Southern History*
LC	Library of Congress
LCDR	Lieutenant Commander
LD	*Literary Digest*

LGEN	Lieutenant General
LT	Lieutenant
LCOL	Lieutenant Colonel
LTJG	Lieutenant junior grade
MA	*Military Affairs*
MAJ	Major
MCG	*Marine Corps Gazette*
MDLC	Manuscript Division, Library of Congress
MGEN	Major General
MHS	Massachusetts Historical Society
MR	*Military Review*
MS	Manuscript
MVHR	*Mississippi Valley Historical Review*
NA	National Archives
NAN	*Naval Aviation News*
NAR	*North American Review*
NARG	National Archives Record Group (number)
NARS	National Archives and Record Service (location)
NCAB	*National Cyclopedia of American Biography*
NHD:OA	Naval History Division, Operational Archives
NNR	*Niles' National Register*
NWR	*Niles' Weekly Register*
NYHS	New York Historical Society
NYPL	New York Public Library
OCMH	Office of Chief of Military History
OPNAV	Office of the Chief of Naval Operations
OFSECNAV	Office of the Secretary of the Navy
ORN	*Official Records of the Union and Confederate Navies in the War of the Rebellion*
PHR	*Pacific Historical Review*
pt.	part
RADM	Rear Admiral
RET	Retired
rpt.	reprint
Rpt.	Report
SA	*Scientific American*
SAC	Strategic Air Command
SASC	Senate Armed Services Committee
SCA	Senate Committee on Appropriations
SECA	Secretary of the Army
SECAF	Secretary of the Air Force

SECDEF   Secretary of Defense
SECNAV   Secretary of the Navy
SEP   *Saturday Evening Post*
SUPPL   Supplement
USAS   *U.S. Air Services*
SNP   Papers of the Secretaries of the Navy
USECNAV   Under Secretary of the Navy
USNIP   United States Naval Institute *Proceedings*
USNWCR   *U. S. Naval War College Review*
USNWR   *U. S. News and World Report*
VADM   Vice Admiral
WPLC   Welles Papers, Library of Congress
WW   *World's Work*

AMERICAN SECRETARIES OF THE NAVY

JOSEPHUS DANIELS

5 March 1913–5 March 1921

PAOLO E. COLETTA

Born on 18 May 1862 in Washington, North Carolina, Josephus Daniels left school at the age of eighteen years to become an editorial writer. When he was twenty years old, he bought the *Wilson* (North Carolina) *Advance*; at twenty-six, while publishing both the *Raleigh State Chronicle* and the *North Carolinian*, he married Adelaide Worth Bagley. She bore him four sons.

After a two-year stint in the Appointments (personnel) Division of the Department of the Interior in Washington, D.C., he acquired the *Raleigh News and Observer* in 1894 and made it the largest daily newspaper in the state. As an editor, Daniels propagandized the New South, progressive reforms, prohibition, and white supremacy; as a Democratic national committeeman from 1896 to 1916 he supported the candidacy and administration of Woodrow Wilson.[1]

After his nomination in 1912, Wilson rewarded Daniels with a cabinet appointment as Secretary of the Navy. William Jennings Bryan, the patriarch of the Democratic Party, approved of Daniels, as did Colonel Edward M. House, Wilson's alter ego and confidential adviser. Wilson liked Daniels's cheerfulness, energy, and shrewdness; he also saw that he was just the man to conciliate Bryan and his following, who might oppose the New Freedom's legislative program.[2]

On 4 March Daniels, by invitation, called upon the outgoing secretary of the Navy, George von Lengerke Meyer, who briefed him on the work of the department and introduced him to his aides and bureau chiefs. When the two men were alone, Meyer said, "I do not wish to give you any advice, but merely to suggest to you that you keep the power to direct the Navy *here*," and, for emphasis, slapped his desk—advice that Daniels remembered and cherished.[3]

An excellent public relations man, in time Daniels became one of Wilson's most valuable liaison men with Congress because he knew how Congress worked and got along with conservatives as well as with progressives.

525

Wilson avoided meddling with department patronage. When Daniels suggested the thirty-one year old Franklin D. Roosevelt, as his assistant, Wilson readily agreed.[4] Daniels upheld Wilson's policy of ending Dollar Diplomacy yet would use force to support the Monroe Doctrine. In 1913 he sided with Wilson and Secretary of State Bryan in seeking to mollify by diplomacy a Japan angered by California's seeking to bar Japanese from acquiring title to agricultural land. Military men, he said should not decide national policy; moreover, ship movements would lead to war rather than to the peaceful settlement of the dispute. He thus countered the recommendations of the Secretary of War, Lindley M. Garrison, of his Aide for Operations, Rear Admiral Bradley A. Fiske, and of the Joint Army and Navy Board, who wished to concentrate ships from Hawaii and China in Philippine bases, the American bases closest to Japan. In late May 1913, Wilson ordered that the Joint Board's recommendation be suspended and that the board not meet again until it had his permission to do so—permission he withheld until 16 October 1915, when in the light of the European war Daniels suggested that its advice be sought.[5]

Like Wilson and Bryan, Daniels would defend the Panama Canal. He feared especially the establishment of German U-boat bases in the Caribbean. In 1915 he used the Navy and the Marines to restore order from anarchy in Haiti and San Domingo by occupying them. He insisted, however, that the Navy was merely an agency for carrying out policy made by the Department of State and hoped that when the European war ended the Americans would be withdrawn. In 1917 he supported the purchase of the Danish West Indies (now the Virgin Islands) as a site for an American naval base.[6] Thus, by 1915 he had smoothly made the transition with Wilson and Bryan to an interventionist policy based upon the requirements of national security. The best example of this transition, the intervention in Mexico, is discussed below.

Daniels's political progressivism and fundamentalist morality displeased admirals and businessmen, both eminently conservative. He perennially underscored the supremacy of civil over military authority and denied that everything admirals told him was gospel.[7] In consequence, he made administrative changes that irked many officers. He inspected all shore installations, every type of ship, and he flew in aircraft. He wrenched naval tradition by directing that all officers, staff as well as line, use line titles. Moreover, he strictly enforced his policy of 24 March 1913 that no officer be promoted unless he had performed the sea duty required of his rank. The most publicized case was that of Captain Templin Morris Potts, Aide for Personnel, who had spent almost nine years in the grades of commander and captain but had served at sea for only ten months. When Fiske expostulated vehemently with him, Daniels said flatly that since Potts was not ready to command a division of battleships he would not promote him.[8] Moreover, he directed that attendance at the Naval War College be a factor taken into consideration by promotion boards and enjoined all shipboard officers to take the War College courses by correspondence. He also sought congressional approval for promotion based upon merit rather than making room for younger men by "selecting out" senior men.[9] In addition he directed that since the education of Naval Academy graduates was paid by the taxpayers, they could no longer resign at will. As for racial discrimination in the Navy, he said there was none. All Negroes were messmen![10] Anathema to the officers, of course, was his invitation to all in the Navy to write directly to him. Most of the many letters written to him complained about conditions in the service or alleged mistreatment by officers. Daniels had each complaint investigated and often found a solution to the problem.

Daniels concentrated upon improving the lot of the enlisted man. He obtained permission from the Postmaster General to issue money orders aboard ship so that men could send some of their money home, reduced the cost of clothing, increased the variety of goods sold at ships' stores, and authorized married men aboard ship at naval stations and yards to visit their families at night and on Sundays. When some men complained that they were never assigned to sea duty, he directed the startled commander in chief of the Atlantic Fleet to take his battleships on a Mediterranean cruise during the winter of 1913–1914.

Daniels also avidly sought to repair two evils—excessive spare time and meager basic education—among the men by establishing an Academic Department in every ship and at every station. He wanted to "make the Navy a great university, with college extensions afloat and ashore."[11] Effective 1 January 1914, both academic and practical instruction would be given on off-duty time; during the first two years of a man's enlistment, attendance would be mandatory and on a voluntary basis thereafter. Officers meantime would go on from the Academy to postgraduate work in various universities and finally to the Naval War College, "the apex of the Navy system of education."[12] Since he was letting the aide system lapse, he was inconsistent in adding to his staff an Aide for Education. Despite much criticism of the school idea, especially by Fiske, it was eventually adopted by the Marines and also by the Army. By mid-1915, Daniels noted that 60 percent, or about 25,000 of his men, were using their spare time by being instructed.[13]

Visits to the Naval Academy convinced Daniels that it did well in technical subjects and naval leadership but was deficient in the humanities. To stimulate midshipmen to study liberal arts, he violated tradition by hiring a university professor to become the first civilian head of the English Department. Meanwhile he substituted the presidents of technical schools and of liberal arts colleges for Academy alumni on the Board of Visitors and directed that hazing at the Academy cease. For the last step particularly he earned the ill will of the officers, who refused to acknowledge hazing as a criminal action, and of congressmen whose appointees were discharged for hazing.[14]

At the suggestion of Fiske, Daniels visited the Naval War College in June 1913 and found few officers in attendance. When its president said that the Bureau of Navigation would not send officers to the college because they were needed at sea, Daniels retorted that too many officers were at desk jobs. He thereupon directed that two classes of twenty students each be sent to the college and that no senior officer be promoted until he had taken the War College course. In consequence, the college so grew in favor that he evaluated the new outlook as "one of the best contributions I made to Naval efficiency in the first year of my incumbency. . . ." By the end of 1914, seventy officers were in residence and over four hundred officers were taking its courses by correspondence.[15]

Having rectified what he considered to be faults in the educational systems for both officers and men, Daniels set out to cure "the most serious defect in the Navy . . . the lack of democracy." To get rid of "snobbery" he won congressional authorization for one hundred seamen with one year's service in the fleet to compete for admission to the Naval Academy. He directed that the four years spent by the midshipmen at the Academy would count neither for promotion nor retirement. He invited enlisted men and junior officers to the same dinner to mingle with him and the leading admirals. Perhaps the best explanation of his attitude was that he was a congenital democrat who dearly loved his four sons and thought of the younger enlisted men as an enlargement of his family. To most officers, however, he stood charged with "coddling" the men.[16]

Liquor was prohibited to enlisted men in 1899. By a General Order effective 1 July 1914, Daniels wiped out the officers' wine mess also. This order provoked more prolonged and hysterical criticism than that which greeted his other efforts to democratize the Navy, in part because he released it before telling his officers. His major reason for the order was to make the Navy more efficient afloat, the "moving cause" his feeling that officers should have no perquisites denied the "boys" in the Navy. While various irate officers, like Fiske, and many newspaper editorials lampooned his use of military discipline as a cloak for sumptuary despotism, Protestant church circles supported him, and a poll of the press revealed that eighty editors favored the order, forty-four were neutral, and only forty-eight opposed it.[17]

When Daniels assumed office, he faced such constant problems as short-handed ships' crews, slow officer promotion, and variations in retirement pay. Moreover, he foresaw that by 1923 the number of officers provided for by law would be insufficient to man the growing number of fighting ships, let alone the auxiliaries. Because the House Naval Affairs Committee intended to hold hearings on the personnel problem, he made no recommendation on this subject in 1913 beyond asking for 11,500 men for ships being built, whereas the General Board wanted an increase from 51,000 to 101,000. So serious did the problem become late in 1914, however, that he appointed a board to recommend remedial legislation. On 16 February 1914, meanwhile, Congress established a Naval Militia that could be federalized in time of war, and on 3 March 1915 heeded his recommendation and created a Naval Reserve. The same act repealed that part of the personnel act of 3 March 1899 that provided for the enforced retirement of a number of officers annually, but left the promotion problem unsolved. In consequence, a number of officers applied for voluntary retirement. Nevertheless, delays pushed the needed legislation away until mid-1916.[18]

While Daniels refused to increase the number of flag officers, he wanted at least two vice admirals and one admiral, because his officers in foreign waters usually were outranked. Early in 1915 Congress granted the first and second officers in command of a fleet the temporary titles and pay of admiral and vice admiral, respectively. Daniels made the commander in chief of the Atlantic, Asiatic, and Pacific fleets admirals, and gave the rank of vice admiral to the second in command of the Atlantic Fleet but did not believe that, at the time, either the Pacific or Asiatic fleets rated vice admirals.[19] American fleet commanders then had ranks commensurate with those of foreign navies.

While he did not object to retirement pay for officers who had served long years, Daniels did object to the expense of paying three-fourths retirement to younger men who left the service because of impediments that impaired their usefulness to the Navy but did not preclude their engaging in a civilian career. His solution was to distinguish between total and partial disability, and in the latter case to pay retirement based upon grade and number of years in the service.[20]

A subject close to Daniels's heart was the provision of more chaplains for the Navy, which in 1913, with almost 65,000 officers and men, had the same number, 24, that it had had in 1842, when the Navy consisted of 13,500 officers and men. Congress gave him nine additional chaplains so that he could provide one for every large ship and major shore station. Meanwhile he energetically supported the work of the Y.M.C.A. in the Navy.[21]

Daniels attributed a drop in the desertion rate for 1913 to his provision for education, such "proper diversion" as travel abroad, and his creating new avenues for recognition and promotion. He would reform rather than punish deserters. By having deserters sent to disciplinary barracks administered as schools of correction, rather than to prisons, most of them were easily reformed and restored to their ships. In 1913, 72 percent of the inmates "made good," and 85 percent of them in 1914. On the other hand, Daniels did not want the Navy considered a reform school, and he detached those who enlisted to escape prosecution for crime. Furthermore, he opposed judges who "punished" young civilian offenders by having them enlist in the Navy. The combination of purchase of discharge and "detention" rather than imprisonment worked a vast change which enabled the Navy to get rid of chronic offenders, and to reduce the number of prisoners and detainees from 1,835 on 1 April 1914 to 740 on 13 October 1915.[22]

During the administration of Theodore Roosevelt the United States advanced from third to second place as a naval power. Under President William Howard Taft the Navy dropped back to third place. "Get busy, 'Josie,'" a southerner wrote Daniels, "14-inch guns beat bibles in some cases."[23] In his first statement to the press, in March 1913, Daniels advocated a two-battleship-a-year program and other ships that would move the Navy forward to a "navy second to none."[24]

Daniels established a unique record, in that Congress approved every recommendation he made except for completing a large building program after the armistice in 1918. He explained his requests and obtained the advice of the chairman and ranking minority member of each naval committee. Fortunately for him, the chairmen were not only wise counselors but soon became his warm personal friends. If he found Lemuel P. Padgett, of Tennessee, Chairman of the House Naval Affairs Committee, a man of excellent judgment, in Benjamin R. Tillman of South Carolina, the paralytic Chairman of the Senate Naval Affairs Committee, he found a truly kindred spirit. Daniels established similar happy relations after Tillman's death in 1918 with Claude A. Swanson of Virginia, who was known to be a "big Navy" man.

The General Board told Daniels that since 1903 it had recommended the building of forthy-eight battleships by 1920 and the building of sufficient lesser ships and auxiliaries to provide a balanced fleet. Enjoying parity with the major foreign powers, that fleet should be able to support the nation's interests in times of peace and defend it against any enemy. Moreover, the board suggested the creation of a Council of National Defense. Since 1911 Representative Richmond P. Hobson of Alabama, who served on the House Naval Affairs Committee, sponsored legislation calling for such a body. Because of Germany's naval buildup, he advocated the building of three battleships in 1913, and legislation calling for reorganization of the Navy Department and of naval personnel.[25]

Daniels was the first naval secretary to make public the recommendations of the board, but spoke of finding the "golden mean" between what the Navy needed and what the nation could afford. The board, he said, spoke from a professional viewpoint; the administration had to consider national policy as a whole and national revenues. For fiscal year 1914 he favored only two dreadnoughts, eight destroyers, and three submarines, or about half of what the board recommended. Although the board pointed out that the new battleships it wanted would merely replace four built in the 1890s, Daniels adhered to his smaller number because the six battleships and lesser ships under construction would, by 1917, give the United States a "creditable and capable fleet" in both the Atlantic and Pacific oceans. Neither the advocates of more nor of less construction would be pleased, but his was the "middle course of wisdom"; his program was all that the country could afford.[26]

Busy with tariff and currency legislation, Wilson and Congress did not deal with the military and naval estimates until very late in 1913. The House Naval Affairs Committee on 2 December reported out only a bill on the naval militia and requested Daniels to furnish a separate personnel bill. Daniels did so, and in addition testified on appropriations for six days in late January and early February 1914. But the House and Senate version of the bill did not go into conference until 2 June, agreement was not reached until the thirteenth, and Wilson did not sign it until the thirtieth.

To Daniels's pleasure, the second session of the Sixty-third Congress gave him more than he asked when it authorized the sale of the outdated battleships *Idaho* and *Mississippi*, their replacement by two new dreadnoughts, and the building of a third. With the completion of these new ships, the *California*, *Idaho*, and *Mississippi*, he believed that the nation would have a balanced Navy equal, if not superior, to any in the world. However, enlistments were already at the limit Congress authorized.

For fiscal year 1915 Daniels again reduced the number of new capital ships recommended by the General Board and won the agreement of the chairmen of both naval committees to a two-battleship program, all that the nation "could afford." In conference with him on 1 October 1914, the board restated its recommendation for four battleships and four destroyers for every battleship, but he favored more and better submarines. "The department feels that it is upon sage ground," he countered, "in looking to the Board to prescribe the character of the ships to be constructed," thereby indicating that he would decide how many of what types to recommend to Congress—and he asked Congress to provide for additional fleet submarines without reducing appropriations for other ships.[27]

Padgett began work on new personnel legislation on 9 June 1914. Although Daniels sent sixty-three men to testify before his committee in August, nothing was accomplished before the naval appropriations bill of 13 January 1915—

the first influenced by the outbreak of the Great War—was reported in the House. So short was the time before the Congress would end, on 4 March, however, that Padgett let the matter go over.

The appropriations bill reported on 13 January covered a multitude of subjects. In light of the European war its building program was indeed small, but few people worried about how the war could affect the Navy. The bill called for two battleships, six destroyers, seventeen submarines (one of which would be seagoing), and three auxiliaries. Other provisions authorized: the ranks of admiral and vice admiral, as noted above; additional officers for the Marine Corps; the abolishment of the Plucking Board, as Daniels desired; the creation of an office of chief of naval operations, which Daniels did not want; a naval aviation reserve; the granting of medals to Navy and Marine Corps officers who distinguished themselves in battle; engineering duty only; $1 million for naval aviation; doubling the annual $125,000 for the Naval Militia; and the establishment of a naval reserve.

In the general debate which began on the twenty-ninth, "little navy" forces led by Majority Leader Oscar W. Underwood, of Alabama, tried to cut out one battleship, five submarines, and two auxiliaries, lest there be a deficit of $35 million in the Treasury the next year. Daniels's remonstrance and the work of Hobson saved the building program, except for minor changes. However, on a point of order the House struck out all the personnel provisions of the bill except those dealing with the Plucking Board, the creation of the office of the chief of naval operations and of a naval reserve, the additional admirals and vice admirals, and reduced naval aviation to $500,000. Daniels had to try to get the Senate to add those items he desired, such as a naval reserve, and to keep out such objectionable items as an office of chief of naval operations. In part because of pressure he exerted on Tillman, the Senate Naval Affairs Committee on 22 February recommended a total of $153 million for a program consisting of two battleships, six or more destroyers, five seagoing coastal submarines, one gunboat, and two auxiliaries. In addition it provided for an armor-plate plant, urged the end of the Frederick W. Taylor "efficiency" system, upped the naval aviation appropriation to $1 million, demanded an advisory committee for aeronautics, and restored the authority for both an office of chief of naval operations and a naval reserve.[28] Since the provisions finally enacted into law on 3 March gave him almost everything he asked for, Daniels made a mark rarely achieved by any of his predecessors. With respect to the office of the chief of naval operations, however, he got more than he wanted, as will be seen below.

Whereas in 1913 Germany had only three navy yards and Great Britain, six, the United States, with eleven, had less dry-dock capacity than did the single largest British yard. It was apparent that politics was winning its battle with military efficiency and that Congress was operating on the incorrect theory that the fleet existed for the yards rather than the yards for the fleet. Knowing that reform of the navy yards was blocked by congressional log-rolling, Daniels tackled the problem on the basis of national rather than sectional need. In mid-March 1913 he began an inspection tour of installations in the South. As a result of his tour, Daniels wisely decided to retain several of those Meyer had closed. Pensacola, for example, became a training station for naval aviation. His later visit to installations on the West Coast, provoked by changes expected there because of the opening of the Panama Canal, resulted in plans for expansion at Bremerton, San Francisco, Los Angeles (Long Beach–San Pedro), and San Diego. As a result of his subsequent visit to installations in the East, Daniels decided not to scrap the yard at Portsmouth, New Hampshire, as Meyer had recommended, but to authorize the building of submarines there. He also authorized the building of small craft at other yards, and the enlargement of the Philadelphia and Brooklyn yards so that they could build battleships. In this way the yards would be busy the year round, the Navy would be able to build its ships cheaper than it could by private contract, and he would be relieved of some of the constant pressure of congressmen, governors, mayors, and others, who wanted work for men in their states and cities.[29]

Daniels's visits permitted him to learn about yard management and workers' complaints. Most pleasing to the workers was his abolishment of the time-motion studies known as the Taylor system. Although he was friendly with Samuel Gompers, President of the American Federation of Labor, and with the labor reform movement in general, Daniels refused to permit civilians to serve on local navy yard wage boards. The boards could collect facts and statistics, but he would establish wage rates. In addition he decided to separate the military and industrial functions of the yards. Despite the objection of the officers, who wished to retain full control over work at the yards, he directed that those in charge of military matters would report through the Aide for Operations, while the naval constructors in charge of industrial production would report directly to him.[30] To insure an evenness of the work load and of employment, he assigned ships to designated home yards and sought some building for all of them, with new construction to be undertaken when repair work slowed down. What he failed to mention in his annual report for 1913 was that there was so much new construction in some yards, as at New York and Mare Island, that no more work could be done unless their facilities were expanded.[31] At any rate, Daniels enforced recommendations that reduced overhead costs for new construction by 30 percent and promised a sound cost-accounting system. Moreover, he approved the proposal made by the Bureau of Ordnance that cash rewards be given those who suggested money-saving improvements.

The Navy Daniels inherited was woefully short of dry docks. With the authorizing of larger dreadnoughts in 1914 and 1915, he requested dry docks to hold these behemoths. Of particular interest was the situation at Pearl Harbor, Hawaii. On 17 February 1913, the huge cofferdam structure of a new graving dock over one thousand feet long was wrecked by underground pressures. Daniels reported the accident to Congress. In 1914 he spent more time and effort on reaching agreement with the contractor on rebuilding the dock than upon any other single subject. Work finally resumed on the dock in November 1914. A radically different type of construction was used, but the completion day was postponed to June 1918.[32]

Daniels was barely sworn in when the Senate requested information from him on the cost of armor plate, and a House bill called upon all armament makers to submit competitive bids. Daniels suspected collusion among bidders on armor plate contracts. Since only Congress had the power to obtain cost data from the manufacturers, he noted in a preliminary report that the few manufacturers could easily monopolize and that since Theodore Roosevelt's day the government had placed equal orders with the Bethelehem, Carnegie, and Midvale companies "at practically their own prices." He recommended that the government build near the Atlantic seaboard a plant capable of producing half of the Navy's needs, enough to cause private firms to become competitive. If the companies did not lower their prices, he would build a second plant, on the West Coast.[33]

In 1913 Daniels rejected first bids from the three big steel companies and got a reduction of $111,875 on the plate needed for the battleship *Arizona*. In keeping with a provision of the Naval Act of 1914 that no appropriations be spent for anything the Navy could produce for itself, in 1914 he rejected first bids for three dreadnoughts and accepted the second at a saving of $738,648. By some "mental telepathy," the companies then came up with very close bids for battleships Nos. 43 and 44. If Congress refused to authorize the building of a government plant, it at least authorized a committee to investigate the cost of building plants capable of producing 10,000 tons and 20,000 tons annually. Tillman, Padgett, and Rear Admiral Joseph Strauss, Chief of the Bureau of Ordnance, began their investigation when the war in Europe made foreign costs on armor plate unobtainable.[34] The public plant idea won some support in Congress when the price of plate rose to more than $512 a ton. Padgett, Tillman, and Strauss concluded that a 10,000-ton plant could produce armor at $262.79 a ton and a 20,000-ton plant at $230.11. After a conference committee deleted from the naval appropriations bill of 1915 the Senate's provision calling for the building of an armor plant, Daniels renewed the attack. Tillman introduced the necessary bill, got a favorable committee report on it, and obtained President Wilson's pledge of support. After a week of debate, the Senate by a vote of 58 to 23 approved a public plant on 21 March 1916, and the House agreed by a vote of 236 to 135 on 2 June. Wilson signed the conference report on 18 August, and Daniels, having chosen Charleston, West Virginia, as the site, broke ground there on the thirtieth. Paradoxically, because of the great emergencies of the war, the plan never produced armor before he left office, and was abandoned by the Republicans when they returned to power in 1921[35]

With oil fast replacing coal as the principal fuel used by the Navy, Daniels sought to insure its acquisition from private suppliers at reasonable rates (prices had doubled between 1911 and 1913, and by 1914 consumption was 500 percent greater than it had been in 1911) by having the Navy refine oil from its own wells. However, he was unable to develop the two naval petroleum reserves set aside in California by President Taft in 1912. In the first place, he lacked funds and, in the second, several bills that passed the House of Representatives, but not the Senate, permitted private operators on the reserved lands to take out oil or, under a general leasing arrangement, deposit monies obtained from these lands in a Treasury account for use only by the Navy. Meanwhile, private owners with working wells on land owned by the Southern Pacific Railroad near the naval reserves were pumping out all the oil they could. Tillman suggested that representatives of the Navy, Interior, and Justice departments reach agreement on how to protect the naval reserves, and Daniels told Padgett that a law should be passed to this end. More adamantly in 1914 and 1915 he demanded that the Navy should own its oil land and produce, transport, refine, and store its own oil. After a conference between Daniels, the Attorney General, and the Secretary of the Interior, the legal jungle that strangled the Navy's claims in Reserve No. 1 and Reserve No. 2 was straightened out, and on 30 April 1915 Wilson by executive order created Naval Petroleum Reserve No. 3, at Teapot Dome, Wyoming. When Secretary of the Interior Franklin K. Lane, a Californian, in 1916 announced his intention to validate certain private claims in Reserve No. 2, Daniels blocked legislation that provided relief for the California operators until 1920, when he approved a Mineral Leasing Act that was generous to the states in which the mineral lands were located. Thus for eight years he held the line in protecting the naval petroleum reserves. With his restraining hand removed, the oil reserves provided meat for one of the worst of the many scandals of the following Harding administration.[36]

In 1913, when the United States ranked fourteenth in the world on the basis of its aviation expenditures, the Navy Aviation Corps consisted of fourteen aviators and four flying boats. Daniels got Ensign Richard E. Byrd to work under Captain Washington I. Chambers. Chambers had invented a catapult, and Daniels favored his plan to set up a national aerodynamic laboratory. At Fiske's suggestion, Daniels assigned Captain Mark L. Bristol to duty under Fiske and charged him with developing the art of aerial warfare. Also, he approved the use of Pensacola as a Naval Aeronautical Station, really a combined experiment center and flight school. Subsequently in the old battleship *Mississippi*, qualified naval aviators and representatives of the leading aircraft manufacturers sought to learn how aircraft could work with a fleet at sea. Meanwhile Daniels sent an officer to learn about Europe's aircraft programs and tried to coordinate the activities of the Langley Aerodynamic Laboratory and other public and private agencies. For his own office he asked for an additional clerk who would help to handle the paper work for a naval air arm envisioned to include 50 airplanes, 2 dirigibles, 75 officers, and 250 men.[37]

The scouting and spotting performed by the flying boats carried to Veracruz by the *Mississippi* and by the cruiser *Birmingham* in April 1914 deepened Daniels's belief in the worth of aircraft. He ordered some European craft in order to learn their secrets of design, construction, and equipment, but the Great War intervened and no deliveries were made. With the outbreak of the war, he strenuously supported the recommendation of the General Board for an immediate appropriation of $5 million. The first appropriation of $1 million, specifically for naval aeronautics, had been granted by the Sixty-third Congress. Despite Fiske, despite the General Board, and despite the war, in 1914 Daniels asked for only $2 million and settled for half of that in 1915 because he would not have it appear that he was preparing for war.[38]

Throughout 1913 fleet operations were routine, except that from February on, three or four battleships were stationed off the East Coast and a number of armored cruisers off the West Coast of Mexico. This is not the place to go into detail about the operations at Veracruz, but Daniels's connection with them should be related briefly.

Daniels had great confidence in Rear Admiral Frank F. Fletcher's ability to handle the admittedly "delicate . . . Mexico situation" that arose when men from the *Dolphin's* boat were arrested for taking on supplies where landings had been prohibited, and Admiral Henry T. Mayo demanded a formal apology and a 21-gun salute to the American flag from Mexican President Victoriano Huerta.[39] Huerta had no intention of apologizing and demanded that Mayo respond to a Mexican salute gun for gun. Daniels gave Mayo permission to do so, but other incidents so infuriated Wilson that on 21 April 1914 he decided to seize Veracruz and Tampico by force in order to prevent arms from reaching Huerta by sea.

To prevent the German ship *Ypiranga* from landing arms and ammunition, Daniels advised the taking of the customs house at Veracruz. Wilson and Bryan agreed, and Fletcher landed sailors and Marines to seize the customs house and thus prevent the *Ypiranga's* cargo from reaching Huerta. Mexican fire resulted in nineteen Americans being killed and seventy-one wounded by the time the city was quieted on the twenty-third. Mexico suffered 126 killed and 195 wounded. Fletcher then decided that the American army should occupy the city of Veracruz.

Although Wilson's acceptance on 25 April of an offer of mediation by Argentina, Brazil, and Chile soothed Mexico somewhat, Daniels told Fletcher to keep his three thousand men ashore until they were relieved by General Frederick Funston's troops, who were being shipped out of Galveston. At 1500, 30 April, the formal change of command occurred.

As Fletcher relieved Admiral Charles J. Badger as Commander in Chief, Atlantic Fleet, in July, Huerta, bankrupted by the American hold on the customs house at Veracruz, sought exile. Then the outbreak of war in Europe caused all European and Japanese naval ships in Mexican waters to head for home, and on 8 September Wilson decided that American ships should return also. On 25 November, after a Mexican and an American ship had saluted each other gun for gun, signalizing the restoration of amicable relations, the American troops began leaving Veracruz.[40]

Until his resignation in mid-1915, Fiske was the stormiest petrel of Daniels's administration. A member of the Academy class of 1874, and one of the most talented inventors of his day, he had seen action in the Battle of Manila Bay, had commanded various ships old and new, had had charge of the war plans section of the General Board, had written numerous articles for the United States Naval Institute *Proceedings*, and for several years had been president of the Institute. Perhaps bluntly, he told Daniels that he was the only one of ninety million Americans who, because of his position as his chief adviser, could give Daniels the military counsel he needed, and he persistently badgered him to accept his ideas on naval organization, personnel, war plans, and fleet operations.

As things then stood, there was a secretary of the navy and his assistant, Daniels and Franklin D. Roosevelt; a Council of Aides Daniels rarely consulted; a General Board with merely planning and advisory functions; and a Joint Army and Navy Board that Wilson in 1913 had prohibited from meeting. Interservice differences could be resolved only by the President. Separately funded by Congress, the bureaus went their own ways and were very slow in reaching agreements that affected two or more of them. The somewhat vain and militaristic Fiske not only favored a general staff but counseled Daniels

537

to adopt an administrative plan whereby the department could get the bureaus to take steps to prepare for war and also to support a council of national defense.[41] On 24 January 1914, Fiske and the other aides suggested to Daniels that their status receive legislative sanction. Daniels demurred, saying "Absolute control of the Navy by a military head or by a general staff composed solely of naval officers is contrary to the spirit of our institutions."[42]

Important differences between Daniels and Fiske continued. On 19 March 1914, Fiske tried to argue Daniels into approving an administrative plan whereby the bureaus could prepare for war. Daniels refused to do so. Nor would Daniels agree to recall all battleships, except those needed in Caribbean and Mexican waters, to home yards to be docked and readied for war. Relations worsened precipitately, for Fiske decided to use his own staff to develop "a real & practical War Plan, by which we can mobilize if war comes & then handle our forces," and, going over Daniels's head, to seek instead to impress Congress with his views. He wrote out his preparedness plan, gave it to Daniels to read, and then, without telling Daniels, placed it in the official files—a process that was to lead to recrimination by Daniels later on.[43]

On 20 October the Chief of the Bureau of Navigation told Daniels that by cutting down the crews of certain ships and stations there would be more men than required, whereas the General Board and Fiske estimated that 19,600 additional men would be needed to man the ships necessary in wartime. On 14 November, in a "very free and frank talk" with Daniels, Fiske agreed to withdraw the General Board's letter and to suggest that the board omit any mention of the need for more men, because Daniels adamantly opposed an increase. At this point, Fiske believed that he was "liable to be bounced any day."[44]

Fiske was also "exceedingly disturbed" by the "too rosy" character of testimony given by Badger, Fletcher, other officers, and Daniels at hearings held in mid-December before the House Naval Affairs Committee. Knowing that Daniels did not want him to testify, he arranged for Congressman Hobson to have him appear. When he did so, on the seventeenth, he startled the committee by stating that it would take the Navy five years to get ready for war, whereas it should be prepared for war immediately; that a general staff was needed; that the Navy could not be expanded quickly without its efficiency being decreased; and that an intensive aircraft program should be developed. On the next day Daniels sent for Fiske but instead of ordering him, as he had feared, to some place like Olongapo in the Philippines, discussed some other subject and merely asked for a copy of his testimony.[45] Then Fiske and six other officers met secretly with Hobson and prepared legislation calling for a chief of naval operations who would have fifteen assistants. When Hobson, on 4 January 1915, confronted Daniels with the bill, the Secretary said that if it were enacted he would "go home." On the other hand, a subcommittee chaired by Congressman Padgett unanimously approved the measure, and on 6 January it also received the unanimous approval of the full House Naval Affairs Committee and was incorporated into the naval appropriations bill for fiscal year 1915.[46] However, it was stricken out on a point of order. When it was restored to the bill by the Senate Naval Affairs Committee, Daniels had a chance both to modify the powers granted to the office and to delete the fifteen assistants. As amended, the bill passed both houses. Comparison is invited to the wording of the Hobson and Daniels versions. The House Report on the Hobson bill stated that the chief of naval operations, "under the Secretary of the Navy, is to be held responsible for the readiness of the Navy for war and in charge of its general direction." Because he believed that empowering the chief of naval operations with the "general direction" of the Navy would make a secretary unnecessary, the version that Daniels presented to the Senate read that a chief of naval operations would "under the direction of the Secretary of the Navy, be charged with the operations of the fleet and with the preparation and readiness of plans for its use in war."[47]

On 24 and 26 March Fiske was again before the House Naval Affairs Committee, this time arguing for the provision of fifteen assistants to help the chief of naval operations make war plans. He succeeded in convincing the committee, and thus was fashioned the organization that directed the Navy throughout the war and for which Daniels eventually took credit. However, after Fiske's testimony of December 1914 it became clear that Daniels had no further use for him. Fiske nevertheless drove ahead. U-boat warfare stimulated him to make plans whereby the Navy could be used both offensively and defensively, and the General Board supported his conclusion that both active and reserve ships should be ready in fourteen days following a declaration of war.[48]

By law, because of age, Fiske was to retire in June, but the date of decision for his resignation was 1 April. He pointed out to Daniels that he had served his faithfully for two years and that whenever Daniels had followed his advice he had been proved right. Daniels asked when his resignation would take effect. Fiske said as soon as it would be convenient to Daniels. Daniels said he would arrange it and the very next day confirmed the resignation in writing, but without giving any reasons, and asked him to stay on for the present. Then, on 28 April, he informed Fiske that he had chosen Captain William Shepherd Benson to be the chief of naval operations. While Benson was a good seaman, he had never shown the slightest interest in strategy, or been a member of the General Board, or taken the full course at the Naval War College. Hence, in Fiske's mind, he himself or any one of various other senior officers would have been a better selection.[49] At any rate, Fiske made way for Benson at 1100 on 11 May, and in January 1916 the Senate approved a four year term for him.

As long as Fiske was about, Daniels had run the department largely on the advice of two favorites, Victor Blue, Chief of the Bureau of Navigation, and Albert Gustavus Winterhalter, Aide for Material. With his abandonment of the aide system, he turned not to Benson but relied upon weekly meetings of an Advisory Council composed of the secretary, the assistant secretary, the chief of naval operations, the seven bureau chiefs, the judge advocate general, and the major general commandant of the Marine Corps. Rather than supporting Benson, moreover, he identified with him and used him to counter the organization of a general staff. The "bilinear" organization that existed seemed to place Daniels in an enviable position: since the chief of naval operations, representing the military part of the Navy, reported directly to him, as did the civilian part of the Navy, i.e., the material bureaus, he alone could resolve differences between them. As long as the bureaus were separately funded and could not be "ordered" by the chief of naval operations, however, no one could exercise management control over them.

By concentrating on social and moral matters during his first two years in office, Daniels consumed time and effort he might have given to the material and personnel readiness of the fleet and to the preparation of war plans. Hence to advocates of a strong Navy he appeared moralistic, pedantic, and provincial.[50] That he was flexible, however, he revealed by overcoming his pacifistic nature and counseling the use of force against Mexico and by violating his anti-imperialistic beliefs to the extent of intervening in Haiti and San Domingo. Moreover, by 1917 many people considered him the nation's greatest advocate of a large navy.

Once war broke out in Europe, Daniels moved too slowly to suit either Fiske or Assistant Secretary of the Navy Roosevelt, who saw him as so bewildered that he could not grasp the situation. "I am *running* the real work," Roosevelt wrote to his wife "Babs" [Eleanor] on 2 August 1914.[51]

At the cabinet meeting of 4 August it was decided that a neutrality proclamation should be issued and that Daniels should help Americans stranded abroad and transport them home. On 5 August Wilson directed Daniels to censor radio communications to the end that only neutral messages would be transmitted. He also enforced neutrality by barring publication of statements, interviews, and articles by naval officers that were considered to be "prejudicial to the best interests of the service" and even of the singing by naval personnel of the British martial air, "Tipperary."[52]

Anxious to improve the sea-carrying capacity of the United States, Daniels suggested that the Navy be authorized to convert various cruisers for passenger, mail, and freight service to South America and Europe, that the United States acquire ships of German and Austrian registry interned in American ports, and that the United States undertake a shipbuilding program. Congress opposed the first suggestion and the Allies opposed the second; it was not until September 1916 that a huge appropriation was passed to create a United States Shipping Board that would operate ships built by an Emergency Fleet Corporation.[53]

On 18 February 1915, Germany began unrestricted submarine warfare in the waters around Great Britain. On 28 March, an American traveling in an unarmed British passenger liner died as a result of U–boat action. The U–boat problem was exacerbated by the torpedoing of the American tanker *Gulflight* and of the British liner *Lusitania*, in which 124 Americans lost their lives. Daniels and every member of the cabinet, except Secretary of State Bryan, supported Wilson in sending to Germany a protest that Wilson himself wrote, for they did not think that it would lead to war. When that protest, which became known as the "*Lusitania* note," was published on 14 May, Bryan decided that he must resign. Daniels told Bryan he was making the greatest mistake of his life and urged him to stay on. Bryan replied that he did not wish to embarrass Wilson and that Daniels must remain in the cabinet to help Wilson rather than resign also. At any rate, Bryan did resign, thereby leaving Wilson to determine policy with such pro-Allied friends as Colonel Edward M. House. Moreover, Bryan had been the focus of all those who opposed Wilson. With him gone, critics of Wilson's policy, presumably because they were idealists and humanitarians and had pacifistic leanings, loosed their ire instead upon Daniels and, after he became secretary of war, upon Newton D. Baker. Throughout 1915, Wilson loyally defended Daniels from what he termed "the partisan, puerile, and most grossly unjust attacks."[54]

In his annual message for 1914, Wilson described those who demanded increased armaments as "nervous and excited." He preferred to rely upon "a citizenry trained and accustomed to arms," rather than upon a standing army, and upon a "powerful navy" for purposes of defense.[55] He kept the Army and Navy estimates for 1915 close to those of 1914, and Daniels obliged in part by cutting to twenty the forty-eight new ships recommended by the General Board. In the long run, however, various provisions of the naval act approved 3 March 1915, such as those creating the office of naval operations and a naval reserve, were more important than the few ships authorized.

Another step toward preparedness was the establishment of the Naval Civilian Consulting Board, usually called the Naval Consulting Board. Headed by Thomas A. Edison, the board dealt particularly with problems of steam engineering, ordnance, and construction. By the end of the war, the board considered more than 110,000 ideas, inventions, and devices, held upwards of 4,200 interviews, and studied more than 700 models. Daniels told Edison he could have anything except the job of secretary of the Navy if he could discover, as Edison said, how to "put an end to Fritz." Edison among other things devised an underwater listening apparatus, a preservative for submarine deck guns, and a chemical extinguisher for coal and paint fires; he also greatly improved the ability of ships to turn sharply, and provided loud-speaking telephones for shipboard use.[56] Daniels also had the board make an inventory of the country's industrial facilities for preparedness. With that inventory in hand, the government knew not only what companies could be counted upon to produce the materials needed for war purposes but where to place orders that would insure a sufficient stockpile of munitions.[57]

In the appropriations bill for the Army for fiscal year 1917, passed on 29 August 1916, Congress authorized a Council of National Defense "for the coordination of industry and resources for the national security and welfare." Wilson appointed Baker, Daniels, and four of the other eight men in the cabinet members of the council, which, Daniels saw, could take over and carry forward some of the work already begun by the Naval Consulting Board. A most important agency created by the council was the General Munitions Board, whose mission was to coordinate procurement by the armed services. Known as the War Industries Board in 1917, it was not until the Overman Act approved 20 May 1918 that Congress authorized it to activate the powers of the War and Navy departments to requisition and withhold materials. In the meantime, the Baker-Gompers antistrike agreement of June 1917 had been extended to the Navy on 10 August.[58]

By the middle of 1915, Wilson had approved increased defenses only to the extent of permitting summer camps for college students who desired to become army reserve officers. On 21 July, however, he directed Daniels and Secretary of War Garrison to draft an "adequate national defense program" for presentation to Congress in November.[59] Daniels had already called upon the General Board to formulate specific plans that would enable the Navy to defend the national interest. Under the heading "Policy," the Board's report of 30 July asserted: "The Navy of the United States should immediately be equal to the most powerful maintained by any other nation. . . . It should be gradually increased . . . year by year, as may be permitted by the facilities of the country, but the limit above defined should be attained no later than 1925." It then called for a six-year building program to cost $1.6 billion that would give the United States parity with Great Britain in 1921. Although Daniels cut the time to five years, he was the first secretary to adopt more than an annual program.[60] Among the ships to be built were ten battleships, 6 battle cruisers, 10 scout cruisers, 50 destroyers, and 15 fleet and 85 coastal submarines. In addition, $6 million was earmarked for naval aviation.[61] Early in October, Wilson talked with Congressman Padgett, Senator Tillman, and Daniels. Agreeing with Wilson that his five-year plan would be too costly to pay for entirely in one year, Daniels suggested an annual program that would cost $100 million for each of five years. Wilson approved on the fifteenth and submitted the plan to Congress.

Wilson then began his campaign to win Congress over to a billion-dollar program that would increase the size of the Army, give the Navy parity with Great Britain's Navy, and strengthen the national guard. Including an expected operating cost of $100 million a year, the total cost of the five-year program would be $1,017,482,214. In addition, Daniels asked for an increase of 20 percent in personnel.[62] It should be stressed, however, that the building program was designed to achieve parity with Britain, not to produce ship types needed for an essentially antisubmarine war.

Wilson's broaching of this plan to Congress on 7 December was followed by huge preparedness parades in various cities and a cascade of favorable letters. But he was warned by some Democrats that his failure to win congressional approval of the plan might lose their party the elections of 1916. The new, Sixty-fourth, Congress failed to act on his plan, and Wilson spent late January and early February 1916 stumping for it from New York to the Middle West. While in St. Louis he said that the United States should have "incomparably the greatest navy in the world." Upon his return he told Daniels that it was the "soundest utterance" he had made, even though it was changed to read "incomparably the most adequate navy in the world" in the official report.[63] Although many Republicans favored a larger navy than that Daniels recommended and wanted it built more quickly than he suggested, many Southern and Western Democrats objected on the grounds that preparedness was being demanded only by shipbuilders, big industrialists, the armor-plate monopoly, and big-Navy imperialists.

In March, Chief of Naval Operations Benson testified before the House Naval Affairs Committee to the need for the sixteen capital ships Daniels recommended and to his fear that the naval program might not place the United States in first rank by 1925, but fourth, although losses suffered by the belligerent navies might improve its posture. For three days in April Daniels testified in support of the administration's program. However, the House Committee on Naval Affairs on 18 May rejected the five-year plan in favor of the normal one-year plan. Nevertheless, a minority report submitted by eight Republican members denounced the majority report on various points and in three days of debate the minority were able at least to increase the appropriations for aircraft and submarines. Then, on 2 June, the measure was sent to the Senate Naval Affairs Committee, which was delayed in its work by the intrusion of the national conventions. On 20 June, Wilson told Tillman and Swanson in Daniels's presence that he favored a larger building program than that provided by the House. Tillman, Swanson, and Henry Cabot Lodge, all of whom agreed with Wilson, thereupon framed the requested bill. Meanwhile a subcommittee composed of these same three senators worked on the personnel problem as outlined to them in a letter in which Daniels suggested increasing the enlisted force from 54,000 to 74,700 and that the President be authorized in an emergency to raise that number to 87,000. On 22 June the subcommittee wrote a bill calling for a five-year building program to include 153 ships, of which 148 would be combatants, with 7 capital (4 battle cruisers and 3 battleships) and 47 other ships to be begun immediately. A week later the committee agreed unanimously upon a program calling for four battleships and four battle cruisers in 1917 and for the completion in *three* years of the $500 million building program urged by Daniels. It made it amply clear that the Navy must be "second to one" by calling for the beginning of work on fifty-six ships within six months of the passage of the act. The effects of the Battle of Jutland are obvious both upon the reduced time span for building and upon demands for both battleships and battle cruisers.

The House version of the bill also gave the chief of naval operations fifteen assistants; authorized a government armor-making plant, a government projectile plant, and a naval experiments laboratory; earmarked $3 million for naval aviation; applied the principle of promotion by selection to the grades of rear admiral and captain; and augmented shipbuilding facilities at the navy yards. Finally, personnel provisions were added by amendment to the appropriations bill. These provisions raised enlisted strength to 68,700, authorized the President to raise the limit to 87,000 in an emergency, and created a complicated Naval Reserve Force.

The Senate took up the bill, 184 pages long, on 13 July, with Lodge expressing the sentiment of the Republican minority in favor of it, and Swanson, acting chairman of the Naval Affairs Committee during the illness of Tillman, demanding that the United States "become and remain without question the world's second naval Power." After only two days of debate, the Senate by voice vote accepted a three-year building program and, with minor changes, the personnel provisions. On the twenty-seventh, Wilson told Padgett that he would be satisfied with nothing less than the Senate's building and personnel provisions. In the end, on 15 August, the House accepted most of the report of the conference committee, and Wilson signed the bill on the twenty-ninth.[64]

Daniels was very happy that the act finally established a naval policy and provided men as well as ships for the future. Warning that both public and private shipbuilders would compete for men and materials, he also stated that in an emergency he would ask Congress for extraordinary powers to place contracts and to obtain the materials needed to build his ships.[65]

With speed essential, Daniels advertised bids for four battleships, four scout cruisers, twenty destroyers, and twenty-nine submarines on the very day that Wilson signed the naval act. On the same day, too, he directed the navy yards at Boston, Philadelphia, and Charleston to start building specified ships. In all cases he caused lessons learned from the war to be incorporated into new construction. The battleships, for example, were to have better protection against underwater torpedo attack than older ones, and were to carry 16-inch, rather than 14-inch, guns. On 25 October he opened bids for the four battleships (eventually the *Colorado, Maryland, Washington,* and *West Virginia*), and on 1 November those for scout cruisers and submarines. Although he awarded the bids on the twenty-ninth, he considered them to be so excessively high and the building time so long—up to four years for battle cruisers—that he asked Congress for $12 million with which to fit navy yards to build battleships.[66]

Although the United States was rich enough to build a navy as large as it wanted, hearings were held late in 1916 to determine whether naval expenditures for fiscal year 1918 could be kept under $400 million. After Daniels and others testified, the amount was set at $379 million, which the House cut to $352 million, with aviation getting $3.5 million rather than $5.1 million. The hearings showed that heroic measures would have to be taken to obtain the 4,487 officers and 97,160 men needed in the three-year program. In consequence, Congress increased the number of men that the Academy could accept from 900 in 1916 to 1,200 in 1917. It was expected that in 1918 the number would be 1,500, and even more thereafter. Temporarily, the course at the Academy was reduced from four to three years, with the class of 1917 scheduled to graduate on 1 February 1917. Congress also increased the enlisted force to 74,700 men, fixed the number of officers in both line and staff to 4 percent of enlisted strength, and authorized an automatic increase in the number of officers in each grade whenever the number of enlisted men increased. Thus the "hump" in the grades would eventually be smoothed out. Since the promotion of senior line officers would be by selection rather than by seniority, Daniels directed that each December a board of nine rear admirals, by a vote of at least six to three, would recommend to him the number of men to fill the vacancies expected during the next year. Pleased but not satisfied, he hoped that Congress would extend the selection system to all the lower grades. Moreover, after 30 June 1920, an age-in-grade limit would be placed upon promotion in the grades from lieutenant commander through captain. If he were not promoted, a captain reaching the age of fifty-six years, a commander reaching fifty, and a lieutenant commander reaching forty-five years would be retired at a rate of two and one-half percent of his pay for each year of service. Finally, the retirement age was raised from sixty-two to sixty-four years (as it already was in the Army and Marine Corps), and retired officers of or above the grade of lieutenant commander recalled to duty would receive the pay of a lieutenant commander rather than of a lieutenant.[67]

By 1916, because of the war, the price of almost everything the navy purchased increased sharply. By speeding the granting of contracts, Daniels saved considerable sums. Furthermore, he used naval colliers to bring back cargoes of raw materials normally purchased abroad, such as tin from Singapore and hemp from Manila, again with considerable savings. An additional saving of $700,000 was made by using naval colliers, rather than merchant ships, to transport coal to distant naval stations in the Pacific. He cut the enlisted men's ration allowance by over $1,000 a day, yet bragged that he had "the best fed navy in the world." Finally, by recovering metallic scrap in the navy yards he saved many thousands of dollars.[68]

Fleet operations in 1916 were fairly routine. War games nevertheless emphasized the need for battle cruisers, swift scouts, and more efficient hydroplanes.

Neither Daniels nor the General Board was happy in 1916 with the naval aviation program. Yet it was hoped that the appropriation of $3.5 million in 1916 would put things on the mend. Still to be resolved was the mission of army and naval aviation, a subject to be studied by a Joint Army and Navy Board. After the report was issued, coastal air stations for patrol and defense were established, and more emphasis was placed on rigid lighter-than-air craft, the value of whose scouting and spotting had been proved in Europe.[69]

While Daniels was busy with his duties, a determined attempt was made to have him removed from the cabinet. There were two reasons for this action: first, political infighting dealing with the reconstitution of the Democratic National Committee; and second, his opposition to the promotion of Cary Grayson of the medical corps, Wilson's personal physician, to the grade of admiral over the heads of numerous senior line officers. Wilson would not hear of removing Daniels. Pointing toward the Army and Navy Club, Wilson said, "Those are the fellows behind the agitation, and their real grievance is the stand Daniels has taken on contracts and graft. He makes foolish speeches but he does his work well. If I were to change him it would be taken as discrediting him."[70]

As a broker of the politically possible, Daniels had arrived at the correct conclusion that he would have to follow the policies of the administration with respect both to the war in Europe and to the size and character of the American Navy, rather than the suggestions either of professional naval officers like Fiske or of his energetic civilian assistant, Roosevelt. As long as the United States remained neutral, he was caught in a cross fire between those who favored and those who opposed preparedness. Most of the steps he took, under

Wilson's guidance, had a defensive rather than an offensive objective. By the time the United States entered the war, on 6 April 1917, though he was much maligned by numerous critics, he had survived the attempt to oust him from office. Only actual operations would provide the answer as to how well he had prepared the Navy for war.

After a U-boat torpedoed the *Sussex* on 24 March 1916, Germany stopped attacking unresisting Allied merchant ships. Her resumption on 1 February 1917 of unrestricted submarine warfare meant that neutral as well as belligerent merchant ships in zones about Great Britain, France, Italy, and the Eastern Mediterranean would be sunk without warning. However, Germany announced that the United States would be permitted to send one passenger ship a week to Britain, provided she carried no contraband and had three vertical red and white stripes painted on her hull. Wilson thereupon asked Secretary of State Robert Lansing to prepare a note breaking diplomatic relations with Germany. At a cabinet meeting on 2 February, three members demanded an outright declaration of war while four, including Daniels, supported Wilson in devising a policy that would prevent either belligerent camp from winning the war. On the next day, 3 February, Wilson broke relations with Germany.[71]

While waiting for the overt acts that might mean war, Wilson began to prepare for a war he hoped to avoid. At 0300 on 4 February, Daniels and Baker conferred with him at the White House, then set their departments working on plans for full mobilization. On the nineteenth Wilson directed all Navy bureau chiefs to report to him on the status of their forces. Congress acted, too. It increased appropriations for the services and empowered the President to commandeer shipyards and munitions factories in the event of war or national emergency. With conscription impending, Wilson directed Daniels and Baker to "get and keep" the ablest men they could for their departments.[72]

The naval appropriations bill for fiscal year 1918, which passed the House on 13 February 1917 by a vote of 354 to 22, provided $368.5 million, the largest appropriation of its kind in history. The building program for fiscal year 1918 included three battleships, one battle cruiser, three scout cruisers, fifteen destroyers, one destroyer tender, and nineteen coastal submarines. If Daniels could not have these ships built at reasonable cost by private yards, he was empowered to spend up to $12 million to make it possible for public yards to build them. To speed private construction, he was authorized to make contracts on a cost-plus basis. The Senate Naval Affairs Committee, always more generous to the Navy than the House Committee, after only four days of consideration recommended adding $165 million to the House bill, for a total of $531 million, and called for fifty submarines to be added to the eighteen desired by the House, ten of them to be of the fleet type. On 2 March the House agreed to $517 million, and on the fourth, just before the end of the Sixty-fourth Congress, Wilson signed the bill.[73] Within two weeks, Daniels awarded contracts amounting to $100 million, including those for four battle cruisers and six scouts as well as for fourteen capital ships, thirty-eight submarines, fifty-two destroyers, and a "mosquito" fleet of submarine chasers and other small craft. In addition he made joint plans with the army for the air defense of the Atlantic and Gulf coasts.[74]

Because of the U-boat menace, American merchant and passenger ships hugged their harbors, and there arose a strong demand for arming them and protecting them by means of convoy so that they could sail overseas. Wilson said that while ships were at liberty to arm for defense, he would not ask Congress for authority to give them either guns or gunners.[75] Daniels asserted that convoying would be "dangerous" because it might cause war with Germany. When this conclusion was angrily derided by most of Daniels's colleagues, Wilson charged them "with appealing to the spirit of the Code Duello."[76] Soon, however, two events caused Wilson to change his mind. First, he heard that Senate Republican leaders meant to filibuster the important appropriations bills, so as to force him to call the next Congress into extraordinary session. Second, on 25 February Ambassador Walter Hines Page in London sent him the Zimmermann Note, in which Germany urged Japan and Mexico to enter a war against the United States, with Mexico's reward to be the regaining of the territories lost to the United States in 1848. On the twenty-sixth Wilson went before a joint session of Congress to ask not for war, but for support for armed neutrality; specifically, to grant him authority, first, to arm merchant ships; second, to "employ any other instrumentalities or methods that may be necessary and adequate to protect our ships and our people in their legitimate and peaceful pursuits on the seas"; third, to appropriate $100 million for these purposes. The House quickly passed the armed-ship bill, on 1 March by a vote of 403 to 13, but did not give Wilson any of the broad authority he requested.[77]

On 5 March Wilson asked Daniels to prepare a memorandum on arming merchant ships. He also mentioned the possibility of hunting submarines by having each oceangoing ship lower three boats to search for them, a plan Daniels and his naval experts disregarded. At any rate, Daniels forwarded his memorandum on the eighth. It suggested:

> *First*, to reply to the German threat by permitting armed American merchantmen to shoot on sight at German submarines encountered anywhere, on the assumption that submarines would attack all American ships without warning.
>
> *Second*, to permit armed American merchantmen to shoot on sight at German submarines only in the war zones, and to require armed American

merchant ships to grant German submarines the right of visit and search in all other areas of the high seas.

Third, to require armed American merchantmen to submit to visit and search by German submarines everywhere, but to permit merchantmen to resist certain unlawful acts of submarines.[78]

When Wilson questioned the value of these suggestions, Daniels sent him a revised memorandum and a long letter on the ninth, and Wilson asked Lansing to comment upon them. Lansing preferred the second policy but wanted armed guards to be permitted to resist illegal attack outside the war zones as well as inside them. Later in the day, Wilson agreed that the Navy should put guns and gun crews on merchant ships. He also called Congress into special session on 16 April. On the thirteenth Daniels issued secret regulations for arming merchant ships. Armed guards could shoot at submarines that came within torpedo range in the war zones but were not permitted to seek them out or to attack them anywhere else.[79]

Although the first ships under armed guard left American ports on 17 March, Daniels refused to issue orders for full mobilization of the Navy, as his bureau chiefs recommended, because Wilson had not approved such orders. The next day, however, was the day of decision because U-boats had torpedoed three American ships. The "overt act" by Germany ushered in for Wilson a final week of soul-searching that resulted in his reluctant decision to go to war rather than to continue armed neutrality. Aiding him in reaching his decision were the Russian Revolution, for it now could be said that all of the Allies were democratic, and the unanimous advice of his cabinet. On 19 March he went over to the Navy Department to ask Daniels to do everything possible to protect American shipping, for he still hoped to avoid war. On the next day, he bluntly asked his cabinet what course he should follow. Daniels was one of the two members who originally opposed going to war, but he then changed his mind.

After the cabinet meeting, Wilson asked Daniels to talk with the General Board about the submarine menace. Daniels reported that the board had said there was no effective defense![80] On the next day, Wilson issued a call for Congress to meet on the second rather than the sixteenth of April and directed that the Navy be built up to full personnel strength. On the twenty-fourth he recalled American diplomatic and consular officials from Belgium, announced voluntary censorship regulations, and asked Daniels to establish confidential liaison immediately with Great Britain. During the next week Daniels made radio a government monopoly; established policies for censorship; stopped work on battle cruisers and concentrated instead on destroyers and small craft;

and named two captains to serve on the Department of State's Neutrality Board.[81]

On the evening of 2 April, Daniels heard Wilson read his historic war message. The Senate passed a war resolution on the fourth by a vote of 83 to 6, the House on the sixth by a vote of 373 to 50. At 1318 on the sixth, Wilson approved the joint resolution. Five minutes later Daniels telegraphed the fleet to mobilize. Much as he hated war, he confessed that there was "a sense of relief that we were embarked upon a holy crusade." Admiral Henry T. Mayo, Commander in Chief of the Atlantic Fleet, had told him that the Navy had never been in a better state of preparedness, one in which "there was a feeling of confidence in the personnel of being able to cope with any emergency."[82] Time would soon test this assertion.

The American army was in no wise ready to defeat Germany on the fields of Europe. This is not to deny that the army of two million men and the brigade of Marines sent to France contributed to the Allied forces that margin of strength needed to defeat Germany during the period from 12 September to 11 November 1918. These troops, and productive American factories, won the war, for neither air power nor science, with the possible exceptions of the development of an effective underwater sound detector, a direction finder (radio compass), and an antenna mine, played a vital role.

As for the Navy, its preparations could have been better, even though it met the emergency and played an important part in saving the Allies. Had it not been for the fleets of the Allies, the U.S. Navy would not have had the time to prepare in security for war. Rather than providing the destroyer types needed to overcome the U-boats, the building program of 1916 concentrated on battleships. The battleship squadron sent to operate with the British Grand Fleet never fired a shot at the German High Seas Fleet. Moreover, no special study had been given to ways to combat submarines. The official plans for war with Germany envisaged not submarine warfare but a surface fleet engagement in the Western Atlantic, most probably in the Caribbean. Nor did Great Britain have plans for utilizing American naval power. Yet the decision on building plans was not an easy one to make correctly. Should work on the capital ships have been stopped in favor of antisubmarine ships? Should naval ships have been given priority over merchant ships? Daniels's decision to keep working on the capital ships, but not under "forced draught," was a compromise which provided the United States with sufficient naval power to protect its postwar interests. With work stopped on capital ships, the construction of both antisubmarine craft and merchant ships was pushed. Nevertheless, naval policy had not been correlated with foreign policy, or else much more would have been done to develop submarine, mine, and air warfare, to build the necessary training, aviation, and submarine stations, to expand the navy yards, and to devise plans for cooperating with prospective allies. It spoke well for American in-genuity and ability, however, that the base and station construction work originally projected to take three or four years was completed in nine months.

The demands of war evoked stupendous efforts from Daniels. To house his expanded department he had temporary buildings constructed at B and 6th Streets and on Constitution Avenue. He had to direct the expenditure of the $1.5 billion appropriated for the Navy in 1917 alone, or $2 billion if the naval act of 29 August 1916 is counted. He had to concern himself not only with industrial production but with both defensive and offensive operations. The first step was the creation of a coastal patrol charged with the upkeep of anti-submarine nets, with sweeping for mines off the entrances to harbors from Halifax to Key West, and with scrutinizing all ships entering or leaving Ameri-can ports. At the weekly meetings of the Council of National Defense he helped to direct the war effort and to review the progress of the war. With Baker and Lansing he supervised the work of the Committee of Publicity, and he worked tirelessly as chairman of the Interdepartmental Social Hygiene Board. Coordination of effort with the Allies was a supreme consideration. New men had to be enrolled and trained to serve in combatant ships, as armed guard crews on merchant ships, in fighting naval units, and also to service guns placed aboard transports chartered by the Army. In addition, he had to repair certain interned enemy ships taken over by the United States.

As a result of Daniels's labors, 745 ships were in commission by the end of fiscal year 1917, and on 1 January 1918 there were 113 American naval ships in European waters, a total that by October had swelled to 338 ships of all classes. Highest construction priority was given to antisubmarine craft, first to wooden 110-foot submarine chasers, then to 35-knot "flush-deck" destroyers, then to minesweepers and seagoing tugs. Henry Ford made a beginning in December 1917 by manufacturing 200 steel "Eagle" patrol boats. Of the 406 submarine chasers commissioned in 1917 and 1918, 235 went overseas, where they ac-counted for at least two enemy submarines, while one group of submarines was sent to Ireland and another to the Azores.[83]

Significantly, five times more was spent during the war for submarines and antisubmarine ships than for capital ships. However, the vast preponder-ance of ships authorized during 1917 and 1918 were not completed until after the war. For example, 257 of the 273 destroyers authorized were built between 1918 and 1922. Thus, when the war was over, taking account of the ships build-ing, the United States had the largest fleet in the world.

The best indication of the great expansion that occurred in the naval air service, which was given $67.6 million in fiscal year 1917, lies in statistics: for the calendar year 1917 the ratio of increase in material was 1,400 percent, in personnel training 3,000 percent, and in stations and training schools 3,200 percent. Yet this gigantic effort provided only a dribble at the overseas end of the pipeline. When Franklin D. Roosevelt was in Europe during August and September 1918 he found that, mostly for lack of needed parts, few of the 2,100 American aircraft actually flew and that American pilots used French and occasionally British fighters.

Three days following the entrance of the United States into the war, Sims arrived in London to begin work. He was followed shortly by the first American destroyers. Then, at the suggestion of the United States, a conference of Allied naval experts was held in September 1917. Benson himself went over in November as a member of the commission named by Wilson to the Inter-Allied Conference held in Paris. Daniels created a naval transportation service to carry the troops to Europe. Meanwhile, British, French, Italian, and, eventually, Japanese and Russian missions came to the United States. As early as 12 April 1917, Daniels, Benson, and the leading British and French naval commanders in Western Atlantic waters had conferred in Norfolk and in Washington and decided that the U.S. Navy would guard the Eastern and Gulf coasts of the United States and the Atlantic coast of South America, thereby releasing British and French cruiser squadrons that had borne the duty since 1914.[84]

If Fiske was Daniels's naval stormy petrel from 1913 to 1915, Sims filled that role from 1917 to 1921. Although Sims ranked last in the list of thirty rear admirals, Daniels in January 1917 had chosen him to be the President of the Naval War College. On 23 March, Ambassador Walter Hines Page in London cabled President Wilson that the British wanted an American admiral sent over to share his Navy's "plans and inquiries" with them. A telephone call from Daniels brought Sims from Newport to Washington, where he was given oral and then written instructions for his mission in England. None of the men involved, Daniels, Benson, and Sims, could later agree on exactly what was said except that Sims was told to keep Daniels fully posted on conditions abroad, and to advise how the U.S. Navy could best cooperate with the Allied navies in case the United States entered the war. He was also told, they all agreed, that President Wilson was "decidedly of the opinion that ships should be convoyed." At any rate, Benson told Sims he should be very careful about his feelings toward the British, which in Benson's mind arose from the fact that Sims was born in Canada, and gave him a warning: "Don't let the British pull the wool over your eyes. It is none of our business pulling their chestnuts out of the fire. We would as soon fight the British as the Germans."[85]

On 31 March, Sims sailed for Liverpool. As will be seen, distance and poor communications made cooperation with the Navy Department difficult, problems compounded by the fact that Sims could not know the political considerations that swayed the administration. For its part, the administration not only lacked a feel for the military situation but had failed to spell out clearly either Sims's place in the Navy's organizational structure or what his specific duties were. *After* the war, both Daniels and Benson said that Sims had been merely their overseas assistant, a liaison man and transmitter of communications.[86]

Sims, however, demanded the support from the department which he believed he deserved. He found Daniels agonizingly slow in reaching important decisions, and Benson bereft of Naval War College training and lacking a true picture of the war effort he was directing. Fortunately, after June 1917 Benson's assistant was William Veazie Pratt, who had been chief of staff to Sims when Sims commanded the Atlantic Destroyer Flotilla. Knowing what went on both in Washington and London, Pratt served well as liaison between Benson and Sims.[87]

On 10 April 1917, Sims called upon the First Sea Lord, Sir John Jellicoe, who told him that he saw no solution to the U-boat problem. In the first quarter of 1917, U-boats sank 1.3 million tons of Allied and neutral shipping; it was clear that if that rate were maintained, by October the Allies would be short of the tonnage necessary to carry on the war. The British said they had tried everything—mining Germany's ports, arming merchant ships, use of smoke and of decoy ships, and patroling sea lanes with small boats armed with depth charges. Although the government suggested convoying, older heads at the Admiralty refused to adopt it because convoys consumed time, their speed being that of the slowest ships; they overtaxed harbor facilities at arrival and departure times; they called for sailing skills beyond those of merchant ship captains; and they required escorts which could not be spared from the offensive duties in which they were engaged.[88]

On 11 April the British mission in Washington asked Daniels for destroyers to patrol Europe's Atlantic coast and to engage in antisubmarine warfare off the coast of Ireland. The French wanted large numbers of small craft and destroyers with which to patrol such ports as Brest and Bordeaux. However, of the 51 destroyers Daniels had, only sixteen in full commission were with the Atlantic Fleet; others were in commission with reduced complements or were on neutrality patrol in various parts of the world.

In his first cabled report, sent on 14 April, Sims asserted that Allied control of the sea was actually imperiled. He asked for a "maximum number of destroyers, accompanied by small antisubmarine craft," and for merchant tonnage. To supply these ships, he added, auxiliaries would have to be sent and bases established. Finally he warned that U-boats "very likely" would approach the East Coast of the United States in order to divert attention from the strategic center, the waters about the British Isles. In subsequent reports, he continued to demand from Daniels ships, ships, and more ships. At the same time, Sims tried to convince Jellicoe to use convoys. Failing, he turned to David

Lloyd George, prime minister since December 1916. When Lloyd George threatened to overrule the Admiralty, that august body finally agreed, on 30 April.

Daniels meanwhile discussed with Benson and President Wilson the part the U.S. Navy should play in the war. On 17 April Wilson made his decision—"Let destroyers go to the other side"—and on the twenty-fourth Daniels told his diary "Six destroyers sailed for England to aid in the war," and on the twenty-seventh that six more had been ordered to make ready.[89] Sims first learned that destroyers were on their way on 22 April but, hearing nothing more, got Page to cable the Department of State as well as Daniels that "Thirty or more destroyers would very likely be decisive."[90] Unbeknown to Sims, Daniels and Wilson decided on 30 April that they would eventually send thirty-six destroyers and two destroyer tenders to Europe and would try to send over such smaller craft as trawlers, mine craft, and tugs. Sims was not notified of these intentions until 3 May, the day before the first destroyers arrived at Queenstown.

Submarine warfare was a major topic discussed at the cabinet meeting of 4 May, when Wilson stated that merchant shipping should be convoyed, and at a meeting of the Council of National Defense on the fifth, at which the British mission abruptly broached the need for 500,000 American soldiers to be sent to France immediately.[91]

The urgency with which Sims viewed the need for ships is revealed in his asking for them no less than thirty-two times during May, June, and July of 1917. By the end of May, twelve destroyers and the tender *Dixie* had joined him. Ten more and another tender joined him in June, and nine more in July. On 1 August the United States had in European waters thirty-seven destroyers, two destroyer tenders, and eight yachts. There were as yet no tugs to salvage torpedoed ships or cruisers for ocean convoy duty. Sims believed that many more ships could have been sent to him, but despite repeated requests he was unable to obtain from Daniels the cooperation he needed to protect overseas convoys. Not until 20 June did Daniels even mention convoying; not until the twenty-fourth did he promise to send antisubmarine craft "when such craft become available."[92] At Sims's urging, Page cabled Wilson and Daniels in support of his demands, as did persons in high office in the British government and in the Admiralty.

On 2 July, Wilson wrote to Daniels: " . . . the Admiralty has done absolutely nothing constructive in the use of their navy and I think it is time we were making and insisting upon plans of our own, even if we render some of the more conservative of our own naval advisers uncomfortable. What do you think?" On the third he asked, " . . . are the British now convoying *groups* of ships or are they trying the vain experiment of convoying individual craft?"[93]

Daniels replied that the British were using cruisers and small craft to escort as many as twenty ships. Meanwhile he had told Sims that he was accepting his suggestion about convoying but, rather than using the British routing system, would keep this matter in American hands "on account of present sensitive public opinion," a decision Sims observed was "a fundamental military error."[94] Sims correctly concluded that the administration did not heed him because it had not yet developed a policy for cooperating with the Allies. On 4 July President Wilson cabled that the British seemed to be "helpless to the point of panic": they had rejected every plan set forth by the U.S. government while not furnishing plans which, as for convoying, "seem to us efficacious." Wilson asked Sims to disregard the British and furnish his own estimate of what needed to be done to conduct an offensive anti-U-boat campaign and to convoy merchant ships. On the sixth, Wilson asked "why there should not be a single lane for ships to reach Britain, with plenty of patrol boats and hydroairplanes so as to make submarines there impossible?"[95] Not until the tenth did Daniels send Sims a copy of his letter to the secretary of state in which were set forth six basic principles that were to govern U.S. naval efforts:

1. Extension to the Allies of the most hearty cooperation in meeting the submarine threat, subject only to maintaining an adequate defense of home waters.
2. Full cooperation in meeting any future situation.
3. Although the successful termination of the war was the first aim of the United States, "the future position of the United States must in no way be jeopardized by any disintegration of our main fighting fleet."
4. Recognition that the current main military role of the U.S. Navy was to safeguard the Allies' lines of communication.
5. Granted that the dominant note of the Allied Powers would be offensive, the United States was willing to cooperate in any joint action approved by them.
6. The Department of the Navy's promise to send all the antisubmarine craft it could spare from home needs, send the fleet abroad (but not any division thereof) to cooperate in any emergency; and its readiness to discuss more fully any plans for joint operations with the Allies.[96]

In reply to Wilson's cable of the fourth, Sims said that if he were in charge he would prepare the U.S. fleet for distant service; use as many small craft as possible to fight submarines and to escort convoys; send oil and other supplies to France to support heavy ships; build destroyers, light craft, and merchant ships, in that order, and suspend the construction of heavies; use the convoy system; and build up his staff with a number of men he named. His mission, he continued, was to promote maximum wartime cooperation with the Allies, and he had not given consideration to postwar situations. Maximum cooperation meant total effort against the U-boats. These "hornets" could not be crushed in their "nests" because the latter were too well defended; or by mines, for to date 30,000 mines had not prevented U-boats from operating; or by mystery, or "Q," ships, innocent-looking merchantmen that kept their guns masked until a U-boat appeared; or by a constantly patroled single shipping lane. From three years' experience, the British were convinced that mines, nets, and similar methods were mere palliatives. The most effective opposition to the U-boat yet discovered was the use of antisubmarine craft, and the only worthwhile protection for merchant ships was the convoy. As for the defense of the United States, U-boats could not operate three thousand miles from home; as for the Fleet, all or part of it might prove useful. Finally, Sims said that on 1 August he would have been in London for more than three months and he had been sent no staff. His only aide verged upon a nervous breakdown. He had asked for Pratt on seven different occasions, and for certain other officers by name, but Daniels had said they were unavailable. After thirty requests for aid made during the first four months of the war, he was sent exactly six men. Two more months passed before he had a staff of twelve, and Benson did not furnish him three officers for a Planning Section which would work with the British Admiralty until late November, when he asked for eight more. With this limited staff he supervised the operations of 375 ships of all classes, about 5,000 officers and 70,000 men, and 45 bases, including those at Brest, Gibraltar, Inverness and Invergordon, Queenstown, in the Azores, and Malta. Also under his supervision were the five coal-burning battleships of Battle Division Nine, operating since November 1917 as the Sixth Battle Squadron of the British Grand Fleet.

Although Daniels, with Wilson's approval, vetoed Mayo's suggestion that he take the rest of the fleet over to Europe, Benson stated that Sims's conduct of the antisubmarine campaign from April through September had been quite satisfactory.[97] In late December Daniels, too, praised his work.[98] In contrast, Wilson was so unhappy with the conduct of the naval war that on 2 August he suggested to Daniels the creation of a Department of Operations and a more imaginative, bold, and better trained man than Benson to head it.[99] On the eleventh, when Wilson secretly addressed the officers of the Atlantic Fleet at Yorktown, he dared them to discard outmoded doctrines, to be innovative in devising ways of overcoming the U-boat, and to undertake bold ventures just this side of suicide.[100]

To obtain an understanding with the Allies that would enable the United States to pursue its own interests rather than support those particularly of Great Britain, in October Wilson sent Colonel House, accompanied by a group including Benson and General Tasker H. Bliss, USA, to confer with the Allies, who were about to hold an Inter-Allied Conference in Paris to plan their campaigns for 1918. Benson carried with him Wilson's instructions: "All possible cooperation but we must be free."[101] On 12 February 1918 Daniels commented: "Strange feeling between allied nations. One did not know what other was doing & a great Eng. general [?] had said, 'Before this war is over, we will be fighting among ourselves.' "[102] In any event, following its debacle at Caporetto, Italy joined Britain and France in establishing a Supreme War Council which would meet monthly at Versailles and oversee the general conduct of the war. Wilson sought to avoid diplomatic and political entanglement by appointing to the Council only a military representative, Bliss, although House attended the meetings in December 1917 and October 1918, at the latter of which he had some success in getting the Council to accept Wilson's Fourteen Points as the political basis of an armistice.[103]

Another illustration of the independence Wilson and Daniels tried to maintain is their declining to let American naval officers accept honors from the Allies. A special case was that of Sims; the British wished to make him an honorary member of the Board of Admiralty and thus, they said, enable him to listen to Admiralty deliberations although he would not be allowed to speak or vote. "An emphatic NO," exclaimed Daniels, and Wilson promised to veto any congressional authorization for Americans to accept foreign honors.[104]

"Hard nut to crack," commented Daniels with respect to how to conquer the U-boat. He took under consideration the suggestion made late in April by the Bureau of Ordnance to plant mine barrages across the North Sea and the Strait of Dover in order to destroy U-boats and to lower the morale of their crews. The Admiralty considered the plan impractical if not impossible, as did certain American admirals and Daniels himself, but Wilson liked the idea because it appealed to his "desire for aggressive action against the submarine menace"—enough to win Daniels over. Daniels instructed Benson to arrange with the British for the laying of the North Sea Mine Barrage while he attended the Inter-Allied Conference in Europe and selected Captain Reginald R. Belknap to begin work on it. Because England could not provide all the facilities needed, he also directed that a mine station be established in Scotland.[105]

Early in December 1917, Daniels heard the members of Colonel House's mission declare that "conditions are very serious."[106] Whatever had to be done, Daniels told his diary, would have to be done by Americans, who already were patroling the French coast, undertaking harbor improvements, and preparing landing and other facilities.[107]

While Sims was stretching what few ships he had to the breaking point, on 1 June 1917 Daniels told him that he must provide escort for troopship convoys to France. To do so, Sims retorted, he would have to suspend all patrol and escort duties in the Western Approaches. Why not, he asked, let the British control troop convoys? Angry because Sims would protect merchant ships rather than troop ships, Daniels peremptorily reminded Sims that his "paramount" duty was to protect troopships.[108] What Sims did not know was that Washington was anxious to control troop transport as much from a sense of professional pride as out of political considerations. Since U-boats upheld Sims's judgment by concentrating on merchant shipping, the United States was able to send increasing numbers of men abroad, from about 175,000 in December 1917 to over 2,000,000 in November 1918. American ships carried 44 percent of the men and escorted 62 percent of the transports, and not a man under American protection was lost because of enemy action. British ships ferried about a million Americans, and other Allies a few more.

Daniels contributed mightily to the success of the American Expeditionary Force by securing the ships needed by the Naval Overseas Transportation Service, but successful troop movements would not have been possible had not shipping losses to U-boats been cut from about 300,000 tons in January 1918 to 112,000 in October. Built up to 5,000 officers and 29,000 men, the Transportation Service sent a ship to France every five hours. To put it another way, during the summer of 1918 the United States was landing seven soldiers and their equipment in Europe every minute of every day and night.

In mid October 1918, as rumors were heard in Washington about the possible agreement of Germany to peace, Daniels conferred with the General Board on its demand for a seven-year building program that would give the United States the largest navy in the world by 1925. Wilson, however, suggested that it would be unwise to increase the Navy while discussing disarmament as part of the peace settlement and that it would be better to plan another three-year program similar to that of 1916.[108] Daniels thereupon submitted such a plan to the House Naval Affairs Committee: it was to cost approximately $600 million a year and called for the construction of 10 battleships, 6 battle cruisers, and 140 ships of other types. He added, however, that he would prune his requests if adequate peace terms were reached.[109] By the end of October the naval aviation program appeared to be superfluous. It could be cut back. Too, shipping could be returned to private control. High-ranking officers were in general agreement on another three-year building program, but disagreement upon whether to build more battle cruisers became so acrimonious that Daniels cabled Benson at Paris to make a study of them and deferred a decision until his return.[110] A decision also had to be made upon the naval terms of the armistice to be offered to Germany. After consulting with Wilson, Daniels cabled Benson to use his own judgment on defining those terms but that Wilson wanted all German armed ships to be held in trust by the Allies. On 4 November, at the White House, Daniels learned that Great Britain objected to the freedom of the seas, one of Wilson's Fourteen Points, and that Wilson had cabled House, as Daniels told his diary, to the effect that:

"If E[ngland] took course in opposition we would use our facilities to build the greatest navy."[111]

At 0245 on 11 November, Daniels learned of the signing of the armistice. Later that day he heard Wilson give Congress the details of the armistice terms. The shooting part of the war was over.

Congress had been generous to Daniels during the war. Daniels wisely reduced his estimates for fiscal year 1919 to about half of those of 1918, and reduced ship building by one-third. The House Naval Affairs Committee cut his estimates only slightly. More important, it authorized the resumption of building of capital ships of the 1916 program, which had been in abeyance for a year. As passed by the House on 20 April 1918 after two days of consideration, the final sum authorized was $1.3 billion. When the Senate on 22 May appropriated $1.6 billion, the difference had to be resolved in conference. With the acceptance by the House of the Senate's figures, the permanent manpower of the Navy was set at 131,485 and its temporary strength at 181,485. On 1 July Wilson signed the bill, with Daniels pleased less because of the amount of money but more because promotion by selection was extended to the staff, and the old Naval Militia was federalized. Most important, the act provided the officers and men needed for the Navy as it would be increased by the ships of the 1916 program.[112]

Daniels was determined that the end of the war should not stop him from obtaining the naval strength he believed the nation needed, and in this he had Wilson's hearty support. However, with the war over "peace" was the cry on many lips, demands for demobilization were overwhelming, and congressmen rejected advice from military men. At hearings beginning 19 November on Daniels's new program, some members of the House Naval Affairs Committee felt that decisions on appropriations should await the outcome of the peace conference. Daniels said that he would revise his estimates when peace returned. Nevertheless, he argued that the United States must have a navy adequate to protect its interests, to match its status as a power, and to cooperate with Great Britain in policing the high seas in the name of a league of nations.

Sensing that the committee opposed large expenditures, Daniels cut his estimates almost in half but stuck to an annual $600 million for the three-year building program. When the committee opposed any building until the peace conference concluded its work, Daniels again revised his estimates downward; on 30 December he requested $976 million. On 1 and 2 January 1919 he asked for additional funds for a Navy of 250,000 men, for lengthening the Academy course from three to four years, for a Pacific as well as an Atlantic fleet, and for the retention of the Coast Guard in the Navy. By limiting the number of men to 225,000, the committee reduced the number of ships and aircraft that could be operated, and Daniels suspended discharges from the Navy. Finally, on 1 February, the committee recommended only $757 million. The three-year program was saved, yet the committee empowered the President to suspend actual construction in the event the United States became a member of a league of nations. With only the change that no new construction could start until 1 January 1920, the House approved the bill by a vote of 281 to 50.[113]

As Daniels expected, the Senate was more generous. On 26 January its naval affairs committee reported a bill that would increase the number of permanent enlisted personnel, augment pay, and add $17 million for construction that was to be carried out in navy yards. When senators opposed to the League of Nations filibustered and caused the Sixty-fifth Congress to end with much important legislation unfinished, the appropriations bill went over to the extraordinary session which did not meet until 19 May.[114]

The early months of 1919 were filled with private discussions about naval and maritime power between the American and British delegations at Paris. Although Britain's Navy almost equalled the combined navies of the world, she had only four *Hood*-class battle cruisers building. The United States would have supremacy if her 1916 program were completed. Wilson, fully supported by Daniels and Benson, threatened to resort to competitive building if the British would not agree to parity. Knowing of Wilson's obsession with the League, the British demanded agreement on naval competition before they would approve the Covenant of the League and stalled on negotiations. When Wilson directed Daniels to provide a ship to take him home, British dilatory tactics ended—for a while.[115]

Taking advantage of the two months' respite between the old and new congresses, Daniels left New York on 15 March for Paris with the three bureau chiefs who were to design and build the ships of the proposed 1919 program. He and Benson looked upon this program as vitally necessary in itself, while Wilson and House saw it as a useful bargaining weapon at the Peace Conference. When Admiral of the Fleet Sir Rosslyn Erskine Wester-Wemyss called on Daniels to learn why he wanted to increase his fleet and asserted that Britain needed the "largest navy afloat," there began what Daniels called the "Sea Battle of Paris."[116]

In conference with Daniels and Benson, Wemyss stated the British case— that of an insular nation that had to protect colonies throughout the world. Benson replied that the United States had responsibilities from the Philippines to Alaska and, because of the Monroe Doctrine, from the Virgin Islands to the tip of South America: therefore, he would never agree to British supremacy, but he would accept parity. There the discussion ended.[117] Another conference, this one between Daniels and Benson and Wemyss and the First Lord of the Admiralty, Walter Long, resulted in similar deadlock, mainly because

Long revealed that Britain feared loss of commercial supremacy to the rapidly increasing American merchant marine. It thus became clear that the British would not support the League of Nations if Wilson persisted in his building program.[118] After talking with Wilson, Daniels told Long that the President wished to deal first with the establishment of the League and would later take up the disarmament problem directly with Lloyd George. Neither Daniels nor Benson suspected that this meant that Colonel House, rather than they, would conduct the negotiations that really counted.[119]

Daniels left Paris on 14 April to visit American troops and various battle sites before proceeding to England for a tour of British and American naval installations and major ships. On the thirtieth he was received by the King and Queen. On 1 May he called on Long and Wemyss and among others met the former head of the British Navy, Lord Fisher, then retired. He also had a private talk with Winston Churchill, who told him that "Great Britain would build as big ships & guns as any."[120] Soon thereafter Daniels learned that Wilson had reversed himself at Paris and withdrawn his support from the three-year program because Lloyd George promised support for the League.[121]

By the time Daniels returned from Europe, the Republican-controlled Sixty-sixth Congress had only five weeks in which to pass the appropriations bills for the new fiscal year. It had little interest in providing an "adequate" army and navy. Thomas S. Butler, of Pennsylvania, chairman of the House Naval Affairs Committee, was well versed in navy ways and a fiend for economy. In keeping with Wilson's desire, on 27 May Daniels asked Butler's committee only for the completion of the 1916 program, saying that the adoption of the League of Nations and the promise of an end to competitive building no longer required that the United States have the "largest navy in the world." For naval aviation, however, he wanted $45 million, primarily for experimental work, and he stressed the temporary need for at least 250,000 men. When he appeared before the committee for the last time, however, he promised to pare the number to 200,000 by 1 January 1920.[122]

With Butler's committee revealing that economy was more important than naval efficiency, Daniels sought support from the chairman of the Senate Naval Affairs Committee, Carroll Smalley Page, of Vermont. At hearings before Page's committee Daniels and the bureau chiefs urged an increase in the estimates authorized by the House; also, Daniels opposed the creation of a Department for Air, an idea that was vehemently supported by Army Brigadier General William Mitchell. On 25 June 1919 the Senate adopted the committee report but added $44 million to it, with $20 million of this for naval aviation and $21 million for increasing the pay of enlisted personnel. Not until the thirtieth was the report of the conference committee adopted; it gave aviation $25 million out of a total of $616 million.[123]

While the bill awaited the return of President Wilson from Paris on 8 July, Daniels conferred with Benson on how to prevent the "prostration" of the Navy. They lacked men to man ships, let alone to perform shore duties. Nevertheless, until the end of Daniels's tenure the personnel situation worsened. As the new statutory limit of 120,000 men, which was to take effect on 4 January 1921, approached, he ordered recruiting stopped.[124]

For a year, Daniels had prepared his estimates without anyone knowing whether the Senate would approve the Treaty of Versailles. During 1919 he often warned the American people that they faced the choice of accepting the League of Nations or embracing militarism, the same theme Wilson espoused in his September crusade to win support for the League. After Wilson's health broke down and the treaty was defeated by the Senate, Daniels violated Wilson's agreement with Great Britain by proposing a new building program designed to thrust the Navy toward primacy at sea.[125] Yet he had no better luck in getting appropriations for fiscal year 1921 than he had had for 1920. In December 1919 he asked for $573 million and a personnel limit of 131,485. Hinting at the commercial challenge from Great Britain and the possible enmity of Japan, the General Board recommended a building program that would make the Navy the equal of any other by 1925 and the expenditure of $27 million for naval aviation. The latter request sat badly with General Mitchell, who told a House subcommittee that there should be a separate air department and a separate air academy. Daniels, who planned to use obsolete ships as targets for aircraft in order to learn how to build better protection into ships, protested vigorously to Secretary Baker and to the House Committee on Military Affairs because Mitchell had been heard but no invitation had been extended to naval personnel. Part of Mitchell's testimony, he added, was incorrect, incomplete, and misleading; it put the Navy on the defensive before Congress and hindered the development of naval aviation. Baker thereupon directed Army men to speak for their service only—but no one asked for testimony from Navy air experts. In any event, Daniels and Baker on 22 January 1920 agreed on an air policy that left the Army supreme over land and the Navy supreme over water but provided for cooperation in defense of the coasts.[126]

Before the House Naval Affairs Committee on 6 March, Daniels demanded a Navy equal to Britain's and increased to thirty-eight the General Board's recommendation of thirty new ships, including four carriers. Were the Senate to approve the Treaty of Versailles, he would recommend merely completion of the 1916 program; were the treaty defeated, he would duplicate the 1916 program and make the U.S. Navy "incomparably" the greatest in the world.[127] All in vain. On the sixteenth, the committee cut his estimates of $574 million to $424 million, and on the twenty-third the House agreed to $425 million.

On 5 April the Senate Naval Affairs Committee added $30 million to the House bill. After Daniels had appeared before them the following day, they raised the appropriation for naval aviation from $15 million to $25 million and gave him six steel hulls released by the Shipping Board to convert to seaplane tenders. With the House saying $425 million and the Senate $467 million, the final conference figure of $433,229,574 was obviously a compromise. Wilson signed the bill on 5 June. Unhappy, Daniels noted four items he thought the people would disapprove: inadequate provisions for the expansion of naval bases on the Pacific coast; less than a "half-way" provision for naval aviation; failure to appropriate for a single new ship beyond completing the 1916 program; and a $140 million shortage in the funds allotted for keeping the operating ships in fit material condition.[128]

The status of the Navy deteriorated rapidly during what remained of Daniels's tenure. The general public demanded financial relief, a "return to normalcy," and disarmament. Devoted to economy, Congress pulled the purse strings as tightly as possible. Furthermore, it saw no reason to listen to a lame duck like Daniels when Edwin Denby stood ready to relieve him.[129]

More trouble brewed for Daniels in investigations into the administration of Samoa and especially into how the Navy had conducted itself in Haiti and San Domingo. In addition, General Mitchell persisted in his demand for a separate air department. And Roosevelt's resigning on 8 August 1920 to campaign for the vice presidency left Daniels for his last seven months with an inexperienced assistant. Partisan politics also hurt the Navy, for Republicans were anxious to discredit Wilson.

For fiscal year 1922 Daniels asked for $679 million, about a third more than for fiscal year 1921, with the largest increases devoted to aviation and pay. He also took direct issue with Senator William E. Borah's demand for a "naval holiday." There were, Daniels believed, only two courses of action open to the United States: "(1) To secure an international agreement with all . . . nations, which will guarantee an end of competition in navy building; (2) To hold aloof from agreement [and] build a Navy strong enough . . . to command the respect and fear of the world."[130]

On 2 February 1921, the Appropriations Committee reported to the House a bill carrying $395 million including only $90 million to continue construction of the 1916 program, or about half of what Daniels had requested. The report recommended that the number of enlisted men be reduced from 143,000 to 100,000, and slashed naval aviation to less than $7 million. Funds were granted to build up four navy yards on the West Coast but no funds were authorized for several yards on the East Coast or for a naval station at Guam. At the same time, however, approval was given for the creation of a Bureau of Aeronautics in the Navy Department.[131] Except for the authorization to create that bureau, the only possibly heartening events for Daniels were a resolution of approbation of his services adopted by the Naval Consulting Board and praise for his administration at an unprecedented dinner in his honor given by the members of the House Naval Affairs Committee.

Meanwhile, in late January and early February both naval affairs committees heard Army, Air Corps, Navy, and Marine officers discuss national policy, submarines, battle cruisers, aircraft carriers, and naval aviation.[132] On 8 February, the Senate committee promised an adverse report on Borah's measure to suspend naval building. In its view the battleship was still the chief element of the fleet. In the end, the committee recommended $496 million, approved the building of two carriers but the scrapping of twelve destroyers, and set enlisted strength at 120,000.[133] The differences with the House bill were so great, the life of the Sixty-sixth Congress was so short, and the parsimoniousness of the House was so well documented that the chance was good that the Senate would refuse to accept the bill. Although Senator Lodge defended the measure, Borah filibustered against it, and the Congress ended without making any provision for the Navy.

By the end of 1917 Congress had begun investigating the conduct of the war. However, in January 1918, those members who had visited Haiti and San Domingo had nothing but praise for what the Navy had done, particularly in Haiti. Again nothing but praise came for the work during the war of the navy bureaus, the antisubmarine campaign, the Marine Corps, and the shipbuilding program. However, Daniels opposed the suggestion that the Navy Department be reorganized by providing him with additional assistant secretaries.[134]

The battle for private control of radio communications well illustrates, even if in miniature, the strong demand that official wartime control over commercial enterprise be ended, particularly after the elections of 1918 returned a Republican Congress. On 25 July 1919, Daniels suggested that the Navy, which controlled 85 percent of the country's radio facilities, be authorized to handle commercial as well as official traffic. Businessmen strongly opposed the continuation of naval control, however, and in 1920 the commercial part of naval radio was sold to the Radio Corporation of America.[135] Daniels also lost when he sought to keep the Coast Guard in the Navy.[136]

Much more heat was engendered by the medals questions. On 31 July 1917, Daniels vetoed acceptance by American naval personnel of foreign honors. Sims, who accepted a decoration from the British, felt embarrassed, and Daniels did not order its return because he, in turn, did not want to embarrass an ally. However, in February 1919 Congress permitted the granting of the Distinguished Service Medal, the Medal of Honor, and the Navy Cross for specified heroic actions. In consequence, Daniels sent the recommendations for awards he received to a Board of Awards. After they reported, he dissolved the board in October 1919. Upon finding that 68 percent of those recommended for a DSM had served only at desks, he dropped some of them and added those who had laid the North Sea Mine Barrage or served as naval armed guards. Since only 119 out of 500,000 enlisted men had been granted awards, he added 13 DSMs and 68 Navy Crosses for them. Both Sims and Mayo told him they were displeased with his action, and Sims (and later two others) declined to accept the DSM awarded to him on the ground that some of his recommendations had not been followed. On 15 December a feature article in the anti-administration *Washington Post* charged that Daniels had robbed naval heroes of their honors and given them to his friends, including his brother-in-law, David Worth Bagley, to whom he awarded the DSM. Chairman Page of the Senate Naval Affairs Committee, thereupon established a subcommittee headed by Frederick Hale, a Republican and good friend of Sims, to ascertain the facts.

In his testimony, Sims charged that Daniels and the Board of Awards changed the relative merit of those recommended by commanding officers. Second, Daniels rated sea duty above shore duty. Third, DSMs were given to "Many, if not all, of the officers who were defeated in action or whose ships were sunk or seriously damaged by enemy submarines," thus severely lowering service morale. Finally, Daniels provided neither the Board of Awards nor commanding officers with policy guidance upon which to base their recommendations. After three weeks of testimony, including that of Daniels, it was established that lack of policy guidance had enabled commanding officers, the Board of Awards, and Daniels to make subjective judgments and interpretations, and that Daniels had accepted but 41.5 percent of the recommendations, revised others up and still others down, and added names of his own. Daniels then seemed to vacillate by alleging that his published list of medals *awarded* was only tentative and that his awareness of his errors had caused him to reconvene the Board of Awards just before the hearings began. Moreover, he could not escape the charge of nepotism in granting an award to his brother-in-law, who lost his ship.

But Sims did not escape altogether. Other admirals had recommended DSMs for captains of ships torpedoed by U-boats; he had recommended only the Medal of Honor. He himself had recommended Bagley for the Navy Cross and had revealed himself to be vindictive in recommending a DSM for every admiral who had served with him abroad except Henry Wilson. However, Daniels had approved Mayo's recommendation of a DSM for Wilson. That partisanship marred the hearings was clear, for the majority report by the three Republicans on the committee condemned most of Daniels's actions while the minority report by two Democrats upheld them.[137]

Personal altercation between Daniels and Sims over the medals question then flourished into what Daniels characterized as a "Tempest Born in Politics." On the first day of the medals hearing, 17 January, Senator Hale asked Sims to submit "any further correspondence with the Secretary of the Navy about the question of awards and their effect on the morale of the service." Sims offered a long letter he had written to Daniels on the seventh entitled "Certain Naval Lessons of the Great War" and leaked to the press. At Hale's request, Sims read the letter to the subcommittee. Lacking power to investigate all of Sims's charges, Hale postponed the hearings on the medals and obtained the right from the full committee to conduct an investigation into all the matters Sims broached in his letter. Thus, the investigation into the latter began on 9 March.

Sims probably hoped to force Daniels to resign, thereby discrediting civilian control of the Navy, and perhaps to obtain a general staff. In a prepared statement he cited errors made in policy, tactics, strategy, and administration. To substantiate the need for reorganization, he attempted to show that the Navy had been both unprepared for war in 1917 and slow to act in the first six months of the war itself, saying repeatedly, however, that he had nothing but praise for the naval operations of 1918.

Two and a half million words were spoken at the investigation, most of them concerning three major questions Sims raised.

First, had the Navy been prepared for war? Evidence from 1914 to 1917 supported the contrary with respect to personnel.

Second, was the Navy in good material condition to fight the war? Here, also, Daniels was suspect. Testimony brought out that the United States did not have a single submarine ready for war in 1917; that the battleships in reserve were unready; that the destroyers were short of men; that the fleet was unbalanced because it lacked battle cruisers, scout cruisers, light cruisers, and fleet submarines; and that the scouting and screening ships were scattered about the world rather than mobilized with the fleet. Daniels could not support the claim he made in his annual report for 1918 that the Navy in April 1917 was ready "from stem to stern." On the other hand, he and Benson had followed the administration's policy of not preparing for war lest its very preparations be taken as "overt acts" likely to precipitate war and violate its announced policy of neutrality. With a real general staff, argued Sims, Daniels could not have acted as he did because he would have had to accept the advice of his chief professional adviser. But Sims was thinking of a man like Fiske rather than like Benson.

Third, Sims charged that the department "entered the war with no well-considered policy or plans." This was not quite correct. There was a base plan providing for the organization of fleets, bases, communications, logistics, and the like, founded upon the assumption that the Atlantic fleet would meet an enemy fleet somewhere in the Atlantic. More cogent was the charge that the plan had no applicability to the war itself. The General Board had answered Daniels's request of February 1917 for a plan "for operations necessary to conduct the war, taking up the question of submarine warfare among the others," but the reply had been lost. It probably made no difference, for the record showed that Daniels approved and acted upon only six of the forty-five papers on the war sent to him by the board between 1914 and 1917. Captain Pratt had made numerous suggestions about plans, none of which was followed, and Benson admitted that "No definite war plan [was] drawn up on paper. . . ," but he hurriedly added that such a plan would not have been used because, rather than attempting to fight the war alone, the Navy followed plans already used by the Allies for three years. Thus it did follow a plan.[138] It was clear, however, that the department from 1914 to 1917 failed to *prepare* to follow such a plan. One untoward result of that failure was that Daniels and Benson directed ship operations from Washington and Mayo, the Atlantic fleet commander, was left in the dark on the department's war policies. Not until November 1917 were personnel and material conditions improved enough to enable his forces to work as a fleet.[139] Nevertheless, he backed Daniels and Benson by saying that the material unpreparedness of ships in reserve and the shortage of personnel was due primarily to the administration's neutrality policy, one that did not permit war preparations. However, he concluded by saying that a strengthening of the office of the chief of naval operations was needed so that it could force the cooperation of the various offices, boards, and bureaus in the Navy.[140]

Sims had said:

> Owing to [our lack of preparedness] and to the lack of proper organization of our Navy Department . . . we failed, for at least six months, to throw our full weight against the enemy; that during this period we pursued a policy of vacillation, or in simpler words, a hand to mouth policy, attempting to formulate our plans from day to day, based upon an incorrect appreciation of the situation.

Then followed his jarring conclusion that the apathy of the Navy delayed victory for four months and cost the Allied cause 2,500,000 tons of shipping, 500,000 lives, and $15,500,000![141] Of this charge Badger said, "utterly unfounded"; Benson, "an outrage"; Mayo, "a wild statement not at all susceptible to proof"; Rodman, "There are three kinds of lies—lies, damn lies, and statistics"; Strauss, "NO."[147] As his biographer has pointed out, Sims never discovered the difference "between rapping for attention and knocking his audience cold,"[143] and the minority members on the committee took him severely to task.

The Navy Department during the first six months of the war, Sims asserted, neither realized that the critical area was in the submarine zone in the Eastern Atlantic nor that it could not intelligently direct its forces from Washington. To support these assertions he submitted that for a whole year his staff had been totally inadequate, that not all existing naval forces had been sent abroad, that a two-month delay had occurred in the adoption of the convoy system, that more protection had been given to American coastal shipping than to Allied ships serving Europe; that he had not been informed of adjustments made between the department and representatives of the Allies in Washington or of the disposition of the forces sent abroad, and that he had not received any policy guidance from Washington until 10 July. In the meantime he had been asked by the department why he could not undertake such infeasible operations as to blockade the German coast "efficiently and completely, thus making practically impossible the egress and ingress of submarines," or to plant a mine barrage across the North Sea. Only after Benson visited him in London in November and realized his needs did conditions improve, particularly because he was thereafter provided with three officers for a Planning Section to operate with the Admiralty.[144]

Sims supported his allegations by referring to cables and letters he had sent the department, but the opposition interpreted them differently than he did. True, his staff had been inadequate, but Benson would have had to strip his own staff in order to send Sims the officers he wanted. True, the entire naval establishment had not been placed at his disposal because, first, not all the ships and supplies were ready. Second, the Allies did not give the department a complete picture of the desperate status of the naval war. Third, some forces had to stay behind to protect the American coast from U-boats and, should it defeat or escape from the British Grand Fleet, from the German High Seas Fleet, and to show the flag particularly in the waters off Mexico and Argentina, countries suspected of pro-German leanings. What if the Allies were defeated and the United States had to face Germany alone? The delay in accepting the convoy system had resulted from doubt about its effectiveness. True, he had not received policy guidance until 10 July. Furthermore, Sims saw things from his post in London, whereas the department had to take a worldwide view he could not possibly possess. That the war could have been directed from Washington was also possible: since the Allies so believed, it was tenable, Benson suggested, that Sims had an exaggerated idea of the position he occupied.[145]

Benson was not called until 4 May, by which time he had retired. His testimony was of particular importance because, under Daniels, he had been responsible for wartime plans and operations. While he admitted that the Navy had been unprepared for war in 1917 in the material and personnel sense and that the fleet had not been mobilized, he asserted that these shortcomings stemmed from following the policy of neutrality. With some heat, and with obvious reference to Sims's Anglophilism, he added that he himself put American interests first. The department had given Sims as much help as it could in view of the shortage of officers and of all the other tasks it had to perform. Finally, Benson declared that Daniels had been under no compulsion to follow Sims's recommendations.

As Daniels prepared to appear before the committee, the widowed Mrs. Mildred Dewey told him, "Give them hell."[146] To Daniels it seemed that "a few disgruntled officers" and some "partisan politicians" were engaged in a "conspiracy" to try to find "or to invent some flaw in the great work of the armed forces in the direction of the war." Admirals Samuel McGowan, Robert E. Coontz, the Chief of Naval Operations, and others demanded that he court-martial Sims, particularly for his stating that Benson had lacked "the will to win." Daniels refused to establish a court which he believed would have found Sims guilty. Admiral Henry Wilson upheld him, saying: "We want to make no martyrs. Admiral Sims has ruined himself, why not let him stay in the hole he has dug for himself."[147]

Daniels began testifying on 10 May with a strong statement against "certain critics, self-appointed to ferret out the molehills of mistakes which they exaggerate into mountains. . . ." The only thing that really counted, he said, was results. Small mistakes were undoubtedly made during the war, but the record of the Navy "stands untouched today and for all time by criticisms from within or without." As for Sims, he had not measured up to expectations in six ways: 1) he had not got at the U-boats in their bases; 2) he preferred British to American plans; 3) he maximized the British contribution and minimized the American; 4) he coveted British honors and placed a higher value upon them than upon those of his own country; 5) he aspired to become a member of the British Admiralty and complained when denied permission to do so; 6) "He placed protection of merchant shipping, with concentration of destroyers at Queenstown, as the main operation of our forces abroad, failing to appreciate that the protection of transports carrying troops to France was the paramount . . . naval duty until I felt impelled to cable him peremptorily that such was our main mission." Daniels said he had nevertheless granted Sims's request to be returned as President of the Naval War College, and he had recommended that he be made an admiral for life, for like Benson, Mayo, Rodman, and other admirals he had been wholeheartedly animated by the desire to defeat Germany.

Had Sims given his letter dated 7 January 1920 to the General Board for study, some good might have come from it, Daniels continued; but he had made it public, thereby bringing odium upon the Navy. Since Sims lacked all the information he needed to judge certain actions, the result was that his "scandalously unwarranted" charges had cast mud upon only himself. Of the twelve admirals most responsible for the direction of the war, Daniels noted, ten in addition to Sims had testified, and all had denied Sims's charges.[148] Given his position, which was merely that of a liaison officer in London, Daniels continued, Sims had been given all the staff he needed; indeed, although he had only seven officers on 1 July 1917, he had 179 officers and 373 men on duty by November 1918. None of the British admirals he had spoken with would admit Sims's charge that the American Navy had prolonged the war for four months and caused an unnecessary loss of 500,000 lives.[149] Moreover, President Wilson had suggested bolder operations than had either American or British naval officers. Indeed, "If Admiral Sims . . . suggested one important measure the United States Navy put into effect during the war, I can not recall it." And some of these policies were carried out despite Sims's objections to them. Then Daniels added that what Sims wanted was to "Prussianize" the Navy with a general staff and "place the Secretary of the Navy at the top of the Washington Monument without a telephone."[150]

As for Sims's charge that he "procrastinated," Daniels pointed out that within a few weeks after war was declared he had either under construction or under contract every destroyer that American yards had the capacity to build at that time. And destroyer construction time was reduced by 50 percent. Similar records of efficiency were made by all the Navy bureaus, while the Marines had contributed mightily to victory on the Western Front. In sum, "there was never a minute from April 6, 1917, to November 11, 1918, when a ship was ready to sail that the officers and men were not ready to man the ship, and this was true not only of fighting naval craft but also of hundreds of ships carrying troops and supplies and merchant ships. . . ."[151]

Hale began the cross-examination on 20 May by asking whether the Navy had drafted plans for war. Daniels replied that the Navy had basic plans that could be used against any nation bordering either ocean; it also had detailed plans for a war against Germany. Hale then asked for a schedule showing exactly what plans existed at the time the United States entered the war and when they were adopted, only to be warned by Daniels that there was "a great deal of bunk about this plan business." German plans in the Great War, for example, had exploded at the Marne. Plans must be made before a war begins, but they must change as conditions change.

Hale then asked whether the United States had written a plan specifically for antisubmarine warfare. Daniels mentioned a plan of 4 February 1917, but pointed out that at that time the United States was a neutral and could not have received plans from future allies. However, as early as 26 November 1915 he had called for the prepartion of the fleet for war and for the drafting of war plans. Thirteen plans had been written before the United States went to war. Later on, plans had been made for war with Germany. The last of the prewar plans dealt with "Assistance that United States can give Allies upon declaration of war." Additional plans for every possible contingency had been made during the months of April, May, and June 1917. But, persisted Hale, did Daniels "on the 1st day of February 1917, or about that time, [have] detailed plans all prepared so that the Navy could assume the offensive in submarine warfare and especially in areas where that submarine warfare would be carried on?" Daniels replied that the Black Plan covered all types of war, adding that there was no plan for a war in which U.S. naval forces would be used almost exclusively against submarines because every possible contingency had to be covered. That was all Hale could get from him.[152]

Why, continued Hale, did Daniels choose a captain, Benson, to be the chief of naval operations when there were on the active list twenty line admirals. He had first offered the post to Admiral Fletcher, Daniels replied, who had turned it down because he preferred to remain as commander in chief of the Atlantic fleet. It was then that he had offered it to Benson, in whom he had found the combination of character and professional ability that he believed best fitted the post.

Hale then sought to make hay out of Daniels's lack of knowledge concerning a letter on preparedness that he had received from Fiske in November 1914, and out of why he had told the General Board not to recommend 19,600 additional men for the 1915 program. Daniels was explaining that, given a choice between getting more battleships or more men, he preferred the ships, when Senator Key Pittman, of Nevada, intervened by saying that nothing would be gained by this kind of questioning, that Daniels had been cross-examined for four days already, and that the hearings should be closed as soon as possible.

Hale nevertheless tried to rake Daniels over the coals of the unreadiness of the fleet for war. Daniels had had the office of the chief of naval operations send Hale tables showing the status of each ship; whether she was in commission or in reserve; her location; her munitions supply; the number of days it would take to put her into "100 percent" condition in materiel; and the number of additional men needed to furnish her with her wartime complement. Hale had gone over the tables and listed the ships as "fit to fight" or "not fit to fight" in February 1917, but Daniels objected strenuously to those classifications and to Hale's use of his own staff to deduce conclusions from the tables. Hale nevertheless barreled through with the conclusion that the Navy had not been prepared to fight.

Hale asked why Daniels had chosen Sims to command American naval forces in Europe. Daniels replied that his first choice had been Henry Wilson, but he was put in charge of the Patrol Force, and Sims had been selected instead because he had seemed to be very excellently qualified and also knew the leading British and French naval officers.

Hale was still trying to make Sims look good and Daniels bad when the time came for Daniels to be dismissed. The only witness to follow Daniels was Sims, who was appearing for the second time and restated his case but added nothing that had not been in his original testimony. An appendix to the printed hearings contains recommendations from a large number of officers including Coontz, Badger, Mayo, Sims, Fletcher, and Fiske on how the Navy Department might be reorganized.

What did the hearings accomplish? Did the Navy Department need the reorganization Sims implied it did? Should Daniels be forced to leave the cabinet?

Sims did establish the fact that there was room for improvement in the department but failed to prove that its shortcomings stemmed from its administration. His questions served to reveal the "reforms" Daniels had introduced into the Navy and that Daniels had performed "a great job greatly done."

In 1921, when the investigation was almost forgotten, a majority report signed by three Republicans confirmed most of Sims's contentions, while two minority reports written by Democrats rejected his arguments.

On 2 March 1921, Daniels discussed with Edwin Denby the transfer of power. On the third he said goodby to the officers and men at the department. On the morning of the fourth he sent a farewell message to all ships and stations and arranged with a newspaper syndicate to publish a series of articles about the Navy at war. At 1500 on 5 March, at a ceremony in his office attended by the ranking officers of the department, the bureau chiefs, and the assistant chiefs, he watched Denby take the oath of office. He then prepared to return to his newspaper offices at Raleigh.

Daniels, George M. Robeson, and Gideon Welles were the only secretaries of the Navy who served two full terms, with Daniels's tenure eclipsing that of the others by a few days. When Daniels sent Wilson his collected wartime speeches, Wilson wrote him: "I hope that I made you feel throughout the war how completely I approved and supported your administration of the Navy which was, on the whole, the most difficult part of our warring activities. . . ."[153]

The *News and Observer* received most of Daniels's energy until 1933, when he began an eight-year career in diplomacy as Franklin D. Roosevelt's ambassador to Mexico, during which time he gave great strength to the Good Neighbor policy.[154] Although he served as editor of the *News and Observer* during World War II, he also wrote his multi-volume autobiography, the last two volumes of which deal with the Wilson Era, 1910–1923. He died in harness in 1948, in his eighty-sixth year.

NOTES

1. Josephus Daniels, *The Wilson Era: Years of Peace, 1910–1917* (Chapel Hill: University of North Carolina Press, 1944), pp. 110–11; Ben Dixon MacNeill, "Josephus Daniels," AM 29 (July 1933):305.

2. Arthur S. Link, *Wilson: The New Freedom* (Princeton, N.J.: Princeton University Press, 1956), p. 11; MacNeill, "Josephus Daniels," 305.

3. Josephus Daniels Diary, Daniels Papers, MDLC, entry of 5 Mar. 1913 (hereinafter cited merely as Diary); Daniels, *Wilson Era, 1910–1917*, pp. 119–20, 239.

4. Daniels, *Wilson Era, 1910–1917*, pp. 124–28, 148; Frank Friedel, *Franklin D. Roosevelt: The Apprenticeship* (Boston: Little, Brown, 1952), pp. 154–55.

5. B. A. Fiske to Daniels, 29 Dec. 1913, Daniels to Wilson, 4 Apr. 1915, Daniels Diary, 13–17, 20 May 1913; *Washington Post*, 27 Apr. 1913, 28 June, 9 July 1914; Paolo E. Coletta, " 'The Most Thankless Task': Bryan and the California Alien Land Legislation," PHR 36 (May 1967): 163–87.

6. Daniels, *Wilson Era; 1910–1917*; Friedel, *Roosevelt: The Apprenticeship*, pp. 275–85.

7. Daniels, *Wilson Era, 1910–1917*, pp. 257–58, 280, 329; Jonathan Daniels, *The End of Innocence* (Philadelphia: J. B. Lippincott, 1954), p. 47.

8. Daniels to Wilson, (?) Mar. 1913, Daniels Papers; *Washington Post*, 11 Mar., 7, 11, 13, 14 Apr. 1913; ARSN, 1914, p. 19.

9. Daniels to H. B. Rust, 20 July 1914, and Daniels, Diary, 24–26 Mar. 1913; ARSN, 1915, pp. 22–25; *Washington Post*, 2 July 1914; "The 'Plucking Board' on Trial," LD 49 (18 July 1914):92–93; RADM Thomas O. Selfridge, USN, "Plan of Selection," USNIP 42 (May-June 1916):915–16.

10. Daniels to J. J. Adkins, 27 May 1913, Daniels Papers; "Making Over Our Sea Language," *Nation* 96 (24 Apr. 1913):406–07.

11. ARSN, 1913, p. 6; *Washington Post*, 1 Apr., 29 May, 1–3 June 1913.

12. ARSN, 1913, p. 7; RADM Bradley A. Fiske, USN, *From Midshipman to Rear-Admiral* (New York: Century Co., 1919), pp. 351–52, 536–37; Josephus Daniels, "Training Our Bluejackets for Peace," IND 76 (11 Dec. 1913):490–92; Daniels, "The Navy: A Power for Peace," WW 28 (May 1914):62–63; Daniels, "The Navy at School," ARR 63 (June 1921):654–55.

13. ARSN, 1914, pp. 35, 150–51; Daniels, *Wilson Era, 1910–1917*, pp. 253–55.

14. Daniels to The Superintendent, CAPT William F. Fullam, 14 Mar. 1914, Daniels Papers; ARSN, 1913, pp. 23–24; ARSN, 1914, pp. 38–39, 147–48; Daniels, *Wilson Era, 1910–1917*, pp. 267–69.

15. RADM Austin M. Knight to Daniels, 9 Jan. 1914, Daniels Papers; ARSN, 1913, App., pp. 34–36; ARSN, 1914, pp. 39, 44; Daniels, *Wilson Era, 1910–1917*, pp. 260–61, 270–71, 279–80.

16. Daniels, *Wilson Era, 1910–1917*, pp. 273–76; T. H. Price, "Josephus Daniels: The Man Who Has Democratized the Navy," *Outlook* 118 (27 Mar. 1918):484–86.

17. Fiske to Daniels, 27 May 1914, Daniels Papers; ARSN, 1914, pp. 42–45; Daniels, *Wilson Era, 1910–1917*, pp. 386–403; "The Navy and Drinking," *Nation* 98 (9 Apr. 1914): 385–86; "For a 'Dry' Navy," LD 47 (18 Apr. 1914):890, and "Daniels Explains the Wine Mess Order," *ibid.* 55 (27 Oct. 1914):42–46.

18. The congressional naval committees handled appropriations as well as general legislation until the adoption of the Budget and Accounting Act of 1921. In the

Naval Militia, the federal government provided ships and other support for state units, whereas the Naval Reserve was a purely federal organization.

19. B. A. Fiske to Daniels, 13 Jan. 1914, Daniels Papers; U. S. House of Representatives, Naval Affairs Committee, Report No. 377, *Admirals and Vice Admirals USN*, 13 Mar. 1914, 63rd Cong., 2nd Sess. (Committee print).

20. ARSN, 1914, pp. 34–35.

21. Daniels to Lemuel Padgett, 19 Feb. 1914, Daniels to Bruce Barton, 25 Feb. 1914, Daniels Papers; ARSN, 1913, p. 22; ARSN, 1914, p. 48; ARSN, 1915, p. 26.

22. ARSN, 1913, pp. 20, 22, 24, 79–85; ARSN, 1914, pp. 40–42; ARSN, 1915, pp. 26–28, 133–34; Frank Friedel, *Franklin D. Roosevelt: The Ordeal* (Boston: Little, Brown, 1954), pp. 41–46.

23. "Georgian" to Daniels, 21 Jan. 1914, Daniels Papers.

24. Daniels, *Wilson Era, 1910–1917*, pp. 326, 337.

25. U.S. House of Representatives, *Council on National Defense*. Report No. 2078 (6 Feb. 1911), 61st Cong., 3rd Sess. (Committee print); ARSN, 1913, App. pp. 3, 29; Paul Y. Hammond, *Organizing for Defense: The American Military Establishment in the Twentieth Century* (Princeton, N.J.: Princeton University Press, 1961), pp. 64–72.

26. Lemuel Padgett to Daniels, 11 Oct. 1913, Daniels Papers; ARSN, 1913, App. pp. 29–33; ARSN, 1914, pp. 55–56; " 'Two Battleships,' Says Our Persuasive Secretary," ARR 49 (Jan. 1914):8.

27. ARSN, 1913, App. A, p. 53; ARSN, 1914, p. 9 and App. A, p. 63.

28. "Naval Appropriations in the Senate," ANJ 52 (27 Feb. 1915):822.

29. Senator-elect David I. Walsh to Daniels, 26 Dec. 1913, Senator John W. Weeks to Daniels, 27 Dec. 1913, Governor Samuel D. Folker, New Hampshire, to Daniels, 30 Dec. 1913, and Daniels, Diary, 5 Apr. 1913, Daniels Papers; George von L. Meyer, Former Secretary of the Navy, "Are Naval Expenditures Wasted?" NAR 201 (Feb. 1915):250–51; "Navy Yards and Stations," ANJ 51 (25 Oct. 1913):242, and "Conditions of our Navy Yards," *ibid.* 51 (1 Nov. 1913):224.

30. ARSN, 1913, pp. 41–42; ARSN, 1914, pp. 15–16; ARSN, 1915, pp. 125–26; LCDR John W. Adams USN, "The Influences Affecting Naval Shipbuilding Legislation, 1910–1916," USNWCR 22 (Dec. 1969):50.

31. ARSN, 1913, pp. 41–42; ARSN, 1914, p. 40; ARSN, 1915, pp. 47–48; "Report on the Atlantic Navy Yards," ANJ 51 (6 Sept. 1913):18.

32. H. R. Stanford, Memorandum to the SECNAV, 17 Feb. 1917, Daniels Papers; ARSN, 1913, pp. 16–19; ARSN, 1914, pp. 20–21; ARSN, 1915, pp. 51–53; *Washington Post*, 21, 23 May 1913.

33. Daniels to Senator Henry F. Ashurst, 15 Apr. 1913, Tillman to Daniels, 22, 29 May, 28 Aug. 1913, Daniels to Representative William Kent, 9 Sept. 1913, Axel Petre, Midvale Steel Co., to Daniels, 9 Sept. 1913, A. C. Dinkey, President, Carnegie Steel Co., to Daniels, 9 Sept. 1913, E. G. Grace, President, Bethlehem Steel Co., to Daniels, 9 Sept. 1913, Daniels Papers; U. S. Senate, *Cost of Armor Plate and Its Manufacture*, 63rd Cong., 1st Sess. (14 July 1913), S. Doc. No. 129 (Committee print).

34. Daniels to Tillman, 28 May 1914, Daniels Papers; ARSN, 1914, pp. 21–23; ARSN, 1915, pp. 57–58; "Commission on Armor Plate," ANJ 52 (31 Oct. 1914):259.

35. For an account of the entire subject, see Melvin I. Urofsky, "Josephus Daniels and the Armor Trust," *North Carolina Historical Review* 45 (July 1968):237–63.

36. Tillman to Daniels, two letters of 1 June 1914, Daniels to Padgett, 20 July 1914, Daniels to Representative Denver S. Church, 27 July 1914, Daniels Papers; ARSN, 1913, pp. 15–16; ARSN, 1914, pp. 18–19; ARSN, 1915, pp. 62–63; "History of the Naval Petroleum Reserves [1909–1924]," MS compiled by R. G. Tracie in 1937, copy in Daniels Papers; Daniels, *Wilson Era, 1910–1917*, pp. 368–81; Link, *Wilson: The New Freedom*, pp. 132–35; "Government Oil Reserves," ARR 54 (Dec. 1916):596–99.

37. ARSN, 1913, pp. 17–18; J. C. Hunsaker, *Forty Years of Aeronautical Research* (Washington: The Smithsonian Institution, 1956), pp. 241–45; *New York Sun*, 24 Feb. 1914; "Naval Aeronautics," ANJ 51 (10 Jan. 1914):583.

38. B. A. Fiske, Memorandum for the SECNAV, 19 Jan. 1914, and Fiske, Memorandum for the SECNAV, 9 June 1914, Daniels Papers; ARSN, 1914, p. 65; ARSN, 1915, p. 40.

39. Daniels to LCDR Ralph Earle, 10 Feb. 1914, Daniels Papers; F. F. Fletcher to Daniels, 9 Apr. 1914, Washington: National Archives, Department of State Decimal File, 812.00/11497. On 15 Sept. 1916, by adding Article 1648 to *United States Navy Regulations*, Daniels prohibited the issue by a naval officer of an ultimatum to, or demand for service from, a foreign power without first communicating with the Navy department "except in extreme cases where such action is necessary to save life."

40. *New York World*, 21 Apr. 1914; Robert E. Quirk, *An Affair of Honor: Woodrow Wilson and the Occupation of Veracruz* (Lexington: University of Kentucky Press, 1962); Jack Sweetman, *Landing at Veracruz: 1914* (Annapolis, Md.: U.S. Naval Institute, 1967).

41. RADM Bradley A. Fiske, USN, "The Paramount Duty of the Army and Navy," USNIP 40 (July–Aug. 1914):41–42.

42. Fiske, *From Midshipman*, p. 533; "Proper Control of the Navy," ANJ 52 (24 Oct. 1914):227.

43. Fiske, *From Midshipman*, pp. 540–45, 548–53.

44. *Ibid.*, pp. 553–58, 561, 562, 599–601.

45. *Ibid.*, pp. 564–65.

46. U.S. House of Representatives, Naval Affairs Committee, *Chief of Naval Operations*. Report to Accompany H.R. 21257 (to create Office of Chief of Naval Operations), 2 Feb. 1915, House Report 1344, 63rd Cong., 2nd Sess. (Washington: GPO, 1915); U.S. Senate. *Naval Investigation Hearings before the Subcommittee of the Committee on Naval Affairs*, 66th Cong., 2nd Sess., 2 vols. (Washington: GPO, 1921), 1:268; 2:1793, 1881–82 (hereafter cited as NIH); Fiske, *From Midshipman*, pp. 567–70; Hammond, *Organizing for Defense*, pp. 71–77.

47. Daniels, Diary, 26 Jan. 1915; Fiske, *From Midshipman*, pp. 570–71.

48. Fiske, *From Midshipman*, pp. 573, 577–78.

49. *Ibid.*, pp. 584–85; interview with COMMO Howard H. J. Benson, USN (RET), Annapolis, Md., July 28, 1966. Among other newspapers, the *New York Times*, *New York Tribune*, and the *Army and Navy Journal* favored Fiske for the new post.

50. Among many items critical of Daniels, see Burton J. Hendricks, "The Case of Josephus Daniels," WW 32 (July 1916):281–96; By the Editor [George Harvey], "The Rt. Hon. N.C.B. [North Carolina Boy], Our First Lord of the Admiralty," NAR 201 (Apr. 1915):481–500, and [Harvey], "Preparedness a Political Issue," *ibid.* 203 (Apr. 1916):481–92; "Warships Considered as Universities," ANJ 51 (13 Sept. 1913):48–49; "Civilianizing the Navy," *ibid.* 51 (July 1914): 1114–15; "Daniels in the Lion's Den," LD 50 (24 Apr. 1915):941–42, and "Daniels at Bay," *ibid.* 52 (8 Apr. 1916):955–56. For Daniels's rebuttal, see "What's Been Done for the Navy Since March 4, 1913," Ms. dated 19 Feb. 1915, Daniels Papers; "Secretary Daniels' Defense," LD 50 (8 May 1915):1067; Josephus Daniels, "A Navy Prepared and Efficient," IND 84 (6 Dec. 1915):382.

51. F. D. Roosevelt to Mrs. F. D. Roosevelt, 1, 2, 5 Aug. 1914, 10 June 1915, in Elliott Roosevelt, ed., *FDR: His Personal Letters*, 4 vols. (New York: Duell, Sloan and Pearce, 1947–1952), 2:233; F. D. Roosevelt to Daniels, 1, 4, 18 Apr., 12 July 1917, Daniels Papers.

52. See for example Daniels to Hamilton Holt, 28 Aug. 1914, Daniels to RADM F. E. Chadwick, 25 Aug. 1915, Daniels to CAPT W. S. Sims, 21 July 1916, Daniels to Fiske, 16 Dec. 1916, 25 Mar. 1917, Daniels Papers. Also, on 5 Nov. 1914 Daniels wrote to ADM George Dewey, President of the General Board of the Navy, that the board must treat as "strictly confidential" any discussion of "our naval policy in connection with the present situation in Europe." (Washington: NHD:OA, GB Series, 429–2, GB Records).

53. Daniels, Diary, 26 Jan., 2 Feb. 1915, Daniels Papers; Arthur S. Link, *Wilson: Confusions and Crises, 1915–1916* (Princeton, N.J.: Princeton University Press, 1964), pp. 36, 321, 339–40; Richard Lowitt, "The Armed-Ship Bill Controversy: A Legislative View," *Mid-America* 46 (Jan. 1964):38–47.

54. Wilson to Daniels, 27 Jan. 1915, Ray Stannard Baker, *Woodrow Wilson: Life and Letters*, 8 vols. (Garden City, N.Y.: Doubleday, Page, 1927–1939), 5:15.

55. Ray S. Baker and William E. Dodd, eds., *The Public Papers of Woodrow Wilson*, 6 vols. (New York: Harper and Brothers, 1925–1927), 1:223–27.

56. Matthew Josephson, *Edison* (New York: McGraw-Hill, 1959), pp. 446–55; George S. Bryan, *Edison: The Man and His Work* (New York: Knopf, 1926), pp. 228–41; Lloyd N. Scott, *Naval Consulting Board of the United States* (Washington: GPO, 1920); Thomas Parkes Hughes, "Early Government Research and Development: The Naval Consulting Board During World War I," MS, courtesy Professor Hughes.

57. Daniels to Benson 20 Apr. 1916, Daniels to Padgett, 20 Apr. 1916. William S. Benson Papers, MDLC (used by permission of COMMO H. H. J. Benson, USN (RET).

58. ARSN, 1916, p. 70; Grosvenor B. Clarkson, *Industrial America and the World War: The Strategy Behind the Lines, 1917–1918* (Boston: Houghton Mifflin, 1923), esp. pp. 11–12, 27–49, 316–17; Louis B. Wehle, *Hidden Threads of History: Wilson Through Roosevelt* (New York: Macmillan, 1953), pp. 3–30.

59. Baker, *Wilson*, 5:8.

60. Report of the GB, 30 July 1915, in *New York Times*, 25 Dec. 1915; Link, *Wilson: The New Freedom*, pp. 585–93; "The Naval-Increase Program," LD 52 (8 Jan. 1916):53–55.

61. ARSN, 1915, pp. 5, 74–76; ARSN, 1916, p. 81.

62. ARSN, 1916, pp. 6–9, 61–62, 305–06; "Naval Legislation in Prospect," ANJ 53 (23 Oct. 1915):144.

63. *New York Times*, 4 Feb. 1914; Baker, *Wilson*, 5:25–31, and 6:29n; Link, *Wilson: The New Freedom*, pp. 185–86; "The President's Preparedness Tour," IND 85 (14 Feb. 1916):216–17.

64. *New York Times*, 27 June, 30 Aug. 1915; *New York World*, 6, 20 Oct., 6 Nov., 8 Dec. 1915; Josephus Daniels, "Comments on Naval Appropriations Bill as Passed by Congress, 29 Aug. 1916," MS, Daniels Papers; "A Rush Order for a Big Navy," LD 53 (15 July 1916):117–18.

65. ARSN, 1916, pp. 4–5, 11, 75–76.

66. Benson to Daniels, 28 Oct. 1916, Daniels Papers; ARSN, 1916, pp. 9–11, 82, 84, 288, 293–94, 309; "The Shipbuilding Bids," ANJ 54 (20 Jan. 1917):653.

67. ARSN, 1916, pp. 2, 38–39, 83, 217, App. H., pp. 139–41; ARSN, 1917, pp. 29, 32–33, 45–47, 77, 759.

68. ARSN, 1916, pp. 60–64.

69. *Ibid.*, p. 90; "Report from the Director of Gunnery Exercises," CAPT C. P. Plunkett, 10 July 1916, Daniels Papers; "Atlantic Fleet Games," ANJ 53 (2 Sept. 1916):19.

70. E. M. House, Diary, entry of 6 Apr. 1916, E. M. House Papers, Sterling Memorial Library, Yale University; John Blum, *Joe Tumulty and the Wilson Era* (Boston: Houghton Mifflin, 1951), pp. 110–22; Jonathan Daniels, *The End of Innocence*, pp. 188–92; Norman Hapgood, *The Changing Years: Reminiscences* (New York: Farrar and Rinehart, 1930), p. 233.

71. Daniels, Diary, 1–3 Feb. 1917; Daniels to Wilson, 2 Feb. 1917, Woodrow Wilson Papers, MDLC; *New York Times*, 3 Feb. 1917.

72. N. D. Baker to Daniels, 7 Feb. 1917, 3 Mar. 1921, Daniels to McAdoo, 19 Feb. 1917, Bernard Baruch to Daniels, 22 Mar., 16 May 1917, Daniels Papers; Baker, *Wilson*, 6:464; Josephus Daniels, *Our Navy At War* (New York: George H. Doran, 1922), pp. 22–23.

73. "The Naval Bill for 1918," ANJ 54 (17 Feb. 1917):795; "Navy Bill in the Senate," *ibid.* 54 (24 Feb. 1917):826.

74. "Speeding Naval Construction," *ibid.* 54 (10 Mar. 1917):897; "Our Naval Defenses," *ibid.* 54 (17 Mar. 1917):930; "Plans for a Large 'Mosquito' Fleet," *ibid.* 54 (24 Mar. 1917):964.

75. Franklin K. Lane to G. W. Lane, 9 Feb. 1917, Anne Wintermute Lane and Louise Herrick Wall, eds., *The Letters of Franklin K. Lane: Personal and Political* (New York: Houghton Mifflin, 1922), pp. 234–35; David G. Houston, *Eight Years With Wilson's Cabinet*, 2 vols. (Garden City, N.Y.: Doubleday Page, 1926), 1:230–34; *New York Times*, 8 Feb. 1917.

76. Daniels to Wilson, 10 Feb. 1917, Wilson Papers; Daniels, Diary, 25 Feb. 1917; Lane and Wall, eds., *Letters of Franklin K. Lane*, pp. 239–40; Houston, *Eight Years*, 1:234–37; Arthur S. Link, *Wilson: Campaigns for Progressivism and Peace* (Princeton, N.J.: Princeton University Press, 1965), pp. 310–13, 340–41.

77. Daniels, Diary, 6 Mar. 1917.

78. Daniels to Wilson, 8 Mar. 1917, Wilson Papers.

79. Daniels, Diary, 8, 11–13 Mar. 1917; Daniels to Wilson, 9 Mar. 1917, Wilson

Papers; The Secretary of the Navy to the Secretary of State, 11 Mar. 1917, U.S. Department of State, *Papers Relating to the Foreign Relations of the United States, 1917, Supplement 1*, p. 171; *New York Times*, 13 Mar. 1917; "To Arm Our Merchantmen," ANJ 54 (17 Mar. 1917):929.

80. Daniels, Diary, 20 Mar. 1917; Daniels to Wilson, 30 Mar. 1917, Wilson Papers.
81. Daniels, Diary, 27, 29 Mar. 1917; Daniels typescript, "The Night of April Second a Historical Occasion,"; George Creel to Daniels, 4 Apr. 1917, Daniels Papers.
82. Josephus Daniels, *The Life of Woodrow Wilson, 1856–1924* (Philadelphia: John C. Winston, 1924), p. 286.
83. Daniels, Diary, 15 May 1917; ARSN, 1917, pp. 6–7; 11–17, 32–33, 157; ARSN, 1918, pp. 9, 17–18, 30–35, 66–70, 74, 511, 545–49; Allan Nevins and Frank E. Hill, *Ford: Expansion and Challenge, 1915–1933* (New York: Charles Scribner's Sons, 1957), pp. 69–76; CDR J. A. Furer. C.C., USN, "The 110-Foot Submarine Chasers and Eagle Boats," USNIP 45 (May 1919):743–52; Carroll Storrs Alden, "American Submarine Operations in the War," *ibid.* 46 (June 1920):811–50, and 46 (July 1920):1013–48.
84. Daniels, Diary, 11–12 Apr. 1917; Albert Gleaves, *History of the Transport Service: Experiences of U.S. Transports and Cruisers in the World War* (New York: George H. Doran, 1921); Lewis P. Clephane, *History of the Naval Overseas Transport Service in World War I* (Washington: GPO, 1969): Edward N. Hurley, *The Bridge to France* (Philadelphia: J. B. Lippincott, 1927).
85. NIH, 1:268, 1793, 1881–82; 2:1913, 1917, 2003.
86. *Ibid.*, 2:1913, 1917, 1995, 2003.
87. Elting E. Morison, *Admiral Sims and the Modern American Navy* (Boston: Houghton Mifflin, 1942), pp. 395–96; Gerald E. Wheeler, "William Veazie Pratt, U.S. Navy: Silhouette of an Admiral," USNWCR 21 (May 1969):41–42.
88. CAPT Thomas Frothingham, USNR, *Naval History of the World War*, 3 vols. (Cambridge, Mass.: Harvard University Press, 1924–1926), 3:33–35; Morison, *Sims*, pp. 344–45, 349–50; David Lloyd George, *War Memoirs of David Lloyd George*, 6 vols. (Boston: Little, Brown, 1933–1937), 3:93–94, 107; Henry Newbolt, *History of the Great War Based on Official Documents*, vol. 5. *Naval Operations* (London: Longmans, Green, 1931), 1–19.
89. Daniels, Diary, 17, 24 Apr. 1917.
90. Burton J. Hendrick, *The Life and Letters of Walter H. Page*, 3 vols. (Garden City, N.Y.: Doubleday Page, 1924–1926), 2:278–79.
91. Daniels, Diary, 9 Oct. 1917.
92. ARSN, 1918, p. 15; Morison, *Sims*, p. 356.
93. Wilson to Daniels, 2, 3 July 1917, Daniels Papers.
94. Sims to Daniels, 3 July 1917; Morison, *Sims*, p. 358.
95. Daniels, Diary, 4, 6 July 1917; Wilson to Sims, 4 July 1917, Morison, *Sims*, pp. 407–12; RADM William Sowden Sims, USN, in collaboration with Burton J. Hendrick, *The Victory at Sea* (Garden City, N.Y.: Doubleday, Page, 1920), pp. 122–41.
96. Morison, *Sims*, p. 359.
97. "Admiral Benson on Submarines," ANJ 55 (29 July 1917):153, and editorial, *ibid.* 55 (18 Sept. 1917):57.

98. Daniels to Sims, 15 Dec. 1917, Daniels Papers; ARSN, 1918, pp. 8–9.

99. Wilson to Daniels, 2 Aug. 1917, Daniels Papers.

100. Daniels, Diary, 11 Aug. 1917; Daniels, *Wilson Era, 1910–1917*, pp. 42–45, 47, 68, 89.

101. Daniels, Diary, 28 Oct. 1917; Daniels to Benson, two telegrams of 28 Nov. 1917, Daniels Papers. See also ARSN, 1918, p. 14, and David F. Trask, *The United States in the Supreme War Council: American War Aims and Inter-Allied Strategy, 1917–1918* (Middletown, Conn.: Wesleyan University Press, 1961), pp. 15–19.

102. Daniels, Diary, 2 Feb. 1918.

103. ADM W. S. Benson, "Naval Conference of 29, 30 November 1917," and "Proceedings of the Inter-Allied Council," n.d., Benson Papers.

104. Daniels, Diary, 26 Nov. 1917, 1 Jan., 2 Feb. 1918; NIH, 2:1984.

105. CAPT Reginald R. Belknap USN, *The Yankee Mining Squadron* (Annapolis, Md.: U.S. Naval Institute, 1920); Navy Department, Office of Naval Records and Library, *The Northern Barrage and Other Mining Activities* (Washington: GPO, 1920), pp. 9–37; CAPT Reginald R. Belknap, USN, "The North Sea Mine Barrage," *National Geographic Magazine* 35 (Feb. 1919):85–110.

106. Daniels, Diary, 8, 16, 17 Dec. 1917.

107. *Ibid.*, 20 Dec. 1917.

108. Daniels to Sims, 10 June 1917, Morison, *Sims*, pp. 419–21; Daniels, Diary, 24 Feb. 1918; Josephus Daniels, *The Wilson Era: Years of War and After, 1917–1923* (Chapel Hill: University of North Carolina Press, 1946), p. 95.

109. Daniels, Diary, 8, 14, 15 Oct. 1918; Daniels to Wilson, 14 Nov. 1918, Wilson to Daniels, 18 Nov. 1918, Daniels Papers; "More Naval Folly," *Nation* 107 (30 Nov. 1918):637.

110. Daniels, Diary, 21, 22, 24 Oct. 1918; Planning Section Memorandum No. 6 [Building Program], to Benson, 21 Oct. 1918, Benson Papers; Benson to Daniels, 23 Jan. 1919, Daniels Papers.

111. Daniels, Diary, 3, 4 Nov. 1918.

112. RADM Ralph Earle to Daniels, 31 May 1917, RADM Parsons to Daniels, 4 June 1917, Daniels Papers: LT Charles C. Gill, USN, "Naval Power in the Present War," CH 6 (June 1917):490–95; "Secretary Daniels on the Naval Act," ANJ 55 (6 July 1918):1730.

113. *New York Times*, 4 Dec. 1918, 31 Jan. 1919; "House Passes Naval Bill," ANJ 56 (15 Feb. 1919): 859.

114. "Naval Appropriations in the Senate," ANJ 56 (1 Mar. 1919): 929. Daniels had written to Benson, who was in Europe: "We are all moving on well here. I envy you the privilege but this fight for our three year program is not easy and my imperative duty is here." (Letter of 26 Nov. 1918, Benson Papers.)

115. Pratt to Benson, 25 Oct. 1918, Benson Papers; Daniels to Wilson, 4 Mar. 1919, Daniels Papers.

116. Daniels, *Wilson Era, 1917–1923*, p. 374.

117. House, Diary, 30 Mar. 1919; ADM W. S. Benson, "Notes Relating to the International Conference on the Limitation of Armaments, 26 September 1921," Benson Papers.

118. E. David Cronon, ed., *The Cabinet Diaries of Josephus Daniels, 1913–1921* (Lin-

coln: University of Nebraska Press, 1963), p. 384n; "Our Navy for Security," ARR 59 (Mar. 1919):230–31.

119. Daniels, Diary, 7 Apr. 1919; House, Diary, 8–10, 12, 19 Apr. 1919; Rolland A. Chaput, *Disarmament in British Foreign Policy* (London: Allen and Unwin, 1935), pp. 72–74; Daniels, *Wilson Era, 1917–1923*, pp. 367–69, 382.

120. Daniels, Diary, 1 May 1919.

121. *United States Naval Activity in Connection with the Armistice of 1918, and the Peace Conference, of 1919* (Prepared by the Division on Naval Intelligence, United States Navy Department, 31 Mar. 1944, GB 429-2, GB Records.

122. U.S. House Naval Affairs Committee, *Hearings on Estimates Submitted by the Secretary of the Navy*, 66th Cong. 2nd Sess. (Washington: GPO, 1919), pp. 2217–19; Daniels, *Wilson Era, 1917–1923*, pp. 306–09.

123. Daniels to N. D. Baker, 14 Jan. 1920, Daniels Papers; "The Sixty-sixth Congress," ANJ 56 (21 June 1919):1474; "Navy Against Aeronautics Department," *ibid.* 56 (1 Mar. 1919):929; BGEN William Mitchell, Air Service U.S. Army, "Aviation over the Water," ARR 62 (Oct. 1920): 391–98.

124. "Personnel Situation in the Navy," ANJ 56 (2 Aug. 1919): 1673; "Mr. Roosevelt Asks Relief of Navy," *ibid.* 57 (13 Sept. 1919): 50; "Reducing the Navy Personnel," CH 16 (Apr. 1919): 137; Archibald Douglas Turnbull, "Economy and Naval Personnel," NAR 215 (Apr. 1922):459–63.

125. Daniels, *Wilson Era, 1917–1923*, pp. 451–82.

126. Daniels to N. D. Baker, 5 May, 12 Nov. 1920, 7 Feb. 1921; ADM R. E. Coontz to Daniels, 23, 28 Feb. 1921, Daniels Papers. See for example CDR D. E. Cummings, USN, " 'Aviation' or 'Naval Aviation': Which?" USNIP 46 (Feb. 1920): 177–80; CAPT T. T. Craven, USN, "Naval Aviation and a United Air Service," *ibid.* 47 (Mar. 1921):307–22; BGEN William Mitchell, "Air Power vs. Sea Power," ARR 63 (Mar. 1921):273–77.

127. "Secretary Daniels Urges Big Navy," ANJ 57 (13 Mar. 1920):843–44.

128. "Naval Appropriations Bill Analyzed," *ibid.* 57 (12 June 1920): 1263–64; "Japan's Growing Navy," *ibid.* 57 (24 July 1920):1437; Thaddeus V. Tuleja, *Statesman and Admirals: Quest for a Far Eastern Naval Policy* (New York: Norton, 1963), pp. 23–27.

129. ARSN, 1920, pp. 211, 216; *New York World*, 26 Dec. 1920; "Decline of Preparedness," ANJ 58 (27 Nov. 1920):360–61; "Secretary Daniels' Attitude [Toward Naval Disarmament]," ARR 63 (Feb. 1921):117; Josephus Daniels, "Why the United States Needs a Big Navy," SEP 193 (19 Mar. 1921):8–10.

130. U.S. Congress. House. *Hearings on Sundry Legislation Affecting the Naval Establishment, 1920–1921*, 66th Cong., 3rd Sess. (Washington: GPO, 1921), p. 86; Daniels, *Wilson Era, 1917–1923*, pp. 584–85; "Naval Building Holiday Before House Committee," ANJ 58 (15 Jan. 1920):561, 572.

131. "Naval Appropriations Bill Reported," ANJ 58 (5 Feb. 1921):646, and "Hampering Naval Aviation," *ibid.* 58 (12 Feb. 1921):697; Thomas W. Ray, "The Bureaus Go On Forever," USNIP 94 (Jan. 1968):54–55.

132. "To Suspend Naval Building Program," ANJ 58 (29 Jan. 1921):622, and "Fleet Elements Hearings," *ibid* 58 (12 Feb. 1921):664–65, 671–72.

133. *Hearings on Disarmament: Its Relation to the Naval Policy and the Naval Building Program of the United States,* reprinted in *Hearings on Sundry Naval Legislation, 1920–1921.*

134. "The Navy Investigation," ANJ 55 (18 Jan. 1918):744, and "Notes on the Navy," *ibid.* 56 (23 Feb. 1918):953.

135. "Navy Radio Plan Opposed," *ibid.* 57 (6 Sept. 1919):6.

136. Carter Glass to Daniels, 30 June 1919, D. F. Houston to Daniels, 3 Mar. 1920, Daniels to Carter Glass, 27 June, 7 July 1919, Daniels to Houston, 18 Feb. 1920, Daniels Papers; "Coast Guard Returned to Treasury," ANJ 57 (6 Sept. 1919):7.

137. Daniels, *Wilson Era, 1917–1923,* pp. 497–98, 505–07; NIH, 1:328–430.

138. NIH, 1:328–40, 369.

139. *Ibid.,* 1:586–99. See also CAPT Joseph Taussig, USN, "A Study of Our Navy Personnel Situation," USNIP 47 (Aug. 1921):1155.

140. NIH, 1:613–15.

141. *Ibid.,* 1:23; Tracy Barrett Kittredge, *Naval Lessons of the Great War: A Review of the Senate Naval Investigation of the Criticisms by Admiral Sims of the Policies and Methods of Josephus Daniels* (Garden City, N.Y.: Doubleday, Page, 1921), pp. 92–116.

142. Daniels, *Wilson Era, 1917–1923,* pp. 501–02.

143. Morison, *Sims,* p. 455. Morison has also written (p. 194) that Sims had "a gift for overstatement which at times amounted to real genius."

144. NIH, 1:28–328; Kittredge, *Naval Lessons,* pp. 117–40.

145. NIH, 1:294.

146. Daniels, *Wilson Era,* 1917–1923, p. 502.

147. *Ibid.,* pp. 503–04.

148. This was not quite so. Some officers, like Pratt, walked a tightrope between Daniels and Sims. On balance, however, most upheld Sims. A poll of the newspaper editors of the country on who should be Harding's secretary of the navy put Sims far in the lead among Republicans. ("The Next Cabinet," LD 67 [16 Oct. 1920]:10–11.)

149. NIH, 2:1981–2009.

150. *Ibid.,* 2:2009–77, 2099–2100.

151. *Ibid.,* 2: 2459, 2476–2644.

152. *Ibid.,* 2: 2719–20.

153. Wilson to Daniels, 27 May 1922, Daniels Papers. See Josephus Daniels, *The Navy and the Nation: War-Time Addresses by Josephus Daniels, Secretary of the Navy* (New York: George H. Doran, 1919).

154. See E. David Cronon, *Josephus Daniels in Mexico* (Madison: University of Wisconsin Press, 1960); MacNeill, "Josephus Daniels," 297–306.

EDWIN DENBY

6 March 1921–10 March 1924

GERALD E. WHEELER

The selection of Edwin Denby as Secretary of Navy by Warren G. Harding surprised a great many political pundits, for the President-elect had approached several big names such as Governor Frank Lowden of Illinois. Lowden had tried for the Republican presidential nomination, however, and an offer to associate with "the best minds in America" (Harding's description of his cabinet choices) was a poor consolation prize. Thus a former congressman, automobile manufacturer, and Detroit politician received the nod on 23 February 1921, for purely political reasons. Michigan had become an important industrial state and Denby was expected to help maintain Republican strength in the upper Mississippi Valley. That he had a record of service in the Navy and a rudimentary knowledge of its structure was pure chance.

Denby was born in Evansville, Indiana, on 18 February 1870. His father had been American Minister to China in the 1880s and young Denby had worked for the Chinese Customs Service. During the 1890s he attended the University of Michigan, starred at football, and graduated in law in 1896. Later he was admitted to the Michigan bar. As a member of the Detroit Naval Militia he served in the Spanish–American War and emerged as a Gunner's Mate Second Class. After the war he returned to Detroit, entered politics, and served one term in Michigan's lower house. Between 1904 and 1911 he was three times elected to the House of Representatives from Detroit's First Congressional District. In 1910 the House of Representatives went Democratic and Denby entered into private practice and marriage simultaneously. His wife, the former Marion Bartlett Thurber of Detroit bore him a son and a daughter.

In April 1917, following the United States's declaration of war against Germany, a somewhat overweight and overage Denby "pulled a few strings" and was accepted as a private in the U.S. Marine Corps. He survived the rigors of "boot camp" and progressed steadily through the ranks. Assigned to training and morale work at Parris Island, he lectured on citizenship, the flag, and the spirit of *semper fidelis*. At war's end he was separated as a major, but he continued his affiliation with the Marines by accepting a reserve commission.

While the Chief Probation Officer of the Recorder's Court for the City of Detroit and Wayne County, Denby stumped Michigan for Harding in 1920 and in February 1921 he was asked to join a cabinet containing such luminaries as Charles Evans Hughes as Secretary of State, Andrew Mellon in the Treasury Department, and Herbert Hoover in Commerce. Among these worthies, Denby was almost obscure. Most of the cabinet nominees were wealthy; Denby was not.[1]

The Senate confirmed Harding's cabinet choices on 4 March 1921. The next day Denby was sworn in as Secretary of the Navy. Warmly welcomed at the Navy Department and by those interested in naval affairs, he reciprocated by stating that he stood for a navy "equal to any other" and supported the current building programs.[2]

When Denby moved from the War-State-Navy Building to the Navy Department Building on Constitution Avenue, many feared that his moving away from the seat of civilian supremacy would result in his capture by his admirals, whereas he believed that his work would be eased by being close to the offices of the Chief of Naval Operations and the bureau chiefs, none of whom were changed except for retirements and normal rotation of duty billets.

Theodore Roosevelt, Jr., the new Assistant Secretary of the Navy, a son of President Theodore Roosevelt, had served with distinction in France during the World War and had left the service as a lieutenant colonel. He liked the Navy and thoroughly enjoyed those rare occasions when Denby was absent and he was "Acting Secretary."

Denby's Navy reminds one of the traveler in Mathew Arnold's "Grand Chartreuse" who was caught between two worlds, one dead and the other powerless to be born. Were the 1916 building program completed, the U.S. Navy would be "second to none." But the chances of its completion were rather remote. When Denby took office ten battleships were still incomplete and six battle cruisers were merely keels. Ten scout cruisers were approaching completion, more than fifty destroyers had been built, and the sixty-seven authorized submarines were mostly built or laid down. However, to many congressmen the postwar construction race among the British, Japanese, and American navies seemed absurd and wasteful. Indeed, Senator W. E. Borah of Idaho, on 14 December 1920 introduced a joint resolution calling for the President to convoke an international conference to reduce naval armaments.[3] Borah knew that President Woodrow Wilson would not respond to his legislative invitation, but he hoped to initiate a nationwide grassroots movement that would force Harding to act.

Once Harding was in office, Borah increased his activities to force him to call an arms limitation conference. In part because of Borah, the Sixty-Sixth Congress had adjourned without passing a naval appropriations act for the fiscal year 1922, and the naval reduction advocates gave evidence of preventing naval legislation in the special session of the Sixty-Seventh Congress unless their wishes were heeded. On 11 July 1921 the President extended invitations to Great Britain, Japan, France, and Italy to meet in Washington to discuss the reduction of armaments and problems of the Far East. Later the conference was broadened, because Far Eastern questions were to be discussed, by the inclusion of China, Portugal, the Netherlands, and Belgium. The convening date was set for 11 November 1921.[4]

Secretary of State Charles E. Hughes insisted that the conference be an assemblage of diplomats and not naval ministers. Harding agreed that Hughes should lead the American delegation and passed Denby by. Hughes expected the Navy Department to supply technical information and assistance. Because naval officers were not among the delegates, Assistant Secretary Roosevelt became the principal liaison between the delegation and the Navy Department. He worked consistently with the Chief of Naval Operations, Admiral Robert E. Coontz, and his assistant, Captain William V. Pratt. In the background, evaluating proposals and attempting to protect the Navy's interests as it saw them, was a very fretful General Board.[5]

Several naval limitation plans were submitted to Hughes's group by the Navy Department, but since they all proposed completion of some of the sixteen capital ships from the 1916 Act, they were rejected. Finally Hughes asked for evaluation of his proposal that a "stop now" approach be taken, including a capital ship building holiday for ten years. The General Board objected strenuously, but Hughes won over his delegation and the President as well. Hughes's proposal gave the United States parity in capital ships with Great Britain and Japan 60 percent of parity. The General Board had insisted that Japan should have no more than 50 per cent, but again Hughes prevailed. On 12 November, at the first plenary session of the conference, after dispensing the usual felicitations and greetings, Hughes presented the full American plan for naval reduction.[6]

The secretary sought three primary objectives: to satisfy the demand of the American public that heavy naval spending cease, to protect American Far Eastern interests, and to end the Anglo-Japanese Alliance.[7]

The first major treaty to emerge from the conference was the Four-Power Pact, signed on 13 December 1921 by the United States, Great Britain, Japan, and France. In it the signatories agreed to "respect their rights in relation to their insular possessions and insular dominions in the region of the Pacific Ocean," and that the Anglo-Japanese Alliance concluded on 13 July 1911 would end with the exchange of ratifications. America's other Far Eastern interests, the preservation of the Open Door and China's political and territorial integrity, were taken care of by the Nine-Power Treaty, signed 6 February 1922.

The most important treaty to come out of the conference was the Five–Power Naval Treaty signed on 6 February 1922 by the United States, Great Britain, Japan, France, and Italy. The following were the more important provisions for the U.S. Navy:

1. *Capital Ship* (battleships and battle cruisers) tonnage was limited to 525,000 tons for the United States and Great Britain; 315,000 tons for Japan; 175,000 tons for Italy and France. Capital ships limited to 35,000 tons maximum displacement; guns no more than 16-inch calibre. No new capital ships, except as allowed in the treaty, would be laid down until 12 November 1931.
2. *Aircraft Carrier* tonnage limited to 135,000 tons for the United States and Great Britain; 81,000 tons for Japan; 60,000 tons for Italy and France. Aircraft carriers limited to 27,000 tons maximum displacement; each nation, within its total aircraft carrier tonnage allowance, may build two carriers not to exceed 33,000 tons displacement each; a maximum of eight guns of 8-inch calibre may be placed on aircraft carriers.
3. *No Fighting Vessel* except capital ships shall exceed 10,000 tons, nor shall such a vessel carry guns in excess of 8-inches calibre.
4. *Insular Possessions* of the contracting powers in the Pacific Ocean, with certain exceptions (viz. Hawaiian Islands), shall not be further fortified and their remaining defenses shall remain in the *status quo*.[8]

Although not particularly pleased with the Five-Power Treaty, Denby defended Hughes's handiwork. If a Japanese Navy 60 percent the size of America's did not deeply disturb the General Board, the nonfortification provision (Article XIX) was a shocker. Utterly gone was the possibility of developing major naval bases on Guam or in the Philippines to support operations against Japan. Hence naval war plans must be radically altered because Guam and the Philippines could not be defended against a determined naval attack; and the U.S. Fleet could not operate successfully in Far Eastern waters from Pearl Harbor. On the other hand, continental America was safe from the Japanese fleet. America's Far Eastern interests were to have parchment defenses—the Four-Power and Nine-Power Treaties.[9] However, the United States had won parity with Great Britain and, in theory at least, laid Anglo-American naval rivalry to rest.

While Denby had little to do with the drafting of the Five-Power Treaty, he had the herculean task of protecting what little navy the diplomats allowed to remain and of bringing the fleet to treaty strength. Modern combat auxiliaries, particularly cruisers, fleet submarines, destroyer leaders, aircraft carriers, and modern supply ships were needed to "round out the fleet." Despite these needs, so evident to Chief of Naval Operations Coontz and his bureau chiefs, Congress began hearings in the winter and spring of 1921–1922 to see if the Navy could not be further reduced. To many congressmen the obvious starting place was personnel. If the naval treaties had reduced the Navy's ships, should not its manpower be reduced?

Since the close of the World War the Navy's personnel strength had diminished steadily. On 1 December 1918 there were 32,208 officers and warrants on active duty, 494,358 enlisted men, and 1,362 vessels in commission. A little over three years later, on 1 January 1922, this force had shrunk to 6,163 commissioned officers, 100,000 men, and 900 ships. By law (the 1916 naval bill) the "authorized strength" of the Navy had been set at a maximum of 137,500 enlisted men in peacetime and an officer corps of four percent of the enlisted strength—5,500 line and staff officers. Department policy was to keep the officer strength at the maximum number possible and to allow available appropriations to determine the size of the enlisted force, which in emergencies could be augmented quickly.[10]

From February through May 1922, Denby, Coontz, and the Chief of the Bureau of Navigation, Rear Admiral Thomas Washington, defended their appropriations request for fiscal year 1923 on Capitol Hill. Denby wanted 106,000 enlisted men, but because of congressional hostility he asked for only 90,000 plus 6,000 apprentices and 4,160 officers.[11] Not convinced that the Navy had truly examined its personnel needs with economy in mind, both the House Naval Affairs Committee and the naval subcommittee of the Committee on Appropriations asked Denby to describe the naval establishment resulting from an enlisted corps of 81,000, 65,000, and 56,000 men.[12]

To meet the minimum figure and yet keep 18 battleships, 103 destroyers, and 84 submarines in full commission, Denby would have to eliminate the Special Service Squadron in the Caribbean, the Yangtze and South China Sea Patrols, 35 eagle boats, 44 submarine chasers, and even the Naval Academy's *Reina Mercedes*. When congressmen objected to removing the trade protection squadrons, Denby tried another approach. With 65,000 men (50,000 afloat and 15,000 ashore) he would keep 12 battleships in commission, reduce the size of the squadrons and patrols, and cut the destroyer and submarine forces radically.[13]

Denby and the bureau chiefs explained that the capital ships of the postwar years were larger, more heavily gunned, and technologically more complicated than the prewar vessels. Electric propulsion machinery, antiaircraft batteries, aircraft handling devices, improved fire control systems, and larger rifles with more complicated projectile handling mechanisms inevitably required more enlisted men and officers. The larger destroyer force was absorbing a disproportionate number of officers and required over 17,500 men; but destroyers were acting in place of cruisers and were absolutely necessary. Naval aviation required officer pilots and the number of aircraft in the fleets would increase steadily through the years. Where the average battleship might operate with 1,000 enlisted men, the aircraft carriers allowed by the 1922 naval treaty (*Saratoga* and *Lexington*) would absorb 3,000 men apiece.[14] From the Navy's point of view, legislators like Thomas S. Butler, Chairman of the House Naval Affairs Committee, with a primitive understanding of naval problems, were a positive menace to national security.

In the end public opinion forced the budget trimmers to reconsider and authorize a navy of 86,000 enlisted men and a line officer strength of approximately 4,500. During the next decade, despite an increase in cruisers and carriers, the enlisted strength of the Navy was to shrink further, although the number of line officers was to increase slightly.

The 1922 hearings strikingly revealed the many facets of the problem of officering the Navy. The upper echelons in the Department posited that the officer corps of the Navy had to come from the Naval Academy. During 1921 approximately 650 ex-enlisted men and 200 wartime officer reservists were granted regular commissions, but this was to be the last major addition to non-Academy officers to the regulars before World War II. Between 1921 and 1933, because attrition and officer input were almost in balance, there was very little overall growth in officer strength. Thus, as demands for pilots increased through the years, particularly after aviation squadrons were organized in 1926 for the *Saratoga* and *Lexington*, the number of officers assigned to the rest of the fleet decreased proportionately.[15]

Congress's answers to the Navy's problem were often more damaging than useful. In the fiscal 1924 appropriation act (approved 22 January 1923) Congress cut the size of future Naval Academy classes by reducing congressional appointments from five to three. In May 1928 the number of appointees per Senator and Representative was raised to four to assure a supply of officers for the cruisers under construction. However, on 28 February 1931 the number of appointees was again reduced to three. Throughout these years the naval secretaries and the top service officers argued that it was uneconomical to operate the Academy at 60 percent capacity and that the nation would gain were a portion of each class not commissioned but returned to civilian life with a reserve commission. To fill the gap in future officer ranks that would result from smaller Naval Academy graduations, some congressmen suggested the substitution of warrant officers, the use of enlisted pilots in naval aviation, and the addition of reserve naval officers to the fleet for both general service and aviation duty. In deference to congressional wishes 30 percent of the naval aviators were enlisted men, but again the Bureau of Navigation could see no possibility of reducing the Navy's officer needs by this accretion. In the 1920s it was assumed that flying was "a young man's game" and that by age thirty a naval aviator would be back at general service duties in the fleet. But what could you do with an enlisted naval aviator who was "overage" at 30 and still had eight or ten years service ahead before retirement?[16]

The squeeze on naval personnel appropriations reflected budget-cutting throughout the Navy during Denby's years. Though welcomed to the Department as a "big Navy man," Denby soon revealed that he could not live up to his press notices. In fairness to him, his problems were shared by all executive departments because of pressures from the Bureau of the Budget, headed first by General Charles Gates Dawes and then by General H.M. Lord. These men were ordered by Presidents Harding and Coolidge to reduce government spending. While doing so the Directors of the Budget established monetary limits in many areas, including shipbuilding, personnel recruitment, and fleet operations. To the Navy and a few congressmen it therefore appeared that naval policy was being set by a new and powerful bureaucracy over which they had no control. For the Secretary of the Navy this was occasionally embarrassing; for Congress, jealous of its policy-setting prerogative, this was insufferable.

As a member of President Harding's executive "team," Denby felt that he could not fully present the Navy's financial needs. Before passage of the Budget Accounting Act of 1921 the bureau chiefs had gone directly to Congress for their money, and the Secretary's main role was to set the stage and introduce his admirals. Now Denby had to have a budget drafted in the Department, submit it, and defend it before the Bureau of the Budget, and then defend before the House and Senate committees the sums allowed to the Navy by the Director of the Budget. It helped him little that the budget directors said that the cuts were made because his requests "were not compatible with the President's budgetary plans."

The results of being a good "team" player are painfully evident in Denby's annual reports and the testimony he gave the congressional naval committees. Heavily reduced budgets left little money for maintenance and repair of the fleet. Appropriations for repairs to ships, alterations, and repairs to equipage declined steadily in Denby's years: from $44 million in fiscal year 1921 to $23.6 million in 1922, to less than $17 million in 1924, and $22 million in 1925. In each annual report Denby noted that repairs and overhauls of vessels were being deferred. Despite a great deal of self-maintenance the overall condition of the fleet was deteriorating. Moreover, as ships aged their repair costs soared.[17]

Privately Denby fought a hard but losing battle. In September 1923 he sent General Lord a blistering letter protesting budget cuts. His bureau chiefs had asked for $416 million for fiscal year 1925; he had pared this to $361,694,592, but Lord would allow only $292 million. To Denby it appeared that Lord now commanded the Navy and determined national defense policy.[18]

What is evident here is that Denby's attempt to abide by the administration's fiscal policy resulted in loss in morale and deterioration in materiel. Alternatives, not all of them politically feasible, would have been to take the Navy's case to the press, seek relief through the Democrats in Congress, try to educate the President, and try to influence the Bureau of the Budget. Denby shrank from battling Congress and he knew better than to open up a press campaign against his boss—President Harding. He was given a little assistance from the Navy League and the Hearst newspapers, but this was not enough. He found Lord and his underlings beyond education. Being controlled by the Bureau of the Budget was to have even greater consequences when the Navy Department sought to "round out the fleet."

In some respects, the Navy had suffered at the Washington Conference because it lacked a long-term naval policy. The closest the General Board had come to a genuine construction policy or fleet plan in the pre-Conference years was to insist on completion of the 1916 naval construction act. With the close of the Washington Conference, the board remedied this gap in its thinking by publishing a "United States Naval Policy" under the date of 29 March 1922.[19]

Central to the board's new policy was the maintenance of "A Navy second to none." By the Five Power Treaty the capital ship strength of Great Britain and America was to be equal. But the navies were unequal: in cruiser strength the British Navy far outclassed America's; in destroyers, the United States was more powerful; if the submarine forces were roughly equal, the British Merchant Marine was predominant. On balance, then, American sea power did not match Britain's, and for a decade the Navy's leaders used this disparity as a prod to get money from Congress and the Budget Bureau for ship construction and modernization.

During the 1920s the battleship fleet claimed the constant attention of Congress and the Navy Department. From 6 February 1922, when the Five-Power Treaty was signed, the Navy Department was forced to fight hard first to keep its battleships in commission and in a decent state of repair, and then, as they aged, to obtain funds to modernize them. Throughout these years the principal mission of Denby and his successors was to educate the President, Congress, the Bureau of the Budget, and the taxpayer to the facts of naval life—ships do rust; boilers will burn out; and naval technology, particularly in Japan and Great Britain, was not at a standstill.

The 1922 treaty left the Navy with eighteen battleships whose dates of completion ranged from 1911 (the *Utah* and *Florida*) to 1923 (the *Colorado* and *West Virginia*). The six oldest vessels (the *Utah, Florida, Wyoming, Arkansas, New York,* and *Texas*), which antedated the World War, were coal-burners, and all of them, except the *New York* and *Texas*, mounted 12-inch-gun main batteries. The last two carried ten 14-inch rifles. The next nine battleships, chronologically speaking (the *Nevada, Oklahoma, Arizona, Pennsylvania, Mississippi, New Mexico, Idaho, California,* and *Tennessee*), were armed with 14-inch batteries, had oil-fired boilers, and incorporated the Navy's latest thinking, in terms of armor and firepower, that had derived from the battle of Jutland. The last three vessels (the *Colorado, Maryland,* and *West Virginia*) were products of the 1916 naval construction act and inaugurated a new era of capital ship construction. They were armed with eight 16-inch guns, heavier armor, and new techniques for underwater protection. To the Navy, these eighteen battleships were *the fleet*. It became dogma for the Navy that the battleships had to be kept in full commission and all had to have similar steaming and fighting capabilities. This meant that the coal-burners had to be modernized and converted to oil; and all ships antedating the *Maryland* (1921) had to have their decks strengthened against extreme long-range plunging fire from 16-inch guns or aircraft bombs. Blisters were to be added to these vessels for protection against torpedoes; and all vessels, including the very newest, would need constantly to improve their antiaircraft armaments. Finally, as long-range battle practice ("LRBP" in reports) became *de rigeur* in the 1920s, newer fire control systems would be required. All of this, of course, meant money. It is little wonder that the budget directors blanched at the expenses and congressmen argued earnestly for more naval limitation.

Radical expense paring, necessitated in large measure by the battleship fleet, began with the opening of fiscal year 1922. Money for fuel was so severely limited by Congress that fleet steaming was sharply curtailed.[20] Even the traditional winter maneuvers in the Caribbean were abandoned. Then, with the scrapping of many battleships, imminent in consequence of the Five-Power Treaty, Congress began to press the Navy to lay up a portion of the battleships retained. Denby, Admiral Coontz, and his relief, Admiral E. W. Eberle, had to answer the question of why the battleships could not be treated like destroyers, that is, rotated between the active and reserve fleet. The admirals explained that crews were trained to operate a particular ship and that operational inefficiency would result when a major portion of a crew was transferred to another vessel.[21] Meanwhile economy forced the Navy to do the best with what it had.

On 12 July 1921 Rear Admiral R. S. Griffin, Chief of the Bureau of Engineering, directed all ship captains to perform as much maintenance work as possible with the crews of their vessels. The result in the following year was a 50 percent reduction in labor costs at the navy yards and a 30 percent cut in materiel expenses. The performance of maximum crew maintenance continued into 1931, when the policy was reversed in order to give business to depression-ridden yards.[22]

But savings through self-maintenance could not hide a major problem endemic in the entire fleet. Major overhaul expenses were building up because a crew could not re-boiler a battleship or replace a main shaft on an antiquated cruiser. The state of disrepair in the older coalburners, battleships and armored cruisers alike, was such that the Navy was forced to ask Congress to raise the statutory limit on the cost of repairs to individual vessels to some figure above the legal $300,000. The inevitable result of postponed or partial repairs to the major fleet units was impairment of operations.[23]

While no breakthrough on this problem occurred in Denby's term, he set the stage for success in December 1924. Before Congress in January 1923, and in his annual report for fiscal 1923, he reported the need to modernize the six coal-burning battleships and estimated the cost at $30 million. His testimony notwithstanding, General Lord believed the coal-burners, particularly the four oldest (the *Florida, Utah, Arkansas,* and *Wyoming*), would never serve in a line of battle, even if modernized. These could be used for coast defense in wartime and in peace were good midshipmen cruise ships. Could not the Navy get by with a million dollars to handle urgent repairs on the four oldest ships and then simply forget the whole business of modernizing them? Nevertheless, on 21 March 1924 Lord told Assistant Secretary Roosevelt that President Coolidge had agreed that the Navy should request Congress for the modernizing funds.[24] The bill finally authorizing the desired improvements was signed on 18 December 1924.

Denby's and the General Board's concern about the battleships was matched by an equally strong belief that the Navy needed a substantial increase of modern cruisers for fleet operations. Cruiser building had been deferred in favor of antisubmarine craft during the war. In 1921 the Navy had ten modern scout cruisers (7500 tons, 6-inch guns) on the ways and a mixed bag of operational coal-burning armored cruisers and light cruisers that could barely keep up with battleships when fleet speed was 18 knots, let alone serve as the "eyes of the fleet."

Congress, to blame for this condition, had to be educated, to be convinced that destroyers could not operate at high speeds in heavy seas and, more importantly, stood little chance of penetrating a protective cruiser screen once brought under fire from 6- or 8-inch guns. What was needed, said the General Board, were 10,000-ton cruisers armed with 8-inch guns.

This new class of "heavy cruisers" was a direct response to wartime cruiser construction in England and to a new situation of tension with Japan. To match the 9,750-ton, 7.5-inch British cruisers developed in the *Hawkins* class, and to provide a type capable of sailing the enormous Pacific Ocean distances to Far Eastern waters and outfighting the Japanese, the General Board called for larger cruisers.

The "United States Naval Policy" of 29 March 1922 called for the completion of ten *Omaha*-class light cruisers then building, for sixteen modern 10,000-ton, 8-inch cruisers, and for no other small cruisers. Optimum cruiser size thus was the upper limit allowed by the Five Power Treaty.[25] While Denby pressed Congress for funds to complete the 1916 vessels under construction, he also informed the President that the fleet exercises of 1922, 1923, and 1924 demonstrated repeatedly the need for more fleet scouts.[26]

With the commencement of fiscal year 1924, Secretary Denby opened the Navy's campaign for authorization to complete ships already begun and also to construct at least eight 10,000-ton cruisers as well as six new submarines and six gunboats. Throughout the balance of 1923 and again in January 1924 the Budget Bureau reviewed the Navy's needs. Not until 29 January 1924 did Lord inform Denby that he could have the eight cruisers if Congress authorized them, but that no money could be spent to begin construction until 1 July 1925 at the earliest.[27] Convincing Congress that the Navy desperately needed the new cruisers became a major chore for Denby's successor and Assistant Secretary Roosevelt.

While little change occurred in the designs of destroyers and submarines during Denby's tenure, he did try to obtain some destroyer flotilla leaders because the small "four-piper" classes simply were not large enough to accommodate the flotilla commodores and their staffs. When Congress responded by calling upon him to reduce his number of operating destroyers, Denby explained to President Harding that in addition to multifarious duties these ships did the work of light cruisers.[28] Denby's forthright approach, and the too obvious lack of cruisers, convinced Congress that 102 destroyers operating with 90 percent complements were not excessive.

A similar story can be told about submarines. While the United States in the 1920s possessed the largest submarine fleet in the world, many of the boats had been constructed before or during the World War. By 1925, there were "R" and "S" types and also three decommissioned "T" fleet-type boats that were total failures. Finally there were three "V"-boats (the V-1, *Barracuda*; V-2, *Bass*; and V-3, *Bonita*) under construction. These were the prototypes of the fleet submarines which operated so successfully during World War II. The "V"-boats were designed to operate with the battle fleet. Unfortunately, the Navy was to receive just three more of this class in the 1920s, and Congress lacked interest in minelaying boats. Moreover, torpedo shortages so plagued the fleet that in the late 1920s ships in reduced commission were robbed of their "fish" so that the operating submarines could continue practice.[29]

In great contrast to destroyers and submarines, naval aviation made great progress: aircraft carriers were added to the fleets, rapid changes were made in naval aircraft, and an expansion occurred in the number of aviators and ground personnel detailed to naval aviation. The 1920s also witnessed the titanic struggle between Brigadier General William "Billy" Mitchell and his adherents and those who did not believe that air power had superseded navies and armies. It was Denby's fortune to guide the Navy as it came to grips with the new weaponry of aviation; and it was likewise his most important task to rally support for the Navy as Mitchell's forces dove to the attack.

General Mitchell's drive for a "United Air Service" and the various ship-bombing tests that took place between 1919 and 1923 have been related often, but the results do need a bit of analysis. The various bills, hearings, and propaganda in support of a single aviation department that would control civil and military aviation, or a single military department to direct Army and Navy aviation and create a United Air Service, received almost no support from the Navy. The views of most naval aviators and the deck officers were rooted in service conservatism and a sense of pragmatism. Despite Mitchell's florid writings and the glorious achievements of pursuit aviation in the World War, it was perfectly obvious that air power had not been a decisive factor in the Allied victory. It was also clear to the Navy that Mitchell's prophecies were based on aircraft that would rise from the drafting boards a decade later.[30] From the study and discussion that did result from Mitchell's activities emerged a realization within the Navy that a new bureau for aviation was necessary and that the naval aviator had to pursue a different career pattern than his deck-bound compatriot. But these ideas were slow to gain acceptance.

The nadir for naval aviation enthusiasts was reached in August 1919 when Admiral W.S. Benson, the Chief of Naval Operations, eliminated the Office of Aviation, distributed its functions and responsibilities among the various bureaus, and left Captain Thomas T. Craven with the empty title of Director of Naval Aviation. Pressure was already mounting, however, for an aviation bureau; when Captain William A. Moffett replaced Craven the pressure was directed toward Congress. Using Lieutenant Commander Richard E. Byrd, a retired officer with good political connections, and flag officers like Coontz (Benson's replacement as Chief of Naval Operations), William S. Sims, David W. Taylor, and Bradley A. Fiske (retired), Moffett convinced a number of congressmen that a Bureau of Aeronautics was absolutely necessary.[31] Harding's call for an aviation bureau was answered in April 1921 when a Bureau of Aeronautics was authorized as a part of the fiscal 1923 Naval Appropriations Act, approved 12 July 1921. Moffett was appointed chief on 25 July 1921 with the rank of rear admiral. The propaganda of General Mitchell and his acolytes had forced the Navy to close ranks and support Moffett, and by June 1919 the General Board was saying that " . . . fleet aviation must be developed to the fullest extent."[32]

Moffett enjoyed the confidence of Denby, Assistant Secretary Roosevelt, and Chief of Naval Operations Coontz. Because he had worked his way up through fleet commands, he knew instinctively the temper of the shipboard Navy and the admirals in command. His basic theme was that naval aviation was a vital adjunct of the operating fleets. As he told Denby during the summer of 1922, "The Navy is the first line of offense and naval aviation as an advance guard of this first line must deliver the brunt of the attack. Naval aviation cannot take the offensive from shore; *it must go to sea on the back of the fleet.*"[33] At all congressional hearings, and among officers in BuAer, Moffett never deviated from this theme.

Moffett persistently pressed the development of carrier aviation. Captains Noble E. Irwin and Craven had studied naval aviation progress abroad, particularly in England. Based on their reports to the General Board, authorization for conversion of the fleet collier *Jupiter* to an aircraft carrier was obtained from Congress in July 1919. From the *Langley* (ex-*Jupiter*) the Navy was to learn about handling aircraft at sea, operating with the fleet, and what improvements would be needed in future carriers as they were built. At the same time that the *Langley* was commissioned and began operations in March of 1922, the Navy commenced planning the conversion of the battle cruiser hulls for the *Lexington* and *Saratoga* into 33,000-ton aircraft carriers.

In many ways it was fortunate that congressional parsimony delayed the conversion of the *Lexington* and the *Saratoga* since neither naval aviators nor aircraft would have been available in sufficient numbers had the vessels been commissioned before late 1927. Between July 1922 and July 1925 the number of naval aviators merely increased from 314 to 382 and the number of enlisted aviation ratings (non-pilot) declined from 2,209 to 1,711. In the fiscal year 1924 the net gain in pilots was two.[34] Obviously the eight new squadrons for the two carriers could not have been properly manned, particularly since aircraft were being added to all battleships and cruisers. Proposals to send Naval Academy graduates directly to flight training after graduation were resisted in the Bureau of Navigation (Naval Personnel); such a move would prevent shipboard qualification of the new ensigns. One answer to the problem was to increase the number of enlisted pilots, but there were limits here. Another was to bring reserve pilots into the fleet for a year or two of duty. This expedient, begun in fiscal year 1927, provided a body of transient flight ensigns in the squadrons and left room for the regulars to hold the more senior billets.[35]

Despite the slowness of completing the *Lexington* and the *Saratoga*, the Navy in Denby's time was able to move forward in making naval aviation a true adjunct of the fleet. Until the spring of 1925 carrier aviation was represented by "constructive carriers"—battleships or cruisers designated as carriers —and single planes represented a bombing squadron. To avoid turret platforms, which interfered with the use of the big guns, Moffett proposed in 1921 to install turntable catapults on all battleships and cruisers. By 1922 catapults had been developed that could launch the battleship and cruiser planes. Moffett then went to Congress for funds to equip all battleships and eight light cruisers with catapults. By mid-1924 most of the battleships and cruisers either catapulted their planes or hoisted them over the side for take-off from the water. Aviation indeed had gone to sea "on the backs of the fleet."

Moffett also experimented in the field of lighter-than-air (LTA) aviation. The United States was due to receive three dirigibles as a part of the World War settlements. Germany and England each provided one rigid airship; a third would be built in America from German Zeppelin plans with technical assistance from the Germans. The ZR-1, christened the *Shenandoah*, first flew on 4 September 1923 and was accepted by the Navy. The British-built ZR-2 broke up on her fourth flight, 24 August 1922, killing sixteen of the Navy's key airship personnel. The German-built ZR-3, the *Los Angeles*, arrived in America on 15 October 1924 and began a long period of highly successful operations.[36]

While Moffett emphasized the experimental nature of LTA, and noted the familiar scouting role for dirigibles, he stressed that they should not be used in tactical situations. Dirigibles were so useful in antisubmarine patrol operations that he believed they might even replace seagoing submarine chasers. However, the Admiral directed that they avoid contact with naval antiaircraft fire.[37]

While Denby fought to round out the fleet and stave off budgetary cuts, he made a lasting contribution in fleet reorganization and war planning. The period from 1919 to 1922 was one of worsening relations with Japan and intense naval rivalry with Great Britain. The Washington Conference, however, laid most of the rivalry to rest. More important, a gradual reorientation in American strategic thinking occurred as Admiral Benson retired as Chief of Naval Operations and new men entered the Operations office and its many subdivisions. Great Britain became less important for long term planning; Japan became the most important theoretical "enemy" of the United States. Stated differently, the U.S. Navy turned to the Pacific Ocean as the Atlantic receded in importance.[38]

In April 1921 Denby told Secretary of State Hughes that "It is time our keels became acquainted with the western ocean and our navy yards and bases on the west coast receive their crucial test."[39] Answering on 31 May, Hughes stated that neither he nor the President saw any diplomatic objections to a fleet reorganization, but that Harding wanted such a reorganization delayed until a more propitious time, apparently after an arms limitation conference.[40] Rather than wait, Denby secretly ordered the Navy to operate as if it were reorganized. Admiral Hilary P. Jones took command of the Atlantic Fleet and Admiral Edward W. Eberle of the Pacific Fleet. What created confusion was the fact that Vice Admiral John D. McDonald was privately ordered to command the Atlantic Fleet. Jones now commanded, as Commander in Chief U.S. Fleet (CinCUS), both fleets plus the Fleet Base Force and the Control Force. He admitted, in the summer of 1921, that it was hard for him to explain his four star flag. Gradually, however, the various commanders learned that there was a U.S. Fleet under Jones, a Battle Fleet under Eberle, and a Scouting Fleet under McDonald.[41] With the Washington Conference completed, Denby finally issued General Order No. 94 on 6 December 1922. The Battle Fleet and the Fleet Base Force would operate from the West Coast and the Scouting Fleet and the Control Force would be in the Atlantic; all would be under the Commander in Chief U.S. Fleet. Not assigned to the U.S. Fleet and operating as separate commands were the Asiatic Fleet, Naval Forces Europe, Special Service Squadron, Naval Transportation Service, and vessels on special duty. The Battle Fleet had the twelve most modern of the Navy's eighteen battleships and in time would be strengthened by the new 33,000-ton carriers. It was no accident of terminology that the term "Battle Fleet" was given to those ships in the Pacific.

Fleet reorganization revived interest in the Navy's war plans. Before the World War, quite general "color" plans had been drafted for naval operations against various enemies. An Orange Plan for war against Japan, a Red Plan for Great Britain, and a Black Plan for Germany had received most attention, but none was kept current. Nevertheless, in preparing for the Washington Conference, Assistant Secretary Roosevelt gave considerable thought to national policies and the necessary naval strength to support them. With American naval strength set by treaty, on 13 June 1922 he ordered the General Board to study the grand strategy of the Pacific under peacetime and wartime conditions and to report what it considered would be the necessary organization to support its principal analyses.[42] The study, dated 26 April 1923, provided the War Plans Division with a basic guide for revising the color plans.

The board's report opened with the premise that the only foreseeable war in the future would be with Japan. Therefore the United States should maintain a 5–3 naval ratio with Japan, develop Pearl Harbor, strengthen Guam and

Manila to the legal limit possible under the Five Power Treaty, and direct all war plans toward operations in the West Pacific. Because it was implicit that Guam and the Philippines would be captured by Japan in a war with the United States, it was therefore necessary to possess a fleet that could operate across the Pacific from Pearl Harbor. It was also premised that the Imperial Navy would have to be decisively defeated in Japanese waters before the pressure of blockade or invasion could be applied.[43] With this report in hand, Roosevelt pressed for full revision of the Orange Plan by 1926 at the latest, even if the modernization of the Battle Fleet to operate transpacifically and the accumulation of a long-legged cruiser force could not keep pace with the war planners.[44]

With the Battle Fleet based in the Pacific and new thought being directed to the Orange Plan, Denby sought to acquire requisite fleet base facilities. Between 1917 and January 1923 four separate studies made of the West Coast facilities agreed on the need for fleet bases, at least one of which should be in San Francisco Bay.[45] The most important study, directed by Rear Admiral Hugh Rodman in the fall of 1922, concluded that primary consideration should be given to developing a base at Oahu capable of handling the whole Navy. Once a Hawaiian base was developed, then the pressing need was for a fleet-sized naval base in San Francisco Bay and an enlarged base in Puget Sound.[46] The Rodman report stirred little interest in Congress. Between 1922 and 1925 little more than $2.5 million was spent to increase naval facilities, and domestic politics prevented the beginning of a base in San Francisco Bay.

Meanwhile Congress was pressing Denby to reduce his expenditures. The congressmen believed that fuel costs were exorbitant and wondered if they could not be reduced by limiting fleet maneuvers. Denby and Coontz eliminated joint fleet maneuvers in fiscal year 1922, but insisted upon holding them in fiscal 1923.[47] Funds were allowed for U.S. Fleet maneuvers in the Caribbean and Panama areas in fiscal 1923 and more than seventy-five congressmen enjoyed a winter cruise in the tropics. After conducting additional exercises, Coontz, now CinCUS, reported that the lack of cruisers and shortage of destroyers, due to severe budget cuts, made Battle Fleet operations most difficult. He also noted that three of the battleships were in such poor repair that they could not finish the maneuvers with a round of port visits for "flag-showing" purposes.[48]

With the omniscience of hindsight, it is clear that Denby's tenure as Secretary of the Navy was headed for a tragic denouement from its beginning. Forces he little understood in the end harried him from office and into political obscurity. One group, exemplified by Secretary of the Interior Albert Fall, was determined to reverse the conservationist philosophy of the previous years and open the natural resources of the United States to private development. Another body of equally determined men, best represented by Gifford Pinchot and Senator Robert LaFollette, was dedicated to preserving the nation's resources that had been set aside by Presidents Theodore Roosevelt, Taft, and Wilson. They wanted carefully regulated exploitation of the nation's forest and mineral resources, and preservation of certain proven oil-rich lands for future defense needs. A third group, including both conservationists and plunderers, were political partisans seeking to drive the Republicans from office. The clash of these conflicting interests occurred over the question of private leasing of the Navy's oil reserve lands in California and Wyoming. While the Elk Hills reserve in California was larger and more important, the nation was to follow the story in the press under the journalistic rubric of the "Teapot Dome (Wyoming) Scandals."[49]

Denby's enmeshment in the oil story began early. In April 1921, when barely a month in office, he agreed to transfer the Navy's oil reserves to Secretary Fall against the advice of his highest officers and some junior officers who had been administering the reserves. Denby knew that the reserves would be opened to private leasing by the E.L. Doheny interests in California and those of Harry Sinclair in Wyoming. However, his decision was based in part on information that the naval oil reserves were being drained by private wells adjacent to the fields. Also the contract would give the Navy oil certificates as royalties which could be cashed for refined oil, and oil would be stored above ground in new storage tanks to be constructed by Doheny in Hawaii and on the Pacific Coast. Rear Admiral J. K. Robison, Chief of the Bureau of Engineering, who managed the fleet's fuel, encouraged Denby to transfer the reserves, saying that the continuing strained relations with Japan required that the Navy have fuel in tanks in the Pacific and not just crude oil underground. Finally, seeing trouble ahead, Denby believed that the Interior Department had the staff and experience to handle the many legal challenges to the government's right to hoard its natural resources. Finally, the President apparently wanted the transfer and a good "team player" must follow the leader's signals.[50] Neither Denby nor Harding knew that Secretary Fall had received over $400,000 in bribes to encourage leasing in Elk Hills and Teapot Dome.[51]

The investigation of Senator Thomas J. Walsh for the Senate Public Lands Committee, Fall's unmasking, the cancellation of the leases, and the return of the oil reserves to the Navy is an often recounted story. Denby and many naval officers were questioned closely but no taint of corruption was laid to the Secretary. But the political partisans were to have their day. On 11 February 1924 the Senate resolved by a vote of 47 to 36 to request President Coolidge to demand Denby's resignation. On 17 February, Denby complied and set 10 March 1924 as his day of departure. In a press statement the following day he said he had three weeks left in office and dared the politicians to impeach him. "I challenge investigation before any unprejudiced tribunal. My actions to safeguard the interests of the Government and the Navy were undertaken openly and in good faith and were based upon the best obtainable information."[52]

There were, of course, no impeachment proceedings. Three weeks later, on March 19, he hauled down his flag and issued the traditional ALNAV to the fleet: "Goodbye and God bless you."[53] Upon his return to Detroit, he reactivated his reserve commission in the Marine Corps and reentered business. At the recommendation of General John Lejeune, he was promoted to lieutenant colonel in January 1928. A year later, just ten days before his fifty-ninth birthday, he died in his sleep of a heart attack. He was a thirty-third degree Mason and was buried with full rites.

Historians through the years have accepted Senator Walsh's judgment that Denby was a man of integrity. Some have concluded that the job was too big for him; others that he was credulous, ingenuous, and ignorant. The Navy's contemporary judgment of its chief was probably best stated in the *Army and Navy Journal* of 15 March 1924:

> Whatever may be the opinion of the country respecting Mr. Denby's practically forced resignation from the Cabinet, the Navy will always regard it with great regret and indignation. Mr. Denby stands out as one of the very few Secretaries the Navy has ever had who understood the Service, was in strong sympathy with it, and worked diligently and effectively for its highest and best interests, regardless of politics. That such a Secretary should himself be made a victim of political expediency is especially deplorable.

NOTES

1. *New York Times*, 9, 23, 24 Feb. 1921; DAB, s.v. "Denby, Edwin."
2. ANJ, 12 Mar. 1921.
3. Harold and Margaret Sprout, *Toward a New Order of Sea Power: American Naval Policy and the World Scene, 1918-1922* (Princton, N.J.: Princeton University Press, 1940), pp. 116-18.
4. *Ibid.*, pp. 122-48; Merlo J. Pusey, *Charles Evans Hughes*, 2 vols. (New York: Macmillan, 1952), 2:453-57.
5. Sprout, *New Order of Sea Power*, pp. 164-68; Pusey, *Hughes*, 2:459-60.
6. William Howard Gardiner, comp., "Memorandum on Naval Matters Connected with the Washington Conference on the Limitation of Armament 1921-1922," New York, 25 Oct. 1924, Hilary P. Jones Papers, MDLC. See also Gerald E. Wheeler, *Prelude to Pearl Harbor: The United States Navy and the Far East, 1921-1931* (Columbia: University of Missouri Press, 1963), pp. 53-56, and Roger Dingman, *Power in the Pacific: The Origins of Naval Arms Limitation, 1914-1922* (Chicago: University of Chicago Press, 1976).

7. U.S. Navy Department, *Report of the General Board on Limitation of Armaments* (Washington: GPO, 1921), pp. 1–14; Sprout, *New Order of Sea Power*, pp. 130–33, 144.

8. "Treaty for the Limitation of Armament, 6 Feb. 1922," in William Malloy, ed., *Treaties, Conventions, International Acts, Protocols, and Agreements between the United States of America and Other Powers 1910-1913* (Washington: GPO, 1923), pp. 2100–16.

9. Dudley W. Knox, *The Eclipse of American Sea Power* (New York: The Army and Navy Journal, 1922), pp. 135–36; Earl S. Pomeroy, *Pacific Outpost: American Strategy in Guam and Micronesia* (Stanford: Stanford University Press, 1951), pp. 81–88; Wheeler, *Prelude to Pearl Harbor*, pp. 25–28, 68–69, 81–82.

10. "Statement of Hon. Edwin Denby, Secretary of the Navy, 13 Feb. 1922," in U.S. House Committee on Naval Affairs, *Hearings on Sundry Legislation Affecting the Naval Establishment, 1922-1923*, 67th Cong. 2nd Sess. (Washington: GPO, 1923), pp. 229–30, 242–46 (hereafter cited as HCNA, *Hearings Sundry, 1922-1923*, 67th Cong.).

11. *Ibid.*

12. U.S. House, Subcommittee on Naval Affairs of the Appropriations Committee, *Hearings on Naval Appropriations Bill for Fiscal 1923*, 67th Cong., 2nd Sess. 10, 13 Mar. 1922 (Washington: GPO, 1923), pp. 347–64 (hereafter cited as HSNAAC, *Hearings on the 1923 Naval Appropriations*, 67th Cong.).

13. *Ibid.*, HCNA, *Hearings Sundry, 1922-1923*, 67th Cong., 2nd Sess., 1 Mar. 1922, pp. 221–22.

14. HCNA, *Hearings on Sundry, 1922-1923*, 67th Cong., 2nd Sess., 13 Feb. 1922, p. 230; HSNAAC, *Hearings on 1923 Naval Appropriations*, 67th Cong., 7 Mar. 1922, p. 298. See also HSNAAC, *Hearings on 1929 Naval Appropriations*, 70th Cong., 2nd Sess., 18 Feb. 1928, pp. 186–87.

15. U.S. Senate, Subcommittee on Naval Affairs of the Appropriations Committee, *Hearings on Naval Appropriations Bill for Fiscal 1926*, 68th Cong., 1st Sess., 20 Dec. 1924, pp. 78–88 (hereafter cited as SSNAAC, *Hearings on 1926 Naval Appropriations*, 68th Cong.).

16. ARSN, 1924, pp. 164–65, 226–28, 622–23; HSNAAC, *Hearings on 1925 Naval Appropriations*, 67th Cong., 21 Dec. 1923, pp. 140–44, and similar hearings for fiscal years 1926, 1927, 1928, and 1929.

17. ARSN, 1924, pp. 12–14.

18. Secretary Edwin Denby to the Director of the Budget, 15 Sept. 1923, NA, Navy Department File 29370–140–27.

19. ARSN, 1922, p. 2.

20. *Ibid.*, pp. 6–7.

21. HCNA, *Hearings Sundry, 1922-23*, 67th Cong., 2nd Sess., 16 Feb. 1922, pp. 299, 301; HSNAAC, *Hearings on 1926 Naval Appropriations*, 68th Cong., 18 Nov. 1924, pp. 80–82.

22. ARSN, 1922, pp. 227–28.

23. "Secretary Denby to Senator Carroll S. Page, 8 Jan. 1923," in HCNA, *Hearings on Sundry, 1922-1923*, 67th Cong., pp. 1513–20.

24. ARSN, 1923, pp. 75–77; "Navy Department: Vessels-Repairs," NA, BOB Files.

25. GB No. 420–2, Ser. 1108, 29 Mar. 1922. NHD:OA.

26. ARSN, 1922, p. 38; ARSN, 1923, p. 77.

27. Director of the Budget to Secretary Edwin Denby, 29 Jan. 1924, BOB Files.

28. Secretary Edwin Denby to President Warren G. Harding, 5 Apr. 1922, NA, Department of State Decimal File 500.A4b/42.

29. SSNAAC, *Hearings on 1924 Naval Appropriations*, 68th Cong., 1st Sess., 28 Mar. 1924, pp. 150–55.

30. Gerald E. Wheeler, "Mitchell, Moffett, and Air Power," *The Airpower Historian* 8 (Apr. 1961):79–87.

31. Richard E. Byrd, *Skyward* (New Haven: Blue Ribbon Books, 1931), pp. 100–16.

32. Quoted in Archibald T. Turnbull and Clifford L. Lord, *History of United States Naval Aviation* (New Haven: Yale University Press, 1949), p. 161.

33. Quoted in Edward Arpee, *From Frigates to Flat-Tops: [Life of William A. Moffett]* (Lake Forest, Ill.: Privately printed, 1953), pp. 98–99.

34. ARSN, 1924, pp. 613–14; ARSN, 1925, p. 593; ARSN, 1926, pp. 601–02.

35. HSNAAC, *Hearings on 1927 Naval Appropriations*, 69th Cong., 2nd Sess., 22 Dec. 1925, pp. 678–706.

36. Richard K. Smith, *The Airships Akron and Macon, Flying Aircraft Carriers of the United States Navy* (Annapolis, Md.: U.S. Naval Institute, 1965), p. 3; Turnbull and Lord, *Naval Aviation*, pp. 173, 219–22.

37. HSNAAC, *Hearings on 1926 Naval Appropriations*, 68th Cong., 1st Sess., 2 Dec. 1924, p. 566.

38. Wheeler, *Prelude to Pearl Harbor*, pp. 47–69.

39. Secretary Edwin Denby to Secretary of State Charles E. Hughes, 15 Apr. 1921, DS File 811.30/133.

40. President Harding to Secretary of State Hughes, 27 Apr. 1921, DS File 811.30/132; Secretary Hughes to Secretary Edwin Denby, 31 May 1921, DS File 811.30/129.

41. ARSN, 1921, p. 4.

42. Theodore Roosevelt, Jr., to the General Board, 13 June 1922, in GB No. 425, Ser. 1136, NHD:OA.

43. GB No. 425, Ser. 1136, 26 Apr. 1923, *ibid*. See also Louis Morton, "Germany First: The Basic Concept of Allied Strategy in World War II," in Kent Roberts Greenfield, ed., *Command Decisions* (Washington: OCMH, 1960), pp. 14–15.

44. CAPT W. T. Cluverius to CNO, 2 Oct. 1925, NA: Navy Department, Alphabetical File of Assistant Secretary, Box 2.

45. Wheeler, *Prelude to Pearl Harbor*, pp. 75–79; Pomeroy, *Pacific Outpost*, p. 60.

46. "Report of the Special Board on Shore Establishments, 12 January 1923," in HCNA, *Hearings on Sundry, 1922–1923*, 67th Cong., 1st Sess., pp. 1577–96. See also Joint Board to Secretary of War, 11 Oct. 1923, NARG 94, Joint Board, No. 304, Ser. 218.

47. HSNAAC, *Hearings on 1924 Naval Appropriations*, 67th Cong., 1st Sess., 14 Nov. 1922, pp. 4–5.

48. Robert E. Coontz, *From the Mississippi to the Sea* (Philadelphia: Dorrance, 1930), pp. 434–35.

49. On the Teapot Dome scandal see especially J. Leonard Bates, *The Origins of Teapot Dome: Progressives, Parties, and Petroleum, 1909–1921* (Urbana; Uni-

versity of Illinois Press, 1963); Burl Noggle, *Teapot Dome: Oil and Politics in the 1920s* (Baton Rouge: Louisiana State University Press, 1962); and Mark Sullivan, *Our Times: The United States 1900–1925*, 6 vols. (New York: Charles Scribner's Sons, 1926–1935), vol. 6.

50. Bates, *Origins of Teapot Dome*, pp. 228–32.
51. *Ibid.*, p. 239.
52. ANJ, 23 Feb. 1924.
53. *New York Times*, 11 Mar. 1924.

CURTIS DWIGHT WILBUR

19 March 1924–4 March 1929

ROGER K. HELLER

Edwin Denby's resignation as Secretary of the Navy, on 18 February 1924, gave President Calvin Coolidge three weeks in which to find a successor. He sought a man who, while utterly free of even the slightest implication of unrighteous conduct such as had tainted Denby, would bolster the Republican party in the elections of 1924.[1] Unable to find a suitable industrialist, business-man, or lawyer, he publicly asked for suggestions. In this quest he surprised a handful of newspaper reporters at his weekly White House press conference by asking for suggestions for a Secretary of the Navy. Among the twenty men recommended were former attorney general and senator William S. Kenyon, of Iowa, Judge of the Eighth U.S. District Court, and Curtis D. Wilbur, Chief Justice of the California Supreme Court. Wilbur was recommended by a Los Angeles newsman and this was strongly supported by his own congressman and friend from Southern California. To the President he was a completely un-known person. At any rate, Coolidge summoned both men to Washington. Kenyon, who was of sufficient stature to warrant consideration as a presiden-tial candidate, could placate the progressive wing of his party, and Coolidge offered him the post. Kenyon took counsel with his old friends in the Senate and declined on the ground that he did not possess the qualifications. On 12 March, Coolidge wired Wilbur that "You seem to be the man I need for the Navy. I am drafting you today. Please answer." Wilbur promptly replied with "Thank you, yes."

Opinion on Wilbur's nomination varied. He had graduated third out of the thirty-five men in the Naval Academy class of 1888 and was Chief Justice of the Golden State. While progressives moaned that Coolidge had selected an-other conservative Republican for his administration on the very eve of the party's national convention, conservatives predicted that Wilbur would be

Coolidge's running mate in 1924, or that he was on his way to a seat on the U.S. Supreme Court, and the like. All Californians were nevertheless pleased when the Senate confirmed his appointment, on 18 March.[2]

The eldest of the six children of well-educated parents, Curtis was born on 10 May 1867. When he was sixteen years of age, the family moved to Dakota territory, where his father became the general land agent for the Northern Pacific Railroad at Jamestown, now North Dakota. Here Curtis met Olive Doolittle, a native New Yorker and local school teacher who would become his wife in 1898.

Nominated from the Territory of the Dakotas, Wilbur entered the Naval Academy in 1884 and did well in leadership, sports, and academics. A big boy —he was 6 feet 3 inches tall—he was such an outstanding football player that he was nicknamed "Magic." As a senior he became President of the Y.M.C.A. and also Senior Company Cadet Captain. However, he resigned upon graduation from the Navy to become a lawyer. Since the family had moved to Riverside, California, he went west. While he taught for two years in Los Angeles at McPherson Academy, then the preparatory step to Occidental College, he studied law and in 1890 was admitted to the bar. After nine years of independent practice, he was appointed a deputy district attorney of Los Angeles County. From 1903 to 1918 he won election to the Superior Court of the county; in 1918 he was appointed to fill out an unexpired term as Associate Justice of the California Supreme Court and then went on to win a full term of twelve years. In 1922 he became Chief Justice.[3]

To familiarize himself with the naval establishment, Wilbur in 1924 inspected all kinds of naval activities—navy yards, ammunition depots, the naval oil reserves in California, naval training stations and Marine barracks, and naval air training stations. While on the West Coast he described Japanese civilization as hostile to the United States, flayed pacifists for opposing naval preparations and maneuvers, declared communism a menace to world peace, and for good measure soundly criticized the noble experiment of prohibition. Coolidge hastily recalled him to Washington lest he further embarrass him in an election year.[4]

From his inspection tour Wilbur concluded that the material condition of the fleet was unsatisfactory, construction work ashore had practically ceased, funds were far too short to properly maintain public works, and the Navy Nurse Corps was far short of its authorized strength.[5] Similar tours in 1925, 1926, and 1927 merely confirmed his first impressions.

From his peregrinations Wilbur nevertheless saw some progress being made. In 1924, for example, he noted that the introduction of higher steam pressures and temperatures called for the rewriting of general specifications for propulsion equipment and auxiliary apparatus of new construction, the Diesel engine heralded a new era in engineering because of its low fuel consumption, and that new sonic depth-finding equipment would soon be put on all ships. So important did the depth finder, or fathometer, appear as an instrument for mapping the ocean depths that Wilbur invited all government departments and related scientific institutions to a Conference on Oceanography, beginning 1 July 1924, that would offer recommendations for naval research in oceanography. He recommended increased appropriations for the newly established Naval Experimental and Research Laboratory, and also praised the work of the Navy engineering experiment station at Annapolis. On the other hand he warned that surplus engineering materials acquired from ships being scrapped or decommissioned was rapidly disappearing and that $40 million in new funds must be appropriated to replace them, and that design, equipment, and armament changes made in many ships lowered the habitability of them below an acceptable degree of comfort. He therefore suggested the experiment of substituting bunks for hammocks on two capital ships. Meanwhile litigation in connection with companies that threatened to deplete the Navy's Western oil reserves consumed a great deal of his time and energy.[6]

Wilbur viewed his new job as one which involved obtaining naval appropriations, establishing policy, and above all advising the President. Getting the money in a period devoted to economy in government, tax reduction especially for big business, peace, and disarmament, particularly when cynicism and indifference replaced wartime idealism, proved difficult for him. Appropriations for the Navy for 1921 were over $1 billion; for 1922, only $536,930,000. They were $378,160,000 for 1923 and $339,720,000 in 1924, when Wilbur took office.

Many questioned whether the Five-Power Treaty of the Washington Conference provided sufficient national security. The United States could not fortify anything west of Hawaii, construction of capital ships was suspended for ten years, and the capital ship fleet totaled only 500,000 tons. Moreover, capital ships replaced after a twenty-year life could not exceed 35,000 tons or have larger than 16-inch guns; cruisers could not exceed 10,000 tons or carry larger than 8-inch guns; total aircraft carrier displacement was limited to 135,000 tons and to 27,000 tons for a single ship, although special arrangements permitted the building of two carriers to displace 33,000 tons. No limit, however, was placed on the building of auxiliary warships, submarines, or aircraft.

Given the terms of the Five Power Treaty, the General Board late in March 1922 recommended that the United States "create, maintain and operate a Navy second to none and in conformity with the ratios of capital ships established by the treaty for the limitation of naval armaments." Its intention was to build to treaty strength in all categories with the largest, best armed and armored, and speediest ships that could be built.[7] Although many destroyers and submarines were fairly new, having been built during or following World War

I, it was extremely doubtful that Congress would respond favorably to Wilbur's recommendation that it fund cruisers and auxiliary ships the fleet needed to achieve treaty strength even though other powers were building them in large numbers. While Coolidge, such favored advisers as Secretary of the Treasury Andrew Mellon and Secretary of Commerce Herbert Hoover, and the public lacked a good perception of what the Navy needed, there were few officers imbued with the insurgent reform spirit of a Bradley A. Fiske, William F. Fullam, or William S. Sims. Furthermore, there was still no adequate machinery for providing a national defense policy, or even a good definition of roles and missions.

Coolidge gave Wilbur ample latitude in decision-making and freedom of action. In turn, Wilbur used his position to furnish a low-key education on seapower to the Chief Executive. In his first appearance on the Hill, in 1924, Wilbur recommended building the Navy to "the full treaty ratio."[8] Many congressmen had observed the Atlantic Fleet maneuvers of 1924, the first in which the newly-organized Scouting Fleet was tested. One conclusion was inescapable: five coal-burning battleships reduced considerably in speed by worn-out boilers were no substitutes for a fast battle cruiser force, yet they were the only big-gun ships available after the scrapping of the uncompleted battle cruisers. But to obtain funds from the incoming Sixty-eighth Congress presented an awesome challenge.

The House Naval Affairs Committee had begun hearings during the first week of February 1924, some seven weeks before Wilbur's arrival at Washington. With no measure forthcoming after forty days, the impatient Burton L. French (Rep., Idaho), Chairman of the Appropriations Committee, offered a naval bill for fiscal year 1925 reduced by $35 million over that of 1924, justifying the cut on the basis of the lack of authorizations from the Naval Affairs Committee and because no other treaty power had authorized the building of ships not covered in the Five Power Treaty. Ignoring some fifty cruisers of varying displacements built or building by Japan and France, French's committee concluded that American building was neither needed or desirable lest it disturb the other powers.[9] After Representative James Byrnes (Dem., S.C.) requested the President to enter into negotiations with the treaty powers for an agreement limiting construction of "all types and sizes of subsurface and surface craft of 10,000 tons standard displacement or less, and of aircraft," French retorted that the President did not think the time for further disarmament propitious.[10] The House, however, adopted Byrnes's suggestion to hold a new conference and then passed a naval appropriations bill for 1925 totaling $345,890,000. The latter passed the Senate in April with only one change—to build a new type of submarine instead of experimenting with a new German diesel in one of the "T" type boats.[11]

In spite of evident congressional desire for a second naval limitations agreement, on 24 May the Chairman of the House Naval Affairs Committee, Thomas S. Butler (Rep., Pa.), called for building eight 10,000-ton cruisers and modernizing the six oldest battleships by providing them with blisters for protection against torpedoes, stronger armored decks to resist air attack, and converting their coal-burning to oil-burning machinery. Although he would not increase the elevation of their guns—an improvement some members believed violated the Five Power treaty—he would provide new fire control systems for the *New York* and *Texas*. In addition he called for the construction prior to 1 July 1927 of eight scout cruisers and six gunboats.[12]

Little opposition developed to the battleship provisions of the "Butler bill" or to the call for gunboats for use in China. Some members supported the cruisers provision because the Navy had no adequate scouts, others because the threat of building them might cause the treaty powers to agree to a 5:5:3 ratio on auxiliaries. Opposition came from pacifists and from those who could not see how building ships could lead to greater disarmament.[13]

While the bill passed, it was amended to read that the President could suspend all or part of it if a disarmament conference was held. The Senate, however, delayed acting on it for five months. The bill represented the most important military act of the Coolidge years and set a course from which neither naval advocates, pacifists, President, Congress, or the public was able to change for another decade. Nevertheless, it passed only because it might provide a paper navy useful for bartering purposes.

To obtain funding for the eight cruisers and six gunboats was another story. Although Wilbur wished to build to treaty limits, public opinion favored the holding of another conference.[14] The fiscal year 1926 appropriations gave the Navy $311,720,000 but no money for new ships, and Coolidge was much more interested in economy than in obtaining naval parity. Without his support, moves to finance the eight cruisers in a Deficiency Appropriations Bill for fiscal year 1925 and supplemental legislation for funds for fiscal years 1925 and 1926 failed. Wilbur then asked for deficiency funds to modernize six old battleships, continue conversion work on the aircraft carriers *Saratoga* and *Lexington*, provide aircraft and accessories for these carriers, and to build two of the eight cruisers and six gunboats. To his great pleasure, his request passed the House easily, took only minutes to go through the Senate, and was promptly signed by the President.[15]

The naval appropriations bill for fiscal year 1927 of $357,710,000 gave Wilbur only $27 million more than in 1926. It provided for plans and estimates for three submarines and funded the beginning of three more of the cruisers authorized in 1924. Wilbur selected the name *Northampton* for one of them to honor the President, a fact Coolidge appreciated. Such niceties, however, could not hide the fact that the funds were so small that the ships could only be started near the end of the fiscal year, when continuing funds would have to be made available or construction would stop. Clearly both the administration and the House Naval Affairs Committee expected that the long-promised second conference for naval limitations might overtake even this need. However, a provision of the act allowed the President to start building the last three cruisers without consulting Congress "if he deems it wise" in the light of possible "future conferences on armament limitations," and the Senate restored nineteen destroyers the House had cut out.[16]

By issuing an eight hundred page report of the subcommittee of the Naval Affairs Committee the night before the naval appropriation act for fiscal 1928 was to be considered, it was clear that French wished to rush it through without much debate. Although it contained $385,270,000, the largest sum recommended since 1922, he promised two additional supplemental acts, one to continue work on the *Saratoga* and *Lexington*, the other to modernize several more of the older battleships. So far so good, but on the sensitive area of cruisers he rode into a gale and caused trouble for the administration. By refusing to accept a 5–5–3 ratio in cruisers because no such treaty provision existed, he countered Wilbur and was dealt a blow by Coolidge. With talks under way for holding a naval disarmament conference at Geneva, he thought it would be "unfortunate" to start building three cruisers—Wilbur and the strong Navy group represented by Butler nothwithstanding. Coolidge's objecting to an appropriation for the three remaining cruisers of 1924 but stressing the need for ten additional ones stimulated the House to revolt. An amendment to add $3 million to begin construction on the three last ships of the 1924 program lost to a substitute raising the amount to $14.5 million and was passed by a vote of 122 to 117 on a division of the House. When French demanded tellers in an effort to save the administration and buy time for reinforcements, the balloting swung against the insurgents by a mere two votes, 135 to 137. The House then passed the original bill by voice vote and staved off an attempt by a Republican member to recommit. The vote this time was 161 to 183, with Midwestern Republicans saving the day for the administration.[17]

The last vote was one of the most significant actions in naval affairs to occur between the two world wars. This first major party revolt since 1910 involved such party leaders as the Speaker, majority leader, chairman of the Naval Affairs Committee, and seventy-three other Republicans backed by a number of Democrats—and was turned back by only two votes. Some newspapers ascribed the victory to the President, who had "asserted his leadership,"[18] but Coolidge's "victory" was short-lived. The Senate Appropriations Committee, led by Frederick Hale (Rep., Me.), amended the naval bill to include the three cruisers so narrowly lost in the House. The committee vote,

49 ayes to 27 noes, thus continued the revolt against the White House. The entire appropriations bill then passed easily by a voice vote and was sent to conference, where it was expected that administration supporters would have enough strength to strike out the unwanted Senate additions.[19] But now international affairs intervened in decisive fashion.

Seeing no serious challenge to world peace in the rise of fascist governments in Italy and Spain, on 10 February 1927 Coolidge invited the naval powers to hold a second limitations conference. Britain and Japan accepted; France and Italy declined. Coolidge therefore decided to go ahead with a three-nation conference and suggested that it agree upon extending the Washington Treaty limitation of 5–5–3 on capital ships to auxiliaries and propose what types of ships France and Italy could have given their "special situations."[20] In consequence, the House group that demanded a second conference before continuing the cruiser program would no longer sustain the administration against House insurgents. Nor would the House check the Senate. Indeed, the refusal of Italy and France to attend the conference caused such a shift in votes that the Senate amendment was approved, with 240 members voting aye and only 115 nay. On the administration's "last stand," a roll-call vote of 208 to 173 defeated "King Cal." Although 51 members were present but had not voted, 99 Republicans had voted against their president.[21]

Coolidge wanted a conference to establish ratios for all types of warships not covered by the Washington Treaty and further reductions in ships if possible. He therefore wished to keep the last three cruisers of the 1924 program as paper ships or, as Wilbur desired, to stretch out their construction to fit budgetary plans.[22] While Congress funded the last three cruisers the House, at least, refused to take seriously a bill that would provide for the ten additional 10,000-ton cruisers requested by the President or to agree that the United States would have to build twenty-one cruisers in order to attain parity with Great Britain.

The American delegates at the Geneva conference, which opened on 20 June, insisted upon a limit of 8-inch guns for cruisers, parity with Great Britain at no more than four hundred thousand tons in cruisers, no increase above the 5–5–3 ratio for Japan, and no further limitation of Pacific fortifications. The conference failed in its attempt to find a common ground for the peculiar needs of the three powers. It was impossible particularly to meet the cruiser needs of the British Empire and of the United States with a figure that would guarantee superiority over Japan in both numbers and weapons. If Japan's eight 8-inch gun cruisers presented the outstanding problem for the other two nations, Japan appeared to be so cooperative at the conference that American public opinion came to see Great Britain as a greater threat than Japan to the security of the United States.[23]

The State Department had viewed the Geneva meeting merely as an avenue to reach agreements helpful to the ongoing League Preparatory Commission, which was planning for a General Disarmament Conference. Coolidge saw the latter as capable of handling the "peculiar problems" of France and of Italy while the Geneva conference considered only the problem of the three participants. As a result, naval technicists headed by Rear Admiral Hilary P. Jones rather than diplomats had been selected as the American delegates to Geneva. Following the conference, American pacifists placed the blame for its failure upon these naval officers. It may well be that these officers were not disposed to accept compromises to the degree that diplomats would have. They were also bereft of the kind of secret intelligence that had been available to the American delegates at the Washington Conference. But the fault was not altogether theirs, for subsequent exposure revealed that American shipbuilders had hired a William B. Shearer to lobby at Geneva against disarmament.[24]

Failure at Geneva drove Wilbur and Coolidge to support an "adequate navy" in keeping with new conditions. When Coolidge asked for advice in determining upon a new policy, Wilbur quickly suggested building the fleet to treaty strength and the Chief of Naval Operations, Admiral Edward Eberle, stated that we should build a fleet that would serve our needs rather than merely achieving parity with Great Britain.[25] With Coolidge's approval Wilbur asked the General Board to formulate a five-year building program. The board recommended building 5 battleships, 5 aircraft carriers, 25 cruisers, 9 destroyer leaders, 28 destroyers, and 35 submarines between 1929 and 1933. In December, in his annual message to Congress, Coolidge recommended a "large" building program, and Wilbur subsequently suggested seventy-one ships to cost $740 million. Of the forty-three cruisers the General Board wanted, ten were of the *Omaha*-class 6-inch gun ships commissioned between 1923 and 1925; the remaining thirty-three would be 10,000-ton, 8-inch gun types, the first of which could not enter service before the end of Wilbur's term. The seventy-one ship program, though still not providing parity with Great Britain and Japan in all classes of ships, was incorporated into a bill by Butler and sent to his House Naval Affairs Committee—where it remained for almost two months. It provoked such a heavy storm of protest from anti-navy and pacifist elements that Coolidge and Congress cut their demands. In consequence, a modified House bill of February 1928 provided for fifteen rather than twenty-five cruisers, one carrier instead of five, and no destroyer leaders or submarines. However, it provided for the modernization of two battleships. The debate was both long and bitter in yet another election year, with opponents asserting that world conditions "do not require a large Navy . . . armaments are the cause of war." Piqued at critics of his "new" Navy program, Coolidge charged that some members of the press were exerting "their influence in behalf of foreign interests."

Amended under heavy pressure from organized labor to have only alternate cruisers built in government yards, the "15 Cruiser Bill" passed the House very easily in March. Although Coolidge spoke several times in its favor, the Senate was too busy considering tax reductions to take it up until after the elections and the covening of the second session in December. Because of the protracted debate, and because negotiations resulting in the Kellogg–Briand Pact to outlaw war drew attention away from the Navy's needs, it did not clear the upper house until 5 February 1929. Coolidge signed it on the thirteenth, only three weeks before the inauguration of Herbert Hoover. Funding was even a closer call and included only the first year of the program—it arrived on Coolidge's desk with only four days remaining in his administration.[26]

Wilbur faced the problems of replacing the obsolescent battleship fleet beginning in 1931 and rounding out a fleet based upon treaty ratios but lopsided because of the delivery of ships from previous building programs. This was particularly true in those classes in which the United States had a marked superiority. Submarines of the "S" type of 1916–1918 continued to come into service through 1925, as did three fleet boats of the "B" type of 1920 and one minelaying "A" type of 1924. With no new destroyers to be authorized until 1931 and the battleship replacement problem deferred in terms of priority until the 1928–1932 time period, the emphasis was on cruisers, aircraft carriers, modernization of older battleships, specific types of auxiliaries, and gunboats for the rivers of China. Wilbur was also concerned because the four private yards that could build cruisers and carriers would soon be reduced to three and he believed that a navy must include not only combatant ships but also a strong merchant marine and the requisite yards, industry, and resources to meet any construction or repair demands.

Leaning heavily upon the teachings of Mahan, Wilbur and his advisers wanted a navy capable of achieving command of the sea in the event of war. While the backbone of the fleet was the battleship, a balanced fleet required many lesser vessels.

There were twelve battleships in the Pacific, and six in the Atlantic, but cruiser squadrons kept on the European and Asiatic stations could not concentrate rapidly. Only the Special Service Squadron based at the Panama Canal Zone could swing quickly in either direction. The Scouting Fleet, in the Atlantic, was a poor and unbalanced organization containing six old battleships, eight cruisers, thirty-nine destroyers and no airplane carriers, flotilla leaders, or fleet submarines. With an eye on the vast Pacific, naval leaders stressed the need of additional cruisers and took the 10,000-ton, 8-inch gun maximum established in the Washington Conference as the ideal. Wilbur agreed that the Battle Fleet should be in the Pacific and recommended that Congress enlarge the facilities needed for its support.[27]

Eleven capital ships under construction were sold as scrap in 1924, and fifteen older battleships in 1925, except for three that would be used for experimental bombing exercises. Two battle cruiser hulls, however, would be used to build aircraft carriers. The backbone of the U.S. Battle Fleet—the generic name for the concentration of the Battle Fleet, Scouting Fleet, Base Force, and Control Force—thus consisted of twelve of the eighteen battleships allowed by the treaty and of twenty-six of the forty-three modern cruisers. Two other cruisers would serve as destroyer squadron flagships, nine would protect strategic geographic points, and the remaining six would be used for escort of convoy. Since the active and reserve ship lists for 1928 named 311 destroyers and 128 submarines, numbers in these types were never a problem, but the specific need for destroyer leaders was not met by new construction. Nor was that of fleet submarines met, for the six boats of the "T" and "V" types proved to be inadequate. For proper organization, eighty-four of the destroyers should have been assigned to the high seas fleet alone, but Wilbur could afford to operate only 103 during his tenure. What the Navy needed after eight heavy cruisers were authorized in 1924 was twenty-five additional cruisers and the previously-mentioned destroyer leaders and fleet type submarines.

When Wilbur took office, naval planning compared unfavorably with Army planning, which had as its base the National Defense Act of 4 June 1920, in two respects: the Navy had no framework legislation, and it accepted the recommendations of the Bureau of the Budget instead of those of the General Board. Therefore, after several conferences with the President, and by his direction, Wilbur in 1924 created a special board headed by Admiral Edward W. Eberle to recommend general naval policy for the next ten years.

While the Eberle Board cogitated, Wilbur supported naval aviation not only within his department but by opposing the combined military air service being called for by Representative Charles F. Curry (Rep., Calif.), Major General Mason M. Patrick, USA, Chief of the Air Service, and Brigadier General William "Billy" Mitchell, its handsome and dynamic Assistant Chief. When the Chairman of the House Committee on Military Affairs said that he had time to hear only two of the twenty witnesses Wilbur offered, Wilbur himself testified. He claimed that the committee was being misinformed and flatly contradicted Mitchell on the effectiveness of air attack on combatant ships. Apparently dissatisfied with the impression he had made, he returned several days later to deliver a death blow—he had been authorized to say that President Coolidge disapproved the unified air service provided for in the Curry bill.[28]

In October 1924, the House had created a special committee of seven members headed by Florian Lampert to look into all aspects of naval and military aviation. After hearing many witnesses, including Mitchell, retired Rear Admiral William F. Fullam and retired Admiral William S. Sims, and Rear Admiral Hilary P. Jones, chairman of the executive committee of the General Board, on 14 December 1925 the committee report recommended the establishment of a department of national defense but not a unified air service.[29] When the House Committee on Military Affairs in January 1925 began hearings on two bills providing for a Department of Aeronautics, Wilbur again called attention to Mitchell's erroneous and misleading statements. While the committee issued no report, it aired the heightened ill feeling that existed between Mitchell and his followers and the Navy and War Departments.[30]

The Eberle Board met between September and December 1924. Wilbur attended many of its sessions to hear what witnesses suggested not only with respect to ship types and weapons but also on how naval aviation should be developed. He agreed with the recommendation for battleship modernization and became convinced that the Bureau of Aeronautics was keenly alive to the importance of naval aviation and that American aircraft were as good as foreign ones. The Navy held world speed records for both seaplanes and land planes. Because of the lack of funds, Wilbur withdrew the Navy from further competition, but he intended to recommend appropriations for aviation sufficient not only to provide aircraft for training and fleet maneuvers but liberal funds for experimentation and development of new designs because he saw aviation as an integral and "vitally essential" part of naval activities in future wars. In addition he would recommend that the aircraft carriers under construction be completed at the earliest possible date and that experiments be continued with the rigid airships *Shenandoah*, built by Americans, and the German-built *Los Angeles*.[31]

On 3 September 1925 it was Wilbur's duty to order an investigation into the tragic loss of the *Shenandoah* during a violent storm in Ohio. He was then chagrined when only two of the three new long-distance airplanes, two Navy-built PN–9s and a Boeing craft, left San Francisco for Hawaii; one subsequently had oil line failure and had to be towed three hundred miles back to San Francisco; and PN9 No. 1, with flight leader Commander John Rodgers aboard, landed two hundred miles short because it ran out of fuel. After nine days, Rodgers and his crew managed to reach the island of Kauai by rigging the wings of the plane as sails![32]

Having become persona non grata to the War Department, Mitchell had been transferred from Washington to San Antonio, Texas. On 5 September he unleashed a tremendous public blast against naval aviation and for good measure against his War Department superiors as well. By ascribing aviation accidents as due to "the incompetency, criminal negligence, and almost treasonable administration of the National Defense by the War and Navy Departments," he opened the way for his subsequent court martial. By hitting the Navy when it was down, moreover, he made an implacable enemy of Rear Admiral William A. Moffett, Chief of the Bureau of Aeronautics, who was no less devoted than Mitchell to the cause of aviation. Although genuinely irked by Mitchell, Wilbur decided not to dignify him by public reply. However, Moffett called Mitchell a liar and ascribed his criticisms to hallucinations or delusions of grandeur.[33] On 11 September, moreover, Wilbur and the secretary of war jointly asked President Coolidge to appoint a board to study both Army and Navy aviation. Agreeable, Coolidge chose an Amherst College classmate, Dwight F. Morrow, to head a board of nine men. Morrow opened hearings on 21 September. While some naval witnesses opposed a separate department of aeronautics and favored a semi-autonomous corps within the Navy like that of the Marine Corps, some of them, like Harry Yarnell and John Rodgers, favored a single department of defense. In any case, the unanimous report offered the President on 30 November pleased Wilbur by disapproving a separate air service or department of defense and recommending that both the Navy and War Departments create assistant secretaries for air, that aviation be granted fuller representation on high departmental levels, and that the name Army Air Service be changed to Army Air Corps. Danger that all military and civilian aircraft design, development, and procurement would be placed under a single agency disappeared when a recommendation was also made to establish a bureau of air commerce in the Department of Commerce.[34] In 1926 Congress used the Morrow Board report as a base for the Air Corps Act and the Air Commerce Act, the latter of which placed responsibility for promoting aviation directly upon the shoulders of the government. For the next generation, bills calling for unification of aviation and the Army and Navy got nowhere.

On 24 June 1926, Congress adopted Moffet's Five Year Plan, which authorized construction which gave the United States the world's largest naval air arm by the 1930s. A bill introduced by Butler that incorporated Moffet's plan provided for a five-year naval aviation program ending 30 June 1931 of 1,614 airplanes, spare parts, and equipment, two rigid airships of about six million cubic feet capacity, and one two hundred thousand-cubic foot metal-clad experimental airship, with all three airships to be built in the United States and begun before 1 July 1927. To Moffett this was "A conservative and yet adequate plan, keeping in mind the necessity for economy urged by the President."[35]

Naval aviation progressed rapidly in Wilbur's day. New air-cooled engines reduced the weight per horsepower of the power plant by about one-third, used 10 percent less fuel than water-cooled engines, cut both the time and cost of maintenance, and were becoming increasingly dependable—by 1926 they were 400 percent more dependable than those of World War I. A 200 horsepower engine was used for training craft, but 400 and 500 horsepower engines were being developed by Pratt & Whitney and the Wright companies. The PN-10s that were replacing the PN-9s, used in the Hawaii flight of 1925, had extended cruising ranges that permitted patrol work with the fleet. In consequence of such improvements, Lieutenant Commander Richard E. Byrd had flown from Spitzbergen to the North Pole in the spring of 1926—a nineteen-hour flight covering twelve hundred miles—and in 1927 Charles Lindbergh was the first to cross the Atlantic Ocean non-stop from West to East. As a member of the official committee designated to welcome Lindbergh upon his return, Wilbur seized the opportunity to express the hope that Lindbergh's dramatic exploit would sway Congress toward liberal treatment of aviation appropriations.[36]

In May 1925, meanwhile, Wilbur had approved substantial changes in the curriculum at the Naval Academy. The Department of Engineering became the Department of Engineering and Aeronautics, and the Department of Seamanship the Department of Seamanship and Flight Tactics. All new ensigns would be given three months of special instruction and flight work at Annapolis immediately after graduating. In the first two years after graduating, every physically capable officer would seek to qualify as a naval observer or naval aviator. Beginning in 1926, midshipmen of the first class would get flight training during the summer.[37]

To meet legislative intent, Wilbur also insisted that the number of enlisted pilots be increased substantially. On 22 September 1926, he ordered one hundred and fifty enlisted men to Pensacola for training. As the program developed, an excessive "washout" rate proved a genuine stumbling block, but the Assistant Secretary for Air, Edward P. Warner, stated on 16 August 1927 that the naval air arm in the period from 1 July 1923 to 1 July 1927 had increased the number of commissioned pilots from 326 to 470 and the enlisted pilots from a "small number" to 108. To use this output Captain Joseph M. Reeves, Commander Aircraft Squadrons, Battle Fleet, manned Fighter Squadrons Two and Six exclusively with enlisted pilots. Thus the department was well on the way to reaching the 1 July 1928 goal of 30 percent enlisted naval aviators.[38]

By his selection of officers and by creating a favorable administrative atmosphere for them, Wilbur made his greatest contribution to the naval air arm. Although he originally planned to limit bureau chiefs to one term, he reappointed Moffett to a second tour as Chief of the Bureau of Aeronautics because his work was as yet "incomplete," and then gave him an unprecedented third tour. Moreover, he recommended to Coolidge that Edward W. Eberle become Chief of Naval Operations because Eberle had headed the board to investigate the future of seapower in terms of the battleship and the airplane and was favorably inclined toward air. Both as Chief of Naval Operations and then as a member of the General Board, Eberle in turn profoundly affected Wilbur's views toward air.

Wilbur's appointment in 1925 of Joseph M. Reeves as Commander Aircraft Squadrons, Battle Fleet, also brought far-reaching changes to the Navy, for Reeves developed the tactical doctrine for air combat at sea and had carriers recognized as major combat units as a result of exercises running from Fleet Problem VII of 1927 to Fleet Problem IX of 1929. Wilbur, Moffett, and other Navy men also made it clear that the Navy proceeded on a functional, or task force, concept and must have the sea, land (Marines), and naval air forces needed to execute its mission.[39]

In addition to rejecting the concept of a separate air service, the report of the Eberle board, dated 17 January 1925, described the bombing experiments on the *Washington* and called for a three-year building program. Although bombed extensively from the air, the super-dreadnought survived and had to be sunk eventually with torpedoes and naval gunfire. The experiments nevertheless pointed up the need of bulges to provide cushions against both bombs and torpedoes and to serve for oil storage, deck strengthening, improved armament and fire control equipment, the replacing of coal-burning with oil-burning machinery, and elevating the heavy guns so that they could fire at greater ranges at targets aircraft reported but gun crews could not see.

The three-year building program consisted of seven major items. Coolidge accepted them but cut their cost below the requested $80 million for each of three years. He also requested that the report show the relative priorities of the seven items under several lesser scales of annual expenditures. The resulting supplemental report, of 31 January 1925, contained the following itemized priorities for the period 1926–1928: the modernization of six coal-burning battleships and of seven additional ones of more recent vintage; speedy completion of the carriers *Lexington* and *Saratoga* and the provision of aircraft for them; the building of the eight 10,000-ton cruisers already authorized by Congress; $20 million in the first year to provide modern aircraft; the laying down of the three remaining fleet submarines during fiscal 1927; and the building of a 23,000-ton aircraft carrier as soon as possible. Coolidge approved modernizing the coal-burning battleships but not the others, the completing of the *Lexington* and *Saratoga* and furnishing their air groups, and requested funds for two cruisers. He disapproved the rest.[40]

One of Wilbur's important tasks was to recommend appointments to the President for the position of Chief of Naval Operations. Two of his Naval Academy classmates, Admirals Edward W. Eberle and Charles F. Hughes, served in this post, the first for three years, the latter for two. During the last two years Eberle served on the General Board. The important post of Commander in Chief U.S. Fleet was retained by Admiral Robert E. Coontz until August 1925, when he was succeeded first by another Wilbur classmate, Admiral S. S. Robison, then by Hughes. Still another Wilbur classmate, A. H. Robertson, was given command of the Scouting Fleet. The service of another Wilbur classmate, Major General John A. Lejeune, as Commandant of the Marine Corps throughout the Coolidge administration, gave Wilbur even greater pleasure. Bureau chiefs and fleet commanders were changed as retirements and normal rotation required.[41]

Wilbur was aided considerably by his Assistant Secretary, Colonel Theodore Roosevelt, Jr., an appointee of the previous administration, who provided continuity and concentrated on the shore establishment and naval reserve, testified before Congress, and expedited planning by the General Board. Particularly important was the Orange War Plan against Japan. According to this plan, the U.S. Navy would go on the offensive in the Far East only after the Japanese had consolidated their initial gains, a procedure Roosevelt opposed. When the colorful colonel resigned in 1924 to run for governor of New York —a race he lost—Coolidge chose as his successor Roosevelt's cousin, Theodore Douglas Robinson, a son of President Theodore Roosevelt's sister and an active figure in Republican politics in New York State.

Neither Colonel Roosevelt nor Robinson was to escape political infighting or a hostile press. One Representative charged that Roosevelt was unfit for office because his wife held a thousand shares of Sinclair Oil and only returned them after the Teapot Dome Lease was made, and Robinson was attacked by the press in November 1927 for supporting Rear Admiral T. P. Magruder in the latter's fight against the Navy Department and Wilbur with charges that there were too many bases and poor navy yard administration. The persistent Magruder wanted a personal interview with the President as Commander in Chief to present his case against Wilbur—a move pleasing to the press but not to Coolidge. The meeting did not occur.[42] On the positive side, however, was the creation in July 1926 of the post of a second Assistant Secretary of the Navy, for aviation, a move resisted by Wilbur as an unnecessary separation of aviation problems within the Department. The President appointed to this post Edward P. Warner, a product of Harvard, professor at the Massachusetts

Institute of Technology, and a leading aerodynamics expert. Warner embraced projects related to service or government aeronautics and aerodynamics and worked closely with Moffett throughout his administration.[43]

The work of two assistant secretaries, particularly that of Roosevelt in the early months of 1924, produced substantial advances in war planning, with primary emphasis placed upon the Orange Plan. That plan, often revised, in 1924 recognized Japan as the most probable enemy, took account of the numerous islands mandated to Japan which lay astride our line of communications with the Philippines, considered the terms of the Five-Power Treaty—which made it doubtful if the U.S. Navy could meet Japan on equal terms in the Far East— and originally gave supreme command of all forces in a "United States Asiatic Expeditionary Force" to one supreme commander assisted by a Joint Army and Navy Staff. At the insistence of the Joint Board of the Army and Navy, the supreme commander was deleted in favor of "thorough cooperation" and "the closest mutual cooperation" between the two services. When questions arose respecting action, "the requirements of the service having paramount interest should govern."[44] In case of war, the Army would have to hold Manila Bay until the arrival of the American fleet, which would then contribute to the defeat of Japan by isolating and harassing her. Wilbur approved the plan on 16 August, the Secretary of War on 3 September 1924. To keep the plan current, it was modified at least six times between 1924 and 1928. Among the changes was one that made the seizing of islands a major war mission for the Marine Corps. The planners of Wilbur's day had not only a Red Plan for war with Great Britain but a Red–Orange Plan for war against both Great Britain and Japan. Although the plan was unrealistic in terms of the international situation of the moment, "as a strategic exercise" it was of great value, for it forced the military planners to consider seriously the problems presented by a war in which the United States would have to fight simultaneously in the Atlantic and Pacific Oceans. These plans of the Coolidge era laid the seed for "Germany first" as the basic Allied concept for World War II in a plan known as Rainbow 5.[45]

Personnel problems perennially plagued Wilbur. Authorized enlisted manpower strength was set at 137,485, but pay appropriations funded only about 86,000. Battleships therefore operated with from 90 to 95 percent of their complement, destroyers 90 percent, and the newest cruisers 95 percent at a time when an additional three thousand men must be found for the *Saratoga* and *Lexington*, which would be commissioned in 1926, and also men for their air crews. Moreover, the naval appropriations act for fiscal year 1924 reduced the number of congressional appointees to the Naval Academy from five to three.

With officer separations and resignations reaching a new high of 4.7 percent compared with the prewar 3.5 percent, Wilbur in 1925 appointed a board to assess the needs of personnel in the rapidly expanding aviation program and to recommend a plan whereby more aviation officers could return to general line duty and thus make room for younger officers coming from training stations. He also pointed out that it was false economy to reduce the number of midshipmen to 1,900 when the Academy was geared to serve 2,500, and that attempts should be made to fill the quota of one hundred enlisted men permitted the fleet.[46]

Since more than half of the officers had entered the service after 1917, only training at sea could overcome their inexperience. Yet Wilbur's new policy of assigning graduating midshipmen to battleships and cruisers meant that these ships must operate largely as training schools and that a large turnover of personnel would occur as these ensigns were then transferred to smaller ships, submarines, aviation, or postgraduate schools, and another draft came aboard. However, the Naval Reserve Officers Training Corps, established in July 1924, and bad times came to his rescue. On 25 February 1925, Congress abolished the old Naval Reserve Force, as of 1 July, and authorized the NROTC within the provisions of the National Defense Act of June 1916. The Navy was allotted twelve hundred students, of which 80 percent would be Navy and 20 percent Marines. So popular was the NROTC that by the opening of the academic year 1926 additional naval units were established at Harvard, Yale, Northwestern, University of California at Berkeley, and Georgia School of Technology.

By late 1927 Wilbur had the number of officers permitted by law, 5,499, when he stated that the Navy needed an additional seven hundred line officers. Similar shortages but eventual stability also marked the enlisted personnel. An extraordinarily high reenlistment rate in 1925, of 72 percent, also resulted in an improvement in quality, and desertions dropped from 3,161 in 1924 to 692 in 1926.[47] That economy reached the civilian employees of the Navy is clearly illustrated by the dropping of 11,000 workers in 1924 alone, leaving about 30,000 on duty. By 1926, however, Wilbur had increased the number to approximately 40,000, a number retained for the rest of his term.

When tension increased with Japan because of our Immigration Act of 1924, which excluded Orientals, the Diet allocated funds for special maneuvers in October and November and placed all reserve ships of the Imperial Navy into commission. Although the Western Allies said they lacked the wherewithal to pay us their World War I debts, money was somehow available for extensive naval maneuvers, especially in the Mediterranean, in 1925. Furthermore, Great Britain sent a Special Service Squadron on a good will cruise to the Dominions which caused it to circumnavigate the globe, including calls at San Francisco and Hawaii. No doubt these events stimulated Congress to furnish increased funds for the American naval maneuvers for 1925, including a cruise to Australia. Although the maneuvers were part of a four-year training cycle established in 1921, pacifists mistakenly concluded that the cruise to Australia was an attempt to apply Theodore Roosevelt's dictum, "Speak softly and carry a big stick," to Japan. Had these pacifists known of the conditions that existed in our Navy, they might not have made the charge.

Just before Wilbur took office, the Chief of Naval Operations, Robert E. Coontz, had written his report on maneuvers recently held. Among other things, he indicated that our only carrier, the *Langley*, though supposed to have fifty-eight aircraft, had six. Improvements were needed in arresting gear, deck lighting for night flying, and in communications on both ships and planes. Carriers needed more destroyer escorts. The catapults on our battleships did not work well and the boilers on most of the older battleships were worn out. In war problems involving twelve thousand miles of steaming it had been demonstrated that the Train Squadrons of the Base Force had been limited to a speed of 7½ knots. Among other improvements he suggested that 10,000-ton, 8-inch gun cruisers were needed "as supports for the screen and as linking vessels and that submarine operations were worst of all combatant ships." Press accounts of the sad conditions of the fleet and publication of parts of Coontz's report, on 30 April, stimulated some of Wilbur's advisers to ask him to issue a counteracting statement. Instead Wilbur testified before the Senate Naval Affairs Committee that "Coontz had given a true picture of the fleet."[48]

In the summer of 1924 Wilbur strongly supported "Defense Test Day," designed to try out the adequacy of emergency plans for the regular forces, National Guard, Organized Reserves, and civilian components to assemble locally throughout the United States. The Navy supported the day admirably with a fleet attack against the coastal defenses of San Francisco Bay while Marines joined the Army in defending local communities. However, after pacifists and anti-militarists both within and without Congress loudly denounced this march towards "German militarism," Defense Test Day disappeared.[49]

The 1925 maneuvers, the most extensive carried out during the 1920s, involved exercises off Hawaii in conjunction with the Army and a cruise by the fleet to Australia. Unfortunately, the jingoistic press both in Japan and the United States tried to picture these maneuvers in a crisis light.

At any rate the critique following the Hawaiian exercises demonstrated an interesting difference of opinion. Commander Harry E. Yarnell, Commanding Aircraft Squadrons of the Scouting Fleet, admitted that the Navy learned a great deal about aerial tactics, formation flying, and combat work. Major Gerald C. Brant, Army Air Service, held that the isolation of the United States had been destroyed "because the airplane and its carrier can bring an aerial menace very quickly to any place on the globe not adequately protected by its own air forces. . . . To the Army Air Service the first and primary defense of our coastline lies in the air." In his annual report, Wilbur stressed the weakness of defensive installations and the need to improve almost every facet of amphibious techniques. In any case, the Battle Fleet—11 battleships, 1 old cruiser serving as flagship, 5 light cruisers, 26 destroyers, and 13 auxiliaries—covered 13,000 miles to New Zealand and Australia and proved its ability to cross the Pacific sustained by its own service support.[50]

Maneuvers for the year 1927 involved Wilbur to a much greater extent than normal. Fairly in line with the Red war plan, the entire fleet would operate jointly with the Army in the Narragansett Bay area for three weeks in May. So important was this operation that a planning conference was held in November between Wilbur, the Chief of Naval Operations, and the commander in chief Atlantic Fleet. When the War Department failed to obtain funds from Congress, however, Wilbur announced that the Navy would go it alone. But even this truncated plan could not be followed through because of troubles with Mexico. At the moment, the Special Service Squadron, normally responsible for this area, was tied-down off Nicaragua; the Battle Fleet was at San Diego scheduled to go south on maneuvers the next month; the Scouting Fleet was exercising at Guantánamo Bay; and the destroyer tender *Holland* was standing by at San Diego with an expeditionary force of 400 Marines. Instead of sending a punitive expedition like Pershing's into Mexico, his diplomatic, Army, and Navy heads advised Coolidge to use the Navy to blockade Mexico's ports and land Marines and bluejackets while Army troops simultaneously moved in force across the border.

Whatever President Coolidge's plans were, Congress sought to limit his freedom of action. While the Senate adopted a resolution advising arbitration of all controversies with both Mexico and China, the House Foreign Affairs Committee favored the reporting of a resolution requesting the negotiation of reciprocal treaties with the Republic of China and seemed willing to do the same for Mexico. Fortunately passions quickly cooled and by the end of January 1927 a return to peacetime maneuvers was possible. But the crises and scare headlines changed some attitudes in this country; when the Army said it was ready to participate in the Narragansett Bay joint maneuvers, Congress readily appropriated funds for this particular exercise.[51]

Wilbur could now turn his attention to the first major maneuvers to be held in the Atlantic since 1920. Assistant Secretary of the Navy Robinson, who observed the Scouting Fleet off Cuba, reported a desperate need for light cruisers and fleet type submarines to keep contact with the Scouting Fleet and communicate course bearings and location of an enemy. The point was driven home when one light cruiser, the *Trenton*, had to simulate the entire Light Cruiser Divisions Scouting Fleet. When the Battle Fleet combined with the Scouting Fleet as the United States Fleet, the *Trenton* represented the cruiser divisions of the assembled fleet. Little wonder that Robinson was impressed with the shortage of such ships.[52]

With Wilbur and Major General Hanson Ely, USA aboard, the second phase began when the fleet sailed from New York on 16 May to storm the shores of Narragansett Bay. The Navy, representing a major enemy fleet escorting across the Atlantic some seventy-five thousand troops, succeeded in landing a part of this force under what the umpire ruled was a heavy loss.

Wilbur's duties in 1928 involved an entirely new arena. Invited to do so by Gerardo Machado of Cuba, Coolidge decided to be the first U.S. president to attend an International Conference of American States. His personal party, including Wilbur and Mrs. Wilbur, went by train from Washington to Key West, Florida, then boarded the cruiser *Memphis*, which transferred them when six miles out at sea to the battleship *Texas*, which was suitably escorted by six destroyers and supported by the tanker *Conoocook*.

By the time he went to Havana, Wilbur was deeply involved in Nicaragua, where a revolt had broken out in 1925. While the Navy was not heavily engaged at first, Wilbur clashed with non-interventionists and those who opposed his use of force. Coolidge would not recognize a government that came to power by unconstitutional methods but provided no policy to follow, with the result that Wilbur and the secretaries of State and of War made policy as events transpired. Moreover, Mexico recognized insurgents Coolidge would not, and Mexico itself created enough of a problem by threatening to expropriate foreign-owned oil properties. Not only must a watchful eye be kept on the Panama Canal, stability in all of Central America seemed to hinge upon the success of the United States in maintaining the status quo therein. When the "legitimate" government of Nicaragua approached collapse in the winter of 1925–1926, Coolidge decided upon direct support. Wilbur thereupon dispatched the Special Service Squadron as reinforced by ships from both the Battle and Scouting fleets, the Second Marine Brigade, and a substantial number of Marine Corps aircraft. For the first time, Marines faced guerrilla tactics. Although the Stimson Agreement of 11 May 1927 enabled Wilbur to reduce his forces to those needed to protect American lives and property, such was the opposition clamor that an amendment was almost added to the 1929 appropriations bill that would have cut off all funds to maintain even the Marine legation guard in Nicaragua. Coolidge left the Nicaraguan stalemate for his successor, Herbert Hoover, to cope with.[53]

Half way around the world, momentous events in China meanwhile threatened our treaty rights and directly endangered American citizens and property. When civil war broke out on 1 September 1924, American, British, French, and Japanese naval forces responded, but only the British and French landed forces to protect their nationals. Although the Army had its 15th Infantry Regiment at

Tientsin, American military power in China rested largely upon the Asiatic Fleet and the Marines. To protect American lives and property, Congress authorized the building of six new gunboats in Shanghai. After conferring with Secretary of State Kellogg in June 1925, Wilbur directed Admiral Thomas Washington, Commander in Chief Asiatic Fleet, to use his own judgment in handling the situation. Within a month Chiang Kai-shek's launching of his northern drive exacerbated the situation. As American warships in the Shanghai area were hit by gunfire, and fired in return, the rest of the Asiatic Fleet under Admiral C. S. Williams rushed from the Philippines to Chinese waters. Still unable to cope with the situation, these forces were strengthened by Light Cruiser Division Three of the Atlantic Scouting Fleet and General Smedley Butler assumed command of Marines landed in the various treaty ports. Hard put to furnish Marines for both Nicaragua and China, Wilbur recruited more men, activated additional units and sent them to China, and asked Congress to enlarge the Corps. Once Chiang Kai-shek had apparently unified China, however, in late 1928, Marine forces in China were greatly reduced, the Asiatic Fleet returned to the Philippines, and gunboats were left to deal with whatever minor problems ensued.[54]

By the time of the elections of 1928, Wilbur had served five years during which he received more criticism on the one hand and praise on the other than any peacetime Secretary of the Navy. This may seem paradoxical, for today his name is almost unknown within or without the Navy.

Hostile reports blamed Wilbur personally for the almost unbelievable string of disasters that occurred during his tenure: the loss of the *S-4* and *S-51*, costing 51 lives; loss of aircraft engaged in stunt flying, international races, attempts at altitude records, and long-distance flights; the breaking apart of the dirigible *Shenandoah*, which "Billy" Mitchell said Wilbur had ordered out to cover failures in Navy air operations; the tragic explosions set by lightening at the Naval Ammunition Depot, Lake Denmarck, New Jersey, unchecked for days and resulting in heavy loss of life; and turret explosions on the battleship *Mississippi* and the cruiser *Trenton*. The *New York World* placed the blame for these disasters on Wilbur and demanded that he "Must go." Although Coolidge supported Wilbur, *Time* magazine in February 1929 poked fun at Wilbur's teaching of a Sunday School class and writing of children's bedtime stories—the only naval secretary ever to do so.[55]

Various other activities kept Wilbur in the public eye. In 1924 he sponsored the holding of a government-wide conference on oceanography. He strongly supported the National Geographic Society and its Arctic Expedition organized by Commander Donald B. MacMillan, USNR, including the use of Commander Richard E. Byrd and his Navy flying unit which in 1926 made the first flight over the Pole. Stemming from this same scientific thrust was the naval expedition to observe a solar eclipse in Sumatra in 1926, and in 1929 the first aerial observation of an eclipse and the sending of a naval exhibit to an Ibero–American Exposition.[56]

Wilbur was also in the public eye for his genuine interest in athletic events. Colonel Robert M. Thompson, frequent visitor to the Naval Academy, founder of the Navy League, and President of the U.S. Olympic Association, appointed him Assistant President in 1924 in time for the VIII Olympiad in Paris. Wilbur wrote an article in 1926 on the subject of "Boxing Big Benefit to U.S. Navy Personnel"; while noting that almost every state had laws against prize-fighting, he instructed the Navy to hold such affairs on federal property outside local jurisdiction. As with any sea-faring man he attended the annual regattas on his official yacht, the *Sylph*, but it was with the Naval Academy and football that he attracted the most press attention. In late 1927, one of the sensational sport page stories was the break in athletic relations between the two service academies over eligibility rules. Seven Army players had had up to four years of competition before entering West Point. Navy had a five-year eligibility rule. Wilbur supported his alma mater and Navy scheduled Princeton instead of Army for 1928. The outcry of irate fans was capped when two congressmen took the matter up directly with the President. Princeton was not removed from the schedule,[57] and it was several years before Army and Navy played football again.

Wilbur represented the Navy before the public in various other ways. He was personally concerned with efforts to save and restore the frigate *Constitution* and made a trip to Boston to watch the docking of "Old Ironsides" as the first step in that process. When Charles A. Lindbergh completed his historic flight to Paris, Wilbur invited him to return home on an American warship and Coolidge asked him to serve on the official welcoming committee.

Wilbur spoke to all kinds of fraternal and national organizations, made his Washington home a center for entertainment, and used his official yacht for social as well as political purposes.[58]

Wilbur's relations with Coolidge did not go unremarked. The President was highly pleased when Wilbur selected the name Northampton, his home town, for the cruiser built at Quincy. In the drive to save "Old Ironsides," Wilbur sold print number one of the famed Gordon Grant painting to the President in an appropriate ceremony. He also vacationed with Coolidge at Cedar Island Lodge in the Black Hills of South Dakota.[59]

Perplexed when his friend Hoover formally launched his campaign for the presidential nomination in September 1927 without either the support of Coolidge or knowing whether Coolidge intended to run again, Wilbur nevertheless became the first cabinet member to support Hoover. Many thought that he would remain as Secretary of the Navy in the new administration and perhaps go on to the Supreme Court. But the call never came. Although his brother, Ray, became Secretary of the Interior, Hoover did not relish his continual championing of a strong Navy built to treaty strength.[60]

A Navy built to treaty strength had been Wilbur's major objective for five years. Because Hoover disagreed, Wilbur had to leave the Navy Department. But Hoover did not forget Wilbur. Instead he appointed him to the Ninth Federal Circuit Court of Appeals in San Francisco, where he served as presiding judge until his retirement in 1945. During World War II he was an active speaker for the Navy and the nation. He died on 8 September 1954, at Palo Alto, California, at the age of eighty-seven years, thus ending a career devoted to national service.[61]

NOTES

1. Claude M. Fuess, *Calvin Coolidge: The Man from Vermont* (Boston: Little, Brown, 1940), pp. 211, 14, 241, 522; Donald R. McCoy, *Calvin Coolidge: The Quiet President* (New York: Macmillan, 1967), pp. 151-52; William Allen White, *A Puritan in Babylon: The Story of Calvin Coolidge* (New York: Capricorn Books, 1965), p. 267.

2. Howard H. Quint and Robert H. Ferrell, eds., *The Talkative President: The Off-The-Record Press Conferences of Calvin Coolidge* (Amherst: University of Massachusetts Press, 1964), pp. 23-24; *Time*, 24 Mar. 1924, pp. 1-2; *San Francisco Chronicle*, 15 Mar. 1924, p. 3.

3. Edgar Eugene Robinson and Paul Carroll Edwards, eds., *The Memoirs of Ray Lyman Wilbur, 1875-1949* (Stanford: Stanford University Press, 1960), pp. 3-35; *Time*, 24 Mar. 1924, pp. 1-2. ANJ, 22 Mar. 1924, pp. 714-15, 3 Apr. 1924, p. 763.

4. LD, 27 Dec. 1924, pp. 6-8; *New York Times*, 9 Sept. 1954, p. 31; ANJ, 6 Sept. 1924, p. 1293, 30 Sept. 1924, p. 1345, 27 Dec. 1924, pp. 1677-78.

5. ARSN, 1924, p. 3.

6. ARSN, 1924, p. 3; ARSN, 1925, pp. 15, 32, 35, 59-60; ARSN, 1926, pp. 55-56.

7. GB Records, File 420-2, Serial 1108, of 29 Mar. 1922, NHD:OA.

8. ARSN, 1924, p. 2.

9. CR, 68th Cong., 1st Sess., p. 4258.

10. *Ibid.*, p. 4673.

11. *Ibid.*, pp. 4675, 4682.

12. *Ibid.*, p. 9746.

13. *Ibid.*, pp. 9749-58, 9761-62.

14. *Ibid.*, pp. 9761-62; LD, 20 Dec. 1924, p. 1.

15. CR, 68th Cong., 2nd Sess., pp. 857, 4771-85, 4982.

16. *Ibid.*, 69th Cong., 2nd Sess., p. 2387; ANJ, 2 Mar. 1929, p. 526.

17. CR, 69th Cong., 2nd Sess., pp. 1084-1101, 1125-50, 1227-29, 1252-54.

18. LD, 22 Jan. 1927, pp. 8-9.

19. CR, 69th Cong., 2nd Sess., pp. 2060-80, 2430-50, 2667.

20. LD, 26 Feb. 1927, p. 6.

21. CR, 69th Cong., 2nd Sess., pp. 4692, 4699.

22. "The Cruiser Bill," in Curtis D. Wilbur Papers, Stanford University Library, Palo Alto; Roger K. Heller, "Factors Influencing Naval Construction in the United States, 1922–1929" (M. A. thesis, University of California, Berkeley, 1952), p. 133.
23. "The Geneva Three Power Conference," Wilbur Papers; "British Once Feared Drift to U.S. War," *The Washington Post*, 22 Mar. 1973, G7; Gerald E. Wheeler, *Prelude to Pearl Harbor: The United States Navy and the Far East, 1921-1931* (Columbia: University of Missouri Press, 1963), pp. 139-57; Ernest Andrade, "United States Naval Policy in the Disarament Era, 1921–1937" (Ph. D. diss., Michigan State University, 1966), pp. 129-55.
24. George V. Fagan, "Anglo-American Naval Relations, 1927–1937" (Ph. D. diss., University of Pennsylvania, 1954), pp. 51-53.
25. "Naval Developments since 1921," Wilbur Papers; *The Congressional Digest*, Jan. 1, 1929, p. 3. See also CAPT Ben Scott Custer, "The Geneva Conference for the Limitation of Naval Armament-1927" (Ph. D. diss., Georgetown University, 1948).
26. For the House debate, see CR, 70th Cong., 1st Sess., pp. 4908-24, and for the Senate debate and vote, CR, 70th Cong., 2nd Sess., pp. 1050-61, 2183, 2310-38, 2355, 2526-31, 2591-99, 2607-55, 2760-62, 2839-40, 2846-47, 3347.
27. ARSN, 1924, pp. 3-4.
28. ANJ, 28 June 1924, p. 1054, 12 Sept. 1925, p. 28.
29. *Inquiry into Operations of the U.S. Air Services*, Hearings before the Select Committee of Inquiry into Operations of the U.S. Air Services, House of Representatives, 68th Congress, on Matters Relating to the Operations of the U.S. Air Services (Washington: GPO, 1925).
30. Laurence J. Legere, Jr., "Unification of the Armed Forces," (Washington, OCMH, 1950), pp. 117-19.
31. ARSN, 1924, pp. 2-3, 31-32; ARSN, 1925, p. 36. Although the *Saratoga* was launched on 7 Apr. and the *Lexington* on 3 Oct. 1925, these ships were not commissioned until 14 Dec. and 16 Nov. 1927, respectively. See Archibald Turnbull and Clifford L. Lord, *History of United States Naval Aviation* (New Haven: Yale University Press, 1949), pp. 243-45.
32. ARSN, 1925, pp. 10-11, 40-41.
33. Eugene E. Wilson, *Slipstream: The Autobiography of an Aircraftsman* (New York: Whittlesey House, 1950), pp. 56-70; "Colonel Mitchell's Statements on Government Aviation," *Aviation* 19 (4 Sept. 1925):317-19; "Admiral Moffett Replies to Accusations," *ibid.* 19 (21 Sept. 1925):353.
34. *Department of Defense and Unification of Air Service*, Hearings before the Committee on Military Affairs, House of Representatives, 68th Cong., 1st Sess. (Washington: GPO, 1926).
35. ANJ, 30 Jan. 1926, editorial page, 20 Feb. 1936, p. 587, 5 June 1926, p. 968, 26 June 1926, p. 1027, 26 Feb. 1927, pp. 601-03.
36. *Ibid.*, 28 May 1927, p. 878, 4 June 1927, p. 909, 18 June 1927, p. 949.
37. *Ibid.*, 9 May 1925, p. 673, 12 Apr. 1926, p. 796, 18 June 1927, p. 942.
38. *Ibid.*, 9 May 1925, p. 2137, 13 Feb. 1926, p. 572, 6 Mar. 1926, p. 651, 25 Sept. 1926, p. 85, 20 Aug. 1927, p. 1119, 20 Jan. 1927, p. 448, 1 Sept. 1928, p. 1.

39. *Department of Defense and Unification of Air Services*, pp. 205-715.
40. ANJ, 27 Sept. 1924, p. 1365, 21 Feb. 1925, pp. 1871-72.
41. *Ibid.*, 12 June 1926, p. 983; "Assignment of Officers," Wilbur Papers.
42. *New York Times*, 16 Mar. 1924, pp. 1, 4; ANJ, 1 Oct. 1927, pp. 82, 90, 22 Oct. 1927, p. 150, 29 Oct. 1927, pp. 161, 163, 171, 5 Nov. 1927, p. 188, 17 Dec. 1927, p. 301, 7 Jan. 1928, pp. 367, 375.
43. ANJ, 23 Jan. 1926, p. 511, 30 Jan. 1926, editorial 3 July 1926, p. 1070.
44. Legere, "Unification of the Armed Forces," pp. 145-46.
45. "Memo-White House, 11 Nov. 1924," Calvin Coolidge Papers, MDLC; *Time*, 22 Nov. 1924, pp. 4-5; ANJ, 15 Nov. 1924, p. 1, 22 Nov. 1924, p. 1561; Wheeler, *Prelude to Pearl Harbor*, pp. 79-83; Louis Morton, "Germany First: The Basic Concept of Allied Strategy in World War II," in Kent Roberts Greenfield, ed., *Command Decisions* (New York: Harcourt, Brace and Co., 1959), pp. 3-9.
46. ARSN, 1924, pp. 4-5, 18-19; ARSN, 1926, pp. 14-15; ARSN, 1927, pp. 18-19.
47. *Ibid.*, 1926, p. 19.
48. ANJ, 3 May 1924, pp. 857, 865, 17 May 1924, p. 909, 6 Feb. 1926, p. 539; *Time*, 12 May 1924, p. 5.
49. ANJ, 9 Aug. 1924, p. 1197, 30 Aug. 1924, p. 1272, 6 Sept. 1924, pp. 1213, 1294, 13 Sept. 1924, pp. 1317, 1327, 20 Sept. 1924, pp. 1344, 1346.
50. ARSN, 1925, pp. 72-73; ARSN, 1926, pp. 64-65; Robinson and Edwards, eds., *Memoirs of Ray Lyman Wilbur*, p. 320; ANJ, 18 July 1925, pp. 2373-74.
51. Donald Marquand Dozer, *Latin America: An Interpretive History* (New York: McGraw-Hill, 1962), pp. 512-13; Henry Bamford Parkes, *A History of Mexico* (Boston: Houghton Mifflin, 1938), pp. 385-87; McCoy, *Coolidge*, pp. 354-56; Samuel Flagg Bemis, *The Latin American Policy of the United States: An Historical Interpretation* (New York: Harcourt, Brace, 1943), pp. 217-18; ANJ, Oct. 1926, p. 103, 6 Nov. 1926, p. 223; 5 Dec. 1926, p. 291, 27 Jan. 1927, p. 512.
52. ARSN, 1927, p. 93; ANJ, 9 Apr. 1926, p. 725.
53. ARSN, 1926, p. 51; Jeter A. Isely and Philip A. Crowl, *The U.S. Marines and Amphibious War: Its Theory and Its Practice in the Pacific* (Princeton, N. J.: Princeton University Press, 1951), p. 28; Neill Macaulay, *The Sandino Affair* (Chicago: Quadrangle Books, 1967), pp. 19-142; ANJ, 22 Aug. 1925, p. 2497, 23 Oct. 1926, p. 169, 12 Mar. 1927, p. 650, 7 May 1927, p. 818, 15 Oct. 1927, p. 5, 27 Oct. 1928, p. 171.
54. ARSN, 1927, pp. 2, 1193; John K. Powell, *My Twenty-five Years in China* (New York: Macmillan, 1945), pp. 161-69; Barbara W. Tuchman, *Stillwell and the American Experience in China, 1911-1945* (New York: Macmillan, 1970), pp. 103-07; ANJ, 6 Sept. 1924, p. 1299, 13 Sept. 1924, p. 1317, 18 Apr. 1925, p. 2064, 12 Sept. 1925, p. 29, 22 Jan. 1927, p. 481, 1 June 1927, p. 415.
55. *Time*, 11 Feb. 1929, p. 5.
56. *Almanac of Naval Facts* (Annapolis, Md.; U.S. Naval Institute, 1964), pp. 6, 174; ANJ, 5 July 1924, p. 1084, 8 Aug. 1925, p. 2447, 22 Aug. 1925, p. 494, 6 Jan. 1929, p. 426.
57. *New York Times*, 28 Mar. 1924, p. 11; ANJ, 2 Oct. 1926, p. 97, 24 Oct. 1925, p. 178, 26 Nov. 1927, p. 256, 30 Jan. 1926, p. 516, 31 Dec. 1927, pp. 344, 358, 11 Feb. 1928, p. 478.

58. ANJ, 21 June 1924, p. 1051, 18 Apr. 1925, p. 2064, 17 July 1926, p. 1114, 13 Nov. 1926, p. 257, 8 Jan. 1927, p. 449, 18 June 1927, p. 949, 17 Dec. 1927, p. 320, 20 Oct. 1928, p. 157, 1 Dec. 1928, p. 266.
59. *Time*, 30 July 1928, p. 5; ANJ, 8 Jan. 1927, p. 439, 22 Jan. 1927, p. 487, 17 Nov. 1928, p. 238, 8 Dec. 1928, p. 286.
60. George H. Mayer, *The Republican Party, 1854–1964* (New York: Oxford University Press, 1964), pp. 402–05; White, *Puritan in Babylon*, pp. 401–02; Robinson and Edwards, eds., *Memoirs of Ray Lyman Wilbur*, p. 398.
61. *New York Times*, 9 Sept. 1954, p. 31.

CHARLES FRANCIS ADAMS

5 March 1929–4 March 1933

GERALD E. WHEELER

Lacking a New Englander or Southerner among his tentative choices for cabinet posts, President-elect Herbert Hoover sought his Navy Secretary from the Northeast. Not unexpectedly, he particularly desired a person with such traits as public esteem, rigid integrity, success as an administrator, general efficiency, and sympathy with his own ideas.[1] The search finally turned up the Treasurer of Harvard University, a fairly recent convert to the Republican faith, and the direct descendent of two presidents—Charles Francis Adams III. Probably bemused, but always ready for public service, Adams accepted.[2]

Adams was born in Quincy, Massachusetts, on 2 August 1866. Like all in the Adams family he was a Harvard graduate, class of 1888, and then had studied law there until 1892. From 1898 until 1929, when he had served as treasurer of the Harvard Corporation, his prudent management had increased the University's endowment from $12 million to $100 million. He also served on the boards of directors of numerous New England banks and corporations. Although he had inherited a comfortable income, he lived modestly and indulged himself in yachting as a hobby. In 1920 he gained international fame when he skippered the racing yacht *Resolute* to defeat Sir Thomas Lipton's *Shamrock IV* in the famed *America's* Cup Races. Until the election of 1920 he had been a registered Democrat, but in that year he supported the Republican ticket.[3]

It was easier for Hoover to find a secretary than assistants to help Adams manage the Navy Department. Adams had recommended that F. Trubee Davison, the War Department's Assistant Secretary for Aeronautics, be "promoted" to Assistant Secretary of the Navy, but the President preferred to leave him with the Army and turned instead to Ernest Lee Jahncke, a New Orleans shipbuilder, good administrator, and yachtsman.[4] Because the Assistant Secretary for Aeronautics, Dr. Edward P. Warner, had resigned to return to the Massachusetts Institute of Technology, this position needed to be filled too. Again President Hoover found an able appointee in David S. Ingalls, of Ohio. Only thirty years of age, Ingalls had been naval aviation's only "ace" in the World War. Following graduation from Yale and law school, he entered Ohio politics and won a seat in the lower house. A man of wealth—he was married to a Standard Oil heiress—he brought his own fleet of aircraft to the position.[5]

While the top civilian positions in the Navy Department were named by President Hoover, Adams inherited from Curtis Wilbur a "slate" of admirals to man the fleet and bureaus. With the President's concurrence, he released the names of those who were to command the U.S. Fleet and its subordinate units in the years ahead. In May, Admiral William Veazie Pratt would become Commander in Chief U.S. Fleet (CinCUS); Vice Admiral Louis M. Nulton would "fleet up" to Admiral and relieve Pratt as Commander in Chief Battle Fleet (ComBatFlt); Admiral Charles B. McVay would become Commander in Chief Asiatic Fleet; and Mark L. Bristol would return to Washington, in his permanent rank of rear admiral, to become Senior Member of the General Board. Vice Admiral Lusius A. Bostwick took over Nulton's position as Commander Battleship Divisions, Battle Fleet; and Vice Admiral W. Carey Cole relieved Vice Admiral Montgomery M. Taylor as Commander in Chief Scouting Fleet. In the Department itself, Admiral Charles F. Hughes continued as Chief of Naval Operations (CNO) and Rear Admiral Richard H. Leigh remained as Chief of the Bureau of Navigation. Most of the bureau chiefs had time to serve on their four year appointments, though Rear Admiral William A. Moffett shattered all modern precedents by being reappointed to a third term as Chief of the Bureau of Aeronautics. Adams learned very early that, besides managing the Naval Establishment, his role was to interpret the President's desires and naval policies. However, the admirals in the department and the fleet were the means by which policy was effectuated or frustrated.

Adams inherited problems dating back to 1921. The official "U.S. Naval Policy" of 1922, up-dated in 1928, stated that general naval policy was "To create, maintain, and operate a navy second to none and in conformity with treaty provisions." The Secretary immediately could see that the Navy was not at parity with the British Navy and was being rapidly overtaken by the Japanese Navy, because the United States had not kept up its allowed naval construction.[6] Trying to bring the Navy to treaty strength would be his dominating problem. In addition to problems of naval construction, within the framework of naval limitation treaties, Adams was concerned with the operational readiness, materiel condition, and efficiency of the fleet, all greatly affected by the Great Depression, the worsening status of Japanese-American relations, and President Hoover's personal attitude toward the Navy.

As Secretary of Commerce for almost eight years, Hoover had expanded American foreign trade, particularly exports, and private investment abroad. With a "Naval Policy" that proposed to "support the national policies and commerce" and also "support American interests, especially the development of American foreign commerce and the merchant marine,"[7] it seemed logical that as President he would bring the Navy to treaty strength. In accepting his presidential nomination he had promised that a Republican victory would "assure national defense."[8] In a major campaign address in early October 1928, he had stressed the need for a Navy that would give "complete defense to our homes from even the fear of foreign invasion."[9] After his good-will trip to South America, in which he used the battleships *Maryland* and *Utah* for transportation, he left a very positive impression on the naval officers he met.[10] Finally, at the end of January 1929 he had endorsed President Calvin Coolidge's 15-cruiser bill.[11]

On the other hand, as he put it in his inaugural address, "Peace can be contributed to by respect for our ability in defense. *Peace can be promoted by the limitations of arms* and by the creation of instrumentalities for peaceful settlement of controversies."[12] Three weeks later he told Secretary of State Frank B. Kellogg that "this Government has . . . consistently advocated the lowest levels of armament that could be arrived at on a relative basis."[13]

During his first month in office, Hoover obtained financial data from his Director of the Budget that influenced his attitude toward the Navy throughout his administration. From information supplied by the Navy Department, the Budget Director presented the following table:

Needed to Round Out The Fleet: Fiscal Years 1932–1944		
Aircraft Carriers	4	$ 80,000,000
Destroyer Leaders	9	45,000,000
Submarines	32	160,000,000
Destroyers	19	58,600,000
Tenders, repair ships, etc.		10,000,000
New authorizations needed:		353,600,000
Battleship replacements	15	$ 555,000,000
Total new authorizations		908,600,000
Balance due on 15 cruisers and 1 carrier authorized 13 February 1929		262,200,000
Cost of Contemplated 12-Year Program		$1,170,800,000

To meet these requirements the Director's annual appropriations estimate for "Increase of the Navy" called for between 100 and 150 millions of dollars annually for ten years.[14]

To avoid increasing naval appropriations, Hoover sought further international agreements that would reduce the world's navies. Were he unable to convince the world to settle its problems by means other than expensive armaments, he could try to convince his nation that it needed only a Navy capable of defending its own shores: protection of foreign possessions, overseas investments, and its foreign trade were luxuries not worth the maintenance of an expensive Navy. Unfortunately for him, and Adams, these alternatives had to be faced between 1929 and 1933.

While well acquainted with the sea, Adams quickly discovered that a secretary could help or hinder the Navy but was not absolutely necessary. Were he and his assistants absent, the Chief of Naval Operations was empowered to act and thus preserve continuity of operations.

In 1929 the sea-going Navy was divided into a U.S. Fleet and three independent aggregations: the Asiatic Fleet, based on the Philippines and operating along the Asiatic littoral; a Special Service Squadron that maintained the peace and protected American lives and property in the Caribbean and Gulf of Mexico; and a few vessels collectively designated Naval Forces Europe. Despite the impressive rank of Admiral Mark L. Bristol, the Asiatic Fleet was little more than a collection of maritime antiques; the same was true of Rear Admiral David F. Sellers' Special Service Squadron. Naval Forces Europe, a vestigial trace of Admiral William S. Sims's World War command, had the principal duty of "showing the flag" and was commanded by Vice Admiral John H. Dayton in a modern light cruiser. Except for a few other vessels on detached duty, the rest of the Navy's vessels were organized into the U.S. Fleet commanded in March 1929 by Admiral Henry A. Wiley as CinCUS. Though Commander in Chief, Wiley actively exercised sea command only when fleet concentrations were held. The rest of the year he visited the drill grounds of his various subordinate units. Frustrated in his attempts to reorganize the fleet into a single fighting unit and to command it actively, he shuffled papers and concluded that the cocked hat of CinCUS was another "hollow crown".

Admiral William V. Pratt held one of the most powerful naval commands in the world as ComBatFlt. The Battle Fleet, based on the Pacific Coast in 1929, consisted of the most modern battleships organized into three battleships divisions, a destroyer force, cruisers, and the new aircraft carriers *Lexington* and *Saratoga*. When actively operating, the Battle Fleet also drew minecraft from the Base Force and submarines from the Control Force. Integral to the mission of the Battle Fleet in 1929, to carry a naval war into the Western Pacific if necessary, was the Fleet Base Force commanded by Rear Admiral Walter S. Crosley.

In the Atlantic Ocean Vice Admiral Montgomery M. Taylor commanded the Scouting Fleet. With two divisions of the Navy's oldest battleships, plus the cruiser divisions, a destroyer force, and aircraft squadrons based on the *Langley* and some tenders, his job was to train his fleet for strategic and tactical scouting missions when the U.S. Fleet assembled. Everyone knew that these old ships were useless for scouting and that they should be concentrated in a single fleet, but their repair and overhaul provided a significant amount of employment for the Atlantic Coast Navy yards. Also based on the East Coast was the command center for the Control Force, the submarines of the U.S. Fleet. While submarine headquarters was at New London, Connecticut, squadrons were scattered around the world with important concentrations in the Canal Zone, Pearl Harbor, and Manila Bay. With the U.S. Fleet parceled out into four major subdivisions, two of them commanded by a "commander in chief," one can understand why both Admirals Wiley and Pratt sought to reorganize the United States Fleet into "forces" all commanded by a single CinCUS[15] In accepting Admiral Pratt's recommendation in 1931, Adams made the one major contribution in administrative reorganization that is associated with him.

Adams knew enough about leadership to realize that he had to be seen by the Navy if he was to command its respect. Because of his small stature and Puckish humor he was good "copy" for newsmen. He enjoyed wandering into various offices in Main Navy just to see what the officers did with their time. He regularly ate in the cafeteria, carrying his own tray, and praised the quality of the traditional bean soup.

As might be expected, Adams's first visits to naval activities were to the Naval Air Station Anacostia and the Washington Navy Yard. Rear Admiral Moffett personally conducted him about Anacostia so that he could inspect the types of aircraft currently in service. At the Navy Yard he inspected the yacht *Sylph*, normally used by the secretaries, and decided it was unfit for further service. A few days later President Hoover ordered his yacht, the *Mayflower*, to be put out of commission.[16] Adams then visited the Scouting Fleet and inspected the naval station on Guantánamo Bay. During the spring and early summer he visited almost all the East Coast and Gulf naval yards and stations and also San Francisco, Honolulu, Seattle, and Alaska. He took a submerged run in the submarine V-4 and later landed on board the *Lexington* off San Diego. After short-range battle practice with the *Texas* in September, he visited Naval Air Station Lakehurst for a day's cruise in the dirigible *Los Angeles*. By the end of his first nine months in office, he had seen a good portion of the Navy, and it had seen him.[17]

Meanwhile Hoover and Secretary of State Henry L. Stimson were engaged in negotiations they hoped would lead to further naval limitation and possibly to reductions. For the President there were two interests involved: first, reduction of armaments that would help further the cause of peace; second, and of equal concern, avoidance of new construction costs in all classes and particularly in replacing capital ships. To support these interests, Hoover sent Ambassador Charles G. Dawes in June 1929 to London to seek a new naval agreement that would limit combatant auxiliaries (cruisers, destroyers, submarines). These, not limited by ratios in the 1922 Five Power Naval Treaty, had spawned a new naval race. Agreement, quite obviously, would be cheaper than meeting the Navy Department's $1 billion replacement and new construction program.

While the administration asked the General Board for information, the board was not asked to develop a position paper outlining the limits that should not be exceeded by any naval agreement. It did design a "yardstick" that permitted comparisons of cruisers differing in gun calibers, age, and displacement. While few in the Department believed the "yardstick" possessed any genuine military value, the administration, without consulting Adams, used it to convince itself that America's cruiser fleet could be smaller in numbers than the Royal Navy's.

Dawes's discussions ended, Prime Minister J. Ramsay MacDonald visited Washington in October 1929 and agreed with Hoover to convene a naval conference at London in January 1930. It was also agreed, by using the so-called "yardstick," that the American Navy could accept a tonnage inferiority in cruisers—339,000 tons for the United States. But the most difficult issue remained unresolved. While the British wanted 15 8-inch gun cruisers among their 50, they wanted America to have no more than 18 of these larger ships. When the General Board said that 21 8-inch gun cruisers was an absolute minimum, Hoover and MacDonald were sure the conference could bridge the difference between 21 and 18.[18]

Adams played an insignificant part in these negotiations. Called by Hoover to attend several special budget discussions, he was indoctrinated with the administration's positions: naval reductions could lead to construction curtailments that would save money and permit tax reductions. Dawes, too, got his instructions—to seek a reduction in the cruiser program to between 200,000 and 250,000 tons.[19] Then, on 25 July, Hoover told the American people that "The hope of tax reduction lies, in a large degree, in our ability to economize on the military and naval expenditure and still maintain adequate defense." He believed spending could be reduced because "there is less real danger of extensive disturbance to peace than at any time in more than a half century."[20] To demonstrate his confidence that naval limitation efforts would succeed, in early

August he suspended construction on three of the five heavy cruisers then on the ways.[21]

Hoover of course had put Adams in a most ambivalent position by having the State Department control the planning for the London Conference. Because Hoover and Secretary Stimson believed that naval officers could not seriously plan for naval limitation or reduction, they gave the civilian side of the government the task. Adams's job was merely to make the Navy understand and support what the President was doing. Such professionals as the retired Rear Admiral Hilary P. Jones, who was on active duty assisting the General Board with its planning, failed to convince Hoover and Stimson that the Navy Department was the proper agency to handle naval negotiations. In consequence Jones felt that "our State Department seems to be bent on reducing our program and are inclined to make proposals, or admit proposals, which seem to me wholly impracticable, dangerous and impossible of execution."[22] Exasperated but unable to alter the situation, Adams had to keep quiet since Hoover determined the goals to be achieved, relied upon a supportive State Department, and avoided him.

However, the State Department gradually brought the Navy Department into the planning for the naval conference. In September, Hoover named Admiral William V. Pratt, then CinCUS, to be an advisor and to head the Naval Technical Staff. The General Board preferred Rear Admiral Jones for this position, probably because Pratt had supported the 1922 naval treaty, but it had to be content with Jones's role as an advisor and member of the staff. Pratt chose the rest of the naval advisory group. Most important, from the Navy's viewpoint, Adams was named as one of the seven delegates, hence could counter Pratt's internationalist views.[23]

While the treaty resulting from the London Naval Conference of early 1930 met the expectations of Hoover and Stimson, it appeared disastrous to the General Board and to most American naval officers.[24] The price of agreement with the British was to have fewer heavy cruisers and accept an increase in light cruisers. To make the treaty acceptable to Japan, the United States could not complete its last two allowed heavy cruisers until after the treaty expiration date, 31 December 1936, and numbers 16, 17 and 18 could not be laid down until 1933, 1934, and 1935. Finally, the 10–10–5 ratio of the 1922 treaty, while continued in capital ships and aircraft carriers, was modified radically in the combatant auxiliaries categories. The ratio would be 10–10–6.6 in heavy cruisers, 10–10–7 in light cruisers and destroyers, and parity in submarines.

Although Adams and Pratt had fought for a better ratio between the United States and Japan, in the end they had supported the various compromises that led to the agreements in each category. Rear Admiral Jones, however, had resisted in the name of the General Board and left early when his health failed. While all of the civilian delegates spoke often on behalf of the final treaty both in London and upon returning to America, Adams gave only one major address. On 2 March 1930, when it appeared that the nation's interest in the negotiations was languishing, he stressed that international regulation was better than mindless competition and called for construction of all vessels finally allotted the United States.[25]

Both Adams and Pratt defended the treaty on the assumption that Hoover would use it as a basis for new construction. During hearings held by the Senate in May and June 1930, however, representatives of the General Board unanimously rejected the agreement. They argued that accepted policy had been ignored, the Navy did not want or need more light cruisers, and Japan had gained too much. America's interests in Asia, particularly the Open Door in China and the Philippine Islands, would now be indefensible against an aggressive Japanese Empire. Ignoring the international relations question, and the *amour propre* of the General Board, Adams then pointed out that the American delegation had had four objectives in going to London: 1) to cooperate in terminating naval construction competition; 2) to assure naval combatant equality with Great Britain; 3) "to arrange a satisfactory relation between our Navy and that of the Japanese"; 4) to reduce category tonnages wherever possible. He believed the London Treaty met these goals. Most important, he believed the treaty would make it possible to develop a building and appropriations program that would place naval construction beyond partisan politics.[26] On the same day, 14 May 1930, Pratt placed his prestige and reputation on the line in support of the treaty. Like Adams, Pratt considered the document a positive gain because it mandated a future naval construction program, saying, "Now for the first time in our history we can lay down a definite program extending over a period of time and visualize a Navy which is not a creature of great ups and downs in the matter of a naval building program."[27]

By sincerely supporting the treaty, Adams and Pratt carried out Hoover's expressed wish. If they dissembled at all in their arguments, it was in leaving the impression that Hoover would bring the Navy to treaty strength. By the spring of 1930 they probably knew Hoover had no intention of doing so. For the remaining three years of Hoover's administration there developed a "credibility gap" between its professed interest in maintaining national defense and its performance.

In May and July 1930, and again in January 1932, bills authorizing the building of the Navy to the limits allowed by the London Treaty failed. To assuage the Navy's feelings, Hoover approved the spending of $30 million to modernize the battleships *New Mexico, Mississippi,* and *Idaho.* Given a choice between new construction and capital ship modernization, Adams opted for the latter.[28]

In 1931 and early 1932 Hoover exerted maximum pressure on Adams to reduce spending and turn back appropriated funds.[29] When Representative Carl Vinson in January 1932 sought to authorize building the Navy to treaty strength, Adams and Pratt, the latter then CNO, supported him. Vinson's bill passed the Senate in May 1932, but never came to a vote in the House largely because its cost, $616 million, was impossible to meet in that depression-ridden year.[30] Because of his support for Vinson's measure, Adams's loyalty to Hoover was questioned sharply by several Republican congressmen, and for a time it did appear that he might resign. In the end it was recognized that he was too valuable to the President to be set aside by congressional whim. Besides, the Vinson bill had failed.[31]

Rather than build the Navy to London Treaty strength, Hoover sought further arms reductions through another international conference. In September 1930 the League of Nations finally set the date of 2 February 1932 for the opening of the long planned Conference for the Reduction and Limitation of Armaments (World Disarmament Conference) to be held in Geneva.[32] During the late summer and fall of 1931 the State Department and the Navy considered the issues and planned the U.S. position. Again the State Department named the American delegation and controlled the planning process. In September Senator William E. Borah, of Idaho, and Hoover separately proposed naval building holidays to last until the Disarmament Conference reached some conclusions.[33] In the same month, Signor Dino Grandi, the head of the Italian delegation to the League, called for a year's moratorium on naval construction to commence 1 November 1931. On 29 October the United States accepted the League resolution which incorporated the Grandi plan.[34]

In 1931 as in 1929, Hoover determined the American approach, but in 1931 the stakes were much higher. Success at Geneva might mean naval reduction, budget savings, and a record of achievement to take before the voter in November 1932. To avoid any conflict with his administration, Hoover clearly outlined his position: seeing no threat to America, the Navy and Army needed only sufficient forces to prevent an enemy invasion of American soil.[35] He ordered Adams to see to it that active duty officers did not publicly challenge his argument.[36] Already forced to plan for a $61 million reduction in the fiscal year 1933 naval budget under consideration in Congress, Adams also wisely decided to eschew public discussion. In fact, all naval appropriations data were removed from public circulation by labeling them "secret."[37]

During November, Hoover invited Adams to name a small naval advisory staff for the U.S. delegation to the Disarmament Conference. Without consulting the General Board, Adams asked Pratt to select the group. Pratt's choices angered the General Board because three of the five men, including Pratt, supported 6-inch versus 8-inch gun cruisers.[38] As in the case of previous arms limitation conferences, the naval staff quickly discovered that it was expected to supply data and advice but that the important decisions would be made by Secretary Stimson and the Western European Division of the State Department. Because of his involvement in deliberations concerning the Japanese invasion of Manchuria, in mid-September 1931 Stimson left the Conference details in the hands of various subordinates and to Hugh Gibson, the Acting Chief Delegate who was also Ambassador to Belgium. The latter, a close friend of Hoover's, probably was the best informed American civilian on naval disarmament matters.

While Adams was not left out of the planning, he did little beyond transmitting messages between the State Department, the CNO, and the advisory staff. At meetings of the delegates with the naval advisors in early January 1932, he and Pratt took the position that the Navy was already limited and what it needed was approximately one hundred and twenty new ships to reach treaty strength. As the State Department saw it, the Navy was disinterested in any further cuts and Adams was leading the resistance. Stimson thereupon commented that "With the Army it was essential to convince Secretary Hurley who would then convince the Generals; with the Navy it was necessary to convince the Admirals who would then convince Secretary Adams."[39] As Drew Pearson put it, "Charles Francis Adams is God's answer to the admiral's prayer . . . . For Charles Francis advocates as big a navy as any admiral, can sail a ship better than most of them, and has reputedly risked his Cabinet job for them."[40]

The World Disarmament Conference came to nothing. It tried to encourage arms limitation at a time when Japan was renovating the status quo in Asia and Chancellor Adolf Hitler was pressing to change the limitations on Germany riveted into the Versailles Treaty. In June 1932, Hoover tried to galvanize the conference into action by calling for an across-the-board one-third reduction of navies. While everyone politely applauded the concept, it was quietly buried under an avalanche of disinterest.[41] Later in the year the delegation and its naval advisors toyed with the idea of reducing battleships in numbers and their armament to 12-inch guns, while limiting future replacements to 25,000 tons; but again this led to nothing.

Much attention has been paid to these naval limitations conferences because, although Adams was not a vital participant in them, they show why he was unable to develop a navy he knew was too weak to support the nation's interests. And this at a time, moreover, when Britain and Japan were building to treaty limits. Yet he was also a member of a larger "team," the President's cabinet. He understood that priorities had to be set and that the Navy was merely one of many departments competing for a slice of the annual budget. If he and Stimson could not convince Hoover that a full "Treaty Navy" was vital to the defense of the nation's interests, then he had to be content with less. Unfortunately, Hoover was playing that dangerous game deplored by military strategists—planning on the basis of the intentions of potential challengers rather than on their measured capabilities. By giving the Philippines their independence and retreating from the Open Door he expected Japan to accept naval limitation on American terms and not to endanger the peace in Asia. Rational man that he was, he also overestimated badly the willingness of Europeans to disarm in an era of international depression. What he could not, or would not, understand was the depth of French insecurity, German nationalism, and British realism. To him, military disarmament appeared terribly logical.

The small amount of naval construction begun in the Hoover administration came nowhere close to bringing the Navy to its allowed strength. All eight of the heavy cruisers authorized in December 1924 were finally commissioned in the Hoover years. Seven of the fifteen heavy cruisers authorized on 13 February 1929 were laid down during 1930 and 1931, and two were commissioned. The aircraft carrier *Ranger* (CV-4) was laid down on 26 September 1931 and christened on 25 February 1933. A few submarines and destroyers were also begun in these bleak years, but that was all. The lack of any serious attempt to create a treaty Navy can be attributed to two major factors: the shortage of funds due to the depression, and the higher priority given to naval limitation efforts rather than to construction. Despite the obvious menace to the Open Door posed by Japan's occupation of Manchuria in the fall of 1931, Hoover preferred to believe the World Disarmament Conference of 1932 would further reduce armaments and somehow solve the problem of Japan. By the end of his administration it was obvious that the League of Nations could do nothing about Japan and that the disarmament sessions had proved abortive. On 4 March 1933, when Hoover left office, American-Japanese relations were at a nadir and the U.S. Navy had not been built to treaty strength. The same could not be said of the Japanese Navy.

Adams's inability to convince Hoover or Congress that the Navy should be brought to treaty strength was part of an even larger problem—the fleet was becoming run down and there were serious problems in the area of personnel. Here again Adams was a victim of his ambivalent position. He recognized the danger signals and tried his best to catch the attention of the Commander in Chief, but the financial situation of the early 1930s created too much static. When he did receive the undivided attention of the President, it only resulted in orders to cut back expenses, reduce personnel, and take ships out of commission.

643

Reading Adams's annual reports between 1929 and 1933 is somewhat akin to perusing a tragedy. Certain phrases appear regularly: "inadequate funds," "deteriorating condition of the vessels," "longer periods of overhaul," "cracked boilers" in destroyers, "persistent oil leaks" and "weakening storage batteries" in submarines.[42]

To meet the problems of deterioration and not sacrifice operating funds to shipyard charges, self-maintenance became the watchword of all fleets. When not actually at sea, the ships' crews worked steadily to keep their vessels in decent condition. The procedure so reduced the need for civilian labor in the Navy yards that Congress began to pressure Adams to ease off on self-maintenance.[43] Regular shipyard overhauls, including drydocking, were normally required annually for the cruisers and battleships. To reduce costs, an eighteen-month interval between major overhauls became policy. Again the Navy yard lobbyists, in and outside Congress, argued that the Navy was creating unemployment. When Adams proposed closing certain East Coast yards or reducing them to caretaker status, the howls became even shriller. Adams's request that the Charleston yard be closed was met with broadsides of opposition from the South's congressional delegations lest its closing set a dangerous precedent.[44]

Because the fleet was aging, and showing it through an increasing incidence of engineering casualties, it became inevitable that certain vessels would be forced out of commission. By mid-1930 thirteen old cruisers were sold to ship-breakers. The 122 destroyers with Yarrow boilers, commissioned between 1918 and 1921, were proving impossible to maintain and 58 were replaced with other destroyers laid up in Philadelphia and San Diego.[45] The London Treaty saved the Navy the further embarrassment of trying to keep the battleships *Florida* and *Wyoming* in repair. Neither had been able to steam at Scouting Fleet speeds for many years and they were scarcely useful for training midshipmen during their summer cruises.

In order to save operating expenses and to improve the material condition of the fleet, Admiral Pratt during his first year as CNO proposed a "rotating reserve" plan of operation. Approximately a third of the fleet would be in reduced commission with minimum operating schedules and reduced crews, a third would be in reserve commission with skeleton crews, and a third would be in full commission. During the period of reduced commission, crews would do all of the maintenance within their capabilities; when in reserve commission the vessels would receive their heavy overhauls, including drydocking, at a navy yard.[46] Theoretically naval personnel could be reduced, ships could continue to operate, and the badly rundown fleet would have its material condition improved. The General Board opposed the whole idea, particularly if it were to be applied to ships larger than destroyers. Its logic was irrefutable when the senior member wrote to Adams that "a Treaty Navy of which 33 per cent is in reduced or reserve commission is not in reality a 'Treaty Navy,' unless the navies of the other signatories to the limitation treaty are maintained on the same basis."[47] Adams permitted Pratt to continue planning, but the scheme was never fully implemented.[48] The fleet continued to deteriorate.

The Navy was experiencing equally severe problems in manning its ships. In the years since the Washington Conference the heart of the operating fleet had consisted of 18 battleships, 10 scout cruisers, approximately 100 destroyers, and 60 submarines, and from 1928 there had been three aircraft carriers in commission. During Adams's tenure 10 heavy cruisers entered service, replacing a handful of overage pre-World War cruisers, and two battleships were decommissioned. If the Navy was fairly stable in terms of ships, its personnel needs should have remained steady, but this was not the case because the growth of aviation in the fleet created a steadily increasing demand for naval aviators and enlisted personnel to maintain the aircraft. With the commissioning of the *Saratoga* and *Lexington* in late 1927, the number of operating aircraft squadrons jumped from 8 in August 1926 to 27 in June 1928 and finally to 32 at the close of Adams's term.[49] As aircraft squadrons were organized, the number of officer naval aviators rose from 426 in 1926 to about 850 in 1933 and enlisted men assigned to aviation duties rose from approximately 5,600 to 13,000 in the same period.[50] At the same time, however, the total number of line officers, including aviators, remained quite constant and enlisted personnel was reduced. The result was a decrease in officers and enlisted men available to the fleet, outside of aviation activities, while the number of surface vessels increased. Creating even greater consternation in the Bureau of Navigation, charged with personnel detailing, was the fact that equipment furnished surface vessels, particularly for fire control and antiaircraft tasks, was becoming increasingly complex and required the care of larger numbers of officers and men.

In his first annual report Adams noted that the fleet was becoming badly undermanned because the maximum number of line officers allowed (5,499) was insufficient. Officer strength had been set at 4 percent of enlisted strength back in 1916, before aviation was significant in the fleet, and it was clearly unrealistic in 1929. To meet current and future officer needs, including pilots, Adams asked Congress to raise the number of congressional appointments to the Naval Academy from four to five and increase the line officer allowance by at least 700. He also requested funds to raise the number of enlisted men on active duty from 84,500 to almost 97,400.[51] Unfortunately, as the country slid into the depression Congress was more inclined to reduce than to augment naval personnel.

Disappointed that all navies were not drastically reduced by the London Treaty, Congress forced economy on the Navy Department by cutting the funds available for enlisted pay, thus perhaps also forcing the decommissioning of ships, and by reducing Naval Academy congressional appointments from four to three.[52]

Although severely circumscribed by Hoover's desire to reduce spending, Adams opposed reductions in officer strength and cuts in Naval Academy appointments because he believed the time necessary to train line officers was too long to risk shortages were war to occur. His annual reports noted regularly that the battleships, cruisers, and destroyers were operating with reduced officer and enlisted complements because of the numbers needed in aviation. In January 1933, when testifying before the House subcommittee on naval appropriations, he noted that ships operated with a complement of 87.5 percent in 1931 but would have only 74.7 percent in 1934, and he asked for additional men.[53]

Congress objected. Adams was not, as expected, decreasing the number of ships in full commission as a means of utilizing the reduced enlisted force. Congress therefore canvassed alternatives for cutting operating funds and enlisted personnel. They liked Pratt's "rotating reserve" scheme and wanted it applied to battleships and carriers. When pressed to take one of the new 33,000-ton carriers out of commission, however, CNO Hughes replied "It would be a catastrophe!"[54] Adams and Hughes's successor, Admiral Pratt, vigorously resisted similar moves. Congress then pressed Adams to increase the percentage of enlisted men designated as naval aviation pilots. The Department for a time was required to have at least 30 percent of its student aviators come from the enlisted ratings.[55] Another approach, favored by Congressmen Burton L. French and James V. McClintick, was to bring a number of Naval Reserve flight ensigns on active duty for one or two years. This would almost eliminate the need to use Naval Academy graduates in the lower ranks of aviators, thus making younger officers available for regular shipboard duty, and it would strengthen the quality of the Naval Air Reserve as the flight ensigns were released to civilian life after their active duty tours. By 1931 the Department found it necessary to accept at least sixty reserve ensigns in the fleet annually to meet its manning needs.[56]

Only one gain for the Navy during Adams's tour is directly traceable to the hard times "on the outside"—the improved quality of the Navy's enlisted men. With rising unemployment among civilians, reenlistments rose from 72.8 percent in fiscal year 1929 to 93.3 percent in 1933. Because the total enlisted force dropped from 85,300 to 79,200 during the same period, the Navy accepted only one out of twenty-eight applicants for a first enlistment. By being highly selective in accepting recruits, the Navy received enlistees with higher average G.C.T. (General Classification Test) scores than ever before in its history and almost all had one or more years of high school. Paralleling this rise in quality came a drop in desertions and those sentenced to summary and general courts-martial trials.[57] There was good reason for Adams to be generous in his praise of the Navy's enlisted men—they were the nation's finest.

Adams had to pay attention to officer morale, which sagged badly in those depression years. There had been no change in the military pay schedules since 1908 and everyone had suffered a bit during the slight inflation of the 1920s. The depression brought an improvement in buying power for the serviceman, but in 1932 officer pay was reduced 15 percent and many of the usual allowances were eliminated. Adams took every opportunity to insist that the services needed a pay rise, but the Bureau of the Budget could not allow it.[58] Another problem plaguing the more senior officers came from the rigid percentages which controlled the number of officers in each rank. Under current legislation only 7 percent of the total number of line officers could be commanders and 14 percent could be lieutenant commanders. By 1931 there were too many officers eligible for promotion to lieutenant commander and commander for the number of anticipated vacancies. Because of this situation there would be a very low percentage selected and an unreasonably large number of excellent officers would be "passed over" and forced to retire. Part of the problem came from the fact that many officers had been advanced rapidly during the World War and were now filling the commander and captain billets. Despite some stiff opposition, again from Congressmen French and McClintick, this "hump" problem was relieved by changing the rank percentages to 8 percent for commander and 15 percent for lieutenant commanders; this opened up 119 new vacancies for the two ranks.[59] The same law eased tensions in another area by providing that the whole Naval Academy class of 1932 should be commissioned. This saved 50 percent of them from graduating without commissions due to lack of vacancies. The depression years, however, had reduced normal attrition in officer ranks that came from resignations and thus squeezed the classes of 1932 and 1933. The latter, unfortunately, could not be saved in a similar manner. Adams again had pressed heavily for this "hump" legislation and carried the day. The larger number of senior officers were needed for the new air squadrons commands that were developing and the new ensigns, if physically qualified, were allowed to enter flight training directly from the Academy rather than first serving a tour of duty at sea.[60]

Possibly because of the constant struggles to build the Navy to treaty strength, operate the fleet economically, keep it in decent condition materially, and maintain an effective level of manning, Adams had little time or energy left to think about a major reorganization of the Navy Department. Basically the *status quo* continued, accompanied by the usual annual fight against congressional proposals to create a unified Department of Defense. In the fleet there did occur a major reorganization, one proposed by CNO Pratt. If the shore establishment changed little during the Hoover years, improvements in air operations came at a nearly geometric rate of progression.

Adams persistently opposed a separate unified air force or a consolidated Department of Defense. The issue of unification acquired additional appeal during the Hoover administration with the lure of economy. To proposals for a unified air service, Adams replied that carrier aviation, probably the best in the world, was greatly improving the effectiveness of the battleship and cruiser divisions. Rear Admiral William A. Moffett, who opposed unification,[61] was backed by Pratt as CinCUS and later as CNO. In early 1932, when unification and a single air force again became live issues, Pratt provided studies for Adams to use at congressional hearings dealing with unification. Adams's testimony was direct and totally opposed.[62]

On the other hand, Adams readily approved Pratt's proposed reorganization of the U.S. Fleet, one that would stress the training mission of the Navy and create subordinate commands within the fleet that would more easily develop unified doctrines and tactics for the whole Navy. On 15 November 1930, effective 1 April 1931, Pratt signed the administrative chart that reorganized the U.S. Fleet into four "Forces". (1) The Battle Force, commanded by an admiral, consisted of those vessels that normally operated in the Pacific as units of the Battle Fleet. Included in this Force were the battleships, commanded by a vice admiral (Commander Battleships, Battle Force) who for training and administration was also Commander Battleships, U.S. Fleet. Rear admirals commanded the destroyers, minecraft, and aircraft of the Battle Force and also served as "type" commanders for the U.S. Fleet. (2) The Scouting Force was commanded by a vice admiral. Subordinate to him was a new vice admiral billet for Commander Cruisers, Scouting Force, who also served as cruiser "type" commander for the U.S. Fleet. Other rear admiral commands included the Commander Destroyers, Scouting Force; Commander Aircraft, Scouting Force; and Commander Training Squadron. (3) The Submarine Force commander was a rear admiral who also controlled the submarine bases in New London, Coco Solo, and Pearl Harbor. (4) The Base Force rear admiral commanded Train Squadrons 1 and 2, which were associated with the Scouting Force and Battle Force, respectively.[63] As for the financial savings Adams expected from the reorganization, they never materialized. Neither did Pratt's "rotating reserve" scheme. However, Pratt's reorganization remained intact until the new Atlantic Patrol was established in 1940.

Until June 1932 Adams had the very active support of Assistant Secretary Ingalls in pressing ahead naval aviation developments. His resignation on 1 June

1932 to campaign for the governorship of Ohio was a real loss to the Navy. As a measure of economy, Hoover did not replace him and the position remained vacant until President Franklin Roosevelt appointed Artemus L. Gates Assistant Secretary for Air.[64]

To relieve his administrative activity, with the help of his wife, Frances Lovering, Adams made his "R" Street home a center where administration leaders could relax and enjoy good food and his famous wit. While he declined to participate in physical fitness workouts held at the White House, spring and summer found him grasping every opportunity to pursue the sport which had first brought him national prominence—sailing.[65]

Adams loyally served Hoover in a political as well as administrative sense. Though disagreeing personally with the many Hoover economy measures that damaged the Navy, Adams backed them forthrightly before Congress and the press. During the congressional elections of 1930 and in the presidential canvass of 1932, he spoke for the Republican cause.[66] Concerned that senior naval officers on Navy Day 1932 (27 October) might create a negative impression of the President's concern about national defense, he ordered them to speak on nonpolitical topics—preferably George Washington, since 1932 was the bicentennial of his birth.

Franklin Roosevelt's victory in November 1932 created mixed feelings within the Navy. Rear Admiral William D. Leahy, for example, hoped that Roosevelt would be more concerned about the United States and its Navy and less about foreign nations than had been the case with Hoover.[67] All naval hands, however, were sorry to trade Adams for Senator Claude Swanson of Virginia, even though the latter had supported the service down through the years.

During his years in the Hoover cabinet, Adams received the usual number of honors appropriate to his office. In June 1929 Harvard University bestowed an LLD upon him.[68] The next year, in special recognition for his service at the London Naval Conference, New York University awarded him another,[69] and in 1932 Amherst College granted him his third honorary degree.[70] But the recognition he probably appreciated most came from the Navy itself. To his complete surprise, on 23 December 1932 Acting Secretary Jahncke named the next cruiser to be built the *Quincy*—the home of the Adams family—as a Christmas present.[71] The Navy's final tribute came five years after his death. On 8 September 1959, the *Charles F. Adams* (DDG-2) was launched at Bath, Maine.

Adams returned to the world of business and finance and in his first year out of government he became President of Boston's Union Trust Company and a director of various manufacturing corporations. His ties to his alma mater continued strong, and in October 1933 he became President of the Harvard

Alumni Association.[72] Four years later, in his seventy-first year, he accepted the presidency of the University's board of overseers and served in this capacity for six years.[73]

Adams never lost his interest in the Navy nor his fondness for the sea. He became a member of Boston's Navy League chapter and occasionally offered counsel to the national organization.[74] As Europe descended into war, he spoke publicly about the need to strengthen the Navy and the rest of the nation's defenses.[75] Despite advancing age and the pressures of his business responsibilities, he continued his yachting activities. In 1939 he amazed the sailing world when at the age of seventy-three he won the King's Astor, and Puritan Cups in a single season.[76] At eighty-five years of age, he still enjoyed a stiff breeze and a trick at the wheel.

Adams died at his Back Bay home in Boston on 10 June 1954 but was buried at Quincy. With typical New England sparseness, Boston's *Christian Science Monitor* paid tribute and summarized his long life of service to others:

> The 20th century Charles Francis Adams was known internationally as a yachtsman and a successful rival in that role of Sir Thomas Lipton. Nationally he was known as the able Secretary of the Navy of the Hoover administration and a negotiator of the London Naval Treaty of 1930. Locally he was acclaimed as Boston's first citizen—a leader in civic enterprises, education, philanthropy, business, and finance. Personally he was unostentatious, individual, conservative, and world minded—the epitome of what is best in the "old Yankee strain."[77]

NOTES

1. Herbert Hoover, *The Memoirs of Herbert Hoover: The Cabinet and the Presidency*, 3 vols. (New York: Macmillan, 1952), 2:217–18.
2. Editorial, "An Old Salt," *New York Times*, 22 Feb. 1929.
3. ANJ, 9 Mar. 1929, p. 549.
4. Charles F. Adams to Herbert Hoover, 6 Feb. 1929, Herbert Hoover Papers, Herbert Hoover Presidential Library; William Hard, "Hoover Picks His Men," ARR, Aug. 1929, pp. 46–51.
5. Hard, "Hoover Picks His Men," 48; John Meredith Wilson, "Herbert Hoover and the Armed Forces: A Study of Presidential Attitudes and Policy" (Ph. D. diss., Northwestern University, 1971), pp. 41–43.
6. U.S. House, Naval Subcommittee of Appropriations Committee, *Hearings on Naval Appropriations for Fiscal Year 1931* (Washington: GPO, 1930), pp. 83, 800.
7. "U.S. Naval Policy of 6 October 1928," in U.S. House. Naval Subcommittee of Appropriations Committee, Hearing on Naval Appropriations for Fiscal Year 1930 (Washington: GPO, 1930), pp. 36–38.
8. Hoover, *Memoirs*, 2:195.

9. Wilson, "Hoover and the Armed Forces," pp. 7–10.

10. See CAPT Adolphus Staton to CAPT Donald C. Bingham, 9 Jan. 1929, Adolphus Staton Papers, Southern Historical Collection, University of North Carolina.

11. Herbert Hoover to President Calvin Coolidge, 28 Jan. 1929, Calvin Coolidge Papers, MDLC.

12. Wilson, "Hoover and the Armed Forces," p. 5.

13. FR, 1929, 3 vols., 1:77.

14. Gerald E. Wheeler, *Prelude to Pearl Harbor: The United States Navy and the Far East, 1921–1931* (Columbia: University of Missouri Press, 1963), pp. 118–20.

15. Henry A. Wiley, *An Admiral From Texas* (Garden City, N.Y.: Doubleday, Doran, 1934), pp. 303–04.

16. William C. Murphy, Jr., "President Hoover's Cabinet: Intimate Sketches," CH, May 1929, pp. 269–75; *New York Times*, 14 Mar. 1929.

17. ARSN, 1930, pp. 1–2; *New York Times*, 9, 26 Apr. 1929; ANJ, 20 Mar. 1929, p. 609.

18. Wheeler, *Prelude to Pearl Harbor*, pp. 162–65; Raymond G. O'Connor, *Perilous Equilibrium: The United States and the London Naval Conference of 1930* (Lawrence: University of Kansas Press, 1962), pp. 40–51.

19. FR 1929, 1:163; *New York Times*, 28 Aug. 1929.

20. "Three Jolts for Mars," LD, 3 Aug. 1929, pp. 5–6.

21. "A Big Disarmament Fight Looms in Washington," LD, 10 Aug. 1929, pp. 5–6.

22. RADM H. P. Jones to Hugh Gibson, 19 July 1929, Hugh Gibson Papers, Hoover Institution.

23. *New York Times*, 21 Nov. 1929.

24. "U.S. Naval Policy of 6 October 1928," p. 40; Samuel Flagg Bemis, *A Diplomatic History of the United States*, 5th ed. (New York: Holt, Rinehart and Winston, 1965), p. 705; Wheeler, *Prelude to Pearl Harbor*, pp. 181–84; Stephen E. Pelz, *Race to Pearl Harbor: The Failure of the Second London Naval Conference and the Onset of World War II* (Cambridge, Mass.: Harvard University Press, 1974), pp. 2–3.

25. "Radio Address to the United States by Secretary Adams, 2 March 1930," in U.S. Department of State, *Conference Series, No. 6*, "Proceedings of the London Naval Conference of 1930" (Washington: GPO, 1931), pp. 270–73.

26. U.S. Senate, Committee on Naval Affairs, *Hearings on the London Naval Treaty of 1930* (Washington: GPO, 1930), pp. 3–4.

27. U. S. Senate, Committee on Foreign Relations, *Hearings on Treaty on the Limitation of Naval Armaments* (Washington: GPO, 1930), p. 66.

28. See NA, BOB Files, "Navy Department Alteration of Vessels #1."

29. ARSN, 1932, pp. 2–4; *New York Times*, 1 Aug., 16 Oct. 1931.

30. *New York Times*, 6 Jan. 1932.

31. *Ibid.*, 7 Jan. 1932; Wilson, "Herbert Hoover and the Armed Forces," pp. 66–67.

32. Merze Tate, *The United States and Armaments* (Cambridge: Harvard University Press, 1948), pp. 101–08; Fred Herbert Winkler, "The United States and the World Disarmament Conference, 1926–1935" (Ph. D. diss., Northwestern University, 1957), p. 359; David Cornelius DeBoe, "The United States and the Geneva Disarmament Conference, 1932–1934" (Ph. D. diss., Tulane University, 1969), p. 203.

33. Armin Rappaport, *The Navy League of the United States* (Detroit: Wayne State University Press, 1962), pp. 141–43.
34. FR 1931, 1:440–71.
35. Ray Lyman Wilbur and Arthur Mastick Hyde, *The Hoover Policies* (New York: Charles Scribner's Sons, 1937), p. 617.
36. ANJ, 24 Oct. 1931, p. 169.
37. *New York Times*, 16 Oct. 1931.
38. Diary of J. Pierrepont Moffatt (carbon), 6–16 Nov. 1931, in Hugh Gibson Papers.
39. Nancy Harvison Hooker, ed., *The Moffatt Papers: Selections from the Diplomatic Journals of Jay Pierrepont Moffatt, 1919–1943* (Cambridge: Harvard University Press, 1956), pp. 50–51.
40. Drew Pearson and Robert S. Allen, *More Merry-Go-Round* (New York: Liveright, 1932), p. 229.
41. Robert H. Ferrell, *American Diplomacy in the Great Depression: Hoover-Stimson Foreign Policy, 1929–1933* (New Haven: Yale University Press, 1957), pp. 212–14.
42. See for example ARSN, 1930, p. 37.
43. See letter of ASECNAV (Jahncke) to Chairman House Committee on Naval Affairs, 3 Mar. 1930, NA, BOB Files, "Ship Construction #1, 1930–1938."
44. Editorial, "Closing Navy Yards," *New York Times*, 4 May 1932.
45. ARSN, 1930, pp. 11, 113–14.
46. CNO to SECNAV, 8 Sept. 1931, NARG 80, Conf., SC File P16–1.
47. GB to SECNAV, 8 Sept. 1931, GB No. 420, Ser. 1552, NHD:OA.
48. ANJ, 21 Nov. 1931, p. 270.
49. William T. Larkins, *U.S. Navy Aircraft, 1921–1941* (Concord, Calif.: Aviation History Publications, 1961), pp. 48–50, 64–65, 124–25.
50. Figures from ARSN, 1926–1933.
51. *Ibid.*, 1930, pp. 155–58.
52. U. S. Congress, PL 745, 71st Cong., 1st Sess., 28 Feb. 1931, pp. 11–12.
53. U.S. House, Naval Subcommittee of Appropriations Committee, *Hearings on Naval Appropriations for Fiscal Year 1943* (Washington: GPO, 1933), pp. 24–25.
54. U.S. House, Naval Subcommittee of Appropriations Committee, *Hearings on Naval Appropriations for Fiscal Year 1931* (Washington: GPO, 1930), pp. 49–54. See also NA, BOB File, "Navy Department Alteration of Vessels #1: *Saratoga* and *Lexington*."
55. Archibald D. Turnbull and Clifford L. Lord, *History of United States Naval Aviation* (New Haven: Yale University Press, 1949), pp. 264–65.
56. See Chief BUAER statistics in ARSN, 1929–1933, and U. S. House, Subcommittee of Appropriations Committee, *Hearings on Naval Appropriations for Fiscal Year 1932* (Washington: GPO, 1931), pp. 227–29, 485–87.
57. See Chief BUNAV statistics in ARSN, 1929–1933.
58. Naval Appropriations Subcommittee, *Hearings on Naval Appropriations for Fiscal Year 1934*, pp. 24–25.
59. ANJ, 31 Jan. 1931, p. 518, and 7 Mar. 1931, p. 633.
60. ARSN, pp. 46–47.

61. William Adger Moffett, "Air Service Versus Air Force," *Forum*, Feb. 1926, pp. 179–85; Edward Arpee, *From Frigates to Flat-Tops* [Life of William A. Moffett] (Lake Forest, Ill.; Privately printed, 1953), pp. 108–12; Turnbull and Lord, *History of United States Naval Aviation*, pp. 249–58.

62. COMBATFLT (Pratt) to CNO (Hughes), 12 Apr. 1929. William V. Pratt Papers, NHD:OA: Memorandum to All Bureaus and Offices from CNO, 16 Jan. 1932, NARG 52, File A3–1/A16–1 (122–31); *New York Times*, 31 Jan. 1932.

63. U.S., House, Naval Subcommittee of Appropriations Committee, *Hearings on Naval Appropriations for Fiscal Year 1932* (Washington: GPO, 1931), pp. 89–91; ANJ, 29 Nov. 1930, pp. 289, 291.

64. Rufus Fairchild Zogbaum, *From Sail to Saratoga: A Naval Autobiography* (Rome: Privately Printed, ca 1961), pp. 421–25; Elretta Sudsbury, *Jackrabbits to Jets: The History of North Island, San Diego, California* (San Diego: Neyenesch Printers, 1967), pp. 147–48.

65. Irwin H. Hoover, *Forty-Two Years in the White House* (Boston and New York: Houghton Mifflin, 1934), p. 189; Ray Lyman Wilbur, *The Memoirs of Ray Lyman Wilbur, 1875-1949*, edited by Edgar Eugene Robinson and Paul Carroll Edwards (Stanford: Stanford University Press, 1960), pp. 536, 542–45; *New York Times*, 29 May, 21 June 1930. An inside view of the whole Adams family at play is found in Abigail Adams Homans, *Education by Uncles* (Boston: Houghton Mifflin, 1966), pp. 117–36.

66. *New York Times*, 13 Feb., 3 Nov. 1932.

67. William D. Leahy Diaries, MDLC, vol. 1, 4 Mar. 1929; vol. 2, 20 Dec. 1932.

68. *New York Times*, 21 June 1929.

69. *Ibid.*, 12 June 1930.

70. *Ibid.*, 21 June 1932.

71. *Ibid.*, 23 Dec. 1932.

72. *Ibid.*, 11 Oct. 1933.

73. *Ibid.*, 13, 17 Oct. 1937.

74. Rappaport, *Navy League*, p. 192.

75. *New York Times*, 2 May 1939, 14 Oct. 1940.

76. Leonard M. Fowle, "Charles Francis Adams," *Yachting*, July 1954, pp. 3, 146–47.

77. Editorial, "Charles Francis Adams," *Christian Science Monitor*, 15 June 1954.

CLAUDE AUGUSTUS SWANSON

4 March 1933–7 July 1939

ALLISON SAVILLE

Claude Augustus Swanson was born on 31 March 1862, in the small town of Swansonville, near Danville, Pittsylvania County, Virginia, Confederate States of America, where his parents, John and Catherine Swanson, tilled a small farm. He attended the local school and helped out on the family farm until his parents were able to afford tuition for two semesters at Virginia Agricultural and Mechanical College (later Virginia Polytechnic Institute), but he then had to leave because of financial difficulties. After working for about two years, he entered Randolph-Macon, where he won honors as a debater and orator and earned his A.B. Entering the University of Virginia Law School, in the fall of 1885, he came away with an LL.B. in 1886.

Swanson began his legal career and received his introduction to politics in Chatham, fourteen miles north of Danville. With his flair for oratory, he attracted the attention of the state Democratic machine, and in 1892 he was elected to the U.S. House of Representatives from Virginia's Fifth District. He served in six succeeding Congresses until 1906, when he became the Governor of Virginia and the head of the State's Democracy. On 1 August 1910, he was appointed to fill a vacancy in the Senate that would expire on 3 March 1911; in 1912 he was elected in his own right. He would win three additional elections until he resigned from the Senate to accept a cabinet portfolio.

In 1914, at the age of fifty-two years, Swanson became a member of the Committee on Naval Affairs. He subsequently served as the ranking Democrat on this committee and on the Foreign Relations Committee as well. While earning a reputation as one of the shrewdest hands at practical politics in the Senate, he also became that body's recognized authority on naval affairs. As a supporter of a navy "second to none," he came into close contact with Franklin D. Roosevelt while the latter was Assistant Secretary of the Navy from 1913 to 1920.[1]

Since Roosevelt knew the sea better than any president before his time and had a knowledge of naval matters superior to most Americans, one wonders why he chose the aged and ill Swanson to be his Secretary of the Navy in 1933. There are two probable answers. First, moving Swanson into the cabinet would provide a Senate seat for another old friend, former Governor Harry Byrd. Second, with Swanson in office, despite his evident intellectual qualifications for it, Roosevelt could be his own Secretary of the Navy.[2]

Swanson became Secretary of the Navy on 4 March 1933, just twenty-seven days before his seventy-first birthday. As his Assistant Secretary, President Roosevelt chose Henry Latrobe Roosevelt. Henry had attended but not graduated from the Naval Academy. Instead he had joined the Marine Corps in 1899 and served the Corps until 1919, when he entered business. To his office he brought a military bent and some administrative skill.

Swanson honored the tradition of having bureau chiefs and assistant chiefs serve four-year terms and of assigning only outstanding officers to these billets. Although he removed no chief when he assumed office, he was served by three Chiefs of Naval Operations between 1933 and 1939. Admiral William Veazy Pratt served until July 1933; Admiral William H. Standley, from 1933 to 1937; and Admiral William D. Leahy, thereafter.[3]

Continuity was also marked in the congressional naval committees. The Senate chair Swanson vacated went to two old friends and naval supporters; first to Park Trammel of Florida, who had served on the committee since 1917, then to David I. Walsh, in 1936. The Chairman of the House Naval Affairs Committee was the Georgia fireball, Carl Vinson, destined to rule the committee for a quarter of a century after 1931.[4] Variously known to friends as "the Admiral," "the Swamp Fox," or "Uncle Carl," Vinson probably knew more about the Navy in general and in particular than any man in his generation, got things done, and usurped Swanson's unofficial role as the administration's prime naval spokesman.

The apparent concentration of power in the Naval Affairs Committee was, however, a chimera in the 1930s because the power of the purse lay with the House Appropriations Committee, which required justification of every detailed item in the naval budget.[5] Moreover, although it supported the administration's large naval program, it inquired sharply into various matters, as into the academic standards of the Naval Academy and the malfunctions of American submarine diesel engines.[6] James Byrnes, of South Carolina, who headed the Senate Appropriations subcommittee, had little trouble in keeping his colleagues in tune with the administration.

Despite the support offered him by the congressional naval committees and the leaders of the naval bureaucracy, Swanson's attempt to overcome opposition to building the Navy up to the strength allowed it in the Five-Power Treaty of 1922 failed in great part because his frequent illnesses made his leadership intermittent. In fact, the Navy he inherited could not possibly undertake its primary wartime missions. Fleet strength was 65 percent of that allotted by the Five-Power Treaty; all fifteen battleships were rapidly approaching obsolescence (and four of them were in inactive reserve status); cruisers and aircraft carriers, were manned at less than 79 percent of normal complement. There was virtually no service force; funds permitted the commissioning of only half of the Naval Academy class of 1933. The Navy had an antiquated organizational structure, and its war plans were woefully outdated.[7] In morale, in material, and perhaps morally, too, the Navy of 1933 needed radical repair and overhaul.

In addition to facing these problems, Swanson must try to keep the Navy attuned with novel requirements dictated by changes in foreign policy and technological progress. He had confidence in himself, was interested in his work, and to his credit he would start again when his health permitted. Yet three debilitating illnesses, the last of which resulted in his death, meant that others had to carry the load. While ill from 16 December 1933 to 2 March 1934, for example, he had no hand in Henry L. Roosevelt's investigation into the need for reorganizing the Navy Department, had no part in putting together the elements of the great Vinson-Trammel Naval Bill of 1934, and also missed the congressional debates on the budget for fiscal 1935.[8] In early February 1936 he fell and broke a rib. Pleurisy set in, and he did not again return to duty until 12 September. Tentative suggestions for replacing him were made after Harry Roosevelt succumbed unexpectedly to a heart attack in late February. Turning aside such overtures, the President directed American interests at the London Naval Conference of 1936 and helped draft the plans for the construction of the *North Carolina*-class battleships. Yet he had the courtesy to ask Swanson's advice on the appointment of a new Assistant Secretary.[9]

Swanson's last illness began in the winter of 1939, when he was almost seventy-seven. A spring cruise in the Caribbean on board the USS *Houston* brought little relief, and on 8 July 1939 Swanson suffered a heart attack that was fatal.

The extent of Swanson's official activity during his last months is difficult to assess. Josephus Daniels, who talked with President Roosevelt on 14 April 1939, quoted him as saying, "Swanson is too sick a man to do much, but I haven't the heart to let him go," adding that "You know I am my own Secretary of the Navy."[10]

In Swanson's time, the attainment of a "Navy Second to None" was impeded by the Washington and London treaties, the still-powerful disarmament movement, and the economic depression. However, Roosevelt planned to have Swanson oversee large modernization and replacement programs to offset the rapidly approaching obsolescence of 15 battleships, 111 destroyers, and 63 submarines.[11]

Within a week after his inauguration, Roosevelt permitted Secretary Swanson to announce that the Navy would be increased to treaty strength and that the Battle Force would base in the Pacific.[12] At the time, Japan was at approximately 95 percent of her treaty allowance, the United States at 65 percent of hers. Roughly speaking, this put Japan on equal terms with the United States. Less than two weeks after Swanson called for it, Admiral William V. Pratt, the Chief of Naval Operations, provided a prospectus for a "Navy Second to None" that in an eight-year program would cost $944,363,000. New construction alone called for 119 combatant ships and 420 aircraft at a cost of $688,480,000. The prospectus also urged the completion of 22 ships under construction or authorized for $62,736,000, various ship replacements at $64,400,000, the construction of ships not limited by the naval treaties at a cost of $56,849,000, and shore-establishment projects for $71,898,000.[13]

Pratt was particularly worried about replacing the battleships, most of which would be obsolete by the end of 1940. He also knew that the administration would be unwilling to spend large sums for battleships when the Navy also hoped to get up to treaty strength in other ship categories. Since all the destroyers would be overage on 1 September 1934, they were tabbed "urgent" and in "first priority." Then came aircraft carriers, light cruisers, submarines, a heavy cruiser, and gunboats. The construction schedule followed the priority list with the fiscal 1934 program setting the pace: two carriers, four light cruisers, four destroyer leaders, sixteen destroyers, four submarines, and two gunboats.[14] Battleships must wait.

Pratt's recommendations, forwarded by Swanson to Roosevelt on 15 June 1933, met their first test in the great National Industrial Recovery Act of 1933, Roosevelt's attempt to help surmount the depression. Swanson had requested $253,282,000 for 32 new ships and aircraft for them: two carriers, four light cruisers, four destroyer leaders, sixteen destroyers, four submarines, and two gunboats—precisely the program Admiral Pratt had recommended for fiscal year 1934.[15] On 16 June Congress passed what Swanson hailed as the "outstanding event of the year for the navy," for the National Industrial Recovery Act committed $238 millions to the Navy for its 1934 construction.[16] The Navy would have to scrape up elsewhere another $15 million for the aircraft in the program.

While the thirty-two ships were but the first step forward toward the 119 ships the Navy wanted over the next eight years, the 1934 funds provided two of the three carriers, four of the seven light cruisers, twenty of the eighty-five destroyer types, and four of the sixteen submarines it wanted. To help private industry and to relieve unemployment, private rather than previously favored navy yards were to receive 85 percent of the work.[17] With the NIRA program and normal construction, by 1937 the fleet would be below treaty allowance by one carrier, sixty-five destroyers and thirty submarines. By comparison, Swanson noted, the Imperial Japanese Navy was almost up to treaty strength in 1933 and had authorization from the Imperial Diet to replace any tonnage that became overage up to 1936.

In its budget of just over $300 million for Fiscal Year 1935, however, the Navy planned to allocate little more than $12 million, approximately the cost of one heavy cruiser, to new construction. In Swanson's absence because of illness, Harry Roosevelt carried the day in Congress and the Navy was able to order the last of the heavy cruisers allowed by treaty obligation the following August.[18]

Congress helped, too, by passing significant supplements to the appropriations. One such supplement, H.R. 6604, authored by Vinson and Trammel, was in the offing for 1934. The vital Vinson–Trammel Act, which passed on 27 March 1934, "authorized construction of vessels and aircraft to bring the Navy to the prescribed treaty strength, and to replace ships as they became overage."[19] Subsequent money bills soon provided for the construction of two 1,850-ton destroyer leaders, twelve destroyers, and six submarines during Fiscal Year 1934, and twelve 1,500-ton destroyers and six submarines for Fiscal Year 1935.[20] Moreover, the Vinson–Trammel Act also provided authority for constructing two new replacement battleships, but with the stipulation that we would construct them only if one of the other signatories to the 1930 London Naval Agreement laid down replacement tonnage in this category—and that could not occur before 1936, according to treaty restrictions.[21] And while the Navy had to wait until 3 June 1936, just after Great Britain announced construction of her *King George V* class replacement battleships, to get an appropriation for the replacements, Swanson had sensibly ordered up the designs for the future *North Carolina*-class battleships in 1935.[22]

The 1936 appropriations bill, with authorization coming from the Vinson–Trammel Act, provided funds for the third and final carrier (the *Wasp*) permitted by the treaty, two more light cruisers, fifteen destroyers, and six submarines in a year that witnessed the abrogation of all existing naval treaties.[23] For the next year and a half, however, the United States continued to abide by the limitations of the treaties.

With treaty limitations ended and Congress willing to pay for new construction, shipbuilding authorizations followed quickly. The 1938 appropriations bill provided for eight more destroyers and four more submarines, that of 1939, passed 4 April 1938, allotted funds for two battleships, two cruisers, eight destroyers, and six submarines.[24] On 17 May, Congress provided a new impetus with P.L. 528, which authorized a 20 percent increase in active vessels (discounting those that were overage) and up to 3,000 naval aircraft.[25] On 25 June the Second Naval Deficiency Act provided for two additional battleships, another aircraft carrier, two light cruisers, and numerous auxiliaries, in which last category the Navy was woefully deficient. The regular appropriations bills for the next two fiscal years, 1939 and 1940, reflected identical construction increments: two battleships, two cruisers, eight destroyers, and six submarines in each bill.[26] The congressional support for the Navy came not from Swanson, but from Vinson in the House and David I. Walsh in the Senate. Moreover, Congress, the administration, and popular opinion preferred to vent their anger against such Japanese insults as the *Panay* incident, of December 1937, by replying not with war, as Swanson reportedly advocated, but with symbols of naval power.[27]

Operational combatant ships in commission increased from 155 to 235 during Swanson's tenure. The initial goals of reaching treaty allowances and of offsetting obsolescence were met in the cruiser and carrier categories but not in those of destroyers and submarines. But after 1936 the treaties were dead; hence the Navy geared itself to meeting obsolescence dates by constructing six new battleships of the *North Carolina* and *North Dakota* classes, scores of new destroyers, and more than two dozen submarines. With a eye also on the pressing Far Eastern problem, it ordered an additional carrier (the *Hornet*) and eight new light cruisers. The program for a "Two Ocean Navy" was still a year off when Swanson died in July 1939. Nonetheless the Navy had embarked upon an expansion that in a few years made the United States the largest naval power in the world, for the major ship types of the war years were coming off the drawing boards by late 1939: the *Iowa*-class and *Montana*-class battleships, the *Alaska*-class battle cruisers, the *Essex*-class carriers, the *Baltimore*-class heavy cruisers, the *Fletcher*-class destroyers, and the 1,500-ton fleet-type submarines.[28] And there was even a new fleet service force in the making.

In 1933 the U.S. Navy was not only greatly behind treaty strength but was woefully undermanned. It had 5,929 officers and 79,700 enlisted men on active service. In 1939 the figures had risen to 6,877 officers and 110,110 enlisted. But the manning needs for 80 new combat ships so offset these increases that, for example, in 1933 the Navy was forced to hold four battleships, ten destroyers, and one submarine in permanently reduced commission status, and another nineteen destroyers and eleven submarines in rotating reserve. As set by Congress, 85 percent of normal complement was allowed the 155 combatant ships in 1933, and only 45 percent of peacetime complements for ships in reduced commission or in rotating reserve.[29]

Shortly after he entered office, Swanson began a campaign to bring fleet manning up to peacetime requirements so that it could perform its missions and also to restore the 15 percent pay cut forced upon the Navy by the Hoover administration. To bestir Congress, in his annual report for 1934 he noted that the 14 battleships and 15 heavy cruisers in commission averaged 77.6 percent of normal peacetime complement, ten light cruisers 77.4 percent, 70 destroyers 85.7 percent, 41 submarines 100 percent, and four aircraft carriers 78.6 percent.[30] In addition to warning Congress of the ultimate calamity that might result in battle or in emergencies, he told the President about the "unsatisfactory operation condition of the fleet" because the ships were undermanned.[31]

Swanson's proposals for alleviating the manning problem were quite realistic. With the nation in depression and many claims on scarce resources, he forwarded to Roosevelt on 9 November 1934 the results of studies that showed that 85 percent of peacetime complement was required to enable large ships to enter battle "with a reasonable chance of success."[32] This meant that the Navy would need 6,915 additional enlisted men in 1935, and not the 18,000 required to bring the ships of the fleet up to full complements. Because the appropriations for Fiscal Year 1935 would not permit the increases in that fiscal year, and the number of men needed increased with every new ship placed in commission, the net gain was only 1,900 men in Fiscal Year 1935. In consequence, the manning percentages on board the battleships, carriers, and cruisers of the Fleet reached approximately 81 percent during that fiscal year,[33] an increase of about 3 percent. However, even this was remarkable because the Navy had to crew four new heavy cruisers, a destroyer, and two submarines commissioned before the end of 1934.

Paradoxically, despite the shortage of officers, especially of aviators, the Navy had an excess of some four hundred over allowance in mid-1933. In fact, only half of the Naval Academy class of 1934 could be commissioned because of the excess, even though the Navy anticipated a further heavy drain upon officers of the line because the newly established Staff Corps (Civil Engineer, Supply, and Construction Corps) had to be supplied, and there was an increasing demand for naval aviators. Moreover, Swanson realized by 1934 that the new Treaty Navy would require more than 7,000 officers. In 1935, the figure was set officially at 7,941. Finally, in response to his recommendations, Congress restored 10 percent of the 15 percent pay cut in 1934 and in 1935 the last 5 percent as well.[34]

Largely because of Carl Vinson, during the early winter of 1935 Congress approved an increase of almost 8,000 men and set a new manning ceiling of 88,000, one that permitted an 85 percent minimum manning level on all combatant ships.[35] More prodding by Swanson and more work by Vinson brought still further increments— to 96,500 men in Fiscal Year 1937, 102,500 in 1938, and 107,550 in 1939. However, the increases went largely to new ships, for even doubling the 1939 manpower figure barely sufficed to achieve 100 percent peacetime complements for the vessels of the Fleet, to say nothing of auxiliaries and lesser craft. To provide full wartime complements in 1940 would have required 10,000 officers and 244,606 men.[36]

To overcome the officer number deficiency, in late November 1934 Swanson asked Vinson to introduce a bill increasing officer strength by 20 percent, from 5,500 to 6,531.[37] The bill easily passed in the Seventy-fourth Congress as part of the Fiscal Year 1937 budget. In 1939, another bill provided a small increment. Meanwhile Swanson got Congress in 1935 to raise from three to four the number of Naval Academy appointments allotted each congressman. Because the Naval Academy could not fully provide for the Navy's needs, he recalled 233 naval officers assigned earlier to the Civilian Conservation Corps and, in 1935, to alleviate the career drain on the line, he had Congress authorize a Naval Reserve Aviation Cadet program under the terms of which cadets had to go on active duty for three years after graduation from Pensacola.[38]

On the other hand, Swanson contributed to the lack of officers by having Congress pass a bill in August 1935 approving *selection* for promotion, instead of automatic promotion, for the grades of lieutenant commander and lieutenant. As a result, in 1936 a large number of "passed over" officers began preparing to leave the service. This drain in the junior grades was corrected, however, in a Vinson bill of 1938 that permitted the Navy to retain those passed over for promotion. Finally, Congress came to the rescue in 1939 and raised the corps limit to 7,562 members, about 1,100 below the estimated peacetime requirement.[39]

Swanson was only moderately successful in solving the critical personnel problem in the Navy. He did get the Congress to allow the Navy to meet the manning schedules for new construction and simultaneously to raise to 85 percent of normal peacetime allowances the manning of combat ships. He at least kept up with the problem concerning enlisted men, though admittedly he did not solve the officer number problem to his satisfaction. Had he lived another year, however, he would have witnessed "the personnel miracle of 1940," when the officer corps increased in size from 6,877, some 300 over the allowance when he died on 7 July 1939, to 10,817 on 30 June 1940. Swanson also had the foresight to do something about the sad condition of the Naval Reserve. In 1938, at his urging, Congress passed the Naval Reserve Act, which permitted a modest though meaningful buildup of the Reserve over a ten-year period (in 1939 that force numbered 12,986 officers and 41,985 enlisted).

The realism with which the administration, Congress, and the Navy approached the problems of how to build up and to man a Navy "Second to None" disappears when it comes to plans for dealing with the major potential enemy of the 1930s—Japan. During the last half of the decade, plans called for abandoning the Philippines, Wake, Guam, Samoa, and Midway except for face-saving local defense in the event of hostilities with Japan. The basic war plan for fighting Japan, "Orange" (o–1), was ambivalent. Navy planners maintained that they could not defend the Philippines for lack of strength, because the Japanese-mandated islands controlled the main lines of communications to the Western Pacific, and because Congress refused the Army funds to provide adequate defenses for the Philippines. Although Plan "Orange" required the Army to hold the Philippines until the Navy arrived, it was expected that it would take the Navy from two to three years to fight its way across the Pacific![40]

Swanson and Secretary of War George H. Dern requested a reappraisal of Plan "Orange" in November 1935, just after their departments had completed redrafting and modifying the basic Pacific Defense Plan, FTP 155 (*Joint Action of the Army and Navy 1935*).[41] By 1939 War Plan "Orange," revised several times, emerged as a defensive as well as offensive plan. The Philippines were realistically written off, save for a "face-saving" defense, and the new Pacific defense line was pulled back to Panama and the Aleutians, with Hawaii as its advanced center.[42] Yet even after the February 1938 revision which, at Admiral Leahy's suggestion, substituted eventual victory for perpetual defense, the Navy, despite its rapid growth in size, refused to consider itself capable of undertaking even an island-hopping offensive back across the Pacific.[43] How much of a hand Secretary Swanson had in all of this can only be guessed from present evidence. He favored the recommendation of the 1938 Hepburn Board of Investigation to build a major base at Guam, but Congress vetoed the $65–million item.[44] If Swanson, known for his sharp anti-Japanese views, opposed this strategy of despair, it must have been because he was up against pressures and realities too great to be overcome.

Swanson may have lost the battle at the war strategy table, but he and the President defeated three attempts by high-ranking naval officers to extend military control over the Navy by creating naval war staffs and extending control of the Chief of Naval Operations over the bureaus. The first move occurred in 1933 or 1934, when the depression could be used as a basis for reorganizing the Navy as an economy measure. Admiral Standley, the Chief of Naval Operations, taking a cue from a suggestion of his predecessor, Admiral Pratt, masterminded calling a Board of Investigation to examine the organizational structure of the Navy. The Roosevelt Board, named after its president, Assistant Secretary Harry Roosevelt, recommended that no drastic changes be made.[45] Standley, who sought to have the bureaus placed under his direct control instead of continuing them under the Secretary, objected to the board's recommendation.[46] Having concurred with the board's findings, Swanson deferred to the President. On 2 March, the President told Harry Roosevelt that he concurred with the Board; there would be no Naval General Staff, no change in bureau control, the Chief of Naval Operations was and would remain a secondary administrative official, and the Navy would remain under strong civilian control.[47] Swanson's action belied that he was a creature of the admirals.

Two bills introduced during the winter of 1939 showed that the admirals had asked Congress to establish a Naval General Staff with vast powers of control. Swanson's sharp rejection of the proposals, doubtless with the President's blessing if not his order, killed the bills.[48] The admirals tried again in June, just a month before Swanson's death, by seeking Vinson's support, which was not forthcoming. Hence Roosevelt remained commander in chief in a very real sense. Swanson was second in command. Vinson vied with the Assistant Secretary to be third and the admirals remained way down the chain of command, where they doubtless belong in a democracy.

Swanson figured prominently in the four major naval areas reviewed herein—fleet construction, manning, war plans, and reorganization. With the exception of solving the dilemma over national policy and war planning, the Navy emerged considerably stronger as the result of strong civilian leadership and cooperation between the President, Swanson, and Vinson. Possibly no one of these men could have accomplished what was done without the help of the others. Despite his physical setbacks, Swanson was diligent, vocal, and absolutely loyal to his chief. It is probably also true that Roosevelt led Swanson more often than he followed him.

In addition to the major matters already mentioned, Swanson handled thousands of private bills, most of them for the relief of enlisted men or naval families, which Congress asked him to verify and approve or not. He also repeatedly tried to prepare Pearl Harbor as a suitable base for the Fleet and to strengthen the other Pacific outposts. On the other hand, the Marine Corps did not grow during his tenure. Nor did the Navy develop any amphibious landing craft worthy of the name before 1940, even though the war plan required taking enemy islands.[49] The President was permitted to have his way in insisting upon the construction of the *Alaska*-class battle cruisers in answer to the German "pocket battleships" though they had no hope of success in any meeting with a ship of the *Bismarck* class.[50] Likewise the President was largely responsible for the Navy's addiction to the outmoded concept of the antisubmarine patrol in place of the convoy. No evidence readily at hand shows what role Swanson played in the development of shipborne radar, or whether he knew of the persistence of inadequate torpedo-testing techniques. And what of the commendable program that gave the nation the F4U and F4F carrier fighters, developed in the late 1930s, and the remarkable change in quality of American submarine construction that gave us the dependable fleet type boats of World War II? These were more than minutiae and perhaps beyond his area of circumscribed cognizance. But in those areas in which he did figure, he was no front man.

Swanson worked for the "Second to None" Navy and helped guide its creation while Secretary from 1933 to mid-1939. During these years a Navy, originally hard-pressed to meet its peacetime tasks and unable to undertake wartime missions, had grown in material strength because of the end of naval disarmament treaty limitations, new constructions undertaken in part as an economic recovery measure, and favorable personnel action pushed by Vinson in Congress. The 5,929 officers and 79,700 enlisted men of 1933 had increased to 6,877 officers and 110,110 enlisted men in 1939 for a fleet enlarged by eighty combatant ships, many aircraft, and a service force. Service morale had been boosted by a restoration of pay cuts suffered in 1933, an increase in normal peacetime complement, a 25 percent augmentation in the number of midshipmen authorized for the Naval Academy, a naval aviation cadet program, and the provision of such fine naval aircraft as the F4U Corsair. Despite three attempts by admirals to subject the Navy to the general staff system, civilian control was retained. Even if departmental organization and war plans were not adequate for war purposes, the Navy was much better prepared for war in 1939 than it had been in 1933. Swanson had carried out his duties to the best that his health and hoary age permitted.

NOTES

1. DAB, s.v. "Swanson, Claude Augustus"; Frank Freidel, *Franklin D. Roosevelt: The Ordeal* (Boston: Houghton Mifflin, 1954), pp. 32, 43–50.

2. James MacGregor Burns, *Roosevelt: The Lion and the Fox* (New York: Harcourt, Brace, 1956), p. 177.

3. Elliott Roosevelt, ed., *F.D.R.: His Personal Letters*, 4 vols. (New York: Duell, Sloan and Pearce, 1948–1950), 1:329; Ernest J. King and Walter Muir Whitehill, *Fleet Admiral King: A Naval Record* (New York: W. W. Norton, 1952), p. 261.

4. Robert G. Albion and Robert Connery, *Forrestal and the Navy* (New York: Columbia University Press, 1962), pp. 138–45; Robert G. Albion, "The Naval Affairs Committees, 1816–1947," USNIP 78 (Nov. 1952):1227–37.

5. Albion and Connery, *Forrestal and the Navy*, p. 143.

6. U.S. Congress. *Hearings in the House and Senate, Naval Appropriations Bill, 1935*, 73rd Cong., 2nd Sess., December 1933 (Washington: GPO, 1934); *Navy*

Department Appropriations Bill for 1936: Hearings before the Subcommittee of the House Committee on Appropriations, 74th Cong., 1st Sess. (Washington: GPO, 1935); *Navy Department Appropriations Bill for 1937. Hearings before the Subcommittee of House Committee on Appropriations,* 74th Cong., 2nd Sess. (Washington: GPO, 1936), pp. 547-50; *Navy Department Appropriations Bill for 1938. Hearings before the Subcommittee of the Committee on Appropriations, House of Representatives,* 75th Cong., 1st Sess. (Washington: GPO, 1938).

7. ARSN, 1934, p. 13.
8. *Hearings in the House and Senate, Naval Appropriations Bill, 1935,* p. 648: Harold L. Ickes, *The Secret Diary of Harold L. Ickes,* 3 vols. (New York: Simon and Schuster, 1953-1954), 1:132, 151.
9. Elliott Roosevelt, ed., *F.D.R.: His Personal Letters,* 2:565, 570.
10. Carroll Kilpatrick, ed., *Roosevelt and Daniels* (Chapel Hill: University of North Carolina Press, 1952), p. 184; King and Whitehill, *King,* p. 292.
11. U. S. Navy Department. *The Naval Establishment: Its Growth and Necessity for Expansion.* NavExos-P-1038 (Washington: GPO, 1951), p. 3.
12. Cordell Hull, *The Memoirs of Cordell Hull,* 2 vols. (New York: Macmillan, 1948), 1:287.
13. Pratt to Swanson, 15 Mar. 1933, SNP. The 119 new combatant ships asked for plus the 22 under construction consisted of 3 carriers, 1 heavy cruiser, 7 light cruisers, 9 destroyer leaders, 76 destroyers, 23 submarines, 1 CV (*Ranger*), the 7 *Astoria*-class heavy cruisers, the first 4 *Porter*-class DDLs, the 8 *Farragut*-class destroyers, and the last 2 of the ill-performing V class submarines (the *Cachalot* and *Cuttlefish*).
14. Pratt to SECNAV, c 15 Mar. 1933, SNP.
15. Swanson to Roosevelt, 15 June 1933, *ibid.*
16. ARSN, 1933, pp. 2, 7; ARSN, 1934, p. 6.
17. ARSN, 1934, pp. 2, 17-19. The contracts for the two carriers, the *Hornet* and *Yorktown*, went to the Newport News Shipbuilding and Drydock Co., in Swanson's home state.
18. ARSN, 1934, p. 19; James C. Fahey, *The Ships and Aircraft of the United States Fleet.* Two-Ocean Fleet Edition (New York: Ships and Aircraft, 1941), p. 10. The keel for the *Wichita* was not laid until Oct. 1935 and the ship was not commissioned until Feb. 1939.
19. ARSN, 1934, p. 2.
20. ARSN, 1934, p. 18; ARSN, 1935, pp. 19-20.
21. ARSN, 1936, p. 20.
22. ARSN, 1937, p. 21; King and Whitehill, *King,* p. 297.
23. ARSN, 1936, pp. 18-19.
24. ARSN, 1938, p. 1.
25. *Ibid.*
26. ARSN, 1938, p. 1; ARSN, 1939, p. 1.
27. ARSN, 1933, p. 9; ARSN, 1939, pp. 3, 6, 9; Ickes, *Secret Diary,* 2:273-74.
28. King and Whitehill, *King,* p. 297; Fahey, *Ships and Aircraft,* pp. 7, 11.
29. ARSN, 1933, p. 9; ARSN, 1939, p. 17.
30. ARSN, 1934, p. 13.
31. Swanson to Roosevelt, 9 Nov. 1934, SNP; ARSN, 1934, p. 14.

32. Swanson to Roosevelt, 9 Nov. 1934, SNP; ARSN, 1934, p. 14.

33. ARSN, 1935, pp. 3, 14.

34. ARSN, 1934, pp. 14–15; ARSN, 1935, pp. 4, 14, 16.

35. ARSN, 1935, p. 14; ARSN, 1936, pp. 14–15.

36. ARSN, 1939, pp. 6, 17; ARSN, 1940, p. 6; ARSN, 1941, pp. 2–3.

37. Swanson to Roosevelt, 19 Nov. 1934, SNP; ARSN, 1935, p. 14; ARSN, 1936, p. 15.

38. ARSN, 1934, p. 14; ARSN, 1935, p. 14; ARSN, 1937, p. 16.

39. ARSN, 1934, p. 14; ARSN, 1936, pp. 15–16; ARSN, 1938, p. 15; ARSN, 1939, p. 17.

40. Louis Morton, "War Plan Orange," *World Politics* 11 (Jan. 1959):221–50.

41. *Ibid.*, 241; U.S. Navy Department, *Narrative Statement of Evidence at Navy Pearl Harbor Investigations*, 3 vols. (Washington: GPO, 1945), 1:80.

42. Morton, "War Plan Orange," 245–49.

43. *Ibid.*, 246.

44. Navy Department, *The Naval Establishment*, p. 5.

45. U.S. Navy Department, *Naval Administration: Selected Documents on U.S. Navy Department Organization, 1915–1940* (Washington: Navy Department, 1945), pt. 5:2–3.

46. *Ibid.*, 5:3–4.

47. *Ibid.*

48. *Ibid.*, 6:14.

49. Fahey, *Ships and Aircraft of the U.S. Fleet*. Victory Edition (New York: Ships and Aircraft, 1944), pp. 78–79. It is true that the prototype for the wartime LCVP, the Higgins-built, 36-foot *Eureka* (LCP(L)), came out in 1936.

50. *Ibid.*, p. 14. Julius Augustus Furer, RADM, USN (RET), *Administration of the Navy Department in World War II* (Washington: GPO, 1959), p. 47.

CHARLES EDISON

2 January 1940–24 June 1940

ALLISON W. SAVILLE

In February 1936, with Assistant Secretary of the Navy Henry La-trobe Roosevelt dead and Secretary Claude Swanson so ill that fear was held for his life, President Franklin D. Roosevelt sought a new assistant secretary. "How about Charles Edison—the son of Thomas A. Edison?" he asked Swanson. "He is an excellent businessman, has familiarity with government methods, has a sense of humor, and, best of all, is wholeheartedly devoted to our cause."[1] Roosevelt got the man he wanted, but he wisely waited until two weeks after his reelection before announcing Edison's appointment. Edison assumed office on 18 January 1937 and held the position for exactly three years.

Charles Edison was born at Llewellyn Park, West Orange, New Jersey, on 3 August 1890, the son of America's best known scientist-inventor of the day, Thomas Alva Edison, and his wife Mina (nee Miller). Charles attended some of the nation's exclusive prep schools—Dearborn–Morgan, Carteret, and Hotchkiss—before entering M.I.T. Four years later, in 1913, he joined the powerful Edison Illuminating Company. His talents reflected little of his father's scientific and inventive genius, but he was gifted with considerable managerial ability. In 1916, at the age of twenty-six, he became chairman of the board for Edison Illuminating. The next year brought him into close association with the Navy for the first time. When President Woodrow Wilson named Thomas A. Edison chairman of the wartime Navy Consulting Board, Charles became his father's assistant. As a result, the Edisons spent considerable time with such senior naval administrators and luminaries as Secretary of the Navy Josephus Daniels and Assistant Secretary Franklin Delano Roosevelt.[2]

After the war, Charles Edison returned to the business world, but in 1933 he threw his energies into the anti-depression campaign in his home state of

New Jersey, first with the New Jersey State Recovery Board, then with the regional labor board of the NRA program. Noting his excellent work, Roosevelt appointed him regional representative on the National Emergency Council for his state. During 1934 he also labored in the Federal Housing program for New Jersey, and finally in April 1935, received a presidential appointment to the National Recovery Board.[3]

Except for acting in Swanson's absence, Edison concentrated on management of the navy yards, including construction schedules, contracts, materiel, base operations, public works, labor, and personnel administration. In 1938, his duties were increased when he was named Coordinator of Shipbuilding in order to bring together the "activities of all bureaus and offices involved in shipbuilding"[4] for the greatest naval construction program undertaken since World War I. More than once he felt the sting of presidential reproach for recurring delays in construction schedules.[5] By 1939, however, he had set up a system for inspecting and reporting on construction that greatly improved the shipbuilding program.[6] For the first time since 1918, one of the most ineffective and costly facets of the American naval establishment was subjected to some semblance of close fiscal and labor management.

As Assistant Secretary, Edison gained experience in naval administration that stood the Navy in good stead. On numerous occasions he and his able assistant, Lewis C. Compton, appeared before the House subcommittee on Appropriations and the Senate and House Naval Affairs committees and their numerous subcommittees.[7] He also learned how to parry with the master of the White House. While on occasion Roosevelt wounded him with words, Edison learned never to beg the question, and his letters show a writing skill rarely achieved by engineers.[8]

Edison, who was Acting Secretary of the Navy, *ad interim*, during the period of Swanson's terminal illness, represented the Navy at the funeral services and interment at Richmond. The President sent his own final and touching salute.

After 7 July 1939, when Swanson died, Edison's name was mentioned as his successor. Also mentioned was the High Commissioner of the Philippines, Paul V. McNutt, while Josephus Daniels, the Ambassador to Mexico, let the President know he would like the job.[9] Roosevelt, who preferred Frank Knox, the Republican Chicago newspaper publisher, or Robert Jackson, the Solicitor General of the United States, merely confirmed Edison as Secretary of the Navy *ad interim*, on 5 August and had Edison's special assistant, Lewis C. Compton, become Acting Assistant Secretary.[10]

In addition to maintaining the ship construction schedules and securing additional naval personnel to man the expanding fleet, three other problems arose with the outbreak of the European war. First, the nation had to decide what to do following the abrogation of the existing naval treaties. Within the year the Congress voted funds for an enormous increment in naval strength. Second, on 5 September, Roosevelt ordered the establishment of the Neutrality Patrol, which was to engage the services of almost all the existing Atlantic Squadron. Third, the admirals, seeking to muscle in on civilian control of the Navy, pressed Edison for a revamping of the bureau structure.[11]

In 1939, new construction was forthcoming under the 1934 program and the large 1938 program. On 14 June 1940, however, just before Edison left office, Congress increased the Navy by 11 percent, and on 19 July it voted a 70 percent augmentation in the composition of the combatant fleet, thereby greatly adding to the duties of the Secretary of the Navy. During his last year in office, Edison had 39 new ships commissioned and also supervised the construction of 138 other ships including almost every class that saw action in World War II, not to mention small craft and auxiliaries.[12] Roosevelt at the close of 1939 complimented Edison on the progress he had made in ship construction programs even though he continued to cry for "lower costs, more ships."[13]

Three months after Congress had ordered the 70 percent augmentation of the combatant fleet, President Roosevelt declared a limited national emergency on 8 September, and then issued an executive order for the addition of the 29,000 enlisted men needed for the new construction, bringing to 145,000 the number of men added to the Navy in fiscal year 1940.[14]

While the construction program represented the greatest single domestic issue that faced the Navy during Fiscal Year 1940, at sea the Atlantic Neutrality Patrol, ordered by the President on 5 September, challenged the skills and the resources of the Navy as they had not been tried since the First World War. With a patroling force of 4 heavy cruisers, 4 new destroyers, 12 "four-pipe" destroyers of World War I vintage, and a score of patrol planes, the U.S. Navy undertook the most unrealistic task of reporting on belligerent air, surface, and underwater forces in the waters southward from Placentia Bay, Newfoundland, to a point some four hundred miles east of Cape Horn.[15] In early October, the multilateral Act of Panama warned belligerents against conducting warlike operations in the ocean areas staked out by the United States in the Atlantic and a similar area in the Pacific. However, the lifting of the arms embargo in November and the adoption of a "cash and carry" policy meant that merchant ships leaving American East Coast ports loaded with war materials would need the protection of British and French warships, which in turn would attract German raiders and possibly result in combat in violation of the Panama "Safety Belt." Displeased with the initial deployment of the Neutrality Patrol, on 9 October Roosevelt sharply directed Edison to speed up its operations.[16] Then, knowing that two German pocket-battleships were loose in the Atlantic, he ordered Edison to bolster the patrols by deploying an additional forty destroyers.[17] Edison might better have suggested to the President an augmentation of the Patrol rather than wait for him to take the initiative.[18]

Whether Edison's dilatoriness in this instance determined Roosevelt to remove him remains unknown. In December 1939, however, Roosevelt asked Colonel Frank Knox about his taking over the Navy portfolio.[19] Knox declined, but Roosevelt left the door open. He told Knox on 29 December that "On January first I am putting Edison into the Navy Portfolio, but he understands perfectly that I may make changes of many kinds if things get worse."[20] Edison thus operated on merely a day to day basis.

Yet Edison had time to make one highly significant contribution to the development of the Naval Establishment in proposing and sponsoring a bill to integrate the bureaus of Engineering and of Construction and Repair into a new Bureau of Ships.[21] He maneuvered the proposal through congressional hearings that ran from late February until 19 April 1940,[22] and by 1 July the Navy had its first Chief of the new Bureau of Ships. One study of naval administration cites Edison's effort in this matter as "one of the rare cases of effective leadership between the World Wars."[23]

Edison's last acts seem almost anti-climactic. He supported creating the billet of undersecretary of the navy, which would coordinate procurement and material. Roosevelt approved graduating the senior class at the Naval Academy a whole semester early because of a near-critical shortage of officers for manning the naval vessels rapidly being commissioned. During his last ten days in office, from 14 June to 24 June, Edison witnessed the approval of the third and fourth Vinson bills, which created the great "two-ocean Navy."[24]

The *Wehrmacht* finally pushed Edison out of the cabinet. On 10 May Hitler began his invasion of France and the Lowlands. Disaster followed for Europe. For Roosevelt this was the moment to declare America's intent and to prepare the nation for war. On 10 June he publicly declared the United States in the Allied camp; and on 20 June, the day Germany drafted the armistice terms for France, he announced that Henry L. Stimson was relieving Harry Woodring as Secretary of War and Knox was replacing Edison as Secretary of the Navy. At the same time, however, he arranged a deal with the Czar of New Jersey politics, "Boss" Frank Hague of Jersey City, to have Edison nominated as Democratic candidate in the fall gubernatorial election.[25] On 24 June, Edison concluded his three and one-half years of labor in the Navy Department. Since Knox did not take office until 11 July the Assistant Secretary, Lewis Compton, served as Acting Secretary *ad interim*.

Though Edison pales when measured against such a Secretary as James V. Forrestal, his worth has not passed unnoticed. The extensive study of wartime naval administration by Rear Admiral Augustus Furer gives Edison part of the credit owed him by noting that he performed many of Swanson's duties since 1937 and had "excelled in the understanding of engineering and technology," as applied to the general administrative work of the Navy.[26] Albion and Connery applauded his reorganization of the bureau structure.[27] Moreover, shortcomings in naval strategy, war plans, promotion, flag-officer selections, war operations, and even tactics must be laid at the feet of the President and his *naval* advisors, for Roosevelt effectively cloistered off these areas from the normal prerogatives and cognizance of his civilian naval administrators. From Edison, of whom, according to Harold Ickes, the President once said was "too deaf to be effective," Roosevelt received a full measure of loyalty and effort.[28] Materially this took the form of substantial increases in new combatant ships of notable design and fighting efficiency, in timely manpower allotments to man them, and in an effective wartime bureau system.

NOTES

1. Elliott Roosevelt, ed., *F.D.R.: His Personal Letters*, 4 vols. (New York: Duell, Sloan, and Pearce, 1948–1950), 1:613.
2. *Ibid*. On 27 Mar. 1918, Edison married Carolyn Hawkins of Cambridge, Mass.
3. NCAB, s.v. "Edison, Charles"; Elliott Roosevelt, ed., *F.D.R.: His Personal Letters*, 1:613.
4. ARSN, 1938, p. 2.
5. Elliott Roosevelt, ed., *F.D.R.: His Personal Letters*, 2:843.
6. ARSN, 1939, pp. 27–28.
7. U.S. House, Subcommittee of the Committee on Appropriations, *Hearings on Appropriations Bill for 1938*, 75th Cong., 1st Sess. (Washington: GPO, 1938), and similar hearings for 1939 and 1940.
8. Edison, Memorandum to the President, 8 Sept. 1938, 16 Jan., 1 Mar. 1939, SNP.
9. John Morton Blum, *From the Morgenthau Diaries*, 2 vols. (Boston: Houghton Mifflin, 1965), 2:165; Harold L. Ickes, *The Secret Diary of Harold L. Ickes*, 3 vols. (New York: Simon and Schuster, 1954), 2:679; Carroll Kirkpatrick, ed., *Roosevelt and Daniels* (Chapel Hill: University of North Carolina Press, 1952), pp. 129, 186.
10. *Biographical Dictionary of the American Congress, 1774–1961* (Washington: GPO, 1961), p. 31; Ickes, *Secret Diary*, 2:692, 718.
11. U.S. Navy Department, *Naval Administration: Selected Documents on U.S. Navy Department Organization 1915–1940* (Washington: Navy Department 1945), pt. 6:2,3; Robert G. Albion and Robert H. Connery, *Forrestal and the Navy* (New York: Columbia University Press, 1962), p. 45; Ernest J. King and Walter Muir Whitehill, *Fleet Admiral King: A Naval Record* (New York: W. W. Norton, 1952), pp. 295–96.
12. The combatants included the first of the *Iowa*-class battleships, all those of the *Indiana* class, and the *South Dakota*; the *Atlanta*-class light cruisers, the *Cleveland*-class light cruisers, and the *Fletcher*-class destroyers. Plans and designs were

also drawn for the *Montana*-class super battleships, the *Alaska*-class battle cruisers, the *Essex*-class heavy carriers and *Independence*-class light carriers, and the *Baltimore*-class heavy cruisers. (ARSN, 1940, pp. 20–22; James C. Fahey, *The Ships and Aircraft of the United States Fleet*. Two Ocean edition. [New York: Ships and Aircraft, 1941], pp. 4, 7, 9, 11, 13, 14.)

13. Elliott Roosevelt, ed., *F.D.R.: His Personal Letters*, 2:977–79.
14. ARSN, 1940, p. 16.
15. Samuel Eliot Morison, *History of United States Naval Operations in World War II*, 15 vols. vol. 1, *The Battle of the Atlantic, September 1939–May 1943* (Boston: Houghton Mifflin, 1954), pp. 13–16.
16. *Ibid.*, p. 13.
17. Elliott Roosevelt, ed., *F.D.R.: His Personal Letters*, 2:936.
18. *Ibid.*, 2:963.
19. *Ibid.*, 2:975–77.
20. *Ibid.*, 2:977.
21. *Naval Administration: Selected Documents*, pts. 1:4, 6:2–3; Albion and Connery, *Forrestal*, p. 45.
22. King and Whitehill, *Fleet Admiral King*, pp. 295–96.
23. Albion and Connery, *Forrestal*, p. 45.
24. Edison, Memorandum to the President, 10 June 1940, SNP; ARSN, 1942, pp. 11–13; Robert G. Albion, "The Naval Affairs Committee, 1816–1947," USNIP 78 (Nov. 1952):1227, 1234–36.
25. Elliott Roosevelt, ed., *F.D.R.: His Personal Letters*, 2:1031–32, 1041.
26. Julius Augustus Furer, RADM, USN (RET), *Administration of the Navy Department in World War II* (Washington: GPO, 1959), p. 40.
27. Albion and Connery, *Forrestal*, p. 45.
28. Ickes, *Secret Diary*, 3:718.

FRANK KNOX

11 July 1940–28 April 1944

GEORGE H. LOBDELL

In a front page editorial in his *Chicago Daily News*, 11 May 1940, an alarmed Frank Knox declared that "The German invasion of Holland strikes the hour of decision for the United States." He then called for new defense efforts including the building of "The Most Powerful Fleet in the World as Soon as is Humanly Possible." Exactly two months later he was sworn in as President Franklin D. Roosevelt's Secretary of the Navy and had the opportunity to make his words good with deeds.

Knox was born on New Year's Day, 1874, in Boston, Massachusetts. (He was christened William Franklin Knox but adopted the shortened version of his name—Frank Knox—early in life.) During his boyhood he moved to Grand Rapids, Michigan, where his father was a grocer. He left high school at the end of his junior year to become a traveling saleman; when he lost his job during the depression of 1893, he enrolled at Alma College. The Spanish American War interrupted Knox's senior year at college and he fought in Cuba as a Theodore Roosevelt Rough Rider. He admired his colonel without reservation and for the rest of his life expounded Roosevelt's ideas and ideals.

During the war many of the letters Knox wrote were published in the *Grand Rapids Herald* and brought him an offer to become a reporter. By accepting, he started his remarkably successful career in journalism. He ended the year 1898 by marrying his college sweetheart, Annie Reid, on 29 December. Several years later, after completing a special reading course, Alma granted him a bachelor's degree.

Knox's journalistic career was brilliant. With printer-partner John Meuhling, he bought a paper in Sault Ste. Marie, Michigan, in 1902. In 1912, they moved to Manchester, New Hampshire, and started another successful paper. Knox, meanwhile, held honorary appointments as a major on the staffs of

677

the governors of both Michigan and New Hampshire. Although he was forty-three years old when the United States entered World War I, he volunteered for Army service. He earned a captain's commission at an officer's training camp and served as a major in command of the 303d Ammunition Train, 78th Division, in France, participating in the St. Mihiel and Meuse–Argonne offensives. He was only nominally active in the Army Reserves after the war, but he did earn promotions to lieutenant colonel and colonel in field artillery before he retired completely from military activities. Though he never served on extended active duty at highest rank, he was popularly addressed as Colonel during the last two decades of his life. Knox's grave marker in Arlington National Cemetery bears the title "Major" which was his highest military rank during his active service in World War I.

Following World War I, Knox earned such a reputation as an effective editor and publisher that William Randolph Hearst invited him to join the Hearst papers, a position he resigned in 1930 when he and his boss disagreed about management policies which seemed necessary to meet depression conditions. In 1931, Knox reached the climax of his career by purchasing the well known *Chicago Daily News* and making it thrive despite intense competition and business problems generated by the Great Depression.

Knox's accomplishments as a journalist were not matched by similar achievements when he turned to politics. He did, however, manage the winning gubernatorial campaign of Michigan progressive Chase Osborn in 1910. He then served as a Roosevelt lieutenant in the abortive Bull Moose campaign of 1912 and was a floor manager for General Leonard Wood's unsuccessful bid for a Presidential nomination at the Republican National Convention in 1920. After he himself lost a primary campaign for the Republican nomination for the governorship of New Hampshire in 1924, he vowed that he was through with politics. But in 1932 he served President Herbert Hoover as the director of a brief, vigorous drive to bring money out of hoarding, and thereby gained a measure of national prominence. He won much more attention as one of the first prominent journalists to mount a sustained and strident editorial attack on Franklin D. Roosevelt's New Deal. By 1936 he was a contender for the Republican presidential nomination, but he lost that prize to Governor Alfred Landon of Kansas. To his surprise, though, he was chosen as Landon's vice presidential running mate. After conducting what he called a "slashing frontal attack" against President Roosevelt, he and Landon went down to overwhelming defeat in November. Once again he swore that he was done with politics.[1]

After his defeat in the 1936 election, Knox paid increasing attention to the steadily deteriorating international situation. Although unusually well informed by the *Chicago Daily News*'s outstanding corps of foreign correspondents, he broadened his insights into foreign affairs by trips to Europe in 1937 and South America in 1939.

Although an active critic of the New Deal after 1936, Knox gave strong support to Roosevelt's foreign policy. He thought that the President's October 1937 "Quarantine the Aggressors" speech was magnificent. A few weeks later he wrote Roosevelt privately of his admiration "for the vigorous and courageous way" the administration met the crisis of the sinking of the U.S.S. *Panay* by Japanese bombers.[2] After Austria fell to Hitler in 1938, he urged that the President's billion dollar naval expansion be approved. The nation needed the protection, he argued, and the increased influence such strength would give the United States in world affairs.[3] When war finally broke out in Europe in September 1939, Knox wrote front page editorials calling for universal support of Roosevelt's leadership in foreign affairs, the repeal of the neutrality laws, and a bipartisan cabinet.[4] Very soon all three matters involved him intimately.

The creation of coalition cabinets in Great Britain and France at the start of the war prompted Roosevelt to ask Secretary of the Interior Harold Ickes what he thought about an American bipartisan cabinet which would include the titular heads of the Republican party, Landon and Knox. Ickes approved and gave Roosevelt some background information about Knox, whom he had known since 1912. A few days later Roosevelt invited Landon and Knox to the White House along with influential congressional leaders of both parties to solicit support for repeal of the neutrality laws. Knox, completely innocent of the fact that he was being considered as a candidate for a cabinet post, sought a private conversation with the President before the conference. He told Roosevelt that repeal of part or all of the neutrality laws would receive greater bipartisan consideration if he would take some Republicans into his cabinet and also announce that he was not seeking a third term. The President agreed with the first suggestion but, understandably, was noncommittal about the second.[5]

Knox impressed Roosevelt favorably at both the private interview and the conference that followed, but Landon did not. Two days later Landon diminished his chance for a cabinet post when he demanded publicly that the President announce that he would not be a candidate for a third term.[6]

By December, when Roosevelt must confirm Acting Secretary of the Navy Charles Edison as Secretary or choose someone else, he invited Knox to another private meeting. After a few minutes of pleasant conversation, the President surprised Knox by offering him the Navy post. Knox protested that since the country was not then feeling any sense of crisis he would be branded "a political Benedict Arnold" if he accepted. Roosevelt disagreed, and Knox then argued that more than one Republican should be invited into the cabinet to make it a real bipartisan body. They then talked briefly about other cabinet positions and possibilities, but Knox left without accepting the offer.[7]

The President's invitation to Knox leaked to the press, but when Roosevelt confirmed Edison as Secretary of the Navy, in January 1940, rumors about a coalition cabinet subsided. According to Mrs. Knox, her husband erased the cabinet proposal from his mind and turned to other pressing matters of business and politics.[8]

The "phony war" came to a sudden end in April and May 1940 with Hitler's assaults on Denmark, Norway, the Netherlands, Belgium, and Luxembourg. As the German armies overwhelmed these small nations, Knox renewed his editorial pleas for military preparedness and confessed, in a letter to his wife, that "I am terribly afraid France will be conquered and then will come England's turn. I dread to think much beyond that." Moreover, in early June he let Roosevelt know that he would accept a new offer to be the Secretary of the Navy.[9]

Meanwhile Roosevelt was planning to fill two cabinet positions with Republicans. During April and May he arranged for Edison to run for the governorship of New Jersey and for Secretary of War Harry Woodring to resign. At the suggestion of Supreme Court Justice Felix Frankfurter, he considered Henry Stimson for Secretary of War. Stimson had held that office under President William Howard Taft and more recently had been Hoover's Secretary of State. On June 19, Roosevelt offered both Knox and Stimson a cabinet post. Knox accepted immediately but asked Roosevelt if he could postpone serving until after the Republican National Convention, in which he intended to oppose an isolationist foreign policy plank. The President thought delay unwise, saying that if Knox were placed in the cabinet after the convention and the Republicans had taken an isolationist stand his acceptance would appear to be "political sour grapes." Knox agreed to let Roosevelt select the time of the announcement, endorsed Henry Stimson as Secretary of War (though his own personal nominee was William F. "Wild Bill" Donovan), asked for and received assurances that he could select his own subordinates, and said nothing about a third term. The very next day, somewhat to his surprise, Roosevelt sent the Knox and Stimson nominations to the Senate and the news was out.[10]

An informal poll taken two days after Knox's nomination was announced indicated that the majority of the Senate Naval Affairs Committee, headed by isolationist Senator David I. Walsh, of Massachusetts, opposed his appointment. However, the meeting of the Republican National Convention brought about a congressional recess that gave Knox twelve days in which to prepare for his appearance before the committee and allowed Roosevelt time to bring pressure to bear on some of its members.

Coming just a few days before the opening of the Republican Convention, the Knox and Stimson appointments surprised and angered members of the Republican National Committee, who immediately resolved that the two men "were no longer qualified to speak for the Republican organization."[11] In spite of this attempt to read Stimson and Knox out of the party, further proceedings in the convention helped their cause. The Republicans not only refused to adopt an isolationist foreign policy but nominated Wendell Willkie, whose views on foreign affairs and military preparedness were quite similar to those of Knox and Stimson. After the convention, press comments, editorials, and public opinion polls generally favored confirmation of both men.

William Donovan, one of Knox's 1936 campaign managers, and Senator Scott Lucas from Illinois, who was assigned the task of managing Knox's appointment, coached the publisher on what to expect while being questioned by the Senate Naval Affairs Committee.[12] Since Lucas was a member of the committee, he was able to give Knox insights into such men as California's Hiram Johnson, a long-time and staunch isolationist; Millard Tydings, an anti-Roosevelt Maryland Democrat; and Rush Holt, an articulate and vitriolic Roosevelt opponent and isolationist who had just lost his bid for reelection in a West Virginia primary.

In testimony extending over two days, Knox established that he did not have any commitment that the President renounced a third term, he and the President agreed "in reference to the Navy and its future," he believed in a Navy second to none to protect the nation from any invasion, he was opposed to sending United States troops to fight in Europe, and what he stood for was "selfish security" rather than collective security. "I am not advocating aid to the allies short of war because of my love or regard for Great Britain," he declared, "but wholly out of my concern for American safety."[13] Privately, Knox was decidedly friendly to the British and in favor of aiding the Allies short of war, including the escort of convoys if necessary. However, he was forced by questions put to him by isolationist members to take a contrary stand on some issues. For example, one senator got him to agree that as Secretary of the Navy he would not advocate government aid to the Allies in the form of either credits or arms and supplies presently belonging to the armed forces. Knox stated explicitly that he would not permit the use of American bases or ports by British warships and also implied that he was opposed to any convoy escorting by the U.S. Navy in time of peace.[14]

After the hearings, Senator Walsh declared he was satisfied that Knox was not an interventionist and, after some discussion, the committee endorsed his nomination by a nine to five vote. After two days of debate in the Senate, on 10 July both Knox and Stimson were confirmed, with the vote on Knox being sixty-six yeas to sixteen nays. The next day, in the President's office, Supreme Court Justice Felix Frankfurter administered the oath of office and Knox became Secretary of the Navy.

While some questioned Knox's motives for taking the new position, Mrs. Knox offered the excellent reason that "Patriotism was a living fire of unquestioned belief and purpose."[15] He had sacrificed graduation from college to enlist in the army in 1898 and left his demanding business to join the army again in 1917. Now, in 1940, he sensed that the United States might be at war again, soon. At the age of sixty-six he was too old for military duty, but he would serve his country again even if it cost him friends, political standing, and business losses. When his nomination was announced in June, he released a statement to the press: "National defense is not a partisan question. We are in danger now because we are inadequately prepared. The President has said that I can help him. If I can help him prepare us for any emergency I must do so."[16] These phrases, which sounded trite to many people, summed up his attitude succinctly. Knox's family and close friends knew he meant exactly what he said.

Once escorted to his headquarters on the second "deck" of Main Navy by Assistant Secretary of the Navy Lewis Compton and Captain Morton L. Deyo, his naval aide, Knox immediately began to acquaint himself with his new associates, including the members of the General Board and the chiefs of bureaus. His associates in turn found that it was easy to engage him in conversation, he was frequently profane, and he said what was on his mind bluntly, positively, and honestly. His fine physical condition and his robust energy, moreover, made him seem younger than his sixty-six years.

Harold Ickes described Knox to the President as "impetuous and inclined to think off the top of his head at times." Knox was impetuous; he abhorred indecision and considered action a virtue. The speed with which he reached a decision and then acted upon it, a trait developed while "fighting the clock" in journalism, made him seem rash to many people. Yet he usually reached decisions only after considering all the facts available to him. If the facts were few or the time was short, he might decide abruptly, relying on instinct and giving a measure of truth to the allegation that he thought "off the top of his head."[17]

Ickes also observed that Knox was a responsible and effective business executive, one who concentrated on making policy decisions instead of exercising detailed supervision over his subordinates. He delegated responsibility to those under him, and trusted them to carry out their duties. He wisely admitted that he knew very little about technical naval matters and that he needed expert advice on many matters. If more than one viewpoint on some subject were presented to him, he was capable of selecting among alternatives or of making a synthesis of several suggestions as a basis for any action that might be necessary.

Surrounded as he was by professional officers, New Deal administrators and politicians with whom he had little in common, and by experienced cabinet members, Knox was often uncomfortable. Nevertheless, his unabashed patriotism and intense allegiance to the Navy soon won him many naval friends.

Knox was charged with administering his headquarters in Washington; operating forces including 2,000 ships and 1,750 aircraft; the Marine Corps; and a shore establishment including numerous bases, yards, air stations, and other installations in the United States, the Caribbean area, Hawaii and the Philippine Islands. When Knox assumed office he exercised authority over approximately 161,000 naval officers and enlisted men, 28,300 marines, and 124,500 civilian employees.

Knox entered office at a time when the possibility of a British defeat left the United States, with a one-ocean navy, to confront strong and hostile fleets in all oceans. Responding to this potential danger, Congress in June 1940 passed an 11 percent naval expansion act and a naval aviation law that provided for nearly 25,000 tons of new ships—mostly combat vessels—and 10,000 airplanes. Eight days after Knox became Secretary, moreover, the President signed the immense "Two Ocean Navy" bill which called for the construction of 1,325,000 tons of combat ships, the purchase or conversion of 100,000 tons of auxiliary craft, and a naval aircraft strength of 15,000 units. The increase of naval strength by 81 percent created unprecedented planning and procurement problems for Knox.

Some help for Knox came on 20 June, the very day his appointment was announced, in the Naval Reorganization Act of 1940. This statute consolidated the Bureau of Construction and Repair and the Bureau of Engineering into a single Bureau of Ships and also created the office of Under Secretary of the Navy. Eight days later, procurement procedures were eased when the Navy was authorized to negotiate many contracts without advertising for competitive bids, and to make advanced payments up to 30 percent on defense contracts to aid suppliers to finance intial costs of production.

One of Theodore Roosevelt's naval secretaries once remarked, "I do not believe that any man can understand the Navy Department in less than two years of earnest application."[18] Knox knew that he lacked the luxury of time. If Roosevelt were not reelected, as Mrs. Knox told him, "You have six and one-half months to work and make a record."[19] Knox, therefore, hurried to learn his job so that he could contribute to the rapid expansion of the desperately needed navy. By "earnest application" he learned enough by November to believe he could function confidently.

As in Chicago, so in Washington, Knox delegated authority and trusted his subordinates to do their work without minute supervision. He thus obtained time needed to attend to matters requiring his personal attention, to discharge his social obligations, and to take some physical exercise.

During his first months in Washington, Knox started his day aboard the USS *Sequoia*, the yacht reserved for the use of naval secretaries, by bending, twisting, deep breathing, and jogging around the deck. He would reach his office about 8:30 and spend most of the morning answering mail, conferring with individuals, and signing papers. Not until after Pearl Harbor did he allow the use of a signature facsimilie machine that disposed quickly of a mass of paper work that required his endorsement but not his attention. In the late afternoon, if meetings, conferences, and mail allowed, he would play a round of golf. His work day ended between 5:30 and 6:00 p.m., when he left his desk as clear of obligations as possible, thus setting an example for his subordinates to follow.

At a weekly Secretary's Council Meeting attended by his principal civilian and military executives, Knox heard reports and discussed policies and matters of general interest. Weekly, also, he held press conferences alternating between mornings and afternoons in order to be fair to both morning and evening newspapers. On Friday afternoons at 2:00 p.m., when the President was in Washington, he attended cabinet meetings. Once each week starting in October 1940, moreover, he, Stimson, and Secretary of State Cordell Hull met to discuss matters of foreign policy and national security. This regular schedule was often interrupted by the need to testify before Congress, make inspection trips, or deliver speeches, so that he might be away from his desk for hours or even days. The longer he was Secretary the greater was his number of memberships on committees and boards, with each assignment consuming precious time.

Fond of impromptu dinner parties, Knox invited to the *Sequoia* navy department officers and civilians, congressmen, acquaintances from other government offices, members of the diplomatic community, and old friends from the business and newspaper world. To mitigate the hot summer weather, he would have the yacht sail along the Potomac river. If he were not on the *Sequoia*, he was usually a dinner guest at some embassy or at the home of one of Washington's important people, continuing over cocktails, dinner, and cigars to discuss naval matters. Once back on the *Sequoia*, he would study the latest edition of the *Chicago Daily News* and discuss the paper's functioning with his secretary, John O'Keefe.

Favorably impressed though he was with most of the men working closely with him, Knox quickly saw the need not only for more manpower and for a greatly expanded navy, but for improvement in administration. While he would not make wholesale changes in personnel or organization, he believed that the merger of two former bureaus into the Bureau of Ships was a step in the right direction. However, he would begin his reforms in his own office, then tackle other naval agencies.

In July 1940, the Office of the Secretary was manned by merely seven civilians and seven naval officers. Knox's closest naval associate was his aide, Captain Morton L. Deyo. Deyo not only introduced Knox to naval organization and tradition but traveled everywhere with him. The two men developed a genuine liking for each other; even after Deyo returned to sea and made flag rank they kept in touch through a cordial correspondence.

Marine Sergeant–Major John D. Dillon, who had served secretaries Claude Swanson and Charles Edison ably as Confidential Assistant, continued in his post under Knox. In addition to taking care of classified material, he served as a valuable source of information on the workings of the Navy Department. Knox had him commissioned as a captain, and then had him promoted to major so he could discharge his duties with greater authority and ease. Dillon, whose long service provided continuity in the secretary's office, in the postwar years served the Defense Department as an important civil servant.

Knox brought John O'Keefe, his loyal and efficient personal secretary, from Chicago and installed him in an office nearby. Arthur J. Bulger, a contract specialist loaned to Knox by Ickes, soon joined O'Keefe in the secretary's suite. These two became the first of many to bear the title of Special Assistant to the Secretary of the Navy.

Lewis Compton, the Assistant Secretary, was the only high-ranking civilian when Knox entered the department. Although he probably knew that the President had promised Knox that he could name his own under secretary and assistant secretary, Compton stayed on until early 1941, meanwhile sharing his experience with his new chief during the first critical months of getting under way.

For the newly-created office of under secretary Knox chose William Donovan, who declined. Two Chicago friends—Raleigh Warner, Vice President of Pure Oil Company, and Ralph Bard, an investment banker, also declined. Knox was thus very receptive when Ickes mentioned James V. Forrestal, a New York investment banker.[20]

Moving with characteristic speed, Knox had Forrestal as his guest aboard the *Sequoia* twice and as a golf partner once within four days. He asked Warner, who knew Forrestal both from Princeton and from the business world, for an opinion of the man and received a favorable endorsement. Knox then offered Forrestal the job. Since Forrestal had only come to Washington in late June as one of a new corps of administrative assistants to the President and was unhappy with his poorly defined job, he needed only a little encouragement to accept Knox's invitation. His nomination cleared the Senate easily and on 22 August he was sworn in as the Navy's first under secretary.[21]

Knox had completed six weeks as Secretary when Forrestal joined him. By then, through briefings, experience, and some inspection tours he had gained sufficient understanding of the functions of his department to endorse a memorandum assigning duties and responsibilities to himself and to his two civilian associates. The memorandum, dated 23 August 1940, divided the duties as follows:

The Secretary of the Navy

The Budget; The Joint Board; The General Board; Naval Petroleum Reserves; Legislation (Policy); Public Relations; Technical Aide (Naval Research Laboratory).

The Under Secretary of the Navy

Liaison with Departments and Industrial agencies other than the Budget, Army, Material and Labor; Legal Matters (Routine Legislation); Judge Advocate General; Contracts; Tax Questions; Compensation Board; Naval Examining Board; Naval Retiring Board; Board of Medical Examiners.

The Assistant Secretary of the Navy

Commissioned and Enlisted Personnel; Shore Establishment Division; Civil Employees; Labor Liaison; Shore Stations Development Board; Army and Navy Munitions Board; The Chief Clerk's Office.[22]

As Knox gained in experience and his department burgeoned, he shifted some responsibilities around. For example, he himself assumed responsibility for commissioned and enlisted personnel. Moreover, the addition of an under secretary enabled him to lighten his own load. By assigning the under secretary jurisdiction over liaison with industrial agencies and supervision of contracts, he deliberately placed Forrestal in the mainstream of responsibility for industrial mobilization and procurement at the very time unprecedented naval growth made these two areas of endeavor of paramount importance.

Procurement matters had disturbed Knox from his second day in office, when he was presented with $120 million worth of contracts to approve. Faced with this awesome responsibility, and feeling that he knew little about what he was doing, he asked his friend Ickes for help. Ickes, who had an outstanding reputation for the honest handling of billions of dollars, sent Knox a contract expert, Arthur J. Bulger. Knox immediately had Bulger search for possible "crookedness or unwise provisions" in the Navy's contracts.[23] However, given his own duties and the need to handle contracts rapidly lest they become a bottleneck in the procurement program, Knox soon told Forrestal, "Jim, this is yours; it is too big a job for a man to undertake in my position with all the other responsibilities I have."[24]

Knox's confidence in and respect for his under secretary was matched by Forrestal's high regard for Knox. Together they formed the strongest part of a team which gave firm and dedicated civilian leadership to the Navy Department through a period of critical years.

Knox's chief military partner was Admiral Harold R. "Betty" Stark, the Chief of Naval Operations. Knox and Stark started out on a cordial basis and developed a warm friendship that continued even after Stark moved to London as Commander of Naval Forces in Europe in April 1942. As Chief of Naval Operations, Stark was a dedicated advocate of naval expansion, favored full cooperation with the British during the "short-of-war" period, and was devoted to the task of promoting cooperation among the many components of the Navy and between the Navy and outside agencies.[25] Since Knox shared these same goals, it is not surprising that the two men got along so well together.

Upon entering office, Knox asked all bureau chiefs and heads of offices who had mail requiring his signature to bring it to his office personally and to be prepared to explain the significance of each item.[26] This request was a deliberate device to become acquainted with each highranking officer personally and to learn about his problems. Within a short time he became acquainted with the key officers and acquired a good general understanding of who was responsible for what.

Knox came to know some officers better than others. Questions concerning production put him in constant touch with Rear Admiral Samuel M. Robinson, Chief of the new Bureau of Ships, and Admiral William R. Furlong, Chief of the Bureau of Ordnance, both of whom he liked and respected. Because the personnel problems of a growing navy interested him personally, he saw a great deal of Rear Admiral Chester W. Nimitz, Chief of the Bureau of Navigation (Naval Personnel). Impressed by Nimitz's clear thinking and decisiveness, he marked him as one who could assume other major responsibilities. Knox was attracted to Rear Admiral Ben Moreel, Chief of the Bureau of Yards and Docks, not only because both were closely involved in the expansion of the Navy's facilities, but also because both took the same view of the preciousness of time and the stultifying effect of red tape. Each genuinely admired the other.[27] Knox also respected Rear Admiral John H. Towers, Chief of the Bureau of Aeronautics, but since he did not concern himself often with naval aviation, he did not spend much time with the Navy's senior aviator.

Knox probably shared Forrestal's assessment of Rear Admiral Ray Spear, Chief of the Bureau of Supplies and Accounts, and Rear Admiral Walter B. Woodson, the Judge Advocate General. When both resisted his attempts at reforms in their areas of cognizance, Forrestal regarded them as obstructionists.[28] In any dispute between Forrestal and an admiral, Knox's instinctive response was to support Forrestal, especially if the naval officer seemed to be resisting change or was challenging civilian authority. However, Knox was careful to avoid alienating a highly-placed admiral, especially one who was technically well qualified or had enough autonomous authority to make his dismissal difficult.

During his early days in office, Knox admitted he could not make judgments about most substantive matters because he lacked technical knowledge. However, his long experience as a business administrator enabled him to make valid observations about some procedural matters. Noting how slowly paper work moved, on his first Saturday morning on the job he called the bureau chiefs to a meeting to discuss office procedures. The chiefs agreed, as he told Mrs. Knox, that "the entire operation of the department was slowed down by lack of sufficient clerks and stenographers and minor help, and approved his proposal that "an immediate quick survey [be made] by an expert and the prompt expansion of the force so that routine work could be dispatched promptly."[29] With the President's approval, Knox called his friend Edward Booz, of the Chicago management consulting firm of Booz, Allen, and Fry. With the arrival of Booz on Monday, there began the management studies which, over the next three years, surveyed the administrative functions of every bureau and several department offices and eventually led to the establishment of a permanent office of the Management Engineer.

On the evening of 1 August 1940, Knox's dinner was interrupted by a call from Lord Lothian, the British Ambassador, inviting him to come to the Embassy that evening "to discuss a very important matter."[30] Lothian's call alerted Knox to the fact that there was more to his job than the administration of a complex organization, that the Navy was an instrument of foreign policy, and that its secretary could, therefore, become involved deeply in matters of foreign affairs, especially in time of crisis.

The month of August 1940 was one of continuing crisis, and the "very important matter" Lord Lothian wished to discuss with Knox was the question whether the United States could transfer to the British fifty over-age destroyers. The first request for these destroyers had been made twelve weeks earlier by Prime Minister Winston Churchill, but the President and his associates, aware of significant legal, political, and military problems attendant their transfers, had failed to act on Churchill's appeal. Both Knox and Roosevelt were sympathetic to the British plea for naval help, however.[31]

The Ambassador described to Knox recent British destroyer losses and the critical shipping situation off the English coasts. He then urged his guest "to exhaust every means that he could before giving him a negative reply" on his renewed request for destroyers. Knox replied that the transfer required legislation beyond the administration's power to obtain unless it could show that the United States would receive something of real value in return. Since the British owned lands from Newfoundland to the Caribbean and the United States needed new air and naval bases for the protection of the American east coast and the Panama Canal, Knox asked if Great Britain would consider selling the United States western hemisphere sites for bases, with the price being fifty old destroyers. Lord Lothian replied that he personally favored such a deal but must confer with his government before making a commitment. The men parted with the Ambassador promising to send Knox's suggestion to the Prime Minister that night and Knox promising to lay the whole matter before the President at the scheduled cabinet meeting the next afternoon.[32]

When the cabinet session opened on 2 August, Knox related the details of his meeting with Lord Lothian. Although he had won the support of Stimson and Ickes, he must have been gratified when the President and the rest of the cabinet members endorsed the proposal and the discussion turned to the practical problems of implementing it.[33]

Roosevelt and Hull pointed out that the United States would have to lease the base sites rather than buy them because a recently negotiated Pan American treaty forbade title transfers of the kind suggested. Everyone also agreed that before any destroyers were released the British must promise that no part of their fleet would be allowed to fall into German hands in the event of defeat. Since all then believed that a destroyers-for-bases exchange required special legislation, they spent much time discussing how to avoid making the matter a partisan issue. Finally it was agreed that Roosevelt should ask Kansas editor William Allen White, an old friend of Knox's, to solicit Willkie's support for the transaction before any legislation was introduced.

After the decision to approach Willkie, the cabinet adjourned. It was "one of the most serious and important debates that I ever had in a Cabinet Meeting," Henry Stimson recorded in his diary.[34] Knox's first major contribution to a cabinet meeting had been so well received that he had good reason to be pleased with the outcome.

The destroyers-for-bases negotiations dominated Knox's life for the rest of August. He took William Donovan to the President so that Donovan could report that his recent detailed observations in England confirmed that the British really needed the American destroyers.[35] He accompanied Roosevelt on a weekend cruise aboard the *Potomac*, during which time the President apparently failed to win Senator Walsh's support for the destroyer deal. In various other conferences he helped with the details of the negotiations and contributed to decision-making. He sensed with gratification the development of popular public support for the transaction and was pleased when Willkie decided not to make the question a political campaign issue. He shared with Roosevelt, Hull, Stimson, Morgenthau, and others a sense of relief when Attorney General Robert Jackson assured them that the trade could be made without new legislation. And he experienced frustration when Churchill proposed alternatives which prolonged the negotiations.[36]

The destroyers-for-bases affair, which for Knox started with an invitation to the British Embassy, ended for him at another meeting with Lord Lothian, this time aboard the *Sequoia*. Lothian, Stark, and Knox cruised on the Potomac the evening of 27 August while working out the final phrasing of the agreement. Unable to agree on some phraseology, they returned to Washington and drove to Hull's apartment. There the four men conferred for more than an hour and resolved their differences.[37] "Now it is up to Churchill, and I hope finished," Knox wrote his wife the next day.[38] Indeed, his part in the transaction was done, and his role in the affair had been one of consequence. The President, the British Ambassador, and his cabinet colleagues had come to know him better and to respect his abilities because of his participation in the negotiations.

When the destroyers-for-bases exchange was made public, on 3 September, Knox was flying westward on his longest and most important inspection trip of the year. During his first two weeks in office, he had visited the nearby Naval Research Laboratory, the proving grounds and experimental station at Dahlgren, Virginia, and the Naval Air Station at Anacostia. At the end of July he had traveled with the President, Congressman Carl Vinson, and others aboard the Presidential yacht to Norfolk, Virginia, and spent a busy day touring the naval installations, the Newport News Shipbuilding and Drydock Company, and the Army's Langley Field. The next day Knox flew to the Pensacola Naval Air Station in Florida. Early in August, again as the President's guest, he toured bases and navy yards at Portsmouth, New Hampshire; Boston; and Newport, Rhode Island. By the time he took off westward on 3 September, he had become familiar with shore installations and was anxious to inspect the Navy afloat.

At Pearl Harbor, Knox was the guest of Admiral James O. Richardson, Commander in Chief, United States Fleet, but he did not spend much time at the Admiral's quarters. In order to inspect the seagoing navy he spent the week beginning 7 September at sea with the fleet. He made it a point to travel on as many ship types as possible, transferring from one to another while they were under way. He climaxed his visit by climbing into the observer's cockpit of a scout bomber and flying from the aircraft carrier USS *Enterprise* to Pearl Harbor.[39]

While Knox enjoyed his adventures with the fleet very much, he was not stunting. A secretary who wished to function properly must know his men and ships, he told reporters at the Royal Hawaiian Hotel. Americans should be proud of the quality of the officers and men who man the ships, he continued, and he finished by declaring with unembarrassed pride that he had just inspected "the greatest and most powerful and most efficient fleet anywhere in the world."[40]

For the most part Knox was pleased with what he saw on the trip. He also met many officers who impressed him favorably, including Rear Admiral Husband E. Kimmel. "I thoroughly enjoyed meeting you," he wrote Kimmel afterward, "and learned much from the several fine talks we had while I was on the *Boise*."[41]

Although his escorts made certain that he saw installations and ships at their best, Knox was aware of various shortcomings. At his press conference, for example, while he mentioned deficiencies in antiaircraft protection for the ships, he assured the reporters that steps were being taken to correct this situation. Privately he was disturbed about the unhurried and complacent atmosphere that he found at Pearl Harbor. "By flying out and back I emphasized the value of time, and I think succeeded in stepping up the tempo," he wrote Rear Admiral Robert L. Ghormley when he returned to Washington. "A large part of my time was devoted to inculcating all of the officers and men I met with the imminence of war and the high likelihood that we would be involved before it was over. There was too little appreciation of how near war was in the Fleet as I found it."[42]

Though Knox could warn officers of the fleet privately that the United States might soon be a participant in the war, he had to suppress such utterances in Washington. By mid-September the nation was involved in the presidential campaign, with both major parties dedicated to keeping the nation out of war. In vain did old friends try to entice a political declaration from him. "I was fully aware that my assumption of the post [of Secretary of the Navy] under the circumstances would prevent me from taking part in the campaign," he wrote to one. To another he steadfastly declared that he was "maintaining an entirely neutral attitude in the present campaign."[43]

Though Knox was outwardly neutral, his *Chicago Daily News* was not. On 12 August his name as editor and publisher disappeared from the paper's masthead and it was announced that a three-man board of control had taken over its management. A week later, when he declared that he had taken leave of absence from the paper, the *Daily News* endorsed Willkie for President. Even the fact that he was in Roosevelt's cabinet was insufficient reason to change the paper's long established political orientation.[44]

Knox approved the support for Willkie, yet he wanted Roosevelt to win the election. He was dismayed by the strength of isolationism among Republicans and he did not know or trust Willkie. He did know and trust Roosevelt, however. "You touched the very peak of greatness last night," he wrote the President after the third-term nomination acceptance speech. "In such times as these, partisanship has no place." He sent Roosevelt other privately written assurances of his loyalty and confided to Ickes that he "had come to have a great deal of affection for the President."[45]

The election over, Knox publicly approved Roosevelt's reelection and sent the President a warm congratulatory telegram.

During the campaign, Ickes confided to Knox that Roosevelt was pleased with his service as Secretary of the Navy. Knox was happy, for he enjoyed the position and hoped that he would continue in office if Roosevelt won the election. Apparently he received such assurance, for shortly after the election he left the *Sequoia* and asked Mrs. Knox to move to Washington, where they rented an apartment in the Wardman Park Hotel.[46]

The election and his apprenticeship over, Knox faced the future as the self-confident executive head of the Navy. It was good that he had learned as much as he had, for between election day of 1940 and the attack on Pearl Harbor he was involved in major events.

During 1941, the Navy burgeoned in consequence of legislation passed in 1940. In February, Ralph Bard replaced Lewis Compton as assistant secretary. Bard, an old friend of Knox's, was cautious in offering advice and reaching decisions. He thus balanced Knox's tendency toward impetuosity. Bard also provided continuity in Knox's office by remaining in it for four years, becoming under secretary in 1944.

The office of Assistant Secretary of the Navy for Air had not been filled since 1931, and some political sparring occurred over renewing the post in 1941. Thomas Corcoran, an exuberant Roosevelt assistant, hoped to be selected. But when Roosevelt suggested him, Knox "objected strenuously because of the political implications."[47] Roosevelt, who had promised Knox that he could choose his own civilian secretaries, thereupon withdrew his suggestion.

It was Forrestal who recommended Artemus L. Gates for the Air job. Gates, a World War I naval aviator and a prominent New York banker, was a stranger to Knox. He therefore turned to Warner and Bard for advice. When both men endorsed Gates, Knox installed him in September 1941. Because the Bureau of Aeronautics supervised the naval aviation program, and Knox, Forrestal, and Bard had already divided civilian supervision among themselves, Knox delayed in defining Gates's duties. Lacking specific assignments, Gates soon applied his talents in his own ways.

A personal friend of Stimson's three civilian secretaries, Gates was able to extend liaison with the War Department beyond the cordial dimensions already developed between Stimson and Knox. Already on a first name basis with many other Washington officials, Gates also used these connections to broaden his service to the Navy beyond the apparent narrow limits indicated by his title. He, too, stayed in the Navy Department for several years and in 1945 became under secretary of the Navy.

Knox's personal staff changed and grew even more than did his secretarial group. When Captain Deyo returned to sea duty in April 1941 he was succeeded as Knox's naval aide by Captain Frank E. Beatty, who proved to be a devoted and able assistant.

Joseph W. Powell and Frank E. Mason, so-called "dollar-a-year" men, became special assistants to Knox during 1941. Powell was an Annapolis graduate and Spanish-American War hero who resigned from the Navy early in his career to become one of the leading shipbuilders in the United States. He served Knox as a personal technical advisor on naval construction matters. Mason left a vice president's position with the National Broadcasting Company to help Knox organize the radio activities of the Navy's expanding public relations program.

Just before the Pearl Harbor attack, Knox decided to send John O'Keefe back to Chicago to supervise the operations of the *Daily News*. O'Keefe was replaced by one of Knox's 1936 campaign managers and one-time National President of the American Legion, Edward A. Hayes, who as a lieutenant commander filled the post of personal secretary.

Adlai Stevenson was an important addition in 1941 to the small group of men around the Secretary. Knox had met Stevenson in Chicago some years earlier and was favorably impressed by the personable young lawyer. After he had been in Washington for more than a year, Knox realized that he needed the services of a personal legal advisor. Stevenson, who joined Knox in August, served not only as an attorney but also as a traveling companion and speech writer. Soon Knox was sending him to meetings as his representative and was using him as personal emissary in situations that required integrity, resourcefulness, and intelligence.[48] Stevenson stayed with the Navy Department until the end of 1943, when he was loaned to the Foreign Economic Administration and sent to Italy to help prepare policy for administering and rehabilitating that country. Shortly after he returned from that mission in 1944, Knox died and Stevenson resigned his naval post.

As new men took up new functions within the growing Navy Department, Knox felt the need for some more reorganization of the offices and agencies supervised by the civilian secretaries. In March 1941 a second contract was awarded the Booz firm for a survey of the secretary's office operations and services. After reviewing the reports, Knox divided his immediate jurisdiction into the Secretary's Office proper (SO), and the Executive Office of the Secretary (EXOS). The civilian secretaries and such immediate associates as naval aides and special assistants made up the secretary's office. EXOS embraced the boards, offices, and agencies which were directly under the secretary or one of his civilian deputies and did not belong to a bureau, to Naval Operations, or to the Marine Corps.[49]

During the year before Pearl Harbor both SO and EXOS grew significantly. The *Official Register of the United States, 1940,* lists seven civilians and seven naval officers in Knox's office. The same publication for 1941 shows twenty-five civilians and nine naval officers in the SO, with Forrestal, his naval aide, and fourteen of his special assistants accounting for the greatest increase in Knox's immediate official family.

The first important addition to EXOS came in December 1940 when the Statistical Division under the Chief of Naval Operations was transferred to the Secretary's direct authority. Having relied upon the immediate availability of statistics in making business decisions when he was a publisher, Knox felt that as Secretary of the Navy he would function with greater confidence if he had a statistical agency under his supervision. Later this division lost its separate identity though its elements remained a part of EXOS. Other accretions to EXOS before Pearl Harbor included the Office of Public Relations, a Coordinator of Research and Development, a Procurement Legal Division (directed by Forrestal), a Lend-Lease Liaison Office, and an Administrative Office. The last replaced the Navy Department's oldest administrative agency, the Office of the Chief Clerk, which had existed since 1798, and had accumulated a variety of housekeeping functions which by 1940 were scattered, neglected, and badly supervised.[50]

The Secretary's Office was only the first naval activity reviewed by management consultants. Between the time the first contract was let and Pearl Harbor, four contracts for management studies totaling $95,000 were signed with the Booz firm. The Office of Naval Intelligence and every bureau except Medicine and Surgery were examined during this period. The reforms and reorganizations that resulted improved naval administration significantly just at the time when the stress of war made improved efficiency a valuable asset.

Knox encouraged these surveys and contributed to their importance by urging the bureaus and offices studied to apply the consultant's recommendations. The management studies continued after Pearl Harbor and by June 1942 the Bureau of Medicine and Surgery, Office of Naval Operations, and, for a third time, the Secretary's office were surveyed. The utility of continuing reviews of administrative organizations, methods, working conditions, and services were emphasized when the permanent Office of the Management Engineer was created in April 1942. Knox's introduction of management programs was one of his significant contributions as Secretary.[51]

Knox approached the Navy's press and public relations organization with aplomb because journalism had been his profession for forty-two years. However, he encountered frustrating obstacles that quite baffled him. He could not, for example, publicize confidential information about either the Navy or the administration. Believing, however, that conservative Navy officers cloaked many matters in undue secrecy, he struggled with the problem of the over-classification of Navy information and time and again asserted that it was "vitally important" to get the Navy's story "into current discussion and reading" if that service were to have widespread popular support.[52] Accordingly, he believed that one of his most significant duties was to be the Navy's chief publicity agent.

Knox's primary means for spreading information about the Navy was his weekly press conference, which was attended by from twenty to sixty reporters. After a public relations officer distributed news releases, Knox might read a prepared statement, introduce any visiting officials, and then open the floor to questions.

In order to be ready for queries on sensitive or controversial matters, Knox often had his public relations officers prepare pre-conference notes indicating the limits to answers he provided. He usually referred inquiries on technical matters to the officers present, and he refused to answer questions about ship movements, naval strength, inventions, industrial production figures, or pending appointments. The sessions were often enlivened by good humored exchanges between Knox and the reporters, many of whom he knew personally. However the happy ship atmosphere sometimes disappeared when he learned of reports criticizing him, his newspaper's editorial policies, the Navy, or the administration. Particularly difficult was his old Chicago competitor and adversary, Colonel Robert McCormick, publisher of the *Chicago Tribune*, who jabbed at Knox not only in the *Tribune* but also in the columns of the McCormick-Patterson combination of the *New York Daily News* and the *Washington Times—Herald*.

Actually, Knox had a large reservoir of good will among his fellow journalists. On the last day of 1940 he asked a long list of "American press, magazine, radio and photographic agencies" for their voluntary cooperation "in the avoidance of publicity unless announced or authorized by the Navy Department"—of ship, aircraft and personnel movements, "secret" technical weapons, new Navy ships and aircraft, and Navy construction projects ashore.[53] The response pleased him immensely because four hundred and forty publishers and broadcasters supported his request for journalistic self-discipline, and his request was endorsed at the February convention of the American Newspaper Publishers Association. A few skeptical editors wondered if the Secretary were trying to impose censorship; a few others, including the publishers of the McCormick-Patterson newspapers, did not respond at all.[54]

Soon after the Lend-Lease law was passed, its provisions were extended to cover the reconditioning and repair of British warships in American shipyards. On 24 March 1941 Knox added the presence of such ships in America to the list of proscribed news items. Two weeks later the torpedoed British battleship

Malaya limped into the Brooklyn Navy yard for repairs. Although *The New York Daily News* featured her arrival complete with photographs of her and her crew, most other newspapers both in New York and the nation did not run the story. Knox praised the editors "who cooperated at (*sic*) my request in not reporting the recent arrival of a British warship in this country," and the President similarly applauded at his next press conference. When *The New York Daily News* called for outright press censorship so that editors could not be criticized for what they printed, Knox said that he opposed censorship and reaffirmed his earlier stand. He also arranged for damaged British warships to arrive at night.

During 1941 Knox occasionally published articles on naval topics in popular periodicals because he considered magazines as one more outlet of naval publicity available to him. The articles were usually ghosted for him by Navy public relations men, but he would split the pay between the ghost author and the magazine's staff writers or send the check to the Navy Relief Society.[55]

When Knox became Secretary, the Public Relations Branch was supervised by the Director of Naval Intelligence. In April 1941 he announced the appointment of Rear Admiral Arthur J. Hepburn as the Director of Public Relations (the post had been held by a captain, previously), the upgrading of the function to the status of "office," and its transfer to his own jurisdiction. In May the Naval District commanders were ordered to shift public relations from Intelligence to their own cognizance. In Washington, meanwhile, Knox brought in civilian newspaper and radio executives to help reorganize and expand public relations activities.[56]

At the end of July, Knox told a conference of naval public relations officers that the public should be "thoroughly informed" about the Navy within the guidelines he had established and that it was wrong for naval officers to keep mum lest they get into trouble. His philosophy made some officers nervous while others heartily disagreed with him. Nevertheless, the volume and quantity of information given to the media improved. In Main Navy, Commander Robert W. Berry presided over a newsgathering operation similar to that of a newspaper office. One officer served as managing editor, another as city editor, three others as reporters with assigned beats. If some old Navy hands were skeptical about the Secretary's new press and public relations policies, they had to admit that he had infused the old conservative publicity system with new vitality.[57]

Knox's innovations in management and public relations paled before much more exciting news in the months before Pearl Harbor. He himself was often in the news as a participant in many spectacular events and also by making many militant anti-Axis, pro-British speeches which expressed his own vigorous viewpoints and supported what he conceived to be the President's policies.

Any reticence Knox may have had about speaking publicly vanished with the reelection of Roosevelt in November 1940. On Armistice Day of 1940, for example, he proclaimed that America was willing to keep out of war, "but not at the price of cowardice and dishonor."[58] Three days later he characterized the war in Europe as an irreconcilable conflict between democracy and totalitarianism, adding that "We are going to give Great Britain every possible degree of aid we can short of leaving ourselves defenseless." Though the main part of this speech called for support of America's defense program and increased seapower, newspapers the next morning featured Knox's sensational anti-Hitler charge that Europe was the victim of "a thoroughly unwarranted war conducted by a greedy fanatic."[59]

Having spoken thus without prior clearance from Roosevelt, Knox wondered how the President had reacted. Roosevelt, however, said nothing. Though one editorial writer reported that Knox had been "mildly scolded," he did not act as if he had been reprimanded in any way. Instead he continued to make what Stimson called "astonishingly frank" speeches at the average of two a month throughout 1941.[60]

Isolationists were enraged at Knox's forthright pronouncements. After he told a governor's conference on 30 June that "the time to use our Navy to clear the Atlantic of the German menace is at hand," Senator Burton K. Wheeler demanded that he "should resign or be thrown out of office," and Representative Hamilton Fish suggested that he be impeached.[61] On the other hand, Knox had many supporters. On 2 July Felix Frankfurter wrote him that "When you're impeached can I leave the bench and become one of your counsel?" After Knox addressed the American Bar Association in October 1941 on the topic "World Peace Must Be Enforced," Walter Lippmann of the *New York Times* congratulated him and said, "It is the speech Woodrow Wilson should have delivered in 1917." Stimson and Ickes were also both delighted with his straightforward talk.[62] Apparently Roosevelt was also pleased. When Knox did occasionally send a speech draft to the President before he made some particularly strong statement, Roosevelt suggested very few changes.[63] Indeed, Knox's aggressive assertiveness gave Roosevelt many opportunities to judge popular reaction to explicit interventionist expressions.

In the meantime, Knox was privately exploring means by which British convoys on the Atlantic could be made more effective. Such an inquiry pursued with Stimson soon led both men to conclude that "the only thing that can be done, and the thing we eventually shall do, will be to convoy that Atlantic lifeline . . . with our own destroyers."[64] They knew, though, as 1940 ended, that neither Congress nor public opinion would support their conclusion, and that Roosevelt was not yet ready to order aggressive naval operations in the Atlantic. However, Roosevelt was in a position to give direction to events which could and would require the Navy's participation in the battles then raging in the Atlantic. From the President's "Arsenal of Democracy" fireside chat of 29 December 1940 Knox sensed that if the United States became a producing arsenal for the British, Americans would then have a direct stake in seeing to it that the supplies were delivered safely, and that such delivery meant convoys. The old Rough Rider was delighted and deeply moved by the speech. "Your courage is magnificent," he wrote the President the next day. "No one ever built a great and useful policy on any other foundation."[65]

Upon reading an early draft of the Lend-Lease law, Knox realized that the proposal provided an explicit means of accomplishing all that he hoped for in the way of direct aid to the British. He was kept informed of every stage of the law's development and was an enthusiastic supporter of it.

"We still have a one-ocean Navy," he told the House Foreign Affairs Committee. Completion of a two-ocean Navy was still six years away; in the meantime the British who were defending the Atlantic were in grave danger. "They need our help to survive," he explained, and concluded that "with our unstinted help, I firmly believe that Britain cannot be defeated." Before the Senate Foreign Relations Committee he warned that Nazi Germany was a menace. He overdid the thesis, however, and caused a mild sensation by hinting that Hitler was considering the use of poison gas. He also became involved in an unpleasant exchange with isolationist Senator Gerald P. Nye, who tried to embarrass him by reading excerpts from old editorials and speeches that attacked Roosevelt. He took Nye's bad manners good naturedly and ended the episode by remarking to the Senator, "I'm not a damned bit ashamed of having been a Republican all my life, but I'm not functioning as a Republican now." "Neither am I," Nye retorted, and turned to other matters.[66]

Once the Lend–Lease law was passed, Knox became involved in implementing it. He quickly approved the British request to have damaged warships repaired in American navy yards. He also supervised filling British orders for naval aircraft and other equipment. However, he opposed the transfer of any more destroyers to the Royal Navy because the expanding American fleets were critically short of such ships. He understood clearly that if the United States would not give the British more fighting ships the alternative was to use the Atlantic Fleet for convoying if Lend–Lease cargoes were to be protected adequately from German submarine attacks.

During March and April both Knox and Stimson pressed Roosevelt to authorize escort of convoy. Fearing that a joint resolution then before Congress forbidding both convoys and the use of American merchant ships for Lend–Lease shipments might be stimulated to passage if he authorized any explicit naval escorts, Roosevelt deferred a decision. He also rebuffed Stimson's demand that the bulk of the American fleet be moved from the Pacific to the Atlantic. At first Knox favored such a move, but when Roosevelt and Hull argued against it he became cool to the idea. Soon a compromise was reached on this matter when three battleships, an aircraft carrier, four light cruisers, and two squadrons of destroyers were sent from the Pacific to reinforce Admiral Ernest J. King's Atlantic Fleet.[67]

During the spring of 1941, Knox kept in close personal touch with the officers who at the end of March seized German, Italian, and Danish merchant ships berthed in American ports. He participated in the planning that brought Greenland under United States protection on 10 April. His sense of alarm grew when Hitler's armies crashed through Yugoslavia and into Greece in April, and he felt frustrated when the United States could not get equipment, including naval dive bombers, to the Greeks in time to help stem the Nazi onslaught. He shared the shock of his naval colleagues at the sinking of the world's largest warship, HMS *Hood*, by the German battleship *Bismarck* in the North Atlantic, and he rejoiced when the Royal Navy destroyed the *Bismarck* three days later.[68]

Knox participated with other cabinet members and White House advisers who wrote the fireside chat Roosevelt delivered on 27 May. Knox and Stimson, among others, wanted the speech to contain a strong statement of support for the British. Roosevelt declared an unlimited national emergency but did not authorize convoys nor ask for the repeal of the neutrality laws, as Knox wanted him to do.

Gloomy news continued into June. Successfully defying British seapower, the Germans captured the island of Crete, by airborne invasion. A *New York Herald Tribune* article on 8 June reported that a U.S. destroyer had recently dropped depth charges on an unidentified submarine near Greenland—a fact Knox refused to confirm at his next press conference. On 9 June a report arrived in Washington that a German submarine had sunk the United States freighter *Robin Moore* in the South Atlantic three weeks earlier. Knox hoped that the news of the first American ship victim on the high seas would result in the breaking of diplomatic relations with Germany, but Roosevelt was no more ready for such a move than he was for authorizing convoys.

On 20 June, after the submarine o-9 was lost off New England by accident, Knox interrupted his busy schedule to attend the special services at sea for its ill-fated crew. Thus he was absent from Washington when the most important development of the war that summer took place—Hitler's invasion of Russia at dawn, 22 June. The next day Knox returned to the capital and had lunch with Stimson and Harry Hopkins, Roosevelt's confidant and adviser. Stimson reported that the Army War Plan Division "agreed that with

Germany now distracted . . . now was the time to move in the Atlantic."
Hopkins urged both Stimson and Knox to "push the President" for action, and
Knox immediately wrote Roosevelt that "I feel very deeply that I ought to
say to you that, in my judgment, this German attack on Russia provides us
with an opportunity to strike and strike effectively at Germany." He concluded that "The best opinion I can get is that it will take anywhere from
six weeks to two months for Hitler to clean up on Russia. It seems to me that
we must not let that three months go by without striking hard—the sooner
the better."[69] Roosevelt apparently did not reply, and he certainly took no
spectacular action in response to the pleas of Knox, Stimson, and others.

Knox enraged isolationists by repeating publicly what he had been telling
the President privately. Hitler's attack on Russia was "a God given chance"
to send more aid to Great Britain safely. "The time to use our Navy to clear
the Atlantic of the German menace is at hand," he trumpeted. The brigade
of Marines on its way to Iceland to relieve the British garrison and prevent
any German expedition from taking over the island was the kind of help to
the British he had in mind.[70]

When Roosevelt announced on 7 July that the Marines had arrived in Iceland, Knox urged him to authorize convoy escorts from the Atlantic fleet
between North America and Iceland. Reluctantly, on 19 July Roosevelt gave
the necessary orders for the use of escorts, but he refused to publicize his
action, as both Knox and Stimson wanted him to do. Even though convoying
became a fact, neither secretary was elated because the struggle to establish
convoys had been exhausting. Knox, in particular, was discouraged by the
lack of bold Presidential action.[71]

July and August were hectic months for Knox. When the Senate Naval
Affairs Committee demanded an explanation of what the Atlantic Fleet was
doing, Knox satisfied most of the members without revealing fully that convoying was a fact.[72] He gave more and more time to procurement problems
both for the Navy and for Lend–Lease, the latter now including requests from
the Russians which he was reluctant to consider. Then on 7 August, 16,000
workers at the Federal Shipbuilding and Drydock Corporation went on strike
and he had to deal with his first big labor problem.

Since most of Federal Shipbuilding's $450 million in contracts were with
the Navy, and since Roosevelt was away from Washington to rendezvous with
Churchill at Argentia Bay, Newfoundland, Knox found himself in the middle
of labor negotiations and controversy for the rest of the month. When Roosevelt and Churchill announced their Atlantic Charter, Knox was pleased with
it, but his focus was still centered on the strike problem. He sent Adlai Stevenson with a draft proposal that the Navy be authorized to take over the Federal
Shipbuilding facilities to give the President when he landed in Maine. When

Roosevelt returned to Washington he tried personally to settle the Federal Shipbuilding strike. Failing to do so, he adopted Knox's proposal and ordered the Navy to take over and operate the Kearney plant.[73]

Early in September, Knox was forced to take a few days off for minor surgery. On 4 September near Iceland, the destroyer *Greer* was fired upon but not damaged by a German submarine. Six days later, Knox had recovered enough from his surgery to meet with Hull and Stimson; together they were successful in persuading the President to announce "shoot on sight" orders for the Navy against Axis submarines and ships operating in the North Atlantic patrol zone.[74]

U.S. convoys to Iceland and back were no longer secret and soon the Battle of the Atlantic generated American casualties. On 17 October the destroyer *Kearney* was severely damaged by a German torpedo. Two weeks later the destroyer *Reuben James* was sunk by a Nazi submarine near Iceland. Sinking of American merchant ships also increased. On 6 November the German blockade runner *Odenwald*, flying the American flag, was captured by the cruiser *Omaha* in Atlantic equatorial waters. Knox was excited by these dramatic events and gratified that the Navy was playing an active and responsible role in the Battle of the Atlantic. But paradoxically, though the Atlantic war was boiling, by November 1941 his attention shifted more and more toward ominous developments in the Pacific.

From his very first weeks in office, matters concerning the Pacific Fleet or Japanese-American relations often demanded Knox's full attention. In September 1940, it may be recalled, he visited Pearl Harbor and concluded that there was a lack of "war-mindedness" in the fleet and that both the Commander in Chief United States Fleet, Admiral James O. Richardson, and the Commandant of the Fourteenth Naval District, Rear Admiral Claude Bloch, were too socially minded.

At Pearl Harbor, Knox discovered that Richardson disagreed with the President's decision to keep the fleet in Hawaii. He probably did not appreciate the Admiral's blunt suggestion that if the President wanted to do something about increasing naval personnel he had the authority to do it. Richardson gave Knox a frank memorandum entitled "Cooperation Between Executive, State, War and Navy Departments" that raised many questions about how policies were arrived at in Washington that influenced the disposition of units of the Navy.[75] A veteran of the Washington scene, Richardson was undoubtedly correct in alleging poor coordination among top-level policy makers. Knox usually appreciated straightforward language, but in most cases when an Admiral and the President disagreed, Knox sided with Roosevelt. In this instance, he was unsympathetic with Richardson's points of view and gave him scant support in the weeks that followed.

Eight days after Knox returned from his 1940 Pearl Harbor trip, the Germans, Italians, and Japanese announced the signing of the Tripartite Pact. The treaty, which extended the Rome–Berlin Axis to Tokyo, bound the three nations to aid one another in case of attack by a nation not then engaged in the European or Asian wars. Washington officials understood at once that since the United States was the only country of consequence not then involved in either war, the pact was of special importance to America. Shortly after the existence of the treaty was announced, Stimson invited Knox to his office "to get his reaction on the Naval situation in the Far East."[76]

When Stimson spoke of matters which involved either military administration or foreign affairs, Knox listened respectfully. Their talk that early October afternoon ended with Stimson's giving Knox " a little memorandum" which was an historical summary he had written on Japanese–United States relations. Stimson noted in his diary, "Knox was delighted with it and said that it represented his views exactly." The final paragraph of the memo Stimson had entitled "Moral." Both Stimson and Knox used this summary statement as a guide for dealing with the Japanese in the months that followed:

> Japan has historically shown that she can misinterpret a pacifistic policy of the United States for weakness. She has also historically shown that when the United States indicates by clear language and bold actions that she intends to carry out a clear and affirmative policy in the Far East, Japan will yield to that policy even though it conflicts with her own Asiatic policy and conceived interests. For the United States now to indicate either by soft words or inconsistent actions that she has no such clear and definite policy towards the Far East will only encourage Japan to bolder action.[77]

Starting in October, Knox, Stimson, and Hull met weekly at the State Department to discuss major developments in foreign affairs and to review the situation in the Far East. In January 1941, these three men and the President began to receive almost daily English translations of important Japanese secret diplomatic dispatches provided by the Army's and Navy's remarkable cryptoanalysis process known as Magic.

Knox rarely spoke of the Magic material to anyone lest he reveal that the Japanese diplomatic codes had been broken. Since he saw each Magic intercept briefly, only once, made no notes, and discussed what he read with a very limited number of people, he apparently did not see any pattern in Japanese communications. He knew that the Magic messages were also being read by the head of the Office of Naval Intelligence; the chief of the War Plans Division, Rear Admiral Richmond Kelley Turner; and Admiral Stark. He believed that he was included on the distribution list because he should know what was going on, but he felt no need to act upon the messages. Resolved to stay out of technical affairs, he would let Admiral Stark, Turner, and other responsible officers judge what was important in Magic and what response the Navy should make, if any.

One decision that was reinforced by both the Stimson principle of displaying strength in the face of Japanese aggression and by Magic intelligence was the order to base the main portion of the fleet at Pearl Harbor. Admiral Richardson returned to Washington in October 1940 to argue with Roosevelt and others that the Japanese would respect a well-serviced fleet on the west coast of the United States more than they would a poorly-based fleet in crowded and badly protected Pearl Harbor. When Roosevelt disagreed, Richardson said that the senior officers of the Navy lacked confidence in the civilian leadership of the nation that was necessary for the successful prosecution of a war in the Pacific. Richardson shocked Roosevelt, as he intended to do, but the jolt, rather than resulting in a change of policy, contributed to Richardson's relief as CinCUS three months later. When the Admiral insisted that Knox tell him why he had been peremptorily detached, the Secretary replied simply, "Why, Richardson, when you were here in Washington last October, you hurt the President's feelings by what you said to him. You should realize that."[78]

One matter Richardson did raise substantial doubts about during his October Washington visit was the security of Pearl Harbor. Since the Army had the responsibility for land and air protection of the islands, Stark directed him to review with the Army the adequacy of Hawaiian defenses.[79] Richardson's subsequent report revealed startling weaknesses. Moved by the Admiral's communication, Knox's naval advisors prepared a formal letter for him to send to the Secretary of War on 24 June 1941 pointing out defense deficiencies in Hawaii. "If war eventuates with Japan," Knox stated in his first paragraph, "it is believed easily possible that hostilities would be initiated by a surprise attack upon the Fleet or the Naval Base at Pearl Harbor." The dangers the Navy foresaw in order of importance and probability were, first, air bombing attack, and second, air torpedo plane attack, followed by sabotage, submarine attack, mining, and bombardment by gunfire. Knox therefore urged the Army to increase the number of pursuit (fighter) aircraft and antiaircraft guns in the vicinity of Pearl Harbor and to establish an effective air warning net in the Islands, and also suggested other joint measures for defense. Stimson replied two weeks later expressing "complete concurrence as to the importance of this matter." He then outlined a program for sending to Hawaii within six weeks thirty-one obsolescent P–36 pursuit aircraft, fifty new P–40 fighters, and numbers of antiaircraft guns. He also promised that in June aircraft warning equipment would be delivered and installed.[80]

Ten weeks later any personal anxiety Knox may have had about Pearl Harbor's defenses were dispelled. On 22 April Roosevelt presided over a discussion attended by Knox, Stimson, General George C. Marshall, Army Chief of Staff, and Admiral King, Commander of the Atlantic Fleet. King needed more ships for his command and Stimson urged sending the whole fleet into the Atlantic. Marshall, supporting Stimson, stated that Hawaii was impregnable whether any ships were there or not. As far as Knox was concerned, if the Army Chief of Staff declared in the presence of the President and the Secretary of War that Pearl Harbor was adequately defended, then it must, indeed, be secure.[81] He therefore gave little attention to Pacific area matters and in July cancelled a planned trip to Pearl Harbor. He kept up with Far Eastern affairs in his weekly sessions with Hull and Stimson, but not until news arrived that the Japanese government of moderate Prince Konoye had fallen did events in that part of the world command a large amount of his time.

When Premier Konoye's government resigned, on 16 October, Roosevelt immediately cancelled his regular cabinet meeting and called Knox, Stimson, Hopkins, Stark, and Marshall into special conference. Although reporters could get nothing from these men when they left the White House, they received the impression that the meeting was somber. In a letter to the First Lord of the Admiralty, Viscount Halifax, later that day, Knox confirmed that the Far East situation was "acute," but he did not elaborate. A week later he told a group of naval ordnance manufacturers that if Japan persisted in its expansionist program a collision with the United States "was almost certain, and on very short notice."[82] Yet he was not discouraged by the crisis. "Japan has evidently reached the place where she must either fish or cut bait," he wrote John Winant, Ambassador to Great Britain, in a revealing letter on 10 November.

> I have seen the crisis approaching and I am delighted with the firmness with which it is being met by the President and the cabinet. So far as the Navy is concerned, we have anticipated the event and are as thoroughly well prepared for it as it is possible for us to be. Frankly, deep down in my heart, I doubt that the Japs will have the guts to go through with their program of aggression when they find out they are confronted with war with both the United States and Great Britain. It would be tantamount to committing suicide.[83]

In spite of Knox's doubts about Japan's willingness to confront the United States and Great Britain at the same time, intelligence at the end of November worried him. Magic messages informed Japanese diplomats that on and after 29 November "things are automatically going to happen."[84] On 25 November Knox and Stimson received information that the Japanese were embarking a large force of transports and naval escorts—from thirty to fifty ships—from

Shanghai and that the first elements were proceeding south along the China coast. That same day Roosevelt told Knox, Stimson, and Hull that "we are likely to be attacked perhaps next Monday, for the Japanese are notorious for making an attack without warning."[85] All eyes were fixed for the next few days on the inadequately-defended Philippine islands.

Two days later both the Army and the Navy sent their Pacific area commanders the now famous "War Warning" messages. The communication Admirals Husband E. Kimmel and Thomas C. Hart received declared that "This dispatch is to be considered a war warning. Negotiations with Japan toward stabilization of conditions in the Pacific have ceased and an aggressive move by Japan is expected within the next few days." Hart, in the Philippines, knew that he was in danger from Japanese forces at sea. Kimmel, in Hawaii, did not perceive any specific naval threat; nor did his superiors in Washington think that he was in any particular jeopardy.[86]

Knox, Stimson, Hull, Stark, Marshall, and Roosevelt were in constant touch with one another during the last tense days of November. Magic intercepts and other intelligence sources indicated that the Japanese fleet previously reported at sea was approaching the Malay Peninsula rather than the Philippines. The President and his close advisers were convinced that an attack on either Malaya or the Dutch East Indies with their rich resources was a positive threat to the vital interests of the United States. Roosevelt asked Hull, Stimson, and Knox to draft a message to Congress for him that would describe vividly why an attack on British or Dutch possessions in the Far East was so detrimental to America that the President would be justified in asking for a declaration of war. Apparently Knox still believed that the Japanese might not carry out any threatened aggression. On 29 November, when he sent his draft of the requested message to Roosevelt, who was spending Thanksgiving in Warm Springs, Georgia, he wrote, "The news this morning indicates that the Japs are going to deliberately stall for two or three days, so unless the picture changes, I am extremely hopeful that you will get a two or three day respite down there."[87]

Roosevelt ignored Knox's advice and returned to Washington at once to begin what for Knox was one of the most distressing weeks of his life. Almost every day that week he met with the President, Stimson, Hull, and others, and he became convinced that the Japanese were not backing away from a confrontation. At his press conference, when he was questioned aggressively about the Far Eastern situation, he indicated his increasing worry by being unusually evasive in his responses.[88]

Thursday, 4 December, was an unusually grim day for Knox. The McCormick-Patterson newspapers that morning printed accurate extracts of the Army's and Navy's top secret Rainbow Five war plan. Knox was furious. It was bad enough that his old competitor, Colonel McCormick of the *Chicago Tribune*, was publishing parts of the classified plan in order to give congressional isolationists ammunition to use against the President; his added frustration was in not knowing who had given this sensitive material to the press. Since the Navy had a full copy of Rainbow Five it was possible that the Navy's security system had been compromised. (He would never know that the leak came from the Army's offices.)[89]

What started out as a bad day ended just as poorly. That evening Knox attended with a small group of government officials a dinner given by Donald Nelson in honor of Vice President Henry Wallace. After dessert, Knox was invited to make some remarks. "I want you to know that our situation tonight is serious," he told his hushed audience, "more serious, probably, than most of us realize. We are very close to war. War may begin in the Pacific at any moment. But I want you to know that no matter what happens, the United States Navy is ready." As Knox sat down, Robert Wyman Horton, Director of Information in the Office of Emergency Management, asked to speak. He told how he had managed recently to cruise into the Norfolk Navy Yard with friends in a small Coast Guard patrol boat without being challenged. He reported that he had seen the British aircraft carrier HMS *Illustrious* being secretly repaired there and had landed and strolled around the base without being stopped. Scoffing at Navy security, he finished by looking coldly at Knox and declaring, "Mr. Secretary, I don't think your Navy *is* ready."[90]

Knox was angry and embarrassed, but his faith in naval preparedness was not shaken. Horton spoke of a local security matter in the United States which could be serious, of course. Knox was completely confident, however, that war plans were well worked out and that the seagoing Navy would respond impressively and effectively when war came.

With war imminent, Knox nevertheless ceased to worry about Pearl Harbor. In November, he had been concerned about menacing Magic messages which indicated that Pearl Harbor had been divided into specific areas so that Japanese observers could precisely report ship locations. He had sent his naval aide to ask Admiral Turner if Admiral Kimmel was reading the same messages that high officials in Washington were seeing. "Of course he is," Turner told the aide. "He has the same 'magic' setup we have." But because Turner had been misinformed on this point by the Chief of Naval Communications, both he and Knox were unaware that Kimmel was not getting the Magic messages.[91]

As the first week of December drew to a close, Knox had no sense of any threat to Pearl Harbor. On Friday, the day after his unpleasant encounter with Horton, he attended a briefing conducted by the Chief of Naval Intelligence. The location of the large Japanese convoy which everyone present had been following was plotted on a large chart as nearing the Malay peninsula. Other Japanese warships, including aircraft carriers, were posted on the map, but none was anywhere close to Pearl Harbor.[92]

The next day, Saturday, 6 December, at a similar briefing, Knox asked the group, "Gentlemen, are they going to hit us?" A high ranking officer answered quickly, "No, Mr. Secretary, they are not ready for us yet; they are going to hit the British." No one in the room disagreed.[93]

That evening a Navy security officer took the decoded thirteen parts of an important fourteen-part Magic message to Knox at his Wardman Park Hotel apartment. Knox read the message privately and returned it to the courier. Clearly the intercepted Japanese message did not alarm him, for he soon concluded arrangements with John O'Keefe to fly together to Chicago the next day on newspaper business.[94]

The next morning, Sunday, 7 December, Americans read in their morning newspapers that Knox had made his first annual report to the President. "I am proud to report," he wrote, "that the American people may feel fully confident in their navy." And he stated flatly, "On any comparable basis, the United States Navy is second to none."[95] While such statements may have seemed exaggerations to many, Knox believed them wholeheartedly, a belief which contributed greatly toward making that particular day one of the most miserable of his life.

Early on 7 December, Knox postponed his plans to fly to Chicago and instead went to the State Department to meet with Hull and Stimson. There the three Secretaries read part 14 of the long dispatch each had seen the night before. The message ended current negotiations between the Japanese and the United States, but neither broke off diplomatic relations nor made any particular threat. While the three secretaries puzzled over what was going on in the Far East, another Magic message was decoded that revealed that the Japanese envoys were to deliver the 14-part communication to Hull at 1 p.m. that day. Some who read this message in the Navy Department realized that at 1 p.m. in Washington dawn was rising over Hawaii. That important observation did not get to the three conferees at the State Department, who were busy working out plans about what the President should say to Congress when the Japanese attacked British possessions, a contingency that then seemed to be an immediate certainty. Their conference was interrupted by a secretary's informing Hull that the Japanese ambassador and his special envoy had asked for an appointment for 1 p.m., but the menacing significance of the time requested for the meeting did not dawn on anyone present. Stimson recorded in his diary that Hull was "certain that the Japs were planning some deviltry and we were all wondering where the blow would strike."[96]

When Knox left the State Department about noontime he was met by John O'Keefe, who had been waiting to see if their trip to Chicago was to take place. As the two men drove to Main Navy, Knox commented, "I don't know John. The situation is serious. The Japanese are threatening near Indo-China. Maybe I ought not to take this trip." O'Keefe waited while Knox conferred in his office with Admirals Stark and Turner.[97]

About 1:30, Knox, Stark, and Turner came out of Knox's office when a communication watch officer hurried into the suite and handed Knox a message which had just been received from the West Coast. Knox read, "Air Raid Pearl Harbor. This is not drill." Unbelieving, Knox exclaimed to Stark, "My God, this can't be true. It must mean the Philippines!" Stark studied the note for a moment and replied, "No sir. This is Pearl."[98]

Knox rushed into his office and seized the phone which was connected directly with the White House. When he asked to speak with Roosevelt, the operator told him no calls were being taken for him. He exploded with a volley of strong language that convinced the operator that the call was urgent, and she connected him with the President, who was lunching with Harry Hopkins in the Oval Study. "Mr. President," Knox began, "It looks like the Japanese have attacked Pearl Harbor." "NO!" Roosevelt replied with a mixture of surprise and relief in his voice,[99] and immediately called Knox, Stimson, and Hull to the White House. By the time they had assembled, telephone reports from Admiral Stark began to reveal the magnitude of the disaster which was taking place at Pearl Harbor. Knox paled when Stark telephoned the reported losses. By the end of the afternoon it seemed clear that every battleship of the main fleet in Hawaii was either sunk or damaged, that defending aircraft were shot to pieces on the ground, and that Japanese losses were very small.[100]

When the entire cabinet assembled at the White House that evening, Knox and Stimson exchanged the latest news of their services in whispers. The President then gave details about the losses in Hawaii. Later, when congressional leaders came in and were given the shocking information, Tom Connally, Chairman of the Senate Foreign Relations Committee, demanded to know why the Army and Navy had allowed such a calamity to occur. Knox, who could not answer the question, sat silent and embarrassed through Connally's barrage. Roosevelt then observed that it was no time for recriminations and turned to the question of the message he would give Congress the next day.[101]

When the President appeared before both houses of Congress on 8 December and asked for a declaration of war on Japan, Knox listened from a seat in the gallery. Some time during the speech Knox made up his mind "in a flash to go out there [to Pearl Harbor] and get the actual facts" of what had happened. When he proposed his trip to the President, he met only mild objections and quickly overrode them. The next morning he took off for Hawaii.[102]

Knox and a few aides arrived at Kaneohe Bay, Oahu, the morning of 11 December, where he caught his first glimpse of the damage caused by the Japanese. "The Air Station at Kanehoe Bay seems to have been completely devastated," he observed to his companions.[103]

Knox drove at once to the Royal Hawaiian Hotel, where Beatty had made reservations, because Knox did not believe it was proper for him to be the guest of any senior officer while he investigated what had happened. He was met there by Admiral Kimmel and proceeded immediately to Pearl Harbor, where he and his associates looked with dismay at the still smoking wreckage of warships and shore installations.

Knox charged his aides with the enormous task of evaluating the damage done the ships and making recommendations for repairs or disposal; what had happened to a warning message he believed had been sent from the Navy Department on 6 December; and discovering why Army radar had failed to detect the approaching Japanese aircraft. He told them to talk to as many officers and civil authorities as possible to determine what had gone wrong. Damage assessment was quickly accomplished, but the 6 December warning message could not be found, and no one wanted to talk about the failure of radar to pick up the attacking planes. Knox was distressed by the lack of preparedness he found on the part of both the Army and Navy, and he was annoyed by the indecision of Kimmel and his staff over the matter of sending a relief task force to Wake Island.[104]

After thirty-two busy hours during which no one slept much, Knox and his colleagues left for Washington. On the flight across the Pacific, Knox wrote out the results of his interviews and observations. During the flight the report was typed. Immediately upon reaching Washington on the evening of 14 December, Knox rushed it to the White House.[105]

"The Japanese air attack on the island of Oahu," the report began, "was a complete surprise to both the Army and the Navy." The attack succeeded "due to a lack of a state of readiness" by both branches of the service. Both Admiral Kimmel and General [Walter C.] Short agreed that this was "entirely true," the report continued, "Neither Army or Navy Commandants in Oahu regarded such an attack as at all likely, because of the danger which such a carrier borne attack would confront in view of the preponderance of [American] naval strength in Hawaiian waters."

Knox found that the Army had been mainly concerned about sabotage, the Navy about submarine attacks. The report summarized the Japanese methods of assault, the weapons and ammunition employed, the damage sustained by both sides, and the salvage operations under way. He included details regarding the failure of the Army's radar reporting system which he had discovered when he had given an Army major a ride from Texas to Washington. (The major, carrying a special report from Hawaii to Stimson, had shared the information with Knox.) The report ended with a "Summary and Recommendation" that suggested that the use of the Pearl Harbor base "be restudied" and complimented the Japanese on "the meticulous detail of their plans of attack, and their courage, ability and resourcefulness in executing and pressing home their operations."[106]

Knox stayed at the White House only long enough to present his report. After he left, the President studied the account and then outlined a press release based upon it. The next morning the two men went over the draft press release together and discussed what Knox should reveal at his press conference. Knox used Roosevelt's notes almost verbatim in writing the press release and later edited a copy of the release for his use as a script when he went before newsreel cameras. At the crowded press conference on the afternoon of 15 December he was frank but resisted all questions that went any length beyond the press release he had handed out at the start of the session.[107]

The day after Knox returned, he and Stimson agreed "not to get into an interdepartmental scrap, but to keep the thing on a basis of no recrimination." Both men lived up to this resolve, yet since Knox's trip was major news and the information he released focused on the naval features of the tragedy, the Navy's part of the debacle became the center of public attention. Though Stimson publicly admitted the Army's shortcomings at a press conference he held later, his statements received little attention.[108] Because the public did not realize that the security of Pearl Harbor was the Army's responsibility, it did not comprehend the magnitude of the Army's failure in Hawaii. Inadvertently, Knox was the source of the popular notion that the Navy was somehow solely to blame for the failures at Pearl Harbor.

Knox's press release indicated that the President would have the Pearl Harbor calamity investigated immediately. Within two days, Supreme Court Justice Owen J. Roberts agreed to be the chairman and civilian representative on a five-man board including two high-ranking officers from each service. Knox told this commission that he was convinced that the Pearl Harbor tragedy was caused primarily by the failure of Admiral Kimmel and General Short to plan properly and respond realistically to the warnings sent them.[109] Roberts and his colleagues apparently accepted Knox's hypothesis as a conclusion at the start of their investigation. Knox, therefore contributed significantly and unintentionally to the ineffectiveness of their effort.

After consulting the President, Knox relieved Kimmel of his command and ordered Admiral Chester W. Nimitz to Hawaii as his successor. He had worked closely with Nimitz who, as Chief of the Bureau of Navigation, had impressed him as "a vigorous type in whom I have utter confidence."[110]

At the same time, Knox and Roosevelt decided to move the post of Commander in Chief, United States Fleet, from Hawaii to Washington and appoint Admiral King to the command. "Lord, how I need him," Knox wrote to a friend about King. "One of my most important jobs is to transform the mental attitude of a good deal of the Navy from a defensive to an offensive posture," he continued, for he saw in the stern, efficient admiral the type of personality and experience required for such a challenge.[111]

While the Pearl Harbor tragedy pained Knox greatly, it also brought him a great sense of relief. "I am personally glad that actual war has been declared instead of this half in, half out position we have been in for so long a time," he wrote his sister, Emma Fairfield, on 8 December.[112] The restraints which had bound him and the Navy because the United States had not been a full belligerent vanished with the falling of the Japanese bombs.

A major change took place for both Knox and the Navy during the last days of 1941 when Admiral King, CinCUS, (later changed to CominCh) moved into his headquarters on the third deck of Main Navy, for King was the strong, able, respected, experienced, and aggressive leader Knox wanted. However, King's relations with the Chief of Naval Operations, located in the same building, posed a problem. Anticipating difficulty, Roosevelt had prescribed the duties of CominCh and of CNO in Executive Order 8984, dated 20 December 1941. When the order failed to serve its intended purpose, Knox directed the General Board to redefine the duties of the two offices, and with King discussed the problem with the President. In Executive Order 9096, dated 12 March 1942, Roosevelt solved the problem by stating that the duties of both offices "may be combined and devolve upon one officer. He relieved Stark as CNO, appointed him as Commander, United States Naval Forces, Europe and made King both CominCh and CNO.

After Knox signed Stark's new orders, on 2 March, he wrote his good friend that "No one in the Navy has been a greater assistance and help to me in my efforts to be a constructive and helpful force in the Navy than you." Indeed, under Stark's tutelage, Knox had come to understand and to influence the Navy Department as much as any Navy Secretary ever did. Because his civilian associates had also gained experience, he was in a strong position when the nation plunged into war. His major contribution during the war was the effective coordination he developed between the civilian secretaries and the service heads of the Navy, the teamwork essential to successful prosecution of the war.

The first weeks after Pearl Harbor were horrible for America and its Navy. In the Pacific, Guam and Wake Island were lost within days. The Japanese stormed the Philippines, assaulted the Malay peninsula, crippled British seapower by sinking the *Prince of Wales* and the *Repulse* in the South China Sea, and drove the bulk of America's Asiatic Fleet to the Dutch East Indies. In the

Atlantic, although escorts were hard at work, there were not enough warships to combat German submarines off the American coast.

Starting on 12 January 1942, when a British steamer was torpedoed and sunk three hundred miles off Cape Cod, the slaughter of merchant ships accelerated through the winter and spring from the Gulf of St. Lawrence to the tip of Florida. Ships were sunk within sight of spectators on shore and beaches were fouled with oil and debris.

On 26 February 1942 an alarmed and angry Roosevelt signed an executive order directing Knox "to protect vessels, harbors, ports and waterfront facilities," adding that it was a "real disgrace" to have only seven patrol boats, as distinguished from destroyers, between Eastport, Maine, and Key West. He acknowledged that King's decision to put Admiral Adolphus Andrews in complete charge of the Atlantic coastal patrol "is good but it has taken a hell of a long time to get it done," and he suggested that the Coast Guard, which knew "infinitely more" about coastal patrol work and harbor protection than did the Navy, be "put in charge of this work on the whole of the East coast."[113] On the next day Knox reported that he had placed the Coast Guard in charge of protecting shipping and waterfront property. Still, success in the antisubmarine war was slow in coming. Antisubmarine ships and aircraft were in short supply until late summer, and Knox felt the sting of criticism not only from Roosevelt, but from congressmen, the press, and the public as well.

During the dismal first half of 1942, Knox was also criticized because he endorsed the Anglo-American decision to give priority to the war in Europe. Some newspapers pointed out that the Navy's main war would be in the Pacific and that he therefore should consider Japan as the number one enemy, a view held by many naval officers and also by Wendell Willkie. Such criticism, the steady flow of bad news, and awesome wartime duties combined to reverse Knox's practice of maintaining close contact with Washington's reporters. He held only two press conferences in January and one each in February, March, and April. Between 7 April and 2 September he called only one, on 7 June, to announce the Navy's victory at Midway. In September, however, he reverted to two press conferences a week, a practice he held to fairly consistently for the rest of his tenure. In September, too, he resumed speechmaking.

By late summer of 1942, Knox seemed to sense that the worst of the war was behind him. On 7 August, Marines had landed in the Solomon Islands and he knew that the invasion of North Africa was only weeks away. He had no illusions that a long hard war was not still ahead, but he was certain of eventual victory.

With the nation at war, Knox's relations with Roosevelt became slowly but definitely more remote. Before Pearl Harbor, he had often conferred with the President four or five times a week; six months later he visited the White

House only four or five times a month, if that often. King, in charge of conducting the military side of the war, was frequently with Roosevelt and always accompanied him to the several international summit meetings. Knox was a part of Roosevelt-Churchill sessions only when the Prime Minister came to Washington, except that he was invited to Quebec for the last two days of the August 1943 conference. However, at none of these meetings did he play a role of any consequence.

At the weekly State-War-Navy meetings, Knox agreed with Hull and Stimson that it was difficult for them to get to see Roosevelt. Moreover, Stimson thought that Knox was out of touch with the military plans "of his own people."[114] While Marshall kept Stimson completely informed, King did not fully apprise Knox of his plans because he feared that he would divulge sensitive information. In fact King occasionally called security slips to Knox's attention.

Though Knox complained to Stimson about their mutual lack of touch with the President, he never complained to Roosevelt. He understood that military leaders in war time naturally gained more influence than at other times, and he was willing to allow the admirals to exercise freely their professional judgment and authority over such matters as plans, training, and operations. In matters where civilian experience applied, such as procurement, civil personnel, and public relations, he fought to preserve the power of the civilian secretaries. In this effort the President was his ultimate and necessary ally.

For Knox, the main challenge to civilian authority came from King. Although they liked and respected each other and worked well together, by the summer of 1943 Knox came to resent King's frequent efforts to diminish civilian influence in the Navy and even to diminish his prerogatives. Before King had been in Washington a month, Knox had turned aside his effort to obtain from Congress a separate discretionary fund which would have enlarged his freedom of action.[115] Obviously Knox was not worried by this small effort to obtain more power, since shortly afterward he endorsed the proposal that King become CNO as well as being CominCh. Moreover, he realized that King's continuing quest for even more strength stemmed from his conviction that naval officers were best fitted to run the navy, especially in wartime, not from personal ambition. Nevertheless, his expanded authority would diminish the influence of the civilian secretariat. The first argument came when he made Forrestal his main target.[116]

During January 1942, while Stark was still CNO, Knox created the Office of Procurement and Material and placed it under Forrestal's jurisdiction. Until then material procurement had been a stepchild under CNO, and it needed strong, separate attention and leadership. Under Forrestal and OP&M's immediate director, Vice Admiral Samuel M. Robinson, the agency functioned effectively and aggressively. Soon after King became CNO he attempted to get procurement back under direct military control, and in May 1942 he wrote a plan entitled "Reorganization of the Navy Department" that transferred "the general administrative control of the material activities of all the shore establishments" from Forrestal to himself. Forrestal thereupon objected to Knox, pointing out that "operations has obviously all it can do in its own field."[117]

Although Roosevelt vetoed King's plan, King proceeded to put part of it into effect. On 27 May he directed the creation of two new positions: Assistant Chief of Naval Operations (Personnel) and Assistant Chief of Naval Operations (Material). The second post was to be filled by the Chief of OP&M, Admiral Robinson, and therefore place procurement under King rather than Forrestal.

Roosevelt soon found out about the directive and sent for King and Knox so that he could express his dissatisfaction personally. Afterward, Knox tactfully wrote King, "Don't you think in the light of our talk with the President yesterday that you should suspend or cancel the attached orders at least until the President makes that chart of organization he told us he was going to work on this weekend?"[118] King rescinded a part of his plan and, later, after Roosevelt demanded it, he cancelled the whole scheme.

Roosevelt then wrote Knox that he was "disturbed" by the incident and that Knox should scrutinize all directives issued during the last month. The more the President thought about the matter the more "outrageous" it became. He was convinced, he told Knox, that those who had participated were "old enough to know that you are the Secretary of the Navy and that I am Commander-in-Chief of the Navy."[119]

A year later, King drafted another reorganization plan and shared it with Knox. Knox immediately passed it along to his civilian associates and his trusted Chicago friend, Rawleigh Warner, to whom he wrote, "I want to retain exclusively to myself the delegation of the duties of the several civilian secretaries."[120] Since the new proposal diminished the authority of the civilian secretaries, King's aggressiveness in this matter alarmed Knox. When he wrote Warner ten days later, he reported, "The Navy reorganization plan has run into a snag which will considerably delay it and possibly postpone it until after the war is over."[121] The snag included objections not only from the civilian secretariat but also from the bureau chiefs. When Roosevelt reviewed the proposal, he too, protested. "Tell Ernie once more," the President wrote in longhand, "no reorganization of the Navy Department set-up during the war. Lets win it first."[122] Knox was delighted. He gave the note to his wife and asked her to save it. It was a very important note, he explained to her, since "Admiral King is trying to take my job away from me."[123]

When Knox received the President's memorandum, King and Roosevelt were attending the Quebec conference. A few days later the President unexpectedly invited Knox to join him. There Knox expressed his unhappiness with King by proposing that the Admiral as CominCh move to the Pacific and take personal command of the coming Pacific offensive. Surprised, King countered that his presence in the Pacific was entirely unnecessary since Nimitz was "carrying out his duties admirably."[124]

When King returned to Washington he tried to find out why Knox had challenged him at Quebec. Ultimately he blamed Forrestal, who probably did play a role in convincing Knox that King's reorganization plans always threatened civilian authority. When bureau chiefs, the President, and others agreed that King threatened civil supremacy, Knox's impetuous—and unsuccessful—solution to the problem was to get King out of Washington.

During the next few months the relationship between Knox and King was cool, sometimes excessively formal. Knox's suggestion that King take his command to sea was a reflection of a counterattack on his power in which some civilian executives proposed that the CNO and CominCh offices be separated. King and his immediate subordinates responded by continuing to draft proposals which would preserve or increase his authority. By January 1944 Knox was out of patience with King. "After reading them all [reorganization plans]," he wrote the Admiral in pique, "I am oppressed by the fact that evidently I cannot get across to anyone what I want and what the President and I agree should be done. First, [there should] not be any reorganization of the Navy Department." He then went on to explain a proposal that would reduce rather than increase King's authority, concluding that "it is not contemplated that either you or the Chief of Naval Logistics will take over [the] entire management and control of the Navy Department. That will remain as hitherto, just where it is now—in the hands of the Secretary of the Navy."[125] The whole controversy was passed directly to Forrestal, who succeeded Knox when he died three months later.

Knox and King also disagreed on how much current naval information should be released to newsmen and for public relations. Some people in the Navy Department believed that if King could have his way the Navy would issue but one communique at the end of the war that merely said "We won."[126] Such an allegation was an exaggeration, for King was well aware of the need for a good press. From time to time he gave a group of selected reporters authoritative background on current operations. Although Paul Leach of the *Chicago Daily News* was one of the chosen group, it is possible that Knox was not aware of these meetings. Knox's free wheeling press conferences contrasted greatly with King's restrained approach.

Knox had difficulty over public relations not only with King and other officers, but with reporters as well. On the very day Knox announced the exhilirating news of the Navy's victory at Midway, the *Chicago Tribune* published a sensational story which, among other revelations, listed the Japanese ships which had participated in the battle. The secret list had been picked up by a *Tribune* correspondent aboard a Navy ship in the Pacific and sent to Chicago without being seen by Navy censors. Its publication set off wrathful verbal explosions within the Navy. Though some officers were culpable for leaving a secret document unguarded and the correspondent violated regulations regarding the dispatch of classified information, the greatest potential damage from the story lay in the possibility that the Japanese would realize that American cryptographers had broken their naval operations codes.[127]

After some hesitation, Knox decided that Stanley Johnson, the author of the story, and his publisher should be prosecuted, and he urged Attorney General Anthony Biddle to call a grand jury to investigate the affair. Biddle made it clear to Knox that in order to prove that harm had been done to the national security it would be necessary to tell the jury that Americans had broken the Japanese code. Knox told Biddle to go ahead. However, shortly after the proceedings started in August, and after several "extended consultations" with naval officials, he called Biddle and told him that information about the Japanese codes could not be revealed. His apologies did little to calm Biddle's anger over being let down, and Biddle's wrath only increased Knox's frustration and anger over the incident when the grand jury refused to indict anyone.[128]

Repercussions over the Johnson dispatch episode reached into both houses of Congress. Senator C. Wayland Brooks of Illinois denounced the grand jury investigation against his main supporting newspaper as a vicious, malicious attack instigated by Knox to assure his defeat. Representative Clare Hoffman of Michigan introduced a resolution calling for an investigation of Knox to see if he was using his official position for the advantage of his own newspaper. Admiral Arthur J. Hepburn, who had directed Navy public relations for almost a year, immediately sent Hoffman a copy of a directive Knox had issued in February that ordered that "under no circumstances" would *Chicago Daily News* representatives "receive any more favorable treatment" than other correspondents.[129] Nothing came of Hoffman's resolution, and the entire matter was soon eclipsed by other more important events.

Knox did not let the Johnson dispatch fiasco put him on the defensive. Indeed, in September 1942, the month after the case was closed, he resumed biweekly press conferences for the first time since Pearl Harbor. During the controversy, but unrelated to it, Admiral Hepburn left the directorship of public relations to become Chairman of the General Board. He was replaced by

Captain Leland P. Lovette, who had commanded a destroyer division at Pearl Harbor before coming to Washington as the associate director of public relations. As an author in his own right, he understood the need for as generous a press policy as possible. An experienced naval commander who understood the need for security of sensitive information, he served Knox well for almost two years. In October 1942, Knox told Stimson that he was moving to lessen Admiral King's influence over Navy publicity since King "had been rather narrow and shortsighted about it."[130] In December, Knox resumed in a limited way the use of periodical articles over his own name to publicize Navy activities.

Forrestal was the practitioner of one very effective publicity activity. He knew more members of Congress than any other individual in the upper echelons of the Navy Department, and entertained some of them weekly. With Knox's blessing he introduced them to naval heroes who shared their exploits with the delighted legislators. This practice, coupled with all of Knox's other publicity efforts, was certified as successful by Robert A. Lovett, Assistant Secretary of War for Air, who in early 1943 told Stimson that the Navy's public relations "were now getting ahead of us."[131]

All during 1943 Knox and King continued to differ over what news should be released. In October, when relations between the two men were cool because of the Admiral's efforts at Navy Department reorganization earlier in the year, Knox asserted his prerogatives in a forceful fashion. On 2 October King recommended to him in a memorandum "that until Japan has capitulated, no book or article dealing with our submarine combat operations be published."[132] Knox's stinging reply went well beyond the scope of King's memo. He ordered King to cancel any orders "promptly" which might have placed anyone in intelligence in a position of authority over publicity. "To put the matter bluntly and briefly," he concluded, "I know I have the authority and I know I have the experience to handle, without assistance, the question of Public Relations of the Navy. I propose to assume that responsibility and exercise that authority with the sole provision that questions of security will be dealt with by your representative. . . . "[133] King had no choice but to follow Knox's orders, and in early November he appeared conciliatory when the question of more liberal treatment of the news concerning merchant shipping activity was presented to him. In a memorandum to Knox he announced, "I am in accord with such a policy but feel that since the Navy is responsible for the safe conduct of convoys the implementation of information pertaining to such convoys should be controlled by the Secretary of the Navy."[134] Differences between Knox and King over publicity remained, making Knox more cautious about King than he might otherwise have been. However, for the rest of his tenure Knox dominated public relations policy.

Knox's dedication to personal supervision of publicity was matched by his conviction that he and the other civilian secretaries should "get out in the field and see actual conditions." Such trips, he believed, enabled him and his associates to "come back and act far more intelligently" when making decisions. They also were "a definite aid" to the morale "of the men out in the field."[135] In keeping with a practice begun in World War I "that I do not send men where I don't go myself,"[136] he visited Guadalcanal while it was still an active battle front and an army command post in Italy shortly after the Allies invaded that nation. From 7 December 1941 until his death in April 1944, his flight log recorded that he spent 802 hours in the air and flew 141,000 miles. Time and mileage by land transportation went unrecorded.

Knox's first trip away from Washington in 1942 was an eleven-day inspection tour of naval installations on the Gulf of Mexico and the West Coast in early May. His longest and most important journey of 1942, to Brazil, cast him in the role of goodwill ambassador. After Brazil declared war on Germany and Italy in August, it placed its Navy under the operational control of the U.S. Navy, which made logical the selection of the Secretary of the Navy as an official visitor to that nation.

Taking his friend Rawleigh Warner with him, Knox left Washington on 23 September for a trip which lasted seventeen days. On his way out and back he stopped to inspect most of the Navy's important bases in the Caribbean. He arrived in Rio de Janeiro on the twenty-ninth and was greeted enthusiastically by both Brazilian officialdom and the public. He contributed to good relations and cooperation between the two nations, and he was proud of his efforts.

Between 9 January and 1 February 1943, Knox made the longest and most strenuous trip of his career, from Washington to the battlefronts of the South Pacific. Once again Warner was in his party, to which Adlai Stevenson was added. The group traveled to Hawaii aboard the Honolulu Clipper, then continued with Admiral Nimitz to the South Pacific. The PB2Y-2 flying boat carrying Knox, Nimitz, Warner, and Stevenson lost power in one engine during takeoff and lost its port pontoon as it pancake landed in Pearl Harbor. The craft listed badly and the distinguished passengers were ordered through a hatch in the top of the cabin and directed to crawl along the starboard wing to help bring the flying boat to an even keel. Stevenson recorded in his diary that everyone was "sort of gay," with Knox "enjoying it thoroughly."[137]

An hour and a half later they took off in another aircraft for Midway Island and a full day of inspections. They then flew south to Espiritu Santo, with stops at Johnson Island, Canton Island, and Suva Island.

At Suva, Knox left Stevenson and Warner behind and with Nimitz, Vice Admiral William F. Halsey, Commander of the South Pacific Area and Force, and Admiral John McCain, the newly-appointed chief of the Bureau of Aeronautics, and Captain Frank Beatty, his aide, he traveled to Guadalcanal, which was still an active battle ground. Japanese intelligence apparently found out about the presence of the party of high ranking officials and sent over bombers. "The night bombing the night we were at Guadalcanal lasted from 8:30 in the evening until 3:40 in the morning," Knox later wrote his former naval aide. "During its progress, Nimitz, Halsey, McCain and I occupied the same little dugout and it was a lot of fun."[138]

The journey home threaded its way from Efate to Havannah Harbor, Noumea, Pago Pago, Upolo, and Canton Island. Stevenson marveled at Knox's stamina and his unflagging enthusiasm for speaking to groups of sailors or Marines. After 23,000 miles of travel in twenty-four days the tired party landed in Washington. "I think the trip was highly useful," Knox commented in his letter to his former aide, "and Nimitz and Halsey are sure that it contributed materially to morale to have the Secretary of the Navy go to the actual scene of the fighting."[139]

Knox's next trip, an early summer tour of the Gulf and Pacific coasts, covered many of the same installations he had visited a year earlier. One highlight of this trip was his speech at a War Bond rally in the Hollywood Bowl before a crowd of 22,000 people; another thrill came when he took a flight in a blimp around San Francisco Bay.

Knox's last major journey was a combination good will and front line inspection tour through the British Isles to the North African-Mediterranean theater of operations in September and October 1943. Captain Lovette and Captain Lyman S. Perry, his aide, were his only traveling companions on this trip. On 16 September he landed at Prestwick, Scotland, where a special train was waiting to take him to England. He inspected an American naval installation in Northern Ireland and the great British naval base at Scapa Flow. In London he was feted at a round of luncheons and dinners, and on 25 September he called on King George VI. In company with the First Lord of the Admiralty, A. V. Alexander, he visited Nelson's historic ship, HMS *Victory*, which, when he came over the side, broke out the personal flag of the American Secretary of the Navy, an honor that thrilled him. Just before leaving England he journeyed to Chequers, country home of the Prime Minister, where he spent the evening in conversation with Churchill and Lord Louis Mountbatten and stayed the night. "The past 10 days have been truly hectic," he wrote Mrs. Knox, "but most instructive and interesting."[140]

From the United Kingdom Knox flew to North Africa, then on to Sicily and Italy. He arrived in Italy just three weeks after the American invasion at Salerno and was conducted by Lieutenant General Mark Clark to a command post near the front. "I had a good chance to look over the ground," he told reporters later. "It's tough territory to fight over." Next he boarded a motor torpedo boat and watched the battle for Naples from the sea. He reported that he "had a chance to see Naples while the Germans were busy putting finishing touches on demolitions, blowing up things all over the place."[141]

He returned home by flying the South Atlantic to Brazil, where he inspected bases being built by joint American-Brazilian efforts. After several stops in the Caribbean he returned to Washington, having covered over 22,000 miles in twenty-four days.

At his press conference on 10 October he featured praise for American-British cooperation both in the Atlantic and the Mediterranean. He complimented General Dwight D. Eisenhower, whom he had met in North Africa, calling his dexterity in handling diverse forces "an outstanding achievement." He also lauded the skill and courage of the Navy men who handled landing craft in amphibious operations. In the fashion that was customary with him, he summed up his journey to a friend in very general terms saying, "The whole trip was a pretty strenuous one, [and] well worth while."[142]

Knox had always been in robust health, but the pace of his travels and the strain of his Washington duties, relieved by only a two-week vacation in August 1943, took their toll of his stamina. In January 1944, he had an attack of flu complicated by sinus trouble. Surprised when he did not recover rapidly, he yielded to his associates' suggestions and in February, flew to Cuba for a relaxing week in warm sunshine. When he returned he admitted to a friend, "I am still a little shaky, and I am, therefore, limiting myself to the amount of work I do, and am cutting out all evening engagements."[143]

When John O'Keefe saw Knox in March, he noticed how tired he was and suggested that he take a week off and come back to the *Chicago Daily News*. The suggestion was so tempting that Knox could not resist it. For the last week in March he forgot the cares of Washington and happily played the role of editor and publisher of his paper again. While he was in Chicago he had a complete physical examination by his personal physician. The doctor told him his condition was excellent except that his blood pressure was a little higher than usual.[144]

On 19 April Knox's lifelong business partner and friend of more than forty years, John Meuhling, died. It was with great sorrow that Knox traveled to Manchester, New Hampshire, for the funeral. While attending the service on Sunday, the twenty-second, Knox felt ill but started his return to Washington that evening. He flew as far as New York and stopped for the night; he complained of indigestion but he actually had suffered a mild heart attack. The next day he claimed he felt better and took a morning train to Washington. On Tuesday morning he went to his office, but after two hours he felt so ill that he went home. That afternoon he suffered a severe heart attack. Navy physicians decided not to move him from his home, and as they arranged an oxygen tent around his bed he commented to his wife, "This looks serious, Annie."[145]

Indeed, Knox's condition was very serious. The Boston heart specialist, Dr. Paul Dudley White, was called to his bedside for consultation. John O'Keefe arrived from Chicago and such greatly concerned old friends as Ralph Bard called at his home. At 1:08 p.m. on the twenty-eighth he died while his wife and a few friends were at his bedside.

The nation was as unprepared for Knox's death as were his family and friends. Roosevelt, recovering from an illness himself and recuperating in Georgia, was saddened by the news. "Truly he put his country first," the President declared to a mourning nation. "We shall greatly miss his ability and friendship." Admiral King, who had always admired and respected him, observed, "The Nation has lost a great patriot; the Navy a great leader." Bard probably said that which would have pleased him most, "He was a casualty of the War. He fell in the line of duty."[146]

Flags were brought to half mast, not only in America but also on all British and Canadian ships. Dr. Fred S. Buschmeyer, pastor of Washington's Mount Pleasant Congregational Church and a friend of the Knoxes from Manchester days, was assisted by a Navy chaplain in conducting the funeral service on Monday afternoon, 1 May. Then, at Arlington National Cemetery, a Navy chaplain read the commital service; a bluejacket detachment fired three volleys; and a Navy bugler sounded taps.

Frank Knox was an able Secretary of the Navy. His specific achievements included the timely initiation of management surveys, the establishment and maintenance of effective public relations and news dissemination programs, and service as a traveling ambassador for the Navy Department to bases, fleets, and battlefronts.

Perhaps his most important success came in the intangible realm of effective leadership, for his leadership style was one of his outstanding strengths. Utterly devoid of jealousy, he allowed his often brilliant associates to operate freely and gave them his backing when it was needed. He labored hard to make both men in uniform and men in civilian clothes members of an effective team. Rawleigh Warner, his close personal friend and trusted adviser in organizational matters, wrote that "I believe Frank felt his greatest accomplishment in his Navy work was the coordination he effected in the top echelon between the civilian secretaries and the service heads of the Navy. He developed under great pressure what was undoubtedly the greatest teamwork ever achieved in the history of the Navy."[147]

Early in 1942 Knox had written Admiral Stark, "I came to this present task with little besides good intentions, energy and a desire to serve my country in a very grave crisis."[148] These readily acknowledged attributes along with his extensive business experience and his intense desire to provide intelligent and devoted leadership all contributed to his success as Secretary of the Navy. Admiral King, who gave praise only when it was merited, acknowledged Knox's remarkable achievement of mastering his difficult job under trying circumstances. "He understood the Navy, not only its problems, its achievements and its personnel, but its shortcomings," King declared the day Knox died. "He leaves us, secure in the knowledge that his energy and farsighted vision have been responsible, in great measure, [for the fact] that we are so far advanced on the road to victory."[149]

NOTES

1. Frank Knox to Frank Lowden, 14 Nov. 1936, Frank Lowden Papers, University of Chicago, Harper Memorial Library.
2. Knox to F. D. Roosevelt, 15 Dec. 1937, Franklin D. Roosevelt Papers, Franklin D. Roosevelt Library, Hyde Park, N. Y.
3. *Chicago Daily News*, 12 Mar. 1938.
4. *Ibid.*, 2, 7, 12 Sept. 1939.
5. Harold L. Ickes, *The Secret Diary of Harold Ickes*, 3 vols. (New York: Simon and Schuster, 1953–1954), 2:717–19, 3:16.
6. Knox to William Allen White, 25 Sept. 1939, William Allen White Papers, MDLC.
7. Knox, Memorandum of a Conversation with President Roosevelt on 10 Dec. 1939, at the White House, Frank Knox Papers, MDLC.
8. Interview with Mrs. Annie Reid Knox, 12 Aug. 1953.
9. Knox to Mrs. Knox, 5, 11 June 1940, Knox Papers; Louis Brownlow, *A Passion for Anonymity: Second Half* (Chicago: University of Chicago Press, 1958), pp. 445–46.
10. Interview with John O'Keefe, 15 Feb. 1954; Brownlow, *A Passion for Anonymity*, pp. 450–51.
11. *New York Times*, 21 June 1940.
12. Knox to Mrs. Knox, 6 July 1940, Knox Papers.
13. U.S. Senate, Committee on Naval Affairs, *Nomination of William Franklin Knox, Hearings*, 76th Cong., 3rd Sess. (Washington: GPO, 1940), pp. 12, 18.
14. *Ibid.*, pp. 20–22, 50–51.
15. Mrs. Knox to the writer, 12 June 1953.
16. *New York Times*, 21 June 1940.
17. Ickes, *Secret Diary*, 2:717.
18. Robert Greenhalgh Albion, "The Administration of the Navy, 1798–1945," in James Forrestal *et al, The Navy: A Study in Administration* (Chicago: Public Administration Service, 1946), p. 7.
19. Mrs. Knox to Knox, 11 July 1940, Knox Papers.
20. Ickes, *Secret Diary*, 3:334, 391.
21. Knox to Mrs. Knox, 14 July 1940, Rawleigh Warner to Mrs. Knox, 29 Mar. 1949, Knox Papers; *New York Times*, 23 Aug. 1940.

22. Frank Knox to Chiefs of All Bureaus, Boards and Offices, Navy Department, Headquarters, USMC, 23 Aug. 1940, copy in SNP but also published in Julius Augustus Furer, *Administration of the Navy Department in World War II* (Washington: GPO, 1959), p. 61.
23. Knox to Mrs. Knox, 14 July 1940, Knox Papers; Ickes, *Secret Diary*, 3:334.
24. U.S. House, Subcommittee of the Committee on Appropriations, *Supplemental Navy Department Appropriations Bill for 1943, Hearings*, 78th Cong., 1st Sess. (Washington: GPO, 1943), p. 49.
25. U.S. House, Subcommittee on Deficiencies of the Committee on Appropriations, *The Second Supplemental National Defense Appropriation, 1940, Hearings*, 76th Cong., 3rd Sess. (Washington: GPO, 1940), p. 5.
26. M. L. Deyo to Chiefs of Bureaus, Boards and Offices, Navy Department, Headquarters, USMC, 12 July 1940, SNP.
27. Knox to Walter Lippmann, 18 Dec. 1941, *ibid.*
28. Robert G. Albion and Robert H. Connery, *Forrestal and the Navy* (New York: Columbia University Press, 1962), pp. 61–62.
29. Knox to Mrs. Knox, 14 July 1940, Knox Papers.
30. John Morton Blum, ed., *From the Morgenthau Diaries: Years of Urgency, 1938–1941* (Boston: Houghton Mifflin, 1964), p. 177.
31. Ickes, *Secret Diary*, 3:291.
32. *Ibid.*; Blum, ed., *Morgenthau Diaries, 1938–1941*, pp. 177–78.
33. Stimson Diary, 2 Aug. 1940, Henry L. Stimson Papers, Yale University, Sterling Memorial Library; Ickes, *Secret Diary*, 3:291.
34. Stimson Diary, 2 Aug. 1940, Stimson Papers.
35. *New York Times*, 10 Aug. 1940.
36. Stimson Diary, 13, 23 Aug. 1940, Stimson Papers; Blum, ed., *Morgenthau Diaries, 1938–1941*, p. 180; Elliott Roosevelt, ed., *F.D.R.: His Personal Letters*, 4 vols. (New York: Duell, Sloan and Pearce, 1947–1950), 2:1052; Ickes, *Secret Diary*, 3:303–04; Cordell Hull, *The Memoirs of Cordell Hull*, 2 vols. (New York: Macmillan, 1948), 2:838.
37. Knox to Mrs. Knox, 28 Aug. 1940, Knox Papers; Hull, *Memoirs*, 2:838.
38. Knox to Mrs. Knox, 28 Aug. 1940, Knox Papers.
39. *Ibid.*; *Honolulu Star Bulletin*, 14 Sept. 1940.
40. *Honolulu Star Bulletin*, 14 Sept. 1940.
41. Knox to ADM James O. Richardson, 25 Sept. 1940; Knox to RADM Husband E. Kimmel, 25 Sept. 1940, SNP.
42. Knox to RADM Robert L. Ghormley, 16 Nov. 1940, Knox Papers.
43. Knox to Lincoln S. Ferris, 23 Oct. 1940; Knox to Bert Evans Dart, 23 Sept. 1940, SNP.
44. Statement of COL Frank Knox, SECNAV, 19 Aug. 1940, *ibid;* John O'Keefe to the writer, 25 Mar. 1965; *Chicago Daily News*, 19 Aug. 1940.
45. Knox to Roosevelt, 19 July 1940, Roosevelt Papers; Ickes, *Secret Diaries*, 2:352.
46. Knox to Roosevelt, telegram, 5 Nov. 1940, Roosevelt Papers; Annie Reid Knox, Journal, 6 Nov. 1941, Knox Papers; *Chicago Daily News*, 6 Nov. 1940.
47. Knox to Mrs. Knox, 17 Aug. 1941, Knox Papers.
48. Walter Johnson and Carol Evans, eds., *The Papers of Adlai E. Stevenson*, 4 vols. (Boston and Toronto: Little, Brown and Company, 1973–1974), 2:3.

49. Albion, "Administration of the Navy," 8–9.
50. Furer, *Administration of the Navy Department* 71–73.
51. *Ibid.*
52. Transcript, "Comments of Secretary Knox at the Hotel Willard, 31 July 1941, at the 1941 Navy Public Relations Conference," NHD:OA.
53. Knox to media representatives, 31 Dec. 1940, SNP.
54. Navy Department Press Release, "Statement of the Secretary of the Navy Knox, 7 Apr. 1941," Knox Papers; *New York Daily News*, 7 Apr. 1941; *New York Times*, 9 Apr. 1941.
55. Knox Press Conference, 26 Nov. 1941, SNP.
56. *Ibid.*, 23 Apr. 1941.
57. "Comments of Secretary Knox, 31 July 1941," NHD:OA: "Navy Press Branch," ANJ 79 (4 Oct. 1941):126.
58. Knox speech, 11 Nov. 1940, Knox Papers.
59. Knox speech, 14 Nov. 1940, *ibid.*
60. Stimson, Diary, 21 Apr. 1941, Stimson Papers.
61. *New York Times*, 2 July, 1941.
62. Felix Frankfurter to Knox, 2 July 1941, Walter Lippmann to Knox, 2 Oct. 1941, Knox Papers; Stimson Diary, 21 Apr. 1941, Stimson Papers; Ickes, *Secret Diary*, 3:563.
63. Knox to Roosevelt, 19 Apr. 1941, Roosevelt to Knox, 21 Apr. 1941, Roosevelt Papers.
64. Stimson, Diary, 3 Dec. 1940, Stimson Papers.
65. Knox to Roosevelt, 20 Dec. 1940, Roosevelt Papers.
66. U.S. House, Foreign Affairs Committee, *The Defense Aid Act of 1941, Hearings*, 77th Cong., 1st Sess. (Washington: GPO, 1941), pp. 157–58; U.S. Senate, Committee on Foreign Relations, *To Promote the Defense of the United States, Hearings*, 77th Cong., 1st Sess. (Washington: GPO, 1941), p. 215.
67. Stimson, Diary, 22 Apr., 5, 6 May 1941, Stimson Papers.
68. Annie Reid Knox, Record of Luncheons and Dinners, 29 Mar. 1941, Knox Papers; Knox Press Conference, 4 June 1941, SNP.
69. Stimson, Diary, 23 June 1941, Stimson Papers; Knox to Roosevelt, 23 June 1941, Roosevelt Papers.
70. Knox speech, 20 June 1941, Knox Papers; Ickes, *Secret Diary*, 3:563.
71. Stimson Diary, 21 July 1941, Stimson Papers.
72. David I. Walsh to Knox, 10 July 1941, SNP; Knox to Mrs. Knox, 13 July 1941, Knox Papers; *New York Times*, 12, 15 July 1941.
73. Kenneth S. Davis, *A Prophet in His Own Country: The Triumphs and Defeats of Adlai E. Stevenson* (New York: Doubleday, 1957), pp. 230–34.
74. Hull, *Memoirs*, 2:1047.
75. George C. Dyer, ed., *On the Treadmill to Pearl Harbor: The Memoirs of Admiral James O. Richardson* (Washington: GPO, 1973), pp. 379–80.
76. Stimson Diary, 2 Oct. 1940, Stimson Papers.
77. *Ibid.*
78. Dyer, ed., *Memoirs of Admiral Richardson*, pp. 425, 435.

79. U.S. Congress, *Hearings Before the Joint Committee on the Investigation on the Pearl Harbor Attack*, 79th Cong., 1st and 2nd Sess., 39 parts (Washington: GPO, 1945, 1946), pt. 8, 3895 ff. and pt. 9, 3935 ff.

80. *Ibid.*, pt. 1, 279-81.

81. Stimson, Diary, 22 Apr. 1941, Stimson Papers.

82. Knox to A. V. Alexander, 16 Oct. 1941, Knox Papers; *New York Times*, 25 Oct. 1941.

83. Knox to John Winant, 10 Nov. 1941, Knox Papers.

84. *Hearings on the Pearl Harbor Attack*, pt. 12, p. 165.

85. Stimson, Diary, 25 Nov. 1941, Stimson Papers.

86. *Hearings on the Pearl Harbor Attack*, pt. 16, p. 2224.

87. Stimson, Diary, 27, 28 Nov. 1941, Stimson Papers; Knox to Roosevelt, 29 Nov. 1941, SNP.

88. Knox Press Conference, 3 Dec. 1941, *ibid.*

89. See Ladislas Farago, *The Game of the Foxes* (New York: David McKay, 1971), pp. 561-62.

90. Bruce Catton, *The War Lords of Washington* (New York: Harcourt, Brace, 1948), pp. 9-12.

91. Frank E. Beatty, "Another Version of What Started War With Japan," USN-WCR 36 (28 May 1954):50; *Hearings on the Pearl Harbor Attack*, pt. 4, pp. 2019-20.

92. Beatty, "Another Version," 49.

93. *Ibid.* In this account ADM Beatty says he believes that the officer who spoke was ADM Richmond K. Turner. In an unpublished MS written in 1953, he says it was ADM Slack from CNO's office.

94. *Hearings on the Pearl Harbor Attack*, pt. 8, pp. 3902-03; interview with John O'Keefe, 15 Feb. 1954.

95. ARSN, 1941, p. 1.

96. *Hearings on the Pearl Harbor Attack*, pt. 8, pp. 3907-10, pt. 12, p. 245; Stimson, Diary, 7 Dec. 1941, Stimson Papers.

97. Interview with John O'Keefe, 15 Feb. 1954.

98. *Ibid.*, interview with John Dillon, 15 July 1959; *Hearings on the Pearl Harbor Attack*, pt. 8, p. 3556, pt. 19, p. 3556.

99. Interview with John Dillon, 15 July 1959.

100. Stimson, Diary, 7 Dec. 1941, Stimson Papers; Blum, ed., *Morgenthau Diaries, 1938-1941*, 3:1; Ickes, *Secret Diary*, 3:664.

101. Stimson, Diary, 2:664, Stimson Papers.

102. Knox to Albert Lasker, 20 Dec. 1941, SNP.

103. Frank E. Beatty, "Secretary Knox and Pearl Harbor," *National Review* 18 (13 December 1966):1263.

104. *Ibid.*; *Hearings on the Pearl Harbor Attack*, pt. 6, pp. 2835-36, pt. 8, p. 3815.

105. Beatty, "Knox and Pearl Harbor," 1264.

106. *Hearings on the Pearl Harbor Attack*, pt. 5, pp. 2338-45.

107. Knox Press Conference, 15 Dec. 1941, NIID:OA.

108. Stimson, Diary, 14 Dec. 1941, Stimson Papers; Beatty, "Another Version," 50.

109. Stimson, Diary, 16, 17 Dec. 1941, Stimson Papers.

110. Knox to Walter Lippmann, 18 Dec. 1941, SNP.
111. Knox to Rawleigh Warner, 23 Dec. 1941, Knox Papers.
112. Knox to Emma Fairfield, 8 Dec. 1941, SNP.
113. Roosevelt memorandum to Knox, 26 Feb. 1942, *ibid.*
114. Stimson, Diary, 21 July 1942, Stimson Papers.
115. ADM Ernest J. King to Knox, 27 Feb. 1943, NHD:OA.
116. Stimson, Diary, 28 Mar. 1943, Stimson Papers.
117. Memorandum, ADM Ernest J. King, 22 May 1942, cited in Albion and Connery, *Forrestal and the Navy*, pp. 97–98; Forrestal to Knox, 27 May 1942, cited in *ibid.*, p. 99. Furer, *Administration of the Navy Department*, pp. 163–64.
118. Knox to King, 10 June 1942, cited in Albion and Connery, *Forrestal and the Navy*, p. 100.
119. Roosevelt to Knox, 12 June 1942, cited in *ibid.*, pp. 100–01.
120. Knox to Rawleigh Warner, 11 May 1943, Knox Papers.
121. Knox to Warner, 21 May 1943, *ibid.*
122. Roosevelt to Knox, ca 12 Aug. 1943. Mrs. Knox mounted this memorandum on a piece of cardboard to emphasize its importance.
123. Interview with Mrs. Knox, 12 Aug. 1953.
124. Ernest J. King and Walter Muir Whitehill, *Fleet Admiral King: A Naval Record* (New York: W. W. Norton, 1952), p. 629.
125. Knox to King, 23 Jan. 1944, cited in Albion and Connery, *Forrestal and the Navy*, pp. 126–27.
126. King and Whitehill, *King*, pp. 652–53.
127. Francis Biddle, *In Brief Authority* (Garden City, N.Y.: Doubleday, 1962), p. 248.
128. *Ibid.*, pp. 249–51; John Tebbel, *An American Dynasty* (New York: Doubleday, 1947), pp. 163–65.
129. Knox to RADM Arthur J. Hepburn, 5 Feb. 1942, SNP.
130. Stimson Diary, 30 Oct. 1942, Stimson Papers.
131. *Ibid.*, 4 Feb. 1943, SNP.
132. King to Knox, 2 Oct. 1943, *ibid.*
133. Knox to King, 12 Oct. 1943, *ibid.*
134. King to Knox, 2 Nov. 1943, NHD:OA.
135. Knox Press Conference, 11 Sept. 1942, *ibid.*
136. Transcript of an interview of Knox by Critchell Rimington, 5 Apr. 1944, SNP.
137. Johnson and Evans, eds., *Papers of Adlai E. Stevenson*, 2:74.
138. Knox to CAPT Morton L. Deyo, 5 Mar. 1943, Knox Papers.
139. *Ibid.*; Johnson and Evans, eds., *Papers of Adlai Stevenson*, 2:77, 79, 83.
140. Knox to Mrs. Knox, 26 Sept. 1943, Knox Papers.
141. Knox Press Conference, 10 Oct. 1943, NHD:OA.
142. *Ibid.*; Knox to Chase Osborn, 20 Oct. 1943, Knox Papers.
143. Knox to D. J. Mahoney, 14 Feb. 1943, SNP.
144. Knox to Mrs. Knox, 29 Mar. 1944, Knox Papers.
145. Mrs. Knox to the writer, 27 June, 1954.
146. Statements by various notable persons, Navy Department Press Releases, 28 Apr. 1944, Knox Papers.

147. Warner to Mrs. Knox, 29 Mar. 1949, *ibid.*
148. Knox to Stark, 21 Mar. 1942, *ibid.*
149. Navy Department Press Release, "A Statement by ADM Ernest J. King, 28 Apr. 1944," *ibid.*

JAMES V. FORRESTAL

19 May 1944 – 17 September 1947

JOSEPH ZIKMUND

When President Franklin Delano Roosevelt on 9 May 1944 nominated James Vincent Forrestal to be the Secretary of the Navy, Arthur Krock of the *New York Times* spoke for the nation when he wrote that the appointment was "the best thing for the Navy, for the War, and for the country."[1]

Forrestal was born on 15 February 1892, in Matteawan, New York, near the Roosevelt estate at Hyde Park. His father, a building contractor and part-time realtor, also was active in local and state politics and in 1894 became the local postmaster.

James attended the public schools of Matteawan and then both Dartmouth and Princeton. At Princeton he became so deeply involved in getting out the *Daily Princetonian* that he left school when it became apparent that he lacked the necessary credits to graduate with his class. In rapid succession he held jobs with the New Jersey Zink Company, the American Tobacco Company, and the *New York World*. He joined the Wall Street firm of William A. Read and Company (later Dillon, Read and Company) in 1916. With the exception of a short tour as a naval airman during World War I, Dillon, Read and Company and Wall Street monopolized his attention for the next twenty-four years. His career with the company has been called "meteoric." He began as a bond salesman in the Albany area; by 1923 he was a partner in the firm; three years later he was made vice-president; and in 1938, at the age of forty-six, he became president. In financial circles his politics were considered "liberal," and he supported New Deal programs aimed at abuses of the securities exchange.

After ten years as one of Wall Street's most eligible bachelors, Forrestal married Miss Josephine Ogden, an editor of *Vogue* magazine, whose first marriage had ended in divorce. Although the two continued to lead separate—

perhaps even coldly independent—lives, they apparently remained fond of each other. Despite Forrestal's own misgivings, the couple had two children.[2]

Tiring of Wall Street, early in 1940 Forrestal let it be known that he was available for government service in the event of war, which he felt was inevitable. On 22 June 1940, after verifying his liberal credentials through Harry Hopkins, President Roosevelt appointed him an Administrative Assistant and assigned him the task of coordinating the efforts of the special cabinet committee working on plans for a Pan-American Union. The task was neither challenging nor suited to his particular administrative talents.[3] Six weeks later, Roosevelt nominated him to fill the newly-created post of Under Secretary of the Navy.

On 22 August, the day after he entered his new office, Secretary of the Navy Frank Knox assigned to Forrestal "contracts, tax, and legal matters; liaison with governmental agencies other than the Army, the Budget Bureau, and agencies concerned with labor"[4]- carteblanche to make his office the most important coordinating agency for procurement and material in the Navy Department.

By asking direct and often embarrassing questions when requested to authorize contracts, Forrestal realized that the Judge Advocate General's office cared only about the formal legality of the Navy's contractual agreements and that no one apparently was concerned about their financial soundness. On advice from H. Struve Hensel, a leading New York lawyer, Forrestal added a Procurement Legal Division to his office and asked Hensel to head it. Navy procurement henceforth became both more economical and more effective. During Forrestal's first fifteen months in the Department, August 1940 to December 1941, some 1,300 new ships were commissioned and naval personnel about tripled.[5]

During the last months before Pearl Harbor a number of interdepartmental boards wrestled with complex industrial problems attending military expansion. In January 1941 Roosevelt replaced the Office of Production Management with a new War Production Board and gave its chairman, Donald Nelson, the authority to control industrial mobilization. Among others, Forrestal opposed WPB's becoming a national "ministry of supply" for both services. In order to maintain regular cooperation between the Navy and the WPB, Knox created an Office of Procurement and Material (OP&M) and attached it to Forrestal's office. Through OP&M Forrestal could now coordinate the activities of the material bureaus, but not, however, without some friction with the Chief of Naval Operations, Admiral Ernest King, who wished to control procurement as well as operations.[6]

Plans for the Normandy Invasion and for the drive to the Japanese homeland were well underway when Roosevelt chose Forrestal to replace Frank

Knox, who died on 28 April 1944. Forrestal's primary concern as Secretary was to keep the momentum going. To get first-hand information about conditions in the war zones, early in 1944 he visited the Marshall Islands. Later that year he witnessed the Allied landings in Southern France. The last of these trips to see combat, in February 1945, began with an inspection tour of the naval base at Pearl Harbor, included a visit to Saipan just before Vice Admiral Richmond Kelly Turner jumped off for Iwo Jima, and ended with a visit with General Douglas MacArthur in Manila.

Among other reasons, fear that the invasion of Japan would be a long and bloody struggle led President Harry S. Truman to use the atomic bomb. Forrestal learned of the Manhattan Project sometime before 8 May 1945 through Under Secretary Ralph A. Bard, who was a member of an advisory committee under the direction of Secretary of War Henry L. Stimson. Bard, apparently speaking for Forrestal, was the only member of this interim committee to register a formal protest against dropping the bomb without prior warning.[7] Moreover, believing that retention of the Emperor was essential for a quick end to hostilities and for the re-creation of a stable Japanese government afterward, Forrestal opposed the doctrine of "unconditional surrender" and suggested the adoption of a policy that would cause Japan to yield before she was destroyed.[8]

Additional questions besides the Japanese surrender terms occupied Forrestal's mind; most important among these were Russian intervention in China and the distribution of captured Japanese mandated islands after the war. On these issues Forrestal directly opposed President Truman. Forrestal would keep Russia out of China while Truman wanted Russia to attack Japanese troops in China as soon as possible. Similarly, Forrestal would retain American control over former Japanese trust territories for use as advanced Pacific bases for the U.S. Navy, while the President wanted to convert these areas into a United Nations Trusteeship. These differences with the President, plus the question of Japanese surrender, motivated Forrestal to fly, uninvited, to the Potsdam Conference in July 1945 to press his views. Although Truman responded magnanimously to this rash, almost insubordinate act, in the end Forrestal's efforts had little direct impact on the decisions reached at the conference.[9] The Japanese surrender came after Russia invaded Manchuria and after the United States dropped atomic bombs on Hiroshima and Nagasaki.

The war over, Forrestal played a crucial role in the formation of America's postwar security policy. Speaking before the National Geographic Society on 31 March 1944, he argued that the United States should not totally disarm after hostilities ceased and quoted General Jan Smuts's saying that "peace not backed by a power remains a dream."[10] Three months later, at Princeton, he offered a seven point program:

1. Develop a strong, healthy domestic economy.
2. Remember that America can never isolate itself from European or world wars.
3. Maintain an attitude of world involvement which would enable us to aid our friends and neighbors if their peace and security were ever threatened.
4. Support an International Organization which could develop into an active guardian to watch over world peace.
5. Build a strong military force to protect us and to preserve the peace until the International Organization had time to become effective.
6. Develop the educational system within this country.
7. Get well educated people into the government.[11]

At the same time Forrestal began to have serious misgivings about future Soviet–American relations. As he put it on 2 September 1944:

> I find that whenever any American suggests that we act in accordance with the needs of our own security he is apt to be called a god-damned fascist or imperialist, while if Uncle Joe suggests that he needs the Baltic Provinces, half of Poland, all of Bessarabia and access to the Mediterranean, all hands agree that he is a fine, frank, candid and generally delightful fellow who is very easy to deal with because he is so explicit in what he wants.[12]

When trouble developed in the preparations for the San Francisco Conference, Forrestal's attention focused even more sharply on the Soviet Union. He was deeply impressed by Ambassador Averell Harriman's reports from Moscow, and he supported Harriman's pleas for a firm policy against Russian expansion into, or domination of, Central Europe.[13] Furthermore, his frustration with demands to "return to normalcy" showed through in testimony he offered a congressional committee during June 1945.

> America's readiness to accept her responsibilities in underwriting the peace of the world will be the surest guarantee of maintaining peace. . . . If Hitler and Mussolini had known that this country was prepared to fight, I do not believe [either] would have acted as he did. . . . I say quite respectfully to your committee and to the American people that if we do so act [with complacency] we scarcely deserve to survive as a nation.[14]

When asked whom we were going to fight, he responded: "We are going to fight any international ruffian who attempts to impose his will on the world by force. We should make that determination clear—by deeds as well as words."[15]

A tough question confronting government officials at the moment was not whether to demobilize, but how far to demobilize. While before Congress in June 1945 Forrestal tried to develop standards for creating a postwar Navy that would be consistent with his own activist approach to world affairs.

Rather than freezing the fleet at any one particular size, he preferred a flexible fleet concept that would vary the size and composition according to America's needs. For the minimum fleet he listed six criteria: to maintain American commitments to the United Nations; to overpower the strongest single enemy nation; to police and protect all other American interests and commitments overseas; for the coastal defense of the United States itself; for training purposes; and to support the other military services.[16]

In a nationwide radio speech in late August 1945, Forrestal further elaborated his views. He defined the Navy's mission as "control of the sea by whatever weapons . . . necessary." To achieve this goal, he suggested, the Navy would require 400 ships and some 8,000 aircraft (wartime peaks were about 1,200 ships and 29,000 aircraft).[17] The postwar Navy, he added, would consist of a number of mobile carrier task forces, each with a strong complement of Marines, that would cost between $2.8 and $4.0 billion annually.[18]

The war ended. Forrestal bowed to popular demands and promised to complete the transition to peace in twelve months, but he warned of the consequences likely to develop, saying that there is "no better way to ensure a third world war" than to demobilize too quickly.[19]

Before Congress in the spring of 1946 Forrestal defended naval estimates of $5.1 billion for Fiscal 1947. Responding to questions, he conceded that national security was expensive but he added, "'I cannot help but feel that if this country, in the present state of the world, goes back to bed, we don't deserve to survive."[20] The final naval appropriation came to $4.1 billion. Although demobilization was completed by 1 September 1946, the budgetary cut for Fiscal 1947 immediately affected naval preparedness. Navy strength as of 31 December 1946—which included 319 major combat ships, 724 lesser ships, 1,461 combat aircraft, 491,663 naval personnel, and 108,798 Marines—stood well below the goals Forrestal had outlined just eighteen months before, and he again predicted that American foreign policy would suffer accordingly.[21]

Forrestal often rebutted the most vocal critic of the "hard-line" policy toward Russia, Secretary of Commerce Henry Wallace. At a Jackson Day Dinner in 1946, for example, he attacked Wallace's pro-Soviet bias by identifying it with the head-in-the-sand posture that had characterized American policy after the First World War.[22] Wallace paid no attention and eventually was forced from the cabinet by President Truman. By coincidence, the Navy greeted Wallace's dismissal by sending an American fleet to the Mediterranean on permanent patrol. The purpose of this move, Forrestal indicated, was to support American foreign policy in this crucial area of the world.[23] "It is well that we remind ourselves," he said, "that the weight of American influence at the peace tables is in almost direct proportion to the strength and readiness of our armed forces."[24]

The newly-elected Eightieth Congress, dominated by conservative Republicans, was even more budget-conscious than its predecessor. Early in 1947, after the President's fiscal recommendations had reached Capitol Hill, Forrestal testified against further military cuts. The effort failed. Naval appropriations for Fiscal 1948 dropped to $3.3 billion for operating expenses and $248 million for contracts issued in previous years. As a result, military hard times set in just two years after the end of the Second World War. In a quixotic attempt to cope with the situation, Forrestal proposed that one hundred out-of-date ships be sold to our friendly neighbors to help defray the cost of our own military needs. The plan never got off the ground.[25]

In the spring of 1947 Truman began to act with force and determination at several important areas of contact between East and West—Greece, Turkey, and South Korea being cases in point. While Forrestal had not been the only high government official to plead for military forces sufficient to support our newfound world responsibilities, to many Americans he alone symbolized the most rigid military position. Americans wanted peace, not war; they wanted to return to demobilized normalcy.[26]

Forrestal realized that the Navy had various administrative weaknesses. Naval planning often did not coordinate with national policy; organizational operations were decentralized and inefficient; and civilian control was weak.[27] Another problem stemmed from the dual wartime role played by Admiral King, who since March 1942 had been both Commander in Chief, United States Fleet, and Chief of Naval Operations. As Commander in Chief, King was directly responsible to the President; as CNO he was responsible to the Secretary of the Navy. Lines of authority thus muddled and weakened were then exacerbated by King's attempt to acquire control over the bureaus, thereby butting into the office of Procurement and Material while Forrestal was the Under Secretary. The situation was not helped by a strong even if polite clash of personalities.[28]

Both Knox and Forrestal recognized that strategic planning and naval operations belonged to the naval professional. However, both felt that when the implementation of strategic decisions depended upon action in the civilian sphere, consultation and coordination were absolutely essential. Moreover, since the civilians would be held politically responsible for the successes and failures of the Navy, they demanded to be informed on strategic decisions in order to mobilize the civilian efforts necessary to bring the plans to fruition. In other words, Knox and Forrestal wanted civilian control for important practical, as well as policy reasons.[29]

Various proposals for reorganizing the Navy Department were made during the war. King's attempts to increase his own authority within the department were stopped only through the determined opposition of Forrestal and the President.[30] Although Forrestal would separate the office of Commander in Chief of the U. S. Fleet from that of Chief of Naval Operations (Admiral King's joint roles) and give more authority to the Secretary of the Navy, he left King's dual appointment as it was until the war ended. He did make two organizational changes, however. First, he created a civilian fiscal director (later the Office of the Comptroller) to simplify and establish some measure of fiscal responsibility. Second, he established an "Organization Top Policy Group" which, composed of the highest civilian executives and professional officers in the department, replaced the moribund Secretary's Advisory Council set up by Secretary Josephus Daniels thirty years earlier. The real value of this group was in its serving as a clearinghouse for divergent civilian and military viewpoints and in reaching decisions on basic organizational problems. Its efforts incidentally, gave the Navy a head start on postwar reorganization problems.[31]

Four days after the Japanese surrender Forrestal appointed a joint civilian-military board (the so-called "Gates Board") to recommend changes in departmental structure. Results came quickly. On 23 September 1945 General Order Number 223 reorganized the Shore Establishment. The complex area of logistics was divided into two parts. The first, called "consumer logistics" and dealing with the determination of expendable Navy requirements, was assigned to Naval Operations. The second, "producer logistics," was retained in civilian hands. A new procurement agency, the Office of Navy Material, was established for the entire department. The Office of the Chief of Naval Operations was also altered. In the new scheme there were five deputy chiefs of naval operations with functions similar to those of the Army General Staff: Op–01, Personnel; Op–02, Administration; Op–03, Naval Operations; Op–04, Logistics; and Op–05, Navy Air. If these offices did not function in the manner of the general staff because they were not granted the powers to accompany the titles, they did, however, relieve the Chief of Naval Operations of a variety of minor burdens which had prevented him in the past from concentrating upon major policy problems. In addition, all deputy chiefs were made eligible for fleet duty.[32]

Finally, to restructure lines of authority and communications between the Secretary of the Navy and the Chief of Naval Operations, the Navy was in effect divided into three structural parts: the civilian department of the Navy, the shore establishment, and the operating forces. Four centers of power were created: the Secretary of the Navy, the Chief of Naval Operations, the civilian department, and the professional officers. Each of these was responsible for a distinct function—policy making, naval command, logistics, and business administration, respectively. Admiral King's two roles were meshed into the office of CNO. However, Forrestal made certain that the new administrative arrangement made the CNO directly responsible to both the Secretary of the Navy and the President.[33]

These changes opened up new opportunities for younger officers and relieved some of the pressures which had built up between the CNO and the men just below him in the professional hierarchy. This was most important, for at the end of the war the Navy was undergoing a fundamental change in emphasis from a gunnery to an air navy. The major differences between the aviators, led by Assistant Secretary of the Navy for Air, Artemus Gates, and the traditionalists, supported by Admiral King, concerned promotions and money. In 1941 16 percent of the regular line officers and 12 percent of the admirals and commodores had been aviators; by 1945 these figures were 23 and 27 percent, respectively.[34] Thus, administrative reorganization smoothed the way for an important change in the Navy's postwar strategic concept.

The rise of the submarine as a major element in the modern Navy paralleled somewhat the increased importance of Navy Air. Research in the form of advanced submarine technology and atomic energy contributed to this shift in Navy thinking. Forrestal, who always supported research as the only way to develop and maintain a modern fighting force, in May 1945 established a new Office of Research and Invention to coordinate and direct all Navy work in this area. Many outsiders felt after World War II that surface ships had been rendered obsolete by the atomic bomb. Forrestal personally witnessed the Bikini Tests, designed to determine if regular capital ships could survive a nuclear attack. Although the experiment was inconclusive, Dr. Alvin M. Wienberg of the Manhattan Project gave submariners their cue when he observed that the "navy of the future, if there is any such, will consist of submarines which will travel a thousand feet below the ocean [surface]," and as early as February 1946 Admiral Chester W. Nimitz was suggesting that the surest defense the United States could have against atomic bombardment or attack by missiles would be a strong Navy which would use the submarine as the "most successful vehicle for carrying atomic weapons to within short distances of coastal targets and for insuring accuracy in the use of . . . missiles." The upshot of these various forces was a new strategic concept involving the deterrent effect of the Polaris missile.[35]

National security policy, the Navy budget, and departmental reorganization were all critical problems Forrestal tried to solve in the early postwar years. The single most important issue he faced during this period, however, was unification, which to him implied the destruction of everything the Navy held dear. He therefore felt compelled to fight against unification as a matter of self-survival.[36]

Before 1941 the Army and Navy had blocked all proposals for unifying them. By 1943, however, largely through the efforts of the semi-autonomous

Army Air Force, the Army supported unification. Forrestal's opposition was predictable. In November 1943, responding to increasing pressures from both the Army and the general public, Congress approved a full-scale investigation (before the Woodrum Committee) to begin the following March. With Secretary Knox seriously ill, Forrestal carried much of the burden for the Navy, arguing both against the idea of unification and the particulars of the Army's proposal. Noting the tremendous size and complexity of both the Army and the Navy, Forrestal suggested that there "is no human being capable, in my judgment, of sitting on top of all that and assuring that you have the fine integration and efficiency which is presumed would result from that consolidation."[37] After three months, the committee reported against any major changes until the fighting was over. However, Forrestal was not sanguine about the Navy's chances of withstanding future pressures in this direction.[38]

Throughout the war Forrestal maintained a good working relationship with the professional naval officers with whom he had to deal except, perhaps, with Admiral King and his immediate supporters. He also opened his office to combat officers returning to Washington in 1945 and became an active supporter of their cause within the department. However, it was his defense of the Navy during the Woodrum Committee hearings that won him "at the outset the loyalty and devotion of most of the senior officers in Washington . . . [and as the unification struggle progressed,] he was to retain and even increase this strong following among the officer corps although almost every Navy Department policy and action from that time onward was to bear the impress of his thinking and decisions."[39]

Forrestal retained strong support because he, even more than the Navy professionals, planned and carried out the Navy's defense in the unification struggle from 1943 to 1947, when a satisfactory compromise agreement was reached. One of his most important contributions began on 19 June 1945, when he asked Ferdinand Eberstadt, a personal friend and former business associate, to head a study panel and provide an alternative to the Army plan. The Eberstadt Report reached Forrestal in late September 1945. Although he did not support all of its suggestions, the report became the heart of the Navy's counterproposal in the ensuing debate.[40]

Early in October 1945, the Army initiated its second drive for unification with the Collins Plan, which called for one merged Department of Common Defense to be headed by a cabinet-level Secretary and one overall chief of staff for the entire defense establishment. In addition, the Air Force was to become an independent branch, co-equal with the Army and the Navy. The Eberstadt Report and the Navy opposed both the goal and the specific provisions of the Army's new proposal.

Up to this time Robert P. Patterson and Forrestal had worked well together despite the usual amount of interservice competition between them. During the war, when Patterson had been Under Secretary of War and Forrestal had been Under Secretary of the Navy, their goals had been identical. As a result, cooperation "between the Army and the Navy on material matters in World War II was much more effective than in the First World War. . . ."[41] By the end of 1945 each had been promoted to secretary of his respective department, and their long friendship soon began to dissolve over the question of unification. While Patterson supported the Collins Plan, Forrestal led the Navy counterattack, arguing not against unification, but rather against the Collins Plan which, he said, had been put forward without adequate preparation and study. To support his thesis, Forrestal suggested that merger or unification, contrary to Patterson's assertions, would not guarantee either economy or efficiency. Using the War Department's own experience during World War II as an example, Forrestal noted that "the most significant development in departmental organization has not been the merger of many services into one great conglomerate, but the breaking down of larger organizations into manageable and relatively autonomous smaller organizations. The outstanding example, I believe, has been the gradual separation of the Army Air Force from the rest of the Army."[42] In addition he attacked the Collins Plan "because it concentrates power in one Secretary beyond the capacity of any one man to use that power, and certainly beyond his capacity to obtain and digest the knowledge upon which its use could be based. He certainly would be entirely in the hands of his military advisors."[43] In the end, he assured the committee that he was not appearing "'simply in opposition to unification." His own views, he said, were adequately represented by the Eberstadt Report.

From October 1945 to January 1947, when a compromise was finally reached, undeclared verbal war existed between the two services. Congress was the most important battlefield. The tone of the debate in its early stages is best exemplified by the Doolittle incident. In public testimony, General James Doolittle predicted that the carrier-based Navy, which had been so instrumental in winning the Pacific War, was obsolete and that future wars would be fought by the Air Force with only secondary support from the other military branches. Forrestal countered by accusing Doolittle of a gross slur against the Navy and warned Patterson against such "acrimony." Patterson responded by giving Doolittle his fullest support, indicating that service personnel should give their views with "force and vigor." As far as he was concerned, the conflict could not be elevated to a higher, more intellectual plane. While Forrestal cautioned all naval officers to refrain from direct, slanderous attacks on the Army, he suggested that the President create a special commission to study the entire problem before any concrete action was taken.[44]

During these first few months it was impossible for either side to back down or compromise. Debate quickly degenerated into mutual accusation, and misunderstanding was inevitable. One example, in which the two sides talked right past each other rather than to each other, involved the question of civilian control. The civilian leaders of the War Department had worked for years beside the highly efficient General Staff of the Army. The effect of this arrangement, however, was to insulate the Secretary of War from direct control over the professional officers. Forrestal, as noted above, wanted to keep the General Staff system out of the Navy, and he saw precisely this threat in the Army's plan for unification. He did not want the Secretary of Common Defense to be entirely in the hands of his military advisors. Assistant Secretary of War John J. McCloy did not ease Forrestal's mind at all when he suggested that in the proposed organization the Secretary of the Armed Forces would have "the same degree of control now exercised by the Secretary of War in the War Department . . ."[45] Instead, he confirmed Forrestal's worst fears.

President Truman remained quietly in the background during the first six weeks of the formal unification debate. Then, on 20 November 1945 he publically rejected Forrestal's request for a study commission and indicated that he would submit his own plan to Congress. His unification proposal, dated 19 December, followed the general pattern of the Collins Plan. Forrestal had lost the first battle. The President's decision to support the Army position, moreover, left the Navy Department in somewhat of a quandary. Did the President's action require loyal support under penalty of military discipline or were the opponents of the plan still free to express their own feelings? The department's immediate reaction was to order complete silence. When Navy supporters in Congress and in the press complained of censorship, the President quickly denied that he had intended to "muzzle" the Navy. Discussion of the pros and cons, he said, was acceptable as long as individuals stated their own personal opinions. Thus the debate continued through the first few months of 1946 until Rear Admiral Aaron S. Merrill gave his own opinions a bit too vigorously at a public dinner. The President was incensed and threatened disciplinary action. After a hastily arranged meeting between Truman and Forrestal, the latter announced that there would be no further public statements by Navy personnel except when they were called to testify before a congressional committee.[46] Arthur Krock of the *New York Times* looked back on the Merrill incident and concluded that Forrestal, perhaps more than any other man directly involved in the controversy, stood for reason and compromise. In Krock's words, ". . . if the Navy's real interests—which are also the nation's—are preserved in merger, a goodly measure of thanks will be due Mr. Forrestal."[47]

Forrestal's own involvement in the conflict diminished after the President's bill went to Congress. He seemed to be on the defensive. This period of quiet ended on 1 May 1946, when he testified before the highly sympathetic Naval Affairs Committee and reiterated all the old Navy arguments against the Collins Plan, and then shifted to the offensive. For five months the Navy had appeared to the general public as *opposed*—opposed to the Collins Plan, opposed to unification, opposed to the President, and opposed to the national interest. In those five months, however, the Navy had learned one crucial fact: Congress would not pass a unification bill without the assent of the Navy. Forrestal's offensive move, therefore, was to call for compromise. First, he stated that the Navy supported the basic principle or goal behind the President's plan. Second, he accused Patterson and the Army of an unwillingness to compromise secondary considerations, thereby hindering progress toward the President's primary goal. Third, he suggested that Congress ask the Army and the Navy to make a joint statement on their points of common agreement and disagreement.[48] The Navy had nothing to lose; the Army had everything to lose. The President, who had already lost much in terms of personal prestige, announced the following day that he had seen Forrestal's statement before it had been made public.[49]

From this date until a final agreement was reached between the two services in January 1947, Forrestal, with the wavering support of President Truman, led the search for a compromise. On 13 May 1946, the President brought Forrestal and Patterson together to explore the possibility of a mutually agreeable plan of merger. Truman asked the two Secretaries to compose a list of areas of agreement and disagreement and to report their findings by 31 May. When Forrestal and Patterson submitted their report, the consensus was greater than previously had been expected. There had been compromise on both sides.[50]

During the summer of 1946 progress toward further compromise was again stymied. As long as Congress was in session and the President did not officially withdraw his proposal, the Army continued to hope for passage of the Collins Plan. At times Forrestal wondered if the Army were still willing to accept the points agreed to in May.[51] Then Congress adjourned without taking action. On 27 September Eberstadt met with former Assistant Secretary of War McCloy and Assistant Secretary of War for Air Robert A. Lovett. "With their Wall Street backgrounds, all three 'spoke the same language.' "[52] Agreement was reached on a loose "federal" structure for coordinating the three services. A second gathering on 7 November at Forrestal's Georgetown home went over a number of the remaining points of disagreement. Besides Forrestal, those present included the new Assistant Secretary of the Army, W. Stuart Symington, and Admiral Arthur Radford, who represented the two extremes, and Gen-

eral Lauris Norstad and Admiral Forrest Sherman, who took more moderate
positions. A consensus was reached on the need for compromise. A seventeen
point program was developed encompassing the results of the 27 September
meeting, and Sherman and Norstad were asked to work out the rest of the
scheme. These two met regularly through the first of the year. Progress was uncertain, but the lines of communication remained open. Finally, in January 1947
the intellectual and emotional barriers blocking cooperation fell away and
mutual agreement followed quickly. Norstad, Sherman, and Symington agreed
to the last draft on 16 January 1947. Since the final agreement looked very
much like the proposal contained in the Eberstadt Report some sixteen months
earlier, the Navy, at least for the time being, had won.[53]

The "Forrestal style" involved two important elements. First, he conducted a great deal of important departmental business through informal luncheons, gatherings at his home, or yacht trips on the Potomac. Second, Forrestal
went out of his way to build congressional good will for the Navy and for
himself. Besides his official contacts with the appropriate Senate and House
Committees, he tried to keep in constant communication with friends of the
Navy in both chambers. For example, when settlement was finally reached on
unification in January 1947, he refused to allow the news to be made public
until he had notified his principal Navy friends in Congress, saying that "this
was desirable not merely from the standpoint of the Navy's obligation to these
men, but also by way of enlisting their sympathetic cooperation in the future."[54]

While Forrestal's relations with Congress remained good, and perhaps
even improved during the intra-service controversy, his position within the
executive branch became extremely strained. He had opposed the President
before, at the Potsdam Conference for example, but unification was different.
For over a year Forrestal led the opposition coalition against the President,
the Army, and a good deal of the nation's press. It is a measure of Truman's
stature that he tolerated Forrestal's eccentricities and still made the best use
of his many talents and abilities. That the tense relationship did not become
even more severe may be ascribed to the fact that unification was only one of
several important issues facing the nation and that on most other questions
Forrestal ardently backed the President.[55] In addition, Forrestal's opposition
on unification reflected the preponderant views of most high ranking naval
officers and a number of leaders of Congress whose acquiescence would be
necessary for the passage of any unification proposal. As long as he balked, no
merger was possible. By finding a solution acceptable to him, the President's
long-range goal of unification was achieved. Last, Forrestal's symbolic role as
leader of the opposition made him in a sense inviolable. To "muzzle" him
"might have permanently frozen opposition against unification in Congress."[56]

On 26 July 1947, when Truman signed the bill creating a new Department of Defense, he also nominated Forrestal to be the first Secretary of Defense. Senate confirmation came immediately. Two months later Forrestal left the Navy Department to begin his new assignment. He left behind a stronger and better organized Navy that he had inherited in 1944, and won for the Navy a position in the Department of Defense that it could at least live with.

When he agreed to serve as Secretary of Defense, Forrestal said that he would need the "combined attention of Fulton Sheen and the entire psychiatric profession by the end of another year!"[57] Though he joshed, in about two years he was driven to suicide by the combined pressures of his work and a bedridden, alcoholic wife. While the cold war became hotter, as in Greece, Turkey, the Berlin blockade, and the communist coup in Czechoslovakia, Truman's extremely spare defense budgets meant that dollars determined strategy rather than vice versa, thereby placing undue reliance upon strategic air power and exacerbating interservice rivalry. Through meetings in 1948 with the Joint Chiefs of Staff at Key West and Newport he obtained new definitions of service roles and missions, but opposition to his attempts to obtain interservice cooperation particularly from the Air Force determined him to seek stronger controls. Ironically, the power granted in the National Security Act Amendments of August 1949 would not be wielded by him but by Colonel Louis A. Johnson. Following the elections of 1948, in which he had raised funds for Truman's whistle-stop tour, Johnson demanded the Defense post as his pound of flesh.[58] Forrestal left office on 28 March 1949. Rest and good care would soon restore him, his physicians said, but on 22 May he fell to his death from the seventh floor of the Naval Hospital at Bethesda, Maryland. No public servant more clearly deserved the accolade that he was a "victim of duty."

NOTES

1. *New York Times*, 12 May 1944.
2. Arnold A. Rogow, *James Forrestal* (New York: Macmillan, 1963), p. 70.
3. *Ibid.*, pp. 89–91.
4. Robert H. Connery, *The Navy and the Industrial Mobilization in World War II* (Princeton, N.J.: Princeton University Press, 1951), p. 56.
5. Robert G. Albion and Robert H. Connery, *Forrestal and the Navy* (New York: Columbia University Press, 1962), pp. 63–69.
6. Samuel E. Morison, *History of the United States Naval Operations in World War II*, 15 vols. (Boston: Little, Brown, 1947–1972), vol. 10, *The Atlantic Battle Won*, (1956), pp. 35–36.
7. Walter Millis, ed., *The Forrestal Diaries* (New York: Viking, 1951), p. 54; Len Giovannitti and Fred Freed, *The Decision to Drop the Bomb* (New York: Coward-McCann, 1945), p. 31.

8. Millis, ed., *Forrestal Diaries*, pp. 66, 77.
9. Albion and Connery, *Forrestal and the Navy*, pp. 169–72, 176–78.
10. *New York Times*, 1 Apr. 1944.
11. *Ibid.*, 22 June 1944.
12. Millis, ed., *Forrestal Diaries*, p. 14.
13. *Ibid.*, pp. 16, 36, 47, 49, 55–58.
14. *New York Times*, 17 June 1945.
15. *Ibid.*
16. *Ibid.*, 20 June 1945.
17. *Ibid.*, 25 Aug. 1945.
18. *Ibid.*, 20 Sept. 1945.
19. *Ibid.*, 14 Oct. 1945.
20. *Ibid.*, 15 Feb. 1946.
21. *Ibid.*, 22 Jan. 1947.
22. *Ibid.*, 24 Mar. 1946.
23. Millis, ed., *Forrestal Diaries*, pp. 206–11.
24. *New York Times*, 26 Oct. 1946.
25. *Ibid.*, 26 June 1947.
26. W. W. Rostow, *The United States in the World Arena* (New York: Harper & Brothers, 1960), pp. 207–14, 221–22, 225–30.
27. Connery, *The Navy and the Industrial Mobilization*, pp. 433–34; Vincent Davis, *Postwar Defense Policy and the U.S. Navy, 1943–1946* (Chapel Hill: University of North Carolina Press, 1966), pp. 3–9; Paul Y. Hammond, *Organizing for Defense* (Princeton, N.J.: Princeton University Press, 1961), pp. 135, 145–46, 153, 156–58.
28. Albion and Connery, *Forrestal and the Navy*, pp. 11, 92–93; Hammond, *Organizing for Defense*, p. 138.
29. Albion and Connery, *Forrestal and the Navy*, pp. 105–06.
30. Hammond, *Organizing for Defense*, pp. 139–43.
31. Albion and Connery, *Forrestal and the Navy*, pp. 234–37.
32. *Ibid.*, pp. 237–41.
33. *Ibid.*, pp. 238–41. See also CAPT M. R. Browning, "Post-war Naval Organization —the Navy Department," MR 26 (Dec. 1946):34–38, "Post-War Naval Organization—the Shore Establishment," *ibid.* 26 (Jan. 1947):34–38, and "Post-War Naval Organization," *ibid.* 26 (Feb. 1947):16–23.
34. Davis, *Postwar Defense Policy*, pp. 17, 120–31.
35. *Ibid.*, pp. 130, 246; Albion and Connery, *Forrestal and the Navy*, pp. 180–81, 241–42, 246; *New York Times*, 15 Feb. 1946.
36. Demetrios Caraley, *The Politics of Military Unification* (New York: Columbia University Press, 1966), p. 92.
37. Albion and Connery, *Forrestal and the Navy*, p. 259.
38. Millis, ed., *Forrestal Diaries*, p. 60.
39. Davis, *Postwar Defense Policy*, p. 65.
40. Caraley, *Politics of Military Unification*, pp. 38–44; Millis, ed., *Forrestal Diaries*, p. 63.
41. Connery, *The Navy and the Industrial Mobilization*, p. 315; Albion and Connery, *Forrestal and the Navy*, pp. 63, 76–77.

42. U.S. Senate. Committee on Military Affairs, *Department of the Armed Forces. Hearings during the 79th Cong., 1st Sess., on S. 84 and S. 1482* (Washington: GPO, 1945), p. 102.
43. *New York Times*, 23 Oct. 1945.
44. *Ibid.*, 13 Nov. 1945.
45. U.S. Senate, Committee on Military Affairs, *Analytical Digest of Testimony Before the Senate Military Affairs Committee, October 17, 1945 to December 17, 1945* (Washington: GPO, n.d.), p. 55.
46. Caraley, *Politics of Military Unification*, pp. 129–30; Albion and Connery, *Forrestal and the Navy*, pp. 267–69.
47. *New York Times*, 19 Apr. 1946.
48. *Ibid.*, 2 May 1946.
49. *Ibid.*, 3 May 1946.
50. *Ibid.*, 16 June 1946; Caraley, *Politics of Military Unification*, pp. 135–40.
51. Caraley, *Politics of Military Unification*, pp. 137–43, 147–48; Millis, ed., *Forrestal Diaries*, pp. 201–02.
52. Albion and Connery, *Forrestal and the Navy*, pp. 274–75.
53. *Ibid.*, pp. 274–84.
54. Millis, ed., *Forrestal Diaries*, pp. 229–30.
55. Caraley, *Politics of Military Unification*, p. 145.
56. *Ibid.*, p. 146.
57. Millis, ed., *Forrestal Diaries*, p. 300.
58. On Forrestal as secretary of defense, see especially Paolo E. Coletta, "The U.S. Navy and Defense Unification, 1947–1953," MS; Rogow, *Forrestal;* Timothy W. Stanley, *American Defense and National Security* (Washington: Public Affairs Press, 1956); and Harry S. Truman, *Memoirs by Harry S. Truman*, 2 vols. (Garden City, N.Y.: Doubleday, 1955–1956).

JOHN LAWRENCE SULLIVAN

18 September 1947–24 May 1949

PAOLO E. COLETTA

Before leaving Washington early in August 1947 to attend the Inter-American Defense Conference in Rio De Janeiro, President Harry S. Truman nominated six of the twelve civilians who would administer the military departments and joint agencies provided in the National Security Act of 27 July 1947. It was ironic that he chose as secretary of defense the Secretary of the Navy, James V. Forrestal, who had opposed creation of the position. Senator W. Stuart Symington would be Secretary of the Air Force, and the last Secretary of War, Kenneth Claiborne Royall, would be Secretary of the Army. At the time, "unification" was expected by few, "triplification" by many. Moreover, by altering the original appropriations for the services in fiscal year 1948 in favor of the Air Force, Congress in effect adopted the doctrine of strategic air atomic bombing and thus launched the independent Air Force as the dominant element in American military policy.

The National Security Act provided for a National Security Council charged with assessing and appraising the objectives, commitments, and risks of the United States in relation to actual and potential military power. To "insure a sound and adequate intelligence basis for the formulation and execution of national security policies," a Central Intelligence Agency was to be organized under its direction. A National Security Resources Board would advise the president on the coordination of military, industrial, and civilian mobilization. The National Military Establishment consisted of the secretary of defense, who would have three special assistants; the War Council; the Munitions Board; the Joint Chiefs of Staff and their Joint Staff; the Research and Development Board; and the secretaries of the three military departments.

The first "unified" secretary of the Navy would face a particular challenge in adjusting to the new organization, in part because the Navy used a bilinear organization and the Army and Air Force used the general staff system. More-over, the secretary must compete for organizational position, strategic doctrine, and funds with the president, the secretary of defense, the other service secretaries, the Bureau of the Budget, Congress, and the public, which meant that he had to use public relations as a command tool.[1]

Although the National Security Act provided that naval air remain with the sea service and the Marine Corps would include "land combat and service forces and such aviation as may be organic thereto," advocates of strategic bombing demanded that all military aviation be placed in the Department of the Air Force.[2] Indeed, by early October 1947, a subcommittee of the Congressional Aviation Policy Board, chaired by Representative Carl Hinshaw (Rep., Calif.), began hearings on such questions as the number of combat planes needed, and the relation of the Air Force and naval aviation. Advising the group were General of the Army H. H. Arnold, USA (Ret.) and Admiral John H. Towers, USN, Chairman of the General Board of the Navy.

Top level Navy Department leaders prior to the reorganization of the National Military Establishment included Forrestal, John L. Sullivan, Under Secretary of the Navy; W. John Kenney, Assistant Secretary of the Navy; John N. Brown, Assistant Secretary of the Navy for Air; and Fleet Admiral Chester W. Nimitz, Chief of Naval Operations. With Truman's approval, Forrestal was sworn in as secretary of defense at noon on 17 September. At midnight, the unification act took effect. On the eighteenth, Sullivan, who Forrestal suggested to Truman as his successor, was sworn in as the new Secretary of the Navy, Kenney as Under Secretary of the Navy, and Symington as Secretary of Air.

A Roman Catholic with a face as Irish as his name, Sullivan was a hard worker, often able to smooth troubled political waters. He was born in Manchester, New Hampshire, on 16 June 1899 to Patrick Henry and Ellen J. (Harrington) Sullivan. Patrick Sullivan, a lawyer, served as a county solicitor and also as personal counsel to Frank Knox, the newspaper publisher. John L. Sullivan thus grew up in an atmosphere of law and politics.

Sullivan entered Dartmouth College but dropped out in December 1918, when he qualified as an apprentice seaman in the Naval Reserve. As it turned out, his duty lasted for only three months, whereupon he returned to Dartmouth and graduated in 1921. After Harvard Law School, he entered law practice. In 1932, he married Priscilla Manning. The union resulted in three children.

Sullivan was defeated in two bids as Democratic candidate for governor of New Hampshire, in 1934 and 1938. When he went to Washington in 1939 as an assistant to the Commissioner of Internal Revenue, he appealed so strongly to President Franklin D. Roosevelt that Roosevelt moved him to the Treasury Department as Assistant Secretary. Rumor had it that Roosevelt meant to transfer him to some post in the Navy Department. Roosevelt died before the transfer was made, however, and Sullivan resigned from the Treasury and resumed law practice, in Washington, for six months, when he was asked by Truman to serve as Assistant Secretary of the Navy for Air. Edwin W. Pauley, a California oil man, had been nominated originally. As Treasurer of the Democratic National Committee in 1944, Pauley raised more than half a million dollars, hence was a "deserving Democrat," but his interest in tideland oil provoked strong opposition to him. Sullivan, a New Hampshire "deserving Democrat," had no conflicting interests, had some administrative experience, and had no qualms about accepting even though he knew that Truman preferred the views of the Army and especially of the Air Force to those of the Navy, disliked Forrestal because he was almost the only cabinet member to disagree with many of his key policies, and the cyclical wartime military budget "boom" had given way to normal peacetime "bust." He knew too, that because the old European balance of power had collapsed, the U.S. Navy must be maintained in-being in order to help support the foreign-policy interests of the nation. As yet, the United States had a monopoly on nuclear power. If a potential enemy obtained similar power, Sullivan would be the first secretary of the Navy to serve not only in a cold war but a total war environment.

As Assistant Secretary of the Navy for Air, from July 1945 to June 1946, Sullivan witnessed carrier operations in the Western Pacific and was much impressed by their power and versatility. As Under Secretary of the Navy after 17 June 1946, following the resignation of Artemus Gates, he helped Forrestal smooth the wrinkles out of the troublesome transition to the unified National Military Establishment.[3] "This thing is going to work," he said about unification. He would first learn the job of being secretary of the Navy, he added, then delegate certain tasks, thus keeping himself free to reach policy decisions.[4] In the meantime he asked the General Board of the Navy to advise him on the most effective contributions the Navy could make at war within the framework of the National Security Act and on how to bring the Navy to the highest point of effectiveness to make those contributions.[5]

With respect to the building of a flush-deck supercarrier that could handle heavy bombers and thus break the monopoly of the Air Force on atomic weapons, Sullivan was told that Forrestal approved it when he was secretary of the Navy and that it was discussed among other subjects in the War Council.[6] However, Sullivan had to be convinced of its merits. Convinced after sharp questioning of top naval officers of the need, he decided to support its building and to seek funds for it in budget requests.[7]

The projected 65,000-ton carrier would be the largest ship ever built. She would bristle with new type guns, have an armored flight deck, a speed of about thirty-three knots, and a complement of 4,000 men. She would be the seventh U.S. Navy ship too large to pass through the 110-foot locks on the Panama Canal. Among her other aircraft she would carry planes still under design that would weigh 100,000 pounds, have four turboprop or possibly pure jet engines, a top speed of 400 to 450 knots, operating radii of 1,500 to 2,000 miles, and carry atomic bombs. She would cost $124,000,000 and be built in forty-six months.

Soon after moving from "Main Navy" on Constitution Avenue to the Pentagon, on 20 September Forrestal said that he did not expect immediate economy to result from unification, would make no sweeping changes in the armed services, and would deal with individuals instead of issuing numerous directives. He believed that the services were being well administered and would let the secretaries handle their own public relations.

Forrestal would guide the military departments toward unity of purpose rather than of structure. Instead of forcing his ideas upon the services, he would let them "evolve" toward unification under his direction. Nevertheless, he expected the departments to save some money, as by standardizing equipment and supplies, consolidating services, and ending duplications. To this end the heads of the three armed services would attend meetings of the War Council in person.[8]

In his first address to the Navy, Sullivan noted that the Navy of World War II, largest in the world, had shrunk. While he did not mention the Soviet Union, he added that the challenge to American security remained great. The Navy must therefore offset reductions in numbers both afloat and ashore with increased efficiency, and he asked all hands to be vigorous, efficient, tenacious, and imaginative in meeting the challenge while at the same time working together with the Army and the Air Force in a defense team.[9]

Under Secretary of the Navy William John Kenney specialized in procurement, personnel, and administrative and legislative policies, the last of which he now must coordinate with the other two services. His service for eight years, from 1941 to 1949, did much to provide continuity in the office of the secretary of the Navy. To succeed Kenney as Assistant Secretary of the Navy, in January 1948 Truman named Mark Edwin Andrews, a Texas oil man, who was quickly approved by the Senate.

John Nicholas Brown, Assistant Secretary for Air, supervised air research and development and air personnel and was responsible for correlating naval air strength with national air power to the end that the Navy would control the air under which its ships operated. His opening theme was that the Navy had no quarrel with the Air Force "or anyone else." However, he held that the Navy was the nation's first line of defense because carrier-based planes would be the first to strike an enemy. Such remarks, and similar ones by other top-ranking civilian and military leaders, led Forrestal early in February 1948 to direct that any proposed speech or article on a controversial subject must have his prior approval—a directive that provoked a cry of "censorship" from a number of newspapers.[10]

The Navy in Sullivan's day was in transition to a new era of power and capabilities even though no one could foresee the exact nature of a future war. Would traditional navies be outmoded by the atomic bomb, guided missiles, robot planes, and as yet unforeseen weapons? How could that Navy be used against the only potential enemy, the Soviet Union, with its land-locked mass situated in the heart of Eurasia? It was Sullivan's task to adopt new weapons and techniques capable not only of controlling sea communications but wreaking havoc upon an enemy wherever he was.

Following World War II, the American public rejected any weapon that was not atomic or at least electronic but lacked knowledge of the interplay of geography and technology upon which to base a sound strategy. Various naval officers warned against "Pushbutton Philia" and "Jules Verne Neurosis," pointed out that the development of military equipment was outrunning the ability of personnel to use it, and called for the training of enlisted men and of officers in the techniques of an atomic-age Navy.[11]

Among common fallacies Sullivan had to counter was the notion that surface ships and carrier-based air power had lost their value because ships were vulnerable to atomic bombs; that sea power would be unimportant in the next war because it would be an atomic war waged wholly by long-range aircraft or guided missiles or both, and would be over in a week or two, without the movement of major military forces; that a future war necessarily must be fought with atomic weapons; that the atomic bomb, because so destructive, was a quick key to certain victory; that long-range aircraft eliminated the need for surface fleets and sea-going air power; and that the United States did not need a large fleet because no unfriendly power had a large one.[12]

Sullivan had to counter literally tons of Air Force publicity that demanded that the Air Force be the predominant service because its strategic bombing capability would deter war or, if war came, would annihilate the attacker— early statements of the concepts of massive deterrence and of massive retaliation. To such Air Force generals as Arnold, James H. Doolittle, George C. Kenney, and Spaatz, the Air Force supplanted the Navy as the nation's "first line of defense"; all conventional forces including aircraft carriers were obsolete; the Navy need not develop any strategic air capability; the Navy should supinely give up its air arm, about 30 percent of the Navy, to the Air Force; and the Navy should be reduced to a minor auxiliary service dealing with antisubmarine warfare and sea transportation.

The best answer to the Air Force in 1947 is found in a statement in a booklet issued by the office of the chief of naval operations:

It is impossible ever wholly to anticipate war's requirements. . . . Any exclusive adoption of a single weapon or type of weapon immediately limits
freedom of action and greatly simplifies the enemy's problem of defense.
. . . There is danger that investigation of a single aspect of one war may
give rise to an unbalanced interpretation. Limitations are as significant as
accomplishments.[13]

Sullivan, too, opposed a strategy that relied upon a single weapon and single
delivery system, in part because such reliance would cause stagnation in the
development of other weapons and techniques.[14]

Sullivan enjoyed the counsel of Nimitz, the Chief of Naval Operations,
only until 17 December 1947, when he went off active duty. When Truman
asked Forrestal who should succeed Nimitz, Forrestal replied "[Dewitt C.]
Ramsey, [William H. P.] Blandy, and [Louis Emil] Denfeld," adding that
"the President would find Denfeld the easiest of the lot to work with."[15] On
12 November, Truman approved Denfeld for a two year term.

Denfeld, born in 1891, graduated from the U.S. Naval Academy and was
commissioned as an ensign in 1912. After duty on destroyers during World
War I, he served in various capacities until June 1937, when he became an aide
to Admiral William D. Leahy, Chief of Naval Operations. In August 1939
he became the commander of a destroyer division; in June 1940, of a destroyer
squadron. In March 1941 he was Special Naval Observer at the American Embassy in London. For subsequent service as Chief of Staff and Aide to Commander, Support Force, Atlantic Fleet, 7 April to 26 December 1941, he was
awarded the Legion of Merit. Throughout most of World War II he served
as Assistant to the Chief of the Bureau of Navigation, known after 21 May
1942 as the Bureau of Personnel. He then served as the commander of a battleship division that operated in support of the Okinawa landings and attacks on
the home islands of Japan, and as Chief of the Bureau of Naval Personnel;
after 29 September 1945, he had additional duty as Deputy Chief of Naval
Operations (Personnel). On 28 February 1947 he assumed command of the
Pacific Fleet.

The *New York Times* believed that Denfeld had "one of the most inquiring minds and the most engaging personalities in the Navy," while the *Wor-
cester* (Mass.) *Telegram*, *Washington Star*, and *Washington Post* believed he
would well serve the Navy because of his wide experience in personnel and
manpower work. A personnel man rather than member of the "Gun Club,"
he was nevertheless favored by the latter. To prove his friendliness towards
naval aviation, he wisely chose as his deputy the Navy's senior aviator, Arthur
W. Radford.

Sullivan's major tasks were to square his administration with directives
Forrestal issued as he sought to unify the military services, operate the Navy

efficiently under extremely tight budgets provided by the Truman administration, and defend what he considered to be the Navy's proper strategy and roles and missions until these could be redefined to the satisfaction of all three services. Moreover, as a member of the National Security Council he had to deal with foreign policy rather than purely naval matters.

Representatives of Sullivan, Royall, and Symington met often between early October and mid-November 1947 to aid Forrestal in reaching decisions on matters involving budget, finance, legislation, personnel, organization, and administration. Of prime importance was legislation increasing service pay, providing Universal Military Training, and reorganizing the reserve forces.

During 1947, while the Navy continued long-range research and development programs, it also stored $2 billion worth of weapons found to have been most useful in World War II. Many naval bases around the world had been rolled up, however, and the number of operating combatant and auxiliary ships had been reduced drastically. The number of officers was down to 46,000 and the number of enlisted men to 425,000, whereas the naval reserve had grown to 825,000, with 20,000 of them in the ready naval air reserve. Provision had been made for an atomic proving ground at Eniwetok. Additional Marines had been sent to join the carrier *Midway* and her escort ships in the Mediterranean to support the Truman Doctrine, announced on 12 March 1947.

The first session of the Eightieth Congress, which met in January 1947, considered problems of interim relief for Europe and inflation at home rather than service legislation. As Forrestal put it on 8 December 1947, he took a calculated risk in lowering American defense expenditures in order to bolster the security of Western Europe.[16] However the risk was minimal because the United States had a monopoly on atomic weapons.

Forrestal did not involve himself in the preparation of the service budgets for fiscal year 1948 even though he was well aware that Air Force enthusiasts were unhappy with what they said were "disproportionate" funds going to the Navy. It would have been better for the Navy if he had looked into the service budgets, for the Navy considered its budget critical. Although personnel demobilization had long ended, decisions had to be made on which of the now obsolescent ships, planes, and weapons to retain and on how much funding should go to new weapons such as improved submarines, jet aircraft, and a super carrier. The fiscal year 1946 defense budget was $45 billion; that of 1947 only $14.5 billion; and the $11.25 billion recommended by the Bureau of the Budget for 1948 favored the Air Force.

The second session of the Eightieth Congress, which met on 6 January 1948, would consider increasing military pay; the military budget for fiscal year 1949, which would go into effect on 1 July 1948; the report of the President's Commission on Air Policy and of the Congressional Aviation Policy

Board; and assess the progress of service unification. Also to be considered would be legislation involving various Navy public works, to make the WAVES permanent, and to establish a single system of military justice.

Sullivan said little for two months while he familiarized himself with departmental problems. Well timed to influence Congress was his release during the first week in January 1948 of a paper Nimitz wrote before leaving office on 15 December 1947. In this paper, entitled "The Future Employment of Naval Forces," Nimitz alluded to the value of command of the sea and asserted that the United States would use its command of the sea only to assure our national security and to support the United Nations. Naval air-sea forces contributed mightily to the destruction of Germany and of Japan in World War II; these must be maintained in balanced fashion. As he saw it, the Navy would be used defensively against any attacker and offensively by delivering bombing attacks from land- and carrier-bases, occupying selected advanced bases, and destroying enemy lines of communication. These functions, both defensive and offensive, could be undertaken best by the Air Force and Navy, with the Navy carrying the war to the enemy so that it would not be fought on American soil.[17]

At the moment Nimitz wrote, the Air Force wanted a 70-group program to include 55 active and 15 skeletonized groups, and its secretary, Symington, demanded an annual procurement of 3,200 planes while budget makers spoke in terms of providing only 2,000 planes for both the Air Force and the Navy. More specifically Symington called for 6,869 aircraft, including 436 medium and light bombers, some 1,800 trainers, 936 transports, 2,188 fighters, and miscellaneous craft. "But the headline item," Borklund has written, "was a request for 988 heavy bombers. The glamour girl in that category was to be the B–36."[18]

Symington was bolstered by the report of the President's (Thomas K. Finletter) Air Policy Commission, made public on 13 January 1948, which stated that the "military establishment must be built around the air arm." While a Navy and Ground Force would be maintained, "it is the Air Force and Naval Aviation on which we must mainly rely. Our military security must be based on air power." In fiscal year 1948, ground and sea forces had received $7.2 billion and the Air Force $2.85 billion. For fiscal year 1949, the report suggested $7.75 billion for the ground and sea forces and $5.45 billion for the Air Force. It called for a first-line force of 12,400 new planes organized into 70 regular, 27 National Guard, and 34 Air Reserve groups plus 8,100 modern replacement aircraft. Among other items, the report called for the Navy immediately to increase its annual aircraft procurement in order to equip the fleet with modern planes after those of World War II vintage were exhausted, and that the Air Transport Command and the Naval Air Transport Service be consolidated. (The last was accomplished on 4 February with a Military Air Transport Service to be directed by an Air Force General with a Navy Rear Admiral as his deputy.)

The report concentrated on air policy, not military policy as a whole, for the two years or so that the United States was expected to enjoy its atomic monopoly.[19] It did not recommend the augmentation of ground and naval forces needed for a war of limited scale such as might have to be fought in Italy, Greece, Korea, or Palestine. To the public, overwhelmed with Air Force propaganda, air power meant the Air Force. Navy men saw the report as an Air Force document, which it largely was, that provided for only a temporary policy and grossly overlooked both the usefulness of the naval air arm and the fact that there was no defense against the atomic bomb.

Nimitz's ideas, particularly his concept of bombing the heartland of Russia with naval aircraft and his demand for supercarriers, sat badly with Symington, even though Sullivan stated that the Navy had no intention of intruding into the Air Force's responsibility for strategic bombing. While Forrestal questioned whether "the bomber could survive against modern radar defenses and the new jet fighters armed with Rockets," Symington, even though perhaps half of his top officers would cancel the B–36, "cast the deciding vote to push on with the best of a bad deal."[20]

Forrestal left each service secretary free to air his own views even though he disagreed with them. Symington took advantage of this permissiveness and in an article in the *Saturday Evening Post* challenged Nimitz's views on naval aviation. In rebuttal, someone leaked to the press a memorandum written by a strong advocate of naval aviation, Rear Admiral Daniel V. Gallery, who held that the Navy was the service "destined to deliver the atom bomb" and concluded that "It is time right now for the Navy to start an aggressive campaign aimed at proving that the Navy can deliver the atom bomb more effectively than the Air Forces (*sic*) can." After getting Nimitz to sign a statement that the Gallery memorandum did not represent his views, Sullivan reprimanded Gallery and disavowed the memorandum.[21]

On 12 January 1948, Truman asked Congress for an $11 billion defense budget for fiscal year 1949. Of slightly less than $10 billion in new funds for the military departments, 54 percent would go to aviation and 46 percent to ground and surface forces. With $4.7 billion (or $800 million less than the Air Policy Commission suggested), the Air Force would have not 70 but 55 groups. The Army would get $4.7 billion also, about half of which must be spent in support of the Air Force; the Navy $3.5 billion, of which about 40 percent would support naval aviation.

For fiscal year 1949, Sullivan would reduce shipbuilding but increase naval air power. His building program, which would cost a modest $230 million over a five-year period, called for an expenditure of only $16 million in 1949, with $6 million to go toward construction of a supercarrier. Noticeably absent was a request for battleships.

The "supercarrier" Sullivan desired was approved for planning purposes in 1946, with budgeting for it expected in fiscal year 1948. However, its designs were not completed until the cycle of budget preparation for fiscal year 1949 began. It was approved by Forrestal and by the Bureau of the Budget, but the latter agreed to it on condition that Sullivan sponsor legislation to stop construction on thirteen ships and transfer the funds thus saved to the carrier. Sullivan capitulated and sought congressional permission to construct several prototype ships instead of continuing work on converting the cruiser *Hawaii* and the battleship *Kentucky* to guided missile ships, for which $308 million had been authorized, and to belay the construction of seven destroyers, two destroyer escorts, and two submarines.[22]

In the first week in March, the congressional Aviation Policy Board, chaired by Senator Ralph Owen Brewster (Rep., Me.), issued its report. The board severely criticized the Joint Chiefs of Staff for their failure to furnish it with a unified air plan and explained that it must proceed on statements of requirements prepared separately by Symington and Sullivan. It thereby overlooked the great difficulty the chiefs faced in defining roles and missions. It also criticized rotation of duty for naval aviators, noting that in many cases these had to do "deck duty" before qualifying for promotion in certain ranks—a criticism Sullivan rejected because an aviator must know how to command as well as to fly. Whereas the board recommended a 70-group Air Force program, or 20,541 planes, the Air Policy Commission had recommended 8,000 first line planes for the Navy until the Joint Chiefs prepared strategic plans and integrated requirements, and a total of 14,500 naval aircraft. After noting that loyalty to service traditions prevented the services from integrating their air programs, the board set 30 June for the presentation of such plans to the president and Congress. It also had a special statement on naval air: "Existence of opposing weapons in quantity, and carriers to deliver them is a restraint upon any nation contemplating attack. Possession of weapons in quantity, and carriers to deliver them in overwhelming force, if attack comes, is judged the best and surest protection against defeat and slavery." Finally, the board held the Bureau of the Budget in grave error in estimating the costs of the air program. If the program suggested were adopted, Congress must either raise taxes or engage in deficit financing. Better, then, to reduce other than military governmental expenditures.[23]

Forrestal pointed out that an increase from 55 to 70 air groups, to be accomplished between 1948 and 1953, would cost from $15 billion to $18 billion and necessitate a complete realignment of the balanced power concept of the armed forces. If the Air Force expanded, carrier, cruiser, submarine, tanker and other fleet elements must also increase in order to supply and sustain overseas Air Force bases. Nevertheless, even though the Joint Chiefs were still considering the 70-group plan, the House Committee on Armed Services unanimously approved it on the ground that it should be accomplished before Russia acquired the atomic bomb. The committee then endorsed an additional appropriation of $725 million, of which $450 million would go to the Air Force and the rest to the naval air arm, and the House approved. Truman had supported Forrestal's desire for a 55-group Air Force, as had Sullivan and Denfeld. However, Symington had availed himself of the privilege granted service secretaries in the National Security Act to go over the head of the secretary of defense, pressed the 70-group plan on the House, and won his point even though Sullivan noted that the Navy would have to increase from 450,000 to 550,000 men if the Senate and the President approved.[24]

On 12 February, Sullivan met with the National Security Council, which discussed America's position and policy in Greece, Turkey, Italy, Palestine, and China. Secretary of State George C. Marshall put the dilemma extremely well by saying that "the trouble was that we are playing with fire while we have nothing with which to put it out." Unfortunately, the defense establishment was not yet "unified"; there was as yet no really unified military policy or strategic plan to follow; and the demand for a 70-group Air Force undercut the proposal for universal military training Truman wanted and was avidly supported by the Army.[25]

After hearings were held on Sullivan's budget request by the House Committee on Appropriations, 14 February–8 March, Sullivan, Royall, and Symington, without consulting the Joint Chiefs of Staff, concurred on a budget report to Forrestal. They recommended adding 240,000 additional men to the Army, 63,000 to the Navy, 11,000 to the Marine Corps, and 35,000 to the Air Force. Cross purpose was evident when Royall asked for "undisputed air supremacy" and the retention of "our present sea superiority."[26]

While Sullivan was busy with budget and building problems, Congress approved an organization for his department that centralized power more than ever in the office of the secretary of the Navy and in the office of the chief of naval operations. Under its civilian leaders the department would have a chief of naval operations appointed by the president for a four-year term. He would be the principal adviser to the secretary of the Navy and be responsible to him for the use of the operating forces. A vice chief of naval operations, also to be nominated by the president, would have those duties determined by the chief of naval operations. Six deputy chiefs of naval operations detailed by the secretary of the Navy would head the various bureaus, while an undesignated number of assistant chiefs of naval operations could be named by the chief of naval operations. A new office, that of naval inspector general, would inquire into matters relating to the efficiency of the Navy; and the secretary of the Navy could appoint a chief of naval material and a vice chief of naval material. Except for the chief of naval operations and vice chief of naval operations, the secretary of the Navy was thus authorized to name all the bureau chiefs and the chiefs of the two new offices. In consequence, the bureau chiefs lost much of the autonomy they previously enjoyed, and the General Board of the Navy began a decline in importance that resulted in its abolishing itself in 1951. However, its bilinear organization, designed to slow down if not halt the centralizing process of unification, would be supported by the Navy for the next fifteen years.[27]

Forrestal excluded the service secretaries from a secret meeting that with Truman's permission he called with the Joint Chiefs of Staff for three days starting 11 March at Key West, Florida, to determine upon military roles and missions. Among the notes he prepared for the meeting, he wrote: "The Navy ... would keep its own air power, but would have to realize that budget limitations might compel it to 'make-do' with help from others; that it would for example, have to give the Air Force crews training in antisubmarine work and the close support of amphibious landings." Additional quotations from his diary are illustrative:

> 11 March 1948   Notes for Friday [the opening day]
> ... 3. There should be certain studies inaugurated now looking to reciprocal use of personnel in the event of emergency. For example, I doubt if the Navy will require the number of pilots that were in training at the end of the last war. *Question:* Could any of these be made available to meet deficiencies of the Air Force?
>   4. *Question:* What is being done about joint amphibious training operations between Army and Marines and Navy, so that techniques and tactics will be identical?
>   5. *Question:* Are there any plans for the use of Marine commanders with Army units on tactical maneuvers?
>   6. Function of strategic bombing is the Air Force's.
>   7. The Navy is to have the Air necessary for its mission, but its mission does not include the creation of a strategic air force.[28]

To those who demanded putting all air power in the Air Force, however, he replied that assurance for peace could only be obtained through the coordinated efforts of the entire military establishment, not through the atomic bomb or any other single agent.[29]

The paper entitled "Functions of the Armed Forces and the Joint Chiefs of Staff" Forrestal forwarded from Key West to Truman, it was reported early in April, spoke of the assignment of certain hitherto disputed duties as the "primary" responsibility of one of the services while at the same time making them "collateral" functions of certain other services. Strategic bombing, for example, was a primary Air Force function but collateral function for the Navy and Marine Corps. Moreover, Forrestal stated that the Navy would not be prohibited from attacking any targets, inland or otherwise, necessary for the accomplishment of its mission.

As revealed later, Section I of the paper dealt with such principles as integration of the armed forces, prevention of unnecessary duplication, and the coordination of operations. Section II defined the "common functions" of the services. Section III authorized the Joint Chiefs to permit unified commanders to establish subordinate unified commands and, more important, charged the chiefs with preparing "a statement of military requirements" based upon agreed strategic considerations, joint outline war plans, and current national security commitments," to be used by the secretary of defense and the departments in preparing the budget. Sections IV, V, and VI, set forth the primary and collateral functions of the services, and Section VII contained a glossary of terms and definitions.

In addition to the normal ground forces function, the Army was given the function of organizing, training, and equipping antiaircraft artillery units and primary interest in developing airborne doctrines, procedures, and equipment of common interest to the Army and Marine Corps. The Navy should be made ready primarily for prompt and sustained combat operations at sea "and for air and land operations incident thereto." Another Navy primary function was responsibility for the "amphibious training of all forces as assigned for joint amphibious operations." Further primary functions included naval reconnaissance; antisubmarine warfare; protection of shipping; minelaying, including its air aspects; and naval, including naval air, forces for the defense of the United States against air attack. While the Marines could operate with the fleet and seize or defend naval bases, they could also conduct "such land operations as may be essential to the prosecution of a naval campaign." However, it was specifically provided that "these functions do not contemplate the creation of a second land Army."

Primary missions of the Air Forces included strategic air warfare and the air defense of the United States. Collateral functions included the conduct of antisubmarine warfare, protection of shipping, and aerial minelaying.

The Joint Chiefs were to act as single service members who would decide upon the budget authorization needed to perform both primary and collateral functions. Any chief who disagreed with another in a field of primary responsibility could go directly to the secretary of defense for a decision.[30] If the President approved the agreements reached at Key West, he would issue a new executive order placing them into effect and repeal Executive Order No. 9877, dated 26 July 1947, which he had issued soon after passage of the National Security Act. Unfortunately, the Functions Paper did not determine whether a supercarrier or other ship prototypes should be built or even whether the Joint Chiefs must approve their construction. Hence the answer must be found in the National Security Act. However, in reporting to President Truman on 15 March, Forrestal added several points to the Key West decisions, viz., that "Navy not to be denied use of A-bomb" and that "Navy to proceed with development of 80,000-ton carrier and development of HA [high altitude] aircraft to carry heavy missiles therefrom." When Spaatz asked whether there were to be two air forces, Forrestal said that he had to administer the National Security Act as written, and Spaatz agreed that the decision must be made by Congress. In briefing major congressional leaders, Forrestal noted that "while it would be desirable to build up our Air Force, additions to our air power alone without accompanying increase in the components of the Army Ground Forces and the Navy might give us an unbalanced military organization and an illusory sense of security."[31]

In March, Sullivan testified at hearings held by the Senate Committee on Armed Services on Forrestal's defense program. He supported Forrestal especially on the need to augment military manpower, to undertake a limited rearmament program as insurance during the cold war, and to increase the defense budget $3 billion above the $11 billion ceiling Truman had set. On 15 April, the House agreed to Forrestal's aircraft procurement bill but added $822 million to it for starting a 70-group Air Force and sent it to the Senate. Fortified by a unanimous recommendation by the Joint Chiefs, on 21 April Forrestal offered a compromise plan he thought would not "bust the bungs" on the budget. The Air Force would have sixty-six rather than seventy groups, and corresponding increases would be made in the Army and Navy—a fact that cannot be overstressed. The plan would cost $481 million in addition to the initial $11 billion defense budget and $3 billion supplemental appropriation for fiscal year 1948. For fiscal year 1949, Forrestal suggested $14.5 billion. Truman gave only qualified approval to the supplemental appropriation for fiscal year 1948 and directed that it go via the Bureau of the Budget to Congress.[32]

The Budget Director, James E. Webb, started by cutting the extra $3.5 billion Forrestal wanted to $3.1 billion, then suggested that the Air Force be cut to 55 groups and that the Navy's air and antisubmarine components and the Army's re-equipment be deferred. He also made it clear that the defense establishment must be reduced to where it could live for the foreseeable future on a $15 billion budget—thus freezing military spending and strength. When Forrestal went to see Truman, the president said that his budget represented "preparing for peace and not for war," that the Armed forces must not cut too deeply into the civilian economy, and that he agreed with Webb. Although the resulting budget would greatly strengthen the Air Force and deny anything to the Army and Navy, at a meeting held at the White House on 13 May, Truman also set a limit of $15 billion for fiscal year 1950, "about all the economy could stand." He would support the supplemental appropriation for fiscal year 1948, now cut to $3.19 billion, only on the condition that the services not spend it! Truman made his budget program "administration policy" and expected "every member of the administration to support it fully both in public and in private." Not only did Truman and Webb eviscerate Forrestal's compromise program of 21 April, Truman ordered reductions of military personnel and directed that the Air Force not spend the $822 million the House had granted for the 70-group program until he approved. Forrestal's alternatives were to get Truman to raise his limit or to have the services review their plans and get more effective power out of the dollars they received.

Rather than unification, said some press pundits, the National Security Act created a bitter three-cornered controversy. Hanson Baldwin, the military commentator, spoke of unification as a "joke." Others noted that Forrestal and Royall had taken a "severe mauling" from Symington. Calling the unification act a "flop," Wayne Morse (Rep., Ore.) a member of the Senate Armed Services Committee, introduced a bill to abolish the separate military departments and to create a single chief of staff. Symington, meantime, spoke before the Senate Appropriations Committee, which approved the 70-group plan. Truman said that he favored the 70-group plan but added that he would review the entire military program in September and again in December and warned Congress that defense spending must proceed with an eye upon its impact upon the civilian economy. Because the Senate provided only funds to begin procurement for a 70-group program rather than establishing the Air Force as a 70-group organization, Symington and his adherents planned to obtain that goal when the special session of Congress met in late July.

Forrestal finally realized that the budget must include funds for the services and to support strategic plans and also the government's nonmilitary functions. By 23 June he had rough-drafted a memorandum for the service secretaries on the subject. During the next ninety days, he said, the preparation of the fiscal year 1950 budget would be the most important business facing the military establishment. The Joint Chiefs had acceded to his request to advise him on the division of funds within the budget ceiling imposed upon him. If they could not agree on the division, he would detail three high-ranking officers, one from each service, to duty in his office from 15 July to 15 September. Although the men he mentioned were never detailed, the Joint Chiefs created a board of three "budget deputies" including General Joseph T. McNarney, USAF, Vice

Admiral Robert B. Carney, USN, and Major General George J. Richards, USA, who as the McNarney Board worked to rationalize the operations of the military establishment.[33]

The House approved two military appropriations bills, one for the Army and Air Force, one for the Navy, totaling $10.2 billion. This would be the last time a defense budget would be offered in two bills. The Navy was granted $3.7 billion, a reduction of $241 million from the amount requested by the House Committee on Appropriations. Like Forrestal and the Army Chief of Staff, General Omar Bradley, Sullivan agreed to the defense budget only because greater expenditures might unbalance the economy.[34] The bill as finally approved, including regular, deficiency, and supplemental amounts, gave the Navy $3.8 billion. It also authorized Sullivan to stop work on thirteen ships being built and concentrate on others considered more important, especially the proposed supercarrier.

An extremely disquieting note now came from General Spaatz, former Chief of Staff of the Air Force, to the effect that he and Admiral Denfeld, the Chief of Naval Operations, interpreted differently certain actions taken by the Joint Chiefs, while Denfeld was not yet a member of that body, in forwarding the report of the President's Air Policy Commission. It had been said that the Joint Chiefs approved a 70-group Air Force and "the four oversized carriers of which Admiral Denfeld has spoken." The Joint Chiefs did provide the Finletter Commission with figures on national military air requirements but "did not approve in detail the supporting information contained in the report. Specifically, and I wish to make this perfectly clear, the Air Force action did not include approval of new and larger type aircraft carriers." The president had approved building a prototype supercarrier. At Key West, he asked the Joint Chiefs if they also approved. Spaatz replied that the president's decision was acceptable to him as one of his subordinates. However, a demand for such a carrier must be presented to the military branch having primary responsibility for strategic air operations, i.e., the Air Force, or to the Joint Chiefs. Denfeld thereupon asked the Joint Chiefs to formally approve the carrier. The vote was three to one in favor of its construction, with the Chief of Staff of the Air Force, General Hoyt S. Vandenberg, opposed. Bradley later stated that he voted for the carrier only because it was his understanding that it had been approved by those in authority and "I accepted it as a fait accompli."[35]

In his first annual report to the president, for the fiscal year ending 30 June 1948, Sullivan noted particularly how the Navy had worked to implement the National Security Act and paid special attention to research and planning. In cooperation with the other services, a number of unified commands had been established. The number of overseas bases had been reduced to the minimum needed to support current operations. While the number of naval aircraft and their associated personnel had been reduced, the Navy had agreed with the other services on which service would undertake the development of specific guided missiles. The Navy's personnel strength, 951,930 on 1 July 1946, had been cut to 502,747 on 1 January 1947, and to 477,384 on 30 June 1947, meaning that some shortages now existed, especially in specialist ratings, and that a great deal of imbalance marked the various ratings. Although no new ships were laid down during the year, twenty of thirty-three ships building had been completed, and work had been suspended on the *Hawaii*, *Kentucky*, and *Oriskany* (CV-34) in order to permit inclusion of extensive design changes.

Between the end of the second session of the Eightieth Congress and the special session he called for 26 July, Truman issued an executive order calling for "equality of treatment and opportunity for all persons in the Armed Services, without regard to race, color, religion, or national origin"; Forrestal named Major General Wilton B. Persons, USA, to coordinate all legislative proposals reported to him by three deputies from the armed services; and the service secretaries and agency leaders in the National Military Establishment forwarded to Forrestal initial statements of their requirements for the first truly unified military budget, for fiscal year 1950, which, as already indicated, Truman had limited to $15 billion. By this time Truman's niggardly treatment of the armed services provoked Forrestal to a divergence from presidential policies that eventually led to a request for his resignation.

On 31 March 1948, Sullivan, the other service secretaries, and the Joint Chiefs had met with Forrestal and various Department of State representatives to consider alternative courses of action if the Soviets tried to deny the Western Powers access to Berlin. On 24 June, the Soviets halted land traffic to the city. Three days later, Sullivan again joined Forrestal and various high-ranking military officers and representatives of the Department of State to help decide whether the United States would fight, leave Berlin, or seek an accommodation with the Soviets. Not until 15 July did the National Security Council decide to send additional B-29 bombers to Britain, within striking distance of Moscow. Even if the B-29s did not carry atomic bombs, there was no way Russia could prove that fact. Nevertheless, Truman's decision to remain in Berlin while seeking an accommodation with the Soviets highlighted the fact that the only quickly usable military power the United States possessed was the A-bomb. Symington knew this and exacerbated the rivalry between the services by stating publicly that air power should be put in balance not with the Army or the Navy but with that of potential enemies and referring to the "disjointed" defense budget. Forrestal thereupon asked for his explanation of "an act of official disobedience and personal disloyalty" and told Truman he would ask for his resignation if Symington could not satisfactorily explain his statements. At a dinner meeting of 19 July with Symington, Sullivan, and Royall, Forrestal tried to get at the root causes of Symington's conduct and generously glossed over his misconduct.

Disagreement between Symington and Sullivan, however, was deep if not wide. Sullivan conceded primary responsibility to Symington for strategic warfare but denied that the Navy should be limited to the use of atomic bombs upon particular targets. But Royall told Sullivan that the Navy should be "subservient" to the Air Force in the matter of strategic warfare in the same way that the Air Force was "subservient" to the Navy in the matter of antisubmarine warfare. Forrestal thought the matter could be settled by giving the Air Force primary responsibility for strategic warfare, limiting naval use of atomic bombs to targets indicated by the Air Force or upon "purely naval targets," and giving the Navy the right to appeal this settlement to the Joint Chiefs and then to the secretary of defense. In a subsequent talk with Vandenberg, Forrestal mentioned "1) The Navy belief, very firmly held and deeply rooted, that the Air Force wants to get control of *all* aviation; 2) The corresponding psychosis of the Air Force that the Navy is trying to encroach upon the strategic air prerogatives of the Air Force." The Air Force must have primary responsibility for strategic warfare, he went on, but he would not deny another service of the development of a weapon it thought it needed. While he opposed building a fleet of supercarriers, one such supercarrier, capable of carrying the weight of a long-ranging plane, should go forward even if it served only as an interim weapon until guided missile ships could be built. Forrestal concluded that if the Joint Chiefs could not decide the issue, he would. Vandenberg had suggested that the key was "money," that if funds were limited they should go to the strategic air force—which would then control the atomic bomb. Forrestal recalled to active duty the two leading elder statesmen of the Air Force and of naval aviation, General Spaatz and Admiral John Towers, to define the issues for him.[36]

Meanwhile, because of "Soviet aggression, increased international tension, the general deterioration of world relations, and the necessity for National security," early in August Representative Chester E. Merrow (Rep., N.H.), recommended that the 14,500-plane Navy planned for 1954 be realized by 1 July 1949. It was debatable whether Congress would provide the $2 billion needed for the telescoping of a five-year program into one. However, a thorough appraisal of the capabilities of present and future weapons in the light of their cost and capabilities of delivery, and various problems in connection with strategic warfare, would be made when Forrestal met at Newport, Rhode Island, on 20–22 August, with the Joint Chiefs, the service secretaries, and certain others.

As a result of this conference, Forrestal reported that complete agreement was reached on strategic air warfare. As his diary notes, operational control of the atomic bomb was temporarily vested in the Air Force, pending a decision on the organization for the control and direction of atomic operations to be reached by the services and their link with the Atomic Energy Commission, the Military Liaison Committee. The establishment of a weapons evaluation group was "desirable and necessary." In the field of its primary mission, each service "must have exclusive responsibility for planning and programming," but, "in the execution of any mission . . . all available resources must be used. . . . For this reason, the exclusive responsibility and authority in a given field do not imply preclusive participation."[37] The Air Force, thus, must use whatever strategic bombing capabilities the Navy might develop. The compromise stilled the Air Force-Navy dispute only momentarily. Whether the projected supercarrier was included in the decision was moot, but Forrestal was quick to point out that "The decisions themselves reflect neither a victory for the Air Force nor a defeat for the Navy. Neither do they indicate a victory for the Navy nor a defeat for the Air Force." Admiral Denfeld, who tried to maintain interservice harmony, admitted that each Joint Chief had had to withdraw from "an extreme position" he held with respect to his service but that they had adjourned with the feeling that "the Newport Conference spelled out a reasonable basis for making . . . agreements." However, the *Washington News* commented that "If this last division of responsibilities worked out in Newport turns out to be another Key West agreement, we suggest that instead of calling a third meeting Mr. Forrestal lop off a few official heads."[38]

On the first anniversary of the passage of the National Security Act, in speaking before the Baltimore Squadron of the Air Force Association, Sullivan lauded the "superlative job" the Air Force was doing. He was pleased with progress made in the first year of unification, adding that "most of the interservice projects during the past twelve months have worked smoothly and successfully. Most of these were the unpublished, rather dreary, run-of-the-mill operations—the kind . . . that win wars."[39] A week later, in addressing 1,700 members of the Navy Industrial Association at New York, he asserted that American naval ships in European and Mediterranean waters were "a constant stabilizing force in areas where explosive incidents might occur, and bluntly warned communists that the United States would take every step deemed necessary to preserve peace. He then noted that the achievements of aircraft carriers in World War II refuted criticism that they were at the mercy of land-based aviation. Finally, he said that the importance of the supercarrier, on which construction as CVA-58 would begin late in the year, "cannot be exaggerated,"[40] an idea he also stressed in an article honoring the Navy on Navy Day. In this article he emphasized the speed and power with which the Navy could respond to challenges to American national security. It also served as a deterrent to aggression. The Navy was a member of a defense team. The functions and responsibilities of all members of this team were now clearly defined in the unified organization that replaced the shambles created by postwar demobilization.

Sullivan was then shocked when Truman stated that the armed services had asked for $23 billion for fiscal year 1950 but must conform to the $15 billion limit he had set. Whether he would remain as president or give way to his Republican challenger, Thomas E. Dewey, would soon be known. If he were re-elected, Truman said, the $15 billion limit on the military budget could be lifted only if world conditions so indicated. He then prohibited public discussion of the defense budget by officials of the National Military Establishment.

In May 1948, Ferdinand Eberstadt headed a committee to study the National Security Organization for the Commission on Organization of the Executive Branch of the Government, or Hoover Commission. Truman noted that its report, issued in November, indicated that while the National Military Establishment was soundly organized it was not working well—it cited sloppy accounting and poor inventory control, for example—and that the authority of the secretary of defense over the departments and other security agencies and budget should be strengthened. It recommended that the secretary be given an under secretary and that a chairman be added to the Joint Chiefs of Staff. It rejected suggestions to merge the military departments under a single chief of staff and also a plan offered by the Army and Air Force to merge naval aviation with the Air Force, the last in part because Vice Admiral Arthur W. Radford, Deputy Chief of Naval Operations, spoke of the need of a carrier capable of launching aircraft carrying atomic bombs and criticized the B-36 as too slow to penetrate Soviet defenses, adding that the Air Force did not have bombers which could reach targets in Russia.[41]

Forrestal, who had continued to wrestle with the budget problem, received a report from the Joint Chiefs of Staff that they had "come up with a plan. . . . There was only really one major split decision which was on the question of plan of construction of additional new, big carriers. That question I had to resolve myself."[42] In keeping with his decision, in the first week in August a contract to build a supercarrier was given to the Newport News Shipbuilding and Drydock Company.

The McNarney Board report, which suggested a budget of $23.6 billion, reached Forrestal in early October, but the Joint Chiefs asserted that they could not agree on a program within the $14.4 billion limit and dumped the individual requests of their services into Forrestal's lap.[43] Although Forrestal asked General Eisenhower, the new President of Columbia University, for advice, on 15 October he had a long meeting with the Joint Chiefs and others. He admitted that under the President's budget ceiling "You can do a patchwork job. You cannot do a thorough one." But an intermediate figure of $17.5 billion with which to support American policy vis a vis Russia could be supported before Congress and the public.[44] Moreover, he gave his diary a sound answer to most of the inter-service arguments:

> I do not believe that air power alone can win a war any more than an Army or naval power can win a war, and I do not believe in the theory that an atomic offensive will extinguish in a week the will to fight. I believe air power will have to be applied massively in order to really destroy the industrial complex of any nation and, in terms of present capabilities, that means air power within fifteen hundred miles of the targets—that means an Army has to be transported to the areas where the airfields exist—that means, in turn, there has to be security of the sea lanes provided by the naval forces to get the Army there. Then, and only then, can the tremendous striking power of air be applied in a decisive—and I repeat decisive—manner.[45]

Forrestal therefore quickly sought to admonish Admiral Radford for his statements before the Eberstadt Committee in a letter to Sullivan that stated that one could defend the competence of his service to perform its missions but must not attack the competence of another service. He never sent the letter. On 31 October, Admiral Gallery said in public what Radford said in secret. On 8 November, Forrestal used the draft of his letter to Sullivan as the basis for a memorandum to all the service secretaries that stated that "any report or presentation by a responsible official of your Service to an agency outside of the Military Establishment, which involves any criticism of another Service, be submitted to me prior to delivery."[46] *After* Forrestal had issued his memorandum, Symington forcefully asserted to Eberstadt that the testimony given by Radford to the Eberstadt Committee had been "an unwarranted attack upon the Air Force" and added that "Action must be taken to resolve the present conflict resulting from the Navy's continuous attacks, even if the solution means consolidation." The Navy's case remained unpublished, while Symington's letter to Eberstadt gave the Air Force a publicity advantage.[47]

While Forrestal consolidated all sea transport services under the Navy, created a Weapons System Evaluation Group to "provide rigorous, unprejudiced and independent analyses and evaluations of present and future weapons systems under probable future combat conditions," and issued his first annual report, on 3 December 1948, he also decided that the secretary of defense must be something more than a coordinator of a loosely-knit federation. In his report and in legislation he offered the president, he agreed with most of the recommendations made by the Eberstadt Committee. The secretary of defense should be provided with an under secretary to act as his alter ego. The secretary should have "direction, authority, and control" over the departments and agencies of the National Military Establishment. A chairman should be added to the Joint Chiefs of Staff and the Joint Staff should be increased above its ceiling of one hundred. The secretary of defense should have broader authority over personnel matters. And only the secretary, not the service secretaries or heads of other defense agencies, should have membership on the National Security Council. He was undecided, however, on whether to downgrade the service secretaries.[48]

Forrestal had kind words for the Navy, which had always been "a tightly organized, self-contained service." While strategic air was a part of modern warfare, tactical air must be made capable of close cooperation with ground troops. He added: "I likewise hold the view that carriers and naval air will have a part to play in any war of the foreseeable future. The time may come when both the carrier and the long-range bomber are obsolete weapons, but that time has not yet arrived." Furthermore, new developments in submarine warfare, like the snorkel, made the solution of antisubmarine problems "one of the first importance to the Nation's security, and [I] have urged upon the Department of the Navy all possible acceleration in the research and tactical experiments necessary to solve the problem."

"Costs," said Forrestal, "are becoming a matter of concern. The Navy's operating requirements are being met, but only by extensive use of war-reserve stocks and operating inventories, and these are being depleted to an unwise degree." In his conclusion, Forrestal stressed two points: "The atomic bomb does not give us automatic immunity from attack, as some people would like to believe, nor does its mere possession guarantee victory if war should come," and "true unification of the armed might of the United States cannot spring from legislation alone. The spark generated by the Unification Act must be fanned into flame by the thoughts and actions of generals and admirals, ensigns and lieutenants, soldiers, sailors, and airmen, and civilians."[49]

On 9 December 1948, Sullivan, the other service secretaries, the Joint Chiefs, and civilian budget experts presented to Truman a budget they believed fair to both the defense and civilian sectors. The $30 billion originally suggested by the Joint Chiefs of Staff was pared to $16.9 billion. Truman stood by his $14.4 billion ceiling.[50] Several subsequent attempts by Forrestal to get Truman to lift that ceiling proved unavailing.

In his State of the Union message of 10 January 1949, Truman stated that "great progress" had been made toward unification during the past year, demanded universal military training, and allotted $14.4 billion for defense, with the sum almost equally divided among the services. Although the 50-group Air Force would be reduced to 48 instead of being expanded to 70, as Symington still insisted it should be, Symington realized that the budget favored the Air Force. Forrestal did also, for he told Truman that "With reference to the budget . . . the 14.4 billion ceiling limitation we would probably have the capability only of reprisal against any possible enemy, in the form of air warfare, using England as a base."[51] In sum, if war came the total budget would only be enough to enable the Air Force to mount an air counterattack on Russia from the United Kingdom, and nothing else. The Joint Chiefs therefore concentrated on strategic air power. Truman also promised to offer changes in the National Security Act that would speed unification—an offer promptly challenged by Representative Carl Vinson, now Chairman of the House Armed Services Committee, who said that Congress rather than the President had the authority to reorganize the military establishment. Moreover, Vinson shocked the Navy by introducing a bill authorizing a 70-group Air Force and prohibiting the Navy from building supercarriers unless Congress gave its express authorization—a challenge that would not go unanswered by Sullivan and the Navy.

In 1942, William Bradford Huie, a popular writer on military affairs, wrote a book, *The Fight for Air Power*, that denigrated the Navy. In 1946, a second book, *The Case Against the Admirals: Why We Must Have a Unified Command*, alleged that surface fleets had been obsolete since World War I and that strategic air power had won World War II. Using his letterhead, the Army sent a copy to each congressman and congressman-elect to make it appear that it came directly from the author.[52] In the December 1948 issue of *Reader's Digest*, Huie published the first of a series of articles (the others appeared in January, March, and April 1949), written probably with the help of high-ranking Air Force officers, that was extremely critical of naval aviation. The conjunction of Huie's attack and that of the Air Force, and the need to prepare the Navy's counterproposals to additional unification stirred the Navy to action.

Like any other interest group, the Navy battled other interest groups laying claim to scarce resources. Sullivan had his own public relations outlets: he contacted congressmen, appeared before congressional committees, and delivered public addresses. In his own office were the Office of Information, Office of Civil Relations, and Office of Public Relations. The last, however, had to work under Forrestal's directive that service "stories and claims" be brought into "a proper perspective—the perspective of national security, not the perspective of single service advantage."[53] "Backstopping" Sullivan were retired naval personnel, the Navy League, reserve officer organizations, and the U.S. Naval Institute.

Naval officers generally avoided politics, yet in emergencies they resorted to covert operations and *ad hoc* agencies in an attempt to improve the Navy's public image. Thus, when the threat of further service reorganization appeared late in 1948, the task of preparing the Navy's defense was given to the Organizational Research and Policy Section, better known by its CNO office code number OP-23, which was headed by Captain Arleigh Burke. Meanwhile legislation based on the Hoover Commission Report authorized the President to submit to Congress proposals for the reorganization of agencies within the executive branch. Unless both houses of Congress disapproved these changes within sixty days, they went into effect. But the military establishment and six regulatory agencies were excluded from the President's purview, an exclusion Truman deemed "disastrous." Truman thereupon asked Clark Clifford, among others, to prepare new legislation embodying the suggestions of Forrestal and of the Eberstadt committee. The result was known as Reorganization Plan No. 8.

Although the cold war still raged, Truman would keep the armed forces practically at their current strength. He thus provoked the "great debate" over the fiscal year 1950 budget. While Sullivan asked for a naval air arm of 14,500 planes. Truman would cut naval air strength from 8,550 to 7,450 planes.[54] The Navy in fiscal year 1950 would have 281 combatant vessels among its 731 ships and funds to proceed with the construction of CVA-58, to which the Air Force was violently and vociferously opposed. Sullivan offered Truman the names of *Pearl Harbor, George Washington,* and *United States* for the supercarrier, and preferred the last, to which Truman agreed.[55]

On 8 January 1950, by renewing his demand for seventy groups, Symington reopened the Air Force-Navy controversy, thus further undercutting Forrestal. When Forrestal on 11 January handed the President his pro forma resignation in consequence of Truman's reelection, he was asked to stay on. Despite his evident nervousness and frequent unwillingness to make decisions, symptoms of overwork and overstrain, he was happy to do so because of the important military legislation pending in Congress. While Sullivan did not resign, both Assistant Secretary of the Navy Mark E. Andrews and Assistant Secretary of the Navy for Air, John Nicholas Brown, did. On 15 February 1949, the Assistant Counsel General of the Navy, John H. Koehler, was named to succeed Andrews, and on 15 March Dan A. Kimball, executive vice president of the Aero Jet Corporation and vice president and director of the General Tire and Rubber Company, succeeded Brown.

In his first annual report, Sullivan noted that spiraling prices prevented the Navy from financing its programs. On the one hand, he wanted more pay for enlisted men than that granted in pay revision legislation Forrestal was about to submit to the president; on the other, budget limitations forced him to reduce naval and Marine Corps personnel by 30,000 officers and enlisted men, to lose 72 ships, 418 planes, and 12 air stations, and to reduce the scale of activity at naval shore establishments supporting the fleet, including the naval shipyards. Among the ships to be inactivated, he listed fifteen major combatant types, including three attack carriers, nine light cruisers, and three antiaircraft cruisers.

The Hoover Commission report generally followed the conclusions of the Eberstadt committee with respect to strengthening the authority of the secretary of defense. The three service secretaries would not only be downgraded to under secretaries of their departments and serve directly under the secretary of defense, they would be denied the privilege previously accorded them of appealing budgetary decisions of the defense secretary to the president or the director of the budget. The military departments, the report went on, were rigid statutory structures in which the service secretaries operated their departments as almost fully autonomous units. All authority should be given to the secretary of defense, who could then delegate authority to his assistants, including an under secretary of defense. Were the Hoover Commission recommendations adopted, the secretary of defense would have not merely "general direction" over the military establishment but would be responsible for exercising "direction, authority and control over the Departments and agencies of the Military Establishment."

After a "shattering experience" at the White House on 1 March, Forrestal resigned as secretary of defense, effective on or about 31 March. Truman warmly praised his ability, loyalty, and devotion to duty. Asked whether the service secretaries would be changed also, he said they would not. On 28 March, at Pentagon ceremonies, Royall, Sullivan, and Symington congratulated their new chief, Colonel Louis A. Johnson, and promised him support. At a second ceremony, at the White House, Truman pinned the Distinguished Service Medal on Forrestal's coat.

A West Virginia lawyer with experience in the state legislature, Johnson was big (250 pounds), tough, and politically ambitious. He had served as an Army officer in World War I, helped organize the American Legion, of which he was national commander in 1932, and served as assistant secretary of war from 1937 to 1940. Although he had engaged in a running feud with Secretary of War Harry Woodring, who supported neutrality and opposed mobilization, he so improved the industrial preparedness of the United States that it was said he shortened World War II by eighteen months. He had not, however, established himself in the affections and loyalties of the armed forces. Both he and Woodring resigned in 1940, when President Roosevelt replaced them with Henry L. Stimson and Robert P. Patterson, and Johnson returned to practicing law. Long active in Democratic politics, Johnson was particularly effective in raising campaign funds for Truman in 1948 and deserved reward. As that reward he demanded and was given the position of secretary of defense. Whereas Forrestal and Marshall had cooperated, Johnson and the new Secretary of State, Dean Acheson, were unsympathetic, and Johnson erred in trying to rigidly compartmentalize "political" and "military" factors. By directing that no contracts be made between the Defense and State departments except through their secretaries, he made coordinated policy impossible.[56] He was also an outspoken exponent of air power and of unification.

Forrestal had tried to coordinate rather than control the services. After eighteen months, he concluded that the office he was about to leave needed greater authority. Johnson would probably begin his duties with an under secretary and three assistants and a new chairman for the Joint Chiefs of Staff. Could he, even with this help, bring order out of chaos?

Truman urged the prompt enactment of legislation to strengthen the authority of the secretary of defense over the military departments but did not concur with the Hoover Commission proposals that the service secretaries be demoted to under secretaries of the secretary of defense. Instead he suggested that they retain their current titles but administer their departments under the direction and authority of the secretary of defense and be denied their right to appeal to the president or the director of the budget. He praised Forrestal highly at a dinner given in Forrestal's honor by the three service secretaries. At about the same time the Senate confirmed Johnson as his successor. A few days later, Forrestal was being treated at the Naval Hospital, Bethesda, Maryland, for what physicians said was "occupational fatigue." He improved somewhat, but at 3:00 A.M., 22 May, he fell to his death from an unguarded window.

Upon taking office on 28 March, on the same day the North Atlantic Treaty Organization treaty was signed, Johnson was the honored guest at a dinner attended by Truman. He would accelerate the unification time table, said Johnson, eliminate scores of interservice committees, decide soon upon the correct role of naval aviation, and summarily dismiss those "who do not work wholeheartedly for unification." By trying to "show who was boss," he lost the friendship and support of his staff except for the new people, often called "gauliters," he brought in. Close by him at the dinner had sat General Joseph T. McNarney, formerly head of the ax-wielding McNarney Board, now on temporary duty with Johnson as his prime adviser on administration and organization.

On 7 April, when Truman nominated his press secretary, Stephen T. Early, to be the under secretary of defense, Johnson abolished nine interservice boards and directed Sullivan, Royall, and Symington to report by 1 May which others should be abolished. At the end of two months, Johnson had abolished 68 committees; by October, 134; by the end of the year, 141.

While Johnson approved Sullivan's asking Congress for $10.5 million with which to complete two experimental submarines authorized in 1947, the House of Representatives passed a military appropriations bill that gave the Air Force $851 million more than Truman's budget recommended but only slight increases to the Army and Navy. Of the nearly $16 billion approved by the House Appropriations Committee, the Air Force would receive $6.22 billion, the Army $4.5 billion, and the Navy $5.02 billion. In debate on the measure, an attempt to add $300 million to naval aviation was decisively defeated, whereas the Air Force, now that it could operate against Russia from NATO bases, would grow from 48 to 58 groups. In consequence, Sullivan stated that he must cut his operating forces. The Navy would operate 731 instead of 755 ships, 7,765 instead of 10,687 planes, 8 instead of 11 carriers, and 18 instead of 28 cruisers. The number of destroyers, however, would increase from 147 to 180 and the number of submarines from 78 to 80. Last, 29,000 regular naval and Marines Corps personnel would be cut. What the fate of CVA-58, the USS *United States*, whose keel had been laid at Norfolk with appropriate ceremonies on 18 February, would be was not as yet clear, for Johnson said "No comment" to newspaper reporters' questions. The cost of the new carrier, originally set at $124 million, had increased to $152 million, with an additional $36 million required for ordnance and initial ammunition.

On 21 April, Royall resigned, effective the twenty-seventh. Sullivan meanwhile appeared before the House Appropriations Committee to speak about the importance of sea power. Without mentioning potential enemies, geographic areas, overseas bases which he had much in mind, or the Air Force, he asserted that control of the sea was vital to the national economy and to national defense as long as war remained a possibility. The daily well being and the livelihood of many Americans depended upon the uninterrupted flow of various critical materials from overseas. To keep the sea lanes open both in times of peace and times of war was the function of sea power. He concluded that:

> These considerations explain in part why we cannot abandon our naval strength, and why we cannot predicate our naval needs on a mere relative comparison with the navies of other powers. . . .
>
> It is my conviction that today, and in the world as it exists today, the Navy is more important to this country than it has ever been in time of peace in our entire history.[57]

To a Reserve Officers Association conference at Corpus Christi, Texas, on 23 April, Sullivan stated that the armed services "are working in full harmony" and that the Navy proposed to operate strictly within the agreements reached at Key West and Newport. "Unfortunately," he added, "harmony and accomplishment do not make news. Dissention and frustration do make news." At this moment, in Washington, Johnson wrote him a letter. He had received the views of the Joint Chiefs of Staff and of the President on the matter, Johnson wrote, and had given it his careful consideration. He then ordered Sullivan to discontinue construction on the *United States*. The immediate and violent reaction by the Navy to Johnson's order began with Sullivan's flying back to Washington and submitting his resignation to the President. Three days later

Sullivan made public a letter to Johnson in which he complained that neither he nor the Chief of Naval Operations, Denfeld, was consulted about canceling the carrier and that the President had twice approved its building. The carrier had been under intensive study in the Navy Department since October 1945, when it was proposed by the late Admiral Marc Mitscher. Sullivan had surrendered $307 million, which could have gone to complete other ships, in order to fund it. Its construction had been approved by both houses of Congress in June 1948, and Congress had appropriated funds for the first year of construction. Sullivan had then surrendered another $57 million in building funds for its construction; additional funding for it was carried in the budget for fiscal year 1950. On 18 April, Johnson had asked him about the carrier. Before he could say much, Johnson rushed off to some meeting. On the next day, he sent Johnson some data justifying the building of the carrier and a request for a personal meeting. He heard nothing about the subject until the twenty-third, when his office called him in Corpus Christi and told him that Johnson had ordered him to cancel the carrier's construction.

Sullivan continued:

> I am, of course, very deeply disturbed by your action which so far as I know represents the first attempt ever made in this country to prevent the development of a powerful weapon system. The conviction that this will result in a renewed effort to abolish the Marine Corps and to transfer all Naval and Marine Aviation elsewhere adds to my anxiety.
>
> However, even of greater significance is the unprecedented action on the part of a Secretary of Defense in so drastically and arbitrarily changing and restricting the operational plans of an Armed Service without consultation with that Service. The consequences of such a procedure are far-reaching and can be tragic.

Sullivan concluded by noting that he evidently could provide no further useful service to the Navy Department and had forwarded his resignation to the President.

Upon learning of Sullivan's resignation, Johnson said that "Sullivan has joined the aircraft carrier issue on personal grounds, and I believe that he . . . will soon regret his action. . . . " While testifying before the House Armed Services Committee on 10 October 1949, he added that Sullivan had not resigned on 23 April but about a month earlier "because he was unwilling to support unification." The truth was that Sullivan submitted a perfunctory letter of resignation four days before Johnson succeeded Forrestal and that Johnson interpreted it to please himself. By not returning the letter, furthermore, Johnson could blackmail Sullivan into supporting the augmentation of the powers of the secretary of defense.

On 21 October 1949, after Chairman Vinson chided him on the brusque and abrupt manner in which he had cancelled the *United States*, Johnson denied that he had ever been discourteous to Sullivan, adding:

> Mr. Sullivan was not for unification, would not support unification and . . . on March 26 . . . he tendered to the President of the United States his resignation as Secretary of the Navy and knew it was accepted, because he was not in accord with unification and because I had told him there was no room on my team on the civilian side for anybody who wouldn't loyally and enthusiastically support unification.[58]

Johnson's scrapping of the supercarrier was a major victory for the Air Force, which viewed it and its long-range planes as an invasion of its responsibility for strategic air warfare. Moreover, Truman's prompt acceptance of Sullivan's resignation, to be effective at Sullivan's convenience, made it appear that he backed Johnson. Although some representatives on both sides of the aisle criticized Johnson, and Vinson disliked the manner of his action, both Vinson and Tydings, Chairman of the Senate Armed Services Committee, agreed that Johnson had made a "courageous and momentous decision," that he acted under presidential authority, and that the President could retire an appropriation at any time. Tydings added that he would hold no hearings on the matter because the Joint Chiefs of Staff had decided against the carrier by a vote of two to one and the Senate would not go over their heads.

The supercarrier had been a bone of contention between the Navy and Air Force for some time. The President's Commission on Air Policy was told by the Joint Chiefs that they approved building the carrier. When Sullivan asked Congress for authority to suspend construction of thirteen vessels in order to divert the funds to the new carrier and other ships, Denfeld, the naval representative on the Joint Chiefs of Staff, told the commission that the carrier was discussed at Key West "and the members of the Joint Chiefs of Staff said that they would go along with it because it was in the President's program, and had been approved by the Secretary of the Navy and the Secretary of Defense. It was not discussed at great length, but it was tacitly approved by all the members there." In testifying before the House Committee on Armed Services in October 1949, Denfeld repeated that "The construction of the carrier was approved by the Secretary of Defense, the Secretary of the Navy, and by three members of the Joint Chiefs of Staff, on May 28, 1948, the Air Force member dissenting." The Joint Chiefs were asked on 15 April 1949 to review their decision. In their answer, ready on the twenty-second and delivered to Johnson on the twenty-third, General Bradley reversed his decision. Forty minutes after Denfeld delivered the decision into Johnson's hand, an already mimeographed press release on the cancellation of the carrier was being handed out by his office.[59] Air Force leaders and General Bradley later questioned Denfeld's conclusion, asserting that while the Joint Chiefs of Staff had tacitly accepted the carrier they had not approved the long-range planes with which it was to be equipped.[60]

In briefing Johnson before he himself retired, Forrestal may have spoken about the need to build the supercarrier. The fact that NATO bases for long-range land-based planes would soon be available may have helped Johnson decide that it was unnecessary. Moreover, the authorization by Congress in 1948 to permit the diversion of funds from ships already more than 20 percent completed in order that work might be started on the big carrier left the matter to the President's judgment, and Truman expressed surprise upon learning that the carrier's keel was laid. Johnson briefly discussed the supercarrier with Eisenhower and the Joint Chiefs of Staff on 8–11 April. On the fifteenth, after talking with Truman, he asked Eisenhower and the Joint Chiefs by letter for their individual views about the carrier. Sullivan's contacts with Johnson on the eighteenth and nineteenth have already been mentioned. During the week following the fifteenth, Johnson spoke daily with the Joint Chiefs and also conferred six times with Truman. On the twenty-second, armed with the opinions of the Joint Chiefs, who voted two to one against the carrier, he obtained Truman's permission to stop her further construction.[61] The vote by the Joint Chiefs was unimportant to Johnson. First, they never acted by majority vote; any split decision was brought to the attention of the secretary of defense and of the President. Second, as Johnson himself put it: "Whether the Joint Chiefs of Staff vote two-to-one or unanimously, they are only advisers to the Secretary of Defense and the President who do the deciding."[62] It was upon learning of Johnson's action that Sullivan had returned to Washington from Corpus Christi and prepared his angry letter of resignation. Two days later he called on Truman. Despite the rancor in his relationship with Johnson, he parted friends with the President, whom he evidently did not hold responsible for the cancellation of the *United States*.

When it was agreed that work on thirteen ships could be suspended, Sullivan understood that funds thus saved could go toward the carrier and other new ships. With work stopped on the carrier, he could not use the funds to complete thirteen outdated ships and must ask Congress for additional funds for new construction. Denfeld's misunderstanding of the mind of the Joint Chiefs and Sullivan's misunderstanding of the nature of the legislation affecting the construction of the carrier thus exacerbated the Sullivan–Johnson feud. In the end, Vinson came closest to the heart of the problem. He believed a navy was needed to control the seas but that a future war would be with a land power. He added:

It is simply a matter of the proper allocation of war missions between the Navy and Air Force. It is the business of the Air Force to use long-range bombers in time of war. And yet, this carrier was to accommodate such long range bombers. We cannot afford the luxury of two strategic air forces. We cannot afford an experimental vessel that, even without its aircraft, costs as much as 60 B-36 long-range bombers. We should reserve strategic air warfare to the Air Force.[63]

Johnson had peremptorily discontinued the construction of the carrier without first consulting Sullivan, the responsible head of the Navy, who by law had the right to appeal the decision. He thus put Sullivan in such an impossible position that he felt he must resign.

Johnson's cancellation of the *United States* and Sullivan's resigning made Johnson the center of a controversy that emphasized service disagreements, as illustrated by the "revolt of the admirals" which began even before he stopped the carrier's construction, bedeviled his entire tenure, and continued under his successor, Francis P. Matthews.

On 24 May, Sullivan returned to law practice in Washington. At this writing, although he is eighty-nine years of age, he still remains active.

NOTES

1. Samuel P. Huntington, "Interservice Competition and the Political Roles of the Armed Services," in Harry L. Coles, ed., *Total War and Cold War: Problems in Civilian Control of the Military* (Columbus: Ohio State University Press, 1962), p. 184.
2. W. W. Rostow, *The United States in the World Arena: An Essay in Recent History* (New York and Evanston: Harper and Row, 1960), pp. 223-24.
3. Walter Millis, ed., with the collaboration of E. S. Duffield, *The Forrestal Diaries* (New York: Viking, 1951), pp. 317-18, 320, 329, 342.
4. "John L. Sullivan: The Secretary of the Navy," ANJ 85 (25 Oct. 1947):195.
5. "General Board of the Navy," by VADM C. H. McMorris, USN, Chairman, the General Board, *ibid.* 85 (4 Apr. 1948):833, 839.
6. Carl W. Borklund, *Men of the Pentagon: From Forrestal to McNamara* (New York: Praeger, 1966), p. 73.
7. Millis, ed., *Forrestal Diaries*, p. 333; Paul Y. Hammond, "Super Carriers and B-36 Bombers: Appropriations, Strategy, and Politics," in Harold Stein, ed., *American Civil-Military Decisions: A Book of Case Studies* (University: University of Alabama Press, 1963):470 (hereafter cited as "Super Carriers and B-36 Bombers").
8. Borklund, *Men of the Pentagon*, pp. 12-64; Jack Raymond, *Power at the Pentagon* (New York: Harper and Row, 1964), p. 278.
9. Vincent Davis, *The Admirals Lobby* (Chapel Hill: University of North Carolina Press, 1967), pp. 170-74; ANJ 85 (27 Sept. 1947):82.
10. "Inter-Service Controversies," ANJ 85 (14 Feb. 1948):610.

11. *New York Times*, 1 Jan. 1947. See for example CDR John S. McCain, Jr., USN, "Where Do We Go From Here?" USNIP 75 (Jan. 1949):47–52; CDR Edward J. Fahy, USN, "Pushbuttons Need Men," *ibid.* 75 (Feb. 1949):149–53; Walmer Elton Strope, "The Naval Officer and Tomorrow's Navy," *ibid.* 75 (Mar. 1949): 279–87; and MAJ Guy Richards, USMCR, "The Riddle of Combined Arms," *ibid.* 75 (Aug. 1949):881–89.

12. Defense of the Navy against such charges during 1947 and 1948 is well illustrated in LT William H. Hessler, USNR, "Geography, Technology, and Military Policy," *ibid.* 73 (Apr. 1947):379–90; COMMO Ernest M. Eller, USN, "Sea Power and Peace," *ibid.* 73 (Oct. 1947):1161–73; Walmer Elton Strope, "The Navy and the Atomic Bomb," *ibid.* 73 (Oct. 1947):1221–27; MAJ Guy Richards, USMCR, "The Navy's Stake in the Future," *ibid.* 74 (Feb. 1948):183–95; LCOL Robert E. Cushman, Jr., USMC, "Amphibious Warfare: Naval Weapon on the Future," *ibid.* 74 (Mar. 1948):301–07; and LCDR Malcolm W. Cagle, USN, "The Jets Are Coming," *ibid.* 74 (Nov. 1948):1343–49.

13. Office of the Chief of Naval Operations, *U.S. Naval Aviation in the Pacific* (Washington: GPO, 1947), pp. 53–54. See also Davis, *Admirals Lobby*, pp. 206–07, and LCDR H. B. Seim, USN, "Atomic Bomb—the X Factor of Military Policy," USNIP 75 (Apr. 1949):387–93.

14. *New York Times*, 3 Nov. 1947.

15. Millis, ed., *Forrestal Diaries*, p. 325 (entry of 6 Oct. 1947).

16. *Ibid.*, pp. 350–51.

17. "Ad. Nimitz Sees Navy With Air As First Line," ANJ 85 (10 Jan. 1948):472, 495.

18. Borklund, *Men of the Pentagon*, p. 74.

19. U.S. President's Air Policy Commission, *Survival in the Air Age: A Report by the President's Air Policy Commission* (Washington: GPO, 1948).

20. Borklund, *Men of the Pentagon*, p. 76.

21. *Ibid.*, pp. 75–76; Hammond, "Super Carriers and B–36 Bombers," pp. 472, 480.

22. *New York Times*, 24 June 1948; *New York Herald Tribune*, 25 Aug., 12 Oct. 1948.

23. Report of the Congressional Aviation Policy Board, *National Aviation Policy*, S. Rpt. 949, 80th Cong., 2nd Sess. (Washington: GPO, 1948).

24. "Balanced Arms Urged by Defense Secretary," ANJ 85 (10 Apr. 1948):833, 841; "House Approves 70-Group AF and Naval Air Funds," *ibid.* 85 (17 Apr. 1948): 857, 859.

25. Millis, ed., *Forrestal Diaries*, pp. 370–73.

26. U.S. House, Committee on Appropriations, *Hearings on Department of the Navy Appropriations Bill for 1949*, 80th Cong., 2nd Sess. (Washington: GPO, 1949); Editorial, ANJ 86 (27 Mar. 1948):786.

27. *Report of the Committee on Organization of the Department of the Navy—1954* (Washington: GPO, 1954 [Gates Board Report]); *Report on the Committee on Reorganization of the Department of the Navy—1959* (Washington: GPO, 1959 [Franke Board Report]).

28. Millis, ed., *Forrestal Diaries*, pp. 390–91.

29. "Defense Sec. Presses for War Role Clarity," ANJ 85 (13 Mar. 1948):722.

30. "Text of Functions Paper," *ibid.* 85 (20 Mar. 1948):807, 809, 822, 823.

31. Millis, ed., *Forrestal Diaries*, pp. 393–96.
32. *Ibid.*, pp. 401–02, 414–19.
33. Memorandum for the JCS, 26 Aug. 1947, Memorandum by the Director of the Joint Staff to the JCS, 23 Oct. 1947, Memorandum of the CNO to the JCS, 17 Nov. 1947, Memorandum for Admiral [Nimitz], 21 July 1948, JCS Papers, File 1800, NHD:OA (hereafter cited as CNO Papers).
34. Note by the Secretaries to the JCS, 8 Nov. 1948, CNO Papers, File 1800; Warner R. Schilling, Paul Y. Hammond, and Glenn H. Snyder, *Strategy, Politics, and Defense Budgets* (New York: Columbia University Press, 1962), p. 85.
35. Hammond, "Super Carriers and B-36 Bombers," p. 481.
36. *Ibid.*, pp. 451–54, 456–59; Millis, ed., *Forrestal Diaries*, pp. 462–68.
37. Millis, ed., *Forrestal Diaries*, pp. 476–77.
38. "Closer Accord Seen as Result of Conferences," ANJ 85 (28 Aug. 1949):1433, 1435, 1459.
39. "SecNav Praises Air Force," *ibid.* 85 (18 Sept. 1948):70.
40. *New York Times*, 30 Sept. 1948.
41. Dean Acheson, *Present at the Creation: My Years in the State Department* (New York: W. W. Norton, 1969), pp. 243–44; USNIP 75 (Feb. 1949):238–39.
42. Forrestal to Charles E. Wilson, 9, 18 Sept. 1948, in Millis, ed., *Forrestal Diaries*, p. 493.
43. Top Secret. Memorandum on the Correlation of Army, Navy, and Air Force Budget Estimates with Strategic Plan, ADM [William D.] Leahy to SECDEF, 24 July 1948; [Forrestal], Memorandum for the JCS on Allocation of Funds for 1950 Budget, 9 Nov. 1948; Secret. Memorandum for all Service Secretaries and the JCS, Snyder, Lovett, Draper, 22 Nov. 1948, JCS 1800/13, CNO Papers. The top secret paper, JCS 1800/18, of 17 Nov. 1948, contains breakdowns of budgets set at $14.4 billion, $16.9 billion, and $21.4 billion. *Ibid.*
44. Millis, ed., *Forrestal Diaries*, p. 514 (entry of 27 Oct. 1948).
45. Memorandum for the SECA, SECNAV, and SECAF, 8 Nov. 1948, *ibid.*, pp. 516–17.
46. Memorandum for the President, 3 Dec. 1948, *ibid.*, p. 539.
47. Hammond, "Super Carriers and B-36 Bombers," pp. 488–89.
48. U.S. Department of Defense, *First Report of the Secretary of Defense* (Washington: GPO, 1948), pp. 2–4; Forrestal to John McCone, 3 Dec. 1948, in Millis, ed., *Forrestal Diaries*, pp. 539–40.
49. Forrestal, *First Report*, pp. 9–12, 19, 64–66.
50. Note by the Secretaries to the JCS on Allocation of Funds for FY1950 Budget, 18 Nov. 1948, JCS1800/19; Director, Bureau of the Budget to SECDEF, with enclosures, 1 Dec. 1948, JCS 1800/18; SECDEF to the President, 1 Dec. 1948, JCS 1800/19, CNO Papers.
51. Millis, ed., *Forrestal Diaries*, p. 536.
52. Demetrious Caraley, *The Politics of Military Unification: A Study of Conflict and the Policy Process* (New York: Columbia University Press, 1966): pp. 223–24.
53. ARSN, 1947, p. 82; Huntington, "Interservice Competition and the Political Roles of the Armed Services," 194; LTJG P. W. Rairden, USN, "Navy Public Information," USNIP 73 (Jan. 1947):47–53.

54. *New York Times,* 27 Oct. 1948.
55. *Ibid.,* 3 Feb. 1949; Martin E. Holbrook, "Naming the New Carrier," USNIP 75 (Feb. 1949):227–28.
56. For Johnson's boorish actions in connection with the drafting of NSC–68, see Acheson, *Present at the Creation,* pp. 373–74.
57. "Importance of the Sea Power Explained by Secretary," ANJ–86 (23 Apr. 1949): 978.
58. U.S. House, Committee on Armed Services, Hearings before the Committee on Armed Services, House of Representatives, *The National Defense Program: Unification and Strategy,* 81st Cong., 1st Sess. (Washington: GPO, 1949) pp. 622-23 (hereafter cited as NDP); Hammond, "Super Carriers and B-36 Bombers," p. 536; "Documents Leading to the Resignation of Sec. Sullivan," ANJ 86 (30 Apr. 1949):1003.
59. NDP, p. 360.
60. Hammond, "Super Carriers and B-36 Bombers," pp. 474–75.
61. NDP, pp. 619–20.
62. C. W. Borklund, *The Department of Defense* (New York: Praeger, 1968), p. 56.
63. ANJ 86 (30 Apr. 1949):1003.

FRANCIS P. MATTHEWS

25 May 1949–31 July 1951

PAOLO E. COLETTA

John L. Sullivan left the office of the secretary of the Navy on 24 May 1949. Whoever President Harry S. Truman named as his successor would face the problem of raising naval morale from a twenty-five year low,[1] enforcing Secretary of Defense Louis A. Johnson's directive that forbade service personnel to publicize their views about the defense department without prior approval, and administer his department under terms of a new reorganization plan for the armed services that strengthened the power of the secretary of defense and further limited the authority of the service secretaries. He must try to live with an administration which in both the executive and legislative branches made "economy" a watchword. He would also be involved in two major squabbles: over the capability of the B–36 and over whether a supercarrier should be built.

Some naval aviators asserted that the B–36 could easily be shot down by fighters, whereas Air Force leaders insisted that it was practically invulnerable.[2] To show its air capability, the Navy flew a P2V patrol bomber capable of carrying the atomic bomb off the carrier *Midway*, off Norfolk, which reached San Diego after a 4,863-mile nonstop flight—the longest flight ever made from a carrier.[3] Meanwhile various admirals asked the Senate Appropriations Committee to agree to $43 million for a supercarrier approved by the House.[4]

Representative James Van Zandt (Rep., Pa.), member of the House Armed Services Committee and a captain in the naval reserve, tried to interest the chairman of the committee, Carl Vinson, in investigating the Air Force procurement arrangements for the B–36, including Johnson's connection with it as a director of its manufacturer, Consolidated Vultee Aircraft Corporation.

Lest Van Zandt head a special staff of investigators, Vinson decided to undertake the task himself. In mid-June, he offered a seven point agenda for hearings to begin in July: 1) Was it a "sound" decision to have cancelled the *United States?* 2) Was the Air Force putting too much emphasis upon strategic bombing and not enough upon tactical aviation? 3) Should two of the armed services be able to "pass on" the weapons of a third by a two to one vote in the Joint Chiefs of Staff? 4) Were Van Zandt's charges true? 5) Identify sources of rumors and charges against the Air Force, presumably coming from the Navy and steel contractors. 6) Evaluate the performance of the B–36. 7) Evaluate the roles and missions of the Air Force and Navy, especially naval and Marine aviation.[5]

On 24 May 1949 Truman nominated Francis Patrick Matthews as secretary of the Navy. Matthews, born on 15 March 1887 to Patrick and Mary Ann (Sullivan) Matthews, was a graduate of Creighton University, a banker, corporation executive, and attorney in Omaha, a director of the Chamber of Commerce of the United States, and a prominent Roman Catholic layman. In 1946 Truman had honored him for his wartime work with the USO; in 1946–47, Truman appointed him to the President's Commission on Civil Rights. In 1948 Matthews helped swing the Nebraska delegation to Truman and became friendly with Louis Johnson, chairman of the Democratic Party Finance Committee. Completely unversed in the ways of the Navy and of Washington, he broke the chain of competent men James V. Forrestal had trained while he was Secretary of the Navy and then Secretary of Defense.[6] As an "outsider," however, he would be easier to school in the political patterns of the Department of Defense, a point Truman thought important for the progress of national security "unification."

In the presence of Mrs. Mary Claire (Hughes) Matthews, whom he married in 1914, and their six children, Matthews was sworn in on 25 May, at the same time that Dan A. Kimball, the Assistant Secretary of the Navy for Air, was sworn in as Under Secretary of the Navy. Not until November did Truman name as Kimball's successor as Assistant Secretary of the Navy for Air a Chicago lawyer named John F. Floberg, a naval veteran of World War II.

Matthews met Floberg at a party held on a Sunday late in October. He asked Floberg to have lunch with him at his dining room at the Pentagon on the next day. During the lunch, which lasted three hours, Matthews discussed the problems he and the Navy faced and pressured Floberg to join his secretariat.[7] Floberg agreed. Floberg, incidentally, married a sister of the wife of one of Matthew's sons, so that there was a relationship at least by marriage. That fact aside, Floberg was one of the few people closely associated with Matthews in the Navy Department who supported him even though he knew of his various weaknesses.

Matthews was known in the press as the "rowboat secretary" because that was the only craft he had ever sailed. He admitted to the graduating midshipmen of the Naval Academy that he had "little prior training or preparation" to guide him in his new post. However, he expected to learn quickly. He approved legislation strengthening the authority of the Secretary of Defense, and said that while unification was the "big problem" it could be achieved "without impairing Navy prestige."[8]

Soon after Vinson offered his agenda for investigating the B–36, Johnson announced that the President approved his decision to fund the modernization of two additional carriers of the *Essex* class so that they could handle heavy bombers; that the Air Force would be kept at forty-eight rather than the fifty-eight groups, and told Kimball that naval aviation should be "beefed up."[9] Johnson seemed thus to favor the Navy.

After only nine weeks in office, Matthews made a brief annual report for the fiscal year 1948–1949 in which he stated that he had largely followed policies instituted by his predecessor. The First Fleet in the Pacific, the Second in the Atlantic, and Sixth in the Mediterranean supported U.S. interests. Navy transports had evacuated the families of naval personnel from China, torn by civil war. The Naval Air Transport Service had been merged with the Military Air Transport Service on 1 June 1948. With MATS heavily engaged in Operation Vittles, the succor of Berlin during its blockade by the Soviets, Navy squadrons had taken over domestic air transport and also furnished two squadrons for use in Operation Vittles. Also, arrangements had been made for the Navy to assume responsibility for all military sea transportation on 1 October 1949.

"Considerable" progress had been made in antisubmarine warfare, Matthews continued, and in developing electronic devices for communications, navigation, and countermeasures. Three carriers of the *Essex* class were being modernized, and several light carriers were being converted to antisubmarine carriers. Although "various considerations" had led to the cancellation of the *United States*, her design studies were available for future guidance. The Navy was also studying the feasibility of using electronic computers for solving its logistics problems.

An historic "first" during fiscal year 1949 was the appointment of women in the regular Navy, said Matthews. In addition, the Navy was publicizing equal opportunities for all general service ratings and trying to recruit qualified Negroes for them. The number of naval personnel stood at 50,100 officers and 409,900 enlisted men on 1 June 1949, when there were also 1,019,182 men in the Naval Reserve and 123,817 in the Marine Corps Reserve.[10]

Because of the cold war, the State Department had advised the secretary of defense in June 1948 that the "feast or famine" cycle of defense spending must be oriented toward a situation of "permanent crisis." The fiscal year 1950 budget was the first designed in keeping with this advice. The $15.9 billion defense budget approved by the House in mid-march 1949 allotted $4.8 billion to the Army, $6.2 billion to the Air Force, and $5.0 billion to the Navy, thus keeping the services "in balance." When the Senate cut the total below $15 billion, the difference was given to a conference committee to resolve.

As matters stood, naval aviation faced the greatest crisis in its history; in addition to the cancellation of the *United States*, it was cut $36 million in research and development funds and $687 million for new aircraft. A ceiling was thus placed on technical improvements in naval aircraft, for without the supercarrier the Navy had to scrap designs for the new planes she would have carried, abandon plans for five aircraft prototypes, and suffer a year's delay in producing four others. It therefore sought bombers smaller than those planned for the supercarrier to operate from modernized *Midway*–class carriers. The poor status of naval aviation could be ascribed to various factors: the Navy's failure to present its case to the public, as the Air Force did; Johnson's economizing; "black-shoe" or "battleship" admirals who preferred to expand surface forces rather than aviation; and the fact that the chief of naval operations was not an aviator.

Despite the explosion of a nuclear bomb by Russia in August 1949, Johnson meant to spend less money than that provided in the fiscal 1950 and 1951 budgets. He would get rid of "unnecessary" civilians and regular and reserve personnel; insure that military people performed only military duties; stand pat on the number of operating aircraft carriers and the carrier modernization program; get rid of "all waste, duplication, and extravagance," and reduce the Air Force from fifty-eight to forty-eight groups.[11]

Although the Navy would have been happy with a tripartite division of the budget, Johnson and the Army and Air Force disdained this kind of "balance." Moreover, budget reductions made primarily at the expense of the Navy illustrated the concept in which "distributing shortages" effectively substituted financial controls for adequate review of military requirements and therefore dictated strategy.

Johnson's order that reports from the military departments concerning the B–36 controversy be submitted to Under Secretary of Defense Stephen T. Early before being forwarded to Vinson provoked such strong cries of censorship that Johnson rescinded his Consolidation Directive Number 1, on 14 April, and stimulated a reorganization of the public relations work of the department of defense and of the military services.

By 1949, Captain Walter Karig, USNR, had served in Navy public relations for nine years. As he told the chief of naval operations on 21 June 1949, "The be-all of Navy Public Relations is—appropriations."[12] Two days later he suggested the transfer of the Office of Public Relations (OPR) to OP–004 in the office of the chief of naval operations and that OP–004 and OP–23, the special studies group, constitute a planning group for Navy-wide public relations.[13]

About a month later, Karig noted that one man controlled the public relations of the Army, and one man those of the Air Force. "You can't peddle prestige from a push-cart," he said, adding that the Navy put public relations "on a par with garbage collecting." No wonder, then, that "naval aviation is on the way out, the fleet is shrinking to a ferry service, and Admirals are called 'brass hats' and cartooned as pompous nitwits—all products of anti-Navy press agentry, unopposed." The director of OPR, Karig asserted, should be a two or three star admiral nearing retirement, hence lacking any ambition other than to be a press agent, or a civilian assistant secretary who kept much more closely in touch with the secretary of the Navy than had been the case in the last four years. A committee of two admirals, two captains, and Karig had begun fourteen months earlier to try to carry out a national public relations program. It had bogged down in detail and finally ceased meeting. Therefore the "party line" was being established by OP–23. The Navy of the United States, Karig concluded, was what the people wanted it to be. The task of naval public relations was to educate them in what that Navy should be.[14]

Meanwhile the Navy League's support for more naval aircraft and carriers and resistance to the loss by the Navy of the Marine Corps created the impression that the Navy was opposed to everything Truman, Johnson, and Early wanted. Although Matthews told League President Frank Hecht that he was satisfied with Johnson's treatment of the Navy, Hecht refused to be bridled.[15]

In the meantime, also, Representative Van Zandt moved that the House Armed Services Committee set aside Senator Millard E. Tydings's bill for amending the National Security Act except for Title IV, which covered only budgetary and fiscal procedures, lest Johnson still further tighten his control over the National Military Establishment. Vinson thereupon postponed the B–36 hearings and went to see Truman. On 18 July, Truman sent his Reorganization Plan No. 8 for the National Military Establishment, long in writing, to Congress. Truman's plan converted the National Military Establishment into a regular executive department named the Department of Defense. Its secretary would exercise authority, direction, and control over the military departments, which would be administered by their respective secretaries, but he would not have the right to change the statutory assignment of the combatant functions, roles, and missions of the services. A deputy secretary would replace the under secretary of defense, three secretaries would be provided to assist the secretary, and a chairman would be provided for the

Joint Chiefs of Staff. Only the secretary of defense, not the heads of the military departments, would be a member of the National Security Council. The name of the War Council was changed to Armed Forces Policy Council, and a new Personnel Policy Board was established to advise the Secretary of Defense on personnel matters.[16]

On 21 June, when directed by Johnson to determine the feasibility of adopting a system of organization similar to the General Staff of the Army, Matthews turned the matter over to the General Board of the Navy. Vinson, however, warned against adopting a powerful general staff and on 19 August the General Board advised Matthews that the Navy was "emphatically" and "solidly" opposed to having a general staff imposed upon it. Among its reasons for objecting, the board noted that it would cause naval officers to cease striving for sea command—their primary function—and begin to vie for general staff billets. Moreover, no navy used a general staff system, and the Navy might be subjugated to a landlocked theory of defense. The report sat on Matthews desk for months without his taking action on it.[17]

Both Johnson and Herbert Hoover assured Vinson that the Senate's proposed amendments to the National Security Act would save between $1 billion and $1.5 billion per year, but neither man was able to catalogue where the savings would be made.[18] In the end, saying that he would grant the secretary of defense greater authority only under safeguards assuring Congress even greater control over his decisions and operations, Vinson offered fourteen amendments to the bill Tydings had introduced as Chairman of the Senate Armed Services Committee. One amendment would permit the service secretaries and the Joint Chiefs of Staff to have direct recourse to Congress with or without the approval of the defense secretary. Another would require the latter to consult with the armed services committees before ordering any change or consolidation of statutory functions. A third required him to report to Congress semi-annually rather than annually.

At hearings held by Vinson, Representative Felix Edward Hébert (Dem., La.) accused Johnson of going "beyond the law" with respect to Navy finances. Vinson asked whether Johnson would abolish the Navy's bureau system. Johnson replied that Matthews favored the bureau system and denied that he had directed him to initiate a general staff study. Hébert then asserted that Johnson had overruled the Joint Chiefs of Staff "in the matter of the flat-top [the *United States*]." Another committee member wanted details on the cancellation. Johnson replied that "We took the position of the majority [of the JCS] that it did not tie in with global strategy, and therefore we cancelled it." Vinson said he had done well to do so, but Hébert alleged that he had "vetoed Congress." The hearings were to end on 7 July, but the committee extended them to the eleventh so that the Joint Chiefs of Staff and the President of the Navy League could be heard.[19]

On 2 August, Congress approved the new defense reorganization bill entitled the National Security Act Amendments of 1949. In summary:

> The authority of the Secretary of Defense was strengthened by making the National Military Establishment the Department of Defense and demoting the armed services to "Military Departments." The word *general* was removed from "direction, authority, and control," and the concept of powers "reserved" to the services was eliminated. But the armed services still had to be "separately administered." Furthermore, Congress, while strengthening the Secretary's authority also limited it. He was forbidden to transfer or consolidate any combatant function; that is to say, he could not eliminate the Marines or transfer the naval air arm to the Air Force. He was also required to report to Congress any reassignments of a non-combatant function, and was forbidden to merge the administration of the services. They could no longer appeal to the President or the Budget Bureau over the head of the Secretary of Defense, but any service secretary or member of the Joint Chiefs, after informing the Secretary of Defense, could make recommendations to Congress on his own initiative. This meant that Congress was not to be limited to one official channel for military advice. . . .

A Chairman of the Joint Chiefs of Staff was created with a proviso that he "shall have no vote" and "shall not exercise military command," and the Joint Staff was increased from one hundred forty to two hundred ten officers. The secretary of defense was given an alter ego in the form of a deputy, and one of the three assistant secretaries to the secretary of defense which were authorized was designated by Congress as the comptroller. Finally, a new Title IV—"Promotion of Economy and Efficiency through Establishment of Uniform Budgetary and Fiscal Procedures and Organizations"—added comptrollers to each military department and emphasized a "performance budget." The Vice President was added to the National Security Council but service secretaries were deleted from it. Since the latter no longer headed executive departments, they lost prestige and ranked below the under secretary of defense. They also lost the right to bypass the secretary of defense and appeal his decisions to the President or the Bureau of the Budget, although they could still appeal directly to Congress. In sum, they were reduced to middle managers. The War Council, renamed the Armed Forces Policy Council, added the Deputy Secretary of Defense and the Chairman, Joint Chiefs of Staff, to its membership.[20]

After Truman signed the new defense reorganization act on 10 August, he stated that General Omar N. Bradley, USA, would serve as chairman of the Joint Chiefs of Staff for two years beginning 16 August and that Admiral

Louis E. Denfeld would be reappointed, when his assignment ended on 15 December, for another two-year term as Chief of Naval Operations. By a memorandum he sent via Johnson, Matthews reminded Truman that Denfeld was up for reappointment on 15 December and that his reappointment should be decided before Congress adjourned on about 1 August. The customary term of office for chiefs of naval operations had been four years. In 1945, however, Chester W. Nimitz had been appointed for only two years because he would soon reach the mandatory retirement age and because Forrestal believed "that a new Secretary of the Navy should not be obliged to wait a maximum time for a replacement of a Chief of Naval Operations with whom he found it difficult to work." Matthews added that Denfeld was extremely cooperative, his administrative capacity made him valuable not only to the Navy but to the department of defense as well, and his reappointment insured continuity in the Joint Chief of Staff, of which he was the senior member. He then recommended Denfeld's reappointment for another two year period.[21]

To effect maximum savings under the new defense reorganization law was the task Truman assigned to General Joseph McNarney, USAF, who would be chairman of a National Defense Management Committee on which Secretary of the Army Gordon Gray, Under Secretary of the Navy Kimball, and Assistant Secretary of the Air Force Eugene M. Zuckert would be members. That Johnson took "economy" to heart was illustrated by his ordering the armed services to cut their active duty personnel by 12,073 by 1 July 1950—an order by which the Navy would lose 3,129 men.

Bitter bickering between Van Zandt and the Secretary of the Air Force, W. Stuart Symington, and their respective followers had proceeded throughout the late spring and summer. In mid-August, although five days of hearings at the B–36 investigation made it apparent that no political capital could be made out of Johnson's former connection with manufacturers of long-range bombers, angry clashes took place before packed press tables and gallery among Van Zandt, who based his charges largely upon rumors and an anonymous nine-page letter, and Symington and Air Force General Curtis Emerson LeMay, Commander of the Strategic Air Command. LeMay said that no nation had a night fighter capable of attacking the B–36 in darkness or in bad weather above forty thousand feet, thought the cancellation of the *United States* was "a wise decision," and that "There is no Navy plane that can take-off from a carrier deck, deliver an atom bomb to a target, and land again on the carrier."[22] The retired Air Force General Carl Spaatz, now writing on air power for *Newsweek*, was among the witnesses. Regular in attendance was another witness, Vice Admiral Arthur W. Radford, Commander in Chief

Pacific Fleet, flanked by two advisers, Captain Arleigh Burke and Commander Tom Davies, an expert on naval bombers.

Matthews meanwhile applauded Johnson for having done "a phenomenal job in a short time," stated that having three service secretaries encouraged a "healthy rivalry" among their departments, and supported Johnson's decision that there would be only one Armed Forces Day.[23] He also established a court of inquiry to investigate the anonymous document upon which Van Zandt relied. This document, which emanated from Kimball's office, was extremely critical of the B–36 as an aircraft and also alleged that improper influence had contributed to its procurement.

Matthews's court of inquiry, headed by Admiral Thomas C. Kinkaid, began its hearings on 6 September. Kimball confessed to erring when testifying before the House committee investigating the B–36: he was wrong about certain dates and admitted that he had not spoken to men he had said he had spoken to. More important, it was ascertained that the "anonymous document" was prepared by one of his aides, Cedric R. Worth, a professional writer.[24] Worth had not told Kimball that he had written the document "Because it would do him no good. . . . He would have to tell me not to do it." However, he had already confessed before Vinson's committee that he was the author of the document.[25]

On 10 September, Captain John W. Crommelin, a veteran naval aviator and carrier commander due to be considered for promotion to rear admiral within a few months, criticized "potential dictatorship" in the defense department, asserting that the "Navy is being nibbled to death in the Pentagon." He also violated the rule that prohibited the release of information by publishing the statement he had prepared for delivery to Kinkaid's committee, which had recessed the day before. He knew that he was breaking regulations and expected that his career in the Navy would be ended. While the Tydings unification reorganization bill was under consideration, he said he learned that a document on Johnson's desk provided a schedule for the gradual reduction of naval aviation and the absorption of its remnants by the Air Force. Worth, said Crommelin, was prompted by the highest motives of patriotism in exposing what he believed were the implications in the Tydings bill affecting procurement. The bill was passed after only two of the points on the agenda of the B–36 investigating committee were discussed. Had the other points been gone into, the bill might not have been passed. Crommelin concluded that:

> The B–36 controversy and the recently cancelled carrier contract are mere superficial manifestations of the real cause for disagreements between the Armed Services. The basic contention, in my opinion, lies with the area

of the General Staff concept, and will never be resolved until it is thoroughly threshed out in conformance with the principles of democracy (equal
representation and expression from the three services) before the Congress
of the United States. The Navy cannot support an organization whose
methods and principles violate the Navy concept of a Navy man's oath.

He referred specifically here to the Joint Chiefs of Staff, in which formerly
two, now three men "who may have a landlocked concept of national defense"
could vote against the Navy.[26]

Among others, Fleet Admiral William F. Halsey and Rear Admiral Austin
K. Doyle, Chief of Naval Air Reserve Training, supported Crommelin, whereupon Representative Lansdale G. Sasscer (Dem., Md.), a top-ranking member
of the House Armed Services Committee, demanded an inquiry into the roles
of the three military services—an inquiry made even more important by Truman's announcement on 23 September that the Russians now had "the bomb."

Matthews at first said that Crommelin had "obviously disqualified himself" for his billet on the Joint Staff but that he would take no punitive action
against him. Denfeld said and did nothing, but Kimball came to his rescue,
stating that he voiced only his personal opinion and deserved no punishment.
After Truman told reporters on 15 September that he believed "Secretary
Matthews would handle the matter capably," Matthews transferred Crommelin to an office not involved with the other services and said that Crommelin would appear before the Kinkaid court of inquiry and that he should
realize that "unification is a fact" and that "it was the duty of all hands to
respect the action of Congress, to work for harmonious results under existing
laws."[27] On 16 September, moreover, Matthews "requested" naval officers to
stop criticizing the organization of the defense department in public and to
send their complaints via regular Navy channels. When he told an admiral to
stop arguing with the Air Force, the admiral replied, "If you issue that order,
we'll resist it."[28] On 6 October, Matthews suspended Crommelin from duty
and told him that he could write a letter of explanation to the Navy Judge Advocate General, who was preparing charges against him for violating "military
law" in turning over classified naval documents to the press.

Unrest in the Navy was further documented when Vinson resumed hearings on the B–36 on 5 October, as noted below. Symington, General Hoyt
Vandenberg, the Chief of Staff of the Air Force, and other high-ranking
civilians and officers of the Air Force cooperated fully with a lawyer who
prepared the Air Force presentation for the hearings. In contrast, Matthews
cut himself off entirely from the Navy's preparation, even from his own public
relations people. Therefore the preparation of the Navy's case was made
largely by officers headed by Captain Burke in OP–23.[29]

Still more unrest was generated when the Defense Management (Mc-Narney) Committee notified the Navy that its funds for the current fiscal year would be cut by $353 million. Matthews opposed the cut but believed he could work the matter out satisfactorily with Johnson and prohibited naval officers from complaining about the cut to Congress. He contacted Johnson, who assured him that he would be given a full hearing.[30]

As a Johnson man, Matthews failed to win support from naval partisans. Perhaps wrongly, Navy partisans also blamed Denfeld for the part he played in the carrier cancellation by the Joint Chiefs of Staff, for remaining quiet when Sullivan resigned, and for agreeing with the other members of the Joint Chiefs and approving the B–36 in the hearings Vinson held in August. It was also alleged, quite incorrectly, that Matthews's decision to renominate him for a two-year term was conditioned upon his de-emphasizing of naval aviation and emphasizing of antisubmarine warfare and surface vessels.[31]

On 23 May 1949, Denfeld approved the need for the conversion every year of two old *Essex*-class carriers. Ten years earlier, these carriers could handle all carrier-based aircraft; unless they were modernized, however, none was ready for war, and modernization took two years.[32]

Because Denfeld was in Europe much of the summer of 1949 in connection with making NATO a viable military organization, his deputy, Radford, worked with Burke and others to prepare the Navy's case for Vinson's hearings until he became Commander in Chief Pacific Fleet. When Vinson had him returned to Washington in July as a technical consultant, he rather than Denfeld acted as the chief naval spokesman. Thus Denfeld, who should have been that spokesman even if he was not articulate and by temperament was a conciliator, began to lose the confidence of Radford and his followers.[33]

On 20 September, Vice Admiral Gerald F. Bogan, Commander First Task Fleet, Pacific Fleet, wrote a confidential letter in response to Matthews's request of 14 September to comment on Crommelin's statement. The letter was endorsed by Radford as Commander in Chief Pacific Fleet and by Denfeld as Chief of Naval Operations. Some unidentified person gave a copy of the letter to the press. In the letter Bogan told Matthews that he was in "hearty and complete agreement" with Crommelin and that Matthews erred in saying that Crommelin's statement embarrassed the progress of unification and harmony in the Navy Department because "The basic reason behind all of it is a genuine fear in the Navy for the security of our country if the policies followed in the Department of Defense since the National Security Act became law and are not drastically changed, and soon." Following are some of his most important paragraphs:

The creation of three departments or sub departments where formerly there were but two is not unification. Under the present law it can be made to and does operate effectively in the field. But it would be sheer balderdash to assume that there has been anything approaching it among the Secretariat, the Joint Staff, or the high command of all three services. . . .

The morale of the Navy is lower today than at any time since I entered the commissioned ranks in 1916. . . . In my opinion, this descent, almost to despondency, stems from complete confusion as to the future role of the Navy and its advantages or disadvantages as a permanent career. . . . We . . . are fearful that the country is being . . . sold a bill of goods.[34]

In endorsing his letter, Radford stated that Bogan was a man of long experience who reflected the feelings of a majority of the officers in the Pacific fleet as expressed in Crommelin's statement. Denfeld concurred with Radford in the second endorsement, which he wrote on 28 September and forwarded to Matthews. He added words from a report Admiral Ernest J. King made in October 1945: "Seapower will not be accorded adequate recognition, because the [unified] organization contemplated would permit reduction of that sea power by individuals who are not thoroughly familiar with its potentialities, as has happened in several other countries." Denfeld illustrated King's point by alluding to the history of Germany and Japan in World War II and concluded that "It follows that if the Navy's welfare is one of the prerequisites to the nation's welfare—and I sincerely believe that to be the case—any step that is not good for the Navy is not good for the nation." In a public statement he added that he was distressed by the violation of communications security that permitted Bogan's letter to go to the press, that Bogan voiced merely his own personal opinion, that Radford's endorsement did not mean that he concurred with Bogan's views, and that he himself agreed with Radford. He closed by noting that "Unification of the Armed Forces of the United States is the law of the land, the principles and objectives of which I have wholeheartedly endorsed and am striving to make effective. In this effort I am fully supported by a large majority of Naval personnel."[35]

On 3 October, Matthews, Denfeld, Radford, and other naval leaders met with Vinson. Knowing that naval witnesses would talk about the B–36, Vinson suggested postponing the resumption of hearings, slated for the fifth. Matthews agreed but added that he would take up the Navy's budget cut with Johnson and then, if necessary, to Capitol Hill. Denfeld also supported postponement in order that he might study the case the Navy had prepared. Vinson thereupon said he would recommend postponement until early January. But when Radford argued that the question of budget reduction could not wait that long, Vinson agreed to proceed with the hearings.[36] Later that day, Crommelin leaked copies of the Bogan correspondence to the press, which published them on the fourth. Vinson then said that the Navy could air its views at the hearings to begin on the fifth.

Matthews's recommending Denfeld's reappointment suggests that he was satisfied with his performance of duty and support for unification. Denfeld's endorsement of Bogan's letter, however, caused Matthews to tell him that his usefulness as chief of naval operations had terminated. Overlooking the public statement in which Denfeld asserted that his endorsement of Bogan's letter did not indicate agreement with Bogan's views and that he wholeheartedly supported unification, he ordered Denfeld to sound out Admiral Forrest P. Sherman as his relief.

Before Denfeld could find who had leaked the Bogan correspondence, Crommelin admitted that he had done it—and was promptly suspended from duty and told that charges would be drawn against him.

To influence congressional and public opinion, Matthews could contact congressmen and appear before congressional committees, deliver public addresses, meet with the press, and use his Office of Information. There is no evidence that he used any of these methods; whether he knew of the work being done in "OP-23" is questionable.

Burke was not only to "prepare suggested positions for the Navy Department" on immediate short-range issues with respect to impending reorganization but also on the Navy's position in future defense policy. With time short, he concentrated on the impending B-36 hearings. He gathered data to support the Navy's argument for supercarriers and against B-36 bombers, wrote policy papers, ghosted speeches, chose the witnesses, and wrote the testimony they would offer.[37]

After closing his investigation of the procurement of the B-36, on 5 October Vinson stated that he would ascertain the views of the representatives of the Navy, and if necessary, of the other services, on the other points on the agenda not already covered. These included:

Item Number 3—Examine the performance characteristics of the B-36 bomber to determine whether it is a satisfactory weapon.

Item Number 4—Examine the roles and missions of the Air Force and the Navy (especially Navy aviation and Marine aviation) to determine whether or not the decision to cancel the construction of the aircraft carrier *United States* was sound.

Item Number 5—Establish whether or not the Air Force is concentrating upon strategic bombing to such an extent as to be injurious to tactical aviation and the development of adequate fighter aircraft and fighter aircraft techniques.

Item Number 6—Consider the procedures followed by the Joint Chiefs of Staff on the development of weapons to be used by the respective Services to determine whether or not it is proposed that two of the three Services will be permitted to pass on the weapons of the third.

Item Number 7—Study the effectiveness of strategic bombing to determine whether the nation is sound in following this concept to its present extent.

Item Number 8—Consider all other matters pertinent to the above that may be developed during the course of the investigation.[38]

At Vinson's request, on 20 July Matthews had forwarded his ideas on these points in a classified letter most likely drafted by Denfeld.[39]

The Navy testified for the first seven days of hearings on "Unification and Strategy" held between 6 and 21 October, Matthews first, then almost the entire high command of the Navy. Five additional days were given to Air Force and Army representatives, Louis Johnson, George Marshall, and Herbert Hoover among the approximately forty men who testified.

Matthews, who made his first appearance before the committee on 6 October, tried to have the statement to be made by Radford heard in executive session because it would have "a definite effect upon the national security of our country" and "will give comfort to a possible enemy of our country"—a clear dodge to keep from the public the views of the Navy "partisans."[40] Vinson retorted that "We want to find out the cause of all of this unrest" and noted that Radford's statement was unclassified. Representative Sasscer elicited from Matthews that Matthews gave classified security status not only to "security" matters but also to matters involving naval "efficiency," with the result that he could muzzle critics of his administration and that of Johnson.[41] Matthews then read a prepared statement. He would not attempt to censor any Navy man's testimony or prevent him from testifying, he began, but he punctuated his comments with expressions of wounded feelings and a desire to punish traitorious people. The morale of the Navy was good, he asserted, except among a few individuals who violated their oath of office and "deliberately engaged in the indefensible procedure of surreptitiously disclosing to persons unentitled to possess it documentary and other restricted information belonging to the Department of the Navy." These few would be "brought to an accounting for their guilty conduct."

Matthews was convinced that the greatest impairment to naval morale flowed from naval aviators, who felt keenly the reduction in naval aviation following World War II. Among those who testified against adopting the National Security Act of 1947 were Bogan and Crommelin, whose outspokenness had a bad effect upon some members of the Navy. But these men did not monopolize the loyalty, honor, or patriotic devotion of naval men and did not speak for anywhere near a majority of them. After quoting from him at length to prove that Johnson was not hostile to carrier aviation or to Marine Corps aviation, he dealt very briefly with the other items on Vinson's agenda.

Matthews said that he was ignorant of the technical details of the B–36 and that its qualities could best be ascertained by the Weapons Systems Evaluation Group. Johnson's discontinuation of the *United States* did not mean that he opposed either carriers or naval aviation. Matthews did admit that he believed that the Air Force was "unbalanced in favor of strategic bombing." On Item 6 of the agenda, Joint Chiefs of Staff procedures in choosing weapons, Matthews did not believe that a split vote should control the weapon systems of a service. If such a split occurred, the decision should be made by the secretary of defense. On whether strategic bombing was effective as national strategy, Matthews referred the committee to his earlier classified letter. On the organizational structure of the military establishment, he said that "I have the utmost confidence not only in the organizational set-up, but I have the utmost confidence in the men who man this set-up," and he gave to Johnson the highest praise he could bestow. He concluded by asserting that both he and Denfeld would make a good case for the Navy in the budget being prepared for fiscal year 1951.[42]

Having completed his statement, Matthews submitted to questioning. Representative Porter Hardy, Jr. (Dem., Va.), wished to know "what avenue a conscientious believer that a change is necessary in the interest of national security has to make his views known if he runs into a stone wall within his own department or if he gets blocked in the Department of Defense and can't make his position known."[43] Matthews replied, "I don't know how he could become blocked"—at which his audience of naval officers guffawed and jeered.[44]

Vinson suggested that the major problem was in the naval aviation branch. Matthews agreed. The inactivation of various ships he thought also played a part. As to the kind of Navy there should be, naval experts would enlighten the committee— there were too many statistics for him to remember. He opposed the cut in the fiscal year 1950 budget. He also believed that Air Force plans were "unbalanced in favor of strategic bombing." How could morale be improved? he was asked. By good personnel administration, additional compensation, and improving living conditions and the administration of the Navy, he replied. Why had not the cut from seventy to forty-eight groups caused a similar drop in morale in the Air Force? Matthews did not know; he was interested only in the Navy and did not care what funds went to the other services. Was it true that heavy aircraft could fly off modernized carriers but could not land on them? Matthews did not know. Vinson then asked, "Doesn't the drop in morale in the Navy depend on the reduction in ship, aviation, and Marine Corps strength? This goes beyond the argument against unification." Matthews: "I wouldn't be able to explain that." Had Johnson cut the appropriation for naval air provided in the fiscal year 1950 budget? Matthews believed Johnson had, but did not know by how much.

Representative Sasscer rephrased Vinson's question for Matthews: "Isn't the main opposition . . . produced by the manner in which this [unification] act gives so much power to one man is being projected on a course that is gradually clipping the Navy, Navy air, and the Marine Corps?" Most naval officers felt that a man loyal to Johnson could not be loyal to the Navy, but Matthews said he could not answer. Representative Joseph A. Anderson (Rep., Calif.) queried: "Doesn't Denfeld's sitting with the Joint Chiefs of Staff, on which there are three West Pointers, have an effect on the morale of the Navy?" Matthews disagreed. What was Matthews doing about morale in the Navy, especially in its aviation corps? asked Vinson. Said Matthews: "Whatever we can to make the Navy know it is not to be scrapped," probably because Vinson had alleged that Navy and Marine Aviation would lose 50 percent of the number of planes provided in the fiscal year 1951 budget. Vinson then sharply questioned Matthews on whether cuts in most categories of ships and in the number of air groups accounted for the low morale in the Navy. Matthews was not sure. Nor did not know how many naval flag officers opposed unification. Although he had directed that a "study or survey" of the committee's agenda be made, Matthews alleged that he had not set up a "task force" to prepare the Navy's position at the B–36 hearings and did not know whether such a task force had been established. When Representative Van Zandt referred to OP–23 in all but name, Matthews finally admitted that there was a "top policy committee" composed of two civilian assistants and the top military personnel in his office who had "discussed the matter." Crommelin had been suspended from duty and orders had been issued to draft charges against him. "Would that have any effect on future naval witnesses?" Matthews was asked. Said Matthews: "Not the slightest." Nor did Matthews see any correlation between the criticism of the doctrine of strategic air bombing sent to him by his admirals and poor morale in the Navy, for "A man can be very much dissatisfied and yet his morale could be 100 percent."[45]

The committee then rose, after which it heard Radford read his statement. Upon deciding that it did not contain classified materials, the committee asked the Admiral to testify publicly on the morrow.

When he testified, on 7 October, Radford began by denying charges that naval officers were concerned with the future Navy only to the degree that it affected them personally, as in promotion and prestige. An aviator with almost thirty years of service, and a military statesman rather than merely a military expert, he believed that national air power, the sum of land air power and naval air power, was unquestionably the dominant factor in national security. Moreover, by stating that strategic air warfare should be the primary mission of the Air Force he was one of the few witnesses or committee members to see that the hearings were important less because they concerned the B–36 program than because they might determine national strategy both in peace and war. But he had the B–36 much in mind, saying that it "has become, in the minds of the American people, a symbol of a theory of warfare—the atomic blitz—which promises them a cheap and easy victory if war should come." He rejected that conclusion, on which the committee must pass judgment.

The B–36, he went on, was a gamble with national security not only because of its inability to defend itself or to bomb accurately from great heights, but also because it symbolized the unsound theory of atomic blitz warfare. If it was decided that this theory was correct, a more efficient plane was needed. In picking the B–36, the Air Force had made a "billion dollar blunder." In developing its strategic bombers, the Air Force neglected planes suitable for tactical and fighter missions. Pushing the B–36 program undermined unification and prevented mutual trust, understanding, and unified planning. Any service must be permitted to bring an experimental weapon through the development, test, and evaluation stages—as the *United States* should have been by the Navy —but no weapon should be provided in quantity until it was proven. Strategic bombing should be a primary mission of the Air Force, but the United States should not depend upon strategic bombing as a short cut to victory.[46]

When asked by Vinson whether he had official Navy endorsement for his views, Radford said that he expressed his personal opinion, one developed after consultation with several other high-ranking naval officers. How many of the Navy's top officers shared his views? Almost all senior officers and every experienced officer on the active and retired list, replied Radford, and at request he named Fleet Admirals Halsey, Nimitz, King, and Leahy and Admirals Blandy, Conolly, and Denfeld, among others. He added that it was exceedingly difficult for the minority of experienced officers he represented to get their points of view across to "our sister services" and "some of the civilian secretaries" who were inexperienced in naval matters.[47]

Navy witnesses who followed Radford in person on 8, 10, 11, 12, and 13 October or, if ill, sent statements to be read, included a galaxy of World War II leaders—Halsey, King, Burke, Kinkaid, Conolly, Carney, Spruance, Nimitz. All of these upheld Radford against the B–36 as a plane and as a symbol of the misguided strategy of atomic bombing. Then both Radford and Denfeld criticized the Air Force for violating the spirit of unification by procuring additional B–36s without consulting the secretary of defense or the Joint Chiefs of Staff, an at least tangential blow at the Air Force's approval of the cancellation of the *United States*. Although Radford did not question the budget ceiling of the department of defense, he countered Matthews, who stated that morale in the Navy was good, by saying that it was low for legitimate and serious reasons, among them lack of confidence in the intentions, actions, and judgments of the other members of the unification team.

By questioning Rear Admiral Herbert G. Hopwood, the Budget Director of the Navy, and Wilfred J. McNeil, the Comptroller of the Department of Defense, Vinson brought out clearly that Johnson usurped the powers of Congress by changing the appropriations made to the services; by asking Congress for stated funds and then reducing spending, he made it appear that he was saving the taxpayers' money. Vinson angrily asserted that Johnson should economize by reducing overhead and making the department of defense more efficient, not by cutting combat strength. Others challenged the validity of the strategy of strategic atomic bombing and pointed to the need of forces adequate for limited war, with the lack of tactical air power by the Air Force an apt illustration. Admiral William H. P. Blandy, Commander in Chief Atlantic Fleet, not an aviator, helped develop amphibious warfare in the Pacific during World War II and then commanded the Bikini Atoll atomic bomb tests. In contending that the Navy needed both amphibious and atomic forces he contradicted Matthews, who sought to blame only naval aviators for unhappiness in the Navy. He also contradicted Matthews when he asserted that the cuts in the current Navy budget would reduce the operating forces of the Navy "dangerously below the minimum estimate of forces I have submitted to the Chief of Naval Operations as needed at the beginning of a war."[48]

Retired Fleet Admiral Halsey upheld the Navy, as did retired Fleet Admiral King, who was too ill to testify but sent a statement. After Arleigh Burke and other high-ranking non-aviators offered a systematic and complete defense of the supercarrier as a weapon system necessary for the future, the spotlight fell on Denfeld, who would summarize the Navy presentation.

Would Denfeld continue to support Matthews, as he did by trying to keep Radford's testimony from the public, or would he stick by the "radicals"? Would he, as Matthews asked him to, "get him off the hook" with the press with respect to his own testimony? Would he fulfill Johnson's optimism that he would repudiate his Navy colleagues, "toe the Johnson economy line," and stop what Johnson called the Navy's "campaign of terror"?[49] Denfeld was torn between being a member of the Joint Chiefs of Staff and ranking leader of the professional Navy. The tragedy of his position was that a good performance as a naval spokesman would lose him stature on the Joint Chiefs of Staff and, because Matthews was a Johnson man, cause disaffection also with Matthews.

After he supported Matthews's attempt to keep Radford's testimony secret, Denfeld decided—much too late—to stop acting as a conciliator and to support the radicals even though he was aided in the preparation of his testimony by non-aviators. He said that he would "fully support the broad conclusions presented to this committee by the naval and marine officers who have preceded me" and then concentrated upon management in the department of defense that enabled the Air Force to add to its stock of B–36s, to cancel the construction of the *United States*, and to cut the Navy's budget. The Navy supported unification, but unification was not being followed. The Navy's counsel was being excluded by the department of defense; the Navy was not admitted to full partnership. Denfeld made a vigorous but moderate statement; unlike Radford, who had criticized the B–36 and strategic atomic bombing, he saw naval power, including air power, as part of an integrated force. He said, in part:

> The entire Navy . . . is gravely concerned whether it will have modern weapons, in quality and quantity, to do the job expected of the Navy at the outbreak of a future war. We have real misgivings over the reductions that are taking place in the Navy today. . . . It is not so much the reduction in congressional appropriations that worries us. . . . Our concern is with arbitrary reductions that impair, or even eliminate, essential naval functions. It is not so much a question of too little appropriated money, but how we are allowed to invest that money. . . . Limitations are imposed without consultation, and without understanding of the Navy's responsibility in defense of our maritime nation.
>
> I am an advocate of air power. . . . I am also a proponent of strategic air warfare.
>
> There has been no objection raised by the Navy to the development of the B–36 to the point where its value as a weapon might be thoroughly evaluated. . . . However, it is illogical, damaging, and dangerous to proceed directly to mass procurement without evaluation to the extent that the Army and Navy may be starved for funds and our strategic concept of war frozen about an uncertain weapon. The procedure leading up to the cancellation of the carrier *United States* is another exemplification of the improper operation of unification.[50]

As fellow officers congratulated Denfeld when he ended his testimony and welcomed him to the ranks of the radicals, a visibly flushed Matthews hurriedly left the room. On the next day, he told Denfeld that he was "stunned" by his presentation.[51]

General Clifton B. Cates, Commandant of the Marine Corps, paralleled Denfeld in asserting that unification did not work well. He spoke of the "elimination" of the Marine Corps by budget cuts in fiscal years 1950 and 1951 and of the possible takeover of its amphibious function by the Army, the latter not within the scope of the National Security Act. He was upheld by General A. A. Vandegrift.[52]

Beginning in May 1948, an Air Force committee comprised of officers and civilians had begun a study of the capabilities of the Navy in its surface, underwater, and air aspects, particularly of carriers and carrier-borne aircraft. Armed with the extremely perceptive report furnished by this committee,[53] Symington noted that the Navy's ideas had already been rejected by those responsible for deciding national military policy. While he refuted the Navy's charges about the B–36 and the B–36 program and the weakness of Air Force tactical strength, he used his greatest blows to demolish the Navy's criticism of strategic bombing, an instrument of war approved by the Joint Chiefs of Staff and a primary Air Force mission. Characterizing it as being jealous of the B–36, especially at budget-making time, Symington took an uncompromising position toward the Navy.[54]

Vandenberg, who followed Symington, wondered why the Navy could not concentrate on antisubmarine warfare and the control of sea communications and leave strategic bombing to the Air Force. General Bradley said that balanced forces would be needed if war came with a great foreign power, adding that strategic bombardment and large-scale land operations could be foreseen but that large-scale amphibious operations "will never occur again." Moreover, the Navy's denigration of atomic power damaged the nation's security. Last, the Navy failed to teach its people, including aviators, that its role was to wage antisubmarine warfare. It not only opposed unification, it included "fancy dans" who, rather than being team players, would not play unless they could call the signals.[55]

In releasing pent-up emotions, Bradley exhibited service partisanship and engaged in personalities. He insulted the Navy by seeking to restrict it to an antisubmarine role. When he asserted that the Joint Chiefs of Staff did not consider the supercarrier before April 1949, however, Denfeld submitted a paper showing that it was discussed in May 1948. Seeing his error, Bradley countered that while the Joint Chiefs did not make a *formal* decision on it before April 1949, in discussions of late May 1948 he had agreed to its building only because of his "understanding that it had been approved by those in authority, and I accepted it as a fait accompli." In April 1949, when a formal decision was made, he opposed the carrier. Denfeld misunderstood him.[56]

Both Eisenhower and Marshall were conciliatory, with Eisenhower noting that friction came from the unified budget process which forced the services to compete for funds within a budget ceiling.

In his testimony—thirty-five pages full of blunt language—Johnson stated that "Tradition, opposing interests, and fear of losing identity have all played a part in the turmoil on the subject of unification. . . ." He made much of the fact that he would save $1 billion of the fiscal year 1950 budget and $1.5 billion in that of 1951. At his suggestion, the McNarney Management Committee recommended on 8 September a cut in the Army budget for fiscal year 1950 by $357 million, in that of the Navy by $376 million, and in that of the Air Force by $196 million. Since representatives of the service secretaries sat on the committee, the secretaries must have known about the cuts, and Matthews would be granted the hearing he requested to protest them. He alleged that the naval witnesses had an "erroneous picture" of the Joint Chiefs' war plans and that Denfeld erred in describing the cancellation of the supercarrier. He also revealed that Secretary Sullivan had resigned not following its cancellation but by letter a month earlier "because Sullivan was unwilling to support unification."[57]

After the final witness, Hoover, supported Johnson's efforts to promote economy and efficiency in the department of defense, the committee adjourned on 21 October 1949 and promised a report when it reconvened on 3 January 1950.

Although the hearings were held on the wrong subject—the central issue should have been how to reorganize military and diplomatic policy to deal with a Soviet Union possessed of the atomic bomb—the hearings showed that unification was still an emotionally charged and controversial issue. Naval partisans revealed that they resented the Navy's being treated as a junior partner, of having decisions it opposed imposed upon it by the other services. While the committee felt that there was more than one road to unification, disagreement over the road to take did not diminish the role of Congress in determining national defense policies, the need of Congress to have the advice of military men given without fear of reprisal, or the desire of the committee to continue to assist in the progress of unification.

In Vinson's committee naval partisans enjoyed a forum in which to point out that the "economy drive" of the Truman administration kept the services on extremely short rations. The radicals broke with Matthews primarily because the promised reduction in naval aviation favored the Air Force and gave credence to the long-held Navy position that unification would mean gain for the Air Force and loss for the Navy. In point was the charge that the mass procurement of the B-36 began before it had been properly evaluated by the Joint Chiefs of Staff. Moreover, the cancellation of the supercarrier—a weapon needed for future warfare—highlighted the need for a weapons system evaluation group.

Some naval witnesses offered incompetent testimony; others failed to prove some of their major contentions, for example, that the B-36 performed poorly, that its procurement was achieved improperly, that the policy of strategic atomic bombing was inadequate to provide for national security—which could not be done without the test of war—or that the supercarrier was approved by the Air Force and Army at Key West and earlier. Furthermore, the officers in OP–23 had prepared their presentation without the knowledge of Matthews or the asistance of Denfeld, and Denfeld might have improved or tempered important parts of it. Denfeld's testimony soon led to his dismissal as Chief of Naval Operations by Matthews and Truman. The hearings had no real impact upon the fiscal year 1950 budget, in which the Navy felt it was badly mistreated, and the Navy was castigated by Vinson's committee for trying to undercut the authority of the secretary of defense, take over strategic bombing missions, and force disclosure of secret information.[58] In the long run, however, by reducing its identification with the Air Force and listening more sympathetically to the Navy, the committee helped naval morale swing upward from the nadir it had reached during the fall of 1947. Rebelling against the Truman–Johnson defense economy drive, Congress voted funds for a 58-group rather than 48-group Air Force. The Navy eventually got its carrier (and stopped its assault on the efficacy of strategic bombing), and learned the lesson of thoroughly preparing congressional witnesses.

Soon after the Vinson hearings ended, Matthews asked President Truman for permission to transfer Denfeld to another post. He was well aware of naval opposition to unification when he entered office on 25 May and vividly recalled Truman's telling him that the success of unification was vital to the defense of the country and that naval officers in key positions, including the chief of naval operations, must work for unification. He had recommended Denfeld for a second term, Matthews added, largely because of the value he believed would follow in the continuity of his good service. However, he had found it increasingly difficult to work with Denfeld in the "harmonious relationship which should prevail." Denfeld had endorsed Bogan's letter and committed other disloyal acts. He did not mention Denfeld's testimony before Vinson's committee, but it was obvious that he took vigorous exception to it. On 4 October, the day the Bogan correspondence was published, he had told Denfeld that his usefulness as chief of naval operations had terminated. Because of Denfeld's disloyalty, he himself could not properly perform his duties as secretary of the navy. Therefore a new chief of naval operations should be appointed "at the earliest possible date."[59] Truman replied that he was familiar with the problems concerning unification and approved Denfeld's removal "as a move to restore discipline."[60] Denfeld learned of his dismissal from radio reports about a press conference Truman held on 27 October rather than from Matthews.

Vinson asserted that he would tolerate no reprisals against witnesses and that Denfeld was made to "walk the plank" because he was honest enough to voice his opinion that the Navy was not accepted in full partnership in the national defense structure. Some members of his committee evaluated Matthews's action as an "insult to Congress," "malicious retaliation," and "a campaign of terror being initiated in the Pentagon" which the committee would not take "lying down." Frank Hecht, president of the Navy League, added that "Admiral Denfeld is the Number 1 victim to the new thought control in the United States."[61]

On 28 October, a spokesman for three hundred enlisted men told Denfeld that "I want you to know that we feel the Navy is shot, that our morale is shot, that we feel very low."[62] Matthews was to have shared a box with Denfeld at the Navy-Notre Dame football game on the twenty-ninth. By not attending, he missed witnessing the standing ovation given Denfeld by the midshipmen.

Diametrically opposed reaction to Denfeld's dismissal was expressed by the press. *The New York Times*, for example, approved his dismissal because he refused to see that "civilian authority . . . must always be superior to professional military authority." *The Baltimore Sun* asserted that his dismissal would not "make any less apparent Mr. Louis Johnson's inability to carry the responsibility laid upon him in his job. . . . What has been happening in the Defense Department is that decisions are being made without the full information on which issues of such magnitude should be decided. Kicking Admiral Denfeld downstairs won't change that situation."

A similar dichotomy of attitude was expressed toward Matthews. According to *The Washington Post*, Matthews offered Truman the choice of losing him or transferring Denfeld. "Mr. Truman, who is President of a country dedicated to civilian supremacy, had no alternative but to approve Secretary Matthews' action." In contrast, the *Washington News* held that "For the good of the Navy, for the good of Armed Services unification, for the good of the country, Secretary Matthews should resign. . . . Secretary Matthews does not have the confidence of the Navy and has forfeited the confidence of Congress by firing Admiral Denfeld." According to the *Philadelphia Inquirer*, "There is nothing that can excuse the ruthless manner in which President Truman 'fired' Admiral Denfeld. . . . We must have unity in the Armed Forces. And we need the help of the Navy—we need its earnest devotion, its skill and the experience of its commanders. It's no way to get any of that by laying a whip over the shoulders of able officers and gagging them into terrorized silence."[63]

Although Matthews had his way, Vinson promised that Denfeld's removal would be reflected in his committee's report, and four of his committee members, Democrats Hébert and Sasscer and Republicans W. Sterling Cole, of New York, and Leslie C. Arends, of Illinois, vigorously denied the assertion by Johnson and Matthews that Denfeld's removal was not a reprisal and charged that Matthews merely parroted Johnson. Would Denfeld have been removed, they asked, if his testimony pleased Johnson and Matthews? Meanwhile various senators, among them William G. Knowland, (Rep., Calif.) a member of the Armed Services Committee, called for the resignation of Matthews, in whom he had lost confidence as secretary of the navy.

Forrest P. Sherman, Matthews's choice to succeed Denfeld, was an aviator who had commanded carriers in World War II, served as Deputy Chief of Staff to Admiral Nimitz, and helped work out compromises that led to the writing of the original unification act. Since 1948 he had commanded the Sixth Fleet, in the Mediterranean. Quiet, almost shy in manner, he was a studious man who drove himself to the limits of his physical capacity and was widely acknowledged as being an excellent choice for chief of naval operations even though he was eleventh on the Navy's seniority list and was known to have consuming ambition. Here was a man who could win a respectful hearing for the naval point of view. Moreover, his appointment could be considered a concession to the aviators who had led the fight against the Air Force.

After the Senate approved Sherman for an interim appointment, Matthews announced that he had offered Denfeld the post of Commander in Chief U.S. Naval Forces Eastern Mediterranean and Atlantic. Possibly to discomfit Matthews, Denfeld declined, saying that the "embarrassment" he had suffered would place an "undesirable restraint" upon his dealing with other governments."[64] As has been said, "the discord between the Secretary and the Chief of Naval Operations led to a premature ending of the career of one and an inability for any further effective exercise of his office by the other."[65]

Both Johnson and Matthews denied that Denfeld's ouster was prompted by his testimony before the Vinson Committee. Johnson admitted that he had said there would be no reprisals; however, this did not prevent his reassigning officers found unqualified for their current duties. Matthews pointed out that he had told Denfeld that his usefulness as chief of naval operations had ended several days prior to Denfeld's appearance before Vinson's committee; therefore his testimony could not have been the cause of his dismissal. To those who suggested that he resign, Matthews retorted: "I contemplate being here as long as I do a job satisfactory to President Truman. Work is my hobby and right now my hobby is the Navy Department."[66]

Sherman took office when cuts in naval funds obliged him to drop thirty-five aircraft squadrons, inactivate an air facility, reduce maintenance on five air bases, and inactivate sixty-five training ships. When he wrote a public letter of reprimand to Crommelin, the latter asked him either to cancel the letter or give him a general court-martial. Sherman replied that Crommelin had been permitted to make a statement and that the case was "considered closed." While the case remained closed, the unification controversy continued to rage. Representative Cole, for example, made public the replies but not the names of the writers who answered a questionnaire he sent to the three hundred and eight flag officers of the Navy and Marine Corps. Cole, a naval reserve officer, strongly loaded his questions against the department of defense and in favor of Congress and of the Navy, and Matthews authorized his addressees to reply only on condition that they furnish copies to his own office. Cole's summary of the 170 replies, which he furnished to Vinson, included 117 answers which emphatically supported the views of Denfeld, 15 which approved them "in general" or "in the main"; only 26 were noncommital.[67] Matthews, meanwhile, on 30 November told a meeting of the Navy League that the Navy was being "equitably treated," that Johnson and Early had no favorites among the three departments of the military establishment, that officers were not gagged, and that Denfeld had not suffered retaliatory action. He had now had six months in which to learn about the Navy, he added, and felt that he could speak somewhat authoritatively about its problems. The U.S. Navy was stronger than all other navies in the world combined and ready to carry out its roles and missions. Somewhat short on submarines, it was otherwise as prepared as it could be within restrictions imposed upon it because of "the financial limitations of the national economy" to assume command of the sea heretofore held by the British. Although the Navy was in the throes of "contractual spasms" that produced "operational convulsions," the morale of its personnel was "splendid." As for unification, Matthews predicted that "it will ultimately be universally regarded as one of the most constructive developments in the evolution of our system of government."[68]

To the second session of the Eighty-first Congress, which convened on 3 January 1950, Truman sent a defense budget of $13.5 billion for fiscal year 1951, $1.2 billion less than in fiscal year 1950, and suggested that the services transform their "fat" into "muscle." The total included an increase of $300 million for the Army; a cut of $400 million for the Air Force, which would remain at 48 rather than grow to 58 air groups in 1951 and drop to 39 by 1952; and a reduction of $450 million for the Navy. While the Navy figure might be increased in the light of the expansion of the Soviet Navy, the $3.9 billion allotted to it meant that it would have to drop 31,000 men and 15 combatant ships, including a reduction of large aircraft carriers from 8 to 6 and in small carriers from 11 to 8; reduce carrier air groups from 14 to 9, patrol squadrons from 30 to 20, and Marine air squadrons from 16 to 12; and undertake no new ship construction or conversions. However, funds were provided for the development of both defensive and offensive antisubmarine warfare, including an atomic-powered submarine.

At a press conference attended by the service secretaries and the Joint Chiefs of Staff, Johnson stated that the budget was prepared originally by General Eisenhower and was modified slightly by himself and by General

Bradley, Chairman of the Joint Chiefs of Staff. This "Ike" budget, said Johnson, provided "sufficiency of defense for the hour." Matthews added that a proper balance between combat forces and support would be maintained, but that both operations and support would be kept at "a minimum level consistent with military readiness," Symington, however, told Truman that "I can't accept that man [Johnson]. I don't want to make a mess . . . but I want out." Rather than have Symington "make a mess," Truman shifted him to head the National Security Resources Board.[69]

The Senate Armed Services Committee approved Sherman's nomination as chief of naval operations on the morning of 12 January rather than hold it up until Vinson released his report on the B-36 investigation. In the afternoon, Matthews and Sherman appeared before the committee. Matthews stated that when he became secretary he faced two "live questions," the cancellation of the *United States* and unification of the armed services. To inform himself about unification, he read the hearings held by the congressional armed services committees in 1947. He thought very highly of Sherman. Asked about Denfeld, he said that President Truman had changed his mind about a second term for him as chief of naval operations and that he himself was willing to assume full responsibility for his ouster. While an officer should not be punished for testifying before a committee, "he should be ready to take the consequences. . . . If he is out of sympathy with my policies he should be transferred to wherever he can carry out my policies."[70]

When Chairman Tydings sought unanimous consent from the floor for the confirmation of Sherman, Senators William Langer (Rep., N.D.), and Joseph McCarthy (Rep., Wis.) objected, not because they opposed Sherman but because they wished to discuss both the Denfeld and Crommelin cases before agreeing, and Knowland and others got the committee to agree to the preparation of a motion of inquiry.

It was not known when the Congress met whether the House Armed Services Committee would hold hearings on the ouster of Denfeld. At least one member of the committee stated privately that he would file a minority report if the report on the hearings on unification and strategy did not give the Navy "constructive" handling. Vinson's report, issued on 10 January, exonerated the Air Force of any irregularities in the selection and procurement of the B-36 and postponed reporting on the other charges preferred by the Navy until further studies were conducted. However, in talking with Tydings, Vinson intimated that the further studies would involve the ouster of Denfeld.

Shortly before Matthews ousted Denfeld, and without even informing him, Matthews ordered the Navy Inspector General to investigate OP–23. Investigators and Marine guards impounded Burke's files; he and his staff were placed under technical arrest and held incommunicado for a time. Nothing incriminating was found, whereupon Burke went to ask Matthews to charge him with having committed some offense so that he could "enjoy the rights of a criminal" and defend himself in a court-martial. Matthews retorted that Burke was making a mountain out of a molehill and that OP–23 would continue to operate. It did—until Matthews had most of Burke's files destroyed, ordered the group disbanded, apologized to Burke for having had him investigated—and then gave the Navy's public information agency its first major overhaul since 1945 by creating the billet of Chief of Information which would be filled by a rear admiral who would supervise both public relations and the information service and work for *both* the secretary and the CNO.[71] Nevertheless, under the title of Progress Analysis Group, (OP–09D) created by a memorandum of November 1950 from the Deputy Chief of Naval Operations for Administration, the Navy continued its attempt to burnish its image before both Congress and the public, a task made much easier than heretofore because the Navy was proving its utility in the Korean War.

It had been widely rumored that Matthews had deleted Burke's name from the list of captains to be considered for promotion to rear admiral and that at Sherman's objection he restored it. The truth was that Johnson and Matthews had violated the law that required that a selection board's report go directly to the President by reconvening the board that had recommended Burke and causing it to delete Burke's name. When Truman asked his naval aide, Captain Robert L. Dennison, if any "injustice" had been done, Dennison explained what had occurred and Truman directed that Burke's name be added to the list.[72] Burke was promoted and appointed as Navy Secretary of the Research and Development Board in the department of defense. However, upon learning that he would be reassigned as Commander, Fleet Air, Jacksonville, a post currently held by a rear admiral, Vice Admiral Bogan announced his intention to retire. At Matthews's request, he added, he had written a letter regarding current policies under the unification act. "The only consideration I'm positive my letter received from him was that it caused him to refer to me in very derogatory terms in a public statement to the Armed Services Committee of the Congress." Matthews had not kept his promise to reply to his letter. Therefore, he concluded, Navy officers could not expect loyalty from Matthews. Upon being ordered to report to the Commandant of the 11th Naval District, rather than to Jacksonville, Bogan resigned.[73]

When Denfeld announced on 19 January his retirement effective 1 March, various senators struck hard at Matthews. Joseph McCarthy, for example, asked, "who is this man Matthews who says that anyone who disagrees with him on how to run the Navy will be transferred to the Siberia of an inferior post?" Moreover, "I realize . . . that Matthews was a good and loyal supporter of Truman's when his campaign [of 1948] looked hopeless. But why must he pay him off at the expense of our National Security?" He had talked with many officers of all services, concluded McCarthy, and asked if they would testify at reopened unification hearings. Most of them had replied: "I would be willing to testify today only if I were prepared to resign tomorrow." Thus Matthews had made officers so fearful of testifying that Congress could not have access to their views.[74]

On 24 January, the day the Senate unanimously confirmed Sherman for a four-year term, Denfeld mailed his resignation to Matthews. But the "Denfeld affair" was not yet settled, for Tydings invited Matthews to answer questions before his committee in executive session and Vinson said his own committee would give the matter "full treatment." Charging that Matthews was untruthful or incompetent, McCarthy suggested that he be impeached, whereupon Nebraska's two Republican Senators, among various others, staunchly supported Matthews.[75]

Matthews's first full semiannual report, for the period 1 July–31 December 1949, dated 24 February 1950, was not only short but one of the most vapid on record. He waxed optimistic even though he acknowledged that "drastic changes" had caused a "general downward adjustment" that required "a re-evaluation and restatement of some current Navy plans and policies and reduction in both the operating forces and shore establishment." Following a narration of routine matters, he made much of the fact that for fiscal year 1951 the services would use a performance type budget system and that the Navy woud prepare twenty-one instead of forty-eight and eventually only eighteen appropriations. What he failed to state was that naval aviation was forced to assume a new role. No longer prestigious as the quarterback of the defense team and squeezed for three years in a row in its budget, the Navy was forced to shift from large carriers and heavy bombers to an antisubmarine role, to stress quality rather than quantity, to develop speedy medium-bombers and turboprop rather than long-range turbojet aircraft as complements to the intercontinental Air Force bombers, and to develop only prototypes which could be produced in quantity when needed.[76]

Shortly after issuing his report, Matthews testified in an executive session of Tydings's committee. Tydings then announced the Denfeld incident closed. Denfeld was dismissed he said, "because of an honest difference of opinion" between him and Matthews on departmental policies and not as a "reprisal" for testimony he gave Vinson's committee. Vinson, however, said that he would have something to say about Denfeld when he received the report of his policy committee a week hence.[77] Meanwhile, upon learning that the *Missouri*, which had run aground off Norfolk, was refloated, Vinson suggested that she be mothballed and that a carrier be reactivated and added to the fleet in her stead. Johnson approved not only using the *Missouri* as a training ship for midshipmen and naval reserve personnel but retaining an additional carrier in operation. When Vinson asked whether a supercarrier to be named in honor of James V. Forrestal would be built, Johnson replied that there was no immediate prospect of such construction. Moreover, he had conferred with Matthews, who said that established policy for naming carriers was to avoid the use of personal names, the *Franklin D. Roosevelt* being an exception.[78]

Early in February, Matthews directed that internal parallel external unification. He forbade the use of such terms as "black shoe" (non-aviation personnel), "trade school boys" (Naval Academy graduates), "seagoing bellhops" (sailors), "gyrenes" (Marines), and "fly-fly boys" and "airedales" (aviators). Moreover, no discrimination would be made between reserve and regular personnel. The directive was observed at first more in the breach than in the observance, but in November Matthews made it "policy" that no naval man "utter any comment reflecting upon" the Army, Air Force, or Marine Corps. While naval personnel could speak and write freely, they must refrain from "belittling" and "adverse" comments and from speaking on subjects which were "controversial between the services."[79]

In mid-February came the report of a Service Academy Board of which Robert L. Stearns, president of the University of Colorado, was chairman, and of which General Eisenhower was vice chairman. The report urged the establishment of an Air Force Academy but offered no changes in the basic structure of the academies. No evidence of interservice friction or jealousy was found among the students or instructors at West Point and Annapolis, but controversy was noted among higher commanders, particularly those who had not had the benefit of joint education and joint command experience.

The report of the House Armed Services Committee on the B-36 and unification and strategy hearings, issued on 1 March 1950, was fifty-six pages long and contained a thirty-three point summation. The committee agreed on the objectives of the national security establishment but suggested that the National Security Council provide firm statements of principles upon which the Joint Chiefs of Staff and other agencies in the National Military Establishment could undertake their strategic planning. The report took note of the Navy's opposition to indiscriminate atomic bombing as the only strategy to follow in a future war and its demand for conventional forces that were mobile, flexible, and tailored to perform a given task. Read the report.

> Strategic bombing (high-altitude bombing attacks on area targets in the hinterland of an enemy), Navy strategists contended, will not serve any of [a number of] requirements, for the giant, high-altitude bomber cannot defend the United States, seize or hold advance bases, defend western Europe, effectively attack advancing troops in western Europe, or maintain control of the seas. It was held that tactical air power rather than strategic air

power, plus ground troops and sea power, are the only military instrumentalities that can meet these elementary requirements.

Conversely, air power advocates stressed the deterrent effect of long-range, atomic-laden bombers, that strategic bombing could lay waste the productive heartland of an enemy, and that strategic bombing was "the only alternative available to the United States as a balance for the vast numbers of ground troops available to a potential enemy." Because the committee had not heard witnesses on the value of strategic bombing, it reached no "finding" on the point but suggested that the defense department consider the question and reach a conclusion on it "so that all services will have confidence in the decisions rendered and that the Nation may have confidence that the decisions represent a meshing of views, not the imposition of a one-service or two-service concept upon a third service. This committee holds the view that the existing national defense structure does not insure this result. . . . "

The committee agreed that only the test of war could determine the capability of the B-36, that the Air Force was unbalanced in favor of strategic air power, and that errors were made in the cancellation of the *United States*. While the committee accepted the advice of Air Force "experts" that the B-36 was the best weapon for strategic bombing missions, it felt that such "experts" as the Chief of Staff of the Air Force and the Chairman of the Joint Chiefs were not qualified to determine for the Navy the weapon best fitted to control the seas. Johnson had erred in "summarily" scrapping the *United States* without having conferred first with Secretary Sullivan and with the congressional military and appropriations committees, thereby exacerbating debate over the unification of the services, and a supercarrier should be built when the budget permitted. As for the military budget, "This whole process appears to be disjointed and uncoordinated. . . . "

With respect to the ouster of Denfeld, the report asserted that:

> The committee is convinced that this act was a reprisal—that the frank and honest testimony of Admiral Denfeld in respect to national defense planning and the administration of the unification law, not some more distant cause, produced his removal from office. . . . The committee is convinced that the removal of the Chief of Naval Operations by discouraging honest testimony to the Congress, struck directly against the effectiveness of representative government and civilian control of the Nation's defense through the Congress—that it violated promises made to witnesses by the committee and the Secretary of the Navy, and by the Secretary of Defense. . . .

If the committee learned of similar reprisals in the future, it would "ask the Congress to exercise its constitutional power of redress."

Some salve was applied to Matthews's no doubt wounded pride by a dissenting report signed by eight members of the committee that agreed with the entire report except the characterization of the transfer of Denfeld as a "reprisal."[80] New legislation the committee would call for included adding the Commandant of the Marine Corps to membership on the Joint Chiefs of Staff, a cheerful note to friends of the Navy; rotating the chairman of the Joint Chiefs of Staff after a two-year term; and requiring the secretary of defense within certain limits to confer with the congressional appropriations committees before withholding appropriated funds by administrative act. A week later, irked by Johnson's exercising of powers he believed rested in Congress alone, Vinson introduced the necessary bills—all of which Johnson opposed.

Naval men who hoped that the Vinson hearings would reduce budget pressures on their service and improve the status of naval aviation were disappointed. "Radical" naval witnesses, however, had revealed their loss of confidence in the president, secretary of defense, and secretary of the navy. By airing the rivalry and points in dispute among the services at the Pentagon, they cleared the way for closer working relations between the Joint Chiefs of Staff and between Sherman, Matthews, and Johnson. They also tarred Matthews with a breach of faith in removing Denfeld.[81]

The day before the committee report was published, Denfeld was given a nineteen gun salute preparatory to his departure from the Navy, which became official on the day the report was published. Matthews meanwhile said he knew nothing about published reports that Truman would appoint him, Matthews, the U.S. Ambassador to Eire.[82] In testifying in support of the Navy budget for fiscal year 1951, which it may be recalled was cut 11 percent below that of fiscal year 1950, he uttered the platitude that the Navy "is more important than ever before in providing security to our country" and that the $3.8 billion allotted to the Navy, while allowing a balanced program, was "the minimum essential for effective Navy participation in an adequate security program." He highly praised Sherman, saying that he had "restored discipline, reestablished good order and renewed confidence throughout enlisted and officer personnel." He also directed that the Kinkaid report on the Worth investigation be published.[83]

It may be recalled that Matthews wanted to know the genesis of the once "anonymous" B-36 document subsequently known to have been written by Cedric B. Worth. Kinkaid's board convened in August 1949, heard testimony for two months, took two additional weeks to prepare its findings, and sent its report to Matthews in mid-October. When the report, which he approved, was published early in May 1950, it stated that Worth had "incurred serious blame" for violating the trust inherent in his position but implicated no other person.

Since Worth had long left the government service, no disciplinary action against him was recommended.[84]

Having retired from the Navy after forty-one years of service, Denfeld lost no time in striking back at Matthews in three articles written for *Collier's*. In one, entitled "Reprisal: Why I Was Fired," he asserted that he knew he would be the first target of Johnson and Matthews but had not expected the "contemptuous treatment" he received. Loyalty should work down as well as up, and loyalty included "politeness." The supercarrier was canceled, and he was fired in such an arbitrary way that he feared that control of national defense would pass from the people's representatives. Vinson, Matthews, and Johnson had promised that there would be no reprisals—but he had "offended the secretariat."[85]

The purport of Denfeld's second article is clear from its title: "The Only Carrier the Air Force Ever Sank." Men like Bradley and Vandenberg, he asserted, never boarded an aircraft carrier at sea until 1949, yet they, and others equally ignorant of the Navy's vital role, took it upon themselves to decree how naval warfare would be fought in the future. Denfeld added bluntly: "Strategic bombing was never a factor in the plans for the carrier *United States*." However, the Air Force imagined that the Navy posed a danger to its prime function of strategic air warfare and gathered enough pilots and lay supporters to "sink the *United States*." Denfeld had been forced to conclude that the Air Force wanted to abolish or acquire all combat naval aviation and the Army all the amphibious functions of the Marine Corps and reduce the latter to a mere security force. The twin ambitions resulted in a working agreement, the two-to-one votes against the Navy in the Joint Chiefs of Staff.[86]

On 24 May 1950, Matthews completed a year in office. He had begun at a most inauspicious time—immediately following the cancellation of the building of the *United States* and the heated resignation of Sullivan. New to the naval service, he admitted that he knew little about it but was willing to learn. At first he was tense and insecure; his relations with flag officers and with the press were precarious. With grim determination he weathered the trying days that arose out of the Worth document on the B-36, the criticism of unification by Crommelin, the dismissal of Denfeld, and the financial retrenchment within the department of defense. Despite cutbacks both at sea and ashore, with the help of Sherman he restored morale and good order in the Navy. As ever, he was a model secretary when it came to cooperating with Johnson and his fellow service secretaries on the subject of unification.[87]

Among others, Matthews, Bradley, Eisenhower, and the armed services committees were unhappy with "the minimum essential for effective Navy participation in an adequate security program" and with Johnson's "economizing" on defense. Johnson had not "transformed" fat into muscle; he had cut into muscle. Bradley told the Senate Appropriations Committee that the armed forces were insufficient to fight a major war and would not be ready to do so by the end of the next fiscal year, whereupon the committee suggested adding $385 million to the defense budget. Motivated by what it termed a "pressing need" for new naval vessels in the atomic age, the House Armed Services Committee voted unanimously to seek legislation providing $350 million for the construction of 112 new ships and craft and a nuclear-powered submarine (to cost $40 million), and for the conversion of twenty-nine existing types, one of them to be a powerful guided-missile cruiser. The bill "authorized and directed" the president, not the secretary of defense or the Navy Department, to undertake the new construction. Because the 1951 budget was almost ready, the new funds would be sought in the budget for fiscal year 1952. Perhaps in keeping with Eisenhower's suggestion, backed by Vinson, the departing Symington, and Symington's successor, Thomas Knight Finletter, that half a billion extra dollars be provided, Johnson capitulated. On 9 May, the House had voted unanimously to add $385 million to defense funds. Of the total, $100 million would go toward the procurement of ninety-five additional naval aircraft and $50 million for the Navy antisubmarine program.[88] According to Vice Admiral J. H. Cassady, Deputy Chief of Naval Operations (Air), the regular Navy would still be short 435 planes and an additional $650 million would have to be spent to provide first-line planes for the naval air reserve squadrons required upon mobilization.[89]

Although Matthews would neither confirm nor deny the story that the Navy had secretly developed two air squadrons with a primary mission of carrying the atomic bomb, in mid-May 1950 it was publicly reported that this was the case. About half of the thirty-two planes were P2V-3C Neptune patrol bombers, and half AJ-1 attack bombers, the AJ-1 being the first carrier plane able to handle atomic weapons even though it weighed less than half of a B-29.

The House Rules Committee paved the way for early consideration of Vinson's bill that authorized the building of 173 new vessels and the conversion of 291 others at a cost of over $2 billion. Among the new ships were a 57,000-ton carrier to replace the cancelled *United States* and an atomic-powered submarine. Shortly thereafter, on 27 June, elements of the air and naval services were authorized by President Truman to engage in combat against "Red invaders" who crossed the 38th parallel on 25 June into South Korea. On 30 June, Truman authorized the use of ground troops also.

The outbreak of the Korean war not only gave the department of defense its first trial by fire; it provided an acid test for the policy of containment and upheld the contention of those in all the military services who had appealed for a continuing program of military readiness during the cold war. American strategic atomic air power did not prevent the outbreak of war. While the Strategic Air Command could pulverize parts of Russia, American military power found it extremely difficult to check a second-rate foe in a limited war on the ground in Korea. It was time to reconsider the national strategy recommended by the Air Force and to note that conventional forces would be needed if a nuclear stalemate resulted in the fighting only of limited wars, and perhaps to substitute land-based and waterborne nuclear-tipped guided missiles for manned bombers.[90]

With the outbreak of war, Matthews, the other service secretaries, the Joint Chiefs of Staff, and leaders in the Department of State met with Truman to decide what to do. Thereafter the Joint Chiefs prepared directives to the Commander in Chief, Far East, which were dispatched after receiving presidential approval. The service secretaries had no hand in this process. However, Truman invited them to hear the daily briefings given to him by one of the Joint Chiefs, normally General Bradley, and agreed when they voiced strong feelings about re-examining the entire "military posture" for the dark days ahead even though the budget people in the office of the secretary of defense rather than they or the Joint Chiefs "unified" the budget during the war years. Matthews was not involved in the writing of National Security Council paper NSC-68, a "prologue to rearmament," for it was the work of a State-Defense study group.[91]

In his semiannual report dated 18 September 1950, Matthews noted that between 1 January and 30 June 1950 budget limitations caused the Navy to reduce the number of operating combatant ships, auxiliaries, and aircraft; greatly increase self-maintenance afloat; operate ships with about 67 percent of combat complements; inactivate sixty-five Naval Reserve ships, one shipyard, nine nonaviation bases, and eight naval air stations; cut active duty personnel by 33,464; and greatly reduce the research and development program. Both Fleet Marine Divisions and their Air Wings were in reduced strength. Although jet fighters now operated from carriers, the first of the five *Essex*-class carriers to be modernized would not join the fleet until late in the year.[92]

On the brighter side, the conversion of submarines to the snorkel type had moved steadily forward and both aircraft and helicopters were being adapted to antisubmarine warfare; the Navy was the prime developer of the turbo-prop type of plane; rockets and guided missiles were being provided to ships, submarines, and aircraft; enough progress had been made on a submarine nuclear power plant to warrant a request to Congress to authorize the building of a nuclear submarine in fiscal year 1952; and the membership in the Naval Reserve had grown rapidly, with 17,000 of the 1,120,000 reservists on active duty. Nevertheless, Matthews concluded that funds beyond those provided in the fiscal

1951 budget would be needed to bring the fleet to a satisfactory state of combat readiness. Were Korea the only danger zone, the problem would be relatively simple, but the communists might contemplate an attack on the United States "if all our normal forces are occupied elsewhere."[93]

When American warships began bombarding enemy shore positions along the Korean coast, Truman restricted them to territory south of the 38th parallel. Meanwhile General Douglas MacArthur, commander of the forces various countries provided at the call of the United Nations, directed the U.S. Far East Air Force to operate north of that parallel. Truman also directed that the Seventh Fleet, based in the Philippines and Guam, be placed under MacArthur's operational command; its mission was to prevent a communist invasion of Formosa and also a Nationalist Chinese attack upon the China mainland. Vice Admiral Charles T. Joy, Commander of U.S. Naval Forces in the Far East at the moment war came, had only a light cruiser and four destroyers in Japanese ports, but he needed not worry too much about the North Korean Navy, composed only of light craft and fishing boats, and could assure command of the sea to United Nations forces. While Radford, Commander in Chief Pacific Fleet, ordered a carrier task force to proceed from the west coast of the United States to Hawaii, other ships in the continental United States were prepared for extended operations, not only in the Far East but in the Mediterranean as well, and the production of guided missiles was greatly accelerated, for it was assumed by many persons that the attack on Korea was only a *ruse de guerre* designed to draw American power far away from Europe, where the Russians intended to launch a major military thrust. Truman thereupon dispatched four Army divisions to bolster NATO.[94]

American troops sent to Korea from Japan were soon pressed southward by their foe, yet the Joint Chiefs of Staff spurned an offer of troops for Korea made by Chiang Kai-shek, for they as well as Truman wanted to keep the war limited. Before elements of the 1st Marine Division and First Marine Air Wing could arrive from California, Truman ordered a close naval blockade of the entire Korean peninsula. British fleet units quickly joined American naval forces in patroling Korean waters, enforcing the blockade, and in attacking enemy naval vessels and shore installations. Particularly effective were air strikes flown from American carriers and patrols flown by the new land-based P2V-5 "sub-killer" and the new seaplane, the Martin P5M-1. Navy men also conducted commando raids and amphibious landings and provided vital tactical air support for Army and Marine forces on the ground. The Military Sea Transportation Service began funneling huge amounts of supplies to ports in Japan, Okinawa, and Korea, and escort carriers brought replacement aircraft and spare parts. Meanwhile demands from the media for information caused the department of defense to lift the established personnel limits on military public relations services. In consequence, Matthews expanded the work force in the Office of the Chief of Information from fifteen to seventy persons "for the duration."

Truman first removed budgetary ceilings on military personnel strength, then authorized the use of Selective Service to swell the ranks, and finally permitted the service secretaries to involuntarily recall reservists. Matthews thereupon issued a directive, in late July, to effect the involuntary recall of naval reservists and fleet reservists for a minimum of one year and also provided for the involuntary retention on duty of personnel whose enlistments expired at any time during the next year. In mid-August he added that no officer with less than thirty years service could retire. In consequence, by mid-April 1951, 40 percent of the 1st Marine Division in Korea, 30 percent of the First Marine Air Wing, and 25 percent of the men in Navy ships and planes in the Far East were reservists.

U.N. air and naval power soon reigned supreme over and about Korea, but as of mid-July, with a twenty-to-one manpower advantage, the communists continued their march southward. At a meeting of the Joint Chiefs of Staff with the Senate Armed Services Committee, Chairman Tydings commended the Navy for the prompt action it had taken to strengthen American forces in the Far East, in reactivating several escort carriers, and in taking out of storage and rehabilitating a number of carrier-based aircraft.

Tydings' commendation was amply warranted, for the Navy responded quickly in its first expansion since the end of World War II. Ships it had wisely mothballed during the demobilization following World War II proved to be a "secret weapon." To man ships, it asked for both line and staff officer volunteers and for enlisted personnel in all general and emergency rates, and the Marine Corps eliminated enlistment quotas. In the field, Air Force jet fighters operating from Japanese bases could spend from five to twenty minutes over a Korean target area, and their pilots were untrained in the support of combat troops, whereas Navy fighters from nearby carriers could stay over a target for almost two hours and performed well in support of ground units. Marine divisions with their own integrated air support became the bulwark of defense; these were the same Marines that Army leaders had called obsolete a year earlier.[95]

Until the North Koreans crammed into America's consciousness that her security was in danger, the watchword was "economy." Now Johnson informed Congress that he had only enough funds to carry on until 31 July. Although the Senate Appropriations Committee added $383 million to his budget, Johnson said that he would ask for an additional $1 billion for fiscal year 1951. No one spoke about the "crushing burden of a fifteen billion dollar military budget" or suggested that economic collapse would result from military spending. Instead demands were made to make good the deficiencies of the last five years and to expand the industrial mobilization program. Truman greatly outdid Johnson by calling upon an approving Congress to add $10 billion to defense funds—which sum Vinson told the House should be the minimum rather than the maximum—and to remove the statutory limit of two million service personnel. Of the $10 billion, the Air Force would get $4.5, the Army $3.6, and the Navy $2.7 billion.

Until the Korean War started, Matthews had directed the curtailment of most naval functions. He now had to swing in the opposite direction and order an around-the-clock expansion. With the new funds, the Navy planned to de-mothball 48 ships, thereby raising the number of major combatant ships from 237 to 285, and to add 430 minor combatant and auxiliary ships to the fleet and a thousand planes to its air arm. The Navy was given an additional $446 million for new aircraft, the Air Force $2.7 billion even though the Navy was doing most of the aviation work in Korea. As a naval witness before a House committee late in 1950 put it, "The political and public relations position of the Air Force was superb when it came to fighting for money."[96] Truman's signing of Vinson's bill for creating an "atomic Navy" promised the Navy its first atomic-powered submarine and a guided missile cruiser among the approximately 125 new ships to be built in addition to a number of modernizations. Matthews was the first to disclose that the nation was producing guided missiles for any purpose besides experiments, the latter having been carried on by the Navy since March 1949 on a converted seaplane tender, the *Norton Sound*.[97]

When Matthews testified in mid-August 1950 before the House Appropriations Committee, he was pleased when he was asked whether he had demanded enough funds and heard Johnson say that funds would be allocated to the services "on a concept of overall defense" instead of an equal percentage basis.[98] As appropriations and powers tumbled over one another from Congress to the armed services, for the first time in his tenure Matthews reported that morale in the Navy among both officer and enlisted personnel was "high."[99] However, his days in office were numbered.

Truman's major objective with respect to the Korean War was to keep it limited. When General MacArthur suggested that Chiang Kai-shek's troops be used, Truman considered relieving him as field commander in the Far East. In April, after MacArthur suggested spreading the war to China, Truman relieved him of both his U.N. and U.S. commands. Matthews, however, did not take the broad hint and ended his usefulness as Secretary of the Navy by demanding a preventive war in an address at the celebration marking the sesquicentennial of the Boston Naval Shipyard.[100]

Viewing Matthews's departure as certain, Navy airmen hoped he would be succeeded by Dan Kimball. However, Truman "fired" Johnson before he did

Matthews. Johnson, on a West Coast speaking tour, learned from a "White House spokesman" that he was through. He rushed back to Washington to tell Truman that without his backing the Pentagon would not follow his orders. "Well, Louis, if you feel that way about it, in your resignation, mention George Marshall as your successor."[101] Johnson complied. Ironically, he resigned while MacArthur outflanked the communists with the brilliant amphibious landings at Inchon. As Vinson saw it, Johnson was fired less for his misdirection of the military effort at the Pentagon than for such unbelievably crude actions in working with Secretary of State Dean Acheson and other officials on many matters, including the drafting of NCS-68, that Acheson believed that he was mentally ill.[102] (Several years later Johnson underwent an operation for a brain malady that eventually proved fatal.) As a close observer of the events of the day has noted, however, Johnson was beautifully set up as the fall guy or goat. He dominated the Pentagon but not the brilliant Acheson. Moreover, he was responsible for rendering American military forces ineffective just at the time national policy called for the solution of the Korean problem by military power.[103]

In his letter of resignation, dated 12 September, Johnson said that while the unification of the armed forces was accomplished to a great degree and the nation was rearmed to fight in Korea, "the country should have a Secretary of Defense who does not suffer under the handicap of the enemies I have acquired." He then recommended that his successor be General Marshall—"a man of such stature that the very act of naming him will promote national and international unity." Truman specified 19 September as the end of Johnson's tenure.[104] To his credit, Johnson did not backlash at Truman, who had fired him for carrying out presidential orders.

Marshall, sworn in on 21 September, said nothing about bringing new men into the defense establishment. On 28 September, Truman named Robert A. Lovett as Deputy Secretary of Defense. While the Army's Frank Pace and Air Force's Thomas K. Finletter were expected to stay, rumor had it that Matthews would resign in order to accept a diplomatic post. He did not do so. Neither did he say anything about the hope that the end of defense fund cutbacks might permit the building of a supercarrier. Vinson, however, said he would introduce a bill to build one.[105] With White House approval he did so. She would displace 57,000 tons, take three and a half years to build, and would be named after the first Secretary of Defense, James V. Forrestal. When her atomic-laden, long-range bombers were operative, the Navy would break the monopoly the Air Force had upon strategic bombing. But strategic bombing would remain a secondary rather than primary mission.

On 12 November, Matthews began an inspection tour of the Far East. At Pearl Harbor, he was briefed by Radford. After inspecting naval installations at Guam, he went via the Philippines and Okinawa to Japan, where he conferred with MacArthur prior to visiting naval activities in the forward area in Korea, where Chinese troops had recently begun to cross from Manchuria. Shortly after he returned, Truman asked Congress for a second supplemental budget of $17 billion, thereby raising the military budget for fiscal year 1951 to $41.8 billion, and for a doubling of military personnel to 2.7 million by 30 June 1951. He noted that this was not a "war budget" but "a step toward putting the United States in a position to move speedily into an increased state of mobilization if the situation grows worse." With an additional $3 billion as its share, the Navy's funds would go to $11 billion and its personnel would just about double, from 382,000 on 30 June 1950 to 688,971 a year later.[106] The impact of the new funds on the Navy's new construction and conversion program is illustrated by the fact that these funds were $249 million for fiscal year 1948, $218 million for 1949, originally $20 million but revised to $147 million for 1950; and originally $181 million but increased to $404 million for 1951.

While the Navy conducted its remarkably efficient amphibious operation in reverse at Hungnam, on 16 December Truman proclaimed a National Emergency and called for increasing armed personnel strength to 3.5 million "as soon as possible." The declaration of a national emergency provided Matthews with a host of new powers. He could, for example, recall retired enlisted men and officers of the Navy and of the Coast Guard to active duty; authorize contracts without calling for bids and make contracts on a cost-plus basis in certain cases; and disregard limits placed upon the number of admirals of the Navy and of generals of the Marine Corps. Meanwhile he must help plan for the orderly growth of the Navy in a projected five-year preparedness program.

Legislation to provide more than $50 billion for defense in fiscal year 1952, for the increase in military personnel Truman suggested, and for a five-year preparedness program were priority items to be considered by the first session of the Eighty-second Congress, which would meet on 3 January 1951. There was also the suggestion made by Vinson that the Marine Corps be doubled—to four divisions (not more than 400,000 men) and 36 air squadrons.

Testimony on a department of defense request for a Navy shipbuilding and conversion program was offered by Sherman and Admiral David H. Clark, Chief of the Bureau of Ships, not Matthews. Sherman not only persuaded Johnson, before the latter retired, to build a supercarrier; "his getting the Joint Chiefs of Staff to approve the ship after the fracas over CVA-58 was a masterpiece of diplomacy which no one but Sherman could have handled."[107] It took Vinson's committee only two hours to approve a program to cost about $3 billion, and only two hours of debate on the floor before the House approved, on 17 January, by unanimous vote. In contrast to their negative vote on a supercarrier in 1949, the Joint Chiefs of Staff now unanimously supported the building of one. After the House bill was considered by the Senate Armed Services Committee, a conference committee reached agreement and in early March Truman signed a bill that authorized the Navy to build 173 ships, of 500,000 tons, and to modernize 291 additional vessels, of 1 million tons, at a cost of $2 billion. Included were a supercarrier and an atomic-powered submarine. The Navy, thus, would be expanded to 1,066 ships by 30 June 1952, including eighteen large carriers when all modernization work was completed. In addition, it would increase its operating aircraft from 8,161 to 8,739 and its personnel from 664,200 to 735,000, with 204,029 in the Marine Corps.

The detailed military budget Truman sent to Congress for fiscal year 1952 called for slightly more than $60 billion, with the Navy allotted $15.1 billion in new obligational authority and authorized to operate 1,161 ships and raise its personnel limit to 790,000 men. Under Secretary of Defense Lovett told the Senate Committee on Appropriations that the budget was formulated on military requirements and not on an allocation of dollars, as had been the case in recent years. In his testimony, Matthews stated that naval gunfire support had been an important factor in Korea, as at the Inchon landings and Hungnam withdrawal, and that combat action in the Korean "proving ground" had demonstrated "generally successful equipment design policy."[108]

It was at this moment that Matthews reportedly accepted Truman's appointment of him as Ambassador to Ireland. For all practical purposes, Matthews's tenure ended on 28 June when Truman named him as ambassador to Ireland and Under Secretary of the Navy Kimball as Secretary of the Navy.

Matthews was elected chairman of the Nebraska delegation to the Democratic national convention of 1952, but "urgent ambassadorial duties" prevented his attending the convention. However, after about a year in Dublin, he left Mrs. Matthews and a daughter there and in late September 1952 stopped at Washington for routine consultations with the Department of State and then went on to Omaha for a physical examination because he had not been feeling well. At a luncheon there on 18 October, he remarked that he would retire at the end of the year and spend the rest of his days in Omaha. He had less than a day left, for on the next day he suffered a heart attack and died, aged sixty-five years. He has been remembered, if at all, because he was a "rowboat Secretary" who knew nothing about the Navy when Truman appointed him, ousted Denfeld because the latter had "opposed unification," and become *persona non grata* because he opposed administration policy with respect to the Korean War.[109] On the other hand, once he learned his way about the Navy Department and the Pentagon, he could be rated as about an "average" secretary. The most important thing he did was to bring Sherman in as chief of naval operations.[110]

NOTES

1. *San Francisco Chronicle*, cited in ANJ 86 (21 May 1949):1082.
2. *New York Times*, 17 May 1949.
3. *New York Herald Tribune*, 7 Oct. 1949.
4. "Carrier Battle," AW 50 (23 May 1949):7.
5. "Air Strategy Probe Set for July," *ibid.* 50 (20 June 1949):13–14.
6. Robert Greenhalgh Albion and Robert Howe Connery, *Forrestal and the Navy* (New York: Columbia University Press, 1962), p. 224.
7. John A. Floberg to the writer, 31 Aug. 1976.
8. "Secnav Addresses Midshipmen," ANJ 86 (2 July 1949):1266.
9. " 'Beef Up' Naval Aviation," ANJ 86 (2 July 1949):1270.
10. U.S. Department of Defense, *Second Report of the Secretary of Defense and the Annual Reports of the Secretary of the Army, Secretary of the Navy, and Secretary of the Air Force for the Fiscal Year 1949* (Washington: GPO, 1950), pp. 205–35; *Chicago Tribune*, 12 Sept. 1949: *New York Herald Tribune*, 19 Sept. 1949.
11. U.S. House of Representatives. *National Military Establishment Appropriations Bill for 1950*. Preconference Hearings before a Subcommittee of the Committee on Appropriations, House of Representatives, 81st Cong., 1st Sess. (Washington: GPO, 1949), pp. 22, 49.
12. Karig to CNO, 21 June 1949, NHD:OA, CNO Papers.
13. Karig, Memorandum for the CNO, 23 June 1949, *ibid.*
14. Karig to CNO, 25 July 1949, *ibid.*
15. Armin Rappaport, *The Navy League of the United States* (Detroit: Wayne State University Press, 1952), pp. 196–97.
16. "President's Plan for Reorganizing Defense Set-up," ANJ 86 (23 July 1949):1371–72; Timothy W. Stanley, *American Defense and National Security* (Washington: Public Affairs Press, 1956), pp. 89–91.
17. "Navy General Staff," ANJ 87 (10 Oct. 1949):105, 135.
18. "Unification Act Amendments," *ibid.* 86 (2 July 1949):1281.
19. "Powers of Defense Secretary," *ibid.* 86 (9 July 1949):1295.
20. Stanley, *American Defense and National Security*, pp. 92–94.
21. Top Secret. Matthews, Memorandum for the President, 9 Sept. 1949, copy in CNO Papers.
22. AW, 22 Aug. 1949.
23. "Secnav Issues Navy Day Edict," ANJ 86 (13 Aug. 1949):1430; "Encourage 'Healthy Rivalry,' " *ibid.* 86 (27 Aug. 1949):1479.
24. Paul Y. Hammond, "Super Carriers and B–36 Bombers: Appropriations, Strategy, and Politics," in Harold Stein, ed., *American Civil-Military Decisions: A Book of Case Studies* (University: University of Alabama Press, 1963), pp. 502–04 (hereafter cited as "Super Carriers and B–36 Bombers").
25. Walter Millis, with Harvey C. Mansfield and Harold Stein, *Arms and the State: Civil-Military Elements in National Policy* (New York: Twentieth Century Fund, 1958), p. 241.
26. "Court of Inquiry," ANJ 87 (10 Sept. 1949):27; "Kinkaid Report Under Study," *ibid.* 87 (5 Nov. 1949):254.

27. "Capt. Crommelin's Statement," *ibid.* 87 (17 Sept. 1949):51.

28. Carl W. Borklund, *Men of the Pentagon: From Forrestal to McNamara* (New York: Praeger, 1966), p. 78.

29. Vincent Davis, *The Admirals Lobby* (Chapel Hill: University of North Carolina Press, 1967), p. 374; Millis, *Arms and the State*, p. 242; Jack Raymond, *Power at the Pentagon* (New York: Harper and Row, 1964), pp. 199–200.

30. Hammond, "Super Carriers and B–36 Bombers," p. 511.

31. Hanson W. Baldwin in *New York Times*, 15 Oct. 1949.

32. OP–05B/BC, Memorandum to OP–09, 23 May 1949, CNO Papers.

33. Hammond, "Super Carriers and B–36 Bombers," pp. 505–07.

34. VADM Gerald F. Bogan to the SECNAV, 20 Sept. 1949, CNO Papers.

35. "Texts of Documents in Naval Discussion," ANJ 87 (8 Oct. 1949):139.

36. Hammond, "Super Carriers and B–36 Bombers," p. 511.

37. Davis, *Admirals Lobby*, pp. 286–88.

38. "Rep. Vinson" in "Texts of Documents in Naval Discussion," ANJ 87 (8 Oct. 1949):139.

39. Top Secret. Matthews to Vinson, 20 July 1949, CNO Papers.

40. U.S. Congress, *National Defense Program: Unification and Strategy*, Hearings before the House Committee on Armed Services, 81st Cong., 1st Sess. (Washington: GPO, 1949), pp. 2–3 (hereafter cited as NDP).

41. *Ibid.*, pp. 3–4, 23–24.

42. *Ibid.*, pp. 2–12.

43. *Ibid.*, p. 29.

44. *Ibid.; New York Times*, 8 Oct. 1949.

45. NDP, pp. 12–35.

46. *Ibid.*, pp. 39–52.

47. *Ibid.*, pp. 52–54. Radford was invited to continue answering questions at an afternoon session. See *ibid.*, pp. 54–107.

48. *Ibid.*, pp. 126, 201–36.

49. Hammond, "Super Carriers and B–36 Bombers," p. 528; Borklund, *Men of the Pentagon*, p. 81.

50. NDP, pp. 349–64.

51. ADM Louis E. Denfeld, "Reprisal: Why I Was Fired," *Collier's* 125 (18 Mar. 1950):62.

52. NDP, pp. 394–96.

53. NAFI 168.15–25, courtesy Dr. James N. Eastman, Jr., Chief, Research Branch, The Albert F. Simpson Historical Research Center, Maxwell Air Force Base, Alabama.

54. NDP, pp. 397–449.

55. *Ibid.*, pp. 516–37.

56. *Ibid.*, p. 567.

57. *Ibid.*, pp. 606–35.

58. Hammond, "Super Carriers and B–36 Bombers," pp. 538–46; Stanley, *American Defense and National Security*, pp. 94–95; CDR Richard Lane, USN, "The Navy and Public Opinion," USNIP 77 (Mar. 1951):285–88; "Revolt of the Admirals," AF 32 (Dec. 1949):22–27.

59. The text of the letter was published in the *New York Times* and *Washington Star* on 28 Oct. 1949.

60. Harry S. Truman, *Memoirs by Harry S. Truman*, 2 vols. (Garden City, N.Y.: Doubleday, 1955–1956), 2:53.

61. Rappaport, *Navy League*, p. 197.

62. *New York Times*, 29 Oct. 1949.

63. Newspapers cited in ANJ 87 (5 Nov. 1949):250.

64. Denfeld to Matthews, 14 Dec. 1949, in *ibid*. 87 (24 Dec. 1949):435; Denfeld, "Reprisal: Why I Was Fired," 14.

65. Hammond, "Super Carriers and B–36 Bombers," pp. 547–48.

66. "House Committee Members Angered at Denfeld Relief," ANJ 87 (4 Nov. 1949):249–50.

67. *New York Times*, 11 Nov. 1949; *Washington Post*, 11 Nov. 1949; "Survey of Navy Views," ANJ 87 (17 Dec. 1949):413.

68. "Further Navy Reductions," ANJ 87 (3 Dec. 1949):372, 379.

69. Borklund, *Men of the Pentagon*, pp. 85–86.

70. "Admiral Sherman OK'd: House Report Slated," ANJ 87 (14 Jan. 1950):505, 521.

71. Davis, *Admirals Lobby*, pp. 274–75, 288–89; Raymond, *Power at the Pentagon*, p. 200.

72. Transcript of oral interview by Jerry N. Hess of ADM Robert Lee Dennison, USN (Ret) (Independence, Missouri: The Harry S. Truman Library, 1972), pp. 136–40.

73. "Admiral Bogan to Retire," ANJ 87 (7 Jan. 1950):482, and "Admiral Bogan Relieved," *ibid*. 87 (14 Jan. 1950):510.

74. "Denfeld Commission for 2d Term Revealed," *ibid*. 87 (21 Jan. 1950):544, 559.

75. "Senate Unanimously Confirms Sherman," *ibid*. 87 (28 Jan. 1950):561, 584; Denfeld, "Reprisal: Why I Was Fired," 15.

76. *Semiannual Report . . . July 1 to December 1, 1949, pp.* 165–95. See also RADM Julius A. Furer, USN (Ret), "The Structure of Naval Appropriations Acts," USNIP 74 (Dec. 1948):1517–27, and "Navy's New Role in Air Power," AW 52 (27 Feb. 1950):15.

77. "Study Denfeld Case," ANJ 87 (4 Feb. 1950):500, 587.

78. "No Supercarrier," *ibid*. 87 (18 Mar. 1950):754.

79. "Navy Slang Barred," *ibid*. 87 (11 Feb. 1950):627; "Secnav Sets Policy," *ibid*. 88 (11 Nov. 1950):283.

80. *New York Times*, 2 Feb. 1950; "House B–36 Report May Stir New Laws," ANJ 87 (4 Mar. 1950):693, 722, and "Report Urges Restudy of Defense Concepts: Scores Denfeld Relief [complete text of report]," *ibid*. 87 (4 Mar. 1950):708–13, 723–24.

81. Hammond, "Supercarriers and B–36 Bombers," pp. 553–54; Eugene A. Wilson, "A Basis of Unity," USNIP 76 (Sept. 1950):961–67.

82. "Service News and Gossip," ANJ 87 (4 Mar. 1950):707.

83. "Mission of the Navy," *ibid*. 87 (18 Mar. 1950):755, and "CNO's Accomplishments," *ibid*., 759.

84. "Report on Cedric Worth Inquiry," *ibid.* 87 (18 Feb. 1950):555; "Report on Cedric Worth Investigation," *ibid.* 87 (18 Mar. 1950):766, and "End of Cedric Worth Case," *ibid.* 87 (6 May 1950):959.

85. Denfeld, "Reprisal: Why I Was Fired," 14–15, 62. See also "Denfeld Strikes Back," ANJ 87 (18 Mar. 1950):766.

86. ADM Louis E. Denfeld, "The Only Carrier the Air Force Ever Sank," *Collier's* 125 (25 Mar. 1950):32–33, 46–47, 50–51.

87. "Secnav Anniversary," ANJ 87 (20 May 1950):1022.

88. "House Group Backs 112 New Navy Ships," *ibid.* 87 (6 May 1950):957; "House Unanimously Votes More Funds," *ibid.* 87 (13 May 1950):1005.

89. "Naval Aircraft Purchases," *ibid.* 87 (13 May 1950):1001. The B–17 of World War II cost $238,000 each; a B–36 in 1950 cost $5,757,584 each. The B–29 of World War II cost $640,000 each; the Navy's AJ carrier attack plane, which could deliver an atomic bomb, cost $1,105,599–and the Navy ordered 15 of them in 1950 alone. (*New York Times,* 14 May 1950.)

90. W. W. Rostow, *The United States in the World Arena: An Essay in Recent History* (New York: Harper and Row, 1960), pp. 227–30; GEN Matthew B. Ridgway, USA (Ret), as told to Harold H. Martin, *Soldier: The Memoirs of Matthew B. Ridgway* (New York: Harper and Brothers, 1956), esp. pp. 311–16.

91. Dean Acheson, *Present at the Creation: My Years in the State Department* (New York: W. W. Norton, 1969), pp. 402–03; Paul Y. Hammond, *Organizing for Defense: The American Military Establishment in the Twentieth Century* (Princeton, N.J.: Princeton University Press, 1961), pp. 247–52; Truman, *Memoirs,* 2:311–44.

92. *Semiannual Report . . . for 1950,* pp. 109–26; *New York Times,* 8 Feb. 1950.

93. *Semiannual Report . . . for 1950,* pp. 113–35, 139.

94. *Ibid.,* p. 107; ANJ 87 (1 July 1950):1181–83; A. D. Davis, RADM, USN, Director, Joint Staff, Memorandum for SECDEF, 28 June 1950, JCS 1776.7, NHD:OA, JCS Papers; Bernard Brodie, *The Communist Reach for Empire* (Santa Monica, Calif.: The Rand Corp., June 1964), pp. 14–15.

95. For the war in Korea, among others see Malcolm W. Cagle and Frank A. Manson, *The Sea War in Korea* (Annapolis, Md.: U.S. Naval Institute, 1957), and James A. Field, Jr., *History of United States Naval Operations: Korea* (Washington: GPO, 1962).

96. John A. Floberg to the writer, 31 Aug. 1976.

97. *New York Times,* 6 Mar., 13 May 1949; *Christian Science Monitor,* 3, 14 Nov. 1949.

98. "Congress' New Defense Attitude," ANJ 87 (26 Aug. 1950):1410–11, and "Division of Defense Dollars," *ibid.,* 1411.

99. *Semiannual Report . . . for January-June 1951,* p. 183.

100. *New York Times,* 26 Aug. 1950; Acheson, *Present at the Creation,* p. 478; Truman, *Memoirs,* 2:345.

101. Borklund, *Men of the Pentagon,* p. 87.

102. Acheson, *Present at the Creation,* p. 94; Gaddis Smith, *Dean G. Acheson* (New York: Cooper Square Publishers, 1972), pp. 128–29, 155–62, 241, 264–65, 370.

103. John A. Floberg to the writer, 31 Aug. 1976.

104. "Letter Accepting the Resignation of Louis A. Johnson as Secretary of Defense, 12 Sept. 1950" (followed by Johnson's letter), U.S. President, *Public Papers of the Presidents of the United States: Harry S. Truman*, 8 vols. (Washington: GPO, 1961–1966), 1950, pp. 632–33; "Letter to Committee Chairmen Transmitting Bill to Permit General Marshall to Serve as Secretary of Defense, 13 Sept. 1950," *ibid.*, pp. 633–34.
105. "Drive for Big Carrier," ANJ 88 (4 Nov. 1950):251.
106. "Armed Forces Will Reach 2.7 Million," *ibid.* 88 (9 Dec. 1950):385, 391.
107. John A. Floberg to the writer, 31 Aug. 1976.
108. "Korean Proving Ground," ANJ 88 (16 June 1951):1162.
109. *New York Times*, 19 Oct. 1952.
110. John A. Floberg to the writer, 31 Aug. 1976.

DAN ABLE KIMBALL

31 July 1951–20 January 1953

K. JACK BAUER

Born in St. Louis, Missouri, on 1 March 1896, to John H. and Mary Able Kimball, Dan Able Kimball attended the public schools of St. Louis. In 1917 he joined the Army as an air cadet; after winning his wings on 1 March 1918, he was commissioned a second lieutenant. Mustered out in 1920 as a first lieutenant, he joined the Los Angeles sales office of the General Tire Company. In 1925 he wed Dorothy Ames, but that marriage ended in divorce in 1957. The following year he married newspaper columnist Doris Fleeson. Kimball remained with General Tire for twenty-nine years. During World War II he so successfully headed the development program at General Tire's JATO manufacturing subsidiary, the Aerojet Engineering Corporation, in Azuza, California, that he was promoted to vice president and director of the parent company.

When Secretary of the Navy John Sullivan brought Kimball to Washington in February 1949 as Assistant Secretary for Air, he found the Navy Department seething with the upheavals preliminary to the "Admiral's Revolt," that is, the uproar that followed the scrapping of the building of the supercarrier *United States* by Secretary of Defense Louis A. Johnson. Sullivan and Under Secretary W. John Kenney quit in the *United States* dispute, and Kimball would have too, but he was dissuaded by Johnson. After only six weeks Kimball moved up to Under Secretary when Francis P. Matthews replaced Sullivan. Kimball had the knack of getting along with nearly everyone, a particularly desirable attribute in the charged atmosphere of the Pentagon following the Admiral's Revolt. Further, more so than any of his immediate predecessors he had first-hand knowledge of his department and a personal acquaintanceship with his counterparts in other agencies.[1]

Kimball's appointment and confirmation as Secretary of the Navy, late in July 1951, came at a critical time. President Harry S. Truman had enticed Matthews out of the secretaryship with an ambassadorial post. On 22 July, Admiral Forrest Sherman, the very able and immensely respected Chief of Naval Operations, had died of a heart attack in Naples. To replace him was difficult, and Truman and Matthews deferred to Kimball because he must work with him. Admirals Robert W. Carney, William M. Fechteler, and Arthur W. Radford were all strong and able contenders for the billet. Kimball chose Fechteler, with whom he had already worked harmoniously; had much support from the service; was a favorite of Carl Vinson, the strong-willed Chairman of the House Armed Services Committee; and because he had not been involved, as particularly Radford had been, in the revolt of the admirals and was thus unlikely to reopen old wounds.[2]

The second post to be filled, the under secretaryship Kimball vacated, went to Francis P. Whitehair, a forty-nine year old Florida lawyer, businessman, and political hack who had earlier been Chief Counsel of the Economic Stabilization Agency. His appointment was arranged by a friend and fellow Floridian, Donald Dawson, the chief White House patronage dispenser. Whitehair quickly alienated most of the professional naval officers with whom he dealt because of his overbearing attitude and preoccupation with Florida political maneuverings. Moreover, not long after taking office he hired William L. Willett, another of Donald Dawson's proteges, as special assistant for personnel and housing matters. Willett had lost his job on 1 May when the President abolished the Board of Directors of the Reconstruction Finance Corporation. While at RFC, it was rumored, Willett had been a key figure in an "influence web." More important, he was hired without the knowledge or sanction of the higher officials of the Defense Department. When Secretary of Defense Robert A. Lovett demanded Willett's resignation forthwith, Whitehair accepted it "effective at once."[3]

Kimball's main task was to support the Navy as it fought in Korea while simultaneously strengthening its capacity to deter communist aggression elsewhere, yet doing so without upsetting the national economy. Since most of the material and manpower programs had been under way for some time, he had to keep up the momentum and also provide the base for further rapid expansion of production should the need arise. Given the uncertainties of 1951, this was a highly sensible program and one that Kimball directed with success.

At a press conference on 20 August, Kimball discussed construction of the new carrier *Forrestal*, whose building contract had been let 12 July to Newport News Shipbuilding and Dry Dock Co. He pointed out that she "probably did not represent the largest type the Navy would some day build" but denied that the Navy was behind Representative Vinson's proposal for build-ing two more *Forrestals*. The Navy, he said, wanted experience with the pro-totype before ordering others. However, he drastically reversed that when threatened by the block obsolescence of the Navy's carriers. Among other construction and conversion contracts he announced at the same time were those for the building of four prototype minesweepers, outgrowths of concern over Russian use of sea mines and the difficulties which the existing minecraft had experienced in Korea, particularly in the troublesome Wonsan sweep.[4]

On the following day the Bureau of Ships announced the award of a con-tract to the Electric Boat Company for the construction of an experimental nuclear-powered submarine. She would become the *Nautilus*, the world's first nuclear-powered vessel and leadship for a new generation of similarly pow-ered true submersibles. The *Nautilus* proposal antedates Kimball's arrival as Secretary, but it remained for him to oversee her construction and to contend with the very difficult Hyman Rickover.

When before the Joint Committee on Atomic Energy in September, Kim-ball reiterated his intention to develop aircraft carrier capability to deliver atomic bombs. Such development regained for the Navy the offensive role, from which it had been evicted in postwar strategic planning. In turn, the development of bombs small enough to be carried by carrier-based planes would be a powerful argument for the new carriers the Navy so strongly de-sired. He also estimated that the use of nuclear submarines with their longer cruising ranges would reduce by two thirds the number of boats necessary to accomplish the Navy's underwater mission.[5]

During the fall, Kimball spoke of various other naval needs, such as in-creasing speed in both surface and sub-surface vessels. Because the technical bureaus had not kept up with the technological advances, especially in power plants, he advocated atomic-powered surface craft.[6] His listing of the Navy's prime war-time duties as (1) antisubmarine warfare; (2) operations against enemy vessels, aircraft, and bases; and (3) amphibious assault showed that he wished to move forward from defensive to offensive measures. Hence his willingness to experiment with large *Forrestal*-class carriers and nuclear sub-marines.

Concern with the Soviet submarine threat was coupled with developments in the art of combating that threat. During the fall and winter of 1951–1952 the pioneer Helicopter Antisubmarine Squadron (HS–1) was commissioned at Key West, and a new ASW force, the Hunter-Killer Force Atlantic Fleet, was created. The new unit was designed to increase the nation's overall ASW effectiveness by coordinating the training of Hunter-Killer task groups, de-veloping ASW tactics and techniques, and serve also as an ASW force in being. The Hunter-Killer units were intended to counter submarines which evaded more conventional forces.[7]

In September 1951, Kimball had to find a replacement for General Clifton Cates, Marine Corps Commandant, who would finish his tour at the end of the year. The problem was not as difficult as that of finding Admiral Sherman's successor, and the selection of Lieutenant General Lemuel O. Shepherd seemed to be a natural one. He had a brilliant record and was close to Cates. "Uncle Lem's" selection, highly pleasing to most of the Corps, was formally announced by the President on 5 November.[8]

Still another change in senior departmental personnel occurred in September. Herbert R. Askins, a fifty-two year old Phoenix automotive parts dealer without prior government service, replaced John T. Koehler as Assistant Secretary when the latter became chief of the Defense Renegotiation Board. Kimball chose Askins because he wanted the contract letting post filled by a businessman in whose integrity he had complete confidence. Askins, a friend of over thirty years, fitted the requirements admirably.[9]

To increase the efficiency of the department, on 4 October Kimball shuffled the duties of his chief subordinates. The first recasting of duties since 1949, it remained in effect until the Eisenhower reorganization of late 1953. In Kimball's reorganization, the Secretary assumed responsibility for policy control of the naval establishment; relations with the public and senior government officials; morale and the welfare of the Navy; and supervision of the chief of information. The under secretary supervised and coordinated the work of the assistant secretary, assistant secretary for air, and the administrative assistant to the secretary, as well as collaborated with the chief of naval operations. The under secretary's responsibilities included the economy, efficiency, and business management of the naval establishment; legislative and legal matters; manpower and personnel; the Military Sea Transportation Service; petroleum; housing; the Judge Advocate General; the Office of Industrial Relations; and the Office of Management Engineering. To the assistant secretary fell logistic administration and control; procurement, production, and disposition of "hardware" items; and in cooperation with the Chief of Naval Operations, establishment of stock levels. The assistant secretary for air retained his responsibility for all aeronautical matters while the administrative assistant had charge of departmental administration and the executive office of the secretary.[10] Since the reorganization continued the department's "bilinear" forms of separate lines of military and business direction, it merely streamlined and simplified the administrative arrangements rather than causing any large–scale shifts in either responsibilities or relationships.

On 17 September, Robert A. Lovett succeeded George Marshall as Secretary of Defense. One of his first problems was to get a settlement of the

JCS deadlock over the future size of the Air Force. He took the question away from the service chiefs and gave it to the civilian secretaries, who worked out a compromise Lovett then forced the uniformed leaders to accept. This marked not only the end of the domination of purely military considerations in defense policies, it also marked the return of the secretaries to full participation in policy making.[11]

On 1 October, reflecting the Air Force compromise and Lovett's confrontation with $71 billion in service requests for the Fiscal 1953 budget, the National Security Council modified force levels and extended the period of rebuilding. Under the new levels the Navy got 408 active combat ships, while the Marines were allotted three divisions with their accompanying aircraft wings. In part Lovett based his position on the difficulties encountered by the services in spending the money already appropriated and the slippages beginning to appear in defense production and in part a wish to reduce the military's consumption of raw materials. Almost simultaneously, Senator Brien McMahon justified a tremendous expansion of the atomic weapons program on the grounds that it provided "peace power at bearable cost,"[12]—the kind of thinking that culminated in the "New Look" policies of the Eisenhower Administration.

Congressional resistance to large defense appropriations may be seen in the fate of the Fiscal 1952 Defense Department Appropriation Bill. Truman's initial request called for about $60 billion, but by the time it cleared Congress three months later on 12 October it had been cut to $56 billion. The Navy's share, $15,877,891,000, included a third of a billion dollars more in aviation funds than the President had requested. Despite the cuts the Navy retained money to pay for 229,000 tons of new construction. This, with the appropriation for conversions, amounted to 8.59 percent of the total. New vessels included the *Forrestal*, a second nuclear submarine, two radar picket and a conventional attack submarine, 52 amphibious craft, 47 minecraft, an escort, six oilers, and an icebreaker. Most conversions involved replacing 40mm antiaircraft batteries with the new rapid–fire 3-inch/50-caliber gun, but two involved the reconstruction of the heavy cruisers *Boston* and *Canberra* as the fleet's first guided missile cruisers.[13]

During the formation of the Fiscal 1953 budget, the Defense Department disclosed it would ask for funds for a second *Forrestal*-class carrier, two additional carrier air groups, and a continuation of the *Essex*-class modernization program. As finally worked out, the Navy's part of the $52 billion budget was $13.2 billion.

Coincidental with the budget discussions, Kimball launched a campaign to assure the Navy one big carrier a year for ten years. The figure was arrived at by projecting the Navy's needs against the rapidly approaching old age of the *Essex*-class carriers. In January 1952, when he suggested that "some . . . will be atomic powered," *Time* commented that "The Navy last week staked an early claim to a large chunk of the U.S. defense budget for the next decade."[14] These proposals, as we shall see, nearly came to grief as soon as they were made.

As 1952 began, the Marine Corps received the third division called for in the 1 October NSC decision. On 7 January the 3rd Marine Brigade at Camp Pendleton became the 3rd Marine Division. Its aviation counterpart, the Third Marine Aircraft Wing, was reactivated on 1 February. Plans called for shipping the units to Hawaii for further training and possible dispatch to Korea. Delay in legal authorization, however, was caused by a struggle by the congressional supporters of the Corps against the combined opposition of the Department of Defense and the Joint Chiefs. Senator Paul H. Douglas on 25 January 1951 had introduced a bill on behalf of forty-three other senators that authorized a four-division, four-wing Marine Corps of 400,000 men and made the Commandant a member of the Joint Chiefs. Representative Mike Mansfield introduced a similar bill in the House with the support of seventy-six other members. Douglas's bill passed the Senate unanimously on 4 May 1951, but it did not come to the floor in the House for another year. A watered down version finally passed that chamber on 16 May 1952. The compromise worked out by a conference committee called for three divisions, three wings, and the Commandant's meeting with the JCS unless specifically forbidden to attend a meeting. This cleared both houses on 19 June and received the President's signature without comment on the twenty-eighth.[15]

The Defense Department Fiscal 1953 budget submitted by the President on 21 January 1952 called for the expenditure of $52.4 billion. The services had initially requested $71 billion, but Lovett cut this to $55 billion and the Bureau of the Budget sliced another $2.6 billion before forwarding it to the White House. The Navy fared reasonably well in the reduced budget. It got funds for another big carrier, two additional carrier air groups, and the continuation of the *Essex*-class carrier modernization program. The Navy's $13.2 billion also included money to increase the active fleet to 408 major and 783 minor craft and personnel strength from 790,000 to 835,000. The Marines would also grow, from 217,000 to 243,000. The budget contained the first substantial request ($32.6 million) for the acquisition of operational missiles.

In an attempt to strengthen the antisubmarine capabilities of the Navy, "Uncle" Carl Vinson's House Armed Services Committee enlarged the shipbuilding authorization, but this was thwarted by the House's application of what the *Navy Times* called "Meat-Ax Economy." It deleted the funds for the CVA, twenty LSTs, 100 LCMs, a pair of oilers, six DER conversions, and service craft. While the bulk of the vessels deleted were of relatively low priority, the big carrier was the service's most desired item. In addition the Navy lost $150 million in aircraft procurement money. All told the sea services absorbed $1 billion of the $4.2 billion eliminated from the defense budget. budget.

While Kimball led the fight to persuade the Senate to restore the cherished carrier, a noisy dispute occurred between the carrier's proponents and opponents over whether she had been approved by the JCS. Wisely avoiding the largely senseless argument, Kimball concentrated on the delays which budget cuts would make in the delivery of ships and planes.

As part of the pressure on the Senate, the campaign for the 10-year *Forrestal*-a-year program continued unabated. Assistant Secretary for Air John Floberg argued for it in an address to the Navy League, as did Admiral Fechteler in a speech before the Bond Club of New York. Fechteler then told the Senate Armed Services Committee that the Navy would be willing to forego some of the lower priority items to get the CVA, and Kimball increased the pressure by saying in May that the Navy should have four *Forrestals* building "right now" to offset Communist capabilities. The following month, in another address, he said he "would feel more comfortable about the nation's defenses" if he were building two *Forrestals* a year.

The campaign worked, evidently, for the Senate Appropriations Committee reported out a compromise in which the Navy would be authorized to start the second *Forrestal* but would have to absorb the Fiscal 1953 costs by eliminating lower priority vessels. The Navy provisions of the revised bill sailed through both houses with little difficulty and the bill received the President's signature on 10 July.[16]

To get the second CVA the Navy had to drop the ASW carrier, a destroyer, two submarines, three LSDs, and a DE. Another effect of the reduction was a further stretch-out of aircraft procurement that would delay the completion of the re-equipping of Navy squadrons with modern planes until mid-1955. This rather complicated the preparations for the mid-1954 "period of maximum danger" towards which the Truman military planning looked.[17]

While the budget fight was in process, Kimball attacked both inefficient government workers and carping civilians, arguing on one hand that, "If they don't deliver the goods, let them get to hell out of office," but on the other, "If you're not willing to come down, and show us how to do it better, don't sit home and criticize." Following protests from the American Federation of Government Employees, he had some businessmen check the department's operations and was pleased when they assured him that the department was well run indeed.[18]

When some congressmen complained that too much "brass" showed up for hearings, he directed that the number of officers present at committee hearings be held to "the minimum necessary to conduct departmental business.[19]

After completing his testimony on the budget, Kimball left on a tour of units and installations in the Far East. His sometimes pithy comments made good copy in the stateside press. In both Taipei and Tokyo he stressed the continuing American commitment to defend Formosa, saying that if the Chinese Communists attempted an invasion, "we would clobber the hell out of them." He also offered his personal opinion that the United States would "cheer on" a Nationalist invasion of the mainland, an opinion promptly repudiated by the State Department. On his return he suggested a five-fold increase in the training mission of Formosa and an increase in Far East Command strength. He further reported optimism on the part of the truce negotiators in Korea.[20]

Shortly after his return from the Far East, Kimball cleared the first hurdle in his path toward a nuclear-powered carrier. In April the Atomic Energy Commission endorsed the project and let a development contract to Westinghouse for the engines, whereupon Kimball suggested that an atomic-powered plane be developed to go with the atomic-powered carrier.[21]

Another carrier development came in April with the adoption of the British-developed steam catapult. It had been demonstrated by HMS *Perseus* earlier in the year and was scheduled for initial installation in the *Hancock* during her upcoming modernization. The steam "sling shots" were not only safer than the hydraulic ones, but they could better handle the heavier planes with which the carriers were being equipped. The capabilities of the rebuilt carriers were further enhanced by the adoption of a second British innovation, the angled or canted deck, which got its first operational tests on the *Antietam* in January of 1953. The new deck configuration greatly eased the difficulties in handling the heavier planes and drastically reduced the danger.[22]

Because Congress insisted that ship disposals be cleared with Capitol Hill, Kimball in May 1952 asked for authority to restore the *Constitution* and sell or scrap the other four relics (*Constellation, Hartford, Olympia,* and *Oregon*) on the Navy List. In January 1953 he also asked for an appropriation of $100,000 to restore "Old Ironsides." Ultimately, under an Act of 23 July 1954, the Navy scrapped the *Hartford* and *Oregon* and disposed of the *Constellation* and *Olympia* to civic associations. The struggle of the Marylanders to secure the *Constellation* for Baltimore had its comic overtones. In order for the promoters to raise enough money to restore the old sloop they had to get the Director of Naval History to certify that she was indeed the frigate built in Baltimore in 1796–1798. Since the Navy had always maintained the official fiction that this was true, he did so readily.[23]

Of much greater importance was the Armed Forces Reserve Act of 1952, which provided the maximum possible uniformity of treatment among the services by establishing three reserve categories (ready, standby, retired) and defining the conditions under which each would be mobilized. Changes required in Navy and Marine Corps procedures were minimal.[24]

On 14 June Kimball introduced the President to the crowd of 10,000 gathered at Groton, Connecticut, for the keel laying of the *Nautilus*. In his introductory remarks the Secretary called nuclear power the "greatest advance in propulsion since the Navy shifted from sail to steam." After the speeches, President Truman wrote his initials on a plate destined for the bow and a welder burned them into the plate. The President then proclaimed the keel "well and truly laid."[25]

The submarine was largely the product of the driving energy and singleness of purpose of Captain Hyman G. Rickover and his subordinates in the Naval Reactors Branch of the AEC and the Nuclear Power Division of BuShips. Although he soon became the "darling" of the politicians and much of the press, Rickover lacked a similar standing with many of his uniformed superiors. On 7 July, the day preceding the meeting of the 1952 Flag Officer selection board, Kimball in a pointed reminder awarded Rickover a second Legion of Merit for the "unceasing drive and energy" which made him "more than any other individual responsible for the rapid development of the nuclear ship program." Perhaps indicative of the spirit within the department, the ceremony was well attended by civilian administrators but not by military leaders. Although Kimball was greatly surprised when the Selection Board passed over the controversial officer for a second time, he refused to intervene. While the board's reasons for not choosing Rickover remain secret, they undoubtedly reflected the divided service opinion of him. His astringent personality and tactlessness had alienated a sizable group of officers, headed by the Chief of the Bureau of Ships. Others feared his tendency to build the nuclear navy into an autonomous little barony. Implicit in the board's action is the assumption that Rickover was not essential to the nuclear program. Certainly, *Time's* accusation of "Brazen Prejudice" which reflected a "deep seated prejudice against technical specialists" is journalistic oversimplification.[26]

If there remained any question of the Air Force's rancor over the B–36 controversy and the resuscitation of the Navy's air wing as exemplified by the CVA program, it was settled at the 14 July ceremonies marking the keel laying of the *Forrestal* at Newport News. No high-ranking Air Force officials accepted invitations to attend, whereas the Navy's hero of the B–36 fight, former Secretary Sullivan, was much in evidence, and Lovett sent Deputy Secretary of Defense William C. Foster to be the principal speaker.[27]

As the summer advanced and both Congress and the public objected to high defense spending, Kimball stressed the desirability of building two *Forrestals* a year, yet spoke of the approaching stabilization of defense costs at a "comfortable" level as the Korean build-up tapered off. But the awareness of the economy drive did not prevent Kimball from continuing his drive for a nuclear-powered carrier, and in late August he suggested that the third or fourth *Forrestal* be so built.[28]

In his semi-annual report for the second half of Fiscal 1952, dated 22 September, Kimball admitted that the Navy was still dominated by the problems of Korea but that these problems were "a subordinate element of a far broader task—that of building a Naval Establishment which can cope with other threats of world communism, whenever and wherever they may develop." He continued his drive for more carriers so that the Navy could control the sea by moving "our bases to the enemy's shoreline." He believed that at least twelve big carriers were needed. He was giving high priority to the production of air defense missiles, which were replacing guns as the chief antiaircraft weapon, and to improving the Navy's antisubmarine capacity.[29] On 1 October, at a press conference he held in Paris while on a tour of American and Allied installations in Europe, he acknowledged that the Navy's primary task was to neutralize the approximately 300 Soviet submarines. The admission pleased the Air Force, as did his further admission that no naval vessels carried atomic bombs, although some had the capability to do so.[30]

Although Kimball was a "lame-duck" secretary after the November elections, like the remainder of the Truman administration he had to prepare the paper budget to be submitted to Congress in January 1953, one likely to undergo major revision after the new administration took office. Even so, Kimball had a hard struggle to save the third *Forrestal* carrier. Although approved by the Defense Department, she ran into rough seas in the Bureau of the Budget, which was attempting to hold the Defense request under $39 billion, or $7 billion below the Fiscal 1953 figure. When it indicated that the carrier was an expendable item, Kimball and Admiral Fechteler joined other Defense officials in making strong presentations in her favor at the White House. Kimball also continued his campaign for the *Forrestal*-a-year program in his address at the keel-laying ceremonies for the second big carrier, the *Saratoga*, at New York Naval Shipyard on 16 December.

In the final budget, set at $41,535,000,000, $11,367,732,000 went to the Navy and Marine Corps. Although $1.3 billion less than the preceding budget, it permitted maintaining a fleet of 406 combat vessels, 296 auxiliaries, and 496 other craft, an increase of 72. It provided an 800,000-man personnel level for the Navy and a three division, 248,612-man, Marine Corps. And the $1.1 billion asked for construction and conversion projects included the third *Forrestal*.[31]

In his final press conference, Kimball predicted a future atomic-powered and guided-missile Navy. Eight of the new big carriers, in his opinion, should be nuclear powered.

Kimball's resignation took effect 21 January, after which he returned to his job as vice president and director of the General Tire and Rubber Company. On 17 July 1953 he became President of the renamed Aerojet–General Corporation.

Kimball's tour, in his own words, had been an "enjoyable and satisfying" assignment.[32] It had been a very profitable one for the Navy, for he had brought order and purpose to a department shaken by the revolt of the admirals, Johnson's "meat-axe" economy, and weak civilian leadership. A strong individual who insisted on running the Navy Department in the manner he believed most effective, Kimball not only restored the Department's confidence in itself but gave direction to the restoration of the Korean War Navy. Indeed, one of the strongest commendations of his regime is that with all the opportunities that the massive expenditures offered, and the 5-percenter atmosphere that pervaded so much of Washington at the time, the Navy escaped nearly unscathed from the "Truman" scandals.

NOTES

1. *Current Biography*, 1951, pp. 336–37; *Time* 58 (9 July 1951):17; interview with Dan A. Kimball, 3 June 1966.

2. CR, 82nd Cong., 1st Sess., 97, pt. 1, 9717; Kimball interview; Theron J. Rice, "Salt on the Council Table," *New York Times Magazine*, 12 Aug. 1951; ANAFJ, 28 July, 4, 18 Aug. 1951.

3. CR, 82nd Cong., 1st Sess., 97, pt. 7, 9503; ANAFJ, 11 Aug. 1951; *Time* 61 (2 Feb. 1953):18–19. Kimball claimed that Whitehair was recommended by the White House because he had no candidate for the post. He considered Whitehair efficient and a man who did the job required of him although he irritated some people (Kimball interview) and thanked him for having "intensely pursued your duties . . . [his] searching legal mind." Kimball to Whitehair, 19 Jan. 1953. Dan A. Kimball Papers, Box 4, Harry S. Truman Library.

4. See James A. Field, *History of United States Naval Operations: Korea* (Washington: GPO, 1962), pp. 230–42, 372, 402.

5. *New York Times*, 30 Mar. 1952.

6. ANAFJ, 15 Sept. 1951; Kimball interview.

7. Bureau of Aeronautics, *United States Naval Aviation 1898–1956* (Washington: GPO, 1957), p. 53; *Navy Times*, 29 Dec. 1951.

8. ANAFJ, 22 Sept., 10 Nov. 1951; *Navy Times*, 10 Nov. 1951.

9. CR, 82nd Cong., 1st Sess., 97, pt. 9, 11527; *New York Times*, 19, 27 Sept., 4 Oct. 1951; Askins to Kimball, [Aug. 1951], Kimball to Askins, 19 Jan. 1953, Kimball Papers.

10. SECNAV to Distribution List A, Subj: Assignment of duties and responsibilities . . . , 4 Oct. 1951, in Office of the Management Engineer, *The United States Navy: A Description of Its Functional Organization* (Washington: GPO, 1952), Appendix C.

11. Kimball interview.

12. Walter Millis, with Harvey C. Mansfield and Harold Stein, *Arms and the State: Civil-Military Elements in National Policy* (New York: Twentieth Century Fund, 1958), pp. 352–55; John C. Ries, *The Management of Defense: Organization and Control of the U. S. Armed Services* (Baltimore: Johns Hopkins Press, 1964), pp. 149–50; Edward A. Kolodziej, *The Uncommon Defense and Congress, 1945–1963* (Columbus: Ohio State University Press, 1964), pp. 153–54; *Time* 58 (8 Oct. 1951):27–28.

13. Millis, *Arms and the State*, p. 353; *Congressional Quarterly Almanac, 1951* (Washington: Congressional Quarterly, 1951), pp. 129–32; John H. McQuilkin, "No Ships but the Best," Frank Uhlig, Jr., ed., *Naval Review 1962–1963* (Annapolis, Md: U. S. Naval Institute, 1962), pp. 261–63; ANAFR, 15 Sept., 6 Oct. 1951; Kolodziej, *Uncommon Defense and Congress*, pp. 144–50.

14. Kimball interview; *Navy Times*, 20 Oct. 1951; *New York Times*, 13 Jan. 1952.

15. CR, 82nd Cong., 1st Sess., 97, pt. 4, 4857; *Navy Times*, 13 Jan. 1952; ANAFJ, 12 Jan. 1952; Norman W. Hicks, *A Brief History of the United States Marine Corps* (Washington: Historical Branch, U.S. Marine Corps, 1961), p. 45; Robert D. Heinl, Jr., "The Right to Fight," USNIP 88 (Sept. 1962):37–38.

16. U. S. Congress, HAC, *Department of the Navy Appropriations for 1953*, pp. 1967–82; *H. Rpt. 1681*, 82nd Cong., 2nd Sess.; CR, 82nd Cong., 2nd Sess., 98, pt. 3, 3867, 3869; *New York Times*, 23 May, 6 June 1952; *Navy Times*, 26 Jan., 15 Mar., 12, 19 Apr., 3 May, 14 June, 5, 26 July 1952; Kolodziej, *The Uncommon Defense and Congress*, pp. 156–66.

17. *New York Times*, 6 Feb., 6 May 1952; *Navy Times*, 23 Mar. 1952; Paul Y. Hammond, "NSC–68: Prologue to Rearmament," in Warren R. Schilling, Paul Y. Hammond, and Glenn H. Snyder, *Strategy, Politics, and Defense Budgets* (New York: Columbia University Press, 1962), pp. 267–378.

18. *Navy Times*, 9 Feb. 1952; *New York Times*, 24 Jan., 7 Feb. 1952.

19. *New York Times*, 3 Mar. 1952.

20. *Ibid.*, 24 Mar.-10 Apr. 1952.

21. Clay Blair, Jr., *The Atomic Submarine and Admiral Rickover* (New York: Holt, 1954), pp. 188–89; *Navy Times*, 26 July 1952.

22. Adrian O. Van Wyen and Lee M. Pearson, *United States Aviation 1910–1960* (Washington: GPO, 1960), pp. 153, 155; *Navy Times*, 10 May 1952; Dorothy L. Small "Catapults Come of Age," USNIP 80 (Oct. 1954):113, 121.

23. *Navy Times*, 24 Jan., 24 May 1952; ANAFJ, 17 May 1952.

24. *Armed Forces Reserve Act: Hearings before a Subcommittee of the Committee on Armed Services, United States Senate . . . on H.R. 5426* (Washington: GPO, 1952), p. 284; I. M. McQuiston, "History of the Reserves Since the Second World War," MA 17 (Spring 1953):26.

25. Blair, *Atomic Submarine*, pp. 2, 7; *New York Times*, 15 June 1952; *Navy Times*, 21 June 1952.

26. Blair, *Atomic Submarine*, pp. 190–95; *Time* 60 (4 Aug. 1952):18. In retrospect, Kimball believed he should have intervened. (Kimball interview.)

27. *New York Times*, 15 July 1952; *Navy Times*, 19 July 1952.

28. *New York Times*, 5, 29 Aug. 1952; *Navy Times*, 9 Aug., 13 Sept. 1952; ANAFJ, 30 Aug. 1952.

29. "Semiannual Report of the Secretary of the Navy, 1 January 1952 to 30 June 1952," in *Semiannual Report of the Secretary of Defense . . . January 1 to June 30, 1952* (Washington: GPO, 1952), pp. 145, 150, 158, 191–92.

30. *New York Times*, 2–17 Oct. 1952.

31. *New York Times*, 17 Dec. 1952; *Navy Times*, 20 Dec. 1952, 10 Jan. 1953; ANAFJ, 6, 20, 27 Dec. 1952, 10 Jan. 1953.

32. Kimball interview.

ROBERT BERNERD ANDERSON

4 February 1953–2 May 1954

K. JACK BAUER

When President-elect Dwight D. Eisenhower announced the selections for the second level Defense Department appointments on 19 December 1952, the choice for Secretary of the Navy turned out to be Robert Bernerd Anderson, a Texas Democrat-for-Eisenhower and close friend of Governor Allan Shivers, Senator Lyndon B. Johnson, and the Speaker of the House of Representatives, Sam Rayburn. Eisenhower had first met Anderson in early 1951, corresponded with him concerning international finance while he himself was in Europe, and planned to use him somewhere else if Secretary of Defense-designate Charles E. Wilson did not want him in Defense.[1]

Robert was born on a farm near the central Texas town of Bartleson on 4 June 1910, to Robert Lee and Elizabeth Haskew Anderson. His father, a farmer who dabbled in politics, had served as mayor of Bartleson. After attending the local public schools and Weatherford Junior College, Anderson entered the University of Texas Law School and graduated in 1932 at the head of his class. While in law school he took a year off to earn money by teaching Spanish, history, and mathematics, and coaching football at Bartleson High School. In his senior year in law school he successfully ran for the State Senate. Anderson then entered practice in Fort Worth and in 1933 was named an Assistant State Attorney General. Shortly afterwards, he left the state's service to join the faculty of the law school as an assistant professor. When Attorney General James V. Allred was elected governor, he named his former assistant to the State Tax and Racing Commissions. Then in 1936 Allred named Anderson Chairman and Executive Director of the newly created Texas Unemployment Commission.

In 1935 Anderson married Ollie May Rawlings and two years later re-signed his state positions to become general attorney and manager for the W. T. Waggoner Estate, a five hundred thousand-acre farming and ranching trust which he guided to a steady growth in the ensuing years.

A slight limp resulting from a childhood bout with polio kept Anderson out of uniform in World War II, but he served as a civilian adviser to the Secretary of War. Appointed Chairman of the Texas State Board of Education in 1949, Anderson was twice re-elected. Along with his other business and public duties, he served as Deputy Chairman of the Federal Reserve Bank of Dallas and on the boards of several commercial and philanthropic organizations.[2]

The nomination of Anderson as Secretary of the Navy was not universally hailed. The *New York Times*, for example, sniffed that it "seems to be in part a political recognition of the role played by Texas Democrats in General Eisenhower's election. His previous experience . . . would not appear to fit him directly to be Secretary of the Navy."[3] The service press greeted the appointment, as usual, with a wait-and-see attitude.

Before Christmas, 1952, the incoming Defense Department leaders began a series of meetings with outgoing officials. As a result, Anderson absorbed a great deal of information about his new post before taking the reins and was able to make an exceptionally smooth transition into it. Eisenhower formally submitted the nominations on 29 January and Anderson was approved the following day after only three minutes of perfunctory questioning.

To smooth the transfer of power, the outgoing and incoming Defense secretaries retained one experienced senior official in each of the service departments until the new "team" got settled. The choice in the Navy Department was the Assistant Secretary for Air, John Floberg, who would also be Acting Secretary during the interregnum.

As his under secretary, Anderson brought in Charles S. Thomas, of Los Angeles, president of Foreman and Clark, a California store chain, confidant of former Secretary James V. Forrestal, and frequent department advisor. The new assistant secretary was Raymond Henry Folger, President of the W. T. Grant Company store chain; the new Assistant Secretary of Air, James H. Smith, was a veteran pilot and airline executive. Smith had organized Pan American Airway's African Ferry Route early in World War II and then served as a naval pilot and staff officer. After the war, he returned to Pan American and in 1949 moved to Slick Airways, of which he was now a director. John Dillon remained as administrative assistant and senior professional civil servant in the Department.

One of the earliest problems confronting Anderson was a revival of the Hyman G. Rickover case. On 12 February, Representative Sidney R. Yates, of

Illinois, delivered a blistering attack on the "Navy Brass" and their "convoy mentality" for failing to promote the atomic specialist, who approached retirement in July 1953 upon the completion of thirty-one years of service. Yates and Melvin Price in the House and the Senate Armed Services Committee, respectively, applied pressure on the department by postponing consideration of the nominations of the thirty-nine men selected by the Flag Officer Board, then invited the addition of Rickover's name by returning the nominations to the White House with the request that they be concurred in by the new President. Eisenhower, however, refused to intervene and returned the list as it stood. The committee then announced extended hearings beginning 3 March on the nominations, which Senator Estes Kefauver predicted would lead to an investigate of the entire Navy selection system.

Testimony given particularly by Rear Admiral Homer N. Wallin, Chief of the Bureau of Ships, played down Rickover's importance and failed to calm the anger of Rickover's supporters, especially after it was rumored that the Navy had asked Rickover to remain on active duty after retirement to see the experimental nuclear submarine program through to completion. The controversy increased in heat until the *New York Times* reported that it was "beginning to remind veterans of the row over General 'Billy' Mitchell."

Faced with the possibility of a potentially embarrassing investigation into the entire Navy promotion system, Anderson worked out a solution, the calling of a special board to select EDO captains for retention on active duty and to specify that one "be experienced and qualified in the field of atomic propulsive machinery for ships." This could apply only to Rickover. Moreover, his continuation on active duty would make him eligible for consideration by the 1953 Flag Officer Board, which in turn could be directed to select one EDO of similar qualifications. For better or worse, Rickover's friends on the Hill had carried the day. Following his approval by the retention board, Rickover was selected by the June promotion board and nominated for his two stars by the President on 30 July 1953.[4] Although new to his office, Anderson had moved swiftly and effectively to produce a solution that satisfied Rickover's partisans and kept the Navy's selection system intact. Moreover, the solution kept officially alive probably the only officer with the experience, drive, and ability necessary to see the nuclear submarine program so successfully through its infancy.

Anderson's second challenge came in determining the size and composition of the Navy's Fiscal Year 1954 budget. Determined to cut defense costs, Eisenhower directed the Secretary of Defense to develop plans "to give our Nation maximum safety at minimum cost."[5] This was the initial step in the development of what came to be called the Eisenhower Defense Policy or "New Look." In the initial stage, this amounted to little more than a re-examination of the Truman Defense budget with a view to shaving expenditures by $4 billion in Fiscal Year 1954 and $6.6 billion in 1955.

As for the Navy, a lower budget meant that the third *Forrestal*-class carrier was again in doubt and that it would have to absorb manpower reductions and a procurement stretchout. When the cuts were opposed by the Joint Chiefs of Staff (JCS), they were imposed by Secretary Wilson, although not without the services having the opportunity to defend their requests. Because the Navy's cuts were relatively light, Anderson and his service chiefs did not strongly contest them. The resulting budget permitted the Navy to keep the big carrier but change it from nuclear to conventional power. But the budget cut back aircraft procurement by seven hundred planes and sliced sixty-one thousand men from the planned Fiscal Year 1954 strength. The Marines lost an additional seventeen thousand men, while shipbuilding and conversion money dropped by $254,630,000. As finally passed by Congress on 1 August, the law carried $9,438,310,000 for the Navy, the smallest budget since 1951, $2 billion less than Truman's budget, and $344 million less than Eisenhower's. The bulk of the $5.5 billion reduction from the Truman Defense Department requests, however, came at the expense of the projected expansion of the Air Force.[6] The Air Force's loud cries of anguish, backed by those of the Army, made Anderson's quiet acceptance of the Navy cuts highly noticeable and welcome.

Another part of the "New Look," reorganizing the Department of Defense, had little direct effect on the Navy. During his last months as Secretary of Defense, Robert A. Lovett had recommended various reforms, among them that the Joint Chiefs be relieved of the command of their services in order to concentrate on planning and serving as military advisers to the Secretary. The resulting simplified chain of command would then run from the President through the Secretary of Defense and the Service Secretaries to the Service or Theater Commander. One of Secretary Wilson's earliest acts was to appoint the seven-member Rockefeller Committee to investigate this and other similar proposals and recommend improvements in Defense Department organization.[7]

The Rockefeller Committee report served as the basis for Reorganization Plan 6 of 1953 which President Eisenhower sent to Congress on 30 April along with his revised budget. It abolished several interdepartmental boards, provided for six new assistant secretaries of defense, and for the first time brought the Joint Staff directly under the control of the chairman of the JCS. Most important for the Secretary of the Navy, by making the department rather than its JCS member the executive agent for the unified commands, the plan put the Secretary back into the chain of command from which he had been excluded in the Key West Agreement.[8] In the broad sense, then, the reorganization plan strengthened civilian control at the expense of the military.

Eisenhower's military policy was predicated upon relatively simple premises: (1) that the struggle with Russia and China would continue throughout the foreseeable future; (2) that there existed a practical limit on the size of defense expenditures the American economy could support over that indefinite period; (3) that the cheapest and most useful policy, for the long run, was reliance on a freedom of choice in the method of retaliating against any overt Communist attack; and (4) for the immediate future the United States would hold overwhelming superiority in both nuclear weapons and the means of delivering them.

This new policy involved junking the "year of maximum peril" concept that had guided planning after 1950. The Truman rearmament program (NSC–68) assumed that the greatest peril to the United States would come during that year (estimated to be 1954) in which the Russians could first deliver an atomic attack. The main Republican complaint was the high cost inherent in a series of crash programs intended to meet a similar series of crises years in which successive waves of Soviet power threats crested. Further, as the President himself argued: "for anybody on the defensive . . . to base his defense on his ability to predict the exact date of attack was crazy."[9]

The development of improved atomic weapons and the ability to deliver them allowed a limitation on defense spending while at the same time providing the deterrent force necessary to prevent Russian adventures. As envisioned by its originators, the New Look relied upon an overwhelming nuclear capability, or "massive retaliation," to prevent aggression. Lost to the view of most observers was the maintenance of the largest conventional forces ever assembled by the nation in peacetime.

Because land forces outside of Korea no longer represented the prime deterrent to Russian expansion, the New Look called for concentrating the bulk of American land power in the United States as a strategic reserve. In time of emergency this "fire brigade" could be rushed by sea and air to any trouble spot, whereas any trouble too large to be handled by these forces would activate the massive response. To many, like General Maxwell Taylor, this policy looked like "little more than the old air power dogma set forth in Madison Avenue trapping."[10] The administration's reply, as later stated by Admiral Robert E. Carney, was that the policy was a single, unified plan to counter a centralized Communist strategy rather than a "succession of minor strategies to cope with brush fires."[11] In April the new policy received formal National Security Council approval.[12]

In such a policy the Navy came to play an increasing role because it not only contributed to the nuclear deterrence but its easily shifted striking power multiplied the strength of the American and allied troops protecting the perimeter of the free world. But the new policy did not settle what Henry Kissinger called "the inconsistence between a reliance on all-out war and the political commitment to regional defense [that] has been the bane of our coalition policy."[13] As events proved in Southeast Asia, off Lebanon, and elsewhere, the administration found itself engaged in operations well short of all-out war. In retrospect, it appears clear that the lack of a major showdown between the two great powers resulted from factors quite divorced from Secretary of State John Foster Dulles's brinkmanship.

Because the Joint Chiefs of Staff were "tainted" by their association with Truman, Eisenhower ordered them swept out except for Chief of Naval Operations William M. Fechteler, who had served but a short time. However, Republican congressional pressure for a wholly new JCS and Secretary Wilson's desire for advisers of his own selection meant that Fechteler, too, had to be replaced.[14]

On 12 May, two admirals began serving on the JCS for the first time since the resignation of Admiral William D. Leahy in 1949. As General Omar Bradley's successor as chairman, Wilson chose Admiral Arthur W. Radford, the able and driving Pacific Fleet Commander who had tremendously impressed the President-elect during his Far Eastern trip in December 1952. His strategic ideas, particularly as they related to Asia, meshed well with those of the new administration. Further, as an officer with predominantly Far Eastern experience, he balanced the President's greater knowledge of Europe and helped fulfill the Republican promise to correct the Democratic overstress on Europe. The second appointment, of Admiral Robert B. Carney to succeed Fechteler, assured the Navy of a uniformed head known to the President because Carney had served as Commander in Chief, Allied Forces Southern Europe under him. Fechteler moved to Rome to take over Carney's old post as CinCSouth.[15]

One of Anderson's earliest public controversies and one that won him an approving nod from the White House came over his seeking to end what little remained of racial segregation in naval installations in the South. When Representative Adam Clayton Powell raised the issue, Anderson summoned Under Secretary Thomas and Admiral George A. Holderness, the Chief of the Office of Industrial Relations, and sent them to investigate the situation at the two largest southern bases, Norfolk and Charleston. They returned with confirmation of the complaints. The solution was ingenious. "Colored" and "white" signs on drinking fountains and rest rooms vanished while Anderson reissued SecNav Instruction 1000.2 on the equal treatment of minority races. He followed this on 20 August with the public announcement of a policy of "complete elimination of racial segregation among civilian employees" at the forty-three naval installations in the South. To ensure compliance, he demanded a progress report from each local commander within sixty days. By late November he could report that the Navy's non-segregation policy was "completely effective," with only one small exception. Shortly afterwards, he also announced the beginning of planning to desegregate the heretofore all-colored stewards branch.[16]

While the end of the fighting in Korea on 27 July 1953 reduced the strain on the Navy's budget, it also returned the service to peacetime justification of its budget requests. Two personnel changes also involved Anderson. Admiral Wallin's refusal to provide detailed information on his bureau's procurement plans, which Under Secretary Thomas needed for long term planning, stemmed from his concept of the legal independence and freedom of action of a bureau chief. When it became clear that he could not win the argument, and although eighteen months remained in his term, he requested relief and assignment to Puget Sound Naval Shipyard. Anderson approved and directed Rear Admiral Wilson D. Leggett, Jr., his deputy, to succeed him.[17]

Coincident with the departure of Wallin came the need to find a new under secretary, for Charles Thomas in July received appointment as Assistant Secretary of Defense for Supply and Logistics. His replacement was Thomas S. Gates, Jr., a member of the famed Philadelphia investment banking firm of Drexel and Company and a director of the Navy League. The forty-seven-year-old Gates had served as an intelligence officer during World War II and was to prove himself a very effective administrator.[18]

Anderson, whose eye for small but significant gestures to gratify his subordinates was excellent, in September altered the organization table of the Department to reflect for the first time the real position of the Commandant of the Marine Corps. His box moved from the level of the bureau chiefs to that of the assistant secretaries.[19]

During the late summer and fall of 1953, Anderson joined in a move by Defense Department officials to enlist public support for better "conditions of employment, tenure, standards of living, and security" within the services so that they could attract and hold talented men. Indicative of the problem, Anderson told the American Legion Convention, was the failure of the Navy to induce more than eighty-five of the first eight hundred Holloway Plan graduates to take a regular commission.[20] As chief speaker at the keel-laying ceremonies for the second of Rickover's submarines, he gently chided the Navy for its slowness in adopting nuclear power and called for a "long-range co-ordinated ship building and replacement policy" as well as "elimination of the peaks and valleys in our procurement schedules."[21] This call, of course, echoed the basic philosophy behind the New Look policy. The decline of the American shipbuilding industry alarmed him. Since "a healthy private shipbuilding industry is essential to the national security," he announced that "the Navy would be governed, as in the past, not only by cost but by the necessity for obtaining timely and satisfactory completion, by the need for geographic dispersal of naval work and by other considerations important to the national welfare."[22]

Anderson's belief that the next war would be fought with conventional rather than atomic weapons was an interesting one for a member of the Eisenhower administration. He reasoned, however, that the possession of super-weapons by the great powers might cancel out their use and force countries to rely upon conventional weapons. He therefore called for a defense policy based on both conventional and nuclear capabilities.[23] While hardly a break with administration policies, his ideas reflected the Navy's long-established concern over defense policies that relied too heavily upon atomic and other glamor weapons and strategies. Nevertheless, his critiques went to the heart of the dilemma of the New Look: If the atomic-tipped deterrent of "Massive Retaliation" ensured that any future clashes between the super-powers or their surrogates would employ only conventional weapons, how could an adequate capability be maintained with the expenditures the country could sustain over a long period?

Anderson's Semi-Annual Report dated 29 September reiterated the arguments for maintaining an adequate shipbuilding industry as a mobilization base and pointedly spoke of the rapid aging of the bulk of the fleet. Although the new *Forrestal*-class carriers would begin joining the fleet in late 1955, most other vessels had expended about half of their useful life. Unless steps were taken to correct it, nearly the entire fleet would come to the end of its career in the half-decade before 1965. On the other hand, Anderson's report recognized the necessity of "reconciling the requirements for national security with the requirements for a sound national economy."[24] While the end of the Korean fighting somewhat reduced the pressures, it did not remove them from an administration concerned about the soundness of the economy. This in turn complicated the Navy's steps to alleviate block obsolescence. The solution, when it did come, took the form of the stopgap Fleet Rehabilitation and Modernization (FRAM) program instituted in 1959.

Another aspect of the fiscal problem was the inefficient organization of the department itself. Anderson attacked this by appointing a special board headed by Under Secretary Gates on 14 October 1953, to review the organizational structure of the department, identify areas of overlapping or duplicating functions, and recommend reforms that would establish "an effective pattern of responsibilities and authority, proper lines of communication, clear accountability, and adequate liaison, both internal and external."[25]

Gates's committee concluded that the organization of the department remained basically sound even though some reassignments of functions and clarifications of responsibilities were needed. The gist of their recommendations was that the Under Secretary "be designated in charge of business and production activities" and that two new posts be created—an Assistant Secretary of the Navy (Personnel and Reserve Forces) and an Assistant Secretary of the Navy (Fiscal Management). Thus the Secretary would be responsible for legislative liaison and directly control public information while the Under Secretary supervised and directed the other "Civilian Executive Assistants." The Assistant Secretary for Financial Management would act as comptroller while the Assistant Secretary would become Assistant Secretary for Material. The Assistant Secretary for Air would shed his responsibilities for personnel matters in order to concentrate solely upon aviation matters. Within the Office of the Chief of Naval Operations the only changes related to intelligence. The Director of Naval Intelligence received a second hat as Assistant Chief of Naval Operations (Intelligence) and now reported to the Vice Chief of Naval Operations. The proposed changes, the first major ones in administrative alignment within the department since 1940, were approved by Secretary Wilson on 21 April 1954.[26] They remained in effect until the 1961 reorganization.

Anderson's stress upon strong conventional armaments coincided with the annual fall struggle over the upcoming defense budget. In the fall of 1953, that annual donnybrook was complicated by the failure of the new JCS to adopt a set of force levels consonant with those of the administration, which had been spelled out in NSC 162/2, approved by the President on 30 October, which called for the development of a strong air defense of the United States and the maintenance on home bases of highly mobile, strategic retaliatory forces. The policy also anticipated the tactical use of nuclear weapons when their employment would be militarily desirable and a greater reliance on local allies to furnish the initial troop screen.[27]

This policy was popularized by Secretary of State Dulles in his 12 January 1954 address to the Council of Foreign Relations as "Massive Retaliation." Its essence, he said, was that "local defense must be reinforced by the further deterrent of massive retaliatory power." "The way to deter aggression," he argued, "is for the free community to be willing and able to respond vigorously at places and with means of its own choosing."[28]

Within the framework of this rearrangement of American military strength with its concomitant manpower reductions, the Navy was bound to suffer. Initially asked to drop 75,000 sailors and 41,000 Marines, the department resisted cuts larger than 35,000 and 24,000, respectively. The Navy's top officers, moreover, pressed strongly for the fourth big carrier and additional destroyers. The quiet but forceful Navy arguments resulted in a final budget request of 638,980 men for the Navy (a cut of 52,000) and 215,000 Marines (a drop of 25,000 in two stages) and an increase in shipbuilding money of about 3.5 percent over Fiscal Year 1954. The building program included the fourth *Forrestal*, the third nuclear submarine, two conventional submersibles, five destroyers, and eight escorts plus additional amphibious, mine, and auxiliary craft. It also provided for further *Essex*-class carrier modernizations and radar picket escort (DER) conversions.[29] On balance, the Navy had done very well.

Even so, the New Look's preponderant reliance on strategic bombing remained a grave threat to the Navy. While it had to maintain the control of the seas necessary for the strategic retaliatory forces to be deployed, this task was hardly the glamorous role likely to bring increased appropriations or clout in the defense policies of the country. Nor did Admiral Carney help the Navy's case with the sensible and correct argument that the nation must "hedge our strategic bets, ready to rush into the future, but also prepared to react and rely on, the methods of the recent past."[30] On the other hand, the threat of the New Look did hasten the Navy's development of an atomic capability for its carriers and contributed a sense of urgency to the creation of a Navy-employed ballistic missile and ultimately to the Polaris system.

Anderson's concern over the deterioration of the nation's shipbuilding capacity influenced his assignment of two large contracts in February 1954. Though Bethlehem's famed old Quincy yard by the mid-fifties was quite antiquated, it was one of only three private yards capable of building *Forrestal*-class carriers and Anderson wanted its potential maintained. Therefore, when Quincy's bid on the third *Forrestal* turned out to be much too high, he gave the carrier to the low bidder, Newport News Shipbuilding and Dry Dock Company, but disregarded lower bids from Newport News and Bath Iron Works to give the Massachusetts yard three destroyers. Bath had to be satisfied with one LST. Without the contract, Quincy would have been out of work. Some congressional critics caustically noted that Senator Leverett Saltonstall faced reelection while Margaret Chase Smith did not. They forced an investigation, too, and were nonplussed when it failed to produce any juicy scandal.[31]

In March, Anderson approved a request of Admiral Carney and made a final administrative change within the department by splitting the duties of the Deputy Chief of Naval Operations for Operations between two new offices. The planning functions were consolidated under a new DCNO for Plans and Policies while the old office received the now more accurate title of DCNO for Fleet Operations and Readiness. The change was made simply because the diverse duties of the office were more than one man could handle efficiently.

Coincident with the reorganization of DCNO (Operations) came the 1954 atomic tests at Eniwetok. These involved the explosion of two hydrogen bombs, one of which was estimated to have had a force of forty megatons and seriously contaminated a Japanese fishing boat seventy-five miles away. The implications of these tests, together with the earlier American and Russian hydrogen tests, introduced a host of new problems and possibilities for the

Navy, but their solution would rest with a department led by others than Anderson.

The *New York Times* reported on 9 March 1954 that Anderson had been chosen to succeed Roger Kyes as Deputy Secretary of Defense. The choice, correspondent James Reston commented, grew out of Anderson's "knowledge of production problems" and his successful management of the Department, especially his ability to get along with the senior officers.[32] On 11 March Charles S. Thomas was named as Secretary of the Navy.

Anderson's promotion was universally applauded. The *Navy Times*, not noted for its friendship to the administration, cheered his new appointment, while *Time* called him the "real find of the Eisenhower Administration."[33]

The accolades were well deserved. Combining "Texas frankness with remarkable urbanity," to borrow Hanson Baldwin's apt description, Anderson had shown intelligence, patience, and a quick and absorbent mind. Undoubtedly the most effective secretary since James Forrestal, he had tackled the Navy's problems as they arose and worked hard to make friends and gain the respect of the uniformed professionals. Admiral Radford later said: "He is certainly a man who instills confidence in his subordinates and associates by his dedicated effort." Admiral Carney commented that he was "A considerate gentleman but 'his own man' in [his] approach to all problems." That independence showed in such matters as the Rickover and Wallin affairs. In retrospect, his greatest success seems to have been his ability to keep the Navy out of trouble despite its reduced appropriations and significance under the New Look.[34]

Anderson remained at his new desk in the Pentagon until 1957, when he replaced George M. Humphrey as Secretary of the Treasury. Returning to private life after the 1960 elections, he moved to Connecticut and became a registered Republican and a partner in the New York investment banking firm of Carl M. Loeb, Rhoads, and Company.

NOTES
1. Dwight D. Eisenhower, *Mandate for Change, 1953-1956* (Garden City, N.Y.: Doubleday, 1963), pp. 96-97.
2. *Nominations: Hearings Before the Committee on Armed Services United States Senate, Eighty-Third Congress, First Session, on Nominees Designate . . .* (Washington: GPO, 1953), pp. 84-85; *Current Biography, 1953*, pp. 19-21; *Time* 61 (29 Dec. 1952):11; USNWR 36 (19 Mar. 1954):50; *Newsweek* 40 (29 Dec. 1952):17; *New York Times*, 20 Dec. 1952.
3. Editorial, "The Defense Administrators," *New York Times*, 21 Dec. 1952. Anderson himself reportedly quipped that "I have never paced the deck of a battleship and I come from Texas where it doesn't even rain." (*New York Times*, 9 Mar. 1954.)

4. *Nominations: . . . Nominees Designate*, p. 83; *Nominations: Hearings Before the Committee on Armed Services United States Senate, Eighty-Third Congress, First Session, on Nominations . . .* (Washington: GPO, 1953), p. 47; CR 83rd Cong., 1st Sess., 99, pt. 1, 636, 747; *New York Times*, 30 Jan., 3 Feb. 1953.

5. Dwight D. Eisenhower, *Public Papers, 1953* (Washington: GPO, 1960), pp. 17-18.

6. *New York Times*, 7 Apr., 1 May 1953; *Time* 61 (4 May 1953): 23, and (11 May 1953):21-22; ANAFJ, 28 Mar., 16 May 1953; *Navy Times*, 16 May 1953.

7. Walter Millis, with Harvey C. Mansfield and Harold Stein, *Arms and the State: Civil-Military Elements in National Policy* (New York: The Twentieth Century Fund, 1958), pp. 370-71; *Navy Times*, 28 Feb. 1953. The members of the committee were Nelson Rockefeller, Arthur S. Flemming, Milton Eisenhower, Robert A. Lovett, General Omar Bradley, Vannevar Bush, and David Sarnoff.

8. The text may be found in Eisenhower, *Public Papers, 1953*, pp. 225-38. Good discussions of the reorganization are in John R. Probert, "Pentagon Reorganization: Phase Three," USNIP 81 (Jan. 1955):51-62; Eisenhower, *Mandate for Change*, pp. 447-48; John C. Ries, *The Management of Defense: Organization and Control of the U.S. Armed Services* (Baltimore: Johns Hopkins Press, 1964). In the new arrangement, the Department of the Navy was designated executive agent for the Pacific Command, Atlantic Command, and Middle East Forces. (SECNAV Instruction 5430.45, 23 Dec. 1958.)

9. Quoted in Paul Peeters, *Massive Retaliation: The Policy and Its Critics* (Chicago: Henry Regnery Co., 1959), p. 2.

10. Maxwell D. Taylor, *The Uncertain Trumpet* (New York: Harper, 1959), p. 17. Similar caustic comments can be found in Matthew B. Ridgway, *Soldier: The Memoirs of Matthew B. Ridgway* (New York: Harper, 1956), pp. 272-73.

11. Carney, 27 May 1954, quoted in Peeters, *Massive Retaliation*, p. 13.

12. Good discussions of the "New Look" can be found in Merlo J. Pusey, *Eisenhower the President* (New York: Macmillan, 1956), pp. 189-90; Peeters, *Massive Retaliation*, Chaps. 1-2; Taylor, *Uncertain Trumpet*, pp. 17-18; Robert J. Donovan, *Eisenhower: The Inside Story* (New York: Harper, 1956), pp. 17-18; Glenn H. Snyder, "The 'New Look' of 1953," in Warren H. Schilling, Paul Y. Hammond, and Glenn H. Snyder, *Strategy, Politics, and Defense Budgets* (New York: Columbia University Press, 1962), pp. 383-524; and Millis, *Arms and the State*, pp. 377-78.

13. Henry A. Kissinger, *Nuclear Weapons and Foreign Policy* (New York: Harper, 1957), pp. 54-55.

14. See CR, 83rd Cong., 1st Sess., 99, pt. 11, A2726.

15. *JCS Nominations; Hearings Before the Committee on Armed Services United States Senate . . . on Nominations of . . . Radford . . . Ridgway . . . Carney . . . Twining* (Washington: GPO, 1953); Eisenhower, *Public Papers, 1953*, pp. 283, 868; Eisenhower, *Mandate for Change*, p. 449; Donovan, *Eisenhower*, p. 19; Millis, *Arms and the State*, p. 377; Hanson W. Baldwin, "New Team at Pentagon to Review U.S. Strategy," *New York Times*, 17 May 1953; ANAFJ, 16 May 1953; *Navy Times*, 2, 16, 23 May 1953.

16. Eisenhower, *Public Papers*, 1953, pp. 765-66; Donovan, *Eisenhower*, pp. 158-59; *New York Times*, 2 Apr., 21 Aug., 15, 27 Sept., 12 Nov. 1953; *Navy Times*, 4, 18 Apr., 29 Aug., 21 Nov. 1953; *Time* 62 (31 Aug. 1953):10.

17. *Bureau of Ships Journal* 1 (Sept. 1953):47; *Navy Times*, 1, 15 Aug. 1953; *Time* 62 (10 Aug. 1953):18.

18. CR, 83rd Cong., 2nd Sess, 100, pt. 2, 121, 732; ANAFJ, 1 Aug. 1953; *New York Times*, 3, 8 Oct. 1953.

19. Eisenhower, *Public Papers*, 1953, p. 883; ANAFJ, 31 Oct. 1953.

20. ANAFJ, 5 Sept. 1953.

21. *Bureau of Ships Journal* 2 (Nov. 1953):3.

22. *New York Times*, 17 Sept. 1953; ANAFR, 19 Sept. 1953.

23. Ralph E. Williams, "The Great Debate: 1954," USNIP 70 (Mar. 1954):248; *New York Times*, 20 Sept., 27 Oct. 1953.

24. "Semi-Annual Report of the Secretary of the Navy, January 1 to June 30, 1953," in *Semi-Annual Report of the Secretary of Defense, January 1 to June 30, 1953* (Washington: GPO, 1953), pp. 210–12, 240.

25. SECNAV Notice 5420, 14 Oct. 1953, reprinted in *Report of the Committee on Organization of the Department of the Navy, 16 April 1954* (Washington: GPO, 1954) (hereafter cited as *Gates Board Report*), App. A. The members of the board were Gates, ADM D. B. Duncan, LGEN G. C. Thomas, USMC, VADM J. E. Gingrich, RADM R. E. Libby, VADM Earl Mills, Richard M. Paget, and Hobart Ramsey. Kimball had assigned duties among his subordinates on the basis of their individual talents rather than jobs. Interview with Dan A. Kimball, 3 June 1966.

26. *Gates Board Report, passim;* Paul Y. Hammond, *Organizing for Defense: The American Military Establishment in the Twentieth Century* (Princeton, N.J.: Princeton University Press, 1961), pp. 285–86.

27. Hammond, *Organizing for Defense*, pp. 73–74; Snyder, "New Look," p. 414; *Navy Times*, 31 Oct., 12 Dec. 1953.

28. *New York Times*, 13 Jan. 1954; Peeters, *Massive Retaliation*, p. 16. See also Dwight D. Eisenhower, *Public Papers, 1954* (Washington: GPO, 1960), p. 58.

29. U.S. House, Committee on Armed Services, *Hearings on H.R. 4393* (Washington GPO, 1954), p. 927; 68 *U.S. Stat.* 765–66; Eisenhower, *Public Papers, 1954*, pp. 123–24; *New York Times*, 20 Nov. 1953; ANAFJ, 21, 28 Nov., 2, 23 Jan., 20 Mar. 1954; ANAFR, 10 Apr. 1954.

30. CR, 83rd Cong., 2nd Sess., 100, pt. 2, p. 1885.

31. *Ibid.*, pp. 1579, 1997; *Bureau of Ships Journal* 3 (June 1954):5; *New York Times*, 3 Feb. 1954; *Navy Times*, 13 Feb., 6 Mar. 1954; ANAFJ, 6, 13, 20 Feb. 1954.

32. *New York Times*, 9 Mar. 1954.

33. *Navy Times*, 20 Mar. 1954; *Time* 63 (15 Mar. 1954):20.

34. For various comments on Anderson's successful administration of the Department see Hanson W. Baldwin, "The Men Who Run the Pentagon," *New York Times Magazine*, 14 Feb. 1954, p. 32; Ridgway, *Soldier*, p. 283; Pusey, *Eisenhower*, p. 61.

CHARLES SPARKS THOMAS

3 May 1954–1 April 1957

JOHN R. WADLEIGH

Few Secretaries of the Navy were as well qualified by experience and background as Charles Sparks Thomas, who took his oath of office on 3 May 1954. In World War I he trained as a Naval Reserve aviator. In World War II he was a valued assistant to Secretary James V. Forrestal. He then served as under secretary of the Navy and as assistant secretary of defense for supply and logistics before being named as secretary of the navy by President Dwight D. Eisenhower.

The Navy was fortunate to have as its civilian head a man not only with this background but one also proven successful in business as president of a large manufacturing firm. When Secretary Robert B. Anderson left the Navy Department to serve as deputy secretary of defense under Charles E. Wilson, he turned over the reins to one who already knew its major problems as well as the senior officers of the Navy and Marine Corps with whom he would work.

When Thomas assumed the leadership of the world's largest navy and the greatest peacetime navy in history, he had every reason to be proud of and even a bit complacent about his organization. The Korean War was ending; NATO was growing stronger; except for a huge and growing fleet of Soviet submarines, U.S. control of the oceans seemed unquestioned. Nevertheless, he faced two major problems: how to keep the fleet modernized, and how to provide it with enough qualified career manpower. Each problem was vitally affected by Eisenhower's defense strategy, which coupled economic stability with nuclear deterrent power. Thomas approached his problems as a business executive and manager, for he had no preconceived bias for such fixed procedures as the Robert McNamara analytical processes of the next administration.[1]

Thomas was born in Independence, Missouri, on 28 September 1897, the son of Charles Rogers and Della (Rouse) Thomas.[2] In 1911 the family moved to Los Angeles, California, where young Thomas completed his secondary schooling. After a year at the University of California at Berkeley, he transferred to Cornell University in 1916, where in his junior year he joined the U.S. Naval Reserve for aviation training. Called to active duty in May 1918, he took basic training at the University of Washington, won the stripes of a company commander, and stood in the first ten of his class. As the war was ending he reported to San Diego for basic flight training. Shortly after the Armistice he was demobilized and entered the investment business, first with the George H. Burr Co., of Los Angeles, then, in 1925, as a partner and vice president of the expanded firm of George H. Burr, Conrad, and Broom. In this assignment he had charge of all the company operations in southern California, Arizona, and New Mexico. Five years later he became vice president and general manager of Foreman and Clark, one of the major producers of men's and women's wearing apparel in the United States, and won credit for rescuing it from depression.[3] He married Julia Hayward of Los Angeles on 15 April 1920 and sired three sons and a daughter.

Shortly after the United States entered World War II, the Assistant Secretary of the Navy for Air, Artemus L. Gates, took Thomas on his staff as a special assistant. A year later, when Thomas moved up to become special assistant to Secretary of the Navy James V. Forrestal, his major tasks were in the logistics field, first in aircraft procurement, then in inventory management in the rapidly expanding wartime Navy. Although released from service late in 1944, Forrestal called him back to conduct a detailed morale and recreational survey of the Navy's expanding base complex in the Western Pacific. On this assignment he traveled thirty-three thousand miles in order to report on living conditions, recreational facilities, and morale problems of Navy and Marine Corps personnel stationed at various island bases.[4]

Forrestal showed his appreciation for Thomas by awarding him the Distinguished Civilian Service Award on 4 April 1945. This award was followed by another and more important honor, the Presidential Medal for Merit, on 31 January 1947, by President Harry S. Truman. This medal is the highest civilian award for wartime service to the United States.

Soon after returning to Foreman and Clark, Thomas expanded his business interests when he was elected a director of Lockheed Aircraft and of several smaller enterprises in the southern California area. From 1945 to 1950, while serving as airport commissioner for Los Angeles, he was also active in the Navy League as president of its Eleventh Region, a region coterminous with the Eleventh Naval District. As a vice president of the Los Angeles Chamber of Commerce, he watched his city grow to become the nation's second largest.

Meanwhile he sparked the rebirth of the Republican Party at all levels in southern California. Compared to most politicians, he was strictly an amateur, but his personality and salesmanship, and his willingness to work and risk his own finances brought success.[5] Beginning with the Los Angeles County Republicans, he formed a "Campaign Operations Group" headed by a former Navy acquaintance, Ross Barrett, and by 1948 had raised a campaign chest of $175,000 compared with $15,000 in the previous election. Seeking no office for himself, he then became chairman of the California Republican Finance Committee in 1949, and also a member of the party's national finance committee.[6] In the spring of 1952, he was a prime mover in California to get General Dwight D. Eisenhower to seek the Republican presidential nomination. Pressing forward with the state finance committee, he was able to raise $468,000 as California's contribution to Eisenhower's successful campaign.[7]

Soon after his inauguration on 20 January 1953, Eisenhower nominated Thomas as under secretary of the Navy. The Senate acted quickly, and on 9 February he was sworn in as the senior civilian assistant to Secretary Anderson. During confirmation hearings, Thomas told the Senate Armed Service Committee that he had resigned the presidency of Foreman and Clark, disposed of his Lockheed stock, and was resigning from his corporate directorships.[8] As he moved into his office in the old "Main Navy" building on Constitution Avenue, he joined an administration engaged in a cold war.

The fighting in Korea was winding down when Eisenhower took office. Charles "Engine Charlie" Wilson, the secretary of defense, and John Foster Dulles, the secretary of state, would largely dominate the Washington scene during the next four years. Wilson, particularly, supported Eisenhower's tenet that in order to maintain a free world the Western Alliance, and especially the United States, must remain economically solvent.

During the Korean War, the Joint Chiefs of Staff had assessed the year 1954 as the year of maximum danger for war with the Soviet Union. Eisenhower preferred providing a long-haul preparedness program. Immediately after his election, he had met with Dulles, Wilson, and Admiral Arthur W. Radford, Commander in Chief, Pacific, on board the cruiser *Helena* in the Western Pacific. Here the basis for a national strategy was worked out that called for ending the Korean War honorably, providing proper national defense, and keeping the nation economically strong. Thomas thus moved into his naval office just as the new administration was trying to resolve the conflict between its stated goals and the strategy and programs inherited from the Truman administration.[9]

In 1953 the U.S. Navy was at its peak power since World War II. A strong fleet was kept in the Mediterranean and an even stronger force in the Western Pacific. Although carrier aviation had again proved its capabilities off the coasts of Korea, the largest portion of the Truman budget for 1953 was allocated to a buildup of the Air Force to 143 wings.[10] Believing that when a new corporation president arrives there should be a new set of vice presidents, Secretary Wilson completely changed the Joint Chiefs of Staff. Admiral William N. Fechteler, with barely two years in office, was replaced by Admiral Robert B. Carney as chief of naval operations and Admiral Radford was brought back from the Pacific to relieve General Omar Bradley as chairman of the Joint Chiefs. The new chief of staff of the Army was Matthew B. Ridgway; of the Air Force, Nathan F. Twining. On 29 May 1953, after talking with the Joint Chiefs, Eisenhower spoke during a luncheon with the civilian leaders of the services including Thomas.

The civilian emphasis in this luncheon was prophetic of things to come in Reorganization Plan No. 6 for the Defense Department. In this plan, which went into effect on 1 July 1953, greater power was centralized in the Office of the Secretary of Defense, who was also given six additional assistant secretaries. In consequence, the service secretaries were placed in the position of middle managers.[11] Thomas, who had barely had a chance to apply his managerial talents in the Navy Department, was called upon to serve as Assistant Secretary of Defense for Supply and Logistics.

One of Thomas's new tasks was to build up the stockpile of strategic war materials. He soon had over $7 billion of these on order[12] and then proceeded to catalog the capabilities of American firms that could produce war materials in the event of emergency.[13] While he did what he could to benefit small businesses,[14] he also tried to spend appropriated funds on a regular rather than a feast-or-famine basis.[15] In addition he provided standard fiscal and accounting systems applicable to each service, improved procurement regulations, reduced standardized defense items from 4.1 million to .5 million entries, and provided a standard interservice inspection system.

When Thomas assumed his new duties, on 3 May 1954, the basic military strategy of the United States had shifted from a policy of containment to one of massive retaliation. The Navy's new, large carriers played a role in this strategy.[16] Although Thomas devoted most of his energies to the management side of the department, he frequently became involved in the personnel problems of the Navy and Marine Corps and on occasion also spoke out strongly in interservice conflicts.

During Thomas's absence from Secretary Wilson's staff, Navy Secretary Anderson had chosen Thomas S. Gates, Jr., a Philadelphia banker and World War II Naval Reserve officer, to be under secretary. When Thomas returned to the Navy, Gates was working on the reorganization of the department required by Defense Reorganization Plan No. 6. The two naval assistant secretaries soon became three, with the most important of these being William B.

Franke, who began a tour that culminated with his appointment as Secretary in 1959.

An initial task for Thomas was to look for a relief for Admiral Carney, who would be sixty years of age at the end of his two-year term and thus would not normally be reappointed as chief of naval operations. Thomas began looking for the best man to lead the Navy through a nuclear and missile revolution. He wanted an officer who grasped the capabilities of the atom, who knew naval aviation, but most of all "one whom the Navy would be glad to follow into the tomorrow."[17] He chose Rear Admiral Arleigh A. Burke, Commander, Destroyers, Atlantic Fleet, who ranked ninety-second in the seniority list. With Eisenhower's happy blessing, Burke assumed office in July 1955.[18] His selection was one of the most significant events of Thomas's term, for Burke would serve for six years under three different secretaries and soon would be the most experienced member of the Joint Chiefs of Staff, often acting as their chairman. Thomas and Burke formed a close and continuous friendship and worked well together, with Burke being not only technically competent but an able negotiator in the Joint Chiefs and in addition representing the Navy in meetings with Eisenhower and Charlie Wilson.

In discussions involving budget, service roles and missions, and military operations, service chiefs overshadow service secretaries. Two letters show how Thomas felt about Burke. When he retired in 1957, Thomas wrote, "If I did nothing else for the Navy, your appointment should earn me their thanks."[19] In March 1959, when Thomas was president of Trans-World Airlines, Burke received his third two-year appointment. Thomas wrote: "I am not only pleased for you, but it is a complete vindication of my judgment and the risk I took in going down 92 numbers for you."[20]

In 1956 it was reported that Eisenhower had said that Congress was interested in hearing from the top military officers, not from the service secretaries, on national security affairs.[21] Eisenhower may have been expressing feelings colored by his experience as chief of staff of the Army. While few would argue with him on matters of military strategy, this was not true when it came to his budget, for at budget time the service secretaries, including Thomas, were much in evidence before the appropriate congressional committees.

In his first appropriations hearings, Thomas masterfully presented the Navy's requirements for fiscal year 1956. He was ably seconded by Admiral Carney and General Lemuel Shepherd, Commandant of the Marine Corps. In urging congressional support for the Career Incentive Act of 1955, Thomas eloquently outlined basic Navy policy of maintaining an active fleet capable of controlling the seas and also of keeping a reserve fleet manned by ever-better trained naval reservists.[22] Asked by the House Armed Services Committee whether naval testimony was being choked off by the Defense Department,

Thomas assured the congressmen that this was not the case. Yet he realized that such questions reflected congressional concern over increasing centralization in the Defense Department under Charles Wilson. When he ended a week of hearings before the House Appropriations Committee, a senior member said to him, "I do not think I have ever heard a Secretary or the head of any Government agency show a more profound knowledge of his subject."[23] A similar accolade came from Admiral Burke after the hearings for fiscal year 1957.[24]

Each service maintains an extensive congressional liaison organization. Although considered "lobbying" by some, Congress is aware of the value of such organizations. The services thus keep congressmen current on their latest weapons systems, procurement programs, and personnel actions. In March 1956 Thomas conducted a congressional delegation to Guantánamo Bay, Cuba, where they cruised on board the first of the Navy's new "supercarriers," the *Forrestal*, and the recently converted guided missile cruiser, the *Boston*, on which they viewed a firing of the Navy's first operational surface-to-air missile, the Terrier. At Thomas's insistence, the congressmen were routed home via an overnight stay in Havana. Back in Washington there was universal praise by the congressmen and accompanying reporters for the way in which Thomas and the fleet had shown them the latest in naval weaponry.[25] In this instance, and also when he invited senators and representatives to breakfast or lunch in the Pentagon to meet his senior civilian and military assistants, Thomas was making good use of his own political experiences. Without talking down the other services, he put the Navy story across. Reactions from congressmen indicated that they liked what they heard.

When Thomas returned to the Navy Department in 1954, there were 800,000 Navy and 250,000 Marine personnel on active duty. For the next fiscal year, strengths would be reduced to 682,000 Navy and 215,000 Marines. There would be 1,080 ships and 9,941 aircraft in the operating forces. The Navy was requesting 2,766 new aircraft for fiscal year 1955 at a cost of $840 million. To keep the fleet modern, a shipbuilding program of $2.25 billion was required.[26] It should be noted that personnel accounted for 31 percent of the Navy's budget—a percentage that approximated 60 percent in 1977.

Rising shipbuilding costs and appropriation cuts kept the fiscal year 1955 building program from being fully implemented. However, Thomas made substantial progress in starting a nuclear submarine fleet, maintained carrier and carrier aircraft strengths, and began a replacement program for World War II destroyers. He planned to modernize six World War II light cruisers so that they could carry surface-to-air missiles and wanted fast amphibious ships to apply the new vertical assault techniques of the Marine Corps.

The budgets Thomas defended at the Department of Defense and congressional levels contained seven basic elements: deterrent forces, tactical forces, sea supremacy forces, continental defense forces, an expandable Naval Reserve, support for an industrial mobilization base, and research and development projects.[27] That Thomas was not completely successful in his budget requests may be seen by the end-strength for fiscal year 1956, in which there were 657,000 in the Navy and 193,000 in the Marine Corps.[28]

In November 1954, Thomas made an extensive tour of naval activities in Europe and spent some time with the Sixth Fleet in the Mediterranean. The following month he spoke at the launching of the first supercarrier, the *Forrestal*, saying that "This carrier represents the country's most versatile and most desirable weapon in our modern arsenal."[29] He thus challenged advocates of land-based bombers. Four *Forrestal*-class carriers had been authorized at the time; three more, including a nuclear carrier, would be in the programs Thomas defended. Each of these ships was a major part of the year's shipbuilding budget, and each was fought over at length in the Pentagon and in Congress.

In March 1955 Thomas toured South America and was awarded the Grand Merit Cross of Argentina during a visit to President Juan Peron. Early the next year he visited the western Pacific and the Seventh Fleet commanded by Vice Admiral A. M. Pride. That fleet in the previous year had successfully covered the evacuation of the Tachen Islands by assembling one of the greatest concentrations of seapower since World War II—over one hundred ships including six aircraft carriers.[30]

Thomas signed many documents that strengthened the Navy of the future. While he promised his full cooperation to the Maritime Administrator in keeping shipbuilding levels high,[31] he was adamant on the return by the Soviets of World War II lend-lease ships.[32] On the sharing of guided missile and electronic data with NATO allies, however, he took a conservative position.[33] In the same vein he directed the Office of Naval Intelligence to try to keep new or classified information on weaponry out of professional journals, where they were easily available to Russian attachés and embassy personnel.[34]

During the Truman administration, certain older American warships were transferred to the navies of the free world, a cost effective method of increasing free world seapower. Transfers continued under President Eisenhower, with particular emphasis placed on Reserve fleet destroyers and destroyer escorts invaluable for the antisubmarine warfare requirements of the Atlantic area. Thomas approved this dispersal of American seapower and wished to give some ships to various Caribbean nations as well.[35] While he would establish an American naval mission in Argentina, he would not lend an escort carrier to Brazil, because Brazil could not purchase the aircraft required to outfit it.[36]

Although Thomas prided himself on not losing his temper,[37] on occasion he could be caustic. When the first nuclear submarine, the *Nautilus*, developed troubles during her first trials, he told the Chief of the Bureau of Ships to move quickly against those contractors responsible for the failure of the ship's piping.[38] In the following month he sent a sharply worded memorandum to the Chief of Naval Operations complaining about programing documents originating in OP-05, the Deputy CNO for Air, stating that "this is not the type of aggressive thinking that is needed."[39] A compromise of Naval Academy entrance examinations brought a stern warning to the Chief of Naval Personnel.[40] Finally, in a long correspondence during his last year in office, he reprimanded the Navy Inspector General for not looking properly into a stevedoring dispute at Guam.[41]

Thomas always kept in mind that he was working with an organization that was constantly changing. He provided an excellent summary in his last annual report:

> Today's technological advances differ from those of the past in that progress in a few short months may exceed innovations accomplished in the whole span of former decades. Our Navy has made and continues to make accelerating progress in the transition to atomic propulsion; to guided missiles of increasing size and range, accuracy, and firepower; to greater speed, maneuverability, and sea-keeping endurance in surface and submarine operations; and to supersonic speeds and extended range and power of its air arm. These and other changes come simultaneously, posing difficult problems and decisions, but they are being accomplished in a full awareness of the need for instant readiness to fight and win today, if need be, with today's ships, today's aircraft, today's weapons.[42]

Just as Thomas's term was ending a Washington columnist wrote that "Fourteen United States ships plow towards the Middle East. Our Armed Forces divide the chores. Whenever trouble brews, the Navy gets the first assignment, and the Air Force gets the first appropriation."[43] Such a comment was typical of the many made during the Eisenhower years. Eisenhower was no "yes man" to the appropriations requests of his professional military advisers and leaned backward to insure that his administration would never be accused of stressing military matters. He was also imbued with the need of maintaining the economic solvency of the Western Alliance, particularly that of the United States. From this had grown the "New Look" strategy. Because of the divergence between a sound economy and what appeared to be a growing Soviet threat, the solution early in the administration was to rely on nuclear weapons in a major war. Brushfire wars could be fought with conventional weapons, but a major confrontation would carry the implicit threat of nuclear attack.[44] In the competition for appropriations, the Air Force continued to claim the largest share as the Strategic Air Command was built up with new wings of B–52 bombers prepared to smother any Soviet threat.

Eisenhower used the National Security Council as his forum for decision-making. A significant Defense Department lineup was included, with the Joint

Chiefs of Staff and the service secretaries often joining Secretary Wilson. On the other side of the table was the dynamic and at times aggressive Secretary of State, John Foster Dulles, and his advisers from the Foreign Service. Dulles's policies, which included massive retaliation, found support in the Defense Department, particularly from the Air Force and, initially, from Admiral Radford, Chairman of the Joint Chiefs. The Army and Navy instead supported a balance of nuclear and conventional forces, arguing that there can be only a finite amount of nuclear striking power. As Thomas stated in 1954,

> If we channel our military effort to counteraction against only *one* type of possible military aggression—as we had begun to do just prior to Korea—we ignore the threats of other types of military aggression, which can be just as defeating and just as conclusive. Moreover, in doing so, we permit any enemy to concentrate sufficient strength towards neutralizing or circumventing our single strength. Thus in these days of supersonic planes, nuclear weapons, and guided missiles we must still have soldiers and sailors, rifles, tanks, grenades, and bayonets, antisubmarine ships and landing craft as we so recently saw in Korea, as well as global bombers and massive retaliatory weapons. This is especially true when it is remembered that our fundamental philosophy gives to our opponent the initiative of choosing when, where, and what type of war they can launch.[45]

A nuclear- and missile-armed Navy, including the large carriers of the *Forrestal* class, had a definite place not only in a war with the Soviets but also in brushfire wars. Each year the service secretaries and the Joint Chiefs, meeting in the Armed Forces Policy Council, wrestled with the problem of allocating funds among the services so that overall U. S. strategy would be executed successfully. Roles and missions assigned to each service and the budget of that service were interdependent. Two interservice disagreements during Thomas's tenure deserve mention.

After the first U.S. hydrogen bomb was tested in 1954 it appeared that the Air Force would monopolize it because of its size. The Navy was building *Forrestal* class carriers and working to reduce the size of the H-bomb, however, and the Air Force realized that additional carriers would by the early 1960s constitute weapons systems directly competitive with SAC. Such influential congressmen as Senator Leverett Saltonstall stressed that air power advocates forgot the potentialities of the Navy-Marine Corps aircraft, which represented more than a third of the nation's air power.[46] In an effort to block the Navy's carrier program, in late 1954 the Air Force brought British Field Marshal Montgomery to the United States just as the *Forrestal* was being launched. "Monty" toured the country and delivered lectures downgrading the capabilities of carriers. To counter him, Thomas sent his Assistant Secretary for Air, James Smith, to speak in several localities and emphasize the value of the carrier, especially its mobility and flexibility, and that the new carriers were key weapons in the nation's "massive retaliation strategy." It is doubtful that the Navy's air arm realized that in this argument with the Air Force the new carriers were only an interim solution. The real seabased deterrent would follow in the Polaris program.

The second interservice feud erupted in 1956 while the B–52 force was increasing, the Navy's carrier program proceeded at one ship per year, and money was still being spent on conventional forces. Eisenhower, however, would not use his nuclear deterrent, not even during the Tachen Islands evacuation, when the atomic bombing of Quemoy was recommended by Dulles and certain members of the Joint Chiefs of Staff.[47] In a spat between the Army and Air Force that made headlines, staff officers from both services leaked their position papers on the nuclear vs conventional forces argument to enterprising reporters.[48] Secretary Wilson played down the incident at a press conference Thomas attended. Rather than publicizing his points, Thomas instead spoke directly with Wilson. Then, at a meeting of the service secretaries with Wilson, the atmosphere became heated when Thomas questioned "the honor and integrity" of certain Air Force executives in their quest for appropriations. In another instance Thomas laid it on the line with Air Force Secretary Donald Quarles for trying to go directly to Congress for additional funds.[49] The Air Force had strong supporters in Congress, particularly Senator W. Stuart Symington, their first Secretary. Despite administration objections, Symington was able to get $1.1 billion added to the Air Force budget.[50] During hearings on this appropriation, Secretary Wilson bluntly told Symington that even if the additional money were voted by Congress, he would put it in the bank. In turn Symington accused Wilson of bringing on a "grave constitutional crisis" by refusing to bend to the will of Congress.[51]

Closely intertwined with the budgets and roles and missions of each service were the guided missiles being produced by each. Eisenhower acknowledged the existence of interservice differences by saying that he would be frightened if "there were not good, strong disagreements over roles and missions" in times of great technological change.[52] Secretary Wilson moved forcibly to prevent duplication, but he had great difficulty in keeping the competitors apart. During Thomas's term the Navy was given the green light on its surface-to-air Talos and Terrier missiles and could keep the older Regulus. To Thomas, missiles would revolutionize navies as much as gunpowder had.[53]

The strategy of massive retaliation included an effective interservice continental defense. During Thomas's tenure, he extended the Distant Early Warning (DEW) Line a thousand miles at sea along both coasts, using radar picket ships and aircraft he would have preferred to use for other missions. In fact, he told Congress that, considering other tasks, continental defense was assigned too high a priority. [54]

Secretary Anderson had asked Under Secretary Gates to study how the Navy should be reorganized in consequence of Reorganization Plan No. 6. Gates reported on 14 April 1954, just as Thomas succeeded Anderson. He found nothing wrong with the division of departmental responsibility: policy control to the Secretary; naval command to the Chief of Naval Operations; and logistics administration divided between the civilian executive assistants on a consumer-producer basis. He recommended that the Under Secretary be the supervisor of the other civilian executive assistants and that there be four assistant secretaries: Air, Material, Financial Management/Comptroller, and Manpower/Reserve. He further recommended that the Secretary deal with Congress and directly control the Navy's public relations and information programs. He concluded that because the current organization was basically sound it provided requisite civilian control and was therefore compatible with Reorganization Plan No. 6.[55] He did not, however, clear up the relationships between the bureau chiefs, the Chief of Naval Operations, and the Secretary. Indeed, by adding two assistant secretaries he compounded the confusion of how these senior officials were supposed to operate.[56]

Thomas asked Gates to chair a committee that would delineate the relationships between the Navy and the Marine Corps. Gates was assisted by Admiral Donald Duncan, Vice Chief of Naval Operations, and Lieutenant General Gerald Thomas, Assistant Commandant of the Marine Corps.

The Navy-Marine Corps relationship was of great interest to the services and to Congress as well. In 1950, President Truman had sneeringly called the Corps "the Navy's police force," and his Secretary of Defense, Louis A. Johnson, tried to transfer its "soldiers" to the Army and its aviation to the Air Force. Forrest Sherman, the CNO, in 1949 and again in 1950 had tried to interpose his office between the Secretary and the Commandant of the Corps, but he had been blocked by Secretary of the Navy Francis P. Matthews. Although Sherman strenuously objected to Carl Vinson's desire to make the Commandant of the Corps a member of the Joint Chiefs of Staff, Vinson had his way in 1952 —to the extent that the Commandant could meet with the Joint Chiefs when they discussed matters pertaining to the Corps.[57] In 1954, Thomas approved the Gates committee proposal that the Commandant would be the Secretary's assistant in Marine Corps matters and that the Commandant would report directly to him, not via the CNO.[58] Thus was laid the administrative foundation for the nation's Navy-Marine Corps team of the next twenty years.

No further significant organizational changes in the Navy Department occurred during Thomas's tenure. Thomas nevertheless continually stressed the need for additional military and civilian personnel, of decentralizing wherever possible, and of razing "Main Navy" and housing naval functions under one roof. Not until 1968, however, would Main Navy disappear.

Thomas spent much of his time on the problems of the more than one million military and civilian personnel in his department. His choosing of Arleigh Burke as his new Chief of Naval Operations shows how vigorously he entered the personnel arena. He also urged the selection of younger men for flag rank. Further, he applauded President Eisenhower's call in January 1955 for pay increases including hazardous duty pay and for various fringe benefits that would improve the retention rate of the trained personnel needed to handle our increasingly complex postwar weapons systems.[59]

Late in 1954, the reenlistment rate was so low that reenlistment standards were temporarily lowered and incentives for "shipping over" by first enlistment personnel were increased.[60] In February 1955, Thomas stressed before Congress the important part a wife played in making a career Navy man and noted that the trend to make the Navy more and more a married man's organization was increasing.[61] Meanwhile he also did all he could to make naval life attractive to officers as well, taking care, however, that naval personnel and their dependents overseas did not become "Ugly Americans" to their free world hosts and allies.[62] Furthermore, he did all he could to eradicate any remnants of racial segregation in the Navy.[63]

On the material side, Thomas looked into the research and development, budget ramifications, and production involved in a "new age" Navy that included nuclear power, missiles, and jet aircraft. The fleet of the 1960s was spawned during Thomas's term. Although smaller than needed, he believed it adequate to deter any would-be attacker.[64]

Service disagreements continued over roles and missions even as Thomas's term drew to a close. The Air Force, for example, demanded exclusive control over strategic bombing and long-range ballistic-type missiles under development while the Army argued that a long-range missile was merely an extension of its artillery. In December 1956, Secretary Wilson tried to stop the wrangling by giving the Air Force responsibility for developing missiles of over 200 miles range, the Army control over those with shorter ranges, and the Navy control over all ship-based missile development.[65]

An extensive shipboard tactical missile program was already under way. The Terrier, the first surface-to-air missile system, was installed in two cruisers, in the World War II destroyer *Gyatt*, and would also be installed in cruiser conversions and new guided missile frigates. The longer range Talos surface-to-air system was under development; a third and smaller weapon, the Tartar, was being designed. A surface-to-surface missile, the Regulus, was operational in heavy cruisers and in two submarines. This rather ponderous subsonic missile had a nuclear capability. In the field of air-to-air weaponry, Navy aircraft were receiving the new Sparrow as a replacement for the earlier Sidewinder missile used by Air Force and Navy planes in the Korean War.

While developing strategic missiles, the Navy investigated the feasibility of launching a long-range missile from a submerged submarine. Regulus and its follow-on, Regulus II, essentially tactical, required surfacing by the submarine and had limited growth potential. When Thomas entered office, the Air Force and Army were working on longer range ballistic missiles using a liquid propellant and capable of delivering nuclear weapons. The missiles were large, required large, fixed launching sites, and were themselves vulnerable to counterattack. When Admiral Burke became Chief of Naval Operations, he directed Opnav's Missile Division (OP-51), under Rear Admiral John H. Sides, to place a high priority on getting a ballistic missile to sea, where it would be invulnerable. After an abortive attempt by Burke to join with the Air Force in its program and thus save money and time, the Army agreed to set up close liaison with its Jupiter project at Redstone Arsenal, Alabama. In 1955, after Burke assured the Army that the Navy would not encroach on its project for a 1,500-mile missile, Secretary Wilson officially sanctioned this informal agreement.[66]

Since the Navy's missile planners were fully occupied with various guided missile programs for the fleet, a separate group for ballistic missile research, planning, and production had to be organized. In September 1955, Thomas established a Special Projects Office that reported to him, not to any bureau chief. On Burke's advice, he chose an aviator, Admiral William F. "Red" Raborn, to head the new SPO, the first of its kind in the department. Raborn was given extraordinary powers to cut through Bureau and Opnav directives to produce a ship-based, long-range missile. While Thomas gave Raborn this "hunting license" to obtain what he needed, Burke told him that he would delete the project if it was found to be technically infeasible. By 1957, when Thomas left office, the SPO had gone a long way toward marrying the nuclear submarine with a solid-state Jupiter missile, thus providing a true seaborne deterrent. The new weapon, named Polaris, was speeded up in late 1957 because of Sputnik, and by late 1959 the first ballistic missile submarine, the *George Washington*, was ready for sea. In creating the SPO, Thomas set a precedent in naval management, a model for subsequent projects that cut through the complicated processes of the Navy's bureau system.

During the Korean War, Congress authorized the Navy's first supercarrier, the *Forrestal*. For the next six annual building programs, the most expensive item was a *Forrestal*-class carrier. Always in serious difficulty in every budget, until 1959 the Navy succeeded nevertheless in modernizing the fleet by adding new carriers to it.

Although Henry Jackson, Chairman of the Senate Atomic Energy Committee, began calling for nuclear power for *Forrestal*-class carriers as early as 1955, Thomas had to tell him that because of technological difficulties he could not include an atomic carrier in the 1957 building program.[67] In its place a sixth *Forrestal*-class ship, the *Constellation*, was included. In this same program, however, the Navy obtained approval for its first nuclear surface ship, the missile-armed cruiser *Long Beach*. Finally, in the last naval appropriation bill Thomas defended on Capitol Hill, in 1958, funds were also provided to construct the nuclear-powered carrier *Enterprise*. Meanwhile the first nuclear submarine, the *Nautilus*, under construction when Thomas entered office, had been pushed through to completion by Captain Hyman G. Rickover and commissioned in September 1954. Under Commander Eugene Wilkinson, she proved herself a tactical success in the fleet and forecast a revolution in submarine warfare. By the end of Thomas's term there were twenty-one nuclear submarines built, building, or authorized, three of them of the new fleet ballistic missile (FBM) type.

In 1957, when Thomas left office, the thirty-six destroyer escorts, sixteen converted Liberty ships, and various long-range, radar-equipped aircraft assigned to picket duty in the continental defense system were a significant addition to the Navy budget. In addition to supporting continental air defense, the Navy had to defend the coasts from intrusion by hostile submarines, particularly by the new missile-carrying types being attributed to the Soviets. Project Caesar, sonar listening stations along the Atlantic Coast and later in the Pacific, begun during Thomas's term, was soon enlarged to include coverage to the north through a bilateral agreement with the Canadian Navy.[68]

There were various disappointments in naval developments in this period. Since the project was given a low priority, little progress was made on an atomic aircraft before Thomas left the Navy. The P6M seaplane, the largest and fastest of flying boats, was designed for minelaying, long-range reconnaissance, and strategic bombing. Built by Martin under the name "Seamaster," the first model crashed on 7 December 1955 after fifty-two hours of flight time. The second crashed a year later after even less time in the air. With costs for corrections of structural flaws skyrocketing, Thomas reduced the program from twenty-four to eighteen planes, and in 1959 the entire program was scrapped.[69]

The fleet modernization program, uncompleted during Thomas's tenure, was handed on to his successor. While the carrier force was increasing at an even pace, older carriers received angled flight decks and new catapults. A start had been made on a powerful new fleet element, the Polaris force. Even though the conversion of the submarine force to an all-nuclear force was begun, the major portion of the fleet was still of World War II vintage. A few new destroyers, auxiliaries, and amphibious ships had been added, but real improvements in the fleet for the next few years would be through conversions, a stopgap measure less expensive at the moment than the required replacement programs of new ships.

The Navy-Marine Corps team was strengthened when the Marines developed new amphibious techniques and modernized their Korean War equipment. The tour of General Lemuel Shepherd, the first Commandant to sit as a member of the Joint Chiefs of Staff, expired on 31 December 1955. As his relief Thomas picked General Randolph Pate. While the Navy's amphibious ships were inadequate, Pate worked to perfect the tactic of vertical envelopment, using helicopters flying from assault shipping to land deep behind enemy lines. A new type of ship, the amphibious assault ship (LPH) was planned late in 1955, with the first to be commissioned in 1961. As an interim measure three *Essex*-class carriers and one escort carrier were converted and redesignated as LPHs. Another goal in amphibious warfare was the 20-knot assault force. A start was made in Thomas's term when three *Mariner* merchant hulls were converted to assault ships, but not until 1973 would this goal be realized.[70]

The four battleships in commission when Thomas became Secretary were very expensive to maintain and served primarily as gunfire support platforms for amphibious operations. Over Marine Corps objections, Thomas decommissioned them. Ten years later, both Army and Marine personnel in Vietnam would praise the fire support from a 16-inch gun battleship. To date, there is no substitute for this type of firepower.

Although President Eisenhower was never "pro Marine Corps" and the other services suffered significant cuts during his administration, the Corps was maintained at its three division-wing strength. Thomas not only emphasized to Secretary Wilson the need of keeping this strength but prevailed against several moves by the Army to have a Marine division replace an Army division in Korea and thus permit a buildup of the Army's strategic reserve at home.[71] Moreover, the 3d Marine Division, based at Okinawa, provided the Pacific Command with a ready amphibious capability in the Far East. And when Eisenhower ordered Sixth Fleet Marines to land at Beirut, Lebanon, those Marines—as always—were ready.

Nearing sixty years of age, having completed four years of government service in Washington, and feeling that it would be good for a younger man to take his place, Thomas submitted his resignation at the beginning of Eisenhower's second term. His recommendation that his Under Secretary, Thomas Gates, fifty years old, be promoted to Secretary was approved by Eisenhower and also by the Senate. Eisenhower accepted Thomas's resignation "with very real regret," as did the Navy and the nation, for he had done all possible to keep strong a navy he firmly believed had never been more important in the nation's history.[72]

After traveling about for some time, in July 1958 Thomas was named President of Trans-World Airlines by its owner, Howard Hughes.[73] In 1959 he was elected a director of the Air Transport Association of the United States and also a director of Hilton Hotels International. He was called back to Washington in 1959 to receive from Secretary Gates the Navy's Distinguished Public Service Award for "foresighted and responsible leadership in expediting the Navy's modernization program." His last Washington assignment, completed early in 1974, was a two-and-a-half-year tour as Chairman of the Joint Presidential and Congressional National Tourism Resources Review Commission, which undertook the first comprehensive study of domestic tourism in the United States. From a home in California, Thomas keeps active in many ways, including the golf course and the Episcopal Church. At this writing he still feels that maintaining a strong Navy is more important than at any time in history.[74]

NOTES

1. Hanson W. Baldwin, formerly of *The New York Times*, to the writer, 2 March 1974.
2. The Thomas home was next door to the girlhood home of Mrs. Harry S. (Bess) Truman.
3. Kimmis Hendrick in *The Christian Science Monitor*, 13 Feb. 1953.
4. *Current Biography*, 1954, s.v. "Thomas, Charles S."
5. *Time*, 5 Aug. 1946, p. 26.
6. *Ibid.*
7. *Current Biography*, 1954, s.v. "Thomas, Charles S."
8. Testimony by Under Secretary designate Thomas to the Senate Armed Services Committee, Feb. 1953, cited in *ibid.*
9. Harland B. Moulton, "American Strategic Power; Two Decades of Nuclear Strategy and Weapons Systems, 1945–1965" (Ph. D. diss., University of Minnesota, 1969), pp. 66–67.
10. The Fiscal Year 1953 budget allotted the Air Force was $20.7 billion; the Army, $14.2 billion; and the Navy, $13.2 billion. U. S. Department of Defense, *Report of the Secretary of Defense* (Washington: GPO, 1953), p. 5.
11. "Development of Executive Relationships within the Navy," *Navy Management Review*, No. 6, 1961.
12. *New York Times*, 5 Sept. 1953.
13. *Ibid.*, 26 Oct. 1953.
14. *New York Herald Tribune*, 1 Apr. 1954.
15. ANAFR, 12 Sept. 1953.
16. *Time*, 4 June 1956, p. 20.
17. *Ibid.*, 21 May 1956, p. 26.
18. *Ibid.*
19. Secretary Thomas to ADM Burke, 9 Apr. 1957, NHD:OA, Personal Papers of Arleigh A. Burke.
20. Thomas to ADM Burke, 25 Mar. 1959, *ibid.*
21. Debriefing notes, ADM Burke, 21 Dec. 1956, *ibid.*
22. Testimony of Secretary Thomas, 7 Feb. 1955, in U. S. House, Committee on Armed Services, *Hearings Before Subcommittee No. 2 on Career Incentive Act*

of 1955, February 7, 8, 16, 17, 18, 22, 23, 25, 28, March 1, 2, 3, and 4, 1955 (Washington: GPO 1955), pp. 416–20.

23. Testimony of Representative George W. Andrews of Alabama, U.S. HAC, *Department of the Navy Appropriations for 1956. Hearings before the Subcommittee of the Committee on Appropriations, House of Representatives, 84th Cong., 1st Sess.*, 2 vols. (Washington: GPO, 1955), 2:43.

24. Burke to Thomas, 8 Feb. 1956, Burke Papers.

25. Trip report, Congressional visit to Atlantic Fleet, dated 29 Mar. 1956, NHD:OA.

26. U.S. Congress, HAC, *Department of the Navy Appropriations for 1955. Hearings before the Subcommittee of the Committee on Appropriations, House of Representatives, 84th Cong., 1st Sess.* (Washington: GPO, 1955), No. 3, pp. 268–70.

27. Testimony by Secretary Thomas, in U.S. HAC, *Department of the Navy Appropriations for 1956, Hearings before the Subcommittee of the Committee on Appropriations, House of Representatives, 84th Cong., 1st Sess.*, 2 vols. (Washington: GPO, 1955), 1:1–5.

28. U.S. HAC, *Department of the Navy Appropriations for 1957. Hearings before the Subcommittee of the Committee on Appropriations, House of Representatives, 84th Cong., 2nd Sess.*, 2 vols. (Washington: GPO, 1956), 1:305–06.

29. Speech by Secretary Thomas, Newport News, Va., 11 Dec. 1954, copy in NHD:OA.

30. ANAFJ, 12 Feb. 1955, p. 699.

31. Thomas to Maritime Administrator, 11 May 1954, SNP.

32. Thomas to SECDEF, 17 June 1954, *ibid.*

33. Thomas to SECDEF, 17 June 1954, *ibid.*

34. Thomas to Director, Naval Intelligence, 8 Nov. 1954, *ibid.*

35. Memorandum, Thomas to SECDEF, 6 Sept., 7 Dec. 1956, *ibid.*

36. Memorandum, Thomas to SECDEF, 30 Mar., 1 May 1955, *ibid.*

37. *Current Biography*, 1954, s.v. "Thomas, Charles S."

38. Memorandum, SECNAV to Chief, BUSHIPS, 10 Jan. 1955, SNP.

39. Memorandum, SECNAV to CNO, 19 Feb. 1955, *ibid.*

40. Memorandum, SECNAV to CNO, 12 Apr. 1955, *ibid.*

41. Memorandum, SECNAV to CNO, 19 Feb. 1955, *ibid.*

42. U.S. Department of the Navy, *Semiannual Report of the Secretary of the Navy, January 1 to June 30, 1956* (Washington: GPO, 1956), p. 160.

43. Fletcher Knebel, "Potomac Fever," *Washington Evening Star*, 26 Apr. 1957.

44. Moulton, "American Strategic Power," p. 65.

45. Speech by Secretary Thomas to Institute of World Affairs, Riverside, Calif., 14 Dec. 1954, copy in SNP.

46. George E. Lowe, *The Age of Deterrence* (Boston: Little, Brown, 1964), p. 72.

47. *Ibid.*, p. 96.

48. "Charlie's Hurricane," *Time*, 4 June 1956, p. 19.

49. Debriefing notes, ADM Burke, meeting of Service Secretaries and Service Chiefs, 4 Nov. 1956, Burke Papers.

50. "Charlie's Big Thumb," *Time*, 2 July 1956, p. 11.

51. Editorial, "A Grave Constitutional Problem," ANAFR, 7 July 1956.

52. "Charlie's Hurricane," *Time*, 4 June 1956, p. 19.

53. "Firepower Afloat," *Ordnance*, May–June 1955, p. 869.

54. Thomas to SECDEF, 19 Jan. 1955, SNP.

55. "Development of Executive Relationships within the Navy," No. 7, *Navy Management Review*, 1961.

56. *Navy Department Organization, Report of the Dillon Board*, Part II, Study No. 2, 1962, copy in SNP.

57. COL Robert D. Heinl, USMC (Ret), *Soldiers of the Sea: A History of the United States Marine Corps, 1775-1962* (Annapolis, Md.: U.S. Naval Institute, 1962), pp. 529-32.

58. ANAFJ, 11 Apr. 1954.

59. Thomas to ADM Felix Stump, USN, 26 June 1956, quoted in ANAFR, 7 July 1956; "Eisenhower State of Union Message," *ibid.*, 8 Jan. 1955, p. 543; "Eisenhower Message to Congress on Career Service," *ibid.*, 15 Jan. 1955, p. 566.

60. *Ibid.*, 6 Nov. 1954, p. 278.

61. *Ibid.*, 12 Feb. 1966, p. 699.

62. "Join the Navy & See Naples," *Time*, 30 July 1956, p. 14; "The Reactionary," *ibid.*, 8 Oct. 1955, p. 20.

63. *New York Times*, 4 May 1954.

64. Speech by Secretary Thomas to Kansas City Chamber of Commerce, Kansas City, Missouri, reported in ANAFR, 12 June 1954, p. 19.

65. "Decision on Missiles," *Time*, 10 Dec. 1956, p. 25.

66. *Ibid.*, p. 36.

67. Thomas to Senator Henry Jackson, 6 Dec. 1955, SNP.

68. SECNAV to SECDEF, 9 Feb. 1955, *ibid.*

69. CAPT M. J. Stack, USN, "Patrol Planes," *Naval Review 1966* (Annapolis, Md.: U.S. Naval Institute, 1966), p. 61.

70. The first 20-knot attack transports were the *Paul Revere* and the *Francis Marion*; the first 20-knot attack cargo ship was the *Tulare*. All were converted from *Mariner* merchant hulls during Thomas's secretaryship.

71. SECNAV to SECDEF, 19 Jan. 1955, SNP.

72. Thomas to all ships and stations, ALNAV of 1 Apr. 1957, copy in SNP.

73. Charles Thomas to the writer, 5 Mar. 1974.

74. *Ibid.*

THOMAS SOVEREIGN GATES, JR.

1 April 1957–7 June 1959

JOHN R. WADLEIGH

"My years in the Navy Department have been one constant challenge to balance modernization with readiness."[1] With these words Thomas Gates said goodbye to a Navy he had served as an officer afloat, as its Under Secretary, and for two years as its Secretary. His farewell from Washington was suddenly delayed for a year and a half, however, when upon the death of Donald Quarles, the Deputy Secretary of Defense, President Dwight Eisenhower appointed him as his successor in May 1959. Six months later he became the Secretary of Defense, succeeding Neil McElroy, and remained in that assignment until the Eisenhower administration left office in January 1961. Gates left a record of civilian executive service unparalleled at that time in the history of the Department of Defense.

Gates had arrived in the Navy Department in October 1953 as Under Secretary with a background of World War II service that saw him rise to the rank of captain, USNR. He held two Bronze Star medals for combat service aboard aircraft carriers in both the Pacific and Atlantic oceans. As a successful business executive, moreover, he brought to the Navy Department an expertise in the management field that would help it through times of continuing change during his more than seven years of Washington service.

When Gates assumed office he knew both the problems that he faced and was already acquainted with his professional superiors and subordinates. He had seen the Navy shrink since the end of the Korean War; noted the slow pace of programs for atomic power, jet aircraft, and guided missiles; and was well aware of the twin problems of fleet modernization and the personnel retention. Externally he had to face the threat posed by the growing Soviet submarine fleet. Most significantly at this time, he knew, respected, and worked harmoniously with the dynamic Chief of Naval Operations, Admiral Arleigh Burke, whose reappointment he immediately sought after taking over the department.

Gates was born in Philadelphia on 10 April 1906 to Thomas Sovereign and Marie Rogers Gates. The father, a lawyer and investment banker, served as President of the University of Pennsylvania from 1930 to 1944. Marie Gates died when Thomas, Jr., was born. After graduating from Chestnut Hill Academy in 1924, Gates attended the University of Pennsylvania, where he was a Phi Beta Kappa member of the class of 1928. In his senior year, in addition to managing the football team, he was chairman of Pennsylvania's senior honor society, Sphinx.[2]

Upon graduation, Gates entered the investment business with the firm of Drexel and Co., and in 1940 became a partner. During those years he served in the Pennsylvania National Guard as a private.

On 29 September 1928, Gates married Millicent Anne Brengle of Philadelphia. They have three daughters, their only son having died in a tragic ski lodge fire in 1956.

Although Gates left the Pennsylvania National Guard in 1935, when war came in 1941 he resolved to rejoin the Army. However, a friend convinced him that the only way to stay alive in modern war was to be in the Navy. In consequence, in April 1942 he entered the Naval Reserve and began active duty as a student at the Indoctrination School, Quonset Point, Rhode Island, with the rank of lieutenant. From there he went to the Air Intelligence School, also at Quonset. Upon graduating he was assigned to the staff of the Commander in Chief, Atlantic Fleet, in which capacity he organized and became the first commanding officer of the Naval Air Intelligence School, Norfolk, Virginia. During this tour he participated in the Casablanca landings as an observer in the *Ranger,* the only attack carrier in the Atlantic Fleet.

In the summer of 1943 Gates joined the new light carrier *Monterey* as Air Combat Intelligence Officer. As part of the Fast Carrier Task Force, Pacific Fleet, the *Monterey* supported amphibious landings at Tarawa and Kwajalein and participated in strikes against New Britain, New Guinea, and the island of Truk.

Gates returned to the United States in the early summer of 1944 to join the staff of Rear Admiral Calvin T. Durgin as Flag Lieutenant and Air Intelligence Officer. Durgin, who commanded the *Ranger* when Gates was aboard, was organizing a new staff as Commander Escort Carriers, for Operation Dragoon, the planned invasion of southern France. With his flag in the escort carrier *Tulagi,* Durgin commanded five British and American carriers whose planes flew strike missions, provided gunfire observation, and maintained fighter cover for the invading forces of the U. S. Seventh Army.

Upon the successful completion of Dragoon, Durgin's American carriers redeployed to the Pacific, where the admiral hoisted his flag in the *Makin Island* as Commander, Carrier Division 29. During the next eight months, Gates participated in the invasions of Lingayen, Iwo Jima, and Okinawa. At Lingayen, where the Japanese first unleashed major kamikaze attacks, one of Durgin's light carriers was sunk and two were severely damaged. For service in this operation Gates received the Bronze Star Medal.[3] "The worst night of my life" was that of 21 February 1945, when kamikazes sank the *Bismarck Sea* and severely damaged the attack carrier *Saratoga* during the Iwo Jima operation.[4]

After three additional months of combat operations, in support of the Okinawa invasion, Gates completed his service and arrived in San Francisco on V-J Day. Shortly thereafter he was demobilized as a commander. That his wartime experiences made him dedicated to the aircraft carrier as the Navy's primary and most flexible weapons system is not surprising.

Gates resumed civil life as a partner in Drexel and Co. in the fall of 1945. Shortly thereafter he was elected a director of several corporations in the Philadelphia area. In civic activities he served on the local council of the Boy Scouts and was a member of the finance committee of the USO. As a trustee of his alma mater, the University of Pennsylvania, in October 1948 he was elected to head the Development Fund Drive, which raised 32 million dollars. He was also a founder of the Pennsylvania Blue Cross and its first president.

Shortly after the war, Gates was promoted to captain and continued to take an interest in local reserve activities, being a founder of the "Reserve Officers of the Naval Service." In addition to serving as vice president and director of the Navy League of the United States, he served on the naval advisory council of the Bureau of Aeronautics, in Washington.

In the summer of 1953, Secretary of the Navy Robert B. Anderson was suddenly told that his Under Secretary, Charles Thomas, would move to the Defense Department. At Anderson's request, on 2 October 1953 Gates accepted an interim appointment as Under Secretary from President Dwight Eisenhower and was promptly confirmed after the Senate convened.

On 14 October Gates was appointed to head a board to recommend changes in the organization of the Navy Department necessitated by passage of Defense Reorganization Plan No. 6. The board worked for six months and reported on 14 April 1954, shortly before Anderson left the Department. Gates later said that his work on this board "Provided me the greatest training that anyone could ever have had for my future responsibilities."[5] His report concluded that the Navy's organization, as provided in the Organization Act of 1948, was basically sound, insured proper civilian control, and was compatible with the revised Defense Department reorganization. His report recommended that there be four Assistant Secretaries—for Material, Air, Financial Management, and

Manpower—under the direct supervision of the Under Secretary, making him not only an alter ego for the Secretary but also his "civilian chief of staff" in handling the assistant secretaries. The Gates board did not directly address the fact that the service secretaries were gradually becoming implementers under the Secretary of Defense nor the dual role of the Chief of Naval Operations. The latter as a member of the Joint Chiefs of Staff participated in developing plans he would later execute under direction of the Secretary of the Navy, who had no part in their development.[6]

Following the submission of the Gates report, Gates was assigned the task of rewriting General Order 19 to delineate relationships within the Navy Department between the Navy and the Marine Corps. In his second major organizational task he produced a new General Order No. 5 that restated Navy-Marine Corps relationships within the Department to the satisfaction of both services.

As Under Secretary to Anderson and Thomas, Gates substituted for them whenever they went afield or afloat. He himself narrowly escaped serious injury when a plane taking him on an inspection tour of the Naval Air Training Command blew a tire while landing. As for Thomas's deep selection of Burke as CNO in 1955, he heartily approved.[7] He and Burke would work closely together for the next five and a half years.

When Gates assumed the office of Secretary of the Navy on 1 April 1957, the greatest challenge he faced was from Soviet sea power. In his first annual report he acknowledged that the Soviets had outstripped the United States in building submarines by 6 to 1, destroyer tonnage by 9 to 1, and cruisers by 14 to 1.[8] While the Soviet Navy was modern, the U.S. Navy, although larger, consisted principally of World War II ships. This increase in Soviet naval forces, coupled with a growing Soviet merchant marine and ocean-going fishing fleet, convinced Gates that the Soviets would use the oceans as another battleground in the cold war.[9]

Following President Eisenhower's outline to the nation of the policy on which Gates's Navy would be planned and operated, Gates saw his service as engaged in four tasks: to deter war with a nuclear retaliatory capability, provide flexible forces to overcome Soviet attacks on America's free world allies, provide continental defense, and create a reserve strength vitally useful in emergencies.[10]

When Gates became Secretary, there were 677,000 Navy and 201,000 Marine Corps personnel operating a fleet of 967 ships including 409 warships.[11] A year later personnel had been reduced by almost 40,000 and there were 891 active ships. The following year, as he left office, there were 626,000 Navy personnel and 860 ships in the active fleets. As the fleet grew older, increasingly expensive replacement ships could not be programmed on a one-for-one basis.

Therefore each new ship, carrying more sophisticated equipment, must take the place of two or more older ones, many of which were transferred to Free World navies. Moreover, the tempo of fleet operations increased. In 1957, the Sixth Fleet was deployed in the Mediterranean and the Seventh in the Western Pacific. Meanwhile the First and Second fleets conducted major training exercises in the Pacific and Atlantic, respectively. In the latter, the Second Fleet provided the backbone of NATO forces in such Norwegian Sea exercises as Strikeback. In addition, extended ship deployments were required by the blocking of the Suez Canal in the 1956 war, the annual Unitas cruise of a task group around South America, midshipmen's summer cruises, and operations in the Antarctic. In consequence, material readiness and morale of personnel were of increased concern during Gates's tenure.

In 1958, two significant cold war operations involved landings by the Marines of the Sixth Fleet at Beirut, Lebanon, in July, followed closely by the Formosa Straits crisis. Both operations proved the readiness and the flexibility of the Navy-Marine Corps team, with the Second Fleet bolstering the Sixth and the deploying of the carrier *Essex* from the Sixth to the Seventh Fleet via the newly reopened Suez Canal, thus adding quickly to the striking power of our forces in the Pacific.

Great improvements in the Navy's air strike capability were made during Gates's term. Two new *Forrestal*-class carriers, the *Ranger* and the *Independence*, became operational. Modernization of *Essex*-class carriers by installing steam catapults and angled decks continued, so that by the end of Gates's tenure all attack carriers could handle the new jet attack and fighter aircraft. As Gates put it, "A *Forrestal*-class carrier can launch more explosive power than all the CVAs of World War II."[12] Much of this power was concentrated in the new, long-range heavy attack plane, the A3D Skywarrior.

Under constant prodding from Admiral Burke, and with Gates's full support, increased emphasis was also placed on improving antisubmarine capabilities. In the Atlantic, a Hunter-Killer (HUK) Group was organized under the command of Rear Admiral John S. "Jimmy" Thach to concentrate solely on advanced ASW training and improving techniques to hunt down and destroy intruding submarines. This group, comprised of one antisubmarine carrier, a destroyer squadron, and long-range patrol aircraft, spent its at-sea periods on patrol off the East Coast and often obtained submarine contacts reported by aircraft or through underwater searches. When this Task Group Alfa was in port, another HUK Group remained at sea. Gates visited Thach in his flagship, the *Randolph,* and enthusiastically told a reporter that "Task Group Alfa is one of the greatest things we have ever done. The morale there is the greatest I have seen."[13]

While Gates was Under Secretary, the nuclear submarine *Nautilus* had joined the fleet and revolutionized submarine warfare. In 1957 Gates objected to plans to send her to the Pacific—he wanted no publicity stunt. Persuaded by Burke and Rear Admiral Hyman Rickover, head of the Navy's atomic propulsion programs, that the cruise would be operationally worthwhile and that it was not just a means of keeping the Atomic Energy Commission happy, he beamed when the *Nautilus* made all but 200 of the 5,200-mile transit from New London to San Diego under water.[14] A year later the same ship cruised under the polar ice for 1,000 miles and came within 180 miles of the North Pole. Other nuclear boats, the *Seawolf, Skate, Swordfish, Sargo,* and *Seadragon,* joined the fleet during Gates's term, and on 15 April 1959 the *Skipjack* was commissioned. The last named combined nuclear power with the teardrop-shaped, streamlined hull of the experimental submarine *Albacore.* She and her sister ships were forerunners of the attack submarine forces of the 1970s, a vital segment of our defenses against the Soviet submarine threat today.

As in Thomas's day, so in Gates's, a significant portion of the Navy's budget was spent in supporting the Air Force in continental defense. Although static defense was alien to naval thinking, it was an essential element of President Eisenhower's strategy "to keep our home defense in a high state of efficiency."[15]

Again, as in Thomas's day, so in Gates's, old age, overdeployment, inadequate funding for full overhauls, and constantly rotating and therefore inexperienced personnel caused the material condition of the fleet to deteriorate at what Gates said was "an alarming rate" of .7 percent per year.[16] By 1959, when he left office, Gates had had no more success in overcoming the problems of an aging fleet than any other peacetime Secretary of the Navy since the days of President Theodore Roosevelt.

Burke had served as Chief of Naval Operations for almost two years when Gates became Secretary. Although Burke told Gates that he did not seek reappointment, Gates prevailed upon him to stay on.[17] Two years later he teamed up with Under Secretary William B. Franke to persuade Burke to accept a completely unprecedented third two-year term.

While the trend in the Department of Defense was toward greater centralization, Gates preferred the decentralized system of administration which James Forrestal had used. Nevertheless, in 1955 the second Hoover Commission on Department of Defense Reorganization recommended centralizing even more power in the office of the Secretary of Defense. A principal recommendation was to eliminate the large number of Assistant Secretaries of Defense and concentrate their duties under four: Logistics, Research and Development, Personnel, and Financial Management. The Navy already had a similar grouping of the top civilian executives.

Soon after the Hoover Report came the Rockefeller Brothers Fund Study on International Security. This study looked at the major problems that would face the nation in the years 1958–1968. On the subject of defense organization it emphasized that the armed services were competitive, that the Secretary of Defense spent too much time arbitrating, and that resulting plans and programs were too often merely compromises. It recommended eliminating the service departments from the operational chain of command, the assignment of all forces to Unified/Specified Commands receiving orders from the President through the Secretary of Defense and the Joint Staff, a reorganization and strengthening of the Joint Staff on a functional basis under the Chairman of the Joint Chiefs, and the carrying out of logistic responsibilities by the Secretary of Defense through the service secretaries.[18]

A new Defense Reorganization Act incorporating the gist of the Rockefeller study recommendations was submitted to Congress for consideration. The act's support for additional centralization was opposed by many powerful legislators and by the Navy as well. During questioning by the House Armed Services Committee, Admiral Burke mentioned his "misgivings" and "apprehension," noted that specific functions of a service could be eliminated, and expressed the hope that the committee would give serious consideration to the truly important matter of defense reorganization.[19] To Burke's testimony, General Randolph Pate, Commandant of the Marine Corps, added that "Good intentions to preserve the Marines are no insurance against future damage to our usefulness. Only in the law can we find such insurance."[20]

The congressional hearings brought inevitable questions about the "muzzling" of service witnesses by the Defense Department. President Eisenhower had told the Joint Chiefs that they would freely express their views to Congress.[21] When Burke and Pate opposed portions of the Reorganization Act he had already approved, Neil McElroy publicly admitted that he was "disappointed" with the Navy's views.[22] Despite McElroy, naval testimony appears to have been a prime factor in obtaining modifications in the reorganization act that permitted the service secretaries and the Joint Chiefs to retain significant roles.

As finally written into law, the Reorganization Act of 1958 clearly established the Defense Department as a fief of its secretary rather than a "federation" of service departments. It placed the Secretary of Defense in operations as well as in policy-making but insured that he operate through the Joint Chiefs. The Chiefs, supported by an enlarged staff, became directly involved in operations. The law emphasized the new focus required in research and development, given the urgency of modern technology. In the Navy itself, the military command function of the Chief of Naval Operations was de-emphasized, although as a member of the Joint Chiefs he participated in the command function of the Secretary of Defense. Naval forces assigned to Unified and Specified commands, however, no longer came under his command.[23]

The act still left some major questions unanswered. What were the specific relationships between the Secretary of Defense and the service secretaries? Or those between the Secretary of Defense and the Joint Chiefs in the formulation of Defense policy? Or those between the service secretaries and the service chiefs? In testifying on the language changes in his command role, Burke stated that those changes would not stop him from carrying out his duties in the way he always did. One significant point the act did clarify was that assistant secretaries of defense could issue orders to the military departments only on those items specifically delegated to them by the secretary of defense and that such orders had to be transmitted through the service secretaries.[24] To the Navy this was welcome insurance that the Secretary would not be officially bypassed by the staff of the secretary of defense.

When Gates directed Under Secretary Franke to review Navy Department organization in light of the new Defense Reorganization Act, Franke appointed a board including Admiral James S. Russell, Vice Chief of Naval Operations, and Lieutenant General Merrill Twining, Assistant Commandant of the Marine Corps, with his own special assistant, John Dillon, as recorder. The report, issued in 1959, generally followed the Gates Board report of 1954 in stating that despite the trend toward centralization in the Department of Defense the Navy's internal organization and methods of administration were satisfactory.[25]

Franke's board recommended that there be an assistant secretary for research and development in the Navy Department as well as a corresponding deputy chief of naval operations. Previously R&D had been concentrated primarily under the assistant secretary for air. However, the board's recommendation of the formation of a Naval Technical Corps to include engineering, intelligence, and other specialist officers who were not eligible to command at sea was vetoed by Gates on the ground that these officers would have formed another staff corps with distinctive insignia. Finally, the board had good words for the bilineal naval structure.[26]

While Gates liked the bilinear system and worked to improve it, Burke saw the Navy as "the precision instrument of naval policy." Referring to the presence of the Sixth Fleet during the unrest in Jordan and the brief Suez war of November 1956, *Time* called it the "Steel Gray Stabilizer."[27]

If deterrence was Eisenhower's major defense policy, maintaining a sound economy was a close second objective. To achieve strength without spending money caused many of the inter-service disputes that took place while Gates was in the Pentagon.

In the spring of 1957, Gates wished to show the President the latest in naval hardware in a demonstration by units of the Second Fleet off Jacksonville, Florida. Gates accompanied the President and several cabinet members on board the second ship of the *Forrestal* class, the *Saratoga*. The official party watched a modern carrier task group, including missile-armed screening ships, in simulated action against attacking aircraft, surface ships, and submarines. The demonstration went off on schedule and was marred only by an emergency search for a downed fighter and by an unannounced attempt by the Air Force to photograph the operations, with Navy fighters intercepting the B–66 reconnaissance "spy" planes some distance from the task group.[28] It was another example of the intense competition between the Air Force and the Navy, reminiscent in some ways of the B–36 controversy of the previous decade.

Toward the end of his tenure, Secretary of Defense Charles Wilson tended to support naval thinking about service roles and missions.[29] In October 1957, Wilson was succeeded by Neil McElroy, former president of Proctor and Gamble. At that very moment a new element entered the planning and thinking of his department. By orbiting their Sputnik satellite around the earth, the Soviets took the lead from the United States in a new and awesome area of competition. There were near-panic remarks by congressman and a flurry of critical articles in the press. What was wrong with our research and development programs? What was wrong with the military establishment? Why had the Russians surprised us?

At this time the Navy's work in space consisted primarily of Project Vanguard, a research earth satellite that was lightly funded in order to concentrate heavily on ballistic missile programs. By March 1958, however, Vanguard demonstrated its ability to put an earth satellite into orbit. As a result, there was an input for American participation in the International Geophysical Year, but the Russians had taken first place in the propaganda competition.

Sputnik stirred up American missile programs and accompanying service rivalries. By proving that Intercontinental Ballistic Missiles (ICBMs) were feasible, the orbit ended any thought of a doctrine of "limited nuclear war."[30] For Gates's Navy it meant new impetus for the Polaris program. At the time Sputnik flew, Rear Admiral Raborn, project manager, planned to have a submarine on patrol by the spring of 1963. By compromising on a missile with a range of 1,200 nautical miles rather than a longer range one, he had a submarine on station by December 1960.[31] In December 1957, Secretary McElroy, under heavy criticism and congressional pressure after Sputnik, approved an acceleration of Polaris despite skepticism about its success and continuing attempts by the Air Force to downgrade it.[32]

A speedup in Polaris meant extra funding, and early in 1958 Gates went before the House Military Appropriations Subcommittee headed by George Mahon to explain the details of the Polaris acceleration. At this meeting came the first public indications that the new fleet ballistic missile would augment the Strategic Air Command even though Gates, faced with awaiting technological developments, could not at the time specify the number of Polaris boats he could provide.[33]

The Eisenhower administration's answer to Sputnik was to be Polaris, which by 1961 was an operational weapons system admirably fitting the strategy of the new President John Kennedy—a strategy of flexible response.[34]

The Senate Majority Leader, Lyndon B. Johnson, quickly moved into the interservice field after Sputnik by forming a committee to investigate the state of the nation's defenses. By December 1957, his committee began hearing testimony from the Department of Defense and from the services. A special Navy task force was established to prepare testimony and to provide quick answers to questions posed by the committee.[35] While much naval testimony concerned antisubmarine warfare, each service used the committee as a sounding board for its own requirements, particularly for high-priority projects requiring additional funding. Ending its deliberations in February 1958, the Johnson committee issued a report that did not strongly criticize the administration's defense strategy and policies, as it was advocated to do by Senator W. Stuart Symington, the strong Air Force advocate from Missouri. Instead the committee recommended a speedup in modernizing conventional forces, with emphasis on anti-missile missiles and greater imagination in future technology. Defense weaknesses had been exposed in a well-run congressional forum at a critical time.[36]

Gates regularly attended Armed Forces Policy Council meetings and on occasion also attended meetings of the National Security Council. He was a calm but articulate spokesman for the naval service. For example, in a meeting with McElroy when Pentagon reorganization was being discussed, he emphasized the vital importance of maintaining the individual service department organization under a secretary with his present powers of administration and management.[37] On another occasion he personally briefed the National Security Council on the Navy's limited war capabilities when using the new A3D Skywarrior attack aircraft backed up by the deterrent power of the prospective Polaris boats.[38] As quoted in *All Hands*, he said that "As usual the Navy is where the trouble is and is called on first when trouble is brewing. The Navy is an action service rather than an alerted service. If anyone must fight, we fight first, and the atomic age finds us as always, the first line of defense."[39]

Knowing that readiness depends on people, Gates traveled widely to see the people of his service. He visited Europe and the Sixth fleet on several occasions. He went to the Caribbean and Guantánamo Bay, where a change of government in Cuba was turning that tropical naval station into an isolated outpost in a hostile land. He visited the Seventh Fleet, which was keeping watch on the Formosa Straits. He even visited the Navy's small unit in Antarctica's McMurdo Sound.

Early in 1958, a *Newsweek* article entitled "Our Morale Mess" blamed the top level of the Pentagon for a "state of morale in the services that was shockingly low." One third of the Armed Forces were leaving each year; pay was low; a more intellectual enlisted population deeply resented some of the spit and polish directives of former years; and the very small number chosen by the draft brought only malcontents into the defense establishment. Two additional problems that faced the services were a growing schism between line and technical enlisted personnel and the need to retire or separate career officers early, thus providing less security than expected.[40]

The two major personnel needs facing Gates were to reenlist more first-cruise men and to balance the rating structure between line and technicians within each petty officer grade. During Gates's first year, first-cruise enlistments rose from 14 to 21 percent and over one-third of the unbalanced ratings were corrected. When lower force levels permitted more selective recruiting, he stated that for the next fiscal year the Navy would accept no Mental Group IV enlistees.[41] In 1958, when personnel strength again dropped, he released 25,000 draftees from three to five months early. This was also the year in which the new senior enlisted grades of Master (E9) and Senior Chief Petty Officer (E8) were approved, with promotions to these grades starting in 1959.[42] Gates also instituted the Navy Enlisted Special Education Program, which provided for qualified enlisted men to take a full college course at government expense and receive commissions upon graduation. In return the new officers must serve two years for every year of education.

Two major problems involving officers were to retain young officers who had served four or five years and to ease the hump in the senior grades that had existed since the end of World War II. By directing that captains with five years of service who failed to be selected for promotion a specified number of times be screened out, Gates reduced the hump. He also partially alleviated the shortage of aircraft pilots by creating the naval flight officer, one who was trained to carry out many of the non-pilot duties performed by officers in a modern aircraft. In addition he directed that younger officers be selected for flag rank.[43] In 1957 the Navy had no flag officers under forty-five years of age while the Air Force had 49, the Army, 11, and the Marines, 2.[44] Among others, the flag selection board of 1957 picked Captain Thomas H. Moorer, forty-four years old, who served for 18 years, retiring in 1975 as Chairman of the Joint Chiefs of Staff.

Since World War II, responsibility for the administration of aviation officer personnel had been in the office of the Deputy Chief of Naval Operations for Air. Those who believed that Gates's experiences in aviation would cause him to favor aviators were mistaken, for he wished to integrate aviation as part of the Navy into normal servicewide functional divisions. He transferred aviation officer personnel matters from the Deputy Chief of Naval Operations for Air to the Bureau of Personnel and combined the Bureau of Aeronautics with the Bureau of Ordnance into a new Bureau of Weapons. He replaced the post of Assistant Secretary for Air with an Assistant Secretary for Research and Development. That he still thought highly of aviators, however, is clear from his telling Admiral Burke that the next Chief of Naval Personnel would be an aviator.[45]

Although Gates generally had a favorable press, on occasion he was criticized. In August 1957, for example, he missed seeing a delegation that wished to protest Congress's decision to close the Naval Hospital at Corona, California. Poor staff work by his aides also resulted in the failure to invite Rear Admiral Hyman Rickover to a formal White House ceremony at which the President decorated Commander William Anderson, skipper of the *Nautilus*, for his daring voyage under the polar ice cap. For this faux pas, Gates personally apologized.[46]

Although an American Civil Liberties Union report of December 1957 stated that there was "practically no discrimination on board ship," it noted that Negroes were having trouble entering the Naval Academy and NROTC units and attributed this problem to the refusal of qualified preparatory schools to accept Negro candidates.[47]

Concerned about leadership at the lower levels, Gates created a Moral Leadership Program. General Order 21 required the Navy Inspector General to report on the personal example set by officers in each command, the moral atmosphere of the command, and the current standards of personal supervision at each level within the command.[48] The order still stands.

Like secretaries before him, Gates left the Navy Department without solving its foremost personnel problem, the retention of qualified men in an ever more technical organization. On this last point, as Admiral Burke told him as he left, "Your service was in an era marked by the most rapid technological changes in the history of the Navy."[49] Missiles for guns, nuclear for conventional power, and jets for propeller aircraft were changes that continued during Gates's tour, with exploration into space a novel development. Hence Gates could say that "The Navy is in the forefront of the development of new weapons. Nuclear ships, supersonic speed, ballistic and guided missiles set the stage for the golden age of seapower."[50]

For Gates, obtaining the CVAN *Enterprise* was a prelude to the all-nuclear striking fleet of the future. However, the cost of a CVAN was such that the Navy could not hope to include one in each year's program without deleting almost all other ships as well as limiting the nuclear submarine programs. He also knew that the White House was lukewarm toward another CVAN before the first one was proved successful. No such carrier was approved in fiscal years 1958 or 1959. In the meantime, three new *Forrestal*-class carriers had proved their versatility. With their new jet Crusaders and Skywarriors, missile-armed and nuclear capable, they were a significant addition to American sea and striking power.

Just as Gates ordered the decommissioning of the last battleships, the *Iowa* and the *Wisconsin*, the keel of the first nuclear surface ship, the guided missile cruiser *Long Beach*, was laid down. Here was the first real marriage of nuclear power and guided missiles.

When experiments conducted in the *Gyatt* revealed that the conversion of World War II destroyers and destroyer escorts to carry the Terrier missile was inefficient, new and larger destroyers designated as frigates were programmed to carry the Terrier; a smaller missile, the Tartar, was included in the armament of destroyers programmed beginning in 1957. By the time Gates left office, 78 post-World War II destroyer types were built, building, or programmed. He had thus at least made a modest start toward replacing the aging surface antisubmarine warfare potential of the fleet.

The submarine building program, composed entirely of nuclear craft, consisted of two basic types in 1957. Plans called for five or six of the high-speed *Skipjack* class of attack, or antisubmarine, submarines each year. By the time Gates left office, nine Polaris boats had been authorized; for fiscal year 1961, he recommended ten more.

Stimulated by Sputnik, Bureau of Ships designers suggested saving construction time for the first Polaris units by lengthening the hulls of *Skipjack*-class boats under construction and placing the missile tubes and fire control equipment in the additional space. The *Scorpion*, on the ways at Electric Boat Co. in New London, was "opened up" and lengthened by 130 feet. On 9 June 1959, a week after Gates's tour ended, she was launched as the *George Washington*,[51] and Gates paid high tribute to the management processes used by the Special Project Office. Moreover, he took full knowledge of this naval deterrent system with him when he moved up into the office of the Secretary of Defense.[52]

Meanwhile progress was being made in both the techniques and weapons of antisubmarine warfare. Gates was enthusiastic about the Hunter–Killer patrols of Task Group Alfa because they taught how to overcome the Soviet submarine menace. New techniques included the ASROC and SUBROC ASW weapons, improved sonars, and airborne submarine detection systems, and new concepts that came from Project Nobska, a meeting of top scientists at Woods Hole where all phases of the ASW problem with short- and long-range remedies were studied. In addition, Project Argus, conducted by Rear Admiral Lloyd Mustin, yielded significant data about the earth's magnetic surface and the effects of nuclear bursts by exploding nuclear devices at heights of up to three hundred miles.[53]

All of these programs, which Gates pushed and was frequently called on to defend, were expensive. While he asked for more funds for them, he bemoaned the neglect of the Marine Corps, whose problems generally paralleled those of the Navy—cuts in personnel, difficulties in acquiring specialists to handle increasingly complex aircraft and weapons, and the loss of battleships for fire support.[54] However, the Marines were perfecting vertical assault techniques in amphibious landings by using helicopter squadrons operating from *Essex*-class and escort carriers until they were provided with new assault ships (LPH) of the *Iwo Jima* class and a new multipurpose ship, the amphibious landing ship dock (LPD). Both classes, with speeds of over twenty knots, and helicopter and troop facilities, would be the backbone of the amphibious squadrons of the 1970s. Meanwhile Gates blocked the Army's attempt to have the 3d Marine Division, normally in the Western Pacific, replace an Army division in Korea, and an Air Force attempt to have the 3d Marine Air Wing assigned to Korea, thereby freeing tactical air units for duty in the continental United States.[55]

Early in 1959, after five and a half years in the Navy Department, Gates decided that it was time to return to civilian life and submitted his resignation to the President. The illness of his successor, William B. Franke, delayed his departure until 7 June. In the interim, Gates saw the Soviets precipitate a new Berlin crisis and use their fishing ships to break the transatlantic cable off Newfoundland, and a deepening commitment to communism in Castro's Cuba. As unrest continued in various quarters of the globe, the intelligence community predicted a possible war threat in mid May 1959 and the services were directed to improve their readiness.[56] Naval readiness in the Atlantic was increased in part by dispersing ships to home ports other than Newport and Norfolk.

In mid March, Gates thanked Admiral Burke for accepting a third term as Chief of Naval Operations.[57] In early May, President Eisenhower asked Gates to succeed Deputy Secretary of Defense Donald Quarles, who had died. After Gates agreed, the Senate quickly approved, and the Navy was happy to have one of its own as the second man in the Defense Department. The Navy was even happier when Gates was chosen to succeed McElroy as Secretary of Defense, on 1 December 1959.

After fourteen months as Secretary of Defense, Gates left the Pentagon on 20 January 1961 and shortly thereafter was appointed president and a director of Morgan Guaranty Trust Co., of New York. In 1965 he became Chairman of the Board and Chief Executive Officer of this large international banking firm. He was also elected a director of several corporations including the General Electric Co., Scott Paper, and Bethlehem Steel Corporation. In 1969 he returned briefly to public office when President Nixon appointed him to head a board to formulate recommendations for the All Volunteer Armed Forces.

Again, in 1976, Gates was called to government service, this time by a shipmate in the USS *Monterey*, President Gerald Ford, who appointed him head of the United States Liaison Office to the People's Republic of China. The post, which carried the rank of ambassador, had first been held by the veteran diplomat David E. K. Bruce, then by former Republican National Chairman George Bush, whom Gates relieved in May 1976. On arrival in Peiping Gates stated that "my main task will be to work for the normalization of Chinese-American relations."[58] To this end he served until the following May, when President Jimmy Carter's appointee, Leonard Woodcock, succeeded to the assignment. China's Deputy Prime Minister tendered the Gateses a farewell dinner before they left Peiping and Gates, at the age of seventy-one years, once again retired to private life from service to his nation. This service was summed up by Hanson Baldwin, longtime military editor for the *New York Times*, when he wrote that "Gates, lacking any preconceived bias with respect to management techniques and bereft of political ambition, dedicated himself to providing the Navy and later the Defense Department with good leadership."[59]

NOTES

1. J. C. Elliot, "Profile: Thomas S. Gates," *Navy*, May 1959, p. 9.
2. *Ibid.*
3. Secretary of the Navy Citation to LCDR Thomas S. Gates, signed by James V. Forrestal, in personal files of Mr. Gates.
4. Interview with Thomas Gates by the writer, Northeast Harbor, Maine, 22 Aug. 1974.
5. *Ibid.*
6. "Development of Executive Relationships within the Navy," *Navy Management Review*, No. 7, Aug. 1963, p. 19.
7. Interview by the writer with Thomas Gates, Northeast Harbor, Maine, 22 Aug. 1974.
8. ARSN, 1957, p. 170.
9. *Ibid.*, p. 172.
10. President Eisenhower, nationwide radio broadcast, 13 Nov. 1957.
11. U. S. Department of Defense, *Annual Reports of the Secretary of Defense. Statistical Tables, 1957–1959* (Washington: GPO, 1959).
12. "SecNav Gates Says," *All Hands*, July 1957, p. 18.
13. Elliot, "Profile: Thomas S. Gates," 9.

14. Memorandum for the Record, ADM A. Burke, 6 June 1957, NHD: OA, Personal Papers of Arleigh A. Burke.

15. President Eisenhower, nationwide radio broadcast, 13 Nov. 1957.

16. ARSN, 1957, p. 172.

17. Memorandum for Record, ADM. A. Burke, 15 Mar. 1957, Burke Papers.

18. "Development of Executive Relationships within the Navy," *Navy Management Review*, No. 8, Sept. 1963, p. 18, and No. 9, Oct. 1963, p. 19.

19. *Time*, 12 May 1958, p. 19.

20. *Ibid.*

21. Debriefing notes, ADM A. Burke, White House discussions, 25 Apr. 1958, Burke Papers.

22. *Time*, 12 May 1958, p. 20.

23. ADM A. Burke, "The Reorganization Act of 1958," *Judge Advocate Journal*, Oct. 1958, p. 3.

24. "Development of Executive Relationships within the Navy," *Navy Management Review*, No. 9, Oct. 1963, p. 12.

25. Vincent Davis, *The Admirals Lobby* (Chapel Hill: University of North Carolina Press, 1967), p. 165.

26. "Franke Report," ANAFJ, 23 May 1959, p. 6; *Report of Franke Board, 1959*, p. 5, copy in SNP; "Development of Executive Relationships within the Navy," *Navy Management Review*, No. 10, Dec. 1963, p. 15.

27. ADM A. Burke interview with William Hillman, North American Newspaper Alliance, 8 Aug. 1957, Burke Papers.

28. ADM A. Burke, Memorandum for Record, 10 June 1957, *ibid.*

29. ADM A. Burke, Debriefing Notes, Quantico Conference, 10 June 1957, *ibid.*

30. George E. Lowe, *The Age of Deterrence* (Boston: Little, Brown, 1964), p. 153.

31. James Barr and W. E. Howard, *Polaris* (New York: Harcourt, Brace, 1960), pp. 93-95.

32. ADM A. Burke debriefing notes on various Pentagon meetings with the service secretaries and the service chiefs, 1957-1958, Burke Papers.

33. Barr and Howard, *Polaris*, pp. 203-04.

34. Lowe, *Age of Deterrence*, p. 168.

35. CNO Memorandum to various OPNAV Divisions, 11 Dec. 1957, Burke Papers.

36. "Under Control," *Time*, 2 Feb. 1958, p. 15.

37. ADM A. Burke, debriefing memorandum, 22 Mar. 1958, Burke Papers.

38. ADM A. Burke, debriefing memorandum, 29 Mar. 1958, *ibid.*

39. "Secnav Gates Says," *All Hands*, July 1957, p. 18.

40. "Our Morale Mess," *Newsweek*, 17 Feb. 1958, pp. 31-41.

41. ARSN, 1957, pp. 222-23.

42. *Ibid.*, 1958, p. 228.

43. Gates to ADM Jerauld Wright, USN, President of Fiscal Year 1958 Flag Selection Board, 20 June 1957, SNP.

44. "Study of Age of Flag and General Officers," ANAFJ, 20 Apr. 1957, p. 11.

45. ADM A. Burke, Memorandum for Record: Conversation with Secretary Gates, 16 July 1957, Burke Papers.

46. Bob Considine in *New York Journal American*, 20 Aug. 1957.

47. *New York Herald Tribune*, 2 Dec. 1957.

48. "New Leadership Program for Navy," *ibid.*, 1 June 1958.
49. ADM Burke to Secretary Gates, 1 June 1959, Burke Papers.
50. "SecNav Gates Says," *All Hands*, July 1957, p. 18.
51. Barr and Howard, *Polaris*, p. 256.
52. Interview by the writer with Thomas Gates, Northeast Harbor, Maine, 22 Aug. 1974.
53. Hanson Baldwin in *New York Times*, 24 Mar. 1959.
54. ARSN, 1958, pp. 222–30, 233–43.
55. ADM A. Burke, debriefing memorandum, Armed Forces Policy Council Meeting, 13 Aug. 1957, Burke Papers.
56. ADM A. Burke, debriefing memorandum, 4 Mar. 1959, *ibid.*
57. Gates to ADM Burke, 18 Mar. 1959, *ibid.*
58. *New York Times*, 6 May 1976.
59. Hanson W. Baldwin to the writer, 2 Mar. 1974.

WILLIAM BIRRELL FRANKE

8 June 1959–20 January 1961

JOHN R. WADLEIGH

One of President Dwight D. Eisenhower's policies was to promote senior civilian executives of the government within their own departments whenever practical. In the case of William Franke, he promoted him twice, from assistant to under secretary of the Navy and twenty months later to secretary.

Franke was a respected businessman and certified public accountant with Defense Department experience in the Truman administration, for which he had been awarded the Department of Defense Distinguished Service Award in 1952. He joined the Eisenhower administration two years later as assistant secretary of the Navy for financial management and comptroller of the Navy under Secretary Charles Thomas. In April 1957, when Thomas resigned and was relieved by Under Secretary Thomas Gates, Franke became the new under secretary but still retained the assignment of Navy Comptroller. In his new position he headed a major study of Navy Department reorganization, the very one under which he would operate as secretary. As secretary, he served with Eisenhower's last two secretaries of defense, Neil McElroy and Gates.

Franke's eighteen months in office began when the first Polaris fleet ballistic missile submarines took station as major new elements in the nation's deterrent forces. By the time he left Washington, three Polaris submarines had been commissioned and eleven more were in various stages of construction.[1]

Although Franke was primarily a financial and management executive, he came to know the Navy and its personnel ashore and afloat better than his three predecessors who served under Eisenhower. His attitude toward the naval profession was that the Navy would be successful only to the degree that he provided necessary leadership in a constantly changing technical environment.[2]

Franke was born in Troy, New York, on 15 April 1894, the son of William G. and Helen E. (Birrell) Franke. His father, a musician, could not afford to send him to college. After completing high school in Troy, Franke earned enough in various jobs to attend Pace Institute in New York City. Because his mother objected, he declined a congressman's offer of appointment to West Point. During one summer he worked on a newspaper; at other times, for the Cluett and Peabody Co., of Troy, and General Electric in Schenectady. Upon graduation from Pace he became a certified public accountant and in 1924 was elected to the American Institute of Certified Public Accountants and the New York State Society of Certified Public Accountants. After working with the firms of Touche, Niven, and Co., of New York City, and Narramore, Niles, and Co., of Rochester, he organized his own accounting firm, Franke, Hannon, and Withy, in 1929 in New York City.

On 28 June 1919, Franke married Bertha Irene Reedy, of Schenectady. They have three daughters.

During the 1930s and 1940s, when Franke served as a director of various corporations, he exposed inconsistencies in the financial records of several educational institutions, and his unusual abilities in the accounting field came to the attention of federal governmental officials. From 1948 to 1951 he served on the Army Comptrollers Civilian Panel, for which duty he was awarded the Patriotic Civilian Service Commendation. For his year as a Special Assistant to the Secretary of Defense, Robert A. Lovett, he received the Distinguished Service Award.[3]

Although Franke had served with the Truman administration, he was a Republican. When President Eisenhower appointed him as Assistant Secretary of the Navy for Financial Management and Comptroller of the Navy in October 1954, Charles Thomas, the Secretary, and Thomas Gates, the Under Secretary, were completing the Navy's budget for Fiscal Year 1956. Franke became responsible for taking that budget through the Pentagon maze before it went to the Bureau of the Budget and then to Congress. Meanwhile he also served on the "Doolittle Group" that closely examined the operations of the CIA. In his report, Lieutenant General James H. Doolittle gave the CIA a clean bill of health.[4]

Franke joined the Navy Department while revolutionary changes were occurring in the Navy—missiles for guns, nuclear for conventional power, and jets for propeller aircraft—and the policy of deterrence was replacing that of containment. New carriers were part of the last. The 1956 Navy budget provided for the fifth *Forrestal*-class carrier. When the 1957 budget proposed a sixth sister ship, Rear Admiral Hyman Rickover among others recommended that she be given nuclear power. However, cost, lead time, and reactor production problems combined to make a nuclear carrier in the 1957 program impractical.[5] While her cancellation made Franke's budget task easier and allowed thus for other ships, it was looked upon by many as a step backward. Instead of the CVAN, a conventional carrier, the U.S.S. *Constellation*, was authorized and funded.

As the 1957 budget was being prepared, Admiral Arleigh A. Burke, the Navy's new, dynamic Chief of Naval Operations, reported for duty. He and Franke would work together for almost six years.

Franke carried the 1958 budget, which called for a nuclear carrier, to the Secretary of Defense level while Burke took it into the "tank" of the Joint Chiefs of Staff to listen to the inevitable objections from the other services. Although a CVAN would be the most expensive ship in history, it had some congressional support as a prototype and as the backbone of all-nuclear task forces of the late 1960s and 1970s. Unfortunately, nine more years would pass before the second nuclear carrier would be authorized[6]—a victim in part of the inflation that took a continuing toll on the modernization of the United States fleet.

Franke's term as Under Secretary was marked by controversy over Defense Department organization and over the Defense Reorganization Act of 1958, the latter because it granted more power to the Secretary of Defense, while the Navy preferred to retain strong service departments. There was strong congressional support for the Navy's position whereas the President, the Secretary of Defense, and particularly the Department of the Air Force defended the new act.[7] Carl Vinson, Chairman of the House Armed Services Committee, had presided over the "revolt of the admirals" in 1949, opposed additional centralization of power in the Secretary of Defense, and worried lest service representatives who testified before him would again be muzzled. President Eisenhower told the Joint Chiefs of Staff they could testify freely. In consequence, at hearings on the Reorganization Plan, Burke and General Randolph Pate, Commandant of the Marine Corps, spoke strongly against certain parts of it.[8]

In anticipation of changes in the Defense Department, Admiral Burke told his Vice Chief of Naval Operations, Admiral James S. Russell, to draft modifications in the Office of the Chief of Naval Operations and suggested that "we might get the Secretary to start a Navy Department Board."[9] Shortly thereafter, Secretary Gates appointed Franke to head a Committee on Organization of the Department of the Navy. Its members included Admiral Russell; Lieutenant General Merrill B. Twining, Assistant Commandant of the Marine Corps; and John H. Dillon, the knowledgeable Administrative Assistant to the Secretary of the Navy, as recorder. After six months of study in which Franke obtained a firm grasp on problems of his own service, the Franke Board report was submitted early in 1959.[10] However, the board reported it was pleased with the Navy's bilinear organization and recommended that no major changes be made in the department. Instead of seeing the report as his swan song, as Franke put it, he himself would soon be the secretary and thus charged with implementing it. The Franke Report further solidified the under secretary as the business manager of the Department.

The Navy of 1959 was moving ahead in many directions: to advance sea sciences, create new naval weaponry, and provide nuclear propulsion for surface ships as well as for submarines. It was the year of Polaris, but progress occurred in other areas, as in plumbing deeper ocean depths, sailing into polar seas and under the icecaps, probing outer space, and conceiving novel aviation programs, while an orderly Fleet Rehabilitation and Modernization (FRAM) program added from five to eight years to the effective life of a large number of older ships.

When Franke took over from Gates, the Navy had 860 ships (386 warships and 474 supporting types), 16 carrier air groups, and 22 antisubmarine air squadrons. When the Eisenhower administration left office, naval strength had dropped to 812 ships (376 warships and 436 supporting types), the number of air groups had remained the same, and 9 additional antisubmarine air squadrons had been commissioned, an indication of the emphasis the Navy placed on antisubmarine warfare during Franke's term.[11]

Under Franke the fleets remained dispersed on a global basis—the Sixth in the Mediterranean, the Seventh in the Western Pacific, the First in the Eastern Pacific, and the Second in the Western Atlantic, the last two engaged in training.[12]

In May 1960, after the American U-2 pilot Gary Powers was downed and captured by the Soviets, relations with Russia became tense. For a short period Secretary of Defense Gates put his forces in a ready alert status.[13] Based on the results of this test of readiness, Admiral Burke directed Admiral Robert Lee Dennison, Commander in Chief Atlantic Fleet, and Admiral Herbert Hopwood, Commander in Chief Pacific Fleet, to get their respective Striking Fleets (Second and First) into improved states of readiness.[14] In July 1960 the readiness of the latter would again be degraded, however, when Gates, concerned about slippages in the Atlas Ballistic Missile program, requested the Navy to deploy a third attack carrier to each of the Sixth and Seventh Fleets. The Navy responded promptly, its additional nuclear capability filling in until the Air Force Atlas program was brought back on schedule.[15]

Submarine operations during Franke's term were marked by the submerged round-the-world cruise of the USS *Triton*, a record-breaking 46,000-mile voyage completed in eighty-four days. The USS *Skipjack*, first of a new class of streamlined-hull nuclear submarines, completed trials and was accorded a speed of better than thirty knots.[16] The USS *Sargo*, like her sister ship, the *Skate*, penetrated the Bering Straits in February 1960 and went onto the North Pole under the ice, proving that the Arctic route could be used in any season.[17] The day after Franke took office, the fleet ballistic missile submarine, the *George Washington*, was launched at the Electric Boat Co., Groton, Connecticut. A few months later the *Patrick Henry* was launched, followed by the *Robert E. Lee*, at Newport News, Virginia. All three ships were commissioned and the first two had commenced operational patrols by inauguration day of 1961. Meanwhile the converted tender *Proteus* had arrived at Holy Loch in the United Kingdom to start a Polaris base in the Eastern Atlantic and the Polaris missile had been successfully tested by the *George Washington*. As each new Polaris boat was commissioned, a series of firing tests was conducted off Cape Canaveral, Florida.

The Navy operationally entered the space programs by providing support for Project Mercury, the first orbit of a manned spacecraft. From headquarters at Norfolk, plans were made for the Atlantic Fleet to recover manned and unmanned space capsules.

Surface units cruised into distant operating areas in 1959 and 1960: into the Gulf of Guinea near the strife-torn Congo Republic; the Black Sea and the north coast of Turkey where U. S. intelligence sites kept watch on Soviet activity to the north; and the Antarctic. A new South Atlantic Force operated from the U.S. Naval Station in Trinidad, British West Indies, with ships rotated from the Atlantic Fleet. Operation Deep Freeze in the Antarctic seas continued to make extensive progress in hydrographic, meteorological, and oceanographic research.

In the summer of 1959, in New York, Franke reviewed a task force of the Atlantic Fleet that would transit the St. Lawrence Seaway after it was formally opened by President Eisenhower and Queen Elizabeth II. In the next year he visited overseas areas and observed both the Sixth and Seventh fleets at sea.

As with his predecessors, Franke faced the problems of a declining fleet material readiness caused by insufficient maintenance and high operating rates.[18] His attempted solution was to provide thorough overhauls, even if these were spaced at greater intervals, modernize various ships, and continue the FRAM program.[19]

Franke demanded carriers as well as Polaris boats, saying that carriers were vital in a limited as well as in a total war environment.[20]

Some of the men who helped Franke improve his department were old hands, some new. Experienced hands included the Under Secretary, Fred A. Bantz; the Assistant Secretary for Manpower and Reserve Affairs, Richard H. Jackson; and Franke's Administrative Assistant, John H. Dillon. New were Cecil P. Milne, who relieved Bantz, and James H. Wakelin, Jr., the first Assistant Secretary for Research and Development, who would serve for five years under three administrations and make significant contributions particularly in the oceanographic and antisubmarine warfare fields.

When Franke became Secretary he was already well acquainted with a large number of the Navy's flag officers. He strongly endorsed Secretary Gates's recommendation that Admiral Burke accept another and completely unprecedented third two-year term as Chief of Naval Operations. In the rapidly changing Navy and Defense departments as well as the turbulent international arena of the years 1959–1960, Burke's continuity was of inestimable value to the nation. As the successor to General Pate, who completed his second two-year term as Commandant of the Marine Corps when Franke became Secretary, Franke on 1 January 1960 chose Major General David Shoup, a World War II Medal of Honor winner.[21]

One of the most important changes made in consequence of the Franke Board Report on Navy Department reorganization was the new status given to research and development. Coincident with the creation of the post of an Assistant Secretary for this purpose, a new Deputy Chief of Naval Operations for Research and Development was appointed to head a division of Naval Operations, OP–07, that would centralize R&D administration and parallel the new DDR&E in the Defense Department. Under Wakelin and a young and vigorous Vice Admiral, John T. Hayward, the R&D functions previously in Naval Operations and in the various bureaus were concentrated and provided workable guidelines that still remain in effect.[22]

Another change Franke recommended and then implemented was the merger of the Bureau of Ordnance and the Bureau of Aeronautics into a new Bureau of Weapons. He thought this merger of material bureaus sufficient and criticized the 1963 reorganization that brought all the material bureaus into a super-bureau known as the Office of the Chief of Navy Material, in part because he had forecast its employment of thousands of people.[23]

Washington columnist Drew Pearson delighted in taking the Navy to task. In December 1959 his article entitled "Navy Secretary Seen as Pushover" accused Admiral Burke of undercutting his civilian bosses.[24] Burke vigorously denied the accusation and called the article "character assassination."[25] Whether coincidentally or not, shortly thereafter Secretary of Defense Gates reaffirmed civilian control and the naval bilinear chain of command by asserting that the civilian service secretaries would have a greater say in the making of defense policies.[26] Franke took Pearson's criticism and Gates's invitation to participate in high-level decision-making in stride, saying that "I think that we should scrap this expression 'Civilian Control' and substitute 'Civilian Management.' The responsibilities run in both directions—from the bottom to the top and from the top to the bottom. If this is understood and made effective, a capable civilian who becomes the head of a military service need have no concern as to whether or not he is *controlling* his department."[27]

To many Washington observers, Eisenhower's promotion of Gates, as Deputy Secretary of Defense on 15 May 1959, signaled greater naval influence and possible dominance in the operations of the mammoth department. Actually the opposite proved true: on occasion Gates went out of his way to insure that he would not be accused of naval bias.

In the summer of 1959 an interservice disagreement fought out in the press as well as in the Pentagon concerned the amount of deterrent power the United States required. The Army and the Navy argued for a finite deterrent force as part of the nation's strategy. The Air Force clamored for additional nuclear weapons and delivery systems and sought control over Polaris submarines on station. Writers in such publications as the *Air University Quarterly*, *Air Force*, and *Aviation Week* spoke of preemptive war as the only counter to nuclear defeat and national disaster.[28] A possible Berlin crisis in May 1959 evaporated that fall when the Soviet Premier, Nikita Khrushchev, paid a visit to the United States. However, by the spring of 1960, in the wake of the loss of a U–2 over Russia, international tension increased as the Russian leader did his spectacular shoe-pounding act at the United Nations. Through all of this President Eisenhower tried to steer a safe but economically sane course and pledged that he would avoid the "Red spending trap" advocated by some influential congressmen.[29]

Gates made headlines when he became the Secretary of Defense, in December 1959, by stating that he would solve split decisions of the Joint Chiefs of Staff. By exercising his statutory authority, he would thus assert civilian control.[30] He soon took an active part in the Navy-Air Force dispute over operational control of Polaris submarines on station. His solution was to create in Omaha the Joint Strategic Planning Staff headed by the commander of the Strategic Air Command but with a Vice Admiral as Deputy Commander, and direct that it report to the Joint Chiefs of Staff. Further, to improve the command of retaliatory forces and to a lesser extent of limited war forces, in 1960 he integrated overlapping service communications systems into the Defense Communications Agency, first directed by Rear Admiral W. D. Irvin. A special case involved the agency's command posts. The Army had a hardened command post at Fort Ritchie, Maryland, which served as an alternate to the Pentagon for the Secretary of Defense and the Joint Chiefs of Staff. Late in Franke's term other fleet and airborne command posts were established. Assigned responsibility for providing an alternate command post afloat, the Navy created the National Emergency Command Post Afloat (NECPA), soon comprising two command ships, the USS *Northampton* and the USS *Wright*, each prepared on short notice to receive the National Command Authorities and serve as a mobile headquarters, most difficult to target, for the President and his senior advisers.[31]

The nuclear deterrent age provoked the centralization of command and control. Would the need for such control result in a chief of staff system the Navy had always opposed because it would lessen if not end civilian control? To the Navy's relief, Gates as Secretary of Defense saw things as Franke did.

Franke's great interest in personnel was appreciated and reciprocated by those in the naval service, including the writer. Knowing that the Navy's most precious asset is its personnel, throughout his Pentagon career he wrestled with the same problem his predecessors had faced and successors would encounter —how to keep enough trained personnel in an ever more technical Navy.

Naval strength dropped from 626,000 to 617,000 men in Franke's first year, then climbed to 627,000 by the end of fiscal year 1961. Reenlistment rates for first term Navy men averaged 21 percent, not what the Navy desired but somewhat better than in earlier and later years.[32] Unfortunately, reenlistment in the technical ratings was considerably lower, necessitating more training billets and a longer pipeline from schools to the fleet. Officer strength remained fairly constant as the Navy followed the twin programs of earlier retirements for older officers and greater emphasis on the retention of young officers upon completion of their obligated service.

In the summer of 1959, Navy Retention Boards screened out 265 captains, thus making room for additional promotions and paving the way for swifter advancement from the lower ranks. At the same time Congress gave in to Army and Air Force pressure and rescinded the "Tombstone" provision unique in the Navy Personnel Act that authorized officers decorated for gallantry in combat to be advanced one grade upon retirement.[33] Almost coincidentally, congressional committees began investigating the number of retired officers, many in the flag and general officer grades, who were being employed at high salaries by defense industries. President Eisenhower's phrase, "The military-industrial complex," became a catchword in these investigations.

The early retirement of many captains at a time when additional officers of top caliber were needed in the Defense Department put a severe strain on the Bureau of Personnel's detailing system. The captain detail officer of this period once remarked that "My task is simple. I must assign only those officers in the 'top ten per cent' to ninety nine percent of the billets."[34]

Franke's reorganization study of 1958 had recommended that a new Technical Corps be formed to include specialist officers who could not succeed to command at sea. Gates rejected the recommendation. Franke tried in 1959 to differentiate between the command line and technical line by letting officers authorized to command at sea wear the star above their rank insignia on sleeve or shoulder boards and special duty officers to wear a star surrounded by a thin circle. When engineering duty flag officers objected, Franke authorized a "Command at Sea" device for officers in command or who had successfully completed a sea tour in command.[35]

Franke continued the Navy's Moral Leadership program instituted by Gates and like his predecessor wrestled with the reenlistment problem. In the summer of 1960, he inaugurated a new Selective Training and Retention program (STAR) in which qualified first term enlistees were guaranteed formal schooling and specific advancements for at least seven years of service. Hopefully, at the end of seven years the Navy man would consider the service his career. In the program's first year, six thousand applications, primarily in the critical electronic and fire control ratings, were approved.[36]

Besides the "Year of Polaris," Franke's first year could also be called the "Year of the Computers" because the Navy made significant advances in the automatic data processing field both tactically and administratively. In the personnel area the Naval Manpower Information System matured and early in 1961 its operations were extended to include the Naval Reserve.[37]

As Franke's term neared its end, the administration began trying to reduce the number of overseas dependents. Known as the "Gold Dollar Widow" program, it was instituted by Secretary of Defense Gates. Although its purpose was to reduce the unfavorable balance of payments, it immediately aroused a feeling of resentment throughout the services. No other government department had such a policy, and American industries and tourists continued to pour their currency into foreign treasuries. The Navy was less involved than the Army and Air Force, but a continuation of the order would eliminate a real benefit for the Navy's married personnel—a tour overseas accompanied by families. Franke of course obeyed the directive, with the result that after 1 February 1961 few Navy dependents went abroad.[38]

Admiral Burke used to say that Navy people needed to have more fun and enjoy themselves. That this was still possible was revealed on the day of the Army-Navy football game of 1960, when a large "Beat Army" sign was seen hanging from Franke's Pentagon office window and over the window of the office of his Army counterpart two decks below. While the culprits, two yeomen from Franke's office, were congratulated, Burke bemoaned to Franke that the removal of the sign by guards was one of the "signs of the times in which we live."[39] As Franke prepared to turn his office over to John Connally, Burke gave him a farewell party and with due ceremony made him a member of his own Naval Academy Class of 1923, an honor accorded to few.[40]

The list of research and development programs Franke called for in his first annual report laid the groundwork for the Navy's R&D efforts for the next decade.[41] Meanwhile undersea warfare drew closer to antisubmarine warfare as the attack submarines of the *Skipjack* and later classes became primarily antisubmarine submarines. New passive sonars with classification equipment, and a new long-range submarine tactical missile system, SUBROC, were developed. By the end of Franke's term, nineteen Polaris boats were authorized.

Much of the criticism of the Navy's antisubmarine program in the press and in Congress was generated by the Air Force, which wanted the Navy restricted to limited war roles. In September 1959, Franke and Burke met with Secretary of Defense McElroy to discuss countermeasures for a new threat, the Soviet submarine-launched ballistic missile (SLBM), the counterpart of Polaris. Although the Air Force wished to use SAC in the antisubmarine field, Admiral Burke quickly stated that defense against the SLBM was strictly a Navy responsibility.[42] Shortly thereafter Franke directed Burke to form a Navy Antisubmarine Warfare Committee he himself would chair and which would examine all facets of the antisubmarine problem.[43] A nucleus staff for this committee was already working under Rear Admiral Lloyd Mustin in Burke's office. Other members of the committee came from the operational, material, and research segments of the department. A most active member would be the new Assistant Secretary for R&D, James Wakelin, who was backed up by staff members of the new OP-07. Shortly after the committee was formed, Franke directed the establishment of the Atlantic Undersea Test and Evaluation Range at Anders Island in the Bahamas.[44] As the year was ending, Admiral Jerauld Wright, Commander in Chief Atlantic, warned that within the year the Soviets would be able to place missile-firing submarines off the East Coast.[45] Franke questioned this estimate, stating that Congress would be most interested in the new date, which differed from a previous estimate of 1963.[46] Franke took an intense personal interest in the work of this committee as it examined all facets of the problem and looked ahead to future developments. Among the latter were a powerful new surface ship sonar, the SQS-26, improved sonar buoys and aircraft magnetic detection gear, ASROC, a new drone helicopter known as DASH, and new designs for destroyer escorts.

In surface warfare, the Navy program called for developing an inexpensive surface-to-surface missile to replace guns in destroyers and other surface ships. While three frigates, four guided missile destroyers, and four destroyer escorts came onto the building ways during Franke's term, Franke strongly advocated nuclear power for surface ships as well as for submarines. With the cruiser *Long Beach* and frigate *Bainbridge* under construction, in 1960 he demanded additional nuclear frigates. However, the fiscal year 1962 budget, which was approved by the new Kennedy administration, included only one nuclear frigate, the *Truxtun*, and six conventional ships.[47] The construction of the *Long Beach* was delayed by strikes, with the result that she was not commissioned until late in 1961. While the first modernized FRAM destroyers joined the fleet, only one carrier, the *America*, was programmed during Franke's term because Eisenhower suggested waiting for test results from the *Enterprise* before going ahead with additional nuclear power. (The *Enterprise* proved herself during the Cuban missile crisis of 1962 and later off Vietnam.) Franke agreed in general with Eisenhower, but many congressmen and Admiral Rickover objected on the ground that a conventional carrier was a step backwards in modernizing the fleet.[48] The carrier as a weapons system was improved when new aircraft equipped with the Sidewinder air-to-air missile were assigned to fleet carriers, and the first of the WF-2 Tracers, carrier-airborne early warning planes, was completed. Franke vetoed the Missileer program, a ponderous air-to-air missile for fleet air defense to be carried by relatively slow carrier aircraft.[49]

Few logistic support ships had joined the fleet since World War II, and those that remained were inefficient in serving a modernized combatant fleet. A new class of fast replenishment ship, the Fast Combat Support Ship (AOE) began with the USS *Sacramento*. This class carried all types of stores, fuel, and ammunition and had speed enough to operate with fast carriers. A new class of Combat Stores Ship (AFS), with the USS *Mars* as the prototype, would make extensive use of helicopters for replenishment at sea.

Franke objected to the placing of Polaris missiles in the nuclear cruiser *Long Beach* and other cruisers because of costs approximating $60 million per ship and because of the dilution of the primary mission of these air defense/surface defense craft.[50] Overall, Franke's shipbuilding program remained small largely because of Eisenhower's policy of balancing the national economy against our military posture.

The U.S. Marine Corps, 200,000 strong and comprising a quarter of Franke's department, was protected from decimation by Navy General Order No. 5 and by congressional legislation. The Commandant of the Corps, Randolph Pate, displeased McElroy by opposing additional centralization in the Defense Department and irritated some naval and Marine leaders by his traditional staff approach to decision-making.[51] In January 1960, his relief, General David Shoup, brought a new atmosphere to Corps Headquarters with his "cut the red tape" method. However, he raised many naval and Marine eyebrows by supporting the attempt of the Air Force to acquire control over Polaris boats on station.[52]

The Marines normally had two divisions and air wings in the Pacific, one division and air wing in the Atlantic, and three battalion landing teams embarked in ready amphibious shipping. One battalion was with the Sixth Fleet, one with the Seventh, and one operated in the Caribbean, where the new Castro government in Cuba was daily giving the United States concern. As

Franke's term was ending, Castro had whipped his supporters into a frenzy of invasion fears. Franke had the Caribbean Marine Battalion land in Guantánamo Bay for "recreation," sent the carrier *Franklind D. Roosevelt* to undertake "routine training" off Guantánamo, and also instituted a patrol to prevent Castro supporters from landing in Guatemala to promote revolution there.[53] When press reports noted that the Joint Chiefs of Staff had recommended that the United States move into Cuba to protect it from communism,[54] Premier Khrushchev warned the United States to keep hands off.

The Navy–Marine Corps team, proven so successful in the 1958 Lebanon operation, continued training at home and overseas and engaged in such operations as *Solant Amity*, a small force kept off the coast of West Africa in 1960 and 1961.[55]

Marine Corps personnel problems closely paralleled those of the Navy. The cancellation of the "tombstone" law by Congress brought some early retirements of senior Marine officers, and congressional investigators looked carefully at the civilian employment being offered to them, particularly to those in the general officer grades. The moral leadership program prescribed by General Order No. 21 was emphasized throughout the Corps. Although budgetary limitations forced a cutback in the strength of the Marine Corps Reserve, programs to expand the Marine Corps Limited Duty and Warrant Officer rosters in order to retain technical personnel were successful.

Franke took no part in the campaign of Vice President Richard Nixon as he competed for the presidency with Senator John Kennedy. After Kennedy won, Franke forwarded the naval budget for 1962—the eighth budget in which he had been involved—and saw the Navy rather than the Army and Air Force take all the cuts.[56] He and Burke objected to Gates, unsuccessfully, and then told Eisenhower that the cuts would slow down the Navy's modernization.[57] Moreover, $75 million extra was needed to rebuild the new carrier *Constellation*, struck by a disastrous fire as she was fitting out for sea. The problem was left for resolution to Kennedy's Secretary of Defense, Robert S. McNamara, and to Franke's relief, John Connally.

Franke left office on 20 January 1961 and returned to civil life. According to a veteran Capitol Hill reporter, "The Secretary was liked by Congress who thought of him as a fairminded and sound-thinking official who showed a keen respect for the role and the influence of Congress."[58] The *Army and Navy Journal* saluted him with the statement that he "has presented the seapower doctrine to Congress with brilliant skill."[59] Although Kennedy changed the top leadership in the Defense Department, the flag officers who directed fleet operations during the Cuban missile crisis and the Polaris force were those Franke had been instrumental in choosing.

From his retirement in Rutland, Vermont, Franke wrote about his years in the Navy Department for the U.S. Naval Institute *Proceedings*. He believed that judgment was the greatest quality a senior executive must have, judgment to make the difficult decisions brought to him. As he noted, all the easy decisions were made at lower levels: only the hard ones reached the top of his organization. His answer to how one learns the quality of judgment is a good example of the man. He wrote: "The one word more applicable than all others is patience, patience to study, patience to listen to briefings, patience to confer with professional and informed military people. And when all this patience has been exercised, there must be courage to make the decision."[60]

NOTES

1. The *George Washington* (SSBN-598), *Patrick Henry* (SSBN-599) and *Robert E. Lee* (SSBN-601) were in commission; the *Theodore Roosevelt* (SSBN-600) and *Abraham Lincoln* (SSBN-602) were outfitting; and nine ships of the *Ethan Allen* and *Lafayette* classes were on the building ways.
2. Graduation Address, Under Secretary William B. Franke, U. S. Naval Academy, 7 June 1957.
3. *Current Biography*, 1959, s.v. "Franke, William Birrell."
4. *Ibid.*
5. Secretary Charles Thomas to Senator Henry Jackson, 6 Dec. 1955, SNP.
6. Secretary Charles Thomas to ADM Arleigh Burke, 2 Feb. 1956; Burke to Thomas, 27, 29 Mar. 1956, *ibid.* The USS *Nimitz* (CVAN-68) was not authorized until fiscal year 1967.
7. Debriefing notes, Armed Forces Policy Council Meeting, ADM Arleigh Burke, 15 Apr. 1958, NHD:OA, Personal Papers of Arleigh A. Burke.
8. Debriefing notes, White House discussions, 25 Apr. 1958, *ibid.*
9. Memorandum from ADM Burke to ADM James S. Russell, 2 May 1958, *ibid.*
10. James C. Elliott, "Profile: William B. Franke," *Navy*, July 1959, pp. 9–10.
11. ARSN, 1960, 1961.
12. Ships of the Atlantic and Pacific Fleets that were not deployed to Europe or the Western Pacific and were not in overhaul or in basic refresher training, were normally available for assignment to the First and Second fleets, less those assigned to the fleet antisubmarine warfare forces and special missions. Because of upkeep and leave requirements, extra deployments, and slippages in overhauls, more often that not the First and Second fleets were skeleton organizations.
13. "Gates Calls Alert from Paris," *Washington Post*, 17 May 1960.
14. Message from CNO to Fleet Commanders in Chief, 3 June 1960, Burke Papers.
15. Debriefing notes, conference between SECDEF and ADM Burke, 9 July 1960, *ibid.*
16. "To Sea in USS *Skipjack*," *Washington Post*, 1 Oct. 1959.
17. ARSN, 1960, p. 234.
18. *Ibid.*, p. 249.

19. *Ibid.*, p. 205.
20. Speech to National Convention of the Navy League of the United States by Secretary Franke, 6 May 1950, Anaheim, Calif., copy in SNP.
21. "New Marine Corps Commandant," *Washington Post*, 13 Aug. 1959.
22. Memorandum from Secretary Franke to CNO and others, 10 Sept. 1959, SECNAV Instruction of 11 Dec. 1959—Mutual Weapons Development Program, SNP; "Development of Executive Relationships within the Navy," *Navy Management Review*, No. 10.
23. William B. Franke, Comment and Discussion, *"Civilian Control of the Navy,"* USNIP 90 (Feb. 1964):106.
24. "Washington Merry Go Round," *Washington Post*, 19 Dec. 1959.
25. Memorandum for Record, ADM Arleigh Burke, 19 Dec. 1959, Burke Papers.
26. Report on press conference held by the new SECDEF, *Baltimore Sun*, 3 Dec. 1959.
27. Franke, "Civilian Control of the Navy," 109.
28. COL R. C. Richardson, "Do We Need Unlimited Forces for Limited War?" AF (Mar. 1959), pp. 53–56.
29. "Are We Overconfident?" *Washington Post*, 7 Mar. 1959. (President Eisenhower used the term "Red Spending Trap" in connection with Russian moves against Berlin a year before the U-2 incident.)
30. "Capitol Hill," *Navy*, Jan. 1960.
31. Debriefing notes, ADM Arleigh Burke. Discussion by the Joint Chiefs of Staff on a National Emergency Command Post Afloat, 16 Oct. 1960, Burke Papers.
32. ARSN, 1960, p. 260.
33. "Navy to Lose Tombstone Promotions," *Washington Star*, 3 Aug. 1959.
34. CAPT F. M. Radel, USN, personal memorandum to the writer, 6 June 1974.
35. Interview with VADM W. P. Mack, USN, former senior aide to Secretary Franke, 1 May 1974.
36. ARSN, 1961, p. 224.
37. "Washington Merry Go Round," *Washington Post*, 22 Feb. 1960.
38. "Franke Guidance on Dependent Reductions," *Navy Times*, 14 Jan. 1961.
39. Memorandum from ADM Burke to Secretary Franke, 25 Nov. 1960, Burke Papers.
40. Conversation by the writer with ADM Arleigh Burke, 8 June 1974.
41. ARSN, 1960, p. 232.
42. Debriefing notes, ADM Arleigh Burke. Discussion with Air Force Chief of Staff, 3 Sept. 1959, Burke Papers.
43. SECNAV Franke directive to CNO, 9 Nov. 1959, *ibid.*
44. SECNAV Franke directive to CNO and Chief BUSHIPS, 16 Nov. 1959, copy in *ibid.*
45. Speech by ADM Jerauld Wright, Supreme Allied Commander Atlantic and Commander in Chief, Atlantic Fleet, Norfolk, Va., 20 Nov. 1959.
46. SECNAV Franke memorandum to CNO, 25 Nov. 1959, Burke Papers.
47. Interview with VADM W. P. Mack, USN, former senior aide to Secretary Franke, 1 May 1974.
48. Report on press conference with Under Secretary Franke, *San Diego Union*, 8 Feb. 1959.

49. ADM Burke memorandum to Secretary Franke, 9 Sept. 1959, and resultant briefing on *Misseleer* weapons system, SNP.

50. Interview with VADM W. P. Mack, USN, former senior aide to Secretary Franke, 1 May 1974.

51. Debriefing notes, ADM Arleigh Burke, Armed Forces Policy Council Meeting, 20 Nov. 1959, Burke Papers.

52. "Navy-Marine Split," *Washington Star*, 24 July 1960.

53. "Caribbean Patrol," *Washington Post*, 11 Jan. 1961.

54. "Pentagon Report," *Washington Star*, 16 July 1960.

55. ARSN, 1960, p. 254; ARSN, 1961, p. 215.

56. Memorandum from ADM Burke to Secretary Franke, 6 Dec. 1960, Burke Papers.

57. Debriefing notes, ADM Burke, discussions with Secretary Gates and Secretary Franke, 8 Dec. 1960; Debriefing notes, National Security Council meeting, 8 Dec. 1960, *ibid.*

58. "Capitol Hill," *Navy*, Jan. 1961.

59. Editorial, "Changing the Guard in the Pentagon," ANAFJ, 14 Jan. 1961.

60. Franke, "Civilian Control over the Navy," 108.

JOHN B. CONNALLY

20 January 1961–20 December 1961

PAUL R. SCHRATZ

John Bowden Connally was born on Floresville, Texas, on 27 February 1917. He graduated from the University of Texas in 1941 with a law degree. President of the Athenaeum Literary Society and the Curtain Club, he won the Inter-Society Oratorical Contest and was no less persuasive in his courtship of Idanell Brill, whom he married on 21 December 1940. The Connallys have three surviving children.

Commissioned an ensign in the U.S. Naval Reserve on 11 June 1941, he reported for duty in the Office of the Chief of Naval Operations and in January 1942 was assigned to the Office of Under Secretary of the Navy James Forrestal, where he dealt with problems of training and manpower. In February 1943, as a member of the staff of General Dwight D. Eisenhower, he was sent to Algiers to assist in planning the Italian invasion.

Following specialized training in radar, he was assigned to the USS *Essex* (CV-9), which won the Presidential Unit Citation for heroic service in the Pacific during the period 31 August 1943 until 15 August 1945. As Radar and Radio Officer, later Fighter Director Officer of that aircraft carrier, he participated in action in the Gilberts, Marshalls, Marianas, Philippines, Formosa, China Sea, Bonins, Ryukyus, and Japan during the latter period of the war. He was observed to be an "extremely outstanding officer" by Rear Admiral T. L. Sprague, USN, in command of Task Group 38.1, who said "his work was, in great part, responsible for the success of the Task Group."

Connally was awarded the Bronze Star Medal with Combat "V," and the Legion of Merit with Combat "V" "for exceptionally meritorious conduct . . . as Force Fighter Director Officer on board the USS *Essex*, Flagship of Task

Force 58, from 7 July 1944 to 26 June 1945; and later as Task Group Fighter Director of the Staff of Commander Fast Carrier Task Group 39.1, with Flag in the USS *Bennington* during operations against enemy Japanese forces at sea and against the Japanese mainland from 26 June to 28 August 1945."

Detached from the *Essex* in November 1945, he was released from active duty with the rank of lieutenant commander on 3 January 1946. He remained a member of the Naval Reserve (inactive) until 1954.

Returning to Texas, he and several other veterans organized radio station KVET in Austin, Texas, with Connally serving as president and general manager from 1946 to 1949. Here he began a lifelong association with Lyndon B. Johnson, initially as administrative assistant to the newly-elected Senator in Washington. Later in 1949, Connally joined the law firm of Powell, Wirtz and Rauhart, in Austin, where he practiced law until 1952. Under senior partner and former Under Secretary of the Interior Alvin Wirtz, Connally acquired the old-fashioned rural liberalism of Wirtz, suspicious of organized labor but strongly in favor of federal aid for dams, rural electrification, and irrigation. A strong Democrat, Connally in June 1951 refused to attend a banquet held for Douglas MacArthur, who was on a speaking tour seeking conservative Democratic backing for a presidential bid.

Upon Wirtz's death in late 1951, Connally became the attorney and later executor for conservative oil millionaire Sid Richardson. Growing more conservative under Richardson's influence, Connally supported Republican Dwight D. Eisenhower for the Presidency in 1952. He remained with Richardson until his appointment by the Kennedy Administration, in 1961, after having managed the Lyndon Johnson campaign against Kennedy in the primaries. Representing big oil interests of Texas millionaires such as Richardson made Connally a wealthy man; he also possessed the debonair charm and flexibility to adapt to the pattern of the Ivy League or the Boston Irish.

For two years before the election of 1960, Senator Kennedy among others had been critical of American defense strategy and its overdependence on nuclear retaliatory forces. Such a strategy, he stated, left the choice only of "all or nothing at all, world devastation or submission," a choice that necessarily caused hesitation "on the brink," with the initiative in the hands of the enemy. Nuclear weapons had not been used in "brush fire wars" from Korea to Laos. Nor could they "prevent the Communists from gradually nibbling away at the fringe of the Free World's territory and strength, until security has been steadily eroded in piecemeal fashion."[1] Containment of communism therefore required speedy, flexible, and versatile conventional forces that would keep a war limited. The concept and development of such conventional forces for a "flexible response," which General Maxwell Taylor and others had been advocating, became the cornerstone of Kennedy's defense policies.

Herein lay both the opportunity and the need to design new ways of looking at our force structures and weapon systems; of balancing increases in the power and versatility of strategic nuclear forces with the expansion of conventional forces; and of reducing, postponing, or eliminating programs of marginal or dubious effectiveness. The alleged "missile gap" and the "inadequacy" of America's preparedness for dealing with limited war had made lively presidential campaign material in 1960; the Democratic Party platform contained, in addition, a commitment to a complete examination of the organization of the Armed Forces.

The "two primary and related objectives" flowing from the above were, first, to obtain a defense adequate to protect the nation and enable it to discharge its international responsibilities, and second, to obtain such defense "within the framework of a free and solvent economic system." The realization of both objectives depended upon finding a Secretary of Defense and service secretaries who were responsive to the Kennedy style of leadership. His search for "cool" intellectual leaders who could manage rather than be managed by the office was in itself unusual.

The choice of Robert McNamara as Defense Secretary seemed precisely to suit the man to the task. It was also a prelude to revolution. In fact, McNamara wrought two revolutions, one in strategic doctrine, one in the method of making decisions. The first was the "flexible response"; the second, the "cost effectiveness" technique.

McNamara violated tradition by taking an active rather than passive role. Instead of relying upon underlings to make decisions for him, he would decide.[2] In consequence, while the role of the military leadership changed from preoccupation with service problems to a concentration of joint issues, the role of the service secretary changed most of all.

By 1961 the National Security Act, as amended, deleted the service secretaries from the cabinet, the National Security Council, and from the chain of operational command and subjected them to the authority, control, and direction of the Secretary of Defense and Deputy Secretary of Defense. In his *formal* role, a service secretary was limited to a managerial responsibility for organizing, training, and equipping Navy and Marine Corps forces for service in the unified combat commands. He also retained, as a check and balance on military policy matters, the right of direct access to the President and Congress "on his own initiative, after first informing the Secretary of Defense, any recommendation relating to the Department of Defense that he may deem proper." His *informal* role in both executive and operational matters, however, varied widely with the particular skills and abilities of the office holders.

Although McNamara initially viewed the service secretary as somewhat anachronistic, circumstances forced him to recognize him, first as useful, and later as essential, in a wholly unanticipated role. In keeping with his activist role, he insisted on choosing his own service secretaries.

President-elect Kennedy promised Franklin D. Roosevelt, Jr., the Navy office but McNamara did not feel that Roosevelt met the requirements he envisioned. His own talent search had uncovered a great many brilliant young activists soon to be known throughout the world as "whiz kids." Neither Franklin D. Roosevelt, Jr., nor John Connally fitted this image.

While managing Lyndon Johnson's presidential campaign, Connally was responsible for publicizing the rumor that Kennedy suffered from Addison's disease (proved to be untrue) and that Kennedy's father as Ambassador to Britain had been less than completely anti-Nazi in his political beliefs (greatly exaggerated). Contrary to popular belief, Connally was not a Lyndon Johnson nominee; he was one of several suggested for a high office in the administration by Sam Rayburn. However, Connally fitted the McNamara plan for a quite different reason. To strengthen control over the Defense Department, McNamara wanted no "whiz kid" professional manager to head the services. Unification of the military side of Defense was not necessarily in his interest. Contrary to the implication of the 1958 Reorganization, McNamara centralized only the managerial or business side of Defense; he was content with patronage appointments over the services as long as they facilitated his control on a divide and conquer principle.

McNamara also wished to prevent the naval leadership from undercutting his authority via a traditional end run to a sympathetic naval ear in the White House. The naval secretary's chair, therefore, required not a Franklin D. Roosevelt, Jr., nor any other close friend of the President, but the least enthusiastic Kennedy supporter in government. Connally was therefore a natural choice even if it greatly displeased Kennedy.

Connally's path to confirmation met an obstacle in the form of a possible conflict of interest. Senator William Proxmire, a Wisconsin liberal and Armed Services Committee watchdog, vigorously opposed his nomination because his long and intimate association with the Texas oil industries as attorney and lobbyist seemed to be in clear conflict with his leadership of the oil industry's biggest customer, the U.S. Navy. An officer or director in twenty-seven major corporations, he also received $75,000 annually for services as executor of the Richardson estate. (His salary for administering the Navy and its $14 billion annual budget was a modest $22,000. Financial gain was hardly a major inducement to his federal appointment.) On the day of the confirmation hearings on 18 January 1961—two days before the Kennedy inaugural—columnist Drew Pearson castigated Connally for his alleged role in the passage of a natural gas bill. After some delay, however, Connally was confirmed with only the Proxmire vote in opposition and took his oath of office on 25 January 1961, his two close friends, Lyndon Johnson and Sam Rayburn, sharing the honor.

Connally was to serve as naval secretary for less than a year. Like other new Pentagon officeholders, he found no honeymoon in which to become familiar with his duties. Unwilling to act as either judge or spectator amid service problems, McNamara stated on 24 January 1961 his basic thesis that "I'm here to originate and stimulate new ideas and programs, not just to referee arguments." Commencing on Inauguration Day, he raised difficult questions and demanded quantitative answers to them.

Four task forces in McNamara's office went to work on the most immediate and important issues: strategic and continental air defense forces, requirements for limited war situations, a review of all major research and development projects, and an examination of military bases aiming at possible reductions. On the basis of these reports, the first supplement to the 1962 budget was prepared by the services and analyzed in Defense. A program of inquiry and possible reform was spelled out in 99 special projects, later growing to 131. Each raised a question about how things were done in a particular area, and how they could be done better. They ranged from fundamental questions of politico-military strategy to detailed questions of procurement. Many invaded the bone and marrow of service functions and brought serious internal difficulties. The Navy leadership in particular, perennially able to frustrate too close Defense supervision, viewed McNamara with increasing apprehension.

Running strongly contrary to ground rules governing responsibilities long believed to be sacred service preserves, the reception of McNamara's procedures was in many cases less than enthusiastic. Many of the questions needed investigation and were a Defense responsibility; others were believed to be subordinate responsibilities. In these cases, friction was inevitable. Connally and his Army and Air Force counterparts claimed that investigation of such issues by Assistant Secretaries of Defense shortcircuited the statutory authority of the service secretary. Protests were not accepted, however, and Connally soon came into serious differences of opinion with the Defense leadership.

Over sometimes strong objections, McNamara directed that service functions in intelligence, supply, procurement, and communications be unified, combined, or eliminated. Force structures and budgeting processes were to be analyzed on a five-year rather than on an annual planning base; a programming-planning-budgeting system was installed which, with cost-effectiveness procedures, aimed at single manager control. The waxing tide of assistant secretaries eagerly and willingly accepted widespread lines of authority, too often at the expense of the authority of the service secretaries. Whenever service planning faltered over roles, missions, and in particular over force levels or budget, the assistant secretaries constituted an eager alternate source of plans. The mush-rooming superstructure was sanctioned in the law only as "aides and military assistants" for the Secretary of Defense. Equipped with neither administrative personnel nor experience for detailed staff work, the assistant secretaries never-theless developed what soon became a *de facto* general staff numbering 1,600 civilian and military officials. At least potentially, they constituted an alternate source of planning to the armed services and the JCS, an item of particular concern where the respective views of military and civilian leaders might dis-agree. The civilian authority in the Office of the Secretary of Defense took on special significance even with respect to military planning and operations.

The existence of the eight unified commands under direct operational con-trol of the Defense Secretary and his assistants, subject to JCS authority only by delegation of the Secretary, somewhat resembled the War Department and its uncoordinated bureau system before the Root reforms of 1903. The similar-ity can be carried too far, but the absence of a commanding general was the major contrast between the contemporary trend in the Defense Department and the pre-Root War Department.[3]

While the Defense organization was changed slowly by legislative amend-ments in 1949, 1953 and 1958, Kennedy sought to achieve his goals overnight by administrative manipulation, using to the full the authority already granted by the Congress but not previously used. Senator Stuart Symington recom-mended to the President-elect far-reaching changes toward the centralization of Defense, including the elimination of the service departments, granting vast new powers in the Secretary of Defense, creating a highly centralized and uni-fied military staff organization, and adopting a unified budget process under the Secretary of Defense to whom Congress would appropriate all defense funds, some on a multi-year basis.

The Symington recommendations were ignored by the President and Con-gress. Under such a climate of opinion, however, it was no easy task for Con-nally to function effectively in his new role. Nevertheless, from his first day in office he immersed himself in the major and far-reaching changes to the Penta-gon structure then emerging. He visualized himself as "an unbiased person, well enough informed to make judgments, and sufficiently objective not to reject new concepts and ideas." Quick to learn, he soon established an excellent repu-tation with the Navy. Problems with the Defense leadership were of a different order. His coolness with the White House was a matter of record; tempera-mentally he was ill at ease with the liberal idealism and programs of the New Frontier. A conservative by instinct and a moderate by circumstance, Connally had always visualized the Navy as the traditionally conservative yet glamorous branch of the armed services. He saw a clear challenge in his appointment and looked forward to his duties with zest.

The fleet Connally inherited from outgoing Secretary William Franke consisted of 817 ships (of which 383 were combatants) and 6,800 aircraft. These were supported by a network of 222 major U.S. and 53 foreign bases, and served by 619,000 military and 650,000 civilian employees. The glamor of the sea service was epitomized in its blunt, outspoken yet most outstanding Chief of Naval Operations, Admiral Arleigh A. Burke, USN, who was then completing an unprecedented (and final) sixth year in office.

Admiral Burke made an unusual effort to prepare Connally for his duties from the day of his arrival in town. Living at Admiral's House with Burke while househunting in Washington, Connally drove to work with the CNO early each morning and returned with him late at night. Burke was willing to brief him on numerous items which rarely reached the Secretary's ear. After only three days in office, however, Connally informed Burke of his plans to run in the forthcoming campaign for governor of Texas. Burke learned with dismay that his special efforts had been devoted to an interim appointee. The information was not made public, however, and the CNO-Secretary relationship remained harmonious.

Before immersing himself in the supplemental budget already demanding his attention, Connally, with Admiral Burke, made a short, ceremonial visit to naval facilities in the Norfolk Tidewater area, the first of several visits with the operating forces. Connally enjoyed great success with the fleet, creating the impression always as the epitome of the distinguished and knowledgeable civilian leader. But it was in Washington that his innate skills would be thoroughly tested. The Kennedy program supported sizable increases in conventional forces but compensated by cutting in other areas. Insiders soon learned that Connally was a hard fighter for programs he considered worthy, but willing to scrap those he believed impractical. One of the latter was the lighter-than-air fleet. Within ninety days of assuming office, he made the hard choice in a disclosure—even while stressing the importance of antisubmarine warfare—of plans to deflate the blimp fleet, keeping only two for research purposes.

Connally was deeply interested in the Navy's role in the national space effort. In late March 1961, he assured a House committee that he had the support of Secretary McNamara for Navy space programs and told the committee of his opposition to a controversial Pentagon directive assigning most space research to the Air Force. He testified forcefully and effectively that space was not a program but a medium and neither an end nor an objective in itself. When questioned by the committee as to whether he had "resisted" the McNamara directive, Connally said, "I would not use the word 'resist,' but we resisted it, to use your word, by attempting to make constructive suggestions that were not completely in accord with the directive."[4] Whether a slip of the tongue or tongue in cheek, the impact was clear.

The first major Navy development program under Secretary Connally provided a good example of the new Defense methods in making development decisions. It also brought into the open the widening conflict over the traditional role of the Navy Secretary and the Secretary of Defense. The problem was one which persisted throughout and beyond the McNamara era. The issue was the Tactical Fighter Experimental, or TFX.

The need for an ultra-modern fighter for the Navy predated both Connally and McNamara. The Navy had obtained tentative approval from Secretary of Defense Gates in the early part of 1960 to develop a new carrier-based fighter. The Air Force had originated the TFX, its own new fighter, with a separate mission and design. Because President Eisenhower was reluctant to commit the Kennedy administration to a major new weapons system, a directive from Gates halted further work on both projects late in 1960.[5] Given the need of both services for a new fighter, the difficulties began in February 1961 when McNamara decided to develop three structurally identical aircraft which would satisfy the tactical fighter needs of all the services. The principle of "commonality" on which the decision was based soon became a commonplace in Defense language, referring, of course, to use of a single design of an item of military equipment, particularly aircraft, for more than one branch of service.[6]

Yet the requirements of the services were dissimilar. The Army and the Marines needed an unsophisticated, inexpensive, close-support aircraft; the Navy and Air Force, a complex, high-performance craft. The Air Force requirement for long range and supersonic speeds at terrain-hugging altitudes meant a heavy, rugged plane, slim and needle-nosed for greater speed, but therefore too long and too heavy for carrier operations. The Navy needed not high speed at extremely low altitudes for flying behind enemy lines but a combat air patrol able to loiter at high altitudes around the fast carrier forces. This involved a highly computerized missile offense with a five-foot diameter, long-range radar antenna in the nose which the Air Force claimed produced unacceptable drag and speed loss.

A Defense committee on Tactical Air composed of civilian and military officers under Fred Wolcott, Defense Director, Research and Engineering (DDR&E), concluded that the four-service requirements were incompatible and recommended two separate programs, one for the Army and Marines, one for the Navy and Air Force. After eight months of further study, the majority of aeronautical experts in the Navy and the Air Force agreed that an effective common airplane for the two services was not technically feasible.

Although these conclusions were approved by Connally and by Air Force Secretary Eugene Zuckert, McNamara, considering the versatility and capabilities that could be built into a modern aircraft, disagreed. He ordered the two services to get together and to compromise their respective desires until they came up with a common design that could be built for both services.[7] The design compromises proved unacceptable to the Navy, however, and on 31 May 1961 Connally wrote McNamara concurring in the concept of a bi-service fighter but objecting that the compromise design was "too large and expensive and we neither need nor want them on our carriers." If the plane had to be, Connally added, the Navy should be the service responsible for its development to insure that the final design would be suitable for carrier operations.[8]

McNamara found the arguments of the Navy and the Air Force unpersuasive. On 7 June 1961 he chose the Air Force, with requirements for 86 percent of the total production, as program manager for both services. Within a matter of days, Connally appealed the decision on the basis that the dual service version would require major modification to CVA deck structure, catapults, and arresting gear and was infeasible even with modification in the *Midway*-class hull. The smaller wing area of the carrier version reduced the lift/drag ratio and increased its fuel requirements, further increasing takeoff weight. Excess size reduced the number per carrier; excess cost reduced the total number procurable; increased hazards to deck personnel were involved, as was reduced reliability. (Connally himself was not without qualifications in these judgments; he had not forgotten his experience aboard the *Essex* during the war.) As a result of hard negotiating throughout the summer by the two services, the program was near a stalemate by late August.

McNamara, too, was in a difficult position. He originally wanted only one tactical aircraft for the four services. In May, he had been forced to concede that two were necessary; he now faced the unpleasant prospect that there might well have to be three. His reaction was swift. If the two services could not agree, he would decide for them. After instructing DDR&E to establish guidelines for the joint program, on 1 September he directed Connally and Zuckert to develop a joint TFX aircraft and spelled out that "changes to the Air Force tactical version of the basic aircraft to achieve the Navy mission shall be held to a minimum." Both decisions, understandably, caused acute anguish to Connally and the naval aviation leadership. On 1 October 1961, requests for proposals were issued to bidders. Before the end of the year, preliminary design proposals were in hand from eight companies, two of which, one from General Dynamics and one from Boeing, were judged most nearly acceptable.

Even at this early juncture preliminary judgments can be made with respect to the relation of the Secretary of the Navy with the Secretary of Defense. In the TFX case, Connally took a strong position based on entirely valid substantive objections raised by the Navy; second, despite the new and widely proclaimed managerial techniques, the Defense positions were not taken on the strength of sophisticated decision techniques; "systems analysis" was not applied.[9] It was because of the TFX experience that McNamara later developed compilations of experience statistics based largely on the so-called "learning curves." These not being available at that stage of TFX development, he was forced to rely upon his own business experience. We will learn shortly that the selection of the prime contractor was also to be made contrary to the unanimous recommendations of both the military aviation leadership and the Joint Chiefs of Staff—but with the support of the Secretary of the Navy.

Meanwhile, in other areas, Connally seemed to be enjoying greater success as an advocate. The major Kennedy objective, as stated in his message to Congress on 30 January and the first budget directive to the services, was increased combat power. Encouragement was given, under the President's urging, to step up the Polaris program, already moving forward at near maximum effort. Airlift and sealift forces were reexamined and as early as 13 February 1961, again under direct stimulus from the White House, strong emphasis was urged with respect to guerrilla and anti-guerrilla operations.[10] The Bay of Pigs crisis in April 1961, Laos in May, and a new Berlin episode in June 1961 gave visual proof of the need to stimulate further the reawakened interest in conventional forces; the Soviet resumption of nuclear testing on 31 August spurred continuing interest in nuclear forces. The ASROC and SUBROC missiles reached the fleet; the first nuclear cruiser *Long Beach* was commissioned in Boston on 9 September; and the Navy contributed prominently to the manned space program and Commander Alan Shepard's historic 5 May flight.

Just over the horizon, however, another serious problem was arising that would dominate much of Navy thinking for the next several years. This was the fate of the aircraft carrier, particularly of the nuclear-powered version. McNamara seriously questioned the future role of the CVA; partial answers supplied to his inquiries on 28 June, 4 August, and 20 October 1961 proved unsatisfactory. Worse, they were counterproductive in one important aspect. Connally himself concluded that after the USS *Enterprise* there should be no more nuclear aircraft carriers.

As the *Enterprise* joined the Atlantic fleet in ceremonies at Newport News, Virginia, late in November, Connally had high praise for the mammoth nuclear-powered ship. Predicting that the 85,350 ton vessel would reign as "queen of the sea" for a "long, long time," he also used the occasion to emphasize that "his" Navy had no immediate plans to build any more nuclear-powered carriers. The "considerably greater expense" over conventionally-powered ships made the cost prohibitive. This he believed even though he took public issue with the finding of the Navy staff that nuclear power would not reduce the number of ships needed by the Navy. Almost simultaneously with the Connally statement, McNamara cancelled plans for a second nuclear carrier and included a conventional carrier (CVA-67) in his first complete defense budget to be presented to the Congress a few months later, on 1 February 1962.

Connally's lack of enthusiasm for the nuclear carrier did not apply to nuclear propulsion in general. At the *Enterprise* ceremony he had high praise for the Navy's nuclear-powered submarines equipped with Polaris missiles. So concerned was he with the need to expedite the Polaris program that he went to unusual measures to promote key personnel in the program. Levering Smith, a little-known ordnance engineering specialist working behind Admiral William F. "Red" Raborn in the Polaris program, was added to the flag selection list by Connally after action by the selection board but prior to approval by President Kennedy.

When the occasion demanded, Connally could also be a tough taskmaster. In an address to a gathering of a thousand Navy and Marine Corps officers in Washington on 12 April 1961, he denounced officers who hid behind anonymity in opposing Navy policies. "If you are not willing to be quoted by name, you should not be speaking," he declared.

No new operating carriers were added to the fourteen attack aircraft carriers during Connally's year, but the *Kitty Hawk* began her shakedown cruise on 15 July. A tragic fire on the *Constellation* delayed her completion by seven months, to the fall of 1961, when the nuclear-powered *Enterprise* was expected to go to sea. Meanwhile the *Oriskany* was fitted out with the prototype installation of the Naval Tactical Data System; new cruisers, destroyers, and frigates were equipped with Terrier, Tartar, and Talos; the first ship built from the keel up as an amphibious assault ship, USS *Iwo Jima* (LPH-1) joined the fleet during the summer; the new P3V-3 Orion, a land-based ASW aircraft, became operational; eight new submarines, all nuclear powered, joined the fleet; and the first Polaris system replenishment anchorage was established overseas, in March 1961, at Holy Loch, Scotland.

Well aware of the block obsolescence of the World War II fleet, Connally continued the Fleet Rehabilitation and Modernization Program, designed to add five to eight years of life to at least half of the old ships, with thirty-five ships scheduled for 1961. Continuing emphasis on ASW was revealed by the adoption of TENOC—a ten-year plan for studying the ocean environment. Similar emphasis on amphibious operations was revealed by keeping a Marine Corps Battalion Landing Team with the Sixth Fleet, Seventh Fleet, and in the Caribbean, each provided with vertical lift capability.

One can readily conclude that throughout his turbulent tour in office, Secretary Connally was frequently in a difficult position. Calling his year of service a year of "challenge," he tried hard, did his homework, and was a good Secretary. He had a solid knowledge of maritime power and its role in the rise and fall of civilizations. A year and a half before the Cuban missile crisis, he expressed concern at Soviet merchant ships calling at Havana.[11] He worked well with the CNO, Admiral Burke, and with Admiral George W. Anderson, who succeeded Burke in August 1961. They fought hard for Navy programs, often against strong Defense opposition, but frequently received the treatment of second class citizens. In November and December 1961, almost to the day of his departure from office, Connally strongly objected to McNamara's airlift and sealift plans.

Connally's success was clearly greater down than up. Interested in morale and personnel improvement, he attempted new approaches to longer command tours, early promotions, and recognition of outstanding leadership by petty officers. Understandably, he was troubled by his differences with McNamara. He had earned Kennedy's respect but still lacked personal support in the White House. After six months in office, Connally was quoted as being interested in the gubernatorial office. It was not until two weeks before Christmas, however, that he announced his resignation, effective 20 December.

In an editorial tribute noting his departure, the *New York Times* on 13 December praised his "intelligence, warm personality, common sense and political shrewdness" which "established him as the most effective service Secretary in the Defense Department." The *Times* also observed that:

> It was no secret in the Pentagon that Mr. Connally was not in sympathy with some of the plans and methodology of the Department of Defense. This dissent had nothing to do with his departure, but it was clear to all who knew him that Mr. Connally would have difficulty reconciling his private convictions with some of the projects and developments in the Department.

Strong political pressures from his native state were exerted for his return to Texas. His own ambition for a political career was certainly a major consideration. One additional factor must be noted. Connally is in many ways an opportunist. As a son of a poor tenant farmer with an intense desire to make good, Connally sees himself by nature as inherently restless. He likes to get things started, but then seems to lose interest. This pattern has persisted throughout his political life. In his words, "I've been called an opportunist, and I do move from place to place and from thing to thing and I enjoy it."

For all of the above, then, Connally became the first Kennedy appointee to leave the administration. Successful in his gubernatorial campaign, his political career continued to wax. By virtue of having been wounded in the Kennedy limousine at the time of the assassination, his political position in Texas became impregnable, identified in the public mind with a brief and resplendent era for which ironically, he had no sympathy. He never joined the Kennedy bandwagon; while serving as governor, his support of Kennedy in Texas was less than wholehearted. The morning after the assassination, he encouraged President Johnson to replace all the Kennedy people and set aside some of his programs. Gradually shifting his allegiance to President Nixon after 1968, Connally was appointed by President Nixon to be Secretary of the Treasury in 1971, serving again for approximately a year. Mentioned frequently as the Republican presidential candidate in 1976, the movement never gained significant momentum and the opportunity for 1980 seems exceptionally remote.

NOTES

1. John F. Kennedy, *The Strategy of Peace* (New York: Harper & Bros., 1960), pp. 42, 184.
2. Robert S. McNamara, "Managing the Department of Defense," *Civil Service Journal*, Apr.-June 1964, p. 1. Although two management philosophies are specified, McNamara did not like the other to be quoted to him, particularly when it came from below.
3. In Nov. 1961, a special study group appointed by the Secretary of Defense recommended the creation of a commanding general for all unified commands. See John C. Ries, *The Management of Defense* (Baltimore: Johns Hopkins Press, 1964), pp. 191–92; *New York Times*, 29 Nov. 1961; Roswell L. Gilpatric, "An Expert Looks at the Joint Chiefs," *New York Times Magazine*, 29 Mar. 1964, p. 11.
4. U.S. House, Committee on Science and Astronautics, *Hearings*, 87th Cong., 1st Sess., p. 168.
5. Testimony of COL Gregory, U.S. Senate, Committee on Government Operations, Permanent Subcommittee on Investigations, *The TFX Contract Investigation: Hearings*, 88th Cong., 1st Sess., 10 vols. (Washington: GPO, 1963–1964), 3:718 (hereafter cited as *TFX Hearings*).
6. The origin of commonality is attributed to Calvin Coolidge. "If the military really must fly," he asked, "why can't it buy one machine and take turns using it?"
7. *TFX Hearings*, 6:1514.
8. *Ibid.* 6:1387–88.
9. See Alain Enthoven, Assistant SECDEF for Systems Analysis, testimony in U.S. House, Committee on Armed Services, *Hearings*, 1967.
10. The Khrushchev speech promising support for Wars of National Liberation was delivered on 9 Jan. 1961.
11. In an eloquent but somewhat mixed metaphor, Connally stated in New Orleans on Maritime Day, 20 May 1961, that "The single lantern in the old North Church is being hauled down, and two lights are going up, signifying that the enemy is coming by sea. Please saddle up and help spread the alarm."

FRED KORTH

4 January 1962–1 November 1963

PAUL R. SCHRATZ

A Texas lawyer like his predecessor, Fred Korth was a banker and a prominent civic leader. Born in Yorktown, Texas, on 9 September 1909, he graduated from the University of Texas in 1932 and the George Washington University Law School in 1935. While in Washington, he married Vera Connell of Fort Worth, then a student at Fairmont College. They have a daughter and a son. Korth then practiced law in Fort Worth.

Commissioned a second lieutenant in the Army Air Corps in August 1942, Korth served almost wholly within the continental United States. His last assignment was as Chief of Staff for Personnel with the Ferrying Division of the Air Transport Command based at Cincinnati, Ohio. He terminated his active service with the rank of lieutenant colonel in January 1946.

In March 1951, Korth was called to Washington by Secretary of the Army Frank Pace, with whom he had seen war service, and he served a year as Deputy Counselor, Department of the Army. On 22 May 1952, he was nominated by President Truman to the office of Assistant Secretary of the Army (Manpower). For exceptional service during the following year, he was awarded the Distinguished Civilian Service Award by the Department of the Army. In 1953 he was named Counselor to the Secretary of the Army, and again in 1959 he received the Army's outstanding civilian award. From 2 June 1961, until appointed Secretary of the Navy, he served as Civilian Aide to Secretary of the Army Elvis J. Stahr, Jr. One of the three aides-at-large, he was responsible for interpreting Army policy and missions to civilian communities while also advising the Secretary of the Army of civilian views concerning the military service.

Korth entered upon his duties as Secretary of the Navy with the Navy at high tide. The USS *Constellation* (CVA 64) and the first nuclear-powered carrier, the USS *Enterprise* (CVAN 65), had recently reported to the Fleet. Korth, however, found himself squarely in the middle of strong currents of revolution throughout the Defense Department. Under the Secretary of Defense, Robert McNamara, task forces were scrutinizing the operation of every aspect of that department. Permeating the entire Pentagon, also, were new analytical processes for a program budget with common cost-effectiveness procedures to be followed by the services, all aimed at single manager control, and all directed by a waxing tide of eager and energetic young assistant secretaries interposed between the service secretary and the traditional source of executive authority.

Korth's administrative skills were soon put to the test over the TFX problem, the nuclear carrier issue, and adjustments by the Navy to McNamara's managerial structure and procedures.

Four times between October 1961 and November 1962 the Boeing Company and the General Dynamics Corporation submitted, revised, and resubmitted proposals on the TFX. Military experts showed an early preference for Boeing; by May, however, the Chief of Naval Operations, Admiral George B. Anderson, was convinced that chances for obtaining a successful bi-service plane were remote. He therefore advised Korth that the Navy could not use the draft design and recommended that the Air Force be allowed to proceed independently. Korth was sympathetic but not fully convinced. Because McNamara was incontrovertibly committed to joint development, Anderson's advice seemed counter-productive. Korth rejected Anderson's recommendation. Instead, he and the Secretary of the Air Force, Eugene Zuckert, recommended to McNamara that the competitors be given three additional weeks to try to provide satisfactory solutions to the Navy's problems.[1]

Confronted with the prospect that his decision of the previous September to go ahead with the common version might yet be reversed, McNamara instructed his office to do a further detailed analysis, as a matter of urgency. On advice of his staff, he saved the principle of commonality, or common use by the Air Force and Navy, by authorizing last minute changes in the plane to meet Navy demands. On 9 June he concurred in the Korth-Zuckert recommendation. The third Boeing-General Dynamics competition in a three-week interval produced some changes, and on 21 June 1962, the Air Force Council decided in favor of the Boeing plane but agreed that source selection was not an issue. Navy representatives on the council concurred with the reservation that they could not formally commit themselves because time was too short. Both Korth and Zuckert agreed. Significantly, however, the Chief of Naval Operations and Air Force Chief of Staff recommended that Boeing be selected, whereas the two service secretaries recommended that both Boeing and General Dynamics be allowed to continue definition of designs.[2] In the fourth competition, the evaluation group worked directly with both competitors and both companies produced what the services agreed were acceptable designs. Of the two, military analysts agreed that the Boeing designs were superior, offering more airplane for less money. The four service evaluations, the Pentagon Source Selection Board of top admirals and generals, and the military operators unanimously recommended Boeing.

On 21 November 1962, however, a $439 million prototype contract award was made not to Boeing but to General Dynamics. Shock waves of chagrin, surprise, and cynicism reverberated through the Pentagon. The contract was little more than earnest money—the "thin edge of the wedge"—for the largest aircraft contract the United States had ever undertaken. The supporting document, a five-page memorandum of justification, was signed by Secretary McNamara, Navy Secretary Korth, and Air Force Secretary Zuckert. Senator John McClellan of Arkansas, Chairman of the Permanent Subcommittee on Investigations, claimed that the document was full of errors, both technical and factual, including two of simple arithmetic totalling $54 million.[3] Both Admiral Anderson and General Curtis LeMay, the Air Force Chief, professed astonishment.

A few hours before the commitment went to General Dynamics, Senator McClellan requested a delay in order to conduct an inquiry, which was refused. Since both Connally and Korth were Texans and the new plane (now called the F-111) was to be built primarily in Fort Worth, Korth in particular was thrust into a very difficult position. He was still active with his bank, Continental National of Fort Worth, and retained $160,000 worth of stock. General Dynamics had obtained a $400,000 portion of a loan at the same bank at a critical period in its lean months.

In the Senate investigation, Korth insisted firmly that as "a man of integrity" he was not influenced by considerations involving his bank and General Dynamics. When committee investigators discovered correspondence between him and the bank officials on small accounts, he was not disturbed, saying that he meant to return to the bank following his tour as Secretary of the Navy. While use of his office for minor personal and social obligations may have reflected poor judgment, the practice is hardly an isolated example. Asked for an opinion on a possible conflict of interest, the Attorney General saw no legal violation. The incident gained national prominence, however, and the suggestion was made to him by Attorney General Robert F. Kennedy that a resignation was in order.

On the TFX issue, Korth was caught between McNamara and the Navy. Insofar as Defense is concerned, there were admittedly strong domestic political implications in favoring the Texas firm. Texas had gone to Kennedy in 1960, but the President badly needed to increase his support there, support not forthcoming willingly from the newly-elected Governor Connally. President Kennedy was also directly interested in the TFX because McNamara had told both Korth and Zuckert that they would discuss the matter with him. Before the fourth round of proposals had been evaluated, McNamara had told the President that "it looks as if General Dynamics would be chosen." Eight days before the announcement was made, he visited the White House to tell the President of the pending decision.

Although General Dynamics was facing serious economic trouble, McNamara claimed firmly that "Neither so-called nor actual socio-economic factors entered into it," nor had the influence of Vice President Lyndon Johnson. During the McClellan hearings, McNamara identified the grounds for his choice: that Boeing was using titanium in its plane, which was risky and might interfere with the ability to meet contract dates; the General Dynamics proposal appeared to conform more closely than Boeing's to the overriding ideals of low apparent development risk, more realistic cost estimation, and in particular, more identical parts, i.e., more commonality, to the extent that 83.8 percent of the General Dynamics F-111 A (the Air Force version) and F-111 B (the Navy version) were interchangeable. While Boeing's two versions looked almost identical, Boeing was faulted for electing to reduce the weight of its Navy version by substituting similar but lighter-gauge parts. But the commonality factor was judged to be only 60 percent and therefore inferior to the General Dynamics proposal.

Before the contract was signed, McNamara had told Senator McClellan why he had chosen General Dynamics. The Senator appeared satisfied but clearly had to make at least a show of protest if only to allow interested parties on his committee (such as Senator Henry Jackson of Boeing territory in Washington) to justify their positions before their constituents. While the President was both interested and influential, no decision made by McNamara was more exclusively his own than the TFX, with the support of both Korth and Zuckert being an unanticipated bonus. But Korth's support brought his relations with Admiral Anderson and Navy technical staffs into very serious question.

A service secretary is responsible for making procurement decisions. In a policy issue, TFX or whatever, he acts on the advice of his principal military personnel as an essential element in making a sound decision, yet he must ensure that the advice does not take away his freedom to choose among viable alternatives. The military System Source Selection procedure then in use in the TFX case, however, tended to make his authority more apparent than real, for the process gave him a decision rather than advice.[4] It not only evaluated alternative sources but selected a source for a weapon system; the title of the Committee stated as much. Moreover, were a secretary to exercise his statutory power to choose other than the source recommended, the reevaluation required could do little but delay the whole procedure. As General LeMay testified, "In twenty-three development decisions in which I had participated under the System Source Selection procedure [all prior to McNamara and the TFX case], the Secretary had never overruled any of the recommendations that had been presented to him."[5] In addition to reducing his initiative, the system also pressured the secretary to accept decisions based on perspectives not necessarily coincident with his own. Problems of the national economy, even domestic political issues, are a much more legitimate concern to the civilian leadership than to the military. Under the McNamara system, it was the secretary who tried to measure the relative military effectiveness that respective outlays would purchase.

The TFX case, therefore, became a landmark contest in the issue of military vs. civilian domination of procurement decisions. Since McNamara was deeply committed to the joint development principle, each of the four separate recommendations of the military hierarchy on the TFX was examined critically by both the service and defense secretaries. Partly for lack of time, partly because they were sure their recommendations would be accepted, few military leaders even read the fourth phase report on which the final decision was made. The Source Selection Board itself did not receive the 400-page, highly technical report until the morning of the day they made their decision.[6]

When Korth made his choice, he knew that Admiral Anderson and General LeMay in the fourth evaluation had found little to choose between the proposals and therefore had certified that both designs would meet military requirements. Both men recommended Boeing partly because Boeing promised more than it specified in the way of development, which augured for a superior product eventually. Because "development risk" in new and untried systems (such as thrust reversers for tactical use) might levy added cost both in dollars and delay, both Korth and Zuckert favored the more conservative design. The military view naturally was to exceed the requirements; the civilian view to satisfy the requirements. Based on technical advice from the civilian staffs, and in the wider perspective of their offices, both service secretaries supported McNamara's choice of General Dynamics.[7]

Two major results flowed from the TFX decision. First, under the Kennedy system the services allegedly were no longer to receive relatively fixed percentages of the annual budget which they could expend on programs little correlated with either the other services or the defense secretary. The arbitrary budget ceiling was succeeded by the far more sophisticated "program budget." The arbitrary ceiling, based on what the economy can stand, on the surface, is far inferior to the program budget, an integrated plan of what the national defense actually needs without a formal ceiling. The program budget had far-reaching and largely unanticipated consequences for the three services, however. Under the arbitrary ceiling, each service exercised its own priorities. Such a procedure naturally encouraged laying the groundwork for increased shares of future budgets by concentrating on alluring new weaponry, meanwhile protecting existing force levels even at occasional sacrifices of readiness.

With service values deeply institutionalized in the budgeting process, the most important defect in the pre-McNamara budgeting was the almost complete separation between planning and decision-making concerning forces and weapons systems on one hand and budgeting on the other. With guideline dollar totals laid down by the administration on the basis of "what the economy could stand," the result was a mismatch because "required forces" cost more than the administration and the Congress were willing to pay. The resolution of conflicting interests was unsystematic and wasteful, led to unbalanced programs, stimulated new initiatives, and perpetuated old ones.

Unquestionably the new Planning-Programming-Budgeting System (PPBS) and the other elements of the formal McNamara managerial techniques were superior to the pre-1960 budgetary systems in almost every respect. But under the previous system budget cuts were made because, in the Secretary's or President's view, the national economy could not afford more. A budget cut could be accepted by military leaders as necessary within the broader view of the President as to the nation's overall needs. Under the new system, this was not at all the case. As it worked out in practice, when the civilian secretary overruled or cut back military programs, he in effect overruled the professional judgment of the military leaders on military needs. This was one of the principles at issue in the TFX case.

Alain Enthoven, then Assistant Secretary of Defense (Systems Analysis), claimed this was not so, that there was no ceiling dividing the Joint Chiefs on questions of judgment, that only a priority list was set up, not a judgment. The JCS disagreed, however, on the grounds that they never commented on the budget as a whole and hence could not express a view on overall priorities. The Joint Strategic Objectives Plan, or JSOP, the only document that supposedly gave a framework for a broad look at the whole budget, had become meaningless. While the TFX debate was actually in progress, in fact, partly as a concession to the military leaders, partly because only a priority list was set up in any case under the new procedures, the administration reverted once more to a fixed budget ceiling within which the JCS negotiated agreement internally.[8]

Second, and critical to our analysis, is the role of the service secretary and the change in the McNamara conception of the role which came about as a result of the TFX competition.

As a condition of accepting office in 1961, McNamara insisted on picking his own people for the key offices in the Department of Defense. The service secretaries he chose were traditional political individuals rather than "cool" intellectual, RAND and Harvard Business School types common to the Defense staff. McNamara saw a strong, analytical type of service secretary as a rallying point for service loyalties, hence a divisive threat to his own exercise of authority. He demanded a head for figures on his own staff; he was content with a figurehead on the service staff. His own deputy, Roswell Gilpatric, as a member of the Kennedy Task Force just before inauguration, recommended that the service secretaries be abolished. When the TFX case reached the point of decision, McNamara realized that the Source Selection process on major procurement contracts diluted the civilian authority and control and determined to alter it. Thereby he signaled his intention to strengthen the power of the service secretaries in these decisions.[9]

Meanwhile, new problems and events colored the dramatic march of history. During the intensely emotional debate over the TFX, a new Berlin crisis captured the world's interest when young Peter Freuchen, shot in trying to escape to the West, was allowed to bleed to death in agony in full view of West Berlin. Tragedy struck the nuclear submarine force also in the loss of the USS *Thresher* during sea trials 200 miles off Cape Cod on 10 April 1963. In triumph, however, Marine Lieutenant Colonel John Glenn orbited in space in February and Navy Lieutenant Commander Scott Carpenter in May. In February and March the nuclear-powered aircraft carrier *Enterprise* completed her shakedown cruise, and on 22 August the nuclear submarine *Skate* and *Seadragon* rendezvoused at the North Pole. The nuclear frigate USS *Bainbridge* was commissioned in early October, thereby completing the surface nuclear power program.[10]

Dominating maritime events in 1962, however, was the Cuban missile crisis in October, with far-reaching effects upon administration leaders and on the role of seapower and usable force in national crises. U.S. Navy Task Force 136 enforced the Cuban blockade under difficult operational conditions made necessary by the ultra-sensitive nature of the showdown between the United States and the Soviet Union and the imposition of direct White House control over even relatively minor actions on scene. When the tension of the impending confrontation neared its peak, a question arose over whether the blockading forces had been drawn closer to Cuba, under the President's orders, in order to allow Premier Khrushchev more time for decision. McNamara thereupon decided to explore the Navy plans and routines for the imminent interception. He visited Chief of Naval Operations George Anderson in the inner sanctum, the Navy Flag Plot, and questioned him harshly. It was the middle of the night and both men were under severe strain, with tempers shortened by acute loss of sleep and the mounting tension. Lecturing him sternly, McNamara reportedly stated that:

> The object of the operation was not to shoot Russians but to communicate a political message from President Kennedy to Chairman Khrushchev. The President wanted to avoid pushing Khrushchev to extremes. The blockade must be so conducted so as to avoid humiliating the Russians; otherwise, Khrushchev must somehow be persuaded to pull back, rather than be goaded into retaliation.[11]

Witnesses claim that Anderson bluntly accused McNamara of "undue interference in naval matters" and suggested rather firmly that he and his deputy go back to their offices and let the Navy run the blockade. This Anderson later denied, claiming that he had been brought up never to say such a thing even if he felt it. Whatever the literal statements may have been, the incident seriously clouded Anderson's future relations with McNamara and the influence which he may have had on defense policy. It is generally conceded that as a result of the above he was not reappointed to a customary two-year tour the following August, accepting a White House appointment as Ambassador to Portugal at that time. His widely publicized address before the National Press Club, 5 September 1963, expressed his grave concern that "within the Department of Defense there is not that degree of confidence and trust between the civilian and military echelons that the importance of their common objective requires."

Meanwhile, problems in adjusting the Navy to McNamara's new management system were demanding increased time and effort. An unusually broad nine-month review of management processes by the administrative assistant to the Secretary of the Navy, John H. Dillon, had been ordered by Korth on 29 May 1962 and completed in December 1962. Korth's own views on organization and his role in directing the Navy Department were published in the U.S. Naval Institute *Proceedings* in August of the following year.[12]

The article, in large part, attempts to explain the major recommendations of the Dillon Board in unifying the "producer" bureaus under a proposed Chief of Naval Material while continuing the traditional bilinear structure. The CNO and Commandant, Marine Corps, head the operating forces, including the Fleet establishment ashore; and the Chief of Naval Material under the secretary heads the support establishment. Effective 1 July 1963, a limited reorganization was placed into effect with the creation of the Naval Material Support Establishment and the four material Bureaus—Ships, Yards and Docks, Naval Weapons, and Supplies and Accounts—subordinated to the Chief of Naval Material (CNM) and directly responsible to the secretary. Directors of special projects were also placed under the CNM, who thus became a co-ordinating authority and single point of contact for logistics. Simultaneously, the Navy integrated its planning, programming, and budgeting procedures in a manner consistent with the Defense approach.

Problems persisted despite the 1963 reorganization. Modification of the structure did not change its fundamental characteristics. The traditional separation of logistics from naval operations at the highest level had been maintained. This framework was ill-suited either for effective implementation of management procedures, especially the development of weapon systems, or for promoting efficiency. As a possible consequence and before further changes were made, however, Korth himself had left the scene. The cause was the conflict of interest in the TFX case, but near the surface was the smoldering issue of a new atomic-powered aircraft carrier.

The fiscal 1963 budget, the first under McNamara management, went to Congress early in 1962 and included a recommendation for constructing a non-nuclear attack carrier (CVA–67). Contrary to general belief, the recommendation for the carrier in the McNamara statement to Congress was a well-stated argument for the use of sea-based airpower, perhaps the best made to any Congress by a Secretary of Defense.

> There are many trouble spots in the world where the attack carrier is and will continue to be the only practical means of bringing our air striking power to bear. Carrier airpower can be employed without involving third parties, without involving treaties, agreements, or overflight rights. And, as has been demonstrated many times before, the carrier task force is a most effective means for presenting a show of force or establishing a military presence, which often has helped to maintain the peace and discourage hostilities.
>
> There is no reason to expect that the need for this form of airpower will diminish in the future. The fact that they may be vulnerable to attack in a general nuclear war does not detract from their value in limited war.[13]

This excellent statement should be borne in mind in subsequent testimony on the aircraft carrier, primarily—and again contrary to the accepted view—because the Navy itself was neither convinced nor convincing about either the carrier or its propulsion system and was still a long way from making up its mind.

The recommendation for a non-nuclear powered carrier was supported by both Korth and Anderson on two grounds: money and a continuing ambivalence within the Navy about nuclear power for surface ships. Anderson wanted a carrier right away, hence would accept conventional power. McNamara was prepared to back a recommendation either way. Partly because of primitive technology in the surface reactor and partly for a no less primitive planning-programming-budgeting system in the Navy staff, the cost of the nuclear carrier, "one-third to one-half more" than a conventionally-powered vessel, appeared exorbitant. The nuclear attack submarine program, the Polaris program, antisubmarine warfare deficiencies, and amphibious and sealift forces to meet the Kennedy conventional warfare goals had already strained resources to the limit. Therefore Anderson told the House Armed Services Committee it was a simple "lack of money" for a nuclear carrier.[14]

The Cuban missile crisis, however, emphasized the clear superiority of the nuclear-powered *Enterprise*. Vice Admiral John T. Hayward, Commander Task Force 135, reported to Secretary Korth on 2 January 1963 that:

> The *Enterprise* out-performs every carrier in the fleet. . . . My experience convinces me that the military advantages of nuclear propulsion in surface combatant ships more than outweigh their extra cost . . . [and] offers tremendous military advantages that will be sorely needed in the years ahead.

With the support of the Chairman, Atomic Energy Commission, Korth wrote to McNamara on 23 January 1963:

> . . . substitution of an improved . . . nuclear propulsion plant for the oil-fired plan now programmed for CVA-67 is both *feasible and desirable*. . . . I therefore suggest your consideration *as a matter of urgency*.

McNamara replied on 22 February 1963:

> I do not feel that the subject of nuclear propulsion for surface warships has yet been explored sufficiently. . . . I should like you to undertake a comprehensive quantitative study . . . achieving the most beneficial military results for a given expenditure. . . . I am reserving decision on the question of nuclear propulsion for the CVA-67.

The requested study (First Navy Study) was forwarded by Secretary Korth on 4 April 1963, with the statement:

> You stated that the assumption the future Navy will make full use of nuclear power lies at the heart of the matter of whether we should change the CVA-67 to nuclear propulsion. I concur . . . I have concluded that nuclear propulsion does permit a significant increase in the beneficial military results for a given expenditure and that we must exploit and take maximum advantage of it . . . we have come to the conclusion that all new major warships should be nuclear powered . . . I believe that we have sufficiently resolved those major questions you have raised . . . I commend the decision on CVA-67 to your consideration as a matter of urgency.[15]

Apparently indicating that the Navy had finally made its decision on nuclear-powered surface ships, Korth and Anderson released a joint statement four days later that "All major naval vessels of 8,000 tons or more are to be built henceforth with nuclear engines."

McNamara rejected the First Navy Study on 20 April 1963, however, spelling out in considerable detail what he meant by cost effectiveness analysis especially as it applies to comparative merits of nuclear and conventional propulsion for surface warships:

> Your memorandum does not provide me with the information I need in order to reach a decision in this important matter. Specifically, my question concerning the implications of nuclear power for force size has not been answered . . . you have failed to identify the magnitude of the increase in effectiveness or the possible reduction in force. . . . I realize it is difficult to quantify exactly the increase in effectiveness associated with nuclear propulsion, but I would like you and the Chief of Naval Operations to indicate to me the nuclear-powered force which, in your judgment, would be equivalent in effectiveness to a conventional force. Similarly, my question on the implications of nuclear power for the composition of task forces has not been answered . . . while I realize that there are many issues involved here which are not subject to rigorous quantitative analysis, a systematic exposition of issues which are quantifiable is necessary if I am to appreciate fully your position. Let me cite two issues raised in my mind by your memorandum. First, I have been concerned for some time that the steadily increasing size of escort ships may be adding a disproportionate share to the cost of each attack aircraft sortie delivered from our carriers, in comparison with alternative means. . . . The second issue also involved your comparisons of nuclear-powered and conventional task force costs. . . . I should like to know the basis for this assumption (re escort differentials in the two task forces), and the reason why only the replenishment ships associated with the conventional task force require the expensive protection of DDGs.

He then went on to suggest cost-effectiveness criteria by which the Secretary of the Navy was to be guided in his further studies and asked the Navy to work with his Office of Systems Analysis in pursuing these studies.

The Second Navy Study was forwarded to McNamara on 26 September 1963. Comprehensive and detailed, it focused on the lifetime cost differential of nuclear versus non-nuclear propelled task forces—about 3 percent in favor of conventional—and stressed the advantages which make nuclear power superior, concluding that ". . . five nuclear task forces are the equal of or superior to six conventional task forces."

This study, too, was rejected by McNamara, who stated, (without supporting data), "I am absolutely certain of one thing, that the six conventional task forces are superior to the five nuclear task forces . . . proceed with the [nonnuclear] construction as soon as possible."

The reply astonished Korth as much as it did the professional Navy. The following day, 10 October 1963, Korth replied: "I was surprised. . . . I earnestly request that you reconsider. . . ." The letter was hand-carried to McNamara on 10 October. Compounding his difficulties over the TFX (or F–111) issue, appeal was fruitless. Korth thereupon announced his resignation, formally submitting it to the President the following day.

McNamara, on the twenty-fifth, amplified his decision somewhat, saying that:

> Steps should be taken immediately to initiate construction. The real choice . . . is not between a given number of conventional ships for one sum of money and the same number of nuclear ships for a larger sum. The choice is between a given number of conventional ships and a smaller number of nuclear ships at the same total cost. . . . The Navy judgment that five nuclear task forces are as good as six conventional task forces is not generally valid.

Almost simultaneously, McNamara told the Joint Committee on Atomic Energy that "whether any new carrier at all is needed is really the basic question, not what kind of propulsion system it should have."

On 30 October 1963, the JCS recommended approval of the 15 CVA force level. In December, the Joint Committee on Atomic Energy recommended that the "decision on conventional propulsion in the new aircraft carrier, CVA-67, should be set aside."[16]

The resignation of Korth "for pressing business affairs" ended one more episode in the turbulent postwar history of naval aviation involving both the revolutionary F–111 fighter plane and the aircraft carrier. Korth actually resigned over the conflict of interest which arose over the TFX. Along with the Joint Chiefs of Staff, the congressional Joint Committee on Atomic Energy, the Atomic Energy Commission, and the congressional leadership, Korth had warmly supported the Navy position on nuclear power on the basis of its great superiority in performance demonstrated during the Cuban missile crisis. He apparently had fully expected approval even though McNamara had been foot-dragging on his decision for nine months. Korth's resignation was timed presumably because it would be best for his successor from the standpoint of Navy relations with the next session of Congress beginning in January. With his resignation, nevertheless, came the temporary termination of a grave internal controversy on modernization and nuclear propulsion for the surface Navy.

Reflecting also the loss of esteem of the Navy at the Defense level, the same week in which Korth resigned saw McNamara also overrule Navy objections and give the Middle East, all of Africa south of the Sahara, and India to the Strike Command under an Army General (and Air Force Deputy) rather than to two Navy admirals. A carefully calculated ploy to reduce Navy influence and commands, the action struck a severe blow at one of the Navy's cherished concepts—the establishment of an Indian Ocean fleet. Time would show the Strike Command to be of little value except for training. More important, it showed that the Defense leadership did not understand that bombers based in Florida are far less effective military tools in the Middle East and Africa than even a small concentration of force in the area itself.

The Korth stewardship, like that of Connally's, came to a premature end in an atmosphere of frustration and discontent. Throughout a short but stormy tenure, Korth found himself amid controversy both within the Navy and with the larger world beyond. He worked hard for increased Navy benefits, attacking McNamara's proposed military pay raises in early 1963 as inadequate. He was particularly disturbed by the fact that extra pay for proficiency and overseas duty was omitted. He felt strongly the need to accelerate replacement of obsolescent ships in the fleet.

Korth initiated consideration in the Navy of many ideas that were later refined or further developed under Paul Nitze and other secretaries, i.e., the entire management change under the Chief of Naval Material, the office of program appraisal, a central point within the organization of OPNAV for anti-submarine warfare, the input of more naval officers into the nuclear power training program, and a rather remarkable plan on the assignment of flag officers to jobs for which their training and background best fitted them. Yet he was frequently at odds with Anderson, sometimes over the most well-intentioned acts. Without consulting Anderson in 1962, he publicly implied that all departments at the Naval Academy except those which dealt with naval science would eventually be manned almost entirely by civilians. Because of serious opposition from naval officers, the plan did not materialize—but the number of civilians rose 30 percent in the next five years. His significant achievements, unfortunately, were overshadowed by the TFX and the political handling of the conflict of interest.

Korth was properly concerned with the defense budget and its effect on the domestic economy. As secretary it was his responsibility to maintain the balance among parts of the program. Under McNamara, it was he who sought to measure the relative military effectiveness which respective outlays would purchase. In the TFX crisis he convinced McNamara of the need to strengthen the power of the service secretary in weapon program decisions. One can only conclude that his early decisions, primarily the TFX, contributed considerably toward strengthening the relations of the Navy secretariat both with the sea service and with the defense secretary.

Yet in the TFX case Korth achieved the rare and unfortunate distinction of alienating all parties: the Navy by withdrawing his support on the TFX decision; Defense for his previous support of the Navy position; Congress over the alleged conflict of interest in the final decision. Even when he was exonerated and defended by the President for his courage and dedication, Kennedy added a sly aside on his "propensity to write too many letters."[17] All of the above contributed to an enigmatic reputation which has been little resolved in a decade subsequent to his departure from office.

NOTES

1. U.S. Senate, Committee on Government Operations, Permanent Subcommittee on Investigations, *The TFX Contract Investigation: Hearings*, 88th Cong., 1st Sess., 10 vols. (Washington: GPO, 1963–1964), 2:494, 513.
2. Korth statement in *ibid.*, 6:1399.
3. Newsman Henry Trewhitt claims that his scorecard shows the decision to have overruled the judgment of one admiral, five rear admirals, five generals, six lieutenant generals, four major generals, and literally hundreds of lesser rank. (*McNamara: His Ordeal in the Pentagon* [New York: Harper and Row, 1971], p. 139). For an itemized list see Robert J. Art, *The TFX Decision: McNamara and the Military* (Boston: Little, Brown, 1968), p. 3ff.
4. Memorandum, DDR&E to Deputy SECDEF on Bidding and Source Evaluation Procedures, 18 Aug. 1962, in *TFX Hearings* 5:1295–96.
5. *Ibid.*, 3:698.
6. *Ibid.*, 3:650–52; Eugene M. Zuckert, "Has the Service Secretary A Useful Role?" FA 44 (Apr. 1966):473–74.
7. Knowing that McNamara favored General Dynamics and only too well aware of the differences between McNamara and ADM Anderson during the Cuban missile crisis only a few days before, it would have been extremely difficult for Korth, in a nearly equal choice, to have pressed the Anderson recommendation on McNamara with great enthusiasm solely to keep harmony within the Navy family.
8. U.S. House, Committee on Appropriations 1963, *Hearings*, 87th Cong., 2nd Sess., 2 vols. (Washington: GPO, 1963), 2:4–6. Despite the McNamara statement that needs were never examined within an arbitrary ceiling, this is true only in a literal, formal sense. See Robert S. McNamara, *The Essence of Security* (New York: Harper and Row, 1968), pp. 23–24.
9. Art, *TFX Decision*, p. 108. There is direct proof of McNamara's dissatisfaction with the System Source Selection process and the role of the secretary in the process. The Defense Industries Advisory Council, which he formed in June 1962, held its first meeting in the fall of that year to consider ways of giving the civilian secretary more control over Air Force development programs. (See *TFX Hearings*, 5:1299–1300, 1321–31.)
10. The HASC had added a nuclear-powered guided missile destroyer (DLGN) to the defense program in March. This had not been requested by McNamara and it was cancelled in the fall because of delays in the Typhon missile defense sys-

tem. It was reinserted and cancelled once more in January 1964, both instances being of pique rather than of planning.

11. Elie Abel, *The Missile Crisis* (Philadelphia: Lippincott, 1966), p. 155.

12. The Honorable Fred Korth, "The Challenge of Navy Management: A Report from the Secretary of the Navy," USNIP 89 (Aug. 1963):28.

13. U.S. House, Committee on Armed Services, *Military Posture Hearings*, 87th Cong., 2nd Sess. (Washington: GPO, 1962).

14. ADM Anderson statement, *ibid.*, 8 Feb. 1962.

15. Paul H. Nitze, Assistant SECDEF (International Security Affairs) and Korth's successor, looked back on this episode with anguish, especially at the inability to apply "effectiveness values" correctly. See his memorandum to SECDEF, 13 Nov. 1964. Note also that this letter shifts ground from specific consideration of propulsion for the CVA-67 to the question of nuclear power for the Navy's future via a comprehensive study.

16. U.S. Congress, Joint Committee on Atomic Energy, *Naval Propulsion Program*, 87th Cong., 2nd Sess. (Washington: GPO: 1963). The committee denied that the "choice is between a given number of conventional ships and a smaller number of nuclear ships at the same total cost," and sharply questioned references to forces and to the "logistics tail" of the carrier force. For a further discussion of systems analysis and decision techniques with respect to the carrier, see Paul R. Schratz, "The Nuclear Carrier and Modern War," USNIP 98 (Aug. 1972): 18–25.

17. Part of the conflict of interest case was the improper use of official stationery to conduct personal business.

PAUL HENRY NITZE

29 November 1963–30 June 1967

PAUL R. SCHRATZ

Paul Henry Nitze was born in Amherst, Massachusetts, on 16 January 1908, the son of William A. Nitze, professor of Romance languages at Amherst College. He graduated from Harvard University cum laude in 1928 and joined the investment banking firm of Dillon, Reed and Co. in 1929, where he was soon known as a Wall Street prodigy. Here, incidentally, he first met James V. Forrestal. Except for a year when he had his own business, Nitze remained with Dillon, Reed until entering government service. When Forrestal became Under Secretary of the Navy in 1940, Nitze served as his assistant, but in 1941 he was named financial director of the Office of the Coordinator of Inter-American Affairs, under Nelson A. Rockefeller. Nitze subsequently served on the Board of Economic Warfare, with the Foreign Economic Administration, and the War Department. For service as vice chairman of the U.S. Strategic Bombing Survey he was awarded the Medal for Merit.

Nitze entered the Department of State in 1946 as Deputy Director of the Office of International Trade Policy. He then became Deputy to the Assistant Secretary of State for Economic Affairs and Deputy Director and later Director of the Policy Planning Staff, in 1948, in which capacity he served until June 1953. As a Republican in the Truman Administration, he helped draft the European Recovery Program, which shaped the Marshall Plan, and headed the first ERP skeleton staff.

After leaving the State Department, Nitze was elected president of the Foreign Service Educational Foundation, which sponsors the School of Advanced International Studies in Washington and administers it jointly with the Johns Hopkins University. In 1957, when the Democratic National Committee set up an advisory committee on foreign policy, Nitze served as vice-chairman under his close friend Dean Acheson. Later in the same year, he served on the H. Rowan Gaither committee, appointed by President Dwight D. Eisenhower, which warned that the Soviet Union was outstripping the United States in the missile race. A number of articles and a book on foreign policy flowed from Nitze's pen during this period. He also served on a number of national committees and chaired the John F. Kennedy pre-inaugural task force on foreign and defense policy.

In December 1960 Nitze was selected by President Kennedy to serve as Assistant Secretary of Defense for International Security Affairs (ISA) and charged with "coordinating State and Defense policies so that U.S. diplomacy and military power go hand in hand." He remained on the Defense staff under Robert McNamara until appointed Secretary of the Navy. As Assistant Secretary of Defense, he had played a key advisory role in the Cuban missile crisis as a member of the President's Executive Committee. He was active in U.S. disarmament negotiations, in the war in Vietnam, the India–China war, the various Berlin crises, and in measures to strengthen the North Atlantic Treaty Organization.

Nitze is married to the former Phyllis Pratt, daughter of a Republican Representative from New York and granddaughter of Charles Pratt, co-founder of the Standard Oil Company of New York and founder of Pratt interests in Brooklyn. The Nitzes have four children. A vigorous outdoorsman, he plays tennis, rides horseback, swims, and sails. He also plays the piano. He fulfills his love of both physical and intellectual life in trips to Aspen, Colorado, where he skis and participates in "think" sessions at the Aspen Institute for Humanistic Studies.

A stocky, handsome, and well-groomed Easterner, Nitze impresses one as a wise, able, quiet, and charming man. His charm is nevertheless edged with a somewhat Prussian quality of energy and toughness, if not austerity. He is known to be impatient with dullards, but those who have worked with him hold him in the highest regard both personally and for the quality of his work. A former associate—namely the writer—can attest to his sharp intellect, for his mind tends to run ahead of a man who is discussing something. He'll jump to the conclusion and give you the answer before you get through.

Many senior naval officers and members of Congress did not believe Nitze to be qualified to be a Secretary of the Navy because he was on record as favoring exploring the ramifications of unilateral disarmament giving the United Nations substantial control over American military might and defenses. At a conference held in California in April 1960, for example, he proposed:

(1) That we concentrate on building a variety of secure, purely retaliatory systems, (2) that . . . we scrap fixed base vulnerable systems. . . , (3) that we multilateralize the command of our retaliatory systems by making SAC a NATO command and that we will (4) turn over ultimate power of decision on the use of these systems to the General Assembly of the United Nations.[1]

Such views, even though Socratic, made him not only a target for the extreme right but for conservative congressmen, Strategic Air Command generals, and others in and out of public life. Pragmatic critics, noting that the only possible nuclear enemy was the Soviet Union, wondered how the Soviets would vote in the United Nations on use of the American retaliatory system against them.

As Secretary of the Navy, Nitze had his first experience, despite long years of government service, in managing and directing a large organization. He entered office, five weeks after President Kennedy's assassination, in a volatile period.[2] In October 1963 a military coup in Saigon and the murder of South Vietnamese President Ngo Dinh Diem threw Southeast Asian policy into a turmoil; the limited nuclear test ban treaty, negotiated in the fall of 1963, stimulated a mounting effort to move beyond weary cold war dogmas; and key domestic legislation on civil rights and social reform programs lay festering. President Lyndon Johnson continued both the Kennedy people and programs but Johnson's presidential style also made for change. Many saw him only as a "wheeler-dealer" in the Southern Democratic tradition, as a politician motivated only by a sense of where the votes lay and ignorant and uninterested in foreign affairs.

On the day he assumed office, 29 November 1963, Nitze addressed a personal letter to all flag and general officers entitled "Perspective and Current Views of the Secretary of the Navy." Confessing that he had much to learn, and recognizing the abundance of top leaders superbly managing current problems, he pleaded for support and promised a frank and free exchange of views contributing toward a strong, coordinated effort. He pointed out the need for especially close contact with program planning for the years ahead. Drawing upon his two and a half years under Secretary McNamara, whose vital concern for improving the military power of the United States demanded making best use of money and resources available for national security, he expressed the belief that he could assist in presenting, in terms capable of being understood by civilians, the military advantages of weapons systems which the Navy recommended as the best means to exploit sea power in the sixties and seventies. He would carefully evaluate the effectiveness of his department's organization and its personnel. Asking for the full support of the new Commander in Chief, he promised also the closest possible relationship with the senior military leadership in the department and his own support in carrying on the magnificent traditions of the Navy and Marine Corps.

Nitze tried from the beginning to establish a warm and congenial relationship with Navy and Marine Corps leaders. Aware of the misgivings of those who questioned his views of defense matters, of the suspicion among others that he had been sent to accelerate the Navy's indoctrination into the McNamara management techniques, of his reputation for being somewhat distant in dealing with people, and of the pain and turmoil the McNamara reforms were causing in the Navy, he nevertheless soon convinced the doubters. One of his first moves was to establish a close relationship with Admiral David L. McDonald, the Chief of Naval Operations. He even moved the Admiral's office next to his own for greater mutual accessibility.

Having come to the Navy post with a broad appreciation of global strategy and the importance of usable military strength as vividly displayed in the Cuban missile crisis, Nitze immediately impressed the admirals with his knowledge and concern for maritime power. That concern soon expressed itself in echoing McNamara's strong interest in antisubmarine warfare (ASW) as our greatest need. Nitze felt that the Navy was not doing all it should and could in undersea warfare, indeed that it was not able to perform its mission anywhere acceptably.

Despite success in tracking and forcing several Russian submarines near Cuba to the surface during the missile crisis in 1962, problems of detection, identification, location, and tracking still required major emphasis. This was particularly true in the case of the nuclear submarine opponent. Technical advances in weaponry sometimes offered great promise: SUBROC, a submarine-launched antisubmarine rocket; ASROC, the surface-launched equivalent; DASH, the unmanned drone antisubmarine helicopter, and new wire-guided or highly sophisticated homing torpedoes. All too frequently, however, the cruel sea proved a staunch adversary and promises fell far short of realization.

Because the ASW problem required better knowledge of the sea, Nitze stressed oceanographic study, especially in the circulation of ocean currents, acoustics, and bottom topography. Three oceanic survey ships were commissioned in 1963; also put into service was the floating instrument platform (FLIP), a long, cylindrical, 600-ton buoy that can be towed horizontally, then water-ballasted to float upright.

The nuclear submarine made the torpedo problem difficult; defenses were falling far behind offensive capability. Antisubmarine weapons capable of traveling at high speed and great depth needed near-human intelligence in locating, tracking, overtaking, and homing on a deeply-submerged, fast-moving, and maneuverable target. With such sophistication, the unit cost increased astronomically. Nitze was convinced that our antisubmarine forces fell far short in their ability to perform their required mission, largely because of the lack of an effective torpedo. McNamara fully supported his total dissatisfaction with the Mark 43 torpedo production schedule and insisted that the Navy accelerate production in a dual development program to provide competition. The efforts to correct the deficiencies in the SQS sonar system were almost equally important. McNamara prodded Nitze and the Navy on the single source contract. In ASW, both secretaries manifested a deeper concern than many uniformed professionals in the Office of the Chief of Naval Operations. Nitze made detailed, personal reviews of the major ASW weapon systems including studies and proposals for organizational change, means of strengthening managerial and technical direction of the program, increased combat readiness, and a better focused development and evaluation of new weapons systems to minimize problems of introduction into the fleet.

The antisubmarine warfare problem led into the broader problem of modern maritime war. Here Nitze was in a uniquely favored position. His long experience in policy positions in the departments of State and Defense and on special projects for the White House qualified him as perhaps no previous naval secretary in the understanding of war and national strategy. A profound student of strategy, he read carefully and understood papers, including contractor's brochures dealing with technical problems. He personally initiated a far-reaching "War at Sea" project as a logical and feasible alternative to the so-called "spasm war" of nuclear annihilation then much in vogue. "War at sea can be bitter and grim but it seldom results in lasting harm to real estate," he observed. Citing the possibility that the enemy might choose the seas for an all-out war against the United States, he visualized such a maritime war as presenting not only a lesser chance of deterioration into nuclear war against homeland targets, but a wholly plausible alternative on its own merit.

Two of the conflict situations Nitze visualized for the seventies and eighties were a war at sea with the Soviet Union and a limited conventional war without direct Soviet participation. In his view, the Soviets would then have achieved a standard of living close to that enjoyed in the 1960s by the United States, and European allies would have continued to prosper. Neither side could visualize, as a rational act, permitting political crises to deteriorate into a major war in Europe. Rather, it seemed more likely that a proper response to harassment in Europe would be a limited blockade at sea which might in turn lead to limited war at sea. In such a war the major role would be played by our antisubmarine warfare forces and a lesser role by antiair warfare forces. If this were to be the case, American antisubmarine warfare forces would not need to concentrate on defending the continental United States from submarines armed with nuclear-armed rockets; instead they could concentrate on defeating the enemy navy and protecting our own and allied naval and merchant ships from enemy submarines. Against the estimate of 400 operational Soviet submarines, many nuclear-powered, many equipped with underwater breathing devices similar to the snorkel, the conflict offered a serious sense of urgency. In presenting his view to a Naval War College graduating class, he said that although reaction time in a limited war would be less crucial than in a nuclear war, "technical difficulties limit our prospects." However, the NATO nations could impede Soviet submarines by mining and patrolling straits and passages, and their geographical advantages should result in "very great attrition upon enemy submarines in a limited war at sea." Limited wars without Soviet intervention could begin in a number of locations, he continued, with submarines again presenting a serious hazard. In the Pacific, however, the United States and her allies held key positions throughout the entire island chain of the northern and eastern coasts of Asia. Distance and allied command of the sea, moreover, forestalled the waging of limited wars far from Soviet or Chinese territory. He closed by saying that:

> This threat of limited war [requires] maintaining the capability to project power ashore from the sea. . . . Despite our ASW difficulties, [we] have . . . some remarkable tools for this task. By the early seventies this nation will have acquired the capability to mount out and deliver, wherever required, up to two divisions of Marines in 20-knot assault amphibious shipping. [We can] deliver these troops by new and improved techniques of horizontal and vertical envelopment, designed to meet the possibility of escalation from conventional to nuclear weapons. These assault troops will be preceded by greatly improved carrier striking forces, including in my judgment, additional nuclear-powered carriers. These and the conventionally powered attack carriers will be capable of maintaining improved antiwar war environment in sea areas of importance to us. . . . [are] capable of projecting U.S. carrier air power over 90 percent of the non-Soviet land area of the world. Our amphibious and carrier striking forces should be fully competent to meet [any] limited war threat [which we may visualize].[3]

Nitze claimed that numerous major international crises could be resolved entirely by threatening the use of sea forces. Many other actions offered the nation choices for response that minimized actions on or against the enemy homeland and maximized the degree of control so as to prevent deterioration into nuclear war. Such options at sea might include the traditional show of force, surveillance, harassment, pacific blockade, quarantine (of the type used in Cuba), interdiction, interception, reprisal, total blockade, open war at sea with conventional weapons, and a war at sea including nuclear weaponry.

The combinations of circumstances and actions were enormous even in restricted applications, such as in Southeast Asia.[4]

The War at Sea concept led to considerable improvement in the Draft Presidential Memoranda prepared annually by the Secretary of Defense. In consequence, far better integration of overall strategic policy flowed from the increased attention paid to the maritime aspects.

Closely related to his belief in the need for increased attention to ASW inherent in the war at sea concept was Nitze's concern for new construction of both warships and merchant shipping to meet U.S. needs. Senior naval officers were clearly worried about the future of the Navy, believing that the preeminence of U.S. seapower was jeopardized by limited naval construction, a steady decline in the merchant marine, and a general lack of understanding of the naval arm in the Department of Defense. Reflecting "cost efficiency" and domestic political views, the historic Brooklyn Navy Yard, despite a long public debate, was slated to be closed in December 1964 and the Portsmouth Yard (New Hampshire) to be phased out by 1975.

In one area, however, the herald of a new merchant ship era glowed brightly in the nuclear-powered *Savannah*, which made its first transatlantic voyage to Britain and North European ports in 1964. The glimmer soon faded. Superstition concerning nuclear power, labor disputes, high operating costs, and technical training deficiencies, among other problems, brought a premature eclipse. Both the ship and the idea headed for inactivation and early obscurity.

The U.S. Navy, basically of World War II vintage, was worn out from excessive commitments of too many years and too many demands on both people and machines. The inevitable result appeared in a rash of accidents, fires, and other casualties. Serious fires in two aircraft carriers, a submarine grounding off Australia, and the collision of a carrier with the nuclear submarine *Nautilus* during maneuvers in the Atlantic brought a telegram from Representative William R. Anderson of Tennessee, former captain of the *Nautilus*, to Chairman L. Mendel Rivers of the House Armed Services Committee. Calling attention to the Navy's worn out ships and overworked crews, he urged Rivers to rectify the situation independently of Secretary McNamara, saying that "The American people expect to have a modern navy built with space age effiiciency and the least possible dangers to its men."

The shipbuilding program did not develop; nor did the pattern of operations subside. Short, intense flareups such as the Dominican crisis occurred. An amphibious task force was called upon to land 2,300 fully-equipped Marines of the 6th Marine Expeditionary Unit in Santo Domingo in April 1965. Within six days, over 8,000 Marines of the 4th Marine Expeditionary Brigade were landed by sea and air. They established and maintained an international safety zone, assisted in the evacuation of 4,000 civilians, and with other U.S. forces helped restore a semblance of law within the strife-torn country. The whole operation was conducted simultaneously with the major Marine buildup in Vietnam.

Unanticipated demands upon the support services came during the search for the missing hydrogen bomb in 2,800 feet of water five miles off the village of Palomares, Spain, in January through April of 1966. Following the crash of a U.S. Air Force B–52 bomber with a KC–135 jet tanker during inflight refueling, three unarmed H–bombs were found ashore within a short time, but the fourth required 30 ships and 3,000 men for 57 days before it was located on an underwater precipice. Salvage efforts were successful. However, similar efforts incident to the tragic losses of the nuclear submarines, the USS *Thresher*, 220 miles off Cape Cod in April 1963, and the USS *Scorpion* south of the Azores in late May of 1968 failed. Both exercises highlighted the inadequacies of salvage and rescue capabilities at normal deep operating depths of the nuclear submarine forces.

A significant around-the-world demonstration cruise, Sea Orbit, was carried out in October 1964 by the nuclear-powered *Enterprise* and two nuclear-powered escorts, the missile cruiser *Long Beach* and destroyer *Bainbridge*. The 30,500-mile, 65-day voyage was made at a speed of more than 22 knots, without logistic stops. Proceeding eastward from the Mediterranean via the Cape of Good Hope, the Indian Ocean, Australia and 'round the Horn to Norfolk, the task force carried out full underway operations and ultimately launched a simulated attack upon targets in Virginia. The *Enterprise* and the *Bainbridge* shortly thereafter deployed to South Vietnam, where nuclear-powered ships were used in combat for the first time in history. Their operation across the broad reaches of the Pacific demonstrated the logistic extension provided by nuclear power, a lesson as impressive for legislators as for strategists. Yet dramatic expressions of the great mobility and flexibility of modern naval power were too easily forgotten or ignored when problems of budget and the extreme need to modernize an aging fleet again came to the fore. In no case was the enthusiasm in Congress and in certain areas of the Department of Defense more constrained than when the issue was the nuclear-powered aircraft carrier.

Nitze entered office soon after McNamara had decided that the new aircraft carrier CVA–67 would be conventionally powered. At the time of the decision, 25 October 1963, McNamara had given further indications of his attitude toward carriers in general in a statement to the Joint Committee on Atomic Energy that "whether any new carrier at all is needed is really the basic question, not what kind of propulsion system it should have."[5] Nitze had supported McNamara against his own predecessor as Secretary of the Navy, Fred Korth, in the October decision. Almost immediately upon assuming office, however, he had endorsed a statement of Navy plans to retain fifteen carriers until

1970. The Joint Committee on Atomic Energy also entered the fray, recommending that the McNamara decision against nuclear power be set aside. But McNamara on 20 February 1964 told the House Defense Appropriations Subcommittee that "by the early 1970s we plan to make some reduction in the number of attack carriers." Three days later he added that "a reduction would be made in the carrier force because an analysis of the requirement indicated to the Chiefs that [13] was a proper number . . . [although] the Chiefs split on this issue rather widely."[6] In April McNamara forced the Navy to give up its CVA role in the Strategic Integrated Operations Plan (SIOP), the common nuclear targeting plan initiated by Secretary Thomas Gates and implemented by Nitze himself several years earlier. In June, however, President Johnson named the CVA–67 the *John F. Kennedy* and suggested that the carrier planned for the Fiscal Year 1967 program be nuclear propelled. In October Nitze requested advanced procurement funds in the fiscal 1966 budget for the fiscal '67 carrier, to be named the *Chester W. Nimitz*, and in November he wrote McNamara that:

> failure of operations analyses so far has been to place the correct effectiveness on (1) being free operationally of the requirement for logistic fuel support, (2) the ability to operate warships over long periods of time at sustained speeds and (3) the strategic and tactical gain of eliminating a major at-sea replenishment requirement.

The basis for this recommendation is not clear. Since McNamara was aware of these facts and no part of the recommendation offered the quantitative measure of comparison he demanded, the memorandum was counterproductive. In budget hearings held in February 1965, McNamara repeated his judgment that only thirteen carriers were justified while Nitze insisted that fifteen were the minimum required. In April, however, McNamara, with the support of Nitze, the Chief of Naval Operations, and the Joint Chiefs of Staff, recommended to the President and Congress that no funds for the CVAN be included in the fiscal 1966 budget. Admiral McDonald could not be prodded by Congress into a break with McNamara. Asked if he had lost his nerve, he stated he did not want CVA funding "because it must come from the sister services."[7] Angry with McNamara and disgusted with the Chiefs, Congress deliberately and arbitrarily cut $1.6 billion from the defense budget, added funds for the Advanced Manned Strategic Aircraft which Air Force Chief General Curtis LeMay said he could not use, and funded two more nuclear submarines which Admiral McDonald said he could do without.[8]

McDonald, Nitze, and the Joint Chiefs at this time were in a very difficult position. McNamara was at the peak of his power and influence. From early days in office he had told the Chiefs that in testifying before Congress they were not to reveal differences with him unless pressed to do so, and then to give his side also.[9] Violations of either the letter or spirit did not go unnoticed. In June 1963, General LeMay received an unprecedented partial reappointment as Chief of Staff, Air Force (in all likelihood, to remove him from the 1964 Presidential campaign on the Barry Goldwater bandwagon); and Admiral Anderson found himself not Chairman of the Joint Chiefs as he had anticipated but Ambassador to Portugal. On most of the major service programs—the anti-ballistic missile system, the manned bomber, and the carrier—the Chiefs disagreed but decided to present a unified view. Immediately prior to the testimony given to Congress in the spring of 1965, McNamara had instructed his deputy, Cyrus Vance, to put in writing his oral directive concerning the congressional testimony of the Joint Chiefs of Staff.[10]

The following year, in July 1966, initial advance procurement funds were made available for CVAN–69, the *Eisenhower*. Before another budget period came around, McNamara and Nitze had both left office. So far had the loss of confidence of the Congress in McNamara progressed by that time that the House Armed Services Committee noted the "almost obsessional dedication to cost effectiveness" in a decision maker "who . . . knows the price of everything and the value of nothing."[11]

Centered around the continuing problems of material and weaponry was the reorganization of the Navy Department to bring it into line with new managerial procedures installed throughout the remainder of the Defense Department. Both the Army and Air Force had implemented far-reaching reforms in 1961 and 1962, and in 1963 the Navy tried to absorb the new Defense management procedures with a minimum of organizational change. For approximately three years it had functioned remarkably well without a coordinating authority below the secretarial level. However, fundamental changes were now necessary to introduce modern management techniques, and in 1966 it undertook a thorough reorganization. John H. Dillon had made a number of noteworthy recommendations resulting in the limited reorganization of 1 July 1963. The Naval Material Support Establishment created at that time subordinated the material bureaus (Ships, Yards and Docks, Naval Weapons, and Supplies and Accounts) to the Chief of Naval Material, who was directly responsible to the Secretary of the Navy. Problems persisted, however, and a new and further reorganization plan was submitted to Congress on 10 March 1966. In the absence of objection, it was put into effect on 1 May 1966.[12]

The new reorganization broke away from the traditional framework and restructured the Navy largely along functional lines. The old bilinear organization was transformed into a unilinear or vertical structure like that of the other services. The Navy's material, medical, and personnel supporting organizations were placed under the command of the Chief of Naval Operations. The infant Naval Material Support Establishment of 1963 became the Naval Material Command composed of six functional systems commands: Air Systems Command, Ship Systems Command, Electronic Systems Command, Ordnance Systems Command, Supply Systems Command (formerly the Bureau of Supplies and Accounts), and the Facilities Engineering Command (formerly the Bureau of Yards and Docks).[13]

The authority and responsibilities of the Chief of Naval Operations were increased to include command over the Chief of Naval Material, the Chief of Naval Personnel, and the Chief of the Bureau of Medicine and Surgery as well as over the operating forces.[14] In the evolving structure after 1966, therefore, the U.S. military forces for the first time in history came formally under effective unified management and direction. Purpose functions flowed from the administrative head to the unified and specified commanders; support functions flowed to the services.[15] Dualism had returned but at the Defense level, not in the services.

Critics of the unilinear system claimed that placing the entire department under a chief of service who alone is responsible to the secretary tends to make the secretary a figurehead. Franklin D. Roosevelt had resisted the unilinear concept because he had insisted upon full civilian control of the services. The unilinear concept nevertheless does give the Chief of Naval Operations a more realistic position to perform the complex job of supporting the fleet. In a forwarding letter to Congress, Nitze stated that the Navy's material support functions should be so structured as to subject them to more effective command by the Chief of Naval Material under the Chief of Naval Operations.[16] He did not say that he favored the Chief of Naval Operations at the head of both material and operations for the very practical reason that the system worked that way anyhow, no matter what the law stated.[17]

With organizational matters seemingly under control, Nitze could turn his attention to the extremely important problems of personnel. Throughout his tenure he displayed a deep and personal interest in Navy life and the education and welfare of its people that probably exceeded that of the great majority of his predecessors. Perhaps the need was greater also.

Retention of highly trained people demanded serious study because the officer resignation rate in 1964 was twice that of the previous year. Enlisted retention in certain key rates was critical. A call for volunteers produced seventeen thousand men in 1965, but the quality of the average recruit dropped somewhat and shortages appeared in vitally needed non-commissioned officers. In December 1964, Nitze established a Personnel Policy Board, which he personally chaired. A retention task force was set up (the Alford Board) as his fact-finding and analytical body. Spot promotions were offered to a number of junior officers, and personnel management was improved by the adoption of automatic data processing equipment.

The first action concerned pay and allowances. President Johnson on 12 May 1965 had proposed to Congress, effective 1 January 1966, a 5 percent increase in base pay for all except enlisted men with less than two years' service. Of greater importance, the bill provided for a federal salary review commission, for a quadrennial review of the Federal salary system, civilian and military, and for a formal system in the intervening years to make annual pay adjustments without specific action by Congress. The Military Pay Act of 1965 was claimed by Admiral McDonald to be "the act of greatest consequence to military compensation in our history."[18]

In addition, the Navy leadership devoted considerable attention to "focus pay," special compensation in areas where retention was particularly acute or in which services of a particularly valuable nature were rendered. A large cash incentive for personnel reenlisting in critical skills was offered, it being proposed to Congress that a multiple of up to five times the authorized bonus for eligible first term personnel be approved. Hazardous duty pay was pushed through Congress for flight deck personnel; restrictions on submarine pay while not actually serving on board a submarine were eased; and responsibility pay for commanding officers was increased beyond the rates established in the 1958 law.

An extensive military housing and base facilities plan was already in motion in the Defense Department. The Navy planned, for the five-year period beginning fiscal year 1966, 22,000 family housing units, 386,000 barracks spaces, and 14,000 bachelor officers' quarters. Proposed design criteria and architectural standards emphasized livability and individual privacy.

In the way of operations, the "blue and gold" plan of blue ships in port while gold are out exercising, offered promise of more stable operating schedules and predictable periods ashore for fleet personnel. In port, duty requirements were relaxed and consideration was given to civilian custodial forces such as were utilized in certain Air Force units.

Nitze succeeded in lengthening command tours from twelve to eighteen months in both qualifying and major commands. To compensate to some extent for reduced command opportunities, the list of qualifying commands was expanded somewhat to include three-striper command of destroyers, certain LSD commands, and the DLG class (double-enders).

Junior officers were given increased opportunities for promotion and increased responsibilities at sea, and an important and far-reaching change affected flag officers. In an address to Navy and Marine Corps officers in Washington, 7 June 1965, Nitze stated that he was "impressed by the fact that our flag officers are generally older by several years than their counterparts in the other services." He questioned the traditional policy on flag selection and pushed through modifications to existing regulations so as "to produce younger officers who will have time in flag grade to serve six or eight years as three or four star officers." Equally important, qualifications for selection to flag rank were broadened to include specialists skilled as operational analysts, so that officers revealing special managerial talent and the like could be given a fair opportunity to rise to the top.

Last, the Secretary added his personal and direct influence to the problem of advanced education in the Navy. He aimed to bring opportunities for advanced formal degree study at civilian universities up to comparable opportunities in the Army and Air Force.[19]

In these and similar problems, Nitze assumed a role that frequently placed him in the middle of moderate to serious disagreement with either the admirals or the defense leadership, and occasionally with both. Part of the difficulty with defense was the Navy's slowness in adjusting to the new managerial operating philosophy. Another part of the difficulty stemmed from Nitze's choosing of issues in which he challenged the position either of defense or the service.

The War in Vietnam from 1964 onward increasingly dominated administrative, operational, and managerial considerations and placed a heavy burden on the total energy and resources of the Naval Establishment. Although the formal role of the service secretary in operational matters is minimal and often questionable, Nitze for a number of reasons was drawn into the Southeast Asian operations. He had been the primary member of the McNamara team involved in foreign policy matters; he still retained a close relationship with McNamara and John McNaughton, who succeeded him as Assistant Secretary of Defense ISA. Above all, he was keenly interested in the Vietnam situation as it developed. Indeed, during his tenure the involvement of the Navy and Marine Corps in the war became his central preoccupation. The turning point was 2 August 1964, when three Vietcong torpedo boats were reported to have attacked the destroyer *Maddox* in the Gulf of Tonkin in international waters thirty miles off the coast. The torpedo boats had been driven off by gunfire, with the help of fighter planes from the nearby carrier, the *Ticonderoga*. Two days later a second attack was made on the *Maddox* and a sister ship, the *Turner Joy*. With the full support of defense and the Navy and the backing of a nearly unanimous Senate resolution, President Johnson ordered retaliatory strikes by the *Ticonderoga* and the *Constellation* against four North Vietnamese patrol torpedo bases and a fuel depot. These attacks inflicted heavy damage. Simultaneously, U.S. forces in the Far East were augmented by a carrier, an antisubmarine task group, and additional Air Force units.

Following heavy and destructive mortar raids by the Vietcong against U.S.

forces and installations at Pleiku airbase on 7 February 1965, combat operations in Vietnam reached new levels of intensity. Retaliatory raids were again authorized in an operation called *Rolling Thunder*—like thunder, designed to be spasmodic for maximum psychological effect—against carefully planned targeting minutely controlled from Washington. Within a few months, tactical air support missions were added in South Vietnam as well, and the following year most of the bombing missions against North Vietnam were flown by carrier aircraft. By the end of 1965, eighty thousand men in 140 ships and 20,000 Marines were involved in Vietnam.

The strategic concept for the increased tempo of operations in Southeast Asia had been widely referred to as "gradualism"—applying military pressure in small doses—a strategy which was to continue for almost two and a half years until April 1967, interspersed with other self-imposed bombing pauses, self-inflicted restrictions, and self-designated sanctuaries. It was hoped that selective use of overwhelming airpower against North Vietnam would force the enemy to the peace table, that gradual military pressure would "get the signal through to Hanoi," a frequently-used State Department term, and that North Vietnam would be convinced to stop attacking its neighbor. In so doing we would be able to control the conflict within the Vietnamese borders.

When he visited Vietnam in the spring of 1966, Nitze was greatly concerned by the smallness of the secure areas or enclaves controlled by South Vietnam and the enormous resources that would be required for success. Throughout 1966 and into early 1967, Admiral U.S.G. Sharp, Commander in Chief, Pacific, and the Joint Chiefs of Staff repeatedly recommended lifting bombing restrictions against North Vietnam. Sharp saw the necessity of offensive actions to curtail the flow of men and supplies into Laos and South Vietnam necessary to support aggression from the north. In April 1967, however, Nitze, along with John McNaughton and Deputy Secretary of Defense Cyrus Vance, proposed that bombing be pulled back to the 20th parallel, thus limiting it to North Vietnam's southern panhandle. This recommendation, in the absence of enemy willingness to reciprocate, was not only rejected by McNamara, but in mid-April and through May new targets were authorized and heavily attacked.[20]

On 5 July 1967, a crucial briefing was given McNamara and key Defense, State, and military leaders in Saigon—in which Nitze did not participate—which determined the future of the air interdiction campaign. Admiral Sharp again strongly recommended heavy increases in the pace of the bombing. Implemented over the succeeding months, it reached a peak of intensity in October 1967, when the northeast monsoon commenced. Also, mining of inland waterways had commenced in February 1967 and slowly dried up the traffic entering or leaving important rivers.

In another area of the war, a wholly different type of campaign had been carried out with Nitze's generally enthusiastic support. This was the so-called "Riverine Warfare" in the Delta commencing late 1965 under the code name Game Warden. The mission: patrol inland waterways; conduct visit and search; conduct surveillance to prevent Vietcong infiltration, movement, and the re-supply in the Delta and Rung Sat (or "Forest of Assassins"); and conduct mine countermeasures required to get ocean shipping into Saigon. Game Warden grew rapidly into a force of 230 river patrol boats, a growing number of Coast Guard 82-foot WPB patrols and 50-foot PCF or "Swift boat" air cushion vehicles, 4 minesweepers, 6 Seal (underwater demolition) detachments, a half dozen helicopter detachments, miscellaneous landing craft, and five non-propelled mobile bases. Aided by on-call Army aircraft and artillery, a major riverine amphibious assault, Operation Jackstay, took place late in 1966.[21] As a result, the Delta gateway to Saigon, haven of pirates and criminals for centuries and major Vietcong retraining, munition manufacture, and hospital area came under Allied control for the first time. Patrols reached a hundred miles up river and into secondary waterways and bayous near Cambodia. The U.S. Navy became involved in river patrol operations for at least the thirteenth time in its history. Although the skills and tactics of this unusual type of warfare had to be relearned, it soon produced an accomplished, veteran, river patrol force.

As the year 1967 drew to a close, the war had become very much a contest of determination. Extremely poor weather greatly limited air action. When the bombing was drastically curtailed on 31 March 1968 by President Johnson in his dramatic announcement terminating air attacks north of Latitude 20 North, it became the prelude to termination of all air attacks on North Vietnam seven months later. The 37-month effort by Task Force 77 cost over 300 airplanes destroyed in combat over North Vietnam, 1,000 others damaged, 83 pilots and crewmen killed, and 200 captured or missing. The enemy warmaking capacity was wrecked: its airfield and air forces had been destroyed, and its military complexes devastated. But with its capacity to match the numbers of men the United States sent to South Vietnam, and with mainly simple, often captured weapons, Hanoi remained at war.

Throughout the long and difficult war, direct control by civilian authority in Washington was complete, unquestioned, ubiquitous, and detailed not only at higher levels of strategy and political decisions but at lower levels of operations and tactics.[22] In that 37-month period, the enemy had not won a major ground battle and had not succeeded in subjugating South Vietnam. Nor had he ceased his aggression. He had been forced to a peace table but he would not make peace.

Nitze, meanwhile, prepared to step down as Navy Secretary, on 30 June 1967, to become Deputy Secretary of Defense. He served in his new capacity for only a few months when the Defense Secretary resigned and the McNamara era in the Pentagon came to an end.

McNamara initially held the service secretaries in relatively low esteem. The Symington Committee on Defense Reorganization and the Deputy Secretary of Defense, Roswell Gilpatric, both advocated their elimination. In less than a year in office, however, Gilpatric had softened his views that the secretaries were divisive obstacles to progress and McNamara, too, considerably changed his appraisal. Yet McNamara saw each major controversy with the services—in the TFX case, for example—as a direct challenge to his authority. He himself wanted to set defense policies and make the necessary judgments and decisions.[23] With such strongly-held views of his authority, many of his "cost-effectiveness" decisions appeared to be heavy-handed in crushing dissent. Many of his decisions infuriated military officials and sympathetic members of Congress. They also placed the service secretary in a difficult position between him and their departments. His new management procedures directly affected the secretary and, at least at first questioned the future existence of the military departments. Were the service secretaries slated for extinction or would they continue to play a useful role? Clearly there could be no turning back to the days of James Forrestal, of separate services under a paternalistic Secretary of Defense.

If McNamara's successors were in no way bound to follow his activist pattern, they could not evade the structural changes he had made in the Department of Defense. Generally his service secretaries, moreover, had to shape new formal and informal relationships with him, with the result that they developed an effective role unanticipated by either. Far-reaching managerial change gradually brought a new function, a new sense of professionalism to the Navy and Marine Corps. The leadership learned new techniques in developing a requirement, designing and producing a suitable weapon, devising and governing its proper use in battle, then training and supplying the troops to operate the weapon effectively in a familiar medium. But the team effort did not always come easily.

A new and complex middle management role emerged for the service secretary in personnel, procurement, logistics, training, and research and development. The functional conflict with McNamara resolved itself with key responsibilities retained on each side. The service secretary emerged not as a special pleader for a service viewpoint but as an operating vice president presenting a distinct and necessary view. A delicate balance wheel, the civilian head of the service advises the Secretary of Defense and serves as an intelligent advocate of service interests at the Defense level—a job which the military chief could rarely discharge as effectively. The role of the Navy Secretary, as a consequence, appeared to be more stable and challenging at the end of the McNamara era than it had for many prior years. Resourceful, energetic, and determined leadership made the new role possible; the question remained as to whether the gains could be preserved under varying conditions of leadership by future officeholders.

Nitze left the office of the Secretary of the Navy on 30 June 1967 with expressions of sincere regret by the Navy and Marine Corps leadership. No better illustration of the new and close relation of the service secretary to defense is the fact that he left the Navy to return to defense, where he served as Deputy Secretary under McNamara for the latter's remaining days in office, and under his successor, Clark Clifford, throughout the remainder of the Johnson Administration. With a breadth and depth of experience then unmatched by anyone in government, the new Nixon administration quickly recruited his services in a key role as deputy head and senior defense representative of the Strategic Arms Limitation Talks (SALT) during the difficult and prolonged negotiations with the Soviet Union. Basically a hardliner in his attitude toward the Soviet Union, China, and communism, his sense of proportion, knowledge, and sound judgment on matters of both policy and technique found quick rapport within the American delegation as well as respect by his opponents. It was his hard line attitude toward negotiations with the Soviet Union that led in the spring of 1974 to the termination of his services with the delegation.

President Nixon's increasing implication in the Watergate scandal apparently led Nitze to believe, on the eve of a June 1974 Presidential trip to Moscow, that the President would make concessions in the SALT negotiations to take attention from his domestic difficulties. On 14 June 1974, therefore, he submitted his resignation in protest, citing the paralyzing influence of Watergate on the operation of government. Although he continues an active writer, lecturer, and critic of government, his long and distinguished service to the government, at age sixty-seven, had come to an end.

NOTES

1. U.S. Senate, Committee on Armed Services, *Hearings on Nitze Nomination*, 88th Cong., 1st Sess., 7, 14 Nov. 1963 (Washington: GPO, 1963), pp. 1–90. Nitze maintains that in order to provoke discussion he followed one of the less widely accepted definitions of the economist—adroitly to pass over minor inconsistencies the better to press on to the grand fallacy. Nitze's views on nuclear weaponry are found in his *Political Aspects of a National Strategy* (Washington Center of Foreign Policy Research, School of Advanced Studies, Johns Hopkins University, 1960).

2. Some observers thought he added a duplicate set of Johnson men. A nabob accustomed to dealing with the White House growled, "I don't know who to call; it's like Noah's Ark. There's two of everybody." (Eric F. Goldman, *The Tragedy of Lyndon Johnson* [New York: A. A. Knopf, 1969], p. 23.)

3. "Address by the Honorable Paul H. Nitze," USNWCR, Sept. 1964, pp. 1–9.

4. Statement of the Secretary of the Navy Paul H. Nitze and Chief of Naval Operations Admiral David L. McDonald, HCA, *Department of Defense Appropriations for 1967: Hearings*, 89th Cong., 2nd Sess. (Washington: GPO, 1966), pp. 582–90.

5. Later the same day McNamara authorized SECNAV Fred Korth to "take steps immediately to initiate construction" of a non-nuclear carrier.

6. ADM Hyman G. Rickover interpreted the McNamara statement for the benefit of the committee by saying that "It may be that the Secretary of Defense thinks the surface Navy should be drastically reduced and if we were to build this ship as a nuclear carrier, we enhance the chances for a new surface Navy."

7. HCA, 1966. *Hearings*, 3:659.

8. SCA, 1966 *Hearings*, pp. 738, 1029.

9. SCA, 1965, p. 286.

10. HCA, 1966, 3:381.

11. U. S. Congress, House Report No. 1536, *Authorizing Defense Procurement and Research and Development, and Military Pay*, 89th Cong., 3rd Sess., 16 May 1966 (Washington: GPO, 1966), p. 9.

12. Charles H. Donnelly, *United States Defense Policies in 1965*, H. Doc. No. 344, 89th Cong., 2nd Sess. (Washington: GPO, 1966), p. 132; Navy Department General Order No. 5, 29 Apr. 1966.

13. Department of the Navy Fact Sheet, *1966 Reorganization of the Department of the Navy*, 7 Mar. 1966, pp. 2–4.

14. The CNO "command," however, is without statutory authority, it having been removed pursuant to the 1953 Amendments.

15. Scot MacDonald, "How the Decisions Were Made: Exclusive Inside Story of Navy Reorganization," *Armed Forces Management*, May 1966, pp. 74–79; interview by the writer with Paul H. Nitze, Washington, D.C., 8 Sept. 1972.

16. See Letters of Transmittal to the Congress, 10 Mar. 1966, by the SECDEF, *Reorganization of the Department of the Navy* (Washington: GPO, 1966).

17. Interview with Paul H. Nitze, Washington, D.C., 8 Sept. 1972.

18. U.S. HCA, Statement of ADM David L. McDonald, CNO, *Department of Defense Appropriations for 1967: Hearings*, 89th Cong., 2nd Sess. (Washington: GPO, 1967), p. 597.

19. See The Honorable Paul H. Nitze, Secretary of the Navy, "The Place of Higher Education in the Naval Profession," *Naval Training Bulletin*, Fall 1966, pp. 1–5.

20. Nitze's disenchantment with Vietnam continued to fester, erupting after the Tet offensive in a strongly worded memorandum on "the unsoundness" of continuing to reinforce weakness" and arguing for a policy in Vietnam placed within the context of other U. S. commitments in the world. See Townsend Hoopes, *The Limits of Intervention* (New York: David McKay, 1969), pp. 145–46.

21. See LCDR Robert E. Mumford, USN, "Jackstay: New Dimensions in Amphibious Warfare," *Naval Review 1968*, pp. 28–42. Annapolis, Md.: U.S. Naval Institute.

22. Malcolm W. Cagle, "Task Force 77 in Action Off Vietnam," *Naval Review 1972*, pp. 108–09. So ubiquitous was Defense supervision, particularly of the bombing,

that RADM Henry Miller, Commander Task Force 77, in the spring of 1965 estimated that he received more than one message per minute from the Pentagon.

23. Theodore C. Sorenson, *The Kennedy Legacy* (New York; Macmillan, 1969), pp. 416–17.

PAUL ROBERT IGNATIUS

1 September 1967–1 January 1969

PAUL B. RYAN

When Paul R. Ignatius was sworn in as Secretary of the Navy on 1 September 1967, Secretary of Defense Robert S. McNamara praised him as "one of my most trusted and valuable associates."[1] Never one to bestow idle compliments, McNamara had observed Ignatius for the past six years in three demanding assignments wherein he had earned the respect and confidence of his superiors. Ignatius's performance during his next sixteen months in the Navy Department would confirm their collective judgment.

The new secretary, forty-six years of age, was of average height and had a roundish face and dark eyes. A soft-spoken man, he had a reputation for remaining unshakably calm during tense situations.

Ignatius was born in Los Angeles, California, on 11 November 1920, to Hovsep (Joseph) B. and Elisa (Jamgochian) Ignatius, both of Armenian descent. He attended local schools and in 1938 graduated from Hoover High School in Glendale, a suburb of Los Angeles, where he was president of the student body.[2] Ignatius then graduated from the University of Southern California with honors in 1942, having earned an A.B. degree in economics along with election to Phi Beta Kappa.

With the country at war, he volunteered for the Navy, and was commissioned as an ensign.

After Indoctrination School at Fort Schuyler, in New York City, Ignatius attended the General Ordnance School in Washington, D.C., before being sent to the Naval Air Technical Training Center, Jacksonville, Florida, for instruction in aviation ordnance. As a lieutenant, junior grade, he served with Composite Squadron 80 on board the escort carrier *Manila* until 9 October 1944, when he was transferred to the ship's company as an aviation ordnance officer. The *Manila* engaged in the invasion of the Philippines at Leyte Gulf and in the Battle off Samar. After repairing substantial damage inflicted by a kamikaze, she took part in the battle for Okinawa. Following Japan's surrender, she patroled the coast of Honshu and Hokkaido while air-dropping food and clothing to prisoner-of-war camps.[3] Ignatius thus obtained a first-hand look at sea power in action that served him well when he became Secretary of the Navy.

Although he was separated from the naval service on 12 June 1946, Ignatius affiliated with the Naval Reserve until December 1955, when he resigned his commission.[4] In the meantime he resumed his war-interrupted education by entering Harvard Business School and obtaining an M.B.A. degree, in 1946. His distinguished performance resulted in an invitation to remain at the school as an instructor and research assistant. While there he married Nancy Sharpless Weiser, of Holyoke, Massachusetts. Four children were born of this union.

In 1961 Ignatius and several business school colleagues founded a management consulting firm, Harbridge House, that because of its work in defense logistics obtained contracts from both American and Canadian defense agencies and industries. During the ten years he remained with Harbridge House, Ignatius counseled the Army in the establishment of its Management School at Fort Belvoir, Virginia, and its Logistics Management Center at Fort Lee, Virginia, lectured on management and logistics at the Army War College, and also worked closely with large industrial firms on ways to improve their management methods for providing services, material, and equipment to the armed forces. By late 1960, when the Kennedy administration began seeking qualified candidates for high Pentagon posts, his name came to the attention of Army Secretary Elvis J. Stahr, Jr., who asked him to serve as Assistant Secretary of the Army for installations and logistics. Ignatius quickly demonstrated his competence. When Defense Secretary Robert McNamara, for example, asked the Army to save $459 million in his defense economy campaign, Ignatius bettered the goal by saving $736 million.[5] After only a year in office, he was awarded the Decoration for Distinguished Civilian Service, the Army's top award for non-career individuals.

Convinced that McNamara interfered too much in the affairs of the military services, Stahr resigned.[6] To succeed him McNamara chose Cyrus R. Vance, who worked in the Office of the General Counsel in the Defense Department. Impressed with Ignatius, Vance promoted him to Under Secretary on 28 February 1964.[7] Less than a year later, McNamara drafted him as an Assistant Secretary of Defense for installations and logistics, in which post he became a major source of support to him just when the Vietnam imbroglio was turning into a major war.

In managing the overall problem of delivering men and material to Indochina, ten thousand miles away, Ignatius gained an appreciation of the value of sea transport—ships that carried the vast bulk of cargo—and of the need of port facilities.[8] He promptly called for faster port construction and better ship movement control. In consequence, the 120 ships carrying military cargo that awaited unloading in November 1965 were reduced to only 34 in March 1966.

McNamara's plan for fighting the Vietnam war included the special Vietnam Steering Group, headed by Ignatius, whose task was to monitor the complex job of estimating supply requirements and matching them with production and delivery schedules, transport availability, and port cargo-capacities. Another of Ignatius's responsibilities was to inject better planning, control, and management techniques into defense procurement and thus minimize the chances of zooming costs. A third task was to allay congressional and public concern that the huge expenditures for the Vietnam War would not impede President Johnson's goals for his Great Society programs.[9]

In the summer of 1967 a sequence of events resulted in the selection of Ignatius as Secretary of the Navy, his fourth and last assignment under McNamara. The move was triggered by the resignation of Deputy Defense Secretary Cyrus R. Vance, and the appointment of Navy Secretary Paul H. Nitze to the Deputy's post. To take over Nitze's job, McNamara chose another administration veteran, John T. McNaughton, the Assistant Secretary of Defense for International Security Affairs. But before McNaughton was sworn in as Secretary, he was killed on 19 July 1967 in a midair plane collision over Henderson, North Carolina. Faced with a need to find another man who understood his system and spoke in his conceptual terms of management, McNamara recommended Ignatius for the post. Two weeks later President Johnson named him, and on 18 August 1967, the Senate unanimously confirmed him.[10]

Piqued by the feeling that the right to "advise and consent" on foreign policy was being disregarded by President Johnson, the Senate Armed Services Committee, while inquiring into Ignatius's qualifications, asked him whether he was willing to provide Congress with defense information. He assuaged the committee by saying that he would be "responsive."[11] Then, when Senator John Stennis, the chairman, asked him why he would accept the naval post, Ignatius revealed his strong sense of patriotism by saying that "I have stayed on . . . longer than I thought I would because . . . there is a job to do . . . and because we are involved in a number of important things I have elected to stay on for a longer period of time." In appreciation of Ignatius's fine record in the Defense Department, another committee member, Senator W. Stuart Symington, informed his colleagues that he believed Mr. Ignatius "to be a superb public servant." As a former Air Force Secretary, Symington was well qualified to make the evaluation.

Ignatius entered office at a time of national doubt and uncertainty. In October 1967, twenty thousand anti-war demonstrators marched on the Pentagon. McNamara himself was beginning to question the correctness of his previous actions in the war, as revealed in President Johnson's reputedly complaining to a senator that his Secretary of Defense had "gone dovish on me."[12] In the Far East, America's allies—Australia, New Zealand, Korea, Thailand, and the Philippines—had made clear to Clark Clifford during his recent round-robin evaluation visit that they were no longer prepared to support the war and that the United States would be wise to cut back its efforts.[13] There were other straws in the wind, all of which gave evidence that Ignatius would be faced with reduced naval budgets and programs in the year ahead.

On the brighter side, Ignatius's staff was blessed with abundant talent on both the civilian and military side.[14] On the latter were Admiral Thomas H. Moorer, the Chief of Naval Operations, and the Marine Corps Commandant, General Wallace M. Greene, Jr., who was succeeded by General Leonard Chapman, an officer with a splendid record particularly in management. Lower down in the naval hierarchy was a young rear admiral, Elmo R. Zumwalt, Jr., who headed the systems analysis group for Moorer and was strongly supported by Ignatius.[15] Zumwalt left the Pentagon in August 1968 to take command of the U.S. Naval Forces, Vietnam, as a vice admiral. He returned in 1970 to become the Chief of Naval Operations. Another young officer who impressed Ignatius was Captain Worth H. Bagley, Ignatius's executive assistant and aide. Bagley was later promoted to flag rank and became a vice admiral at the age of forty-eight years.

As an old Pentagon hand, Ignatius was familiar with the Navy Department's organization. Since 1966 the material organizations had reported to the Chief of Naval Operations rather than to the Secretary of the Navy. Thus the Chief of Naval Operations, as the principal executive of the Secretary of the Navy, was responsible for administering the Navy and for carrying out the Secretary's policies. Nevertheless, although the Chief of Naval Material now was a direct subordinate of the Chief of Naval Operations, he was also empowered to provide direct staff assistance to the Secretary of the Navy on matters pertaining to contracting, procurement, production, laboratories, and related matters of primary interest to the secretary.

During the McNamara years the Office of the Secretary of Defense (OSD) secured a firm administrative grip on the three services. All major (and some minor) programs emanated in OSD, whence directives flowed forth to the services for "implementation." Under the Defense Secretary, Ignatius was responsible for establishing policies and control in the Navy's organization, logistics, research and development, and personnel. He was not required to be a strategic planner; that was a responsibility borne by the Joint Chiefs of Staff. However, the Chief of Naval Operations and Marine Corps Commandant, when acting as members of the JCS, were required to keep the Secretary of the Navy informed of matters under consideration.

Ignatius saw himself in two roles, as an assistant to the Defense Secretary and also an advocate for the Navy.[16] Because the two functions were often incompatible, opposing pressures exerted on him by both sides were occasionally severe.

Early in his term, Ignatius became involved in the *Pueblo* crisis. On 23 January 1968, while in Wonsan Bay off North Korea, the USS *Pueblo*, a small auxiliary ship engaged in the collection of electronic intelligence, was captured. The ship's electronic equipment was undamaged and undoubtedly ended up in Russian hands. The eighty-three man crew was imprisoned on charges that they were operating a "spy-boat" in North Korean territorial waters.[17]

When news of the capture hit Washington, McNamara immediately asked Ignatius for details.[18] Investigation revealed that although the ship's captain, Commander Lloyd M. Bucher, had radioed for help when his ship was first threatened, no U.S. ship or aircraft arrived on the scene in time because none was within range. That many federal agencies and commands were involved in the ship's covert operations soon became evident. The U.S. government finally gained release of the crew eleven months later (save one who had died) by signing an apology and simultaneously repudiating it.

The *Pueblo* incident resulted in part from poor command procedures wherein responsibility for the ship's mission had been so divided that command accountability for the success or failure of the operation had become blurred.

A naval court of inquiry subsequently recommended a court-martial for Bucher for failure to fight for his ship. By this time Ignatius had left office and the matter was inherited by his successor, John H. Chafee. The new Secretary declined to act on the court's recommendation, stating that those involved had "suffered enough." Bucher's name surfaced again momentarily in connection with his duty in 1973 in sweeping mines from the harbors of North Vietnam planted by the United States there in 1972. He retired shortly thereafter.

If the *Pueblo* crisis eventually faded into the background, the expanding operations of the Soviet Navy caused Ignatius continuing concern, as became clear on 29 March 1968, when he addressed a symposium of senior retired officers at the Statler-Hilton Hotel in Washington. Through such meetings as this one, he sought to benefit from the experience and judgment of these naval elder statesmen. Taking note of the current policy of the Soviet Navy, as set forth by a senior Russian Admiral, to "be prepared for broad offensive operations against sea and ground troops . . . on any point of the world's oceans" and to support Russia's "state interests at sea in peacetime," Ignatius described the impressive capabilities of that navy. For example, during the Arab-Israeli War of

June 1967, the Soviet high command went to great lengths to emphasize its presence in the Mediterranean. Not only was the Russian Mediterranean fleet built up to some thirty-one surface combatant ships and thirteen submarines, but Soviet ships shadowed Sixth Fleet units, sometimes in a manner truculent and at the same time dangerous to safe navigation.

Additionally, Ignatius stated that Soviet naval squadrons had visited Arab ports in Egypt and Algeria in an obvious show of naval power. And all these activities were carried on by an adversary in an area once dominated by the Sixth Fleet and NATO navies.

Ignatius warned that the Soviet Navy was a well-equipped fighting force that posed a serious threat with the surface-to-air missiles deployed in twenty ships; more ships, similarly equipped, were scheduled for construction. The Soviet surface-to-surface missile capability was also impressive; and Ignatius pointed out that a Russian-supplied patrol boat manned by Egyptians had hit and sunk an Israeli destroyer by missile fire in the Mediterranean in 1967. A major arm of the Russian Navy was its submarine force comprising "many cruise missile submarines . . . and a formidable force of over 250 attack submarines." Equally sobering was Ignatius's belief that the Russians were "now improving their ballistic-missile submarine fleet with a construction program of nuclear-powered submarines similar to our early Polaris boats."

The list of new Russian naval developments, Ignatius disclosed, included the construction of two helicopter carriers. One of these, the *Moskva*, was a combination command ship and anti-submarine warfare (ASW) vessel that could also be employed as an assault ship in amphibious landings by carrying Soviet naval infantry (Marines), a branch reactivated in 1964 with much fanfare.

Asked what motivated the Soviets to develop such a large, versatile, and global naval force, Ignatius suggested that the Soviets wished to use naval power to gain political and psychological advantages both in peacetime situations and in periods of tension. There was no doubt, he added, that the movement of Soviet forces in strength to the Mediterranean marked the end of exclusive U.S. and NATO presence in that area and was a potential threat to a vital sea line of communication. Even in Asia and Africa, he observed, the Russians now had a naval force that could be used to support their political interests. In short, it was evident that Russia would use its navy as an implement to support its initiatives in power politics through demonstrations of shows-of-force. Ignatius concluded that only by maintaining American naval power could we defend ourselves against new forms of Soviet attack. Only through a strong Navy could the U.S. government "work for relaxation of tensions between the West and East." While he recognized that the Soviet navy was "here to stay," he left his audience with the generally optimistic picture that "our fleet is far larger, stronger, and more versatile than theirs and we intend to keep it so."[19]

While Ignatius watched Soviet naval expansion with a wary eye, U.S.-Soviet relations began thawing considerably early in 1968. On 13 January, a consular convention was signed. On 21 June, the U.S. Government agreed to a direct airline service between New York and Moscow. Perhaps more important, Russia and the United States on 1 July arranged for future discussions on the limitation of nuclear arms. And if it was true that Russia's invasion of Czechoslovakia, on 20 August 1968, to quell a trend toward liberal rule, temporarily slowed this move toward improved relations, the American public tended to set aside the Soviet Navy as a long-range problem that did not require immediate action.

Ignatius's preoccupation with the Soviet naval threat was well founded. Starting in the 1950s and continuing into the 1960s, the Soviet navy underwent a rapid expansion that changed it from a traditionally coastal-defense force into a tool to support Soviet interests world-wide. By 1968, during Ignatius's tenure, the Soviets possessed a navy of some five hundred thousand men manning a modern fleet that was second in strength only to the American Navy.[20] In 1968, the defense budgets of the United States and Russia (of which their navies received approximately one-third) were $77 billion and $40 billion, respectively. The nearest competitor in terms of defense outlays was mainland China, with $7 billion, followed by France, $6.1 billion, Britain, $5.5 billion, and West Germany, $5.1 billion. Far down the list were Italy, with $1.9 billion, Canada, $1.6 billion and Japan, $1.2 billion. The navies of the two superpowers clearly dwarfed those of the rest of the world.

The intensive Russian shipbuilding program contrasted sharply with that of the United States, where the rising costs of the Vietnam War and urgent domestic programs combined to turn public attention away from the need to replace the Navy's aging World War II ships. In building up its fleet, the Soviet high command had concentrated on strengthening its elite submarine force ever since the end of World War II.

Giving substance to Ignatius's assertion of Russian submarine strength was a force reportedly consisting of some 330 conventional boats and 50 nuclear vessels. Thirteen of the nuclear type and 30 of the conventional class were believed to carry ballistic missiles. And it was quite true, as Ignatius stated, that the Russians were constructing submarines similar to those of the U.S. Polaris class. That the Russians were also closing the gap in naval strategic weapons was evident from a report by the authoritative Institute of Strategic Studies which, in early 1969, estimated that the Russians now had 125 ballistic missiles installed in fleet submarines compared to 656 carried by U.S. Polaris boats and that they were closing the gap. At this time, the U.S. Navy had 41 Polaris boats and 102 other submarines including 40 nuclear attack types.

While the Soviets were far from approaching the unique capabilities of the U.S. carrier task forces (each of 15 carriers had an air group of from 80 to 100 planes), the fact that Soviet naval architects had designed the innovative *Moskva* class foreshadowed their potential to build true aircraft carriers. And already the Russian naval air arm comprised an impressive force of 400 shore-based bombers plus 500 other types of naval aircraft.

Another index that offered a comparison between the two navies was that of combatant surface ships. In this category the United States in 1968 had 337 equipped for antisubmarine warfare (ASW), anti-air warfare (AAW), and other tasks. In contrast, the Russian fleet included 230 cruiser/destroyer/escort type ships, many of them carrying surface-to-surface and surface-to-air missiles to which Ignatius had flagged attention.

One area in which the Russians clearly were deficient was that of amphibious warfare. The U.S. Navy's twenty-six years of amphibious experience in three wars gave it a pronounced superiority in that field of naval warfare. And in 1968 its 165 amphibious assault ships, including eight new helicopter-carrying LPHs (later LPAs), far outmatched the one hundred to two hundred landing ships and craft of the Soviet navy.

When Ignatius stated that the U.S. Navy was more versatile than its Russian counterpart, he had the element of mobile logistic support in mind. Since World War II the U.S. Navy had developed to a fine art the techniques of underway replenishment, maintenance, and repair. In the 1960s, the Navy's approximately two hundred mobile support ships gave the Sixth and Seventh Fleets unsurpassed mobility and endurance in conducting operations at sea. There was no evidence that the Russian navy had attained a commensurate capability. Nevertheless, the Russians had taken steps to correct this weakness. One example was apparent in five large support ships for their nuclear submarine force. Additionally, they had converted certain cargo ships to serve as tenders and replenishment ships. Obviously, they were well aware of the need for mobile logistic support ships in their plans for naval expansion.

In comparing the U.S. and Soviet naval services, one must also take into account their Marines. Here again the differences were marked. The 302,000 U.S. Marines had no equal in their role as the spearhead of amphibious operations. Notwithstanding the fact that they were far behind, the Russians by 1968 had a corps of some 8,000 naval infantry, and indications were that the number of these so-called "Black Berets" would continue to grow.

In summary, during the decade of the sixties, while the U.S. Congress and the public were distracted by war as well as by mammoth domestic problems and international monetary crises, conditions were anything but favorable for the Navy to succeed in obtaining approval of an expensive ship construction program. In the meantime, as Ignatius pointed out, the Soviets now possessed a global naval force that was steadily expanding, making them a strong contender for the position of the world's number one navy in the years ahead.

During the years when the Navy's chief preoccupation was with the war in Indochina, participation in NATO affairs and other multilateral organizations inevitably declined. During Ignatius's term the Navy nevertheless assigned a destroyer to full-time service with a NATO squadron. This move came about in early 1968 in consequence of a decision of the Brussels meeting of the NATO foreign ministers to transform the NATO "training squadron" into the Standing Naval Force Atlantic (StaNavForLant). When the squadron was activated at Portland, England, on 13 January 1968, it comprised a British frigate, a Dutch destroyer, a Norwegian frigate, and a U.S. destroyer, all ASW ships.[21] This move, probably of more political than military benefit, undoubtedly was taken in order that NATO, by presenting a more united front in naval operations, could counter the growing Russian naval presence in the Mediterranean, the North Sea, and the waters around the British Isles.

Other problems arose. In an effort to improve the quality of the Navy's flag officers, Ignatius expressed to Admiral Moorer his interest in the selection of relatively young but talented captains to flag rank. Specifically, he focused on the "head and shoulders" type of officer skilled in modern management techniques as well as having the traditional qualifications for promotion.

As more American business managers such as Ignatius were named to high Defense Department posts, they were drawn to this type of officer, one who "spoke the language" and could manage complex programs. In its own interest, if it were to compete in the system-analysis world of the Pentagon's E ring, the Navy needed officers who could prepare proposals for new weapons systems couched in terms acceptable to OSD.[22]

Rightly or wrongly, this trend toward managership was universally applauded in the service. But one critic observed in 1972 that selection boards now were placing greater emphasis on those who were project managers or technical experts and that the old requirement of maximum command-at-sea was no longer accorded top consideration. Inevitably, he concluded, the unlooked-for result would be a lack of officers possessed of "battle-mindedness," that is, officers who knew how to fight their ships by motivating, training, and leading their men in combat.[23]

However, in 1968 Ignatius had no qualms in counseling the flag selection board to meet the Navy's requirement for experts in systems analysis, financial management, and oceanography. Then, in recognition of the traditional requirements, he commented that "operational proficiency at sea" should be a necessary qualification and that "difficult decisions lay ahead for the board."[24] It would take four more years before the managerial trend would evoke genuine alarm among the "battlemindedness" school.

Another headache for Ignatius was the Arnheiter affair, a matter which had festered since 1966. As did the *Pueblo* incident, the case involved such basic issues as command-at-sea, discipline, and the traditional honor code of an officer.

In the spring of 1966 Lieutenant Commander Marcus A. Arnheiter had been relieved summarily of command of a destroyer escort reportedly because of certain irregular practices detrimental to the morale and efficiency of the ship. Over the next year, press stories criticized the mistreatment accorded a "talented if unorthodox officer."[25] In May 1968, the case reached Capitol Hill when a New York Congressman, Joseph Y. Resnick, held a public hearing in an attempt to force the Service to arrange for a court of inquiry. Resnick, who had made himself Arnheiter's champion was, incidentally, campaigning for senator and reportedly was not averse to the attendant publicity. After calling on the Navy to give Arnheiter his day in court, Resnick demanded the resignation of Ignatius.[26] However, the House Armed Services Committee had studied the case and refused to hold a formal hearing on the ground that the Navy had taken proper action in the affair. Ignatius later recalled that he had spent "untold hours" examining the record to ensure that Arnheiter had received just treatment.[27] He remained convinced that the Navy indeed had decided correctly. Arnheiter retired from the active service in 1971; Congressman Resnick was defeated in his try for the senatorship and died in 1969.

As the Vietnam war rose in intensity, so did the Navy's problem of manpower retention. In the late 1960s young officers were resigning at such a rapid rate as to create an acute shortage. By 1968, in the submarine force alone, 50 percent of its nuclear-trained junior officers were retiring; in the surface ships, middle grade officers were likewise resigning. Moreover, naval aviation was beset by a lack of trained pilots, traceable chiefly to a Department of Defense economy move initiated several years previously in an effort to save funds. The shortage was aggravated by the lure of the airlines, which presented irresistible opportunities to naval aviators.[28] Equally depressing, the enlisted ranks were growing thinner as naval technicians left the Navy for well-paying jobs in industry.

The Navy's apparent difficulty in retaining men could be blamed readily upon the war in Vietnam, with its long deployments. But there were other reasons: stepped-up operations at sea, aging ships requiring frequent repairs, and last, as Ignatius described it, a movement "to denigrate the role of the military man. These unjustified attacks on the military image add to the problem of motivating impressionable young men toward a career in the Navy."[29]

The Navy took several steps to improve the situation. The new Secretary of Defense, Clark Clifford, authorized the Navy to increase its pilot training, and the Air Force and the Army agreed to provide some flight training for Marine Corps pilots. Ignatius approved more postgraduate education for young officers, a shortened first tour at sea for nuclear submarine officers, and improvements in the enlisted men's situation, specifically in college education, individualized assignments, less family separation, and more shore duty. He also expressed satisfaction with the plan to reduce a ship's crew through shipboard automation.[30]

Directly tied to the retention issue was the racial question. In November 1967, the Navy under Ignatius's direction launched a high priority campaign to double the number of black naval and Marine Corps officers. At the time there were 290 Navy and 155 Marine Corps black officers in the naval service. The plan called for recruiting activities at predominantly Negro colleges, of which there were one hundred seven in the nation; an intensified effort to secure more black candidates for the Naval Academy; and the establishment of the first Naval Reserve Officer Training Corps (NROTC) at the predominantly black Prairie State A and M College in Texas.

A year later the Navy could announce that it had almost tripled the ranks of black officers and that its policy was to continue the recruiting program until the number of minority group officers was proportional to their percentages in the U.S. population. The success of the recruiting effort was matched by the excellent retention rate of black officers.[31]

Ironically, the drive to recruit minority group officers suffered from an economy move when in October 1968 the Navy slashed the candidate input to naval and Marine Corps officer training schools by five hundred candidates. The Navy also eliminated a substantial number of educational and training programs, a fund-saving action that realistically took precedence over its desire to improve retention.[32]

Aside from the Navy's efforts, a Defense Department committee charged with attracting and keeping service personnel conducted a review of military pay in 1967. Subsequently Congress enacted legislation increasing the pay scale. Ignatius himself thought that this action would make the military career more nearly competitive with opportunities in civilian life.[33] However, the retention problem appeared insoluble and continued to plague his successors.

To set Ignatius's work in perspective against the backdrop of the late sixties, it is necessary to introduce some basic budgetary and personnel data. Although statistics can be dull, they do provide a sound scale for measuring the Navy's activities within the Department of Defense. The Army's budget went from $22.6 billion in FY 1967 to $26.7 billion in 1969; the Air Force's from

$24.6 billion to $26.7 billion; and the Navy's from $21.3 billion to $22.5 billion.[34] In 1963, the Navy included 663,000 men (74,000 officers and 585,000 men); in 1968, 765,000 men (85,000 officers and 675,000 men).[35] The Marines, similarly, went from 190,000 to 307,000 men. During the same years, the Navy kept pace with increases in the Army while the Air Force actually lost some men.[36]

In sum, the magnitude of the Navy's programs, as part of the overall U.S. Department of Defense's budget, attained new levels. In looking back up on his participation in the preparation of the budget, Ignatius recalled that during the McNamara period, despite the intensity of feelings by individual service representatives, these differences were resolved. As he put it:

> The Secretary [McNamara] was anxious to establish budgetary requirements without the imposition of any prior ceilings or allocation among the services in order to determine the force structure that was needed. He expected the Services to come forward with their requirements and depended upon his own staff for detailed analysis prior to decision making. This imposed an enormous workload on the Secretary and Deputy Secretary as well as upon the OSD and Service staffs, but Mr. McNamara felt that the force structure requirements should be determined without prior budget restraints. Ultimately, of course, budgetary considerations were undoubtedly a factor. ...[37]

But if the "final" decisions on the proposed service budgets were taken by the Secretary of Defense, there still remained the Congressional budget hearings, where airings of different opinions sometimes became heated, as related below.

A bitter controversy between McNamara and certain influential congressmen over nuclear-powered ships exemplified the pressures to which Ignatius was subjected both from the Secretary of Defense's office and the Navy. McNamara, who held that nuclear ships might not be worth the price, based his position on studies by his systems analysis staff, headed by Alain Enthoven. Consequently he urged caution.[38] But the Navy and its congressional supporters argued that a nuclear fleet would have the obvious combat advantages of increased range, responsiveness (speed), staying power, and reduced vulnerability to nuclear attack. Therefore, delay was not prudent.

Where did Ignatius stand on this hot issue? He explained the dilemma confronting him in a Navy Day speech at Chicago in October 1967. The choice was between a complete nuclear fleet or a combination of nuclear ships and conventional vessels. For justifying his selection of the latter he referred to "studies" (apparently the Enthoven systems analysis) that showed that in a major war we would need so many destroyers it would not be economical to have them all nuclear-powered. Why? Because a nuclear escort ship cost twice as much as a conventional ship. Further, Ignatius asserted that we did not have sufficient industrial capacity to produce such a large nuclear program in view of the commercial nuclear-power programs to which our industrial base was already committed.[39]

One of the Defense Department's most controversial and costly procurement programs in which Ignatius was embroiled was that over the F–111 aircraft, a McNamara-sponsored project originated in 1961. The F–111 presumably was an aircraft embodying "commonality" features making it suitable for use by the Air Force and by naval carrier aviation. The Navy's version of the plane was known as the F–111B.

By the summer of 1967, senior naval officers had become alarmed that the F–111B was certain to be crippled by excessive weight, thus disqualifying it for use by the Navy. These fears prompted them to initiate an alternative proposal for another fighter first known as the VFX.

Fully aware of the reluctance of influential members of the Congress (one of whom was Senator John McClellan, Chairman of the Government Operations Committee, who called the F–111B "a flop")[40] but knowing that the Navy's study of proposals for the VFX was not yet complete, Ignatius took an interim position. On 22 January 1968, he and Admiral Moorer issued a statement that, because the assessment would not be available for several months, the Navy would continue to support the F–111B. In the Secretary's view, this course of action would provide insurance for the fighter procurement programs and was worth the cost.[41]

As it turned out, the F–111B was killed by the Senate Armed Services Committee, whose members voted by eleven to two to omit all F–111B funds from the fiscal year '69 defense authorization bill. In a subsequent action, however, Congress approved funds for development of the VFX. Anticipating the congressional vote, Secretary of Defense Clark Clifford on 10 July 1968, authorized the Navy to cancel the F–111B program. When the Fiscal Year 1969 defense appropriations bill was passed, it included $130 million for the VFX project, later named the F–14. As for the F–111, the Air Force continued to have problems with the aircraft.[42]

Ignatius was near the end of his tenure as Secretary when two Washington journalists separately requested interviews to discuss the accomplishments of the past year as well as the problems that lay ahead.[43] During the interviews Ignatius gave a broad overview of the major issues facing the Navy. While he did not minimize such serious problems as the paucity of shipbuilding funds, he made it clear that the service was advancing toward its goal of a modern fleet. To prepare himself for the interviews he had compiled a lengthy memorandum touching on those questions which might be asked.

On the matter of ship construction, he noted that the fiscal year 1969 naval budget allotted only $800 million (4 percent of the budget) for ship-building. In his opinion, this amount was impossibly low to operate a modern Navy. It was the Navy's collective duty, he thought, to gain more support for its ship program.

What was the Navy's number one operational problem? Without a doubt it was antisubmarine warfare, said the Secretary; the Navy should consider not only antisubmarine warfare submarines but other types such as patrol, attack, and missile submarines. While there was no "magic number" on the mix of submarine types, he asserted that there was general agreement on approximately one hundred to one hundred ten submarines, a combination of nuclear and conventional boats. He regretted the inactivation of the antisubmarine warfare carrier *Randolph* and other antisubmarine warfare units. He had concurred reluctantly in the decision because this fund-saving action would have little effect on the Vietnam war. Moreover, he observed, the core of skilled antisubmarine warfare personnel had been reduced and the Navy would certainly suffer in the future. Equally unfortunate, the cutback would place an undue burden on remaining antisubmarine units.

Turning to the attack carrier construction program, Ignatius explained that it was based on a level of four nuclear attack carriers replacing the older *Hancock* type. Two of these new ships had been funded through the fiscal year '68 and fiscal year '69 budgets. Funds for the fourth carrier were planned for the fiscal year '71 budget.

In addressing the submarine program, Ignatius declared that the *Permit/Sturgeon* classes of nuclear attack submarines were two of our most effective antisubmarine warfare systems. The fiscal year '68 budget funded a major conversion program to improve thirty-one of forty-one fleet ballistic missile submarines and to equip them with the Poseidon missile. The Secretary further commented on a new force of specially configured submarines armed with advanced long-range ballistic missiles. This undersea long-range missile system, first known as ULMS, later was designated Trident.

Related to the antisubmarine warfare problem was the program for fleet escort ships, of which there were three types: ocean escort, multi-purpose destroyers, and frigates. Currently, the Navy had seventy-seven ocean escorts, which Ignatius thought enough; hence no more were planned. But the multi-purpose destroyer was a different case. Many of this type still operating were of World War II vintage and obsolescent. Therefore, the Navy planned for a multi-year procurement of a replacement type. As for frigates, he emphasized that construction contracts for two nuclear frigates had been awarded in fiscal year '67 and fiscal year '68. He concluded by stating that "owing to higher investment costs we cannot nuclearize the Navy overnight, but we see the need to construct more of these ships annually. . . ."

Finally, in his summary of the building program Ignatius described the new general purpose amphibious assault ship, the LHA. It was "a significant example of the Navy's continuing efforts to provide maximum military effectiveness at least cost." Not only could it land a Marine battalion landing team by surface assault craft, it could also put the Marines ashore by helicopter. Furthermore, the LHA combined the capabilities of four other amphibious ship-types used in the past. By mid-1968 the Navy had in hand design and production plans and had selected Litton Industries as the contractor. Ignatius expressed satisfaction that this contract offered an opportunity to realize cost savings associated with series production of a sizable number of ships by one shipyard.[44]

Ignatius's concern for a modern fleet was reinforced by Congressman Porter Hardy, of Virginia, in a report released in August 1968. Based on a House Armed Services Committee subcommittee's inspection of the forces afloat, the report stated that the Sixth fleet now suffered from "a marginal state of readiness." Further, it strongly implied a condition of overall degradation and accelerated deterioration of equipment.[45] The congressman recognized that these inadequacies derived from the requirements of the Seventh Fleet in the Far East. Consequently, the absence of the Atlantic Fleet tenders and supervisory enlisted men (sent to Indochina) had created problems of repair and maintenance in the Atlantic and Mediterranean naval forces. None of this information was news to Ignatius, who was very conscious of the aging fleet and consistently pressed for a balanced shipbuilding and ship modernization program.

With the inauguration of Richard M. Nixon to the presidency, Ignatius left the Pentagon to become president of the *Washington Post*. He resigned in 1971 to be the executive vice president of The Air Transport Association in Washington. Subsequently he became president and chief executive officer, positions he held as of this writing (1978).

Ignatius's term, although relatively brief, took place during a time of transition and proved of substantial benefit to the Navy. In an era when many in the Service were mystified and frustrated by the defense policies of the McNamara era, Ignatius brought a calm and stabilizing presence. As a management expert he helped naval procurement programs to gain approval by ensuring that they were presented in a format and terminology preferred by OSD system analysts. Under his direction, the Navy kept alive the nuclear ship program and fought successfully for the electric drive "quiet" submarine. Last and most important, the Navy Department supported, in impressive fash-

975

ion, U. S. operations in Southeast Asia. A significant part of the credit for the management of the Department's resources in this major effort must go to Ignatius.

NOTES

1. *Philadelphia Inquirer*, 3 Sept. 1967.
2. *Glendale* (Calif.) *News-Press*, 13 Feb. 1964.
3. Department of the Navy, *Dictionary of American Naval Fighting Ships*, 5 vols.— (Washington: GPO, 1959–   ), 4:214–16.
4. BUPERS letter "To Whom it May Concern," Pers E24, serial 195868, dated 23 Sept. 1968.
5. Hal Bamford, "Cost Reduction at No Expense to Readiness," *Armed Forces Management*, Dec. 1963, pp. 18–20; *New York Times*, 9 Dec. 1963.
6. *New York Times*, 8 July 1962. For details see James M. Roherty, *Decisions of Robert S. McNamara* (Coral Gables: University of Miami Press, 1970).
7. *New York Times*, 5 Aug. 1967.
8. See "Where the Vietnam Pipeline Begins," *Business Week*, 16 Apr. 1966, p. 188; banquet speech by Ignatius in Defense Supply Association, *DSA Review*, Nov.-Dec. 1966.
9. "Where the Vietnam Pipeline Begins," 190.
10. Weekly Compilation of Presidential Documents, 4 Aug. 1967; *Washington Post*, 5 Aug. 1967.
11. U.S. Senate, *Hearings Before the Committee on Armed Services, U.S. Senate, 90th Congress, 1st Session on . . . Nomination of Paul R. Ignatius to be Secretary of the Navy* (Washington: GPO, 1967), pp. 1–9. On the use by Congress of its investigative powers in 1967–1968, see Francis E. Rourke, "The Domestic Scene," in Robert E. Osgood and others, *America and the World* (Baltimore: Johns Hopkins Press, 1970), pp. 169–71.
12. Townsend Hoopes, *The Limits of Intervention* (New York: David McKay, 1969), p. 90.
13. *Ibid.*
14. Interview with Paul M. Ignatius, Washington, D.C., 12 June 1972 (hereafter cited as Conversation with Ignatius).
15. *Ibid.*
16. *Ibid.*
17. For a full account, see Trevor Armbrister, *A Matter of Accountability* (New York: Coward McCann, 1970); U.S. House, Armed Services Committee, Rpt. No. 91–10, *Inquiry into the USS Pueblo and EC-221 Plane Incidents* (Washington: GPO, 1969); Lloyd M. Bucher, with Mark Rascovich, *Bucher: My Story* (Garden City, N.Y.: Doubleday, 1970); Daniel V. Gallery, *The Pueblo Incident* (Garden City, N.Y.: Doubleday, 1970); Don Crawford, *Pueblo Intrigue* (Wheaton, Md.: Tyndale House, 1969); and Edward R. Murphy, Jr., *Second in Command* [The *Pueblo Affair*] (New York: Holt, Rinehart, and Winston, 1971).
18. Harold Heffner, "Sally Moser—The Secretary's Secretary," *Our Navy*, Nov. 1968, p. 35.

19. News release of speech by Ignatius, No. 278–68, Office of ASECDEF (Public Affairs), 29 Mar. 1968.

20. For an authoritative listing of the naval and Marine Corps strength of the Soviet Union and of the United States that prevailed during Ignatius's tenure, see *The Military Balance 1968–1969* (London: Institute for Strategic Studies, 1968), pp. 7–8, 30–31, 55–56. *Janes' Fighting Ships, 1968–1969* (London: S. Low Marston Co., 1968) agrees closely with the I.S.S. lists.

21. *NATO Letter* (Brussels: NATO Information Service,) Jan. 1968, p. 25, Apr. 1968, p. 16.

22. For a discussion of this trend, see Anthony L. Wermuth, "Youth Wants to 'No.'" USNIP 98 (July 1972):50–55.

23. CAPT R. A. Bowling, USN, "Battle-Mindedness," USNIP 98 (Oct. 1972):42.

24. Letter from SECNAV to the Flag Officers Selection Board, quoted in AFJ, 25 May 1968, p. 15.

25. Neil Sheehan, of the *New York Times*, covered the Arnheiter case for his newspaper and later wrote a thoroughly researched account entitled *The Arnheiter Affair* (New York: Random House, 1971). Sheehan is convinced that Arnheiter was not qualified for command, but he faults the Navy for its handling of his case.

26. Sheehan, *The Arnheiter Affair*, p. 242.

27. Conversation with Ignatius.

28. *Armed Forces Management*, Oct. 1968; AFJ, 21 Sept. 1968, p. 12.

29. Speech by Secretary Ignatius at Navy League banquet, McAlester, Oklahoma, 26 Oct. 1968.

30. *Ibid.*; AFJ, 9 Nov. 1968, p. 21.

31. AFJ, 4 Nov. 1967, p. 8, and 21 Sept. 1968, p. 12.

32. *Ibid.*, 12 Oct. 1968, p. 35.

33. Speech by Secretary Ignatius, McAlester, Oklahoma, 26 Oct. 1968.

34. *1970 Defense Budget and Defense Program: A Statement by Secretary of Defense Clark M. Clifford* (Washington: Department of Defense, 1969), p. 157.

35. *Appendix, The Budget of the U.S. Government, 1965* (Washington: GPO, 1964), p. 241; *Appendix, The Budget of the U.S. Government, 1970* (Washington: GPO, 1969), p. 257.

36. *1970 Defense Budget and Defense Programs*, p. 161; *Appendix, The Budget of the U.S. Government, 1965*, p. 241.

37. Paul Ignatius to the writer, 18 Dec. 1972.

38. *Defense Secretary's Annual Statement on Defense Posture*, in *Hearings Before the Committee on the Armed Services*, 90th Cong., 1st Sess. (Washington: GPO, 1967), p. 839.

39. Speech at Navy League Banquet, Chicago, Ill., 27 Oct. 1967.

40. *Congress and the Nation*, 2 vols. (Washington: Congressional Quarterly Service, 1969), 2:877.

41. Conversation with Ignatius, 12 June 1972.

42. For a comprehensive account of the F-111, see *Congress and the Nation*, 2:875–78.

43. Scott MacDonald, of *Armed Forces Management*, and Orr Kelley of the *Washington Evening Star*.

44. Memorandum in files of Office of SECNAV dealing with 16 issues. (Record of interview with Orr Kelley, 13 Nov. 1968, signed by CAPT W. Thompson, USN, in Secretary's files, The Pentagon); Scott MacDonald, "We Pay a Dear Price for New Ships," *Armed Forces Management*, Oct. 1968.

45. AFJ, 31 Aug. 1968, p. 13; Report of Special Subcommittee on National Defense Posture, "Review of Vietnam Conflict and Its Impact on U.S. Military Commitments Abroad," *Armed Forces Management*, Oct. 1968, pp. 56-60; Committee Report, *The Changing Strategic Naval Balance, U.S.S.R. vs. U.S.A.*, prepared at the request of the Committee on Armed Services, House of Representatives, 90th Cong., 2nd Sess., Dec. 1968 (Washington: GPO, 1968), pp. 21-25.

JOHN HUBBARD CHAFEE

31 January 1969–4 April 1972

PAUL B. RYAN

The Senate confirmed John Hubbard Chafee as Secretary of the Navy on 29 January 1969. A "liberal" Republican allied with a conservative administration, he recently had been defeated for the governorship of Rhode Island. He came to his new job when the Navy was in the midst of a sharp transition, as shown in a worsening maritime posture, a smaller fleet, different ship designs, minority group flare-ups, and shifting social mores. Forty-six years of age in 1969, Chafee had an informal and engaging manner, but fellow Republicans knew of his determination to improve the lot of the personnel in the service, particularly of the underprivileged.[1]

Early in the presidential campaign of 1968 Chafee had alienated certain followers of Richard Nixon by backing Governor George Romney, of Michigan, for the nomination. When Romney withdrew, Chafee not only supported Governor Nelson Rockefeller, of New York, but strongly opposed the selection of Governor T. Spiro Agnew, of Maryland, for the vice presidential post. As Chafee acknowledged after the election, the Nixon team owed him no political favors.[2] To some, therefore, his nomination as Secretary of the Navy was totally unexpected.

Chafee was surprised when Vice President-elect Agnew telephoned to ask what federal office interested him. Chafee preferred a position dealing with domestic problems. But Defense Secretary-designate Melvin Laird then telephoned and persuaded him that the Navy post required his acceptance.[3] Various GOP leaders regarded the placing of key "liberal" East Coast Republicans such as Chafee in the administration as a shrewd demonstration of party unity. President-elect Nixon told Laird that he was free to select whomever he wished for his associates in the Pentagon. After considering several candidates, Laird settled on Chafee. "It was a good choice," said David Packard, the new Deputy Secretary of Defense.[4] Chafee's appointment delivered him from political limbo. But because it did not call upon him to "commit himself for life," presumably, he would be free to run again for political office.[5]

The new Secretary was descended from a long line of New England public servants. Both his great-grandfather and a great-uncle had been governors of Rhode Island. Another great-uncle had served in the U.S. Senate. More recently an uncle, Professor Zechariah Chafee, had been a famous law professor at Harvard. To this distinguished lineage, Chafee was born in Providence on 22 October 1922, the son of John Sharpe and Janet (Hunter) Chafee. The family owned an iron foundry and, later, a firm that manufactured measuring instruments.

After attending Providence Country Day School, in 1938, at the age of sixteen years, Chafee enrolled at Deerfield Academy, Deerfield, Massachusetts, where he played varsity football and lacrosse as well as editing the school paper and being a member of the chess club. In September 1940 he entered Yale.

Following the attack on Pearl Harbor, the nineteen year-old sophomore enlisted in the Marines and in February 1942 began training at Parris Island, South Carolina. By July he was in Wellington, New Zealand, as a member of 5th Battalion, 11th Marines, preparing for combat in the Solomons. Several weeks later, on 7 August, his battalion landed at Guadalcanal. Assigned to a fire-direction team, he immediately engaged in some of the most fierce fighting of World War II. In November 1943, he arrived at Quantico, Virginia, to attend the officer candidate school, from which he graduated in June 1944.[6]

After training in photo-interpretation and combat intelligence, Second Lieutenant Chafee was designated as staff-intelligence officer and ordered to the 6th Marine Division at Guam. Shortly thereafter he was once again in combat, this time on Okinawa. In September 1945, following the Japanese surrender, he was ordered to Tsingtao, the seaport city in North China where U.S. naval and Marine forces formed up to accept the surrender of Japanese troops and to provide for their transportation to Japan. Returning to the United States in December 1945, Chafee was mustered out but retained his reserve commission. In March 1946 he re-entered Yale, graduating in the class of 1947. He then enrolled at Harvard Law School.[7]

At Cambridge, Chafee did well academically, placing in the top 25 percent of his class. In 1950, law degree in hand, he passed the Rhode Island bar examinations and joined a Providence law firm. An equally important event in his life was his marriage to Miss Virginia Coates, of Bayville, New York, whom he had met at a Vermont ski resort after the war.

The North Korean army smashed into South Korea on 25 June 1950. In March 1951, First Lieutenant Chafee was recalled to active duty. By August he was in Korea as assistant staff operations officer for the 1st Tank Battalion, 1st Marine Division. Other assignments with increasing responsibilities followed: executive officer of a weapons company and, later, commanding officer of Company D, 7th Marines. In January 1952, by now a captain, he was ordered to Pearl Harbor for duty in the legal office of the Fleet Marine Force. Soon thereafter he returned to civil life in Providence, having spent six years of his life in uniform.

As his forebears did, Chafee entered local Republican politics. In November 1956 he was elected to the state legislature from the third district of Warwick, on Narragansett Bay, and was reelected in 1958 and 1960. He was then successively chosen as a member of the House Elections Committee, State Chairman of the March of Dimes, and House minority leader. In 1961 he made his bid for the governorship in what appeared to be a lost cause. The state had (and still has) a large percentage of voters of French–Canadian, Portuguese, and Italian extraction. Many were Roman Catholics, members of the so-called blue-collar class, and Democrats. Chafee was the scion of an old Yankee family, an Episcopalian, a member of the educated elite, and a minority Republican, handicaps that would have discouraged lesser men than he. In a notable display of endurance he campaigned by car, helicopter, and plane, and when the votes were counted he had won by a margin of sixty-one votes. A recount gave him a lead of 398 ballots, not exactly a landslide but still an impressive upset. He evidently appealed to the electorate, for he was reelected in 1964 and 1966.

As governor, Chafee met all the constituents he could, meanwhile asking for suggestions for improving the general welfare. True to his word, he subsequently pressed the Democratic-controlled legislature to establish state medicare programs for the aged, more vocational training schools, a "green acres" program for woodlands and parks, and an anti-billboard law.[8]

Chafee's growing prominence won him recognition in national political circles. At the Republican national convention at San Francisco in 1964 he attained notoriety by criticizing those GOP leaders who in his view failed to react responsively to important issues, particularly in the civil rights field. Four years later at the Miami convention he leveled similar charges.[9]

Elected in 1966 as vice-chairman of the Republican Governor's Association, Chafee quickly assumed a leading role in formulating policy relating to the violent race riots wracking the big cities. At the Republican convention at Miami in 1968 he proposed that the GOP platform committee accept a State governor as vice-chairman. The Chairman, Congressman Melvin R. Laird, of

Wisconsin, declined the suggestion, at which point a frustrated Chafee lashed out at the "hostility and divisiveness" apparent in Laird's refusal. He had no way of knowing that Laird would soon be his superior in the Defense Department.

Chafee returned to Providence from Miami to start his fourth successive campaign for the governorship. His surprising defeat in November 1968 by Superior Court Judge Frank Licht stunned many. Ironically, one reason for his loss could be traced to his stand for a personal state income tax, a reversal of a position taken some years earlier. His future political career appeared dark indeed until Vice President-elect Agnew's phone call suddenly changed his prospects.

When Chafee entered the Pentagon in January 1969, it was brimming with a cheerful ambience because President Nixon had said that he intended "to restore ready access of our top military professionals to the President of the United States as contemplated by the National Security Act"—a direct jab at former Secretary of Defense Robert McNamara, who had depended for advice on military matters more upon his system analysts than upon the Joint Chiefs of Staff.[10] The new Secretary of Defense, Melvin Laird, also changed the situation considerably. Laird had served eight terms as a Wisconsin congressman. During World War II he had fought as a naval officer in the Pacific. He had written several books on national security affairs and was referred to by the press as the leading Republican defense specialist. It was predicted that he would advocate a negotiated end of the war in Indochina, a nuclear superiority for U.S. forces, and a stronger, nuclear Navy.[11]

To understand Chafee's relationship with Laird and his deputy, Packard, a brief look at the new Pentagon procedures of 1969 is in order. Laird quickly assured the service secretaries that they would have a strong voice in the planning of force levels and in the formulation of personnel policies. Meanwhile each secretary would keep himself informed of overall defense issues, particularly if he were addressing the Defense Secretary as an advocate of his department.[12] Packard later remarked that Chafee invariably displayed a competent grasp of the national defense and was very successful in conveying his views to congressional committees.[13]

The Laird–Packard team also decentralized controls exercised by the previous administration, particularly in force planning, on the "sizing out" of the military elements of each service.[14] McNamara had not announced budget parameters to the services prior to their annual preparation of recommended force levels because he wished to know beforehand the forces each service considered paramount. Only then, it was said, could he place the various programs in perspective and decide upon their relative merit. This procedure rendered irrelevant any realistic service planning based upon a predetermined budget goal.

Under Laird, the secretaries were notified of their budgetary limits in advance so that they could shape their force levels accordingly.[15] Additionally, Laird assigned the systems analysis group an advisory rather than a reviewing role, thus increasing the reliance he placed on the professional military advice of the Joint Chiefs of Staff (JCS).

While Laird wielded the economy axe on service budgets in response to White House directives, he also gave more guidance and support to his associates, both civil and military, than they had previously received. By saying that a service secretary had to "ride two horses at the same time" he meant that a secretary must represent his service but also recognize the Secretary of Defense as his superior.[16]

For his immediate staff Chafee chose men who were professionally qualified and also knowledgeable in the folkways of official Washington. As Under Secretary he tapped John W. Warner, who had fought as a naval enlisted man in World War II and as a Marine officer in Korea, and who by 1969 was a member of a prominent Washington law firm. To give continuity to his office, he wisely retained two appointees of former President Lyndon B. Johnson: Dr. Robert A. Frosch, the Assistant Secretary for Research and Development, and Charles A. Bowsher, the Assistant Secretary for Financial Management. For the post of Assistant Secretary for Installations and Logistics he selected Frank Sanders, a lawyer who had been staff assistant for the House Armed Services Committee and was especially qualified in military procurement and logistics. As Assistant Secretary for Manpower and Reserve Affairs he chose James D. Hittle, a Marine Corps veteran who had served as a special counsel to the Senate Armed Forces Committee. Last, Chafee welcomed the reappointment of Admiral Thomas M. Moorer to a second two-year term as Chief of Naval Operations (CNO). As a former Marine himself, Chafee enjoyed a congenial relationship with the Marine Corps Commandant (CMC), General Leonard C. Chapman.

As an administrator, Chafee was not involved directly with the preparation of operational plans and operations. These were functions of the Joint Chiefs of Staff, who reported to the Secretary of Defense. However, both the CNO and CMC kept him informed of operational matters wherein he had an interest. In sum, Chafee was responsible for maintaining the readiness of the Navy and Marine Corps for the performance of military missions planned and directed by others and for supporting the Navy and Marine Corps in areas of administration, personnel, material, finance, and technology (including research and development).[17]

Chafee assumed office when the nation was wracked by civic unrest, racial confrontation, rebellion to authority, weariness with the Indochina War, and in addition public dissatisfaction with large cost overruns in defense procurement contracts.[18] To Chafee, however, these problems were peripheral to the main issue: how to build a modern fleet to meet the requirements of the Nixon Doctrine.

The Nixon Doctrine, enunciated by the President at Guam on 25 July 1969, stated that the United States would keep its treaty commitments, provide a nuclear shield, and furnish assistance to its allies when needed, yet pull back its overseas forces from involvement abroad[19]—thus plainly signaling a greater emphasis on sea-based forces.

What was involved in this new ocean strategy? First, the Navy would comprise two basic elements: a strategic deterrent force (missile submarines) and a general purpose (sea control) force. But the administration's desire to cut government expenditures conflicted with the Navy's need for new ships and aircraft, thereby posing a dilemma for Chafee during his entire tenure.

To achieve the build-up of a Navy geared to the new ocean strategy, Chafee set various specific goals. The Navy must accommodate to smaller defense budgets in order that the administration could fund such higher priority domestic programs as urban transit, housing, medicare, and education. Accordingly, on 21 August 1969, Chafee ordered the deactivation of over 100 ships from a fleet of 886, and a 10 percent reduction of personnel numbering 72,000. And more cut-backs were in the offing.[20] Chafee explained that the tremendously high costs of the Indochina war—up from $5 billion to $20 billion in 1967, 1968, and 1969—made impossible any other course of action. Rather than operate obsolete World War II ships, he opted for a smaller navy while investing in new weapons, ships, and planes scheduled for the late 1970s and early 1980s that could match the growing strength of the Russian navy.[21] He was well aware of the difficulty of obtaining funds for such expensive weapons systems as the Polaris and Poseidon missile submarines; yet to ignore these programs would result only in yielding to the Russians an ocean combat superiority, a proposition he found unacceptable. Moreover, he thought there were alternatives to a nuclear war with Russia. If a war of "massive retaliation" was now a remote possibility, conventional naval forces that could fight small wars and keep the peace were as important as strategic forces to the national defense. He thus saw the new ocean strategy as fitting uniquely with the temper of the American people, collectively a nation skeptical of foreign involvements but determined to remain a world power.

Having outlined the Navy's broad mission, Chafee decided to acquaint the Washington naval community with his program by calling together all naval and Marine officers who could be spared from their desks. After briefing his audience on the general issues of budget, ship construction, and the Russian naval threat, he focused on the low retention rate of naval personnel, a situation which also caused Admiral Moorer much concern. The reenlistment rate for first-term sailors declined steadily—from 17 percent in 1968 to 16 percent in 1969 and to 14 percent in 1970—insufficient to meet the Navy's goal of 31 percent. As for overall officer retention, Chafee disclosed that in 1970 it was only 14 percent compared to a goal of 31 percent. Furthermore, whereas the Navy needed to retain 55 percent of its naval aviators, it was keeping only 31 percent. Obviously industry was drawing skilled naval technichians to civilian jobs, naval aviators were leaving in large numbers for the civil airlines, and younger officers were resigning to enter industry or attend graduate schools. But Chafee suggested another cause for low retention—demanding ship employment schedules that wore down the crews by long watch-standing and additional maintenance work. As a possible new approach, he asked the officers to "restore the adventure, the fun of being a Navy man."[22]

Current operational conditions were wearisome to the men in overworked ships. As shipbuilders packed more equipment into older ships, they encroached on living spaces and created overcrowded conditions that lowered morale. To correct these conditions, Chafee urged that each echelon of command do its best to improve general conditions for its people.

With the all-volunteer force scheduled to go into effect in July 1973, Chafee realized that failure to retain top performers would leave the Navy many vacancies begging qualified replacements.[23] To attract and keep good men, he recommended more family housing, motels at naval bases, sea pay, better shipboard habitability, faster petty officer promotion, and bigger housing allowances.

Chafee set an example to his subordinates by his personal efforts. On three different occasions he testified (the only service secretary to do so) before congressional committees on the need for housing as a means to retain men. His efforts paid off, for in fiscal year 1971 Congress authorized the construction of 3,700 new permanent housing units, the largest number approved since World War II. In addition, Chafee authorized travel funds for individuals to make up to three trips to visit their families during a ship overhaul.

The question of retention nevertheless remained a chronic difficulty that engaged Chafee's constant attention. Reenlistment rates slowly rose after fiscal year 1970, but during his tenure Chafee never attained his goal of 31 percent retention. In fiscal year 1972, when the Navy's recruiting quota was 73,000 new enlistees, only 63,000 were recruited. At this writing the Navy has not yet solved its recruiting problem.

The *Pueblo* affair, inherited by Chafee, in a sense demonstrated that with the rise of nationalism after World War II lesser nations were not overawed by American naval or military power. When the ship's company returned home after long confinement in North Korea, a naval court of inquiry was convened, headed by Vice Admiral Harold G. Bowen, Jr. The uncompromising language of Navy Regulation 0730 did not accord with the surprisingly pliant surrender of the *Pueblo* by her commanding officer, Commander Lloyd M. Bucher, to several small North Korean vessels. The regulation states:

> *Search not Permitted*
> The commanding officers shall not permit his command to be searched by any person representing a foreign state nor permit any of the personnel under his command to be removed by such person, so long as he has the power to resist.

Bowen's court recommended general courts-martial for Bucher (for "permitting his ship to be seized while he had the power to resist" and laxness in carrying out various required security drills) and for Lieutenant Stephen R. Harris, the electronics-intelligence officer. Three other officers, one of whom was Rear Admiral Frank L. Johnson, who as Commander Naval Forces Japan, had been Bucher's operational superior, also came under fire. But in his case, as with the other two officers, the court recommended censure rather than a court-martial. The court then sent the record of proceedings through the chain of command to Chafee.

In view of the fact that the ship's company had endured eleven months of cruel treatment in a North Korean prison camp and after discussing the problem with both Laird and Packard, Chafee concluded that he would take no disciplinary action against any of the *Pueblo's* men, for "they have suffered enough."[24] While the charges leveled against Admiral Johnson could also be aimed at others even higher in the chain of command, Chafee considered the incident closed[25]—an astute decision that caused the *Pueblo* story to fade from the front pages of the press and precluded the washing of additional naval linen in public.

However, dissatisfaction over the incident prompted the House Armed Services Committee to name a special subcommittee to probe into the *Pueblo* matter as well as the shooting down of a naval plane by North Korean jets.[26] In its report the subcommittee, headed by Representative Otis G. Pike, charged that "serious deficiencies in the . . . military command structures of both the Department of the Navy and the Department of Defense" existed.[27] It was the sense of the report that the Navy and DOD had become too ponderous to conduct operations effectively. In response to the report, Laird ordered a review of the military-civilian command structure and its capability to cope with emergency situations. Soon thereafter Chafee ordered that the *Banner* and the *Palm Beach*, sister ships of the *Pueblo*, be decommissioned.[28]

Chafee seized every opportunity to alert the public to Soviet advances in ship construction and weaponry in contrast to the American decline in sea power. He told an American University audience in late 1969 that the United States must be watchful of those who "have built 350 submarines, who placed nuclear weapons in Cuba, and who tested atomic bombs while vilifying the United States. To suggest the United States just needs more love seems to me to ignore the lessons of the last 20 years. In fact, of the last 50 years."[29] Again, at Philadelphia on 27 October 1970, he compared the tactical capabilities of the Soviet Mediterranean fleet and of the U.S. Sixth Fleet. Each fleet, consisting of some fifty ships, could show the flag, stage a cruise-by or a fly-over (the Russian naval planes being limited to helicopters), evacuate its citizens from trouble spots, and wage conventional war. Only in the delivery of nuclear weapons to distant targets by carrier aircraft were the Russians deficient; their closest approach to an aircraft carrier was the helicopter–ASW vessel of the *Moskva*-class.

Chafee reminded his audience that the Mediterranean was no longer an American lake, that the Sixth Fleet was forced "to look over its shoulder at missile-armed Soviet warships within easy range and worry about Soviet submarines at the same time." Meanwhile Soviet harassment of NATO ships occasionally resulted in tragedy. In November 1970, for example, two Russian sailors died as a result of a collision between a *Kotlin*-class destroyer and the British aircraft carrier *Ark Royal* during night flight operations in the eastern Mediterranean.

Soviet task forces were operating not only in the Eastern Mediterranean but world wide, even just a few miles off the coasts of Florida and Louisiana. The Soviet merchant fleet, so essential for logistic support in wartime, had long ago left its U.S. counterpart behind. Russian naval intelligence profited from the information collected by eighteen thousand fishing vessels and two hundred oceanographic research ships which lent direct support to the largest force of submarines ever operated by any country in history—350 against 146 for the U.S. Navy. Equally important, these ships operated under the "continuous, absolute, and centralized control of the Soviet state."[30]

Three months later, in January 1971 in San Francisco, Chafee cited the mammoth Soviet naval exercise held in April 1970 and entitled Okean (Ocean). Conducted world wide, this operation involved one hundred fifty surface ships, sixty submarines, and several hundred planes. It therefore exceeded any previous naval exercise in history. There was no doubt that it was designed to counter the U.S. Navy's attack carriers. And even if we were still ahead, the gap was closing. As an example, the Soviets were building fifteen nuclear submarines annually, the United States only four. However, because funds were needed for domestic programs, Chafee's Navy had to achieve a high level of combat effectiveness despite austere budgets that between June 1969 and June 1971 caused a shrinkage of 264,000 men and 189 ships. This latter figure equalled 20 percent of the fleet and included an attack carrier, three ASW carriers, four cruisers, 51 destroyer types, 54 amphibious ships, and 32 auxiliaries.[31]

Although the Navy could not build ships fast enough to replace those retired for old age, Chafee took heart in the progress made in the Polaris/Poseidon submarine system, which had made "outstanding records." Nevertheless, if the present trend continued, the United States in the 1970s could end up second-best to Russia. From 1963 to 1971, the number of major American combatant ships declined from about 350 to 250 while Russian counterparts increased from about 180 to 220. Of attack submarines in 1971, the Russians had about 250, the United States, 90.[32] Chafee wondered whether the American people really wanted a Navy with a creditable combat capability.

Early in 1969 Chafee told the House Armed Services Committee and its Navy-minded chairman, L. Mendel Rivers, of South Carolina, that over the next ten years the Navy would require annual amounts of $3.5 billion or more for ship construction and modernization rather than the $2 billion allocated during the past ten years.[33] His demand evoked some eye-blinking from those who overlooked the Navy's loss of a "generation" of ships because of the lack of a sound building program in the 1950s.[34] Evidently Chafee had not obtained administration support for his demand, for shortly thereafter he suffered a $992 million reduction in his current budget. When Congress appropriated only $2.7 billion, Chafee inactivated fifty ships and eighteen air squadrons and Laird and Packard deferred budget planning for the proposed fourth nuclear carrier, CVN–70, to 1972.[35]

Litton Industries, a conglomerate new to shipbuilding, was encountering difficulties at its shipyard at Pascagoula, Mississippi.[36] When Chafee told Rivers that the Navy needed an additional $600 million to cover "cost increases and escalations" in the Litton contract, he attributed the cause to inflation coupled with long-term contracts and slow material turnover—all of which had put shipyards in an economic squeeze. Rivers was unconvinced.

Seeking new ships at moderate cost, the Navy had signed a contract for nine LHAs (amphibious helicopter assault ships) with Litton, a firm that lacked experience in shipbuilding. Rivers, who took a dim view of the contract, reminded Chafee that new ship or aircraft designs invariably led to large cost overruns and then demanded to know why Litton should be awarded "a nine ship package when they haven't even built the first prototype?"[37] Would it not have been better, he asked, for the Navy "just [to] get the prototype [built] and then see what it is going to cost. . . ?" Admiral Moorer came to Chafee's aid by explaining that Litton had to be given a nine-ship contract in order to make the capital investment necessary to install the modern auto-mated shipbuilding equipment which had proved so successful in Europe and Japan.

Rivers insisted that too many companies had been destroyed by unmanage-able contracts wherein final costs were not—or could not—be foreseen. "I don't want to be clobbered on the floor [of the House] and in the public press," he said. However, he agreed that the Navy needed LHAs and "we will give them to you. Don't let's get killed in the process." As events turned out, the LHAs fell sixteen months behind schedule and held up construction of following ships. Chafee thereupon reduced Litton's contract from nine to five LHAs and left intact a second contract, one that called for sixteen *Spruance*, or DD963-class, destroyers.[38] Moreover, in seeking a way out of this nightmare Chafee authorized fixed-price incentive contracts instead of firm-fixed price contracts which proved impractical in inflationary times. Next, he instituted a project management procedure by which a single officer would be responsible for cost- and change-control, thus reducing the number of costly engineering changes in the original design. Last, he made "selected reductions" that were nevertheless drastic: the laying-up of over 125 ships; cut-backs in personnel totaling 73,000; deactivation of the 5th Marine Division and other Marine units for a total cut of 20,000 men in the Corps; and the closure of eighty-three shore facilities by June 1972.[39] Very clearly Chafee was leading the Navy Department through turbulent times.

Litton's problems were matched by those of the Grumman Aerospace Corporation and its F–14 contract, another example of an agreed-upon price for a "total package" (the Pentagon term for a massive contract to deliver a complete system).

The first new jet fighter in over ten years, the F–14 had been approved by Defense Secretary Laird in early 1969. Subsequently the Navy signed a con-tract with Grumman. Under its terms, a first increment of $388 million would cover the costs of research and development plus six planes for test and evalua-tion. The contract included an option for the Navy to buy 463 additional planes. It was anticipated that the first F–14s would be operational by May 1973 to replace the McDonnell–Douglas F–4. Unhappily, the F–14 encountered design and production difficulties that produced a large overrun. With the cost rising from $11.5 to $16.8 million for a single plane, the Navy reduced its option from 463 to 313 planes.[40]

Grumman's troubles came from greater labor costs and overhead rates, higher material prices, and expensive modifications dictated by the test pro-gram. Additional unexpected expense was incurred in contracts for spare parts, ground support equipment, and personnel training, all of which had failed to remain on schedule and added to the cost. Grumman then looked to the Navy to renegotiate the contract, pleading inability to build more aircraft at the negotiated price without committing corporate suicide.[41]

The Navy and Grumman were still contesting the contract when Chafee left office in the spring of 1972. Early in 1973, with the matter unresolved, the Navy agreed that the company could build approximately fifty F–14s in addition to those already operational. Meanwhile the Navy had commissioned the first two F–14 Tomcat squadrons in October 1972 at the Naval Air Station, Miramar, California. Moreover, tests of the plane with the new, long-range Phoenix missile proved for the first time in naval warfare that a plane could launch multiple missiles against multiple air targets. In support of this achievement, Chafee's persistent efforts to obtain funds for the F–14 played a large part.

Chafee enthusiastically supported the increased participation of minority groups in all levels of government. In May 1970 he visited Prairie View State College, in Texas, to present commissions to thirteen officers from the first Naval Reserve Officer Training Corps unit at the predominantly Negro college. He then opened NROTC units at four more predominantly black colleges and established Junior NROTC units at thirty-two predominantly black high schools. The task of developing his new personnel program he gave to James E. Johnson, the Assistant Secretary of the Navy for Manpower and Reserve Affairs, who succeeded James D. Hittle when he returned to private life. Upon taking his oath of office on 16 June 1971, Johnson became the highest-ranking black official in the Defense Department. Another significant event in the history of minority groups occurred when Captain Samuel L. Gravely became the first black flag officer in the U.S. Navy.

Minority group participation in service life was occasionally difficult. Laird had spoken of the "disharmony [in racial matters] which has the potential of impairing our overall mission." One way to meet the problems, he said, was action to improve "communication and understanding among members of different races through education."[42] Chafee backed this policy wholeheartedly and ensured that selected members of the Navy and Marine Corps attended the seven-weeks course at the Defense Race Relation Institute at Patrick Air Force Base, Florida. On return to their units these graduates became race-relations instructors. Nonetheless, scattered racial incidents increased while Chafee remained in office.

Chafee's zeal to advance participation of minority groups in the Navy eventually focused on the U.S. Naval Academy. To attain this goal, admirable in itself, he allegedly sought to increase the number of minority group midshipmen by lowering the admission standards. Reportedly, he ran into stiff opposition from the Academy's superintendent, Rear Admiral (later Vice Admiral) James Calvert, who felt that a stated level of student ability was necessary in order to train officers competent to serve a modern Navy. While the President of the Alumni Association, Admiral George W. Anderson (himself a former CNO), praised Calvert for refusing to let Chafee dilute the Academy's entrance requirements,[43] the Defense Department mounted a campaign to recruit academically qualified minority-group candidates for all the service academies.[44] That the effort succeeded is apparent in the rise of minority candidates who entered Annapolis. In 1969, 23 minority candidates, of whom 17 were black, entered the Academy; in 1972, 94 minority candidates, of whom 73 were black, entered.[45] Moreover, proof that the midshipmen were above average academically is evident from a profile of the Academy class of 1975 (entering in 1971). Of this class, 81.3 percent had ranked in the top quarter of their high school class as compared to 72.7 percent for private universities and 35.1 percent for all institutions.[46]

Although Chafee intensified the recruitment of minority group members, he also stressed that the service had "no preferred route to advancement other than superior performance in responsible assignments," thus indicating that the modern sailor is expected to be more and more a skilled technician. Consequently, many officers felt that the Navy could not accept for its technical schools those who lacked an elementary knowledge of high school science and mathematics.[47] When the recruiting goals fell in fiscal years 1971 and 1972, enlistment standards were lowered, whereupon the number of recruits who were "school eligible" also fell. Hence many minority members who for various sociological causes lacked the education of white sailors failed to qualify for training schools and found themselves in the deck force, ship's laundry, or galley, where they became prime targets for militants.[48] This development, which Chafee could not foresee, sparked the violent shipboard disturbances that occurred some months after he left office.[49]

Early in 1969, in the customary "guidance" letter to the senior member of the flag officer's selection board, in this case Admiral John J. Hyland, Commander in Chief Pacific Fleet, Chafee asked that special attention be given to the selection of more junior admirals, saying that "in addition to youth we need innovative and searching minds . . . courage of conviction to challenge the *status quo* and accepted doctrines without sinking the ship."[50] He also placed less stress than his predecessors on the traditional requirements of substantial experience in command-at-sea and in senior command posts, a trend some older officers disliked. Moreover, he reversed precedent by selecting a non-aviator, Vice Admiral Isaac Kidd, to command the Sixth Fleet, which included carriers; and an aviator, Vice Admiral Dick Guinn, to head the Bureau of Naval Personnel, customarily a billet reserved for surface or submarine officers.

In the summer of 1970, when Admiral Moorer was appointed Chairman of the JCS, Chafee passed over thirty-three admirals and recommended Vice Admiral Elmo R. Zumwalt, Jr., to succeed Moorer as CNO. At forty-nine years of age, Zumwalt was older than only twenty-one of the Navy's 302 admirals; when confirmed, he was the youngest officer ever to hold the post.

At the time of his appointment Zumwalt was Commander Naval Forces Vietnam. In this capacity he had impressed his superiors with his concern for his men and his imaginative, energetic approach to Vietnamization, the assumption by the South Vietnam Navy of naval missions formerly borne by the U.S. Navy. By setting up a workable training program for the South Vietnam Navy, he made possible a rapid turnover of the river patrol boats and other craft, thus facilitating the early phaseout of U.S. naval personnel. Traveling constantly, he worked closely with other commanders, spoke with young sailors, and gave the impression that he wished to help rather than to interfere.[51] Chafee, forty-seven years of age, reportedly believed that he would feel at home with a forty-nine year old CNO, especially one who he was convinced could cope with the problems arising from a changing Navy in a changing world.

Unlike most former CNOs, Zumwalt lacked experience as a fleet commander or commander in chief, or in a billet closely associated with the operations of the JCS. Equally significant in terms of Chafee's people-oriented philosophy was Zumwalt's saying at the change-of-command ceremony on 1 July 1970 that "personnel management and some personnel procedures must be altered to conform to changing social attitudes." He affirmed his intention "to achieve a balance between the demands we make on our people and the rewards of a naval career."

Zumwalt poured forth a flurry of directives—the 111 so-called Z-Grams issued between 14 July 1970 and 4 May 1972—designed to meet the needs of naval personnel without relaxing the standards of good order and discipline. Changes were immediately visible. Hair grew longer, beards and mustaches proliferated, new styles of uniforms for enlisted men were introduced, and the working uniform could be worn to and from home. At the same time, the Navy's ranks were increased by radicalized youths who were determined to erode discipline by bending, if not actually breaking, established customs and regulations.[52] Worse, a steady increase occurred in the number of cases of willful destruction of property. Additionally, some personnel who took advantage of the less restrictive regulations frequently created the impression that naval discipline had slackened. Coupled with the stresses of the Vietnam war and a fleet operating with fewer ships and men, these circumstances helped to breed the outbreak of riots and free-for-alls on board the carriers *Constellation* and *Kitty Hawk* and the oiler *Hassayampa* after Chafee's departure.[53]

While undoubtedly benefiting from its small size and its reputation as an elite force, the Marine Corps eliminated potential disciplinary problems by maintaining its traditionally rigorous military standards. Even its recruiting slogan advertised the Corps' toughness: "The Marines are looking for a few good men." However they did it the Marines continued to maintain their status as a prestigious fighting unit without serious outbreaks similar to those that plagued the Navy.[54]

While Chafee applauded the "highly effective" direction given to the Navy and to the Marine Corps by Zumwalt and Chapman, respectively,[55] certain high-ranking retired flag officers who had served as fleet commanders and in even more senior billets privately commented on the need to tighten discipline. They also noted the trend to substitute younger and inexperienced flag officers for older and more experienced ones. One even said privately that perhaps matters would have worked out better for the Navy and for Zumwalt himself if Chafee had waited long enough to permit him to gain experience, say as a fleet commander, before appointing him as Chief of Naval Operations. It is certainly too early to make a balanced judgment at this writing.

Early in 1972, when it was openly rumored that he planned to reenter political life in Rhode Island, Chafee reviewed his stewardship and the current state of the Navy in a final appearance before the House Armed Services Committee. As expected, he spoke of the need of a Navy capable of exercising command at sea, of blocking Russia's wish to be "predominant on the world's oceans." In spite of inflation and the war, he reported that the Navy had made substantial advances. It had completed its part in "Vietnamization," and almost all U.S. naval personnel shore-based in Indochina, about thirty thousand strong in 1968, had departed for home. Other goals attained included improved fleet readiness, modernization of weapons systems, better program management, more effective recruiting, and an improved Naval Reserve.

In addition, ten Polaris submarines had been converted to carry the more advanced Poseidon missile, nine more boats were considerably more powerful, carrying twenty-four missiles rather than the sixteen in the Polaris boats. Moreover, the Poseidon missile was fitted with MIRV (multiple independently targetable reentry vehicles).

But much remained to be done, warned Chafee. Rapid turn-over of personnel and long training periods caused material deficiencies. Equally troublesome, the Navy's equipment was so complex that the spare parts problem in some cases was acute. The new construction program, Chafee alleged, was now satisfactory. Shipbuilding authorizations were $1.2 billion for fiscal year 1969, $2.7 billion for 1970 and the same for 1971, but $3.3 billion for 1972. In the fiscal years 1969 to 1972, among the 108 new ships that joined the fleet were the nuclear carriers *Nimitz* and *Eisenhower*, twelve nuclear attack submarines, sixteen destroyers, five amphibious assault ships, and five nuclear frigates. But the unsettling fact remained that the Navy had been forced to retire older ships faster than newer ones were being built. Consequently, the Navy's flexibility to meet worldwide commitments had declined.

Chafee also noted that vastly improved planes were being introduced to the fleet: the long-range ASW P-3C aircraft equipped with a new generation of ASW avionics; the S-3A carrier-based ASW plane; the AV-8A and A-4M attack aircraft for the Marines; the carrier-based F-14 fighter; the EA-6B electronic warfare aircraft; the E-2C early warning plane; and the A-6E/A-7E attack planes. However, because there was not enough procurement money to provide for a one-for-one replacement of older planes, Chafee warned that within several years this deficit would affect the readiness of the Navy's and Marine's air arms.

In addition, major progress had been made in the amphibious forces, Chafee declared. For the first time in the Navy's history all amphibious assault ships could steam at twenty knots and all were configured with a platform to accommodate large helicopters for vertical envelopment assaults. Furthermore, the Marines on board these ships would be equipped with a new family of amphibious tractors to speed the ship-to-shore movement. Unhappily, however, the number of amphibious ships was barely adequate for fleet needs.

In concluding his review of the material program, Chafee spoke of the Mark 48 torpedo, which had a long history of test and production difficulties but was now on schedule.[56] This long-range, high-speed, deep-diving, command-guided torpedo was destined for use by attack submarines against enemy surface ships and submarines. For antiair warfare missiles, the Navy now had the Basic Point Defense Missile system which would be installed on board carriers, amphibious ships, and escort types. The Standard missile for surface-to-surface warfare had been installed on our guided-missile ships and some escort types. Last, the air-to-air missile, Phoenix, which was being produced for the F-14 fighter plane, had been spectacularly successful in tests.

Chafee informed the committee that he had reorganized the Navy's recruiting establishment and assigned to it some of his most talented officers. Next, the Naval Reserve had been reorganized to develop a higher state of readiness, provided more ships, and achieved more operational training. However, the number of regular Navy and Marine Corps officers and men had declined by 286,000 during his tour, the Marine Corps Reserve had also fared badly, and the Naval Reserve had increased by only four thousand.

Chafee also mentioned the drug abuse problem, one that afflicted all the services. To meet this problem, he had instituted rigid recruit screening, information programs, law enforcement, and stepped-up curative measures. Two drug rehabilitation centers were now operating, in Jacksonville, Florida, and Miramar, California. Prospects for ridding the Navy of this problem seemed good.

Aware of the committee's interest in naval contract management, Chafee asserted that he had called for "increased stress on test and evaluation *before* the weapon system is committed to the fleet." This move was related to another of his management actions, the decision to authorize the initial manufacture of a satisfactory prototype of a weapons system before the Navy would sign a large contract. No doubt he recalled the warning in 1969 by Congressman Rivers, recently deceased, that the Navy should require successful prototypes before awarding large contracts.

Chafee concluded his lengthy presentation with his oft-repeated warning that Russia was building up its naval strength far beyond its needs in keeping with an obvious plan to project its political power. It was clear to Chafee that the Navy, in concert with its allies, must remain "capable of maintaining the vital interests of the Free World" by guarding its margin of supremacy at sea.[57] On 4 April, when Chafee submitted his resignation to the President, Pentagon gossip had it that his successor would be Under Secretary Warner.

Chafee should be remembered primarily as one who consistently tried to improve the quality of the service environment. He also will be recalled as one who presided unwillingly over large cutbacks in men and ships. He started with 976 ships; as he left, Navy planners were resigned to a reduction to fewer than six hundred. Yet Chafee always fought hard to convince Congress of the need for fleet modernization and, to some extent, succeeded. As the Navy's advocate in OSD, he deserves credit for winning approval for the funding of such important programs as the F-14, the CVN-70, the 688-class nuclear attack submarine, and the Trident missile submarine, the last of which Laird saw as the most appropriate alternative to the newest strategic bomber, the B-1.[58]

Additionally, Chafee backed the construction of nuclear frigates, DD-963-class destroyers, patrol frigates, and surface effect ships.[59] He had fought to keep sixteen aircraft carriers (a type of ship which Russia had not yet developed), thus ensuring that the Navy's carrier task forces would continue to constitute a unique form of sea power which the Soviets had not yet matched.

In his letter of resignation to President Nixon, Chafee summed up his three and a quarter years in the Pentagon:

> During my tenure . . . the Navy and the Marine Corps have been in transition as a result of our winding down the war in Vietnam and our preparation for the period beyond Vietnam. We are modernizing our forces and they are ready. . . .

> Under your leadership . . . we in the Department of the Navy have participated in the development and implementation of the Nixon doctrine and the national security strategy of realistic deterrence. . . . The Navy and Marine Corps . . . have benefitted from your compassion and interest in the individual Sailor and Marine. . . .

In his reply President Nixon praised Chafee's "superb service," especially his "outstanding efforts in helping to carry out our Vietnamization policy, while simultaneously taking the needed steps to modernize our Fleet. The new, bold program developed under your guidance holds great promise for the future of our naval forces. . . . Well done!"[60]

On 4 May 1972, Laird presented to Chafee the Defense Medal for Distinguished Public Service. The accompanying citation praised his "great emphasis on the needs of the men and women in uniform" and his role in guiding the development and procurement of weapon systems for overall fleet modernization.[61] According to a flag officer who had served in Washington under him, Chafee was a widely respected leader who eased the Navy's transition from the Vietnam era to the new requirements of the 1970s. Various critics, however, sensitive to the need for tightening discipline in the Navy, were convinced that his personnel policies were detrimental to the best interests of the service in that they failed to attract and retain good people.

Still other observers took a more charitable view, recalling that the problems which Chafee faced were not unique. Public esteem for the military usually dropped after every war. As for budget cuts, these were inevitable after a major conflict. It was to Chafee's credit, they held, that in spite of many obstacles, he had fought hard to bring to the public's attention that the world was not at peace and that the Navy must be brought to greater strength.

Secretary Chafee relinquished his office to Under Secretary Warner at a ceremony, fittingly held for the two former Marines, at the historic Marine Barracks at Eighth and I Streets near the Washington Navy Yard. He returned to Rhode Island to oppose the incumbent Senator Claiborne Pell, a Democrat. His campaign for office was unsuccessful and he resumed the practice of law. In 1976 he ran again, was elected, and entered the senate where he serves as of this writing (1978).

In summing up his record, one is struck with Chafee's cast of mind, which showed a predilection for original thinking and for change. He also displayed a propensity for questioning, for not accepting established procedures. These characteristics undoubtedly caused certain senior flag officers to react with something less-than-enthusiasm for some of his programs, fearing that it was simply not enough to identify what was wrong with the Navy; it was also essential to exercise caution not to make matters worse.

When more facts have accumulated it will be the responsibility of future historians to illuminate the story of Chafee's term as Secretary. Whether his leadership might have been more efficacious cannot be determined now; but no one can doubt that John H. Chafee worked hard and unceasingly at his job.

NOTES

1. See profile on Chafee in *Navy Times*, 25 June 1969, p. 5.
2. *New York Times*, 7 Jan. 1969.
3. *Washington Post*, 7 Jan. 1969.
4. Interview with David Packard, 6 Oct. 1972, Palo Alto, Calif.
5. *Time*, 17 Jan. 1969, p. 14.
6. Biography of John H. Chafee, Governor of Rhode Island, by James J. Marshall, Press Secretary, on file in OFSECNAV; Virginia Conn, "Portrait of New Secretary of the Navy," *Navy*, Feb. 1969, pp. 23-25; "SecNav Uses 'People-Minded' Ideas," *Navy Times*, 25 June 1969, pp. 5, 49.
7. At Yale, Chafee majored in history, was a member of the wrestling team, and chaired the Senior Prom Committee. His fraternity was Delta Kappa Epsilon, and he was tapped for Skull and Bones. (*Yale Yearbook*, class of 1947.) At Harvard Law School, he was a member of Lincoln's Inn and the Scott Club. (Information provided by Harvard Law School Library.)
8. As a zealous environmentalist, Chafee, when he was SECNAV, had his official car converted to compressed natural gas, thereby lowering exhaust pollution by 90 percent.
9. *Time*, 17 Jan. 1969, pp. 16-17.
10. *Navy*, Dec. 1968, p. 10, and AFJ, 8 Jan. 1967, p. 7, contain accounts of Nixon's views on defense. For a discussion of the Pentagon budget process see William A. Niskanen, "Defense Management After McNamara," *ibid.*, 8 Feb. 1969, p. 23.
11. AFJ, 1 Feb. 1969, pp. 9-10.
12. For an analysis of Laird's views on defense see *Navy*, Jan. 1969, pp. 16-19, July/Aug. 1969, pp. 26-29, and Apr. 1970, pp. 8-11.
13. Interview with David Packard, 6 Oct. 1972.
14. For a description of Laird's methods see AFJ, 12 Apr. 1969, p. 31.
15. Interview with David Packard, 6 Oct. 1972.
16. The role of the JCS and their relationship with their civil superiors is described in C. Merton Tyrrell, *Pentagon Partners: The New Nobility* (New York: Grossman Publishers, 1970).
17. A description of the responsibilities borne by Chafee and his principal assistants is contained in SECNAV Instruction 5400.13, dated 24 Aug. 1971, OFSECNAV.
18. See William L. O'Neill, *Coming Apart: An Informal History of America in the 1960s* (Chicago: Quadrangle Books, 1971).
19. The Nixon administration moved slowly but steadily to extricate the United States from Indochina. In June 1969, as a start, 250,000 American personnel were withdrawn. They turned their equipment over to South Vietnam.
20. The economy program begun in 1969 was only the beginning. By 1970 the fleet had dropped below 800 ships. The Marine Corps was reduced from four to three divisions. The Navy's personnel was cut to 703,000 and 28 Naval Reserve training installations were closed. See *Navy*, Oct. 1969, pp. 18-22, and Dec. 1969, pp. 37-38. (The name of this publication was changed to *Sea Power* in Sept. 1971.)
21. In 1969, the Navy had about 850 ships with an average age of 18 years. In 1972 it had fewer than 700 ships with an average age of 15 years.
22. Remarks by Secretary Chafee, Departmental Auditorium, Washington, D.C., 9 Dec. 1969. (Copy of speech in OFSECNAV.)

23. ADM Charles K. Duncan, CINC Atlantic Fleet, said that his fleet was 4,500 men short of its allowance, a shortage compounded by serious deficiencies in skill. (Remarks by ADM Charles K. Duncan, Norfolk, Va., 31 Oct. 1972. Copy of speech in file of Public Affairs Officer Atlantic Fleet.) While he was Deputy ASECDEF for Manpower and Reserve Affairs, VADM William Mack stated that "the Services cannot retain people by subjecting them to rigorous deployment schedules," (AFJ, 8 Mar. 1969, p. 9), and Chafee averred that "personnel retention has been helped by all the efforts that ADM Zumwalt has made in his Z-grams." (U.S. House, Committee on Armed Services, *Hearings on Military Posture*, HASC No. 92–45, 92nd Cong., 1st Sess. [Washington: GPO, 1972], p. 9653.)

24. Interview with David Packard, 6 Oct. 1972.

25. *New York Times*, 7 May 1969.

26. For the EC-121 plane incident and President Nixon's action, see *Navy*, May 1969, p. 35.

27. U.S. House, Committee on Armed Services, *Report on the Activities of the House Committee on Armed Services* (HASC No. 91–35, 91st Cong., 1st Sess. [Washington: GPO, 1969], p. 5109). For the congressional investigation see HASC No. 91–10, Mar. 1969, and HASC No. 91–12, July 1969, the latter entitled *Inquiry into the USS Pueblo and EC-121 Plane Incidents* (Washington: GPO, 1969).

28. HASC, 91–10, p. 641; *Navy*, Nov. 1969, p. 37.

29. *Navy*, Nov. 1969, p. 6.

30. Speech on file in OFSECNAV.

31. Address at Commonwealth Club, San Francisco, 15 Jan. 1971. Copy on file in OFSECNAV. Comprehensive accounts of Soviet seapower appear in James D. Theberge, ed., *Soviet Sea Power in the Caribbean: Political and Strategical Implications* (New York: Praeger, 1972); Ernest McN. Eller, *The Soviet Sea Challenge* (Chicago: Cowles Book Co., 1971); David Fairhall, *Russian Sea Power: An Account of Its Present Strength and Strategy* (Boston: Gambit, 1971); and Norman Polmar, *Soviet Naval Power in the 1970s*, 2d ed. (New York: Crane, Russak, 1974).

32. U.S. House, Committee on Armed Services, *Hearings on Military Posture*, HASC 92–45, 92nd Cong., 2nd Sess. (Washington: GPO, 1972), pp. 9469, 9470.

33. HASC No. 91–41, pp. 2751–79.

34. The estimated $3 billion Russia spent on ship construction in 1971 far exceeded American spending. (ADM Zumwalt letter to senior retired officers, ca July 1971; *Navy*, May 1969, pp. 7, 10–13, and Jan. 1970, pp. 7–10; LCDR Terry L. Johnson, "Ship Acquisition: The Lost Generation," USNIP 98 [Nov. 1972]:27–32.)

35. Interview with David Packard, 6 Oct. 1972; *Navy*, Dec. 1969, p. 36; *Sea Power*, Dec. 1971, p. 30.

36. *Wall Street Journal*, 7 Mar. 1973; *Newsweek*, 19 Feb 1973, pp. 12–13.

37. The Deputy SECDEF, Packard, later stated that it was impossible to estimate the cost of total-package-procurement and that this type of contract led to "buy-ins" whereby DOD lost control of the contract. A "buy-in" is a deliberate underbidding of the contract: 1) on the assumption that the Government would bail

out the contractor by adding more funds, or 2) to prevent a competitor from winning the contract.

38. HASC No. 92–45, p. 9385; *Navy*, Jan. 1970, pp. 7–10, and June 1970, pp. 13–16; *Sea Power*, Dec. 1971, p. 30.

39. *Navy*, Apr. 1969, pp. 13–16, May 1969, p. 7, Oct. 1969, pp. 18–22, and Nov. 1969, pp. 24–25; *AFJ*, 19 Apr. 1969, p. 10, and 14 Feb. 1970, pp. 5, 10.

40. *San Francisco Chronicle*, 9 Mar. 1973; *AFJ*, 8 Feb. 1969, p. 9.

41. *AFJ*, 8 Feb. 1969, p. 9, 10 May 1969, p. 13; *Navy*, Mar. 1969, pp. 9–12.

42. "Statement of Secretary of Defense to Senate Armed Services Committee," *Annual Defense Department Report FY 1973* (Washington: GPO, 1972), p. 173.

43. *Shipmate*, Nov. 1972.

44. "Statement of Secretary of Defense to Senate Armed Services Committee."

45. Data furnished by Career Guidance Office, U.S. Naval Academy.

46. See Charles L. Cochran, "Service Academy Myths," *Shipmate*, Nov. 1972, p. 35.

47. Late in 1972 violent riots or free-for-alls took place in the carriers *Constellation* and *Kitty Hawk* and in the fleet oiler *Hassayampa*. CDR John Schaub, the *Constellation*'s executive officer, commented afterward that "the system we have had that encourages the recruiting of educationally deprived personnel, places them in competition with others more fortunate, is poorly conceived and totally unfair." (*San Francisco Sunday Examiner and Chronicle*, 11 Feb. 1973.) In the same article another officer commented: "There are too many recruits—not only blacks—but members of other minorities and underprivileged whites as well—who cannot cope with the technical training. As a result they are forced into menial jobs." See also CAPT Paul Ryan, USN (Ret), "USS *Constellation* Flare-up: Was It Mutiny?" USNIP 102 (Jan. 1976):46–53.

48. Following the shipboard demonstrations of 1972, ADM Zumwalt issued a directive that provided for a "voluntary early release program" for men who were a burden to the Navy and "whose performance did not contribute in significant degree . . . who are considered marginal or non-productive performers." (CNO dispatch 262029Z/231 [26 Dec. 1972], on file in Office of CNO.)

49. A three-man panel of the House Armed Service Committee chaired by Floyd V. Hicks, of Washington, investigated the disturbances. Hicks said that the investigation confirmed what he called "increasing concern over the development of more relaxed discipline in the military services, adding that "We commend the Chief of Naval Operations for those of his programs which are designed to improve Navy life and to maintain good order and discipline." (*San Francisco Chronicle*, 24 Jan., 2 Feb. 1973.)

50. The letter is printed in *AFJ*, 31 May 1969, p. 23.

51. George W. Ashwork, "The 'Big Z' Takes the Conn," *Navy*, June 1970, pp. 17–21. For a description of Zumwalt's relations with Chafee and an account of Vietnamization, see Elmo R. Zumwalt, Sr., *On Watch* (New York: Quadrangle Books, 1976), *passim*.

52. ADM Duncan, CINC Atlantic Fleet, said that "the sooner the Navy is free of this group the better off the country and the Navy will be." He added: "I am talking about the activists, anti-social, anti-military, anti-United States misfits . . . [who] have no place in an environment of stress, responsibility, and danger . . . handling nuclear weapons . . . operating high speed deep diving submarines

. . . [and] dangerous fleet operations in rough seas at night." (Remarks of 31 Oct. 1972, on file in Public Affairs Office, Atlantic Fleet.)

53. On 10 Nov. 1972, ADM Zumwalt told an audience of Washington area flag officers that the incidents on board the *Kitty Hawk, Constellation,* and *Hassayampa* were "not the cause of racial pressures; rather they are manifestations of pressures unrelieved . . . these current racial incidents are not the results of lowered standards, but clearly are due to failure of commands to implement those programs [which Zumwalt had initiated] with a whole heart." (Remarks on file in Office of Information, Navy Department.)

54. GEN Robert E. Cushman, USMC, who relieved GEN Chapman on 1 Jan. 1972, later wrote: "We don't move very far down the path of 'liberalization' of the Armed Forces before we bump into the reality; the fundamental truth that [soldiers, sailors, Marines] are raised and maintained for the purpose of fighting. If they cannot fight, they can neither deter war nor win war." (*Shipmate,* Nov. 1972, p. 17).

55. HASC, No. 92–9, 92nd Cong., 1st Sess. (Washington: GPO, 1971), pp. 3247–48.

56. The Mark 48-Mod 1 torpedo was introduced into the fleet in Feb. 1970. The development cost alone was $680 million. When the costs were added up for a fleet inventory of torpedoes, fire control, and launching systems, the cost estimate in Nov. 1972 was about $2 billion. The Mark 48 bid fair to counter any threat posed by any submarine either operational or projected. (Information provided by Chief of Information, Navy Department.)

57. HASC, 92–45, pp. 9648–69.

58. *Ibid.,* p. 9363; *San Francisco Chronicle,* 17 Feb. 1973.

59. The surface effect ship is a hydrofoil patrol boat (PHM) designed to be a missile-carrying craft for littoral waters.

60. Letters on file in OFSECNAV.

61. The citation, dated 4 May 1972, is in *ibid.*

INDEX

Pages in Volume II are prefaced by italicized *II*.

Abbreviations used:

ADM	Admiral	LT	Lieutenant
ASEC	Assistant Secretary	MAJ	Major
ASECNAV	Assistant Secretary of the Navy	MGEN	Major General
		Pres.	President
ASECDEF	Assistant Secretary of Defense	PM	Prime Minister
BGEN	Brigadier General	Prof.	Professor
BR	British	RADM	Rear Admiral
CAPT	Captain	Rep.	Representative
CDR	Commander	(RET)	Retired
CNO	Chief of Naval Operations	Rev.	Reverend
COL	Colonel	RN	Royal Navy, British
COMMO	Commodore	SEC	Secretary
Cont. Navy	Continental Navy	SECA	Secretary of the Army
CSN	Confederate States Navy	SECDEF	Secretary of Defense
CSS	Confederate States Ship	Sen.	Senator
DOD	Department of Defense	Sp.	Spanish
FADM	Fleet Admiral	USA	United States Army
FY	Fiscal Year	USAC	U. S. Army Air Corps
GEN	General	USAF	U. S. Air Force
Ger.	German	USECDEF	Under Secretary of Defense
Gov.	Governor	USENAV	Under Secretary of the Navy
JCS	Joint Chiefs of Staff		
LCDR	Lieutenant Commander	USMC	U. S. Marine Corps
LCOL	Lieutenant Colonel	VADM	Vice Admiral
LGEN	Lieutenant General	V. Pres.	Vice president